Inspiring a Medico-Legal Revolution

Essays in Honour of Sheila McLean

Edited by

PAMELA R. FERGUSON
University of Dundee, UK

GRAEME T. LAURIE
University of Edinburgh, UK

Routledge
Taylor & Francis Group
LONDON AND NEW YORK

First published 2015 by Ashgate Publishing

2 Park Square, Milton Park, Abingdon, Oxfordshire OX14 4RN
52 Vanderbilt Avenue, New York, NY 10017

Routledge is an imprint of the Taylor & Francis Group, an informa business

First issued in paperback 2020

British Library Cataloguing in Publication Data
A catalogue record for this book is available from the British Library

Library of Congress Cataloging-in-Publication Data
Inspiring a medico-legal revolution : essays in honour of Sheila McLean / by Pamela R. Ferguson and Graeme T. Laurie.
pages cm
Includes bibliographical references and index.

ISBN 978-1-4724-3428-9 (hardback : alk. paper)
1. Medical laws and legislation–Great Britain. 2. Medical laws and legislation–Moral and ethical aspects. I. McLean, Sheila, honouree. II. Ferguson, Pamela R., editor. III. Laurie, G. T. (Graeme T.), editor.
KD3395.A75I57 2015
344.4104'1–dc23

2014045359

ISBN 978-1-4724-3428-9 (hbk)
ISBN 978-0-367-59903-4 (pbk)

Contents

Table of Cases

A v. B [2012] EWCA Civ 285, [2012] 1 WLR 3456
A and B v. SA [2013] EWHC 426 (Fam)
A, B and C v. Ireland [2010] App. No. 25579/05 ECHR 2032
A Local Authority and Mrs A [2010] EWHC 1549
A Local Authority v. K [2013] EWHC 242 (COP)
AB and CD v. CT [2015] EWFC 12
Airedale NHS Trust v. Bland [1993] AC 789 (HL), [1993] 1 All ER 821
Alliance for Marriage and Family v. AA [2007] 3 SCR 124
Alyne da Silva Pimentel Teixeira (deceased) v. Brazil, CEDAW/C/49/D/17/008, August 10, 2011
An NHS Trust v. B [2006] EWHC 507 (Fam)
Artavia Murillo et al. v. Costa Rica, Inter-Am Ct HR (ser C) no. 257 (Nov. 28, 2012)
Attorney General's Reference (No 3 of 1994) [1998] AC 245
Attorney General's Reference (No 6 of 1980) [1981] QB 715, [1981] 2 All ER 1057
Barr v. Matthews (1999) 52 BMLR 217 (QBD)
Birch v. University College London Hospital NHS Foundation Trust (2008) 104 BMLR 168
Bolam v. Friern Hospital Management Committee [1957] 1 WLR 582
Bolitho v. City and Hackney Health Authority [1997] 3 WLR 1151
Brüstle v. Greenpeace eV [2012] 1 CMLR 41
Buck v. Bell, 274 US 200 (1927)
C v. S [1987] 1 All ER 1230, [1988] QB 135
Chartier v. Chartier [1999] 1 SCR 242
Chatterton v. Gerson [1981] QB 432
Cherry v. Borsman (1992) 94 DLR (4th) 487 (Can BC CA)
Chester v. Afshar [2005] 1 AC 134
Davis v. Davis, 842 SW 2d 588 (Tenn Sup Ct, 1992), 842 SW 2d 588 (Tenn 1992)
Department of Health and Community Services (NT) v. JWB (Marion's case) (1992) 175 CLR 218
DL v. Local Authority and Others [2012] EWCA Civ 253, [2012] 3 WLR 1439, [2013] Fam 1
Evans v. Amicus Healthcare Ltd [2005] Fam 1
Evans v. United Kingdom (2007) ECHR 266, (2008) 46 EHRR 34
F v. R (1983) 33 SASR 189
Gibb v. Maidstone and Tunbridge Wells NHS [2010] EWCA Civ 678
Gillick v. West Norfolk and Wisbech Area Health Authority [1985] 3 All ER 402
Gleitman v. Cosgrove, 227 A 2d 689 (NJ Sup Ct, 1967)
Greater Glasgow Health Board v. Doogan and Wood [2014] UKSC 68
Gregg v. Scott [2005] 2 AC 176
Gross v. Switzerland (2013) App. No. 67810/10 (ECHR)
H (A Healthcare Worker) v. Associated Newspapers [2002] EWCA Civ 195
Haas v. Switzerland (2011) App. No. 31322/07 (ECHR)
Hobby Lobby v. Sebelius, 870 F Supp 2d 1278 (WD Okla, 2012)
Hotson v. East Berkshire Area Health Authority [1987] AC 750

Hunter and New England Area Health Service v. A [2009] NSWSC 761
I.G. and Others v. Slovakia [2012] App. No. 15966/04 (ECHR, Final [2013])
In re C (Adult: Refusal of Treatment) [1994] 1 WLR 290
In re T [1992] 3 WLR 782
In re Z (Local Authority: Duty) [2004] EWHC 2817 (Fam), [2005] 1 WLR 959
In the Application of Herrington; Re King [2007] VSC 151
In the Matter of Alice Hughes, 611 A 2d 1148 (NJ Sup Ct App Div, 1992)
In the Matter of Baby M, 537 A 2d 1227 (NJ Sup Ct, 1988)
In the Petition of Mary Teresa Doogan and Concepta Wood [2013] CSIH 36, P 876/11
J v. C [1970] AC 668
J v. G (Parental Orders) [2013] EWHC 1432 (Fam)
Jepson v. The Chief Constable of the West Mercia Constabulary [2003] EWHC 3318 (Admin)
Jones v. North West Special Health Authority [2010] EWHC 178
JP v. LP [2014] EWHC 595
L and R v. W and W [2011] EWHC 2455 (Fam), [2012] 1 FLR 1056
L Teaching Hospitals NHS Trust v. A [2003] EWHC 259 (QBD), [2003] 1 FLR 1091
LA v. SB, AB and MB [2010] EWHC 1744 (Fam)
LBL v. RYJ and VJ [2010] EWHC 2665 (COP)
Lim v. Camden & Islington Area Health Authority [1980] AC 174
Local Authority X v. MM, KM [2007] EWHC 2003 (Fam)
M v. F [2013] EWHC 1901 (Fam)
Malette v. Shulman (1987) 47 DLR (4th) 18 (Can Ont CA)
McFarlane v. Tayside Health Board [2002] 2 AC 59 (HL)
McKay v. Essex Area Health Authority [1982] QB 1166
Messiha v. South East Health [2004] NSWSC 1061
M.S. v. Sweden (1997) 28 EHRR 313
Ms B v. NHS Hospital Trust [2002] 2 All ER 449
Muir v. Alberta (1996) 132 DLR (4th) 695 (Can Alta QB)
Newcastle upon Tyne Hospitals Foundation Trust v. LM [2014] EWHC 454 (COP)
Nicholas v. Imperial College Healthcare NHS Trust [2012] EWHC 591
Office of Public Prosecutions v. Chabot, Nederlandse Jurisprudentie 1994 No. 656
O'Reilly v. BBC and Another (unreported) 2200423/2010
P v. K [2006] NZFLR 22
Paton v. British Pregnancy Advice Service [1979] QB 276
Pearce v. United Bristol Healthcare NHS Trust (1999) 48 BMLR 118
Pratten v. British Columbia (Attorney-General) (2012) 357 DLR (4th) 660 (Can BC CA)
Procanik v. Cillo 478 A 2d 755 (NJ Sup Ct, 1984)
Qumsieh v. GAB and Pilgrim (1998) 14 VAR 46, [1998] VSCA 45
R v. Brain (1834) 6 C&P 349
R v. Brown [1994] 1 AC 212
R v. Catt (Sarah Louise) [2013] EWCA Crim 1187
R v. E (Female Parent: Known Father) [2010] EWHC 417 (Fam)
R v. Human Fertilisation and Embryology Authority, ex p. Blood [1997] 2 All ER 687
R v. Morgentaler (1988) 44 DLR (4th) 385 (Can Sup Ct)
R v. NW Lancashire HA, ex p A, D & G (2000) 53 BMLR 148
R v. Northumbrian Water Ltd, ex p Newcastle and North Tyneside HA [1999] Env LR 715
R v. Poulton (1832) 5 C&P 329

R (Burke) v. General Medical Council [2006] QB 273, (2006) 85 BMLR 1 (CA), [2005] EWCA Civ 1003
R (Condliff) v. North Staffordshire PCT [2011] EWCA Civ 910
R (on the application of Purdy) v. Director of Public Prosecutions [2009] UKHL 45
R (on the application of Smeaton) v. Secretary of State for Health [2002] EWHC (Admin) 610
Rance v. Mid Downs Health Authority [1991] 1 QB 587
Re A Local Authority (Inquiry: Restraint on Publication) [2004] Fam 96
Re B (A Minor)(Wardship: Medical Treatment) [1981] 1 WLR 1421 (CA)
Re B (Role of Biological Father) [2007] EWHC 1952 (Fam), [2008] 1 FLR 1015
Re C (Adult: Refusal of Treatment) [1994] 1 WLR 290, [1994] 1 All ER 819 (CA)
Re D [2006] EWHC 2 (Fam), [2006] 1 FCR 556
Re D (Children) (Surrogacy) (Parental Order) [2012] EWHC 2631 (Fam), [2013] 1 All ER 962
*Re E (*Medical Treatment*: Anorexia)* (Rev 1) [2012] EWHC 1639 (COP)
Re E and F (Assisted Reproduction) (Parents) [2013] EWHC 1418 (Fam)
Re F (Mental Patient: Sterilisation) [1990] 2 AC 1, CA: (1989) 86(10) LSG 42
Re G (A Child) [2013] EWHC 134 (Fam), [2013] 1 FLR 1334
Re G (Children) (Residence: Same-Sex Partner) [2006] UKHL 43, [2006] 1 WLR 2305
Re K (A Minor) (Custody) [1990] 3 All ER 795
Re M (Child Support Act: Parentage) [1997] 2 FLR 90
Re Marion (1990) 14 Fam LR 427
Re MB (1997) 38 BMLR 175 (CA), [1997] 2 FLR 426
Re P (Contact) [2011] EWHC 3431 (Fam), [2012] 1 FLR 1068
Re P-M [2013] EWHC 2328 (Fam)
Re PS (An Adult) [2007] EWHC 623
Re Q (Parental Order) [1996] 1 FLR 369
Re R (A Child) (IVF: Paternity of Child) [2005] UKHL 33, [2005] 2 AC 621
Re R (A Minor) (Wardship: Medical Treatment) [1992] 1 FLR 190
Re SA (Vulnerable Adult with Capacity: Marriage) [2005] EWHC 2942 (Fam), [2006] 1 FLR 867
Re T [1997] 1 All ER 906
Re T (Adult: Refusal of Treatment) [1993] Fam 95
Re W (A Minor) (Medical Treatment) [1992] 4 All ER 627
Re W (A Minor) (Consent to Medical Treatment) [1993] 1 FLR 1
Rees v. Darlington Memorial Hospital NHS Trust [2004] AC 309
Rogers v. Whitaker [1992] HCA 58, (1992) 175 CLR 479 (HCA)
R.R. v. Poland [2007] App. No. 27617/04 (ECHR, decision final as of 28 November, 2011)
Schloendorff v. Society of New York Hospital, 105 NE (1914) 92
Sidaway v. Board of Governors of the Bethlem Royal Hospital [1984] QB 493 (CA)
St George's Health Care NHS Trust v. S [1998] 3 All ER 673 (CA), [1998] 3 WLR 936
T v. B [2010] EWHC 1444 (Fam), [2010] Fam 193
Tabet v. Gett [2010] HCA 12
The Sydney Children's Hospital Network v. X [2013] NSWSC 368
U v. W (Attorney General Intervening) (No. 2) [1997] 2 FLR 282
Vo v. France [2004] ECHR 326
Westminster City Council v. C [2008] EWCA Civ 198, [2009] 2 WLR 185
X v. The Sydney Children's Hospital Network [2013] NSWCA 320
X v. Y (2002) SLT (Sh Ct) 161
X and Y v. St Bartholomew's Hospital Centre for Reproductive Medicine [2015] EWFC 13

Xakmok Kasek Indigenous Community v. Paraguay, Inter-Am Ct HR (ser C) no. 214 (Aug. 24, 2010)
XCC v. AA [2012] EWHC 2183 (COP), [2013] 2 All ER 988, [2013] 2 FCR 401
YL v. Birmingham City Council [2007] UKHL 27
York City Council v. C [2013] EWCA Civ 478, [2014] 2 WLR 1
Zurich Case, Entscheid der 3 Kammer VB Nr 9900145 (1999)

Table of Statutes and Other Instruments

Australia

Acts Amendment (Consent to Medical Treatment) Bill 2006 (WA)
Alcoholics and Drug-dependent Persons Act 1968 (Vic.)
Consent to Medical Treatment and Palliative Care Act 1995 (SA)
Crimes Act 1958 (Vic.)
Criminal Code 1899 (Qld.)
Directions for Medical Treatment Bill 2005 (Tas.)
Disability Act 2006 (Vic.)
Guardianship Act 1987 (NSW)
Guardianship and Administration Act 1986 (Vic.)
Health Services (Conciliation and Review) Act 1987 (Vic.)
Medical Treatment Act 1988 (Vic.)
Medical Treatment (Health Directions) Act 2006 (ACT)
Mental Health Act 1986 (Vic.)
Natural Death Act 1988 (NT)
Powers of Attorney Act 1998 (Qld.)
Public Health Act 2005

New Zealand

Accident Compensation Act 2001
Crimes Act 1961
Health and Disability Commissioner (Code of Health and Disability Services Consumers' Rights) Regulations 1996, under the Health and Disability Commissioner Act 1994
Health Practitioners Competence Assurance Act 2003
Homosexual Law Reform Act 1986
Marriage (Definition of Marriage) Amendment Act 2013

Switzerland

Swiss Penal Code

United Kingdom

Abortion Act 1967
Adoption and Children Act 2002

Adoption and Children (Scotland) Act 2007
Adults with Incapacity (Scotland) Act 2000
Births and Deaths Registration Act 1953
Care Act 2014
Care Standards Act 2000
Child Support Act 1990
Children Act 1989
Children (Scotland) Act 1995
Civil Partnership Act 2004
Contracts (Rights of Third Parties) Act 1999
Data Protection Act 1998
Disability Discrimination Act 1995
Disability Discrimination Act 2005
Equality Act 2010
Family Law Act 1986
Family Law Reform Act 1969
Family Law (Scotland) Act 1985
Family Law (Scotland) Act 2006
Health and Social Care Act 2008
Health and Social Care Act 2012
Health and Social Care (Community Health and Standards) Act 2003
Health and Social Care (Community Health and Standards) Act 2003 Commencement (Wales) (No. 5) Order 2011
Human Fertilisation and Embryology Act 1990
Human Fertilisation and Embryology Act 2008
Human Fertilisation and Embryology (Deceased Fathers) Act 2003
Human Medicines Regulations 2012, SI 2012/1916
Human Rights Act 1998
Human Tissue Act 2004
Human Transplant (Wales) Act 2013
Legal Aid, Sentencing and Punishment of Offenders Act 2012
Marriage and Civil Partnership (Scotland) Act 2014
Marriage (Same Sex Couples) Act 2013
Medicines for Human Use (Clinical Trials) Regulations 2004, SI 2004/1031
Mental Capacity Act 2005
Mental Health Act 1983
Mental Health (Care and Treatment) (Scotland) Act 2003
Mental Health Measure 2009
National Health Service Act 2006
National Health Service Commissioning Board and Clinical Commissioning Groups (Responsibilities and Standing Rules) Regulations, SI 2012/2996
National Health Service (Concerns, Complaints and Redress Arrangements) (Wales) Regulations 2011, No. 704 (W.108)
National Health Service (Wales) Act 2006
NHS Redress Act 2006
NHS Redress (Wales) Measure 2008
NHS Redress (Wales) Measure 2008 (Commencement) Order 2011

Offences Against the Person Act 1861
Patient Rights (Scotland) Act 2011
Prohibition of Female Circumcision Act 2003
Protection of Vulnerable Groups (Scotland) Act 2007
Safeguarding Vulnerable Groups Act 2006
Stillbirth Definition Act 2002
Sunbeds (Regulation) Act 2010
Surrogacy Arrangements Act 1985
Tattooing of Minors Act 1969

International Instruments

American Convention on Human Rights
Commission Directive 2003/63/EC of 25 June 2003 amending Directive 2001/83/EC of the European Parliament and of the Council on the Community code relating to medicinal products for human use
Council of Europe, Oviedo Convention on Human Rights and Biomedicine (1997)
European Convention on Human Rights (1950)
European Directive 93/42/EEC of the European Parliament and of the Council 14 June 1993 concerning medical devices
European Directive 95/46/EC of the European Parliament and of the Council of 24 October 1995 on the protection of individuals with regard to the processing of personal data and on the free movement of such data
Resolution of the Government of the Czech Republic 1424, Nov. 29, 2009
UN Convention on the Elimination of all Forms of Discrimination Against Women (1979)
UNESCO, Universal Declaration on the Human Genome and Human Rights (1997)
United Nations Convention on the Rights of the Child (1989)
United Nations General Assembly Resolution, 11/8, Preventable Maternal Mortality and Morbidity and Human Rights (June 16, 2009)
United Nations International Covenant on Civil and Political Rights (1966)
United Nations International Covenant on Economic, Social and Cultural Rights (1966)
United Nations Universal Declaration on Human Rights (1948)
World Health Organization, Constitution (1946)

Miscellany

Adults with Incapacity (Scotland) Act 2000: Code of Practice (2008)
Charter of Patients' Rights and Responsibilities (NHS Scotland, 2012)
NHS Constitution for England (2013)
Pope Pius IX, decree of 12 October 1869, Apostolicae Sedis Moderationi
Practice Note, The Official Solicitor to the Senior Courts: Appointment in Family Proceedings and Proceedings under the Inherent Jurisdiction in Relation to Adults (March 2013)
Speaking Up Charter (NHS Employers, 2014)

Abbreviations

ACD	advance care directive
ACT	Australian Capital Territory
AIDS	acquired immunodeficiency syndrome
ALSPAC	Avon Longitudinal Study of Parents and Children
ANH	assisted nutrition and hydration
APA	American Psychological Association
AS	assisted suicide
AvMA	Action against Medical Accidents
BMA	British Medical Association
BMJ	*British Medical Journal*
BTE	'Before The Event' (insurance)
CCG	Clinical Commissioning Group
CEDAW	Committee on the Elimination of Discrimination against Women
CMO	Chief Medical Officer
CNORIS	Clinical Negligence and Other Risks Indemnity Scheme
CNST	Clinical Negligence Scheme for Trusts
CPR	cardio-pulmonary resuscitation
DH	Department of Health
DSM-V	Diagnostic and Statistical Manual of the American Psychiatric Association
ECHR	European Convention on Human Rights
ECtHR	European Court of Human Rights
EU	European Union
FIGO	International Federation of Gynecology and Obstetrics
GCA	Generic Conditions of Agency
GMC	General Medical Council
GP	General Practitioner
GTAC	Gene Therapy Advisory Committee
HCP	healthcare professional
HFEA	Human Fertilisation and Embryology Authority
HIV	Human Immunodeficiency Virus
HMSO	Her Majesty's Stationery Office
HTA	Human Tissue Authority
ICCPR	International Covenant on Civil and Political Rights
ICESCR	International Covenant on Economic, Social and Cultural Rights
ICD	International Classification of Diseases
IVF	*in vitro* fertilisation
LASPO	Legal Aid, Sentencing and Punishment of Offenders Act 2012
MAR	medically-assisted reproduction
MHRA	Medicines Healthcare Products Regulatory Agency
NCOB	Nuffield Council on Bioethics

NFCRG	No Fault Compensation Review Group
NHS	National Health Service [UK]
NHSLA	National Health Service Litigation Authority
NPSA	National Patient Safety Agency
NSW	New South Wales
NT	Northern Territory (Australia)
OBR	Office for Budget Responsibility
PAS	physician-assisted suicide
PND	Pre-Natal Screening Diagnosis
PGC	Principle of Generic Consistency
PGD	Pre-implantation Genetic Diagnosis
PHI	Principle of Hypothetical Imperatives of Instrumental Reason
PIP	Poly Implant Prosthesis
QALY	Quality Adjusted Life Year
Qld.	Queensland (Australia)
REC	Research Ethics Committee
SA	South Australia
Tas.	Tasmania (Australia)
UDHR	Universal Declaration on Human Rights
UK	United Kingdom
UKXIRA	United Kingdom Xenotransplantation Interim Regulatory Authority
UN	United Nations
UNESCO	United Nations Educational, Scientific and Cultural Organization
UNFPA	United Nations Population Fund
US / USA	United States of America
VCAT	Civil and Administrative Tribunal of Victoria
VE	voluntary euthanasia
Vic.	Victoria (Australia)
VLRC	Victorian Law Reform Commission
WA	Western Australia
WHO	World Health Organization

List of Chapter Contributors

Deryck Beyleveld, Professor of Law and Bioethics, School of Law, University of Durham, United Kingdom

Margot Brazier, Professor of Law, Centre for Social Ethics and Policy, School of Law, University of Manchester, United Kingdom

Roger Brownsword, Professor of Law, King's College London, and Honorary Professor of Law, University of Sheffield, United Kingdom

Tom Campbell, Professorial Fellow, Centre for Applied Philosophy and Public Ethics, Charles Stuart University, Canberra, Australia

Rebecca J. Cook, Professor Emerita and Co-Director, International Reproductive and Sexual Health Law Programme, University of Toronto, Canada

Bernard M. Dickens, Professor Emeritus of Health Law and Policy, Faculty of Law, Faculty of Medicine and Joint Centre for Bioethics, University of Toronto, Canada

Robin Downie, Emeritus Professor of Moral Philosophy, University of Glasgow, United Kingdom

Anne-Maree Farrell, Australian Research Council Future Fellow and Associate Professor, Faculty of Law, University of Monash, Australia

Marie Fox, Professor of Socio-legal Studies, School of Law, University of Birmingham, United Kingdom

Colin Gavaghan, Associate Professor, Director in Emerging Technologies, Faculty of Law, University of Otago, Dunedin, New Zealand

Vivienne Harpwood, Professor of Law, University of Cardiff, United Kingdom

John Harris, Sir David Alliance Professor of Bioethics, Director of the Institute of Science, Ethics and Innovation, University of Manchester, United Kingdom

Mark Henaghan, Professor and Dean of Law, University of Otago, Dunedin, New Zealand

Emily Jackson, Professor of Law, Department of Law, London School of Economics and Political Science, United Kingdom

Graeme T. Laurie, Professor of Medical Jurisprudence and Director of the JK Mason Institute for Medicine, Life Sciences and the Law, School of Law, University of Edinburgh, United Kingdom

J. Kenyon Mason, Emeritus Professor of Forensic Medicine, University of Edinburgh, United Kingdom

Jean V. McHale, Professor of Health Care Law, Director of the Centre for Health Law, Science and Policy, Birmingham Law School, United Kingdom

Christopher Newdick, Professor of Law, University of Reading, United Kingdom

Kenneth McK. Norrie, Professor of Law, University of Strathclyde, United Kingdom

Loane Skene, Professor of Law, Melbourne Law School, University of Melbourne, Australia

Foreword: In Celebration of the Life and Career of Sheila McLean

Lawrence O. Gostin

This festschrift celebrates the work and life of *Sheila Ann Manson McLean* – a towering figure in the United Kingdom and worldwide in law, ethics and health policy. What makes Sheila an extraordinary human being is her generosity of spirit – to family, friends and colleagues. What makes her extraordinary in her career is that she is a pioneer who literally formed the discipline that is variously called medical law, health law and, more broadly, bioethics and the law.

Sheila began work in this field before it even had a proper name, let alone a claim to be the leading legal discipline that it is today. From the late 1970s, she held a position in the University of Glasgow's Department of Forensic Medicine and Science, epitomising the early origins of the field as stemming from medico-legal analysis in civil or criminal law proceedings – sometimes also termed 'medical jurisprudence'. In this respect, Sheila has a common link with William J. Curran, the American Father of Health Law, who held the position of Frances Glessner Lee Professor of Legal Medicine at Harvard. On both sides of the Atlantic, the Mother and Father of modern health law were publishing innovative work, not only in law journals, but also in medical journals.

I think back to when I was a young activist and budding scholar at MIND (the National Association for Mental Health) in the late 1970s. I became friends with another young scholar working in the field of mental health law, Brenda Hoggett, now famously Baroness Hale of Richmond. Another close friend, Ian Kennedy, gave his seminal BBC Reith Lectures, *The Unmasking of Medicine*, in1981, commonly viewed as the first systematic treatment of the field. But it must be remembered that Sheila in the same year published her *tour de force*, *Legal Issues in Medicine* (Gower). This collection of powerful essays came to define the contours of the discipline. Her tome, *Medicine, Morals and the Law* (jointly with Gerry Maher; Gower) in 1983 influenced a generation of scholars in examining the critical features of the doctor-patient relationship – fundamental questions relating to consent and confidentiality.

Sheila took her doctorate in 1987, with her foundational treatise published as *The Patient's Right to Know* in 1989 (Ashgate). So began a career-long partnership with this publisher, with Sheila leading their medical series and international library to make Ashgate one of the foremost publishers in medical law and ethics globally.

And so Sheila launched a magnificent career spanning four decades of shaping a field. What is remarkable is that over that period, her work has continued to illuminate the most important issues of the day – ranging from criminology, juvenile justice and disability rights to xenotransplantation, human reproduction, the right to die and genomics. When scholars and policy makers think back to all the defining questions at the intersection of health, law and ethics, there is Sheila lighting the way. That is a remarkable legacy of influence and achievement.

In recognition of her towering academic stature, the University of Glasgow appointed Sheila as the inaugural International Bar Association Chair of Law and Ethics in Medicine, where she also directed the Institute of Law and Ethics in Medicine. She became only the second female professor in the venerable Glasgow Law School, appointed shortly after her dear friend Noreen Burrows in European Law. Sheila made it her mission to mentor young scholars, serving as a role model particularly for young women entering the field of law and medicine. Her dedication to students, especially to those taking doctorates at the University, is unparalleled. If one asked scholars in our field who influenced them most, it would most likely be Sheila – touching the academy through personal mentorship, being a role model, or simply by reading her prose.

At the same time, Sheila had deep connections to senior leaders in the field, notably Margot Brazier and Ken Mason – scholars whose perspectives were very different from her own, and yet with whom Sheila has fostered a life-long bond of friendship and deep mutual respect.

The academy, the health professions and government have all showered Sheila with honours, for example, her election as a Fellow of the Royal Society of Edinburgh and the Royal Society of Arts. She has acted as a legal advisor to the House of Commons Select Committee on Science and Technology and to a joint House of Lords/House of Commons Committee. Sheila has been appointed to chair commissions and advise at the highest levels. To mention but a few, she has held senior positions with respect to the Criminal Cases Review Commission (Scotland), the review of the Human Fertilisation and Embryology Authority Act (United Kingdom), the Working Party on Rationing and Health Care (*British Medical Journal*) and the Ethics of Clinical Trials (Department of Health). Internationally, she has served the World Health Organization, World Association for Medical Law and UNESCO, among others.

Although eminent institutions have bestowed Sheila with honours and the privilege of serving, and she has articulately shaped the public discourse through the media, she has remained grounded and humble – so characteristic of Sheila as a person. And although Sheila has walked on the world stage, she has always maintained her pride in and love for her home country of Scotland. From her graduation from Glasgow High School for Girls in 1968, to her education at the University of Glasgow (LLB with Honours, an MLitt. in the Faculty of Social Sciences, and a PhD in the Law School) through to her appointment of International Bar Association Professor, Sheila has led by example.

During the autumn of 2013, the University of Edinburgh (yes, she even soothed the historic rivalry between two of Scotland most eminent academic institutions) hosted a meeting of scholars to debate Sheila's life's work. I sat (mostly quietly) in awe, not merely because such eminent scholars were all vociferously debating her scholarship and the medical law field itself, but because of the grace, keen intelligence and humility of Sheila Ann Manson McLean, whom I am proud to call a dear friend and mentor.

Preface

As is befitting a collection of this nature – honouring the body of work of a distinguished scholar over her entire career – the majority of the contributions in this book offer a panoptic perspective of developments in the field in the 30 or more years that typically make up someone's working life. However, in the case of Sheila McLean this has been no easy task; and this is so for many diverse reasons. First, Sheila has been a pioneer in the truest sense of that word. The discipline of medical law simply did not exist when she began writing in the late 1970s about the importance of valid informed consent to medical treatment and a smattering of subjects loosely connected to the regulation of the doctor-patient relationship. Her first appointment to the University of Glasgow was not to the School of Law, but rather to the Forensic Medicine Unit where she taught for many years and introduced the first dedicated Honours degree programmes in the nascent field. As co-editors of this collection, it was our privilege to be among the early students who undertook that degree. For one of us, it was the principal reason for choosing to study at the University of Glasgow.

Sheila's early contributions were about bringing themes, and people, together. Her 1981 edited collection *Legal Issues in Medicine*[1] addressed a diverse range of topics, from 'collective responsibility in healthcare' to 'the expert witness', via 'live animal studies', 'ante-natal injuries' and 'artificial insemination', while her 1983 series of essays with Gerry Maher – *Medicine, Morals and the Law*[2] – began to take on the mantle of a textbook in medical law *and ethics*: the important qualifier that has always shaped her work since. Thus, while Sheila is first and foremost a lawyer, much of her discipline-shaping discourse has been about the crucial importance of using ethical reflection to guide and inform responsible legal and social practice. Many of the chapters in this festschrift serve as testament to this fact.

These chapters also confirm the challenge mentioned above about doing proper credit to Sheila McLean's work. Not only do they demonstrate, for example, the depth and breadth of her writings over the years – covering such topics as the beginning and end of life, autonomy, care and protection of the patient, and regulation of new and emerging technologies – but they illustrate too the incredible international reach of her influence. We are delighted to welcome contributions from several Anglo-American jurisdictions and to be able to provide accounts of both the temporal changes in the discipline and the comparative responses of legal systems to advances in medicine, patient rights and human social values.

The changes have been without precedent. Many of these are mapped in the chapters that follow. The broad arc that can be identified has become something of a caricature, but remains true just the same: it is the journey from paternalism to patient-focus; from protectionism to empowerment. And yet, a more nuanced reading of developments detailed in these chapters reveals the vital importance of McLean's message always to be alert to the importance of ethical reflection in legal evolution. The central questions have become more refined: not *whether* reproductive choices

1 Gower. Two of the contributors to that volume have also contributed to this festschrift.

2 Gower. Its contents were mirrored in many medico-legal books published thereafter: 'the sanctity of life', 'abortion', 'euthanasia', 'terminating treatment', 'consent', 'experimentation', 'sterilisation and contraception', 'negligence', 'confidentiality' and 'decision-making in medicine'.

should be respected and facilitated, but *which ones*; not *whether* patients should be informed, but *how far*; not *whether* new technologies should be promoted, but *how best to do so*; and not *whether* citizens should be allowed to choose when to die, but *how* to help them to *die well*.

We have, then, a collection of historical, international, comparative and wide-ranging discussions that embody Sheila's incredible contributions in each of these domains. As the above suggests, we have grouped these chapters into discrete themes that typify Sheila McLean's work: (i) beginning of life, (ii) care, (iii) liability, (iv) regulation and (v) end of life.

The collection begins, fittingly, with a chapter by Rebecca Cook and Bernard Dickens, fellow pioneers in the discipline, which maps and analyses developments in the international human rights' protection of reproductive health laws. This reflects Sheila's membership of the ethics committee of the International Federation of Gynecology and Obstetrics (2000–2006), and her many creative contributions to legal and related developments in this area.

Emily Jackson's contribution on 'DIY Abortion' then continues this developmental sweep by considering the downstream consequences of the Abortion Act 1967 and the advent of misoprostol, an abortifacient drug which can be purchased online from offshore 'pharmacies'. This chapter explores the very real challenges of attempting to regulate these practices against a legal framework that could never have imagined the advent of the internet. Far from endorsing the criminalisation approach that the 1967 Act embodies, Jackson argues for the need for more high quality information about the risks of self-medication, and provides a compelling public health reason for liberalising abortion laws.

It is in the field of reproductive health laws that we have seen most legislative activity over the last quarter century, and the United Kingdom has been a prescient test case in this regard, having passed the first such law in the world: the Human Fertilisation and Embryology Act 1990. This Act has been subject to profound changes since its initial iteration, and these are examined by Kenneth Norrie in his chapter on parentage and artificial human reproduction. His analysis considers the enduring notion of 'family' within the changing legislative frameworks, contrasted with shifting social attitudes, notably with respect to homosexual parents. The disjunct is palpable.

The section on 'Beginning of Life' is closed with a contribution from yet another pioneering pair: Margot Brazier and John Harris. Their chapter serves as a perfect bridge to our next section on 'Care', arguing that the legal fiction that a 'bright line' divides the fetus and the baby is a problematic, and increasingly unrealistic, position. This contribution from a lawyer and an ethicist again reflects McLean's message about the centrality of sound moral reflection in regulation: both with regard to technological developments that support increasing numbers of extremely premature infants, and the tenability of a legal rule that suffers under strict ethical scrutiny.

It is undoubtedly in the realm of 'Care' that Sheila McLean made her weightiest, initial mark in scholarship. Her doctoral thesis – *A Patient's Right to Know* – which became her first monograph,[3] argued cogently and convincingly that the long-standing paternalism of law and medical practice had to change. Current students of medical law might now see this as an argument that can be resigned to a textbook footnote, but this would be to ignore the enormity of the change that had to be brought about, against considerable institutional resistance, from courts and healthcare professionals alike. In their chapter on the changing nature of the doctor-patient relationship, Graeme Laurie and J. Kenyon Mason trace the changes that have since occurred, focusing on more recent developments that see the emergence of a new notion in law: the vulnerable autonomous adult. They examine whether this represents a swinging back of the pendulum, and whether it can be defended as the latest twist in the law and ethics of personal autonomy.

3 *A Patient's Right to Know: Information Disclosure, the Doctor and the Law*, Gower, 1995.

Loane Skene then examines what happens when autonomy fails completely, and when states are required to institute protective mechanisms that enable medical decisions to be made by third parties. While this does not mean, of course, that considerations of (prior) autonomy are entirely excluded, it does mean that the challenge of devising fair, transparent, effective and respectful frameworks is one of the most difficult in the medico-legal environment. Skene offers insights from recent Australian reforms, supported by empirical evidence of their effectiveness.

Robin Downie, a former colleague of Sheila McLean at the University of Glasgow, has been a stalwart philosophical collaborator on many of her edited collections and a fellow member of numerous national committees. His chapter draws on these experiences to examine disability and healthcare from a philosophical perspective. In doing so, he highlights the considerable challenge for law in embodying adequate protection against disability discrimination, fuelled by the signal failure to capture robust meanings of 'disability' in law. This is contrasted with medical and social models of disability, and the powerful argument is made that humane policies require not only effective cooperation between all social agencies involved, but also the support of informed public attitudes.

The public accountability dimension of medical law is picked up by Christopher Newdick in his chapter on making difficult decisions in healthcare resource allocation. Shifting the analysis from the purely patient perspective, Newdick offers a meso- and macro- level account of the ethical dilemmas facing systems managers, budget holders and ultimately government itself, in the provision of a public health service. In doing so, he argues for the need for a more inclusive, community-oriented ethical lens with which to view developments in, and provision of, health services.

Part III of this festschrift continues the theme of accountability, focusing on models of redress for patients when things go wrong and they are harmed as a result. It is a sad irony that in the 30 plus years of legal and ethical changes under discussion – which are typified by growing respect for, and recognition of, patients' rights – there has also been a parallel and worrying growth in the number of legal actions for compensation for liability for medical errors. The vagaries of the medical negligence action are well rehearsed in the literature, but a defining feature of Sheila McLean's contributions on the question of 'Liability' has been her work on no-fault compensation. This culminated in the 2011 report and recommendations of the *No Fault Compensation Review Group*,[4] produced under McLean's chairmanship, and which carefully examined the case for no-fault liability in Scotland. It contrasted abstract proposals for reform with concrete experiences elsewhere, notably in New Zealand and Sweden, and more recently in Wales for dealing with low value claims. The ultimate recommendation was in favour of a new scheme based on a modified version of the system operating in Sweden. This report serves as the backdrop for the two chapters considering liability in this volume, by Viv Harpwood and Anne Maree Farrell.

Viv Harpwood offers insights from the origins and earliest development of the Welsh model which attempts to embody the two key guiding principles of both providing appropriate financial compensation and supporting people in care back to the position they were in prior to injury. Albeit tentative, the chapter attempts to evaluate such a model, particularly in light of more recent failures as outlined in the Francis Inquiry Report in 2013 on events at Mid Staffordshire. As a complement to this, Anne Maree Farrell uses the 2011 McLean report as '… a useful and insightful springboard for exploring what principles should underpin the design and implementation of no-fault schemes for medical injury …'. She argues that while the aspiration is admirable and defensible, the actuation might be considerably more challenging, especially in light of experiences internationally.

4 Available here: http://www.scotland.gov.uk/Topics/Health/Policy/No-Fault-Compensation.

Part IV moves to the amplification of health services in new directions. In particular, the section on 'Regulation' focuses on new and emerging treatments and technologies. It begins with a chapter by Deryck Beyleveld and Roger Brownsword that examines the enduring importance of 'informedness' for participants in health-related research. In stark contrast to informed consent in the context of medical treatment – where information must be provided up-front and in advance of any intervention – Beyleveld and Brownsword address the importance of downstream duties of informing participants in research lest any clinically relevant findings subsequently emerge. In this highly topical field, and drawing on their own extensive writings supporting the ethics of Alan Gewirth, they argue that researchers have enduring responsibilities to keep participants informed.

Jean McHale's contribution on the acceptability of cosmetic surgery on children raises important questions about the priorities of our aesthetically self-conscious Western culture, and about the shifting sands of normalcy towards idealised notions of physical perfection. In terms of regulation, McHale asks why the United Kingdom has not yet seen fit to regulate in this area. Drawing on experiences in Australia where legislation has been passed, she offers an account of a range of regulatory options, including outright criminalisation. This is a very concrete illustration of a lawyer struggling with the dilemma of how to respond to a contemporary, ethically contentious issue.

Evidence exists in abundance in this volume of academic partnerships that have contributed extensively to the development of medical law. Jean McHale and Marie Fox are another example of this, and although they have not collaborated on a single piece on this occasion, their separate chapters nonetheless sit perfectly together. Thus, while McHale considers a regulation-free zone, Fox offers an historical insight into abortive and half-hearted attempts to regulate new technologies, using the case study of xenotransplantation in the UK. She teases out the symbiotic nature of the role of regulation and risk in informing debate and (in)action over the years, and ultimately suggests that the fears and concerns which once resulted in clarion calls for legal regulation in the 1990s – led by McLean in her controversial review of xenotransplantation for the Department of Health – might no longer be the most appropriate response to where this particular technology has reached in its development today.

In closing this section, Mark Henaghan from the University of Otago pays homage to another example of Sheila McLean's international contributions through her work on New Zealand's Human Genome Project. In a highly reflective piece on the nature and significance of McLean's role in shaping the New Zealand response, Henaghan offers yet more confirmation of the central commitment to ethics which Sheila's work embodies.

It is very difficult to do justice to Sheila McLean's contribution to the assisted dying debate over the years. This has been prodigious.[5] The debates, however, rage on, and an enduring feature is the international comparison. In the final section of this collection, 'End of Life', we illustrate this with two important contributions. Colin Gavaghan, another graduate from Sheila's programme and now a professor in New Zealand, asks important questions about the impact of mental health, and notably depression, on requests for assisted dying. Set against the literature on the nature of depression and our shifting understandings, Gavaghan argues strongly against allowing untested assumptions to cloud the issues, or the entitlement of all citizens to access assistance, where this has been provided for in law.

The final word is given to one of Sheila McLean's longest-standing colleagues, Tom Campbell. Sheila and Tom worked together from the time when Sheila was in the Forensic Medicine Unit,

5 See in particular: *Death, Dying, and the Law*, Dartmouth, 1996; *The Case for Physician-Assisted Suicide*, Pandora Press, 1997; *Assisted Dying: Reflections on the Need for Law Reform*, Routledge Cavendish, 2007.

and they co-edited (with David Goldberg and Tom Mullen) the seminal collection *Human Rights: From Rhetoric to Reality*.[6] It is apt, then, that in this final contribution Tom considers some of the philosophical aspects of Sheila's assessment of the ethical issues at stake in assisting others to die in a manner and at a time of their own choosing. While this chapter questions aspects of Sheila's autonomy-based moral justifications for a permissive approach to assisted dying – arguing that justifications for change ought to focus primarily on the relief of suffering and only secondarily on the ethical importance of autonomy with respect to assisted dying – it ultimately concurs with the recommendations Sheila has advocated for many years for reform of the requisite legal procedures.

We are very grateful for the research assistance provided by David Ford, and to Jonathan Hoare for his editorial work, in the preparation of this book. We also wish to thank the School of Law, University of Edinburgh, for its support in funding a workshop and dinner in September 2013 that allowed us to bring contributors together to discuss and refine their chapters. It was an honour that Sheila McLean was able to join us. It is a privilege that we deliver this festschrift in her name.

Pamela Ferguson and Graeme Laurie
30 September 2014

6 Blackwell, 1986.

PART I
Issues at the Beginning of Life

Chapter 1
Reproductive Health and the Law

Rebecca J. Cook and Bernard M. Dickens

Introduction

The chapters contributed to this book in tribute to Sheila McLean show how widely, indeed comprehensively, her scholarship and career have spanned and enriched the field at first modestly known as medical law, now often more ambitiously described as health law and policy. Sheila's career vindicates this description, since she has not only advanced legal scholarship through her own writing and in sponsoring and inspiring writing by others, but has also contributed to national governmental, Scottish governmental and international and non-governmental organiation policy-making and advisory agencies. The books she has written, edited and to which she has contributed chapters cover the spectrum of human life, from assisted reproduction to end-of-life care, from choosing children to assisted suicide, and many areas of concern in between, both immediate, such as the right to life, and more prospective, such as xenotransplantation. In this chapter, we draw upon Sheila's contributions to the advance of reproductive health law and policy, and the integration of modern perceptions of bioethics. There are different explanations of the rise of bioethics,[1] but an observer of and participant in this rise, Warren Reich, has recorded that:

> Fertility control was the major issue that spawned bioethics, more than any other single issue – certainly more than any high-technology-related issue in medicine. It was an issue that directly affected hundreds of millions of people; it dealt with quintessentially human suffering and fulfillment ... involving ethical, religious, legal, and social controversy on the levels of social policy as well as personal ethics and ecclesiastical authority. The theologians, who were the first ethicists working in bioethics, cut their teeth on contraception/sterilization and abortion debates; and in a very real sense, much of the great energy that was turned toward bioethics around 1970/71 was energy that was diverted from the then-increasingly futile [Roman Catholic] church debates on fertility control.[2]

From 2000 to 2006, Sheila was a member, among many other activities, of the Committee for the Study of Ethical Aspects of Human Reproduction and Women's Health (The Ethics Committee) of the International Federation of Gynaecology and Obstetrics (FIGO). One of us (RJC) was a founding member of this committee in 1985, serving until 1994, and the other joined the Committee in 2003, and will chair it from 2009 to 2015. As predecessors to, colleagues in, and inheritors of Sheila's contributions to the Committee's work, we want to reflect on how this aspect of her scholarship and guidance illuminates the challenges and prospects for advancement in the reproductive health of populations in general, and of women in particular.

---

1 Jonsen, A., *The Birth of Bioethics*, New York, Oxford University Press, 1998.

2 Reich, W.T., 'The Wider View: André Helleger's Passionate, Integrating Intellect and the Creation of Bioethics' (1999) 9 *Kennedy Institute of Ethics Journal*, 25–51, at p. 37.

The field has been energised not only by Sheila's intellect, analytical rigor and wisdom, but also by her adventurous and vivacious personality. One of us (BMD) will long retain the memory, following an unusually exotic November 2005 FIGO Ethics Committee meeting in Luxor, Egypt, of driving with her into the Valley of the Kings and entering the tomb of Tutankhamen just hours after concluding ethical recommendations on confidentiality and privacy, human cloning and embryo research. This juxtaposition of consideration of a classical past, the pressing present and what may come in the future is an epitome of Sheila's career in health law and policy.

International Recognition of Human Rights to Reproductive Health

The United Nations (UN) International Covenant on Economic, Social and Cultural Rights (ICESCR), a leading human rights instrument, provides in Article 12(1) that parties to the Covenant shall 'recognize the right of everyone to the enjoyment of the highest attainable standard of physical and mental health'. Clause 2(d) requires parties' commitment to 'creation of conditions which would assure to all medical services and medical attention in the event of sickness'. The World Health Organization (WHO) understands 'health' to encompass 'physical, mental and social well-being and not merely the absence of disease or infirmity',[3] but clause 2(d) concerns only medical services and attention. The WHO Constitution observes that '(t)he enjoyment of the highest attainable standard of health is one of the fundamental rights of every human being without distinction of race, religion, political belief, economic or social condition',[4] but, drafted in 1946, the observation did not specify distinction of sex, gender or sexual orientation. Reproductive health is of particular concern to women, however, and the UN Convention on the Elimination of All Forms of Discrimination against Women (the Women's Convention) accordingly provides in Article 12(1) that: 'States Parties shall take all appropriate measures to eliminate discrimination against women in the field of health care in order to ensure, on a basis of equality of men and women, access to health care services, including those related to family planning'.[5] Women's related claims to reproductive rights and reproductive health have become controversial, and bitterly contested, particularly by conservative religious hierarchies and agencies. The Roman Catholic Church, through its unified, singular leadership, has been most outspoken in its condemnation of the concept of 'reproductive health', and opposed the Convention's adoption first at the UN Conference on Population and Development, held in Cairo in 1994, and again at the Fourth World Congress on Women, held in 1995 in Beijing. The Catholic hierarchy, of course, excludes women, but the Holy See, having Permanent Observer status in the UN, is entitled to attend UN meetings, and had the largest delegation at the Beijing Congress. The concept of reproductive health, modelled on the description of 'health' in the WHO Constitution, describes 'reproductive health' as:

> a state of complete physical, mental and social well-being and not merely the absence of disease or infirmity, in all matters relating to the reproductive system and to its functions and processes. Reproductive health therefore implies that people are able to have a satisfying and safe sex life and that they have the capability to reproduce and the freedom to decide if, when and how often to do so.[6]

3 World Health Organization, 1946, preamble to Constitution, para. 1.

4 World Health Organization, 1946.

5 Cook, R.J. and Undurraga, V., 'Article 12' in Freeman, M.A., Chinkin, C. and Rudolf, B. (eds) *The UN Convention on the Elimination of All Forms of Discrimination against Women: A Commentary*, Oxford, Oxford University Press, 2012, pp. 322–3.

6 United Nations Department of Public Information, *Platform for Action and Beijing Declaration*, Fourth World Conference on Women, New York, United Nations, 1995, para. 94. For background, see Cook,

Catholic church leaders, having renounced a 'sex life' of their own and tolerating one for others only within lawful marriage for the purpose of procreation, were actively hostile to the Beijing Declaration in its continuing explanation that:

> Implicit in this last condition are the right of men and women to be informed and to have access to safe, effective, affordable and acceptable methods of family planning of their choice, as well as other methods of their choice for regulation of fertility which are not against the law ....[7]

The reference to family planning has long been understood to embrace contraception and contraceptive sterilisation, but opponents of family planning often seek to add stigma by extending the reference to cover abortion, so that, for instance, family planning centres, such as Planned Parenthood affiliates in the USA, can be condemned, restricted or defunded, and picketed as abortion clinics. However, the Beijing Declaration rejected abortion as a method of family planning. The Declaration included abortion in the subsequent phrase 'other methods ... for regulation of fertility', emphasising their acceptability only when 'not against the law'.

In recent times, family planning has emerged from the negative context of fertility control through contraception and sterilisation to include fertility promotion. In the past, this referred to fertility preservation, but now includes the varieties of overcoming infertility subsumed under the generic description of 'test tube' or *in vitro* fertilisation (IVF). Forms of IVF are now widely available, although often at high individual cost, as a branch of 'luxury medicine', since publicly and privately funded health insurance services may not follow the WHO in characterising infertility as a disease.[8] In 2000, the Constitutional Chamber of the Supreme Court of Costa Rica ruled IVF constitutionally prohibited in the country for violation of an embryo's human right to life from conception, with which fertilisation was assumed to be synonymous, due to the tendency of IVF techniques to leave surplus embryos naturally to disintegrate when not transferred to women's bodies. The prohibition was challenged before the Inter-American Court of Human Rights for violations of the American Convention on Human Rights. The Court's judgment was released in November 2012.[9]

The Court distinguished 'fertilisation' from 'conception', and observed that 'the term "conception" cannot be understood as a moment or process exclusive of a woman's body, given that an embryo has no chance of survival if implantation does not occur'.[10] The Court rejected the claim that 'fertilisation' is included in a reference to 'conception', since the latter is dependent on an embryo's implantation *in utero*, while the former is not. In an extensive review of the jurisprudence of the European Court of Human Rights, the Court noted that 'the regulatory trends in international law do not lead to the conclusion that the embryo should be treated in the same way as a person, or that it has a right to life'.[11] This accorded with the Court's earlier finding that 'the historic and

R.J., Dickens, B.M. and Fathalla, M.F., *Reproductive Health and Human Rights: Integrating Medicine, Ethics and Law*, Oxford, Clarendon Press, 2003, pp. 11–13.

7 *Platform for Action and Beijing Declaration*, note 6, above.

8 See World Health Organization, 'The International Committee for Monitoring Assisted Reproductive Technology (ICMART) and the World Health Organization (WHO) Revised Glossary on ART Terminology' (2009) 24 *Human Reproduction*, 2683–7, at p. 2686.

9 *Artavia Murillo et al. v. Costa Rica*, Inter-Am Ct HR (ser. C) no. 257 (Nov. 28, 2012).

10 *Artavia Murillo*, note 9, above, para. 187.

11 *Artavia Murillo*, note 9, above, para. 253.

systematic interpretation of precedents that exist in the inter-American system confirms that it is not admissible to grant the status of person to the embryo'.[12]

The Court ruled that denying infertile couples access to IVF in order to protect un-implanted embryos, in violation of individuals' human rights to private and family life, and to found and raise families, was disproportionate and unjustified. The Court further found that denial constituted indirect discrimination on grounds of disability and financial means, since those with means could obtain IVF services by travel to other countries, and in particular that it constituted indirect discrimination in effect against women, since the burden of childlessness falls with distinctive impact upon women. The Court shared the view of WHO that 'the role and status of women in society should not be defined solely by their reproductive capacity',[13] and found discriminatory gender stereotyping incompatible with international human rights law.[14] It accepted the evidence of social science, however, that, particularly in Latin America, women outside convent life not discharging duties of motherhood attract some disdain and loss of esteem in family and communal life.

The European Court of Human Rights' (ECtHR) denial of status and rights to human embryonic life is confirmed in its protection of rights to refuse non-consensual parenthood. In the *Evans* case,[15] for instance, one former partner in a couple that had preserved embryos from IVF treatment refused consent to their transfer to the other former partner, although they represented the latter's only chance to have her own genetically-related child due to removal of her ovaries for a precancerous condition. The ECtHR upheld UK legislation requiring gamete donors' consent to embryo transfer, and the consequent wastage of the embryos. The issue of what legal status *in vitro* embryos possess, since they are not 'persons', had been timorously approached in 1992 by the Tennessee Supreme Court,[16] reversing a trial judge who had described an embryo as 'a human being existing as an embryo, *in vitro*', by saying that it was neither a person nor property, but *sui generis*, in an 'interim category' over which there were interests 'in the nature of ownership'. More recently, however, courts have accepted that *in vitro* embryos are a species of legal property,[17] leading to issues of their disposition for instance upon divorce.[18]

The loss or wastage of human embryos is an inescapable incident of individuals' exercise of their human rights to natural reproduction, the loss being quite accurately calculable in IVF. An expert witness before the Inter-American Court of Human Rights estimated '[o]f every 10 embryos spontaneously generated in the human species, no more than 2 or 3 are able to survive natural selection and be born as a person. The remaining 7 or 8 embryos die in the female genital tract, generally without the parents' knowledge'.[19] More significant from a human rights perspective is the rate of avoidable pregnancy-related maternal death and morbidity associated with denial of women's rights to reproductive health.

---

12 *Artavia Murillo*, note 9, above, para. 223.

13 *Artavia Murillo*, note 9, above, para. 296.

14 See Cook, R.J. and Cusack, S., *Gender Stereotyping: Transnational Legal Perspectives*, Philadelphia, PA, University of Pennsylvania Press, 2010.

15 *Evans v. United Kingdom* (2007) ECHR 266, (2008) 46 EHRR 34.

16 *Davis v. Davis*, 842 SW 2d 588 (Tenn Sup Ct, 1992), 842 SW2d 588 (Tenn 1992).

17 See Dickens, B.M. and Cook, R.J., 'The Legal Status of In Vitro Embryos' (2010) 111 *International Journal of Gynecology and Obstetrics*, 91–4.

18 Flannery, M.T., '"Rethinking" Embryo Disposition upon Divorce' (2013) 29 *Journal of Contemporary Health Law and Policy*, 233–82.

19 *Artavia Murillo*, note 9, above, at para. 310.

The estimated rate of maternal deaths worldwide, meaning a woman's death while pregnant or within 42 days of termination of pregnancy, by whatever means,[20] fell to 273,465 in 2011[21] from about 358,000 in 2009.[22] Satisfaction is undermined, however, by recognition of the high proportion of deaths that were avoidable had countries met the responsibilities they have assumed under international human rights conventions, and their own national constitutional and domestic laws, regarding provision of maternal and related reproductive health services.[23] Associated with maternal mortality are deaths of newborns, infants and dependent children.

Underlying many causes of maternal mortality and morbidity is discrimination against women, from their births and throughout their reproductive lives. The UN Human Rights Council has recognised preventable maternal mortality and morbidity as a human rights violation,[24] and in response to its request, the UN High Commissioner for Human Rights has prepared guidelines on applying human rights to reduce preventable maternal deaths and morbidity.[25] Direct causes of these dysfunctions of pregnancy include haemorrhage, infection, high blood pressure, unsafe abortion (frequently associated with illegality) and obstructed labour, which collectively account for an estimated 80 per cent of maternal deaths worldwide, overwhelmingly in resource-poor countries.[26] Indirect causes include malaria, anaemia and HIV/AIDS that complicate or are aggravated by pregnancy, which contribute to the remaining 20 per cent.[27] Further, incentives to promote the welfare of children that hospital administrators intend to be born rather than miscarried may deny women the care they require while pregnant.[28]

Discrimination against female children and women that conditions their vulnerability to maternal mortality and morbidity was long considered so culturally ingrained as to be not just a characteristic but rather a prerequisite of social order. Discrimination was non-justiciable, not least because male-dominated legal systems were at best unaware of or insensitive to such discrimination, and at worst perpetuated or reinforced the discrimination.[29] In recent times, however, courts and

20 Porta, M., Greenland, S. and Last J.M. (eds), *A Dictionary of Epidemiology*, 5th edn, Oxford, Oxford University Press, 2008, pp. 148–9.

21 Lozano, R., Wong, H., Foreman, K.J. et al., 'Progress Towards Millennium Development Goals 4 and 5 on Maternal and Child Mortality: An Updated Systematic Analysis' (2011) 378(9797) *The Lancet*, 1139–65.

22 WHO, UNICEF, UNFPA, The World Bank, *Trends in Maternal Mortality: 1990–2008*, Geneva, WHO, 2010.

23 Cook, R.J. and Dickens, B.M., 'Upholding Pregnant Women's Right to Life' (2012) 117 *International Journal of Gynecology and Obstetrics*, 90–94.

24 G.A. Res. 11/8, UN, HRC, 11th Sess., Preventable Maternal Mortality and Morbidity and Human Rights. UNDoc.A/HRC/11/L.16/Rev.1 (June 16, 2009).

25 United Nations, Human Rights Council, 20th session, *Technical Guidance on the Application of a Human-rights Based Approach to the Implementation of Policies and Programmes to Reduce Preventable Maternal Morbidity and Mortality*, A/HRC/21/22, 2 July 2012; see Yamin, A.E., 'Applying Human Rights to Maternal Health: UN Technical Guidance on Rights-based Approaches' (2013) 121 *International Journal of Gynecology and Obstetrics*, 190–93.

26 Khan, K.S., Wojdyla, D., Say, L. et al., 'WHO Analysis of Causes of Maternal Deaths: A Systematic Review' (2006) 367(9516) *The Lancet*, 1066–74.

27 Shaw, D. and Cook, R.J., 'Applying Human Rights to Improve Access to Reproductive Health Services' (2012) 119 *International Journal of Gynecology and Obstetrics*, S55–9.

28 Freedman, L.R. and Stulberg, D.B., 'Conflicts in Care for Obstetric Complications in Catholic Hospitals' (2013) 4 *American Journal of Bioethics (AJOB) Primary Research*, 1–10.

29 Rhode, D.L., *Justice and Gender: Sex Discrimination and the Law*, Cambridge, MA, Harvard University Press, 1989.

human rights tribunals have been seized with claims of human rights violations due to gender discrimination. Pioneering claims were brought by empowered women who suffered employment discrimination due to demeaning workplace stereotypes and mind-sets,[30] but more recently claims have been presented by and on behalf of women marginalised by poverty and/or minority status in their communities who have suffered discrimination in access to reproductive healthcare.

For instance in 2010, the Inter-American Court of Human Rights, addressing multiple claims of violations of the American Convention on Human Rights presented by an indigenous community in Paraguay, held the state responsible for an avoidable maternal death, observing:

> [T]he Court declares that the State violated the right [to life] provided in Article 4(1) of the American Convention … because it failed to take the required positive measures … within its powers, that could reasonably be expected to prevent or to avoid the risk to the right to life. Consequently, the death of the following individuals are attributable to the State … Remigia Ruiz … who died from complications while in labor in 2005, at 38 years of age, and did not receive medical attention.[31]

This finding represents the first time that this Court has held a state responsible for a preventable maternal death. The Court ordered the defendant state to provide special medical care for pregnant women both pre- and post-natally.

In 2011, the first decision of an international human rights treaty-monitoring tribunal was written holding a state and government accountable for a preventable maternal death. The Committee on the Elimination of Discrimination against Women (CEDAW), monitoring compliance with the Women's Convention, found Brazil in violation of a woman's right to appropriate services in connection with pregnancy, confinement and the post-natal period, and liable for discrimination in her accessing care. In the *Alyne* case,[32] an impoverished Brazilian national of African descent, aged 28, died following the stillbirth of an estimated 27-week-old fetus. On 11 November 2002, in her sixth recorded month of pregnancy, she was treated for severe nausea and abdominal pain at a private clinic, and scheduled for blood and urine analysis two days later. However, her condition worsened, and on 13 November, when no fetal heartbeat was detected, the stillbirth was medically induced, and Alyne became disorientated. On the following day, when curettage surgery removed remaining placental tissues, she further deteriorated, with severe haemorrhaging and low blood pressure, and on 15 November, doctors at the clinic proposed to transfer her to a better-equipped public hospital. That hospital, however, refused to use its only ambulance in the evening to transport her, and her family lacked means to provide private transport, such as by taxi. Alyne waited eight hours, in a critical condition, the last two with symptoms of coma, before reaching the public hospital. There, she became hypothermic, had acute respiratory distress with intravascular coagulation, and was resuscitated when her blood pressure fell to zero. No bed was available for her, and she was placed in the emergency room hallway. Her medical records had not been transferred with her, so the treating physician was given a brief oral account of her symptoms. Alyne died the following day, the official cause of death being recorded as internal bleeding.

CEDAW measured the circumstances of the death against the standards not of medical practice, but of human rights, and took account not just of Alyne's hospital care, but also of the social conditions in which she lived, and died. The Committee also noted that Alyne's family filed a civil

30 Cook and Cusack, note 14, above.

31 *Xakmok Kasek Indigenous Community v. Paraguay*, Inter-Am Ct HR (ser C) no. 214 (Aug. 24, 2010), at para. 234.

32 *Alyne da Silva Pimentel Teixeira (deceased) v. Brazil*, CEDAW/C/49/D/17/008, August 10, 2011.

claim in court for material and moral damages in February 2003, three months after her death, but the claim was either ignored or denied by the time the case came for decision by the Committee, eight and a half years later. The Committee found that, as a matter of law, Brazil was directly responsible for:

a. its failure to monitor private healthcare institutions to which medical services were outsourced;
b. the failure to meet Alyne's specific, distinctive health needs during her pregnancy;
c. failure to address her status as a woman of African descent and her poor socio-economic circumstances; and
d. failure to comply with state obligations to ensure effective judicial action and protection for her or posthumously on her behalf.[33]

In Brazil, the state's responsibility regarding both public and private healthcare institutions is strongly anchored in its Constitution, which professes the right to health as a general human right. The Committee found that the State's failures to take measures to ensure appropriate pregnancy services violated rights to non-discrimination, on grounds of sex, racial origin and poor economic status, and the cumulative failures of Alyne's care finally violated her human right to life itself. Brazil did not contest many of CEDAW's findings of lack of appropriate pregnancy-related care, and accepted the Committee's requirements of detailed remedies to reduce preventable maternal deaths. It remains to be seen whether the CEDAW findings of human rights violations and of remedies required for reform, in Brazil and other countries whose compliance with the Women's Convention CEDAW monitors, will prove effective to promote women's pregnancy care and wider reproductive healthcare.[34]

Fertility Regulation

The exercise of individuals' choice over their reproduction has historically been impaired by the sexual nature of reproduction, and cultural tendencies, reinforced if not more directly conditioned by religious attitudes, to see human sexuality through the lens of sin. In the nineteenth century, sending birth-control information by mail offended obscenity laws, and promotion of contraception was imprisonable.[35] To approach reproduction as a matter of personal choice rather than divine will or intention was seen as an impertinent human arrogation of supernatural design, and courts have been reluctant to treat medical negligence resulting in the birth of a healthy child as other than a blessing.[36] The jurisprudence and academic commentary[37] associated with the House of

33 *Alyne da Silva Pimentel Teixeira*, note 32, above, at paras 7.5–7.8.

34 Cook, R.J., 'Human Rights and Maternal Health: Exploring the Effectiveness of the Alyne Decision' (2013) 41 *Journal of Law, Medicine and Ethics*, 103–23.

35 Williams, G., *The Sanctity of Life and the Criminal Law*, London, Faber and Faber, 1958, ch. 2.

36 Ranous, J.S. and Sherrin, J.J., 'Busting the Blessing Balloon: Liability for the Birth of an Unplanned Child' (1975) 39 *Albany Law Review*, 221–51.

37 See, for example, Mason, J.K. and Laurie, G.T., *Mason and McCall Smith's Law and Medical Ethics*, 9th edn, Oxford, Oxford University Press, 2013, paras 10.20 et seq; Mason, J.K., *The Troubled Pregnancy: Legal Wrongs and Rights in Pregnancy*, Cambridge, Cambridge University Press, 2007, pp. 152–87; Morris, A. and Saintier, S., 'To Be or Not To Be: Is That the Question? Wrongful Life and Misconceptions' (2003) 11 *Medical Law Review*, 167–93.

Lords' 2002 decision in *McFarlane v. Tayside Health Board*[38] reflects moral discomfort in assessing compensation for a couple's unplanned parenthood when they intended to engage in non-procreative sex.

The legality of providing and acquiring contraceptive services has become relatively non-contentious in industrially-developed countries in recent years, although still controversial where restrictive professional, religious and other arguments are socially and/or politically influential.[39] An internationally publicised instance of such influence was the ban on artificial contraception initiated in 2000 by the mayor of Manila, in the Philippines,[40] and more recently in the USA the requirement of contraceptive coverage in health insurance plans under the Patient Protection and Affordable Care Act, from which religious employers were exempted, has triggered litigation by for-profit commercial employers not wanting to provide health services contrary to their personal religious convictions.[41]

Related concerns include sex-education in schools, age-eligibility to receive contraceptive prescriptions, and public provision of or subsidies for contraceptive products. In international human rights conventions, there are no explicit requirements to ensure services to members of low-income populations. Under the Women's Convention, for instance, states accept the obligation, in accordance with Article 12(1), 'to ensure … access to health care services, including those related to family planning', but such access may remain dependent on having the means to pay for them. State provision of unpaid services is limited, under Article 12(2), to 'ensure to women appropriate services in connection with pregnancy, confinement and the post-natal period, granting free services where necessary'. Although limited, this requirement may include post-natal contraception, which may be desirable for birth-spacing between pregnancies. Short birth intervals endanger survival of women, their subsequent fetuses *in utero* and their newborn children.[42]

Long-acting contraceptive means, such as intrauterine, injectable or implantable contraception, are convenient for women who know how to adjust to their use, but raise legal and ethical concerns. Safe removal at times of patients' choices may be unassured in some settings, and contraception by injectable or implanted means can be operator-controlled rather than patient-controlled. That is, they may be applied at the preference of care-givers, for instance for mentally-disabled women or those unable to resist superiors' pressure, rather than by recipients' free choice. They raise a range of legal concerns regarding informed consent, free consent (meaning non-coerced and not improperly induced consent), and capacity to consent or to give assent, by those who lack capacities to give legally effective consent.

In view of women's liability to menopause, usually in their 50s, long-acting contraception can merge into sterilisation, which has raised its own historical controversies,[43] and remains an active

38 *McFarlane v. Tayside Health Board* [2002] 2 AC 59 (HL).

39 Campbell, M., Sahin-Hodoglugil, N.N. and Potts, M., 'Barriers to Fertility Regulation: A Review of the Literature' (2006) 37 *Studies in Family Planning*, 87–98.

40 Manila City Executive Order no.003, 2000 (Mayor Atienza). See *Imposing Misery: The Impact of Manila's Contraceptive Ban on Women and Families*, Center for Reproductive Rights, 2007, available at: http://www2.ohchr.org/english/bodies/hrc/docs/ngos/CRR_AnnexIPhilippines104.pdf (accessed 13 January 2015).

41 The more than 50 lawsuits, led by *Hobby Lobby v. Sebelius*, 870 F Supp 2d 1278 (WD Okla 2012), are discussed in Sepper, E., *Contraception and the Birth of Corporate Conscience*, Washington University in St. Louis School of Law Legal Studies Research Paper No.13-07-01, July 2013.

42 WHO, *Report of a WHO Technical Consultation on Birth Spacing*, WHO/RHR/07.1, Geneva, WHO, 2007.

43 Williams, note 35, above, ch. 3.

focus of human rights litigation in modern times, particularly in Europe.[44] For instance, until the 1970s there was evidence of coercive sterilisation of disabled women in Scandinavian countries.[45] In November 2012, the ECtHR found Slovakia in violation of the European Convention on Human Rights (ECHR) Articles 3 (prohibition of inhuman or degrading treatment) and 8 (right to respect for private and family life) for the involuntary sterilisation of Roma women,[46] the last in a sequence of three cases before the Court on the same topic. In 2009, the Czech government expressed regret regarding illegal sterilisation, largely of Roma women.[47] It is depressing that it is taking so long to end the wave of oppressive eugenic policies that spread across the industrialised world and beyond in the 1920s,[48] now seen through the lens of experience of Nazi racial laws and practice.[49] However, the notorious 1927 judgment of the US Supreme Court in *Buck v. Bell*[50] has not been overruled, and shame is muted in the US and Canada that this judgment and related laws allowing eugenic sterilisations without patients' consent were cited at the Nuremberg War Crimes Tribunal in explanation and defence of German practice.[51]

Attitudes have now evolved to recognise the distinction between sterilisations performed *on* individuals, and those performed *for* patients. The former, often undertaken for punitive or eugenic reasons, are acknowledged to be, and to have been, wrong. In 1996, for instance, the Canadian provincial government of Alberta, when sued for an unlawful sterilisation performed in 1959, accepted the mental competency of the woman sterilised as mentally impaired, acknowledged the human rights violation under its historical laws that authorised the procedure, admitted legal liability, waived an available full defence that the claim was outside the limitation period, and litigated only on the quantum of damages. The judge denied punitive damages, observing that the claim 'was made too late, and the government could have used this delay as a complete answer … This deliberate abandonment of a complete defence is in the nature of an apology. Indeed, it is more than an apology; it is an amendment – a real effort to make things right'.[52]

In contrast to eugenic sterilisations are contraceptive procedures, including vasectomies, that may be performed for patients, on their competent, free and adequately informed consent. Failures of due disclosure, resulting in pregnancy or childbirth, lead to as much litigation as failures to perform procedures in accordance with legally required standards of care. Much legal literature now addresses claims variously described as wrongful conception, wrongful birth and even claims by or on behalf of usually seriously impaired children for wrongful life itself.[53] Sheila McLean

---

44 Zampas, C. and Lamačková, A., 'Forced and Coerced Sterilization of Women in Europe' (2011) 114 *International Journal of Gynecology and Obstetrics*, 163–6.

45 Broberg, G. and Roll-Hansen, N., *Eugenics and the Welfare State: Sterilization Policy in Denmark, Sweden, Norway and Finland*, East Lansing, MI, Michigan State University Press, 1996.

46 *I.G. and Others v. Slovakia* [2012] App. No. 15966/04 (ECHR, Final [2013]).

47 Resolution of the Government of the Czech Republic 1424, 29 November 2009.

48 Kevles, D.J., *In the Name of Eugenics: Genetics and the Uses of Human Heredity*, Berkeley, CA, University of California Press, 1986.

49 Burleigh, M. and Wippermann, W., *The Racial State: Germany 1933–1945*, Cambridge, Cambridge University Press, 1991.

50 *Buck v. Bell*, 274 US 200 (1927).

51 Bruinius, H., *Better for All the World: The Secret History of Forced Sterilization and America's Quest for Racial Purity*, New York, Vintage Books, 2007.

52 *Muir v. Alberta* (1996) 132 DLR (4th) 695 (Can Alta QB), at 735, para. 153.

53 See for example Mason, J.K., *Medico-Legal Aspects of Reproduction and Parenthood*, 2nd edn, Aldershot, Ashgate/Dartmouth, 1998; Mason (2007), note 37, above.

has addressed many issues in this area in journal articles[54] and edited books.[55] Informed consent issues include disclosure of irreducible minimum rates of failure, such as from spontaneous recanalisation of severed fallopian tubes, and times following vasectomy before which intercourse may still transfer motile sperm.

Most legal systems, not only in economically-developed or industrialised countries, have developed jurisprudence on wrongful conception and wrongful birth claims, including the standard tort issues of duty of care, breach of duty, identification and causation of damage and quantification of damage. Most intellectually challenging, however, not only for lawyers but also for philosophers, bioethicists, healthcare practitioners, theologians and others, is the so-called 'wrongful life' action. This may be the description given, and, often by plaintiffs, resisted,[56] when a claim is presented by or on behalf of a person, often a young, severely impaired child, that he or she should not have been allowed to be conceived or, having been conceived, should not have been allowed to be brought to term and born; that is, that he or she should have been aborted. This claim sometimes implies that another person should have been born instead, such as that conception should have been advised to be delayed while the mother carried a temporary transmissible infection.

Apart from a sometimes judicially expressed visceral repugnance that such claims may induce,[57] they raise the complex issue of whether the difference between impaired existence and 'the utter void of nonexistence'[58] can be quantified in monetary terms. With a few exceptions, courts are inclined to dismiss these actions.[59] Even if some measure of perhaps token, representative or non-quantified damages might be awarded, it may be that, as Proctor J ruled, '[s]ubstantial policy reasons prevent [a court] from allowing tort damages for denial of the opportunity to take an embryonic life'.[60] Nevertheless, challenging arguments may be raised in debate,[61] and new perspectives may be offered on how wrongful life claims are best approached,[62] including from outside the Common Law tradition, since the full Chamber of the French Cour de Cassation has allowed a child's wrongful life claim to succeed.[63]

It is difficult if not impossible to disengage responses to wrongful life claims from responses to induced abortion. Although laws on this topic may become relatively settled, powerful forces are committed in many countries to reforming them in favour of their own preferences, either to accommodate women's resort to procedures more liberally or to restrict access more severely. Many legal texts have been produced on abortion, and will continue to be produced,[64] as either

---

54 See for example McLean, S.A.M. and Ramsey, J., 'Human Rights, Reproductive Freedom, Medicine and the Law' (2002) 5 *Medical Law International*, 239–58.

55 McLean, S.A.M. (ed.), *Legal Issues in Human Reproduction*, London, Gower Medico-Legal Series, 1989.

56 See *Cherry v. Borsman* (1992) 94 DLR (4th) 487 (Can BC CA), where the plaintiff successfully resisted a defence argument of a wrongful life action.

57 Perhaps in *Gleitman v. Cosgrove*, 227 A 2d 689 (NJ Sup Ct, 1967), reversed in *Procanik v. Cillo*, 478 A 2d 755 (NJ Sup Ct, 1984).

58 *Gleitman*, note 57, above, at 692.

59 See generally *McKay v. Essex Area Health Authority* [1982] QB 1166.

60 *Gleitman*, note 57, above, at 693.

61 Dickens, B.M., 'Wrongful Birth and Life, Wrongful Death Before Birth, and Wrongful Law' in McLean, note 55, above, pp. 80–112.

62 Burns, T.A., 'When Life Is an Injury: An Economic Approach to Wrongful Life Lawsuits' (2003) 52 *Duke Law Journal*, 807–39.

63 Callus, T., '"Wrongful Life" à la Française' (2001) 5 *Medical Law International*, 117–25.

64 See Cook, R.J., Erdman, J.N. and Dickens, B.M., *Abortion Law in Transnational Perspective: Cases and Controversies*, Philadelphia, PA, University of Pennsylvania Press, 2014.

objective analysis or partisan advocacy, and different orientations may be accepted as self-evidently appropriate. In the UK, for instance, lawful abortion is taken to be best regulated through physicians' assessments of whether legislated criteria are satisfied,[65] whereas the largely comparable society of Canada sees the matter centrally to involve women's own life plans. The Chief Justice of Canada, in a majority judgment finding the Criminal Code provisions on abortion unconstitutional and therefore inoperative, observed: '[f]orcing a woman, by threat of criminal sanctions, to carry a fetus to term unless she meets certain criteria unrelated to her own priorities and aspirations, is a profound interference with a woman's body and thus an infringement of security of the person'.[66] In the USA, abortion politics have exerted such a colonising effect on so many at most indirectly related areas of law that an English court considering the legality of emergency contraception rejected arguments based on US abortion-linked judgments as of no relevance.[67]

Politics and religion come together in the USA in harmony on the right, conservative end of the political spectrum, and in contest and conflict on the left, liberal end. Because so many US hospitals and health centres are under Roman Catholic sponsorship,[68] that Church is heavily involved in healthcare issues. It is in competition with Evangelical fundamentalist Protestant churches for loyalty of the faithful, but makes common cause in opposition to abortion access. The Catholic Church established its opposition to abortion from conception in 1869.[69] However, with the birth of the world's first IVF baby in 1978, the church adopted fertilisation, whether *in utero* or *in vitro*, as the beginning of life, to reinforce its opposition to IVF, although fertilisation is discernible only *in vitro*. In the IVF case before the Inter-American Court of Human Rights, for instance, Costa Rica argued that 'the term "conception" and "fertilization" should be treated as synonyms'.[70] The Court rejected this argument, drawing an important distinction between conception, taking completion of embryos' implantation *in utero* as marking the beginning of pregnancy, and fertilisation, which may occur *in utero* or *in vitro*. It ruled that fertilisation alone does not make embryos 'persons' or accord them human rights. The Catholic Church and Evangelical Protestant Churches may insist that human embryos are rights-bearing persons, however, and in fundamentalist zeal exhibit what may be described as 'embryolatry', a devotion to or veneration for human embryos.

Where abortion is legally restricted, as in most countries in Latin America, women frequently follow the historic practice of self-induction, using traditional herbal and other means, many of which contribute to high rates of maternal mortality and morbidity, but increasingly use modern pharmaceutical products, such as misoprostol and mifepristone, in tablet form. These are considerably safer,[71] and may responsibly be discussed with patients by healthcare professionals to deter use of more harmful methods.[72] Pharmaceutical products are being professionally regularised to induce lawful medical abortion, as opposed to surgical abortion, early in pregnancy, confirming

---

65 Sheldon, S., *Beyond Control: Medical Power and Abortion Law*, London, Pluto, 1997.

66 *R. v. Morgentaler* (1988) 44 DLR (4th) 385 (Can Sup Ct), at 402.

67 *R. (on the application of Smeaton) v. Secretary of State for Health* [2002] EWHC (Admin) 610.

68 Abelson, R., 'Catholic Hospitals Expand, Religious Strings Attached', *New York Times*, 20 February 2012, A1, B5.

69 Pope Pius IX, decree of 12 October 1869, Apostolicae Sedis Moderationi; see Luker, K., *Abortion and the Politics of Motherhood*, Berkeley, CA, University of California Press, 1984, p. 59.

70 *Artavia Murillo*, note 9, above, at para. 168.

71 Sherris, J., Bingham, A., Burns, M.A. et al., 'Misoprostol Use in Developing Countries: Results from a Multicountry Study' (2005) 88 *International Journal of Gynecology and Obstetrics*, 76–81.

72 Erdman, J.N., 'Harm Reduction, Human Rights, and Access to Information on Safer Abortion' (2012) 118 *International Journal of Gynecology and Obstetrics*, 83–6. See also Jackson, E., 'DIY Abortion and Harm Reduction', Chapter 2 of this volume.

women as central decision-makers in termination of their own pregnancies. Products for this purpose usually are legally available only on prescription but women take the products themselves, and, in developing countries, increasingly experience the resulting abortions at home or in locations of their own choice. The emergence of patient-controlled rather than doctor-controlled abortion is not internationally common, even in economically developed countries, but it is a growing trend that seems likely to advance as women acquire greater legal self-determination in their reproduction.

Medically-Assisted Reproduction (MAR)

Artificial insemination attracted fierce religious and medical professional opposition when it became popularised in humans before the 1950s, when artificial insemination (AI) by donor was equated with adultery and resulting children risked the stigma of illegitimacy.[73] It was more common in the US, however, and by the early 1960s had ceased to be generally contentious. Anticipating a widespread experience in use of different MAR techniques, two American gynaecologists writing about AI in the mid-1960s observed: 'Any change in custom or practice in this emotionally-charged area has always elicited a response from established custom and law of horrified negation at first; then negation without horror; then slow and gradual curiosity, study, evaluation, and finally a very slow but steady acceptance'.[74]

Many economically developed countries have enacted legislation to regulate MAR, some addressing only particular MAR techniques, such as varieties of what generically is described as IVF, others going beyond medical interventions to consider consequent issues of family law and the integration of resulting children into families, and the often non-parental status of gamete (sperm and ova) and embryo donors. Nevertheless, even under sophisticated, sympathetic and sensitive legislation, legal problems are prone to arise, some attributable to complexities due to over-regulation and unnecessary restrictions, as Sheila McLean has observed.[75]

An issue on which legal policies are divided is gamete donor anonymity. Some claim that if donors are adequately screened on genetic grounds and are disease-free, resulting offspring are adequately protected and do not need to be able to trace their donors, or siblings of the same genetic parentage. The fear of their future marriage to another child of the donor's raises the incest taboo, but except in small communities the chance is low, and degenerative genetic consequences for children are claimed to be no greater than in marriage in the wider community for first generation offspring. Whether and when children are informed of their origins by donation is a matter that the Nuffield Council on Bioethics in the UK considered best left to children's familial parents, although disclosure is encouraged.[76]

These claims are strongly contested by advocates of children's right to know their genetic parentage, and their arguments have prevailed in several legal systems that now preclude donor anonymity in MAR, although often without retrospective effect. The analogy is often drawn with adoption, where public or quasi-public agencies have records of birth mothers. Some legal systems provide adoptees with rights to trace their birth mothers, while others allow release of data only on a need-to-know basis. The adoption analogy is flawed, however, since adoption is triggered by a

73 Williams, note 35, above, ch. 4.

74 Kleegman, S.J. and Kaufman, S.A., *Infertility in Women*, Philadelphia, PA, F.A. Davis, 1966, p. 178.

75 McLean, S.A.M., 'De-Regulating Assisted Reproduction: Some Reflections' (2006) 7 *Medical Law International*, 233–47.

76 Nuffield Council on Bioethics, *Donor Conception: Ethical Aspects of Information Sharing*, London, 2013.

child wanting a home, whereas MAR is triggered by a home wanting a child. In November 2012, the British Columbia Court of Appeal reversed a trial judgment that applied the adoption analogy, and applied instead the analogy of natural reproduction, in which a child has no legal right to know its genetic father.[77] That is, a woman who becomes pregnant has no legal duty to preserve details of the man by whom she conceived in order to provide them for her child on its reaching adulthood. The Court resolved the conflict between the child's right to know and the donor's right to privacy in favour of the latter, and the Supreme Court of Canada declined leave to appeal.

Many in North America and, through the international range of US news media, no doubt many beyond, were introduced to the phenomenon of surrogate motherhood through the saga of Baby M as it proceeded finally to the New Jersey Supreme Court.[78] Mary Beth Whitehead, the mother of two young boys, responded to a recruitment advertisement to serve as a surrogate mother. On acceptance, she was artificially inseminated, conceived, and surrendered the child on birth, a baby girl, to the commissioning couple, the husband of whom was the baby's genetic father. However, regretting the surrender of her own daughter, she captured the child and proposed to retain custody, naming her Sara. The commissioning couple took judicial proceedings for restoration of their custody rights, having named the baby Melissa (hence Baby M). The lower court awarded custody to the commissioning couple, applying the customary 'best interests of the child' test, but the State Supreme Court reversed this decision in part and ordered joint custody between the now bitterly contesting and mutually antagonistic families. An authority on US children's law described this judgment as 'indisputably the logical, reasoned, and straightforward result of existing legal concepts of parenthood, adoption, baby-selling and the like', but also as 'surely the worst result possible'.[79]

The case, conducted before national and international news media, generated strong reactions, which among the academic community were overwhelmingly hostile,[80] including analogies of baby-selling, commodification of children, exploitation of women, slavery and prostitution. The birth mother of Baby M was her genetic mother, but IVF opened the contrast between 'partial' surrogacy, where the gestating mother is also genetic mother, and 'full' surrogacy, dependent on IVF, in which the gestating mother has no direct genetic link to the child, the ovum coming from the woman to whom the child is intended to be surrendered, or from a third party. Another contrast concerned which of the two women involved with the child is the surrogate, acting in place of another, since gestation is authentic prenatal motherhood, while the woman to whom a child is surrendered assumes the role of mother only on surrender.

As Kleegman and Kaufman anticipated,[81] views have moderated, some finding surrogacy acceptable, even for men in same sex unions, provided that, as much relevant legislation requires, women acting as surrogates are not enriched by commercial arrangements, since motherhood should not be a for-profit undertaking.[82] However, professional fees are earned in many aspects of surrogate motherhood, including by lawyers as well as health service providers and counsellors, and drug companies profit, so that it seems paradoxical or ironic that the only person required to be unpaid in surrogate motherhood agreements is the surrogate mother. International experience shows that monetary rewards are often expressly allowed or are infiltrated into arrangements,

77 *Pratten v. British Columbia (Attorney-General)* (2012) 357 DLR (4th) 660 (Can BC CA).

78 *In the Matter of Baby M*, 537A 2d 1227 (NJ Sup Ct, 1988).

79 Bezanson, R.P., 'Solomon Would Weep: A Comment on In the Matter of Baby M and the Limits of Judicial Authority' (1988) 16 *Law, Medicine and Ethics*, 126–30, at p. 126.

80 See for instance Annas, G., 'Fairy Tales Surrogate Mothers Tell' (1988) 16 *Law, Medicine and Ethics*, 27–33.

81 See quotation in text at note 74, above.

82 Radin, M., 'Market-inalienability' (1987) 100 *Harvard Law Review*, 1849–937.

since between outright prohibition and a free market, in surrogacy transactions and other forms of MAR, may be proposal of a regulated market, governed by transparency and the limits of public tolerance.[83] Even in the UK, where legislation allows reimbursement only of reasonable expenses, evidence shows judicial allowance of quite large payments.[84]

Whether women who act as surrogate mothers are seen as viciously exploited, particularly when they are in poor circumstances in low-resource countries,[85] earning legitimate income to support their own families, or giving children and infertile women a gift of life, is often a matter of individual perception. A social anthropologist has noted regarding surrogacy, but with wider application, that 'an act can be both described (externally observable) and understood (carry an intentionality or meaning). Neither dimension can be reduced to the other'.[86] Describing what parties in surrogacy agreements do can be understood in different ways, including in ways that differ from and oppose the intention and understanding of the actors; that is, their described acts can be misunderstood. If the gestational or birth mother is seen as the true mother, for instance, the recipient woman is the surrogate, but if the rearing woman is considered the true mother because of her intended lifelong commitment to the child's welfare, the gestating woman is the surrogate.

Surrogate motherhood is only one of many MAR processes that can be conducted across national borders. The description 'reproductive tourism' is common, but regrettable. Related to 'sex tourism', the expression trivialises the sacrifices many are willing to bear in order to have their own children, and equates their conscientious motivations with the casual indulgence of spare money and time that allows tourism. Although some cross-border initiatives are compelled by avoidance of restrictive laws, this may be publicly tolerable, and indicated. When, for instance, an English widow took legal action to allow her to have a child through sperm recovered from her dying husband, the Court of Appeal upheld the lower court ruling that UK legislation prohibited this, because his written consent had not been obtained, but indicated that she might be lawfully inseminated in another country of the European Community.[87] She subsequently employed the sperm in Belgium, and over time had two children. When, in light of this experience, the UK government wanted a review of its consent legislation to ensure compatibility with the Human Rights Act 1998, it turned to Sheila McLean, whose report recommended, *inter alia*, that children conceived posthumously should be entitled to birth certification that acknowledges their paternity.[88] Anticipating posthumous use of gametes raises interesting legal issues of estate planning.[89]

---

83 Dickens, B.M., 'Ethical Issues Arising from the Use of Assisted Reproductive Technologies' in Vayena, E., Rowe, P.J. and Griffin, P.D. (eds) *Current Practices and Controversies in Assisted Reproduction*, Geneva, WHO, 2002, pp. 333–48.

84 Blyth, E. and Potter, C., 'Paying for It? Surrogacy, Market Forces and Assisted Conception' in Cook, R., Sclater, S.D. and Kaganas, F. (eds) *Surrogate Motherhood: International Perspectives*, Oxford, Hart Publishing, 2003, pp. 227–42.

85 Shetty, P., 'India's Unregulated Surrogacy Industry' (2012) 380(9854) *The Lancet*, 1633–4.

86 Strathern, M., 'Still Giving Nature a Helping Hand? Surrogacy: A Debate about Technology and Society' in Cook, Sclater and Kaganas, note 84, above, at p. 283, quoting Fenstad, J.E., 'Relationships Between the Social and Natural Sciences' (1995) 3 *European Review*, 61–71, at p. 63.

87 *R. v. Human Fertilisation and Embryology Authority, ex p. Blood* [1997] 2 All ER 687.

88 McLean, S.A.M., *Review of the Common Law Provisions Relating to the Removal of Gametes and of the Consent Provisions, in the Human Fertilisation and Embryology Act 1990*, London, Department of Health, 1998.

89 Carpenter, B.C., 'Sex Post Facto: Advising Clients Regarding Posthumous Conception' (2012) 38 *American College of Trust & Estate Counsel Law Journal*, 187–228.

Cross-border medical care involves issues outside the usual confines of medical law, including those of private international law, often called conflict of laws. An added element is that they may affect the interests or rights of children who are born as a consequence of adults' decisions on exercise of reproductive options. Indeed, the rights of children to the care of parents may be compromised when the children result from arrangements such as of surrogate motherhood in which birth mothers disclaim the genetically-unrelated children they gestated and surrendered to adults from abroad, whose own countries of residence, on their return, will not recognise the children as legally theirs. If birth mothers give the children they deliver neither their names nor nationalities, and the adults to whom the children are surrendered are not recognised as their parents when they try to return with them to their own countries, there is liable to be violation of Article 7(1) of the Convention on the Rights of the Child. This provides that the child 'shall have the right from birth to a name, the right to acquire a nationality and, as far as possible, the right to know and be cared for by his or her parents'. Immigration laws, or punitive official or judicial attitudes when laws have been offended, that obstruct these rights are dysfunctional in that they fail to serve children's best interests.

Cross-border services may satisfy patients seeking services that are unavailable, unlawful, too costly or otherwise inaccessible in their own countries, and satisfy providers in the countries to which patients travel. Concerns arise more of an ethical than a legal nature, however, when scarce resources of professional skills and attention in resource-poor countries are devoted but diverted to the care of visitors from more affluent countries.[90] The concerns of global inequity in allocation of resources to meet legitimate claims to care of infertile couples, particularly where childless women suffer disproportionate impairment of their lives, are not necessarily capable of expression or remedy by processes of the law itself, although remedial or mitigating policies may be implemented by laws.

Legal issues concern basic principles of adequately informed consent, more difficult to achieve when participants in MAR are from different cultures and perhaps understand different first languages, and compliance with standards of care, which may differ between patients' and medical service providers' countries. Under the 'assumption of risk' doctrine (*volenti non fit injuria*), the prevailing legal standard will probably be that of the service provider, to whom the patient goes as a volunteer. Because patients are usually outside any public health service insurance scheme the providers' countries may have, they will usually pay fees for services under contracts, terms of which may in part be implied, of the providers' jurisdictions. Any risk insurance that patients may want will be governed by laws peculiar to the insurance policies' terms, which are usually prescribed by the insurers. Where contracts for MAR transactions are not inherently unlawful or void as against public policy, they may be unenforceable by judicial orders for specific performance, particularly surrogate motherhood agreements.[91] Disputes over who rears resulting children will not usually be governed by the laws of contract as agreed by the parties, but by child custody law, in which the judicially-determined best interests of each child will usually be decisive, unless a judge gives priority to an overriding concept of public policy.

Beyond routine principles of law are issues peculiar to medical care. For instance, drugs used in one country may be unfamiliar or unavailable in another. Providers should be required to

90 Snyder, J., Crooks, V., Johnston, R. and Kingsbury, P., 'Beyond Sun, Sand, and Stitches: Assuming Responsibility for the Harms of Medical Tourism' (2013) 27(5) *Bioethics*, 233–42; Brandon Chen, Y.Y. and Flood, C.M., 'Medical Tourism's Impact on Health Care Equity and Access in Low- and Middle-Income Countries: Making the Case for Regulation' (2013) 41 *Journal of Law, Medicine and Ethics*, 286–300.

91 Drummond, S.G., *Fruitful Diversity: Revisiting the Enforceability of Gestational Carriage Contracts*, Research Paper no. 25/1013, Osgoode Hall Law School, York University, 2013.

equip visiting patients with the information they need to share with their care-givers on returning home. A patient proposing to conceive abroad by gamete or embryo donation will often return home pregnant without necessarily disclosing MAR to her care-provider at home. Accordingly, the original provider may have no follow-up data on the outcome of the pregnancy, and the home country provider may be unaware that the patient's pregnancy involved a prior provider's pharmaceutical or other clinical initiatives.

Similarly, where sperm, ova or embryo donation were involved, the home caregiver may not detect genetic differences between the child and its ostensible parents, unless an incongruity appears in prenatal or postnatal management. While transparency may be most advisable, this may be socially or otherwise dysfunctional, for instance where a patient's religion or culture disallows or discredits gamete or embryo donation, or where children's inheritance rights would be affected by the appearance of illegitimacy. For instance, in Arab cultures where paternal lineage is critical, sperm donation may not be disclosed even if confidentiality is as assured as reasonably possible.

Cross-border healthcare presents perhaps its most publicly engaging issues when its purpose is evasion of criminal prohibitions.[92] Instances include assisted suicide and female circumcision or genital cutting, and more related to reproductive health, MAR, such as for anonymous and/or commercially paid gamete donation, and abortion. The UK Department of Health publication of annual statistics has recorded a decline in abortions undertaken on women giving addresses in the Republic of Ireland: from 6,673 in 2001 to 3,982 in 2012.[93] Irish women have the legal escape from restrictive laws of crossing their national border. Indeed, this was the basis on which in December 2010 the ECtHR upheld Ireland's restrictive provisions. It ruled that 'having regard to the right to lawfully travel abroad for an abortion … the Court does not consider that the prohibition in Ireland of abortion for health and well-being reasons … exceeds the margin of appreciation accorded in that respect to the Irish State'.[94] It may appear incongruous with upholding human rights principles that a country's criminalisation, under severe penalties, of a therapeutic medical procedure undertaken to protect women's health and well-being, may be legally upheld because women may enjoy such human rights' protection provided that they have means to travel abroad.[95]

Protection of Conscience

Delivery of reproductive health services, such as contraception, sterilisation, abortion and MAR, is liable to be contentious, and raises issues of service providers' conscience. Conscience has often underpinned health service provision, since altruism, whether expressed through religious mandates for one's own spiritual salvation or secular inspiration to care for others, is one of humanity's better instincts. In modern times, however, conscientious objection to provision of reproductive healthcare has become the most visible expression of conscience, triggered in large part by liberalisation of prohibitive abortion laws in the 1960s. Opposition to abortion, channelled

92 Cohen, I.G., 'Medical Outlaws or Medical Refugees? An Examination of Circumvention Tourism' in Hodges, J.R., Turner, L. and Kimball, A.M. (eds) *Risks and Challenges in Medical Tourism: Understanding the Global Market for Health Services*, Santa Barbara, CA, Praeger, 2012, pp. 207–29.

93 *Abortion Statistics for England and Wales 2012*, Department of Health, 2013, p. 52, Table 12a.

94 *A, B and C v. Ireland*, App. No. 25579/05 ECHR 2032, [2010] App. No. 25579/05 ECHR 2032, at para. 241.

95 On internationally expected standards, see Erdman, J.N., DePiñeres, T. and Kismödi, E., 'Updated WHO Guidance on Safe Abortion: Health and Human Rights' (2013) 120 *International Journal of Gynecology and Obstetrics*, 200–203.

through religious institutions and influential religious hierarchies, became a legally protected interest. Legal accommodation of conscience is intended for protection of individuals' spiritual well-being, but may be manipulated by religious individuals and, for instance, religious institutions to compel non-believers' *de facto* compliance with their doctrines.[96]

Drawing on language of the Universal Declaration of Human Rights of 1948, the International Covenant on Civil and Political Rights (ICCPR) provides in Article 18(1) that: 'Everyone shall have the right to freedom of thought, conscience and religion. This right shall include freedom … to manifest his religion or belief in worship, observance, practice and teaching'. Human rights to freedom of religion or belief warrant the greatest respect and accommodation, but are not absolute, since Article 18(3) provides that: 'Freedom to manifest one's religion or beliefs may be subject only to such limitations as are prescribed by law and are necessary to protect public safety, order, health, or morals or the fundamental rights and freedoms of others'. To invoke the right of conscientious objection is 'to manifest one's religion or beliefs', which right may be limited to protect the 'fundamental rights and freedoms of others'.

Article 18(1) refers to 'conscience and religion', establishing that conscience is not confined to but separate from religion. Individuals' conscience may be conditioned by their religious beliefs, but religion has no monopoly on conscience, and is subject to individuals' assessments of whether religious doctrines and institutional practices accord with their sense of good conscience, for instance on the status and participation they provide for women. Conscience may be shaped by individuals' social, philosophical, political, professional and other convictions apart from those rooted in religious faith.

On this basis, while some doctors object to participation in such medical procedures as abortion, others may be conscientiously propelled to undertake them.[97] Those who have a conscientious commitment to women's health face the same challenges to provide reproductive healthcare as conscientious objectors.[98] They warrant the same protections against discrimination and sanctions, if conscience is regarded seriously as a right equally available to all healthcare providers.[99]

The implication of respecting all expressions of conscience is that, in the same way that secular hospitals accommodate conscientious objection of religiously inspired health service practitioners, religiously-based hospitals should accommodate the conscientious commitment of practitioners to deliver care they find indicated for patients' well-being, even if contrary to preferences of the hospitals' religious administration. Secular hospitals cannot refuse to recruit practitioners because of the religious faith they hold, and similarly religiously-founded hospitals cannot discriminate in recruitment against practitioners who do not share their faith. Accordingly, practitioners cannot be bound against their clinical judgment by religious directives that would limit the treatments they may recommend to their patients, such as on contraceptive options, including contraceptive sterilisation and emergency contraception, or limit products they may prescribe, such as contraceptive drugs.

Practitioners may refrain from undertaking surgical abortions and comparable procedures that would implicate colleagues, on grounds both of comity and of promotion of mutual respect for conscience, but medical abortion might be prescribed for early termination of pregnancy outside hospital facilities, and referrals might be made for procedures the hospitals cannot

96 Dickens, B.M., 'Conscientious Objection: A Shield or a Sword?' in McLean, S.A.M. (ed.) *First Do No Harm: Law, Ethics and Healthcare*, Aldershot, Ashgate, 2006, pp. 337–51.

97 Joffe, C., *Doctors of Conscience: The Struggle to Provide Abortion before and after Roe v. Wade*, Boston, MA, Beacon Press, 1995.

98 Dickens, B.M. and Cook, R.J., 'Conscientious Commitment to Women's Health' (2011) 113 *International Journal of Gynecology and Obstetrics*, 163–6.

99 Sepper, E., 'Taking Conscience Seriously' (2012) 98 *Virginia Law Review*, 1501–75.

physically accommodate. In the same way that secular hospitals cannot discipline practitioners for their conscientious objection, religiously-founded hospitals cannot discipline practitioners conscientiously committed to best care of their patients, for instance by prompt termination of ectopic or other health-endangering pregnancy notwithstanding detection of fetal heart tones. That is, hospitals cannot enforce religious or other directives that deny practitioners their human rights of conscience.[100] This is no more than an application of 'the Golden Rule', popularly expressed as the 'Do unto others …' rule.

As an individual or personal human right, conscientious objection cannot be invoked by artificial 'legal persons' such as private or public corporations or hospital institutions, as the Constitutional Court of Colombia has ruled.[101] Ecclesiastical and other religious institutions may be granted immunities from compliance with some human rights obligations, such as of non-discrimination on grounds of sex, sexual orientation or marital status, to protect their religious freedoms on such matters as ordination of clergy and celebration of marriage, and Catholic scholars in particular have advocated institutional rights of conscience to protect and justify practices in Catholic hospitals.[102] However, it is no more defensible for a public hospital under Catholic sponsorship to prohibit reproductive healthcare or referrals for care than it would be for a Jehovah's Witness hospital on which a community depends for surgical care to prohibit blood transfusion or use of blood-derived products. Jehovah's Witness doctors and nurses may decline use of such products in their own care, of course, but they do not object to participate in their medically indicated use for patients' care on grounds of their personal conscience. They may risk death for their own convictions,[103] but not compromise the health of others. Similarly, Moslem and Jewish nurses may not refuse to serve meals to patients that do not comply with their own dietary observances.

The balance of mutual accommodation between doctors who object to participate in procedures that offend their conscience, and patients' access to care by such medically-indicated procedures, is in the doctor's duty to refer the patients, in good faith, to where they can receive care. Referral must be timely and be to competent, accessible and available willing providers. In accordance with Article 18(3) of the ICCPR, objecting doctors cannot manifest their religion or beliefs in ways that prejudice patients' fundamental rights to indicated healthcare.

Some objectors claim that referral itself is tantamount to participation on grounds of complicity, perhaps analogous to inchoate offences in criminal law. Less has been made of complicity claims in Catholic advocacy in recent years, however, because of the unrelated issue of management of paedophilia and child abuse by priests. Bishops and senior clergy have been shown to have referred unreformed priests to other parishes, where misconduct was repeated. The bishops' errors have been found by courts and admitted by the church, but it was not accepted nor claimed that the bishops were complicit in the subsequent offences. The bishops did not refer offending priests to new parishes in order for them to commit offences, of course, but equally, objecting doctors do not refer patients they will not treat in order for them to have abortions, sterilisations or the

100 On the defence of (Catholic) conscience, see Pope John-Paul II, 'If You Want Peace, Respect the Conscience of Every Person'; Message for the XXIV World Day of Peace, Vatican City, 1 January 1991, available at: http://www.vatican.va/holy_father/john_paul_ii/messages/peace/documents/hf_jp-ii_mes_08121990_xxiv-world-day-for-peace_en.html (accessed 13 January 2015).

101 Corte Constitucional [CC] [Constitutional Court], febrero 28, 2008, Decision T-209 (Colom.).

102 Sepper, note 99, above, p. 1540, n. 160, and p. 1541, n. 162.

103 Hull, L., Dolan, A. and Newling, D., 'Jehovah's Witness Mother Dies after Refusing Blood Transfusion after Giving Birth to Twins', *Mail Online*, 5 November 2007, http://www.dailymail.co.uk/news/article-491791/Jehovahs-Witness-mother-dies-refusing-blood-transfusion-giving-birth-twins.html (accessed 13 January 2015).

like. Referrals are for consultations regarding care options that may include these procedures, but counselling may result in patients pursuing options other than those to which the referring doctors object.

Discharging the duty to refer does not amount to participation in any procedure that results. Referring doctors do not receive referral fees, and are not party to any negligence, or crime, that the referee doctor may commit. National legislation and national and international codes of professional practice usually require conscientious referral by objecting practitioners.[104] Referral is an element of the duty of care, a term, usually implied, of any doctor-patient contract or relationship, and required by the law of negligence or non-abandonment.[105] Duties of professionalism, negligence law and the law on informed consent also require doctors to disclose treatment options for patients' conditions even when the doctors would object to undertake them. Doctors who satisfy their duty of disclosure but decline referral for patients who seek an objectionable option either continue to treat patients without their freely given consent, or withdraw from treating them, which without referral may constitute unlawful abandonment.

It has been proposed, however, that specialist professional associations may keep records of doctors prepared to perform procedures to which others object, so that objecting doctors can refer their patients to such associations rather than to other individual practitioners.[106] In the same spirit, New Zealand's legislation requires that, when raising a conscientious objection to a reproductive health service, 'the health practitioner must inform the person who requests the service that he or she can obtain the service from another health practitioner or from a family planning clinic'.[107] The reference to 'the person who requests the service' rather than to 'the patient' is significant, since under the general law, the duty to refer applies only to doctors' existing patients, not to persons requesting to become patients.

The widespread understanding in the literature and case law has been that conscientious objection is accommodated to refuse direct participation in procedures, but not in ancillary acts, such as routine nursing care and staff supervision.[108] Surgeons, operating room nurses and anaesthetists, for instance, are direct participants in surgical abortion and related procedures, but not pre- or post-operative attendants. Similarly, doctors prescribing drugs for medication abortion are direct participants, and, controversially, possibly pharmacists filling prescriptions, but not attendant personnel who deliver completed prescription forms to patients or packages containing the drugs. An appellate judgment of the Inner House of the Scottish Court of Session in 2013, which may be *per incuriam*, has, however, challenged that understanding.[109] The case concerned two Catholic midwives employed as Labour Ward Co-ordinators. They were required to supervise midwives who among other functions participated in abortion procedures, but as Co-ordinators did not themselves directly treat patients.

The trial court rejected their application for judicial review of the local Health Board's decision not to exempt them from supervisory duties over midwives who participated in abortion procedures. The Co-ordinators had claimed exemption by invoking protection of their rights to conscientious

104 See the International Federation of Gynecology and Obstetrics (FIGO), *Ethical Guidelines on Conscientious Objection*, 2005, paras 2/3.

105 See *Barr v. Matthews* (1999) 52 BMLR 217 (QBD), at 227.

106 Lynch, H.F., *Conflicts of Conscience in Health Care: An Institutional Compromise*, Cambridge, MA, MIT Press, 2008.

107 Health Practitioners Competence Assurance Act 2003 (NZ), no. 48, s. 174(2).

108 Dickens, B.M., 'The Right to Conscience' in Cook, Erdman and Dickens, note 64, above, pp. 210–38.

109 *In the Petition of Mary Teresa Doogan and Concepta Wood* [2013] CSIH 36, P 876/11.

objection under s. 4(1) of the UK Abortion Act 1967 and Article 9(1) of the ECHR. Section 4(1) allows conscientious objection regarding 'any duty ... to participate in any treatment' authorised by the Act, but the trial judge ruled that the petitioners were not direct participants.[110] Article 9(1) echoes the protection of thought, conscience and religion under Article 18(1) of the ICCPR, but the trial judge dismissed their petition for judicial review because Article 9(2) provides that '(f)reedom to manifest one's religion or beliefs shall be subject only to such limitations as ... are necessary ... for the protection of the rights and freedoms of others'. She held that it is necessary for protection of the rights of patients that their nurses and midwives be properly supervised.

On appeal, the Inner House reversed the trial court, because s. 4(1) of the 1967 Act leaves practitioners who are disposed to object uncertain of what constitutes participation, and the Court favoured an approach 'which avoids, for all levels of nursing staff, the need constantly to make difficult decisions in what might be stressful situations'.[111] The certainty the Court sought to protect is somewhat compromised by s. 4(2) of the Act, which precludes conscientious objection 'to participation in treatment which is necessary to save the life or to prevent grave permanent injury to the physical or mental health of a pregnant woman'. Such necessity is usually determined in the clinical judgment of women's physicians, however, not by nursing staff. The Court accordingly adopted a wide interpretation of the scope of conscientious objection, since '(i)t is consistent with the reasoning which allowed such an objection in the first place that it should extend to any involvement in the process of treatment, the object of which is to terminate a pregnancy'.[112]

The judgment is to be appealed to the UK Supreme Court, but pending the appeal may be of no precedential effect because it was given *per incuriam*, meaning by mistake or flawed by oversight. Its substantive failing is its disregard of the rights of patients, whom it may allow to be denied pre-operative and post-operative nursing care, to be exposed to care by unsupervised nurses or midwives, and so to be treated without regard for their dignity and safety in what for them too 'might be stressful situations'. Its legal failing is disregard of the qualification of freedom of conscience, initially recognised in Article 9(1) of the ECHR, created under Article 9(2). Disregard of patients' rights may have been because the Convention was not introduced into argument on the appeal, but such choice or oversight in advocacy would not allow the Court to ignore relevant law. The UK Human Rights Act 1998 obliges courts to give effect to certain Convention rights, including to security of the person under Article 5, to respect for private and family life under Article 8, when medical care is indicated only for women, such as abortion, to non-discrimination and equality under Article 14, and to conscience under Article 9. By s. 3(1) of the 1998 Act: 'So far as it is possible to do so, primary legislation ... must be read and given effect in a way which is compatible with the Convention rights'.

The expansive interpretation the Court gave to rights of conscientious objection under s. 4(1) of the 1967 Act pays no regard to the limit under Article 9(2) of the European Convention on the right 'to manifest one's religion or beliefs', which may be exercised only consistently with 'protection of the rights and freedoms of others'.[113] The Court addressed only practitioners, without balancing 'the rights and freedoms of others',[114] namely women whose physical or mental health may be endangered by continuation of pregnancy, or by delay or denial of due care, attention or respect. In

110 *Petition of Mary Teresa Doogan and Concepta Wood* [2012] CSOH 32.

111 [2013] CSIH 36, at para. 37, per Lady Dorrian.

112 [2013] CSIH 36, at para. 38.

113 See Campbell, M., 'Conscientious Objection, Health Care and Article 9 of the European Convention on Human Rights' (2011) 11 *Medical Law International*, 284–304.

114 On judicial balancing of competing human rights, see *H (A Healthcare Worker) v. Associated Newspapers* [2002] EWCA Civ 195.

an abortion-related judgment, the ECtHR has held that states are required to 'organise the health services system in such a way as to ensure that an effective exercise of the freedom of conscience of health professionals in the professional context does not prevent patients from obtaining access to services to which they are entitled under the applicable legislation'.[115] The Scottish appellate court allowed the question of balancing the human rights of care providers and of patients for reproductive healthcare to go not simply unanswered, but unasked. Whether patients' rights may be so subordinated will be resolved by the UK Supreme Court,[116] or perhaps on further appeal by the ECtHR according to the European Convention.

Conclusion

This selection of legal issues in reproductive health relates to but one facet of Sheila McLean's scholarly career and accomplishments. As a multi-faceted star in the English-speaking health law firmament, she continues to shine brilliantly through her authored and edited academic publications, governmental and analogous reports, consultations, committee functions and more. Sheila has courageously propelled the historical trajectory that has taken legal regulation of human reproduction from the context of sin prohibited through the retributive punishments of criminal law into the setting of medical and health law, and then into the wider modern framework of human rights.

The regulation of both the control and the promotion of fertility remains contentious, on grounds of pragmatic policy and ethical principle, raising concerns and conflicts within and among legal, political, religious and other communities. As we engage with the spectrum of new legal and ethical challenges in healthcare, from nanotechnology[117] to population[118] and global[119] health, Sheila's rigorous, principled but sensitive analysis, fair and transparent balancing of competing values, wisdom and vision will continue to provide guidance.

---

115 *R.R. v. Poland* [2007] App. No.27617/04 (ECHR, decision final as of 28 November, 2011), para. 206.

116 The Supreme Court reversed the Inner House decision: see now: *Greater Glasgow Health Board v. Doogan and Wood* [2014] UKSC 68.

117 Bowman, D.M. and Ludlow, K., 'Assessing the Impact of a "For Government" Review on the Nanotechnology Regulatory Landscape' (2012) 38 *Monash University Law Review*, 168–212.

118 Krieger, N., 'Who and What Is a "Population"? Historical Debates, Current Controversies, and Implications for Understanding "Population Health" and Rectifying Health Inequities' (2012) 90 *Milbank Quarterly*, 634–81.

119 Benatar, S. and Brock, G. (eds), *Global Health and Global Health Ethics*, Cambridge, Cambridge University Press, 2011; Ruger, J.P., 'Global Health Justice' (2009) 2 *Public Health Ethics*, 261–75.

Chapter 2

DIY Abortion and Harm Reduction

Emily Jackson

Introduction

It is an honour to participate in a book dedicated to the celebration of Sheila McLean's brilliant and foundational contribution to the field of medical law and ethics. Throughout her distinguished career, Sheila's humanism and compassion have been a hallmark of her research, just as much as the extraordinary clarity and rigour of her scholarship. In relation to abortion, as with access to other medical treatments that enable women to control their fertility or infertility, Sheila has always been a strong and uncompromising advocate of women's right to take decisions about their bodies with a minimum of external pressure.[1] At the same time, Sheila has acknowledged the futility of trying to seek agreement on the fundamental moral question of abortion's legitimacy,[2] and suggested that we should look elsewhere if we seek consensual law reform.

On abortion, as Sheila pointed out in a typically elegant and persuasive article in 1990,[3] the pro-choice and the anti-abortion lobbies are effectively talking past each other. Each position has its own internal, albeit value-laden logical consistency, and there is simply no independent logic that can be applied to solve this clash of moral absolutes. Sheila's solution in her 1990 paper was to focus on the middle-ground, and to take a pragmatic approach to rights in order to rescue the debate from the 'swamp into which it seems doomed to sink'.

Unsurprisingly, in 2015 pro-choice and anti-abortion lobbyists continue to talk past each other. Sheila was right to point out that a debate framed in terms of women's rights versus fetal rights cannot ever be conclusively won by one side rather than the other, because neither accepts the other's foundational moral premises. If you believe that an embryo has the same moral status as a child, then you will not be persuaded by arguments to the contrary because your belief in their equivalent moral status is simply not something that could be shaken by evidence of, say, nature's profligacy with newly fertilised eggs.[4] Similarly, if you believe that a woman should have the right to terminate her pregnancy, high-resolution images of fetuses are not going to change your mind, because what the fetus looks like is not the point.

Although debates over the moral status of the fetus are still stuck in the swamp Sheila drew attention to in 1990, there are some aspects of abortion provision that have changed dramatically. First, for example, the licensing of drugs capable of producing what are known as medical abortions means that it is no longer necessary for a woman seeking a termination to undergo a surgical operation. Secondly, the internet has transformed access to information about safe abortion methods. In this chapter, I consider the impact of these two changes on abortion debates, arguing

---

1 McLean, S.A.M., *Old Law, New Medicine*, London, Pandora Press, 1999, at p. 90.

2 McLean, S.A.M., 'Abortion Law: Is Consensual Reform Possible?' (1990) 17 *Journal of Law and Society*, 106–23.

3 McLean, note 1, above.

4 Harris, J., 'Stem Cells, Sex, and Procreation' (2003) 12 *Cambridge Quarterly of Healthcare Ethics*, 353–71.

that their cumulative effect is to facilitate self-abortion, and to make self-abortion potentially much safer than it has ever been before. Rather than being about the rights and wrongs of abortion, or about women's rights versus fetal rights, the rise of DIY abortion is fundamentally a public health issue. While it is never going to solve the intractable debate between the pro-choice and anti-abortion lobbies, a public health framework may help to take some of the political and moral heat out of the abortion debate.

We are all familiar with horrific accounts – often involving gin, hot baths and knitting needles – of women attempting to terminate their own pregnancies. The decriminalisation of abortion, effected in the UK by the Abortion Act 1967, was intended to relegate this sort of practice to the history books. It is undoubtedly true that throughout most of the developed world, safe and lawful termination of pregnancy is available to most women, at least in the early stages of pregnancy. But DIY abortion has not gone away. On the contrary, it is now possible to purchase abortifacient drugs online. Online pharmacies, with websites that generally do not disclose their physical locations, are willing to sell misoprostol to anyone with a Paypal account, rather than a prescription, and ship it worldwide. And we know from the recent English case of Sarah Catt, initially sentenced to eight years in prison (reduced to three and a half years, on appeal) for procuring her own miscarriage,[5] that the use of online pharmacies to purchase abortion pills is not confined to women who live in countries where abortion is against the law.

In countries where abortion continues to be illegal, even given the possibility that medicines bought online might be fake or unsafe, self-medicating with misoprostol is still likely to be safer, on average, than more traditional backstreet abortion methods. If the priority is to reduce the risks to health associated with abortion's illegality, then it is important to ensure that women can access reliable information about how to obtain and take misoprostol safely. Where such information is available, the radical new option of safe, or at least safer, illegal abortion emerges.

This chapter considers the rise of this new species of DIY abortion, and argues that the most appropriate legal response to self-administered misoprostol is not to put women in prison. Instead, women need to understand the dangers of purchasing medicines online and taking them without medical supervision. The growth of online pharmacies means that consumers in general need high quality information about the risks of self-medication with drugs bought online. It is impossible for a consumer to know whether a website is selling cheap generic medicines, which could – if taken according to instructions – be as safe as their branded equivalent, or whether it is selling drugs that are fake and/or unsafe and which therefore pose a risk to health.[6] Women faced with a choice between carrying an unwanted pregnancy to term and taking potentially dangerous termination-inducing drugs purchased over the internet also need access to the safe, lawful abortion services that eliminate the need to make this choice.

In recent years, Conservative politicians in the UK have raised the prospect of restricting access to abortion by, for example, advocating a reduction in the 24-week time-limit;[7] making 'independent' counselling compulsory,[8] and questioning the medical profession's liberal interpretation of the statutory grounds.[9] The ease of DIY abortion, twenty-first-century style, suggests that any further restrictions on access are likely to lead more women to self-medicate with potentially harmful and/

5 *R v. Catt (Sarah Louise)* [2013] EWCA Crim 1187.

6 Gostin, L.O., Buckley, G.J. and Kelley, P.W., 'Stemming the Global Trade in Falsified and Substandard Medicines' (2013) 309 *Journal of the American Medical Association*, 1693–4.

7 Quinn, B., 'Jeremy Hunt Backs 12-Week Legal Limit on Abortions', *The Guardian*, 6 October 2012.

8 Watt, N., 'Nadine Dorries's Abortion Proposals Heavily Defeated in Commons', *The Guardian*, 7 September 2011.

9 Discussed in Bristow, J. (ed.), *Britain's Abortion Law: What It Says, and Why*, London, BPAS, 2013.

or fake medicines. This sort of DIY abortion may look cleaner and less hazardous than the knitting needles of the past, but this chapter argues that the dangers of DIY abortion continue to offer a compelling public health reason for liberal abortion laws.

Abortion Pills

Nearly half of all terminations of pregnancy in the UK are now medical (as opposed to surgical) abortions.[10] Almost all of these are early abortions, in which a woman will generally be given two different drugs a few days apart. Although protocols vary, commonly the woman is first given mifepristone which blocks the hormones that help a pregnancy to continue. Two days later, the woman returns to the clinic where misoprostol is given orally or as a pessary to dislodge the embryo from the lining of the uterus and trigger a miscarriage. In order to satisfy the provisions of the Abortion Act 1967, both drugs must be given to the woman in an NHS hospital or other 'approved place',[11] and the woman's treatment must be supervised by a registered medical practitioner.[12]

Unlike surgical abortion, there is no clinical reason why a woman has to be in a particular place to take the drugs, nor why she has to be supervised by a doctor while she does so. Medical termination of pregnancy is safe and effective, and self-medication is straightforward. Although best practice in carrying out early medical abortions is to give mifepristone and misoprostol separately, misoprostol on its own can be used to trigger a miscarriage. Hence, if a woman can obtain both drugs or even just misoprostol, it will be relatively straightforward for her to terminate her own pregnancy.

Until relatively recently, bypassing the provisions of the Abortion Act by terminating one's own pregnancy would have been difficult. Within the UK, it is a criminal offence to supply a prescription-only medicine without a prescription.[13] Online pharmacies, based offshore, enable consumers to bypass restrictions on the supply of prescription-only medicines. At the time of writing, searching for 'buy misoprostol online without prescription' on google comes up with nearly five million hits. In the most recent global crackdown on the internet trade in fake and unlicensed drugs, in which drugs worth £6.5 million were seized and 18,000 illegal online pharmacies were closed down, mifepristone and misoprostol were found alongside drugs for erectile dysfunction, anabolic steroids and human growth hormone.[14]

With the exception of certain controlled drugs, the penalties for obtaining prescription-only drugs without a prescription are directed at the supplier rather than the purchaser. It is therefore not an offence to buy misoprostol from an online pharmacy. If, however, misoprostol is judged to be a 'poison or other noxious thing', using it to terminate one's own pregnancy would be a criminal offence under s. 58 of the Offences Against the Person Act 1861, to which the Abortion Act 1967 would offer no defence.

In England, Scotland and Wales, comparatively few women will be tempted to terminate their own pregnancies with abortion pills purchased over the internet. In the first months of pregnancy,

10 *Abortion Statistics, England and Wales*, London, Department of Health, 2013.

11 Abortion Act 1967, s. 1(3).

12 Abortion Act 1967, s. 1(1).

13 Human Medicines Regulations 2012, reg. 214.

14 Wise, J., 'Global Operation Tackles Internet Trade in Fake Drugs' (2012) 345 *British Medical Journal*, http://www.bmj.com/content/345/bmj.e6724?hwshib2=authn%3A1421229240%3A20150113%253A14af6725-f749-4233-8cf9-394370500a0d%3A0%3A0%3A0%3AWxpgibju4%2FZDuimqQtqOwA%3D%3D (accessed 13 January 2015).

NHS-funded abortion services are accessible and free of charge. If access to a safe NHS-funded abortion is straightforward, a woman is unlikely to be tempted to pay for drugs from an unregulated online pharmacy instead. It would, however, be a mistake to assume that self-abortion, using drugs bought online does not happen in the UK. In Northern Ireland, where abortion continues to be illegal unless the woman faces a grave risk to her life or health, terminating one's pregnancy with a medicine bought online may be more convenient and affordable than travelling to England, Scotland or Wales for a private abortion. In March 2013, more than 100 Northern Irish women signed an open letter in which they admitted publicly to having terminated pregnancies using pills bought on the internet, and in which they claimed that they 'represent[ed] just a small fraction of those who have used, or helped others to use, this method'.[15]

Within England, Scotland and Wales, there may also be women who are tempted to buy medicines online in order to terminate their own pregnancies. We know that one of the main reasons why people buy medicines online, even when they could obtain them under prescription from their doctor, is shame or embarrassment, and it seems plausible that this might drive some women to seek out self-abortion even when lawful abortion is available. To a frightened and panic-struck teenager, for example, buying a medicine online to trigger a miscarriage might seem preferable to telling her parents about her pregnancy. A woman who is determined to end her pregnancy when to do so would not be lawful under the Abortion Act might also attempt to self-abort. This was the case for Sarah Catt, who bought abortion pills from an internet site in order to terminate her own pregnancy, shortly before she was due to give birth. In doing so, she was said to have 'procured a miscarriage' outside of the statutory defences offered to doctors under the Abortion Act 1967, and committed a crime under s. 58 of the Offences Against the Person Act 1861. Initially Cooke J sentenced Catt to eight years in prison, on the grounds that 'bearing in mind the need for deterrence, a long determinative sentence is required'.[16]

To many observers, this sentence seemed draconian. A woman who has tried to kill her full term fetus in order to deliver a dead baby might appear to be in need of psychiatric help, rather than punishment. Cooke J's reliance on the need for deterrence to justify the long custodial sentence is also noteworthy. For most women, there could be few things more horrific than going through the painful and arduous process of labour and childbirth in order to deliver a dead baby. If a woman is in such desperate straits that that prospect does not put her off, it is hard to imagine that she will be brought up short by the thought of a lengthy prison term. The reduction in Catt's sentence on appeal might look compassionate, but it is at least arguable that psychiatric intervention might be a more appropriate response than punishment to self-abortion in these circumstances.

It is clear that the *Catt* case is by no means an isolated instance of a woman in a country where abortion is lawful attempting to self-abort using drugs she has obtained herself. In the Australian case of *R v. Brennan and Leach*,[17] a woman and her boyfriend were found not guilty of procuring the woman's miscarriage (the wording of s. 225 of the 1899 Queensland Criminal Code is strikingly similar to that of the Offences Against the Person Act) after her partner had obtained misoprostol and mifepristone from a relative in the Ukraine. The couple had decided that, at the ages of 19 and 20, they were too young to become parents and the woman did not want to undergo a surgical abortion. The judge ordered the jury to acquit if they were not convinced that the drugs used were

15 McDonald, H., 'Northern Irish Women Risk Jail by Admitting Use of Abortion Drugs', *The Observer*, 10 March 2013.

16 *R v. Sarah Louise Catt*, 17 September 2012. Sentencing remarks available at: http://www.judiciary.gov.uk/wp-content/uploads/JCO/Documents/Judgments/sarah-louise-catt-sentencing-remarks-17092012.pdf (accessed 13 January 2015).

17 Unreported, District Court of Queensland, 2010.

indeed 'noxious', and reminded them of the testimony of an obstetrics and gynaecology specialist, Professor Nicholas Fisk. According to Fisk, the drugs were not harmful to the person taking them and there had been no ill-effects on the woman in this case. These pills were, he said, taken by thousands of women around the world every year and were listed as an essential medicine by the World Health Organization. Fisk had further pointed out that it could not be proved that the drugs had caused Ms Leach's miscarriage, which could have occurred naturally. This slightly curious interpretation of the word 'noxious' – that it had to be noxious to the woman, and not just to the fetus – meant that Ms Leach and her partner were spared conviction and possible imprisonment. It could nevertheless be argued that there is something odd about prosecuting someone for taking a medicine which represents a safe and effective way to undergo a lawful medical treatment.[18] Women might also be tempted to self-medicate with abortifacient drugs bought online in countries like Canada, where abortion is lawful but mifepristone is not licensed for use.[19] It is impossible to know how common it is for Canadian women to self-abort using drugs they obtain themselves, but given the greater convenience of medical abortion, Canada's failure to issue mifepristone the equivalent of a marketing authorisation might serve to encourage some women to opt for DIY abortion.

In countries where safe, legal abortion is unavailable, demand for self-administered misoprostol is likely to be much greater. It is well established that in countries where abortion is illegal, rates of abortion remain high. Indeed, it appears that the abortion rate is *higher* in countries with restrictive abortion laws than it is where the law is more liberal.[20] Moreover, while abortion rates appear to be dropping in countries where abortion is legal they are increasing in countries where abortion is illegal and unsafe. It is impossible to know exactly how many women have unsafe, illegal abortions each year, but it is thought to be well over 20 million.[21] Each year, about 47,000 women will die from the complications of illegal abortions, and 8.5 million women will require medical attention.[22]

Unsafe abortion is one of the principal causes of maternal mortality worldwide, but it is important to recognise that it is a man-made phenomenon. Abortion itself is an extremely safe procedure, and medical abortions have made it even safer. There is no clinical reason why abortion should be unsafe anywhere in the world. It is laws which restrict access to abortion that are the cause of almost all of the mortality and morbidity associated with abortion. Although there are risks from buying misoprostol online and self-administering it, these are much smaller than the risks associated with more invasive illegal abortions, leading to the rise of a new phenomenon: the 'safe', or at least safer, illegal abortion.

'Safe' Illegal Abortions

Women living in countries where abortion is illegal may decide to purchase abortifacient drugs online entirely on their own, perhaps relying only upon the information on an online pharmacy's

18 Petersen, K., 'Abortion Laws and Medical Developments: A Medico-legal Anomaly in Queensland' (2011) 18 *Journal of Law and Medicine*, 594–600.

19 Erdman, J.N., Grenon A. and Harrison-Wilson, L., 'Medication Abortion in Canada: A Right-to-Health Perspective' (2008) 98 *American Journal of Public Health*, 1764–9.

20 Sedgh, G., Singh, S., Shah, I.H., et al., 'Induced Abortion: Incidence and Trends Worldwide from 1995 to 2008' (2012) 379 *The Lancet*, 625–32.

21 World Health Organization, *Unsafe Abortion: Global and Regional Estimates of the Incidence of Unsafe Abortion and Associated Mortality in 2008*, 6th edn, 2011, at p. 1.

22 Guttmacher Institute, *Facts on Induced Abortion Worldwide: Worldwide Incidence and Trends*, 2012.

website. But this is not the only possibility. On the contrary, two models for the provision of expert advice to women contemplating an illegal self-abortion have been developed. One is that promulgated in Uruguay before abortion was decriminalised, where the medical profession offered advice and support, but without crossing the line into providing illegal abortion services. The second is the '*Women on Waves/Women on Web*' approach, which ensures that advice on obtaining and taking abortion pills is freely available on the internet.

Uruguay

Until recently, abortion was a criminal offence in Uruguay. There were some exceptions, such as rape or risk to maternal life or health, but these were narrowly construed, and lawful abortions were rare. Abortion was nevertheless common, and rates of mortality and morbidity were high. What became known as the Uruguay model, *Iniciativas Sanitarias contra el Aborto Provocado en Condiciones de Riesgo* (Health Initiatives Against Abortion in Unsafe Conditions), was piloted in 2002 in Pereira Rossell Hospital, Montevideo, and was intended to reduce the risks associated with unsafe abortion through the provision of expert information, both before and after termination.[23]

Under the Uruguay model, doctors gave women with unwanted pregnancies information about the risks associated with different abortion methods, and told them how to take misoprostol safely. The doctor did not prescribe the drug, nor did he tell the woman how to obtain it. If the woman chose to terminate her pregnancy – and about a fifth did not – she would be encouraged to return for a follow-up appointment in order to confirm that the pregnancy had been terminated and to obtain treatment for any complications. At that appointment, the woman would be offered contraceptive advice. In seeing women for these two appointments, one before and one after the termination, doctors were not engaging in illegal activity. Instead, the medical profession was said to be fulfilling its duty to promote health and reduce morbidity by offering women advice and support.

Of course, the Uruguay model relied upon women being able to obtain misoprostol themselves. Much of this supply was through the black market, so there was a risk that the drugs were fake, past their 'sell by' date, stored inappropriately, or supplied in an unsafe dosage. Nevertheless, the Uruguay model appeared to be effective: since its introduction, rates of complications were very low and there were no deaths.[24]

Crucial to the Uruguay model was the emphasis upon training healthcare professionals in the 'twin pillars' of respect and confidentiality for women facing unwanted pregnancies.[25] The provision of reliable information and compassionate counselling encouraged women to seek medical advice. And this respectful and confidential consultation with the physician also appeared to serve a broader purpose than simply providing women with information. Women reported that the encounter with the doctor made them feel less marginalised, alone and scared.[26]

Ten years after the introduction of the Uruguay model, abortion was decriminalised in Uruguay during the first three months of pregnancy, provided that the woman satisfies certain procedural

23 Available at <www.iniciativas.org.uy>. Specifically, see: http://www.ips.org/mdg3/uruguay-millennium-goal-on-maternal-health-in-sight/ (accessed 13 January 2015).

24 Erdman, J.N., 'Access to Information on Safe Abortion: A Harm Reduction and Human Rights Approach' (2011) 34 *Harvard Journal of Law & Gender*, 413–62, at p. 457.

25 de Mora, R., *Eliminating Maternal Deaths from Unsafe Abortion in Uruguay: The Experience of Iniciativas Sanitarias*, UNFPA, 2011. Available at: http://www.unfpa.org/public/home/news/pid/8147#sthash.sBbk5UzW.dpuf (accessed 13 January 2015).

26 Erdman, note 24, above.

requirements, such as a mandatory five day 'reflection period' before she is able to consent to the termination (there is an exception to this for cases of rape and incest).[27] In 2013, attempts by anti-abortion campaigners to force a national referendum on the issue failed to attract enough votes.

Women on Waves/Women on Web

The *Women on Waves* website is available in 15 languages. It gives advice about how to obtain misoprostol: brand names are given, as are misoprostol's non-abortifacient uses for the treatment of gastric ulcers and rheumatoid arthritis. These can – the website suggests – be used in order to buy it lawfully:

> To obtain one of these medicines, one could, for example, say that your grandmother has rheumatoid arthritis so severely she can not go to the pharmacy herself, and that you do not have money to pay for a doctor to get the prescriptions for the tablets. If there are problems to get the medicines in one pharmacy, try another pharmacy, or a male friend or partner might have fewer problems obtaining them. Or perhaps you can find a doctor willing to prescribe them. Usually one can expect more luck at the smaller pharmacies that do not belong to a chain.[28]

The website then gives advice on calculating the right dosage. Safe abortion hotlines, staffed by volunteers from local women's organisations, offer advice on how to use misoprostol. These exist in several countries, including Venezuela, Chile, Kenya and Pakistan. Hotline numbers are posted in public places, including public lavatories. When women call the hotline, they are told about the brand names of misoprostol, where it can be obtained and how to use it safely. In addition to practical help, the website also invites women to share their experiences of abortion. The intention is to break down the stigma and taboo that can attach to abortion in countries where it is illegal.

The *Women on Waves* approach is not limited to letting women know how to obtain misoprostol themselves. Through its sister website, *Women on Web*, women can obtain an online consultation with a licensed doctor, who will, provided there are no contraindications, arrange for mifepristone and misoprostol to be delivered so that the woman can terminate her own pregnancy at home. Because the *Women on Web* website is blocked in some countries, the *Women on Waves* website offers alternative weblinks and an email address.

The online consultation service is available only to women who live in countries where access to safe abortion is restricted, and who are less than nine weeks pregnant and healthy. Women are asked to confirm that they are able to get to a hospital or first aid centre within an hour and that they have someone to help them during the abortion process. After the consultation, women are asked to make a minimum donation of 90 euros, more if they can afford it. Women who cannot afford 90 euros are asked to make direct contact, and the website promises that they will 'try to find a way to help you'. In case of complications, women are advised to seek medical attention and to claim that they have experienced a spontaneous miscarriage. Women are advised to have an ultrasound scan 10 days later, or to take a pregnancy test after three weeks. Five weeks after the delivery of the package, an email is sent asking for follow up information about both the outcome and the woman's experience of the process. Although an incomplete response rate means that the data gathered are not completely reliable, self-reported outcomes are similar to those of medical

---

27 Human Rights Watch, *Uruguay: New Abortion Law Breaks Ground for Women's Rights*, 2012.

28 http://www.womenonwaves.org/en/page/702/how-to-do-an-abortion-with-pills-misoprostol-cytotec (accessed 13 January 2015).

terminations of pregnancy conducted lawfully in an outpatient setting. The importance of this cannot be overstated: from the admittedly incomplete data, it appears that women undergoing early medical abortions in countries where abortion is illegal *can* do so as safely as women in countries where abortion is lawful. Of the women who gave feedback, 99 per cent had found medical termination at home acceptable.[29]

Of course, there are reasons why abortions provided in this way are unlikely to be as safe as those provided in countries where abortion is lawful, the most important of which is that the online consultation relies on women self-reporting the various qualifying criteria. Faced with an unwanted pregnancy and the choice between a dangerous backstreet abortion or misreporting how advanced one's pregnancy is in an online consultation with a doctor, it is easy to see why the latter might appear to be the safer option. Young women and girls are especially likely to underestimate gestation. Women might also be tempted to claim that help is accessible in an emergency when it is not, or to report that they do not have contraindications such as chronic adrenal failure.

Because the online consultation is only available to women with access to the internet, it would be a mistake to think that the *Women on Web* approach could eliminate the mortality and morbidity associated with illegal abortions. In Africa, where more than 97 per cent of abortions are unsafe,[30] a minority of the population has access to the internet. Even in countries with higher rates of internet access, this may be largely through public terminals, so it might still be difficult for women to access *Women on Web*'s services. Nevertheless, the option of internet-supplied safe termination of pregnancy is hugely significant. For women who are able to use *Women on Web*'s online consultation, the terrible public health consequences of abortion's illegality can be replaced by internet-assisted safe, early medical abortion.

Empowering Women?

Until recently, illegal abortions were – almost by definition – also unsafe abortions. Giving women advice about how to take mifepristone and misoprostol safely raises the possibility that an illegal abortion could be as safe as a lawful one. Anything that stops women from inserting sharp objects into their vaginas, and dying from the complications, is to be welcomed, but is safer unlawful abortion fundamentally empowering for women, or are there reasons to be ambivalent about both the Uruguay model and the *Women on Web* approaches to the illegality of abortion?

On the one hand, that a country's harsh and restrictive abortion laws might not have to hurt women seems like an extraordinarily progressive development. We know that making abortion illegal does not mean it does not happen. Without access to safe, lawful abortion services, women risk their lives in order to terminate unwanted pregnancies. Until now, the consequences of abortion's illegality have been high rates of mortality and morbidity. Is the possibility of women sidestepping these consequences and undergoing safe unlawful abortions akin to sticking two fingers up at a legal system that values the symbolic protection of fetal life more highly than women's health? It is important to remember that fetuses die in illegal abortions, and so the prohibition of abortion does not save the lives of fetuses. Given that abortion appears to be *more* common in countries where it

29 Gomperts, R.J., Jelinska, K., Davies, S., et al., 'Using Telemedicine for Termination of Pregnancy with Mifepristone and Misoprostol in Settings Where There Is No Access to Safe Services' (2008) 115 *British Journal of Obstetrics and Gynaecology*, 1171–8.

30 Sedgh et al., note 20, above.

is illegal than in countries where it can be lawfully performed,[31] its illegality does not necessarily reduce the incidence of abortion, rather it ensures that women die and are seriously injured as well.

In both the Uruguay model and the *Women on Web* approach, the illegality of abortion need not hurt women. Because self-medication at home can be safe and effective, laws which make abortion illegal do not have to have terrible public health consequences. The criminal law never stopped all women who wished to do so from terminating their pregnancies, but it did prevent them from doing so safely. If this is no longer the case, if unlawful abortion can be as safe as lawful abortion, is the power of those who seek to restrict women's options effectively neutered? If safe access to abortion is possible regardless of abortion's legal status, does abortion law cease to be a way to control women or prevent them from making decisions about their bodies and their pregnancies?

It is almost certainly too soon to draw this sort of radical conclusion. Although illegal abortions carried out after receiving expert medical advice under the Uruguay model *could* be as safe as a lawful abortion in a clinic in the UK, the fact that the woman had to procure her own drugs, perhaps on the black market, meant that in many cases it will have been much less safe. *Women on Web* will supply the drugs, and hence exercises some quality control over the medication which women use to terminate their pregnancies. But for women in whom early medical abortion is contraindicated, perhaps because it is not in fact an early abortion, taking such pills could lead to an incomplete termination and/or complications as serious as uterine rupture. Self-abortion with misoprostol can be extremely safe, but the problem of unsafe abortion does not thereby disappear. It may be preferable for women to take medicines bought online or on the black market than it is to try to self-abort using sharp implements, but there are risks associated with buying medicines from an offshore and unregulated online pharmacy or from a more conventional drug dealer.

It is also interesting to contrast the Uruguay model and the *Women on Web* approach. The Uruguay model medicalised self-abortion in order to make it safer: the doctor gave the woman expert advice on safe self-medication and a follow-up appointment meant that complications were not left untreated. The only difference between the Uruguay model and early medical abortion in a country like the UK was that, until the law changed, women in Uruguay had to obtain the pills themselves and take them without medical supervision. Medical consultations offered counselling, practical advice and some clinical supervision, and they also served to legitimate the woman's decision and make her feel less marginalised.

There is a clear parallel here with the legalisation of abortion in the UK, which adopted a medicalised model in which the abortion decision is not one for the woman to take on her own, but rather is one that requires medical expertise in order to legitimate the abortion decision. It is interesting that Uruguay's medicalised harm reduction approach to abortion in practice acted as the precursor for medicalised decriminalisation in 2012. Might it be possible that 10 years' experience of doctors saving women's lives by giving them advice and support offered persuasive evidence that medicalised decriminalisation could be an effective public health measure? In contrast, *Women on Web* adopts a self-help approach to making unlawful abortion safer. Women access information online and never encounter a healthcare professional in person. Unlike the Uruguay model, which involves a face-to-face encounter with a doctor who is able to check the veracity of the woman's statements about her health and her pregnancy, the woman controls the information she provides as part of the online consultation. A woman who is determined to obtain the drugs will be able to do so, even if no doctor would be prepared to prescribe them to her. Hotlines are staffed by volunteers from women's groups, most of whom will have no medical qualifications. Instead of

31 Sedgh et al., note 20, above.

regarding doctors as the legitimate and legitimising gatekeepers to self-abortion, the *Women on Web* approach enables women to take control of their abortions themselves.

Harm Reduction

What has become known as the harm reduction approach was developed through responses to illegal drug use,[32] and has had particular resonance in relation to the HIV/AIDS pandemic.[33] It has three core principles: neutrality, pragmatism and humanism. Harm reduction is neutral as to the rights and wrongs of an activity, and concerns itself only with the risk of harm. It is pragmatic, insofar as it simply accepts that people will engage in the activity regardless of its illegality, or any stigma attached to it. Its humanism comes from the idea that all people, no matter how marginal or deviant their behaviour, deserve to have their health needs taken seriously. Recognising that people are going to use drugs anyway, a harm reduction approach would focus on measures that enable them to do so safely. Providing clean syringes and enabling the safe disposal of used ones, for example, reduces the likelihood that people will share needles and risk HIV infection. In addition to providing the practical means to reduce risk, a harm reduction approach involves giving people reliable information about the safest way for them to engage in the high-risk and illegal activity.

There are many reasons for embracing a harm reduction approach to abortion. Termination of pregnancy is something that women will do regardless of its illegality. If abortion is going to happen regardless of its legal status, it makes sense to take a neutral and pragmatic approach to the reduction of health-related harms associated with illegal abortion.

Both the Uruguay and the *Women on Web* approaches to illegal abortion represent effective harm reduction strategies. The Uruguay model enabled doctors to do all that they could within the law to make sure women terminating their own pregnancies could do so as safely as possible. The law may have prevented doctors from prescribing the medicines themselves, but it did not stop them from trying to prevent avoidable harm by dating the pregnancy and offering advice, support and follow-up care.

The *Women on Web* approach tries to make sure women who are contemplating terminating their own pregnancies can do so as safely as possible. It provides advice and support, but also will supply the medicines so that women can terminate their own pregnancies without resorting to the black market or potentially fake or unsafe medicines bought online. These alternative approaches to illegal abortion have the potential to transform its associated health risks. Death rates from poorly stored medicines, or from taking the drugs at 11 weeks' gestation rather than eight are likely to be much lower than those that result from the brutal insertion of sharp objects. Crucially, however, risks remain. It would be a mistake to believe that online pharmacies offer an unproblematic solution to the problem of illegal abortion: misoprostone is a prescription-only medicine in the UK precisely because self-medication can be unsafe. Comparatively few women in some parts of the world have internet access. A safe abortion hotline may be life-saving for some women, but for illiterate women without access to a telephone, it will be no help at all.

It is also important to bear in mind that the ease with which abortion pills can be bought online is also likely to lead to an increase in unlawful abortions in countries where abortion is legal.

---

32 Des Jarlais, D.C., 'Harm Reduction: A Framework for Incorporating Science into Drug Policy' (1995) 85(1) *American Journal of Public Health*, 10–12.

33 See, for example, Petersen Z., Myers, B., van Hout, M.C., et al., 'Availability of HIV Prevention and Treatment Services for People Who Inject Drugs: Findings from 21 Countries' (2013) 10 *Harm Reduction Journal*, http://www.harmreductionjournal.com/content/10/1/13 (accessed 13 January 2013).

Women who cannot easily access a lawful abortion in the UK may be more likely to try to self-abort using drugs bought on the internet than they would have been to visit a backstreet abortionist. This includes women like Sarah Catt who are beyond the legal time limit for abortion in the UK, and teenagers who would prefer to 'deal with' their unwanted pregnancies alone.

A harm reduction approach to abortion sidesteps the question of whether abortion is right or wrong, and focuses instead upon the reduction of risk. Where abortion is illegal, there are good reasons for endorsing the Uruguay model, although abortion's subsequent decriminalisation in Uruguay has made it safer still. It is also hard not to be impressed by the solidarity between women embodied by the *Women on Web* model, which brings safer abortion within reach of anyone anywhere in the world with an internet connection and a shipping address (admittedly, not everyone). Yet it is surely obvious that the only failsafe harm reduction approach to abortion is to remove restrictions on access to safe, lawful terminations of pregnancy. The harm that is caused by illegal abortions is wholly avoidable and easily preventable. Women who die avoidable deaths, or suffer avoidable injury as a result of abortion's illegality have been injured by laws whose focus is indubitably not on the reduction of harm. Harm reduction strategies that leave illiberal abortion laws intact may be better than nothing, but they will always be second best to liberal abortion laws.

A harm reduction approach to abortion would emphasise the public health risks of abortion's illegality and would endorse steps to reduce these risks. The most effective way of doing so is to liberalise abortion laws, but in countries where that is not politically feasible, the second best approach is to facilitate access to information, support and advice that enables illegal abortions to be as safe as possible. It is clear that the Uruguay model and *Women on Web* services enable illegal abortions to be much safer than they used to be. It is hard to imagine how anyone could fail to welcome the development of effective strategies to save the lives of women who would otherwise die. Indeed it seems baffling that anyone might consider illegal abortions that kill and permanently maim women preferable to illegal abortions that do not have these terrible consequences.

Conclusion

The safer illegal abortion is an interesting new phenomenon. It is by no means universally accessible, and unsafe illegal abortions are certainly not a thing of the past. Nevertheless, as more of the world's population has access to the internet, explicit harm reduction approaches to the illegality of abortion have the potential to save thousands of lives and prevent millions of women suffering avoidable injuries. It is also worth reflecting on the effectiveness of adopting a public health approach to abortion's illegality. This makes it easier to co-opt the medical profession, as happened in Uruguay. It also makes the subversive approach adopted by *Women on Web* readily defensible: it may enable or even encourage women to break the law in their home country, but it is also likely to save their lives.

In the UK, many of us have criticised the public health approach to the partial decriminalisation of abortion that was adopted in 1967: it left power in the hands of doctors and turned women seeking abortions into supplicants. But while a rights-based approach may have much to commend it to those who are already sympathetic to the pro-choice position – 'it's my body and my decision' – the reality is that the public health consequences of restrictive abortion laws are so grave that a focus on harm reduction may be much more likely to persuade those who feel more ambivalent about abortion's legitimacy. A harm reduction approach to abortion would be explicitly non-judgemental, and could even be consistent with the view that abortion is morally wrong. If women are going to terminate unwanted pregnancies regardless of whether termination is lawful or unlawful, right or wrong, a harm reduction approach would try to make sure that they can do so safely.

Sheila McLean has long been an advocate of reproductive autonomy, but rather than following a slavishly libertarian agenda, her approach has always been more nuanced and attuned to the political realities of law reform. In the UK, the wholesale re-criminalisation of abortion is unthinkable. To the extent that it is unimaginable that the provision of safe, lawful abortion would cease in the UK, it might be argued that the pro-life lobby has lost. Sheila was right in 1990 to point out that reforms which chip away at access to abortion – lower time limits, for example – appear to concede that abortion is *sometimes* legitimate, and hence undermine the absolutism of the pro-life position on the fetus's moral status. Nevertheless, despite the apparent inconsistency of arguing that abortion is always wrong at the same time as advocating a lowering of the time limit for legal abortion to 18 weeks, it is clear that the anti-abortion lobby has realised that chipping away at women's access to abortion is a much more fruitful political strategy than dealing in moral absolutes.

Perhaps at the same time, pro-choice lobbyists might recognise the strength of an approach to abortion law reform that does not frame it as a competition between competing and irreconcilable rights. The medicalised approach to law reform in the UK adopted in 1967 was explicitly paternalistic: the decision should be for calm, professional doctors, rather than for hysterical women, at the end of their tethers.[34] In *Old Law, New Medicine*[35] – surely one of the most incisive and concise books on the legal dilemmas posed by new medical technologies – Sheila explained that the professionalisation of abortion in the nineteenth and twentieth centuries involved wresting control over abortion from women and their (female) friends, relatives and midwives in order to give that control to the (male) medical profession.[36] But while medicalisation has historically been synonymous with endowing doctors with a paternalistic, gatekeeping function over women's access to abortion, it is perhaps possible to emphasise the public health consequences of restrictive abortion laws, without simultaneously undermining the woman as the primary decision-maker.

A public health approach to the termination of pregnancy does not have to infantilise women and endow doctors with power over women's access to abortion. Instead, taking a public health approach to abortion does not rule out also making the parallel claim that illiberal abortion laws are bad for women's autonomy and for their equal participation in the public sphere. Pointing out that illiberal abortion laws are in addition bad for women's health need not detract from the autonomy and privacy-based claim that women should have the right to control their fertility.

It is also important for pro-choice advocates to realise that arguments grounded in women's rights and women's autonomy may be convincing for them but have very little purchase with anti-abortion activists, who do not necessarily care very much about restricting women's reproductive choices. Indeed, most of those who campaign against abortion would view laws that place restrictions on women's reproductive options as wholly desirable. But surely it must be harder for them to defend laws that have as their inevitable consequence the avoidable death and serious injury of millions of women? Framing the debate about abortion as a debate about choice enables anti-abortion activists to avoid admitting that which a public health approach forces them to confront: that the symbolic protection of fetal life may be more important to them than women's lives and women's health.

---

34 Sheldon, S., 'The Abortion Act 1967: A Critical Perspective' in Lee, E. (ed.) *Abortion Law and Politics Today*, London, Macmillan, 1998, pp. 43–58.

35 McLean, note 1, above.

36 McLean, note 1, above, ch. 4.

Chapter 3

Parenthood and Artificial Human Reproduction: The Dangers of Inappropriate Medicalisation

Kenneth McK. Norrie

Introduction

In 1992 Professor Sheila McLean edited a volume of essays entitled *Law Reform and Human Reproduction*.[1] Reflecting her consistent internationalist approach to legal study, the volume contained contributions from Australia, Canada, New Zealand, Czechoslovakia (as it then was), France, the United States and – my own contribution – the United Kingdom. That chapter focused on the Human Fertilisation and Embryology Act 1990, which the UK Parliament had recently enacted as a response to the legal and ethical issues arising from the developing medical technologies that had been explored in the Warnock Committee Report.[2] The major purpose of the 1990 Act was the regulation of medically assisted reproduction, and the licensing of its providers, and many of the issues covered in my contribution to that earlier book are examined in the present volume by Rebecca Cook and Bernard Dickens.[3] As well as dealing with regulatory issues, the 1990 Act, under the headnote 'Status', also set out the legal rules for identifying who were the parents of a child whose existence had been brought about by the processes regulated under the Act.[4] The issue of parenthood certainly does not lie outwith Sheila McLean's broad field of interest, and she has had a direct impact on at least one aspect of the parenthood provisions in the 1990 Act, by chairing a review set up by the UK Department of Health into parenthood after the posthumous removal of gametes: some of the recommendations in her report, published in 1998,[5] were enacted as the Human Fertilisation and Embryology (Deceased Fathers) Act 2003 and then re-enacted as s. 39 of the Human Fertilisation and Embryology Act 2008.[6]

The 2008 Act itself was a response to the substantially increased scientific understandings and capabilities in relation to medically assisted reproduction since 1990, but the opportunity was also taken to update the 'status' provisions in the earlier Act, in light both of the experiences in operating these provisions, which had proved to be much more technically troublesome than had been anticipated, and of the changing social realities of family life that had been experienced since the 1990 Act. The very word 'status', used in the 1990 Act to describe the issue, illustrates perfectly how dated the underlying assumptions of that Act were. A new set of rules, under the less

1 McLean, S.A.M. (ed.), *Law Reform and Human Reproduction*, Aldershot, Dartmouth, 1992.

2 *Committee of Inquiry into Human Fertilisation and Embryology* ('The Warnock Committee'), Cmnd 9314 (1984).

3 See Chapter 1: 'Reproductive Health and The Law'.

4 Sections 27–30 of the 1990 Act.

5 Department of Health, *Review of the Common Law Provisions Relating to the Removal of Gametes and of the Consent Provisions of the Human Fertilisation and Embryology Act 1990*, 1998.

6 This allows a deceased man to be registered as the father of a child brought into existence by the use of his sperm after his death.

recondite heading 'Parenthood in Cases Involving Assisted Reproduction', was enacted in Pt 2 of the 2008 Act.[7]

If anything, the social revolution in attitudes both to family life and family law was even more stark than the revolution in scientific capacity since 1990. A non-discrimination imperative had (none too soon) been embraced by law- and policy-makers, and same-sex couples (long used to constructing for themselves non-traditional families outwith the law's regulation[8]) embraced the technologies that made non-traditional methods of human reproduction possible. But the match was, and remains, ill-fitting. The 1990 Act constructed 'infertility' as a medical problem and offered regulation of medically assisted reproduction as the legal solution. Yet the 'infertility' of same-sex couples is not traced to any physical deficiency amenable to medical intervention: rather it comes from the biological reality that they simply cannot themselves provide all the genetic material necessary to create children. It is no surprise, therefore, that same-sex couples continue to access artificial reproductive technologies by non-medicalised routes. It is the purpose of this chapter to examine the continuing appropriateness of constructing the issue as a medical as opposed to a social problem and to highlight, through the case law, an emerging gender tension to which this has given rise.

The Importance of Parenthood

Why is parenthood[9] important? In the United Kingdom the significance of the question of who a child's parents are to the welfare-based judgments courts are all too often asked to make about the child's upbringing has long been a matter of dispute[10] (typically played out in applications for residence and contact orders[11]) but it has never been suggested that the matter is of no relevance and it is not without significance that parties to disputes about a child's parenting continue themselves to raise the issue of parenthood (in an attempt to strengthen their own case or to weaken that of their opponents). The House of Lords endorsed the use of the word 'parent' to cover persons who were not genetically related to (or had adopted) the child in *Re G (Children) (Residence: Same-Sex Partner)*[12] and though Baroness Hale famously allowed the word 'parent' to mean either a

7 The status provisions in the 1990 Act were not repealed and they continue to determine parenthood for children conceived after the coming into force of that Act (on 1 August 1991), but before the coming into force (on 6 April 2009) of Part 2 of the 2008 Act.

8 See Weston, K., *Families We Choose: Lesbians, Gays, Kinship*, New York, Columbia University Press, 1998; Almack, K., 'Seeking Sperm: Accounts of Lesbian Couples' Reproductive Decision-making and Understanding the Needs of the Child' (2006) 20 *International Journal of Law, Policy and Family*, 1–22.

9 I am using 'parenthood' throughout this chapter in the sense that Callus uses the word 'parentage', that is to say to refer to the biological link between progenitors and their offspring: Callus, T., 'A New Parenthood Paradigm for Twenty-first Century Family Law in England and Wales?' (2012) 32 *Legal Studies*, 347–68. She reserves 'parenthood' for what I describe as 'parenting'. The distinction we both draw is the same, but I adopt the terminology of parenthood and parenting to emphasise that the dichotomy is between 'parent' as a noun and 'parent' as a verb. It also consists with the way the word 'parenthood' is used in the headnote to the relevant provisions in the 2008 Act.

10 Is parenthood neutral to the welfare judgment, as the House of Lords seemed to suggest in *J v. C* [1970] AC 668, or a presumptive starting point, as the Court of Appeal held in *Re K (A Minor) (Custody)* [1990] 3 All ER 795? See further, Everett, K. and Yeatman, L., 'Are Some Parents More Natural than Others?' (2010) 22 *Child and Family Law Quarterly*, 290–309.

11 Or 'child arrangement orders', in the new English terminology.

12 [2006] UKHL 43, [2006] 1 WLR 2305.

genetic parent, a gestational parent or a social and psychological parent, the context in which these comments were made indicate that she had in mind 'parent' as someone who parents a child as opposed to someone with parenthood status:[13] it is to be noted that she never allowed the social or psychological parent in that case the title of 'mother'. In fields not ultimately governed by the welfare of the child, such as succession, child support and maintenance, 'parent' has a more absolutist (generally biological) meaning, irrespective of the social realities of the child's life.[14] It is not, however, crucial that the same people should be identified as 'parents' in every context in which the question arises. And, of course, as Campbell points out,[15] the law's conception of 'parent' may be very different from any individual child's.

Parenthood Disputes Prior to 1990

Parenthood disputes have always been strongly gendered, reflecting the very different interests of each gender. Before the passing of the Human Fertilisation and Embryology Act 1990, such formal law as there was on determining how the parent-child relationship was to be established focused on the identification of the father: the identification of the mother was not perceived to create any room for dispute; it is a truth that has bedevilled the male psyche since the dawn of time that, while women always know who their children are, men never do. Men are reliant on information provided by women. The law has long attempted to provide men with some certainty by creating presumptions of paternity from known facts, the most important, and most wide-spread, of which is that a child born to a married woman is the child of the woman's husband: *pater vero is est, quem nuptiae demonstrant.*[16] This is a presumption of biological connection, drawn from the man's relationship with the mother: fatherhood, in other words, has traditionally been located in a combination of biology and relationship with the mother, though biology is the sole determining factor in the absence of the appropriate relationship.[17]

Maternity disputes are different from paternity disputes, in concept, motivation and outcome. The doctrine in the *Digest*, *mater semper certa est etiam si vulgo conceperit*,[18] reflects the fact that for most of human history there was no basis conceived possible, other than pregnancy

13 Cf. *Alliance for Marriage and Family v. AA* [2007] 3 SCR 124 where the Supreme Court of Canada rejected an appeal (if on a matter of title) against a decision of the Ontario Court of Appeal (2007) ONCA 2 that a child had two mothers (the women who were bringing him up) and a father (the genetic progenitor who played a significant part in the child's life) – the application to be recognised as a mother had been brought by the partner of the genetic mother, with the support of both genetic parents. Interestingly the Ontario Court of Appeal contemplated that this recognition would have effect for succession and immigration purposes as well as granting a status and role in the upbringing of the child. See Harder, L. and Thomarat, M., 'Parentage Law in Canada: The Numbers Game of Standing and Status' (2012) 26 *International Journal of Law, Policy and Family*, 62–87, who suggest that the law's general resistance to multi-parenting models is to a large extent explained by its rejection of polygamy as a legitimate family form.

14 So for example the child in *Re G* (note 12, above) will inherit from its legal parent (the gestational mother) but (absent a will) not from those who parent him, such as the gestational mother's partner.

15 Campbell, A., 'Conceiving Parents Through Law' (2007) 21 *International Journal of Law, Policy and Family*, 242–73.

16 Justinian's *Digest*, II, iv, 5.

17 The European Court of Human Rights is highly suspicious of rules of law whose effect is to prevent the (biological) truth of a child's parenthood from being established: see the cases discussed by Bainham, A. in '"Truth Will Out": Paternity in Europe' (2007) 66 *Cambridge Law Journal*, 278–82.

18 See note 16, above.

and childbirth, upon which maternity could be identified. That ancient certainty was, of course, shattered by the development of medical techniques for creating a child using the genetic material of one woman and the gestational environment of another woman.[19] There was much academic discussion of the question of how, in the face of that possibility, the law ought to define 'mother'.[20] In the absence of legislation, there is no obvious answer to the question of whether a woman's genetic contribution is more important than her gestational contribution: in truth, both are essential to the creation of new human life. The Warnock Committee, faced with two analogies (basing motherhood on genetics as fatherhood is, or basing it on a donation model, as they suggested sperm donation should be) made a pragmatic choice, which the UK Parliament accepted and gave effect to in s. 27 of the Human Fertilisation and Embryology Act 1990, discussed below.

The very fact that such a choice existed in relation to motherhood reveals a deeper truth: that parenthood in the eyes of the law is never, truly, 'natural' but is instead a social or legal construct whereby the law *chooses* to preference one factor over another in the definitional quest to locate parenthood in an appropriate individual. Genetic connection is the factor that is chosen to identify, for legal purposes, fathers and marriage is chosen as the factor that presumes this genetic connection: these are choices made by the law no less than gestational connection is the chosen factor that identifies mothers. If this is so, then the parameters of parenthood are as vulnerable to social change as any other legal construct. It is well-recognised that from a child's perspective those who parent (as a verb) tend to have more significance to the child's wellbeing than those who are a parent (as a noun indicating a genetic connection): it is not a self-evident truth that the noun is more important than the verb. This is not to deny that knowledge of one's 'roots' has importance, but merely to suggest that in ranking genetic background with present upbringing there is nothing 'natural' in concluding that the former is more important, for any purpose, than the latter.

The Human Fertilisation and Embryology Act 1990: Mothers and Their Husbands

There was nothing radical about the Human Fertilisation and Embryology Act 1990: as with the common law, in determining parenthood one first starts with the mother and then one traces fatherhood through the relationship that she is in. 'Mother', as the lynchpin, requires a clear definition and was given one by s. 27 of the 1990 Act, as follows:

> The woman who is carrying or has carried a child as a result of the placing in her of an embryo or of sperm and eggs, and no other woman, is to be treated as the mother of the child.

This has been the law in the United Kingdom ever since: it is replicated in s. 33 of the Human Fertilisation and Embryology Act 2008. This absolutist approach renders the position of women in relation to parenthood far more certain than the position of men: the female provider of genetic material, if different from the gestational provider, is automatically and for all purposes excluded

19 Indeed the development of mitochondrial donation, presaged by s. 26 of the 2008 Act (inserting a new s. 35A into the 1990 Act) will allow the genetic material of two women (if in very different proportions) being used; see the Human Fertilisation and Embryology (Mitochondrial Donation) Regulations 2015 (SI 2015/572).

20 See Rosettenstein, D.S., 'Defining a Parent: The New Biology and the Rebirth of the *Filius Nullius*' (1981) 131 *New Law Journal*, 1095; Stumpf, A.E., 'Redefining Mother: A Legal Matrix for New Reproductive Technologies' (1986) 96 *Yale Law Journal*, 187–208; Douglas, G., 'The Intention to be a Parent and the Making of Mothers' (1994) 57 *Modern Law Review*, 636–41.

while the male provider will be excluded from parenthood only if various conditions relating to his consent are satisfied (and even then, as we will see, he retains an 'interest'). One of the consequences of this, as McCandless and Sheldon point out,[21] is that the position of the gestational mother in a surrogacy situation is made unchallengeably that of 'mother', with the result that she has absolute control over the parental order process and substantial control over the adoption process. By these means, surrogacy arrangements are rendered unenforceable.[22]

Starting from the certainty of motherhood, the 1990 Act follows a centuries-long tradition in filiation by drawing a fundamental distinction between births to married and births to unmarried women. Section 28(2) provides that if a woman was party to a marriage at the time of the placing in her of an embryo, or of sperm and egg, or her (artificial) insemination and her husband was not the provider of the (male) genetic material, then that husband will nevertheless be regarded by the law as the father of the child, though he can avoid paternity by showing that he did not consent to the artificial conception.[23] This has the effect of transferring fatherhood from the man who was the biological progenitor to a man who is not. This is less radical than it might sound, for fatherhood's starting point continues to be the man's relationship with the mother: s. 28(2) is little more, then, than a modern manifestation of *pater est quem nuptiae demonstrant*.

There is, however, an important limitation to the rule in s. 28(2), which is that it is applicable only when the child is conceived through 'artificial' means. So if a married woman becomes pregnant by sexual intercourse with a man other than her husband it is the biological progenitor who will be the child's father, even if the intent of all parties was that the husband would be – would perform the role of – father.[24] This limitation may be a necessary consequence of the fact that the 1990 Act is designed to regulate, and to provide parenthood rules following, medically assisted reproduction, but if so the rule in s. 28(2) is too broad since it applies to self-administered as well as medically assisted artificial insemination. Why a child's legal paternity should turn on the mechanism by which sperm was introduced into the mother is obscure.[25]

The rules are rather different if the mother was not married at the time of her (artificial) insemination. In this case, s. 28(3) of the 1990 Act provides that the mother's male partner will be treated in law as the father of the child if the treatment was provided to the woman and the man 'together'. Paternity, once again, is traced to the mother's relationship with the man. The phrase 'treatment together' proved unexpectedly contentious as a matter of statutory interpretation

---

21 McCandless, J. and Sheldon, S., 'The Human Fertilisation and Embryology Act (2008) and the Tenacity of the Sexual Family Form' (2010) 73 *Modern Law Review*, 175–207, at p. 183.

22 See also Horsey, K., 'Challenging Presumptions: Legal Parenthood and Surrogacy Arrangements' (2010) 22 *Child and Family Law Quarterly*, 449–74.

23 That the man must consent to the actual impregnation using identified genetic material – as opposed to consent to the idea of impregnation – is the result of *L Teaching Hospitals NHS Trust v. A* [2003] EWHC 259 (QBD), [2003] 1 FLR 1091. As a matter of strict statutory interpretation this result is questionable, though the pragmatic answer is, in a case in which the parties were in no genuine dispute with each other, understandable. Consent must be positive and not mere acquiescence, according to *M v. F* [2013] EWHC 1901 (Fam).

24 Such a husband will have the benefit of the *pater est* presumption, though of course that presumption is always vulnerable to rebuttal – made more vulnerable in the modern world by the certainties of DNA profiling.

25 *M v. F*, note 23, above, was decided under the 2008 Act where the rule in s. 35 is the same as that in s. 28(2) of the 1990 Act. The first dispute in that case was whether the pregnancy had come about by sexual intercourse (in which case the biological progenitor was the father) or by artificial insemination (in which case the consenting husband would be the father). The second dispute was whether the husband had indeed consented.

and there followed a substantial amount of litigation on the parameters of the phrase.[26] The importance of the provision, however, must not be overshadowed by its inherent ambiguity. There is no prohibition in the 1990 Act on artificial reproductive technology being made available to persons other than married couples, though there was a half-hearted attempt to encourage treatment providers to preference opposite-sex couples.[27] Children born to unmarried couples, no less than children born to married couples, need clear rules identifying who their parents are, and Parliament accepted that these rules should permit, as they do with married couples, transference of paternity from the biological progenitor to the man intended to play the social role of father.

However, the application of the rule in s. 28(3) is limited to pregnancies that come about by licensed medical assistance. This has the clear effect of pathologising artificial insemination, which is entirely inappropriate for female couples where the need for a third party contribution is not traced to any medical condition. Female couples do not suffer from any disability that needs 'treatment':[28] their practical need is simply for access to sperm, and their legal need (which was not met by the 1990 Act) is a means to transfer parenthood from the provider of the sperm to the mother's partner.

In the end, the result of the 1990 Act was not so very different from the common law. The crucial distinction in determining parenthood continues to be between married and unmarried couples and the right of parenting (in the absence of any further court order) remains exclusively vested in that couple. The provision of a rule establishing non-genetic paternity over a child born to an unmarried mother is better seen as an aspect of the vastly decreased significance of the concept of illegitimacy than of any great shift in legal attitudes towards parenthood itself.

The Human Fertilisation and Embryology Act 2008: From Status to Contract

From around the 1990s, systems of family law across the Western world abandoned the overtly political purpose of preferencing certain forms of family in favour of responding to the functions that families perform irrespective of their makeup. It was becoming increasingly obvious that the traditional family model provided too limited a focus for the law, and especially so in relation to the parent-child relationship.[29] Unmarried couples, though still without comprehensive financial claims against each other in England and Wales, have been permitted to adopt children there since

26 See for example *Re Q (Parental Order)* [1996] 1 FLR 369; *U v. W (Attorney General Intervening) (No. 2)* [1997] 2 FLR 282; *R v. Human Fertilisation and Embryology Authority, ex p. Blood* [1997] 2 All ER 687; *Evans v. Amicus Healthcare Ltd* [2005] Fam 1; *Re R (A Child) (IVF: Paternity of Child)* [2005] UKHL 33, [2005] 2 AC 621.

27 1990 Act, s. 13(5), which required treatment providers to take account of the child's need for a father. For comment see Blyth, E., 'The UK's Human Fertilisation and Embryology Act 1990 and the Welfare of the Child: A Critique' (1995) 3 *International Journal of Children's Rights*, 417–38; Laing, J.A. and Oderberg, D.S., 'Artificial Reproduction: The "Welfare Principle" and the Common Good' (2005) 13 *Medical Law Review*, 328–56. The 2008 Act amended s. 13(5), which now reads that account has to be taken of the child's need for 'supportive parenting'. A critique of the very basis of s. 13(5) in any form is offered by Walker, S.E.P., 'Potential Persons and the Welfare of the (Potential) Child Test' (2014) 14 *Medical Law International*, 157–71.

28 See Robin Downie's discussion of disability in the present volume: Chapter 7: 'Disability and Healthcare'.

29 See Sheldon, S., 'Fragmenting Fatherhood: The Regulation of Reproductive Technologies' (2005) 68 *Modern Law Review*, 523–53.

the coming into force in 2005 of the Adoption and Children Act 2002; increased financial rights and obligations were granted to cohabiting couples[30] in Scotland by the Family Law (Scotland) Act 2006,[31] and joint adoption permitted to cohabiting couples by the Adoption and Children (Scotland) Act 2007 (coming into force in 2009). An even more significant cultural development since 1990 has been the revolution in attitudes towards same-sex couples.[32] The law responded to this development by vastly increasing the protections afforded to such couples in both family law and equality law. The most important legal development in the UK for same-sex couples between 1990 and 2008 was of course the Civil Partnership Act 2004, which created a means by which same-sex couples could register their relationship with the state and acquire thereby virtually all the responsibilities and rights that flow from marriage.[33] These social and legal developments rendered the 'status' provisions in the 1990 Act woefully out of date and so, when that Act was revised by the 2008 Act, the opportunity was taken to amend the parenthood rules to provide (as the adoption legislation had already done) for joint parenthood for same-sex couples. The rules determining paternity were extended to female partners of mothers in two ways: (i) the civil partner of the mother is deemed to be the 'female parent'[34] or 'other parent'[35] of the child on the same basis as the mother's husband would be deemed to be the father,[36] and (ii) the non-registered partner of the mother is deemed to be the 'female parent' or 'other parent' if both she and the mother agreed that she should be treated as the parent.[37]

The clumsy terminology is to be noted. The Act cannot bring itself to allow a child to have two mothers. 'Motherhood' is reserved to the provider of the gestational environment and her partner's 'parenthood', traced to the relationship with her, is something different, and less absolute. Just like its 1990 predecessor, the 2008 Act starts from the solidity of the definition of 'mother' and traces co-parenthood through her relationship with her partner. The mother is unshakeably the child's first parent.

The unregistered partner of the mother will become father or other (or female) parent not, as under the 1990 Act through the fact that licensed treatment has been provided to the couple 'together', but instead through both the mother and the partner consenting to the 'agreed parenthood conditions'.[38] These conditions are, as McCandless and Sheldon point out,[39] deliberately designed to be contractual in nature, which can be seen clearly in the case of *Re E and F (Assisted Reproduction) (Parents)*.[40] Here, the mother's partner was denied parenthood because of a technical deficiency, rather than anything to do with her relationship with the mother, or indeed with the child. The

30 Though of lesser value than those of married couples or civil partners.

31 See Sutherland, E., 'From "Bidie-in" to "Cohabitant" in Scotland: The Perils of Legislative Compromise' (2013) 27 *International Journal of Law, Policy and Family*, 143–75.

32 This change is explored by Norrie, K., 'From Decriminalisation to Marriage: Changing Judicial, Political and Religious Attitudes in the United Kingdom to Gay and Lesbian Families' in Petersen, H., Villaverde, J.M. and Lund-Andersen, I. (eds) *Contemporary Gender Relations and Changes in Legal Cultures*, Copenhagen, DJØF Publishing, 2013, pp. 181–210.

33 And marriage itself was extended to same-sex couples in England and Wales by the Marriage (Same-Sex Couples) Act 2013 and in Scotland by the Marriage and Civil Partnership (Scotland) Act 2014.

34 2008 Act, s. 44.

35 2008 Act, headnote to ss. 42–7.

36 s. 35 of the 2008 Act, replicating the rule in s. 28(2) of the 1990 Act.

37 s. 43 of the 2008 Act, replicating the new rule in s. 36, which replaces s. 28(3) of the 1990 Act.

38 2008 Act, s. 36 for men and s. 43 for women.

39 McCandless and Sheldon, note 21, above, at p. 185.

40 [2013] EWHC 1418 (Fam). But see also *X and Y v. St Bartholomew's Hospital Centre for Reproductive Medicine* [2015] EWFC 13.

forms by which the mother and her partner signified their agreement that the partner be treated as parent were completed just after, rather than (as required) before, the insemination treatment was provided. In addition, the forms were regarded as invalid since they had not been preceded by the required counselling, and so, though signed, had not been signed with 'informed consent'. Though a contractual analysis underpins ss. 36 and 43, the availability of the contract is limited to couples who access infertility treatment through licensed providers. As under the 1990 Act, the unregistered partner will be denied parenthood – whatever the terms of any contract or agreement – if the couple use non-medically assisted means (whether sexual intercourse or self-administered artificial insemination with privately acquired genetic material). As we will see below, it is this exclusion that has caused most difficulties for the courts.

Notwithstanding its extension of the rules to female couples, the 2008 Act is, in its underlying assumptions, as traditionalist as its 1990 predecessor and it creates a limited and exclusive legal parenthood that takes as its template the traditional nuclear family. It reflects what McCandless and Sheldon describe[41] as 'parental dimorphism', that is to say a model that cannot conceive of more than two parents: (i) a mother and (ii) her husband or her civil partner or her non-registered partner. The two parent model may well have reflected both social reality and legal principle when no-one conceived of parenthood in any terms other than biological. Yet once the genetic underpinnings of parenthood are broken – and a central aim of both the 1990 and 2008 Acts was to allow that breaking without the necessity of court process (that is, adoption) – there is no logical reason why parenthood needs to be kept within the bounds of the traditional model. Callus similarly suggests that if the law were to preference parenting over parenthood then the way would be open to multi-party parenting.[42] In truth, this is a plea for the rejection of the distinction between parenthood and parenting but the distinction will remain necessary so long as some issues (such as succession) are unchallengeably governed by the former while other issues (such as parental responsibilities and parental rights) are founded (and increasingly so) on the latter. In any case, multi-party parenting would work only when all parties are able to agree roles without misunderstanding and the case law to be discussed below suggests that unambiguous agreement is extremely difficult to achieve.[43]

One important consequence of the law continuing to trace parenthood through the mother is, of course, that the new extensions of the parenthood provisions could not be applied to male couples. The only option for male couples is court action, either seeking an adoption order or a parental order following surrogacy.[44] The only concession made to male couples by the 2008 Act is its extension of title to seek a parental order to them so that, reflecting the adoption provisions, both male civil partners and male unregistered couples can now seek and obtain parental orders after surrogacy.[45] However, surrogacy itself is not regulated by the Human Fertilisation and Embryology Acts as it is not a practice that requires medical intervention. So medicalisation of parenthood has the effect of offering something to (some) female couples and nothing at all to any male couple.

41 McCandless and Sheldon, note 21, above, at p. 188.

42 Callus, note 9, above, at p. 360.

43 In the absence of a fully researched empirical study it cannot be known the extent to which such agreements work amicably in practice: it is only when they break down that they come to the attention of the courts.

44 The latter is governed throughout the UK by s. 54 of the 2008 Act.

45 The 1990 Act had limited parental orders to married couples (as, at that time, did the adoption legislation in both Scotland and England); the 2008 Act extended this to all couples 'in an enduring family relationship' (following the formulation in the English adoption legislation). The provision requiring that one of the applicants be genetically related to the child remains (s. 54(1)(b)). And parental orders have never been available to single people (s. 54(1)), as adoption sometimes is.

The major legal issue faced by male couples – very different from that facing female couples – is whether the payments they make to the surrogate will be authorised by the court.[46] So, while parenthood has been medicalised for women, it has been monetised for men. Yet contract – made available to opposite-sex couples and female couples as a means of achieving legal parenthood – is withheld from male couples for any surrogacy arrangement they make with a surrogate mother remains, as it has been since 1990, statutorily unenforceable.[47] The practical needs of male couples seeking parenthood are, of course, very different from the practical needs of female couples seeking parenthood but the legislature has found it noticeably easier to accommodate the legal needs of the latter than those of the former.

The Challenges of Same-Sex Couple Parenthood

The 1990 Act ignored same-sex couples (male or female) completely, leaving them with no option but to construct their own families without legal involvement.[48] The 2008 Act, following the absorption of same-sex couples into family law by the Civil Partnership Act 2004 and the reforms to adoption law, attempted to meet the deficiency, by offering same-sex couples access to joint parenthood. As we have seen, however, the 2008 Act is no less traditionalist than its 1990 predecessor, and female couples were offered parenthood recognition under the Act only so long as they conformed to the norms long-ago established by heteronormativity. It is no surprise, therefore, that a large number of female couples continue to see more attractions in private arrangements than through the medicalised and assimilationist options regulated by the Human Fertilisation and Embryology Acts.[49] This, together with the very much more limited options for parenting available to male couples, has led men, in particular, to seek to fashion new styles or forms of parenthood which, by and large, women have resisted.[50] A brave new world for gay and lesbian couples, with non-gendered parenting or role expectations – and with full legal support for their designs – this is not.

There have been a number of cases before the UK courts in which female couples have received sperm from men in return for some involvement in the child's upbringing and in which relationships between the parties – the women on one side, the man on the other – have broken down.[51] Cases that come before the courts, necessarily involving arrangements that have not worked, cannot, of

---

46 See for example *Re D (Children) (Surrogacy) (Parental Order)* [2012] EWHC 2631 (Fam), [2013] 1 All ER 962; *A and B v. SA* [2013] EWHC 426 (Fam); *J v. G (Parental Orders)* [2013] EWHC 1432 (Fam); *Re P-M* [2013] EWHC 2328 (Fam); *AB and CD v. CT* [2015] EWFC 12.

47 Surrogacy Arrangements Act 1985, s. 1A, as inserted by the Human Fertilisation and Embryology Act 1990, s. 36(1). The 1985 Act makes it illegal for solicitors to give (paid) legal advice as to the terms of any surrogacy arrangement: see *JP v. LP* [2014] EWHC 595.

48 See note 8, above.

49 See Smith, L., 'Tangling the Web of Legal Parenthood: Legal Responses to the Use of Known Donors in Lesbian Parenting Arrangements' (2013) 33 *Legal Studies*, 355–81, at pp. 373–4.

50 This may be unfair. A noticeable feature of the cases to be discussed is that the women nearly always envisage *some* role for the man in the child's life – just not as involving as the man envisages. See Smith, L., 'Is Three a Crowd? Lesbian Mothers' Perspectives on Parental Status in Law' (2006) 18 *Child and Family Law Quarterly*, 231–52. And see the co-operating three parents in *Alliance for Marriage and Family v. AA*, note 13, above.

51 US cases with the same factual bases are discussed by Maxwell, N.G., 'The Kansas Case of *KMH*: US Law Concerning the Legal Status of Known Sperm Donors' (2008) 4 *Utrecht Law Review*, 135–61.

course, be taken to indicate the likelihood of such arrangements being successful. Nevertheless, the contentious cases do reveal how the courts respond to families created by non-traditional means, and they provide warnings as to likely sources of tension. The bewildering variety of results in the cases about to be discussed might be explained simply by the fact-specificity of any child law case, but Smith is right to point out that 'the judgments exhibit disagreements and uncertainties on points of principle'.[52] This is caused, she suggests, by the fact that orders relating to parenting are being used to resolve disputes about the meaning of parenthood.

A number of common themes emerge from the cases, the most obvious of which is the differing perceptions of the parties, even when what looks like clear agreement has been reached. Words mean different things to different people. So for example in *L and R v. W and W*[53] the women had advertised for a male couple who, in return for their sperm, would be offered the role of 'father' and 'step-father'. The men with whom they entered an agreement to that effect understood these terms very differently from the women. In *Re B (Role of Biological Father)*[54] the role the women saw for the man was an 'avuncular' one, that of a benign, but distant, uncle; the man saw the chance (and perhaps his only chance) to become a parent in an involving sense. The women felt they could accommodate his desire to be a 'parent', but both sides were using that word to mean very different things. In the end, the judge refused to grant the man parental responsibility on the basis that he was likely to use such an order to interfere disproportionately. The women's position as parents of the child was affirmed, for to allow the man 'parental status' 'would not be consistent with [the women's] autonomy as a nuclear family'.[55] Nevertheless a contact order was made, its level being calibrated to allow the child to come to understand the true link he had with the man, but without developing a relationship of great importance. The judge talked of the father's 'unique biological status', indicating that this was a matter of some importance, but without explaining what that importance entailed.

Another feature of these cases, and one that clearly increases the scope for misunderstanding, is the lack of appropriate vocabulary to capture in words the true nature of the relationships between the parties and the child, and the role each is to play. The failure of the Human Fertilisation and Embryology Acts to provide a satisfactory title for the female parent who traces her parenthood to her relationship with the mother has already been noted. Connected to this problem are the sensitivities that existing language creates. The women often term the man who provided the sperm 'the donor' as opposed to 'the father' and it is sometimes this verbal distancing that motivates the man to seek, by court action, some formal recognition of his role in the child's life.[56] The lack of appropriate vocabulary was addressed by Hedley J, in *L and R v. W and W*.[57] Pointing out that 'father', 'step-father' and similar words developed to describe traditional family arrangements were entirely inappropriate in this type of situation, the judge suggested that the concepts of 'primary

52 Note 49, above, at p. 364.

53 [2011] EWHC 2455 (Fam), [2012] 1 FLR 1056.

54 [2007] EWHC 1952 (Fam), [2008] 1 FLR 1015.

55 [2008] 1 FLR 1015, at 1023.

56 See for example *X v. Y* (2002) SLT (Sh Ct) 161 (discussed in Norrie, K., 'Contact, Welfare and the Right to (Gay) Family Life' (2003) *SLT (News)*, 23–7) and *Re D* [2006] EWHC 2 (Fam), [2006] 1 FCR 556.

57 [2011] EWHC 2455 (Fam), [2012] 1 FLR 1056 and, later *Re P (Contact)* [2011] EWHC 3431 (Fam), [2012] 1 FLR 1068. This case has many similarities to the long-running litigation in New Zealand ending with *P v. K* [2006] NZFLR 22, though the court's approach was very different, founding strongly on the child's 'right to know both parents', which preferences (or at least was assumed by the New Zealand court to preference) the two biological parents. The European Court of Human Rights makes the same assumptions: see note 17, above.

parents' and 'secondary parents' better encapsulated the realities of the situation in such cases. He designed the order he made to ensure that the men had a role, albeit secondary, in the child's life: a role that ensured the child's sense of identity, provided a 'male component in parenting', and a general role of benign parenting. The women would remain as what Hedley J described as 'principal parenters' and the men as 'secondary parenters'. As in *Re B (Role of Biological Father)*, the judge was attempting to structure an order that recognised the women as the nuclear family, with the man as a benign, if always external, presence in the child's life.

Neither the attempt to structure parenthood at different levels nor the terminology suggested by Hedley J found approval in one of the few cases on the issue to reach the Court of Appeal. In *A v. B*[58] the Court of Appeal held that there are no principles to guide such cases, other than that the welfare of the child is the determining feature. The implication of this is that identification of parenthood (primary, secondary or however it is described) is not a significant factor in determining issues of upbringing such as what parental responsibility, or what level of contact, any individual should have in respect of any particular child. Referring to Hedley J's approach in *L and R*, Thorpe LJ said: 'I would not endorse the concept of principal and secondary parents. It has the danger of demeaning the known donor and in some cases they have an important role'.[59] Rather, the Court of Appeal saw the mother and partner as primary carers and the father as being on the threshold of providing secondary care, which did not make him a 'secondary parent'. Thorpe LJ nevertheless found no difficulty in describing all three parties as 'parents'.[60]

The vulnerability of the mother's partner (especially significant in *A v. B* because the man was both the biological father and indeed married to the mother:[61] as such he automatically possessed full parental responsibilities and parental rights, while the partner had none) is a feature underpinning many of the cases. In the Scottish case of *X v. Y* the sheriff exacerbated that vulnerability by conferring parental responsibilities and parental rights on the father but withholding them from the mother's partner. A clear hierarchy of 'parent' is apparent here, with the mother (gestationally defined) at the top, followed by the father and then in what seems a distant, because always artificial, third place the mother's partner. *X v. Y* was of course decided before the 2008 Act, which allows 'parenthood' (as well as parental responsibilities and parental rights) to be conferred on the partner, but given that the partner is usually as closely involved in the child's upbringing as the mother, and more closely involved than the father, it illustrates sharply the law's reluctance to construct the parental hierarchy in a manner that places parenting on equal terms with parenthood. Millbank (in discussing what she called the 'intra-lesbian' disputes)[62] reminds us that parenting of the sort done by the partner has never created 'parenthood', while the man's biological connection to the child historically has done so. This, she suggests, explains why the man's biological status is afforded greater weight than the partner's parenting role.

Courts have often perceived the mother's partner as the interloper in the family, by drawing an analogy with heterosexual breakdown. So in *X v. Y* the sheriff treated the father as if he were a separated parent of a child born to a relationship between the mother and the father. The reality of course was that the relationship into which the child was born was between the mother and her female partner who, having been involved in the decision to create the child, was in a very different position from a step-parent. It was the man and not the partner who was the 'interloper' into the

58 [2012] EWCA Civ 285, [2012] 1 WLR 3456.

59 [2012] EWCA Civ 285, [2012] 1 WLR 3456, at para. 30.

60 [2012] EWCA Civ 285, [2012] 1 WLR 3456.

61 The mother had married him in order to hide her sexuality.

62 Millbank, J., 'The Limits of Functional Family: Lesbian Mother Litigation in the Era of the Eternal Biological Family' (2008) 22 *International Journal of Law, Policy and Family*, 149–77.

child's life. The male claimant in *Re D*[63] argued in exactly the same way – as the child's father he had much to offer the child which the women's (and particularly the partner's) recalcitrant attitudes were denying the child.

The tendency to analyse these disputes as if they were traditional separated heterosexual parent cases may paradoxically be traced to the decision in *Re G (Residence: Same-Sex Partner)*[64] where a new conception of parenthood beyond the traditional was first endorsed by the House of Lords. The judges in that case (which was a dispute between the women themselves rather than one of a man against a female couple) were at pains to present the case as no different from any other residence/contact dispute. While, from an equality point of view, this has some attractions – 'it took sex out of the equation, in a historical legal context in which (homo)sex usually operated as a disadvantage'[65] – it nevertheless runs the risk of failing to recognise, and make appropriate provision for, the complexities of individual families and has bedevilled the quite different type of case (men against women) being considered here.

Perhaps the most interesting feature of these 'known donor' cases is that in each of them men are attempting to create a new form of parenthood where they have recognition and some involvement, though less than that expected (or demanded) of the traditional father. Female couples, by and large, have preferred to replicate the nuclear model of family life (as a means of providing security to the position of the partner) and the courts have been reluctant to move beyond that model. In *Re D*,[66] for example, the judge granted parental responsibility to the man, though removed it of much of its content, in order to give recognition to the man as a 'parent of a very different sort'.[67] Smith suggests that this is a judicial attempt to recognise the differing aims of the parties – the women wanted affirmation that they were the decision-makers in the child's life, the man wanted recognition of his status as father – but criticises the result as being at odds with the existing legal position of distinguishing between parenthood and parenting: an order relating to parenting was used to recognise the man's parenthood.[68] The man's influence over the child's upbringing was again the issue in *R v. E (Female Parent: Known Father)*,[69] where the issue of parenthood once again influenced the decision on a question of parenting. The man's application for a residence order – sought as a result of disagreement that arose between the man and the women about certain aspects of the child's upbringing – was refused, though a contact order was made on his behalf and a joint residence order in favour of the women was also made. Bennett J said that the father had never been a 'co-parent' – meaning it seems he had never adopted the role of social or psychological parent, and though he was the genetic parent who had a real relationship with the child, that was not regarded as giving him any sort of veto over how the women, whom the parties had agreed were the child's 'parents', brought up the child. The man was in no better position than, for example, a concerned grandparent who disapproved of some aspects of his or her grandchild's

63 [2006] EWHC 2 (Fam), [2006] 1 FCR 556.

64 [2006] UKHL 43, [2006] 1 WLR 2305.

65 Diduck, A., '"If Only We Can Find the Appropriate Terms to Use the Issue Will Be Solved": Law, Identity and Parenthood' (2007) 19 *Child and Family Law Quarterly*, 458–80, at p. 461.

66 [2006] EWHC 2 (Fam), [2006] 1 FCR 556.

67 [2006] EWHC 2 (Fam), [2006] 1 FCR 556, at para. [93].

68 Smith, note 49, above, at pp. 364–6. Her point is that it is rare for a father's application for parental responsibility to be refused, even when day to day care of the child is being provided by others. The case may be better explained by the judge at the end of her judgment: at para. [94] Black J pointed out that the practical reality of her order was to ensure that the man's consent would be needed were the mother's partner ever to seek to adopt the child (and cut him off completely).

69 [2010] EWHC 417 (Fam).

upbringing at the hands of the parents. The judge was more influenced by the social realities than biological background, but the reasoning is still fundamentally traditionalist: Callus uses this case to illustrate her contention that the 'two parents and no more' model adopted by the law creates tensions that ultimately detract from the child's welfare.[70] The parties' own attempts to construct a matrix of family relationships beyond a traditional model failed because they were unable to agree its parameters – and the court responded by setting traditionalist parameters for them.

The continuing strength of the biological claim to parenthood is shown starkly in the first case in which the 2008 Act was directly applicable and in which, therefore, the biological link had been rendered legally irrelevant. What is remarkable about *Re G (A Child)*,[71] where the Act effected a transference of parenthood from the men to the women, and revealing how embedded traditionalist ideas of the role of men and women in parenting are, is that the consequences of that transference were effectively ignored by the court. The case involved one male couple, two female couples and three children. The disputes were entirely typical: the men had understood a far greater involvement in the lives of the children than the women had either contemplated or were comfortable with. After some years of disagreement, the men eventually went to court, seeking both parental responsibility (over their own biological children) and contact (in relation to all three children). Their problem was that, both female couples being in civil partnerships and the conceptions having been achieved by artificial (though not medically-assisted) insemination, the female partners of the mothers were 'parents' under the terms of s. 42 of the 2008 Act and the men's parental connections to the children were as a consequence completely severed. The result, in English law, was that the men (as strangers to the children) needed to obtain the court's leave to seek the orders,[72] and the decision relates to the application for leave. The men argued that the children would benefit by knowing who their fathers were (blithely ignoring the legal point that these children had no fathers); the women argued that to grant leave to the men would subvert the policy behind the 2008 Act, which the judge accepted was to allow lesbian couples to be joint – and exclusive – parents. Leave to seek contact orders was granted to both men,[73] and the interesting feature of the case is why: the judge held that the men were, whatever the 2008 Act says, the biological parents of the children and this gave them a clear interest entitling them to seek contact. They might not be legal fathers but they were, when all is said and done, fathers. This reflects, if in starker form since the law had acted to terminate fatherhood, the biological determinism inherent in, for example, Black J's acceptance in *Re D*[74] that she was 'considerably influenced by the reality that Mr B is D's father. Whatever new designs human beings have [including, she may be taken to imply, legal designs] for the structures of their families, that aspect of nature *cannot* be overcome'. Mr B is D's father only if we adhere, whatever the law says, to biology as the 'true' definition of parenthood

The biological connection, therefore, continues to give an interest notwithstanding the terms of the 2008 Act and the cutting of the parental link is not as absolute as it appears. It may, however, be that biology gives an interest in this way only to men, for it is not at all clear that the same result would have been reached in relation to a biological mother who, on egg donation, lost her claim to the status of mother. It is unlikely that such a woman would be held to retain a 'clear interest' even

70 Callus, note 9, above, at p. 353.

71 [2013] EWHC 134 (Fam), [2013] 1 FLR 1334.

72 Scots law does not require court leave in these circumstances: any person 'claiming an interest' may seek an order under s. 11(3)(a)(i) of the Children (Scotland) Act 1995.

73 Leave was denied in respect of residence orders since the children were being perfectly well looked after by their mothers. Seeking residence as opposed to contact is likely to be nothing more than a negotiating tactic in many cases.

74 [2006] 1 FCR 556, at 582.

after the law had cut off her maternity. The egg donor, though biologically linked to the child, is not in any legal sense the 'mother', and perhaps she is not the mother in any socially understood sense either (except in the eyes of the geneticist). Perhaps an explanation for this difference in treatment is to be found deep in our (gendered) psyche: men who donate genetic material seem to need a continuing connection with the products of that material far more than women who donate genetic material. I suspect that, if true, this is a consequence of the fact that, for most of humanity's history, the biological connection (even when presumed) was all that a father had, while a mother had (and is expected to have) a clear nurturing role. It is no mere etymological quirk that the words 'mother' and 'father' carry, when used as verbs, very different connotations – to mother is to nurture while to father is to do no more than to procreate.

All of the cases considered above concerned questions relating to the child's upbringing and each, therefore, required ultimately to be decided on the basis that the welfare of the child – as opposed to who the child's parents are – was paramount. As such, they are all in their fundaments part of the long-running debate around the extent to which a parental relationship, however that is established, affects the welfare judgment.[75] However, parenthood as a matter of fact is sometimes determinative of questions to which the welfare judgment has never been relevant. For example the law of intestate succession operates on the assumption that a child has (at most) two parents, identified in an absolutist sense: parenthood is determinative of succession irrespective of who is parenting the child. There is no doubt that a person identified as a parent by the Human Fertilisation and Embryology Acts 1990 or 2008 will be a 'parent' for the purposes of the law of intestate succession and that the cutting of the parental links embodied in these Acts will be given effect without qualification. The biological fathers in *Re G (A Child)*[76] are, therefore, not the children's fathers for succession purposes, even while they have an interest, traced to their biological parenthood, entitling them to seek some parenting role in the children's lives.

The Child Support Act 1990 similarly limits its obligations to 'parents' as strictly defined by law.[77] Private law claims for maintenance will turn on the interpretation of the appropriate statute. In *T v. B*[78] a female couple had a child after artificial insemination from an unknown donor through a clinic licensed under the 1990 Act. This cut off the male donor's paternity but without (as the 2008 Act would subsequently do) transferring parenthood to the mother's female partner, but the partner nevertheless obtained an order under the Children Act 1989 allowing her to share in the parenting of the child. After the couple separated the mother failed in her attempt to enforce a maintenance obligation against the partner. This obligation was imposed by the Children Act 1989[79] on anyone who was a 'parent' of the child, but that word in that context was held to be limited to biological parents and those who had become parents by operation of the law (such as through adoption) and so did not extend to persons who (merely) had parental responsibility. On the other hand, in Scotland an obligation of aliment (private maintenance) is owed not only by a 'parent' (by which is presumably meant a legal parent) to his or her child but also by a person to a child who has 'been accepted by him as a child of his family'.[80] There is some scope in Scotland therefore for financial obligation to be traced to factual parenting as well as to biological parenthood.

75 Note 10, above.

76 [2013] EWHC 134 (Fam), [2013] 1 FLR 1334.

77 See *Re M (Child Support Act: Parentage)* [1997] 2 FLR 90.

78 [2010] EWHC 1444 (Fam), [2010] Fam 193.

79 Sched. 1 para. 1.

80 Family Law (Scotland) Act 1985, s. 1(1)(d). A similar result is achieved in Canada: *Chartier v. Chartier* [1999] 1 SCR 242.

Conclusion

It is tempting to see the 2008 Act as a radical re-imagining of parenthood, with its move away from genetic definitions and its embracing of gay and lesbian families; the very complexity of the parenthood provisions seems designed to reflect the multiplicity of modern family forms. It is more likely, however, that as Eijkholt suggests[81] the 2008 Act was not designed to embrace personal or procreative autonomy[82] but to do no more than to make certain technologies available for therapeutic reasons only. If this is so then the parenthood provisions in the Human Fertilisation and Embryology Acts are properly to be seen not as liberalising measures but merely as necessary consequences of the regulation contained in the Acts of therapeutic treatment. Neither the recognition of joint parenthood for unmarried couples (the major innovation of the 1990 Act) nor the extension of the rules to same-sex couples (the major innovation of the 2008 Act) alters the conception of 'family' as two parents who live together permanently and exclusively, bringing up their children without interference from any individual outside the nucleus. It is for this reason that the Acts are of such little assistance in resolving disputes arising from attempts to exercise procreative autonomy in a non-therapeutic context.[83]

The focus in the Human Fertilisation and Embryology Acts on mothers explains why they are unable to offer much to male couples, and this suggests a deeply rooted understanding of parenting as a fundamentally female activity. For ostensibly anti-discrimination reasons, the 2008 Act addressed the needs of female couples by providing a mechanism to transfer parenthood from the male progenitor to the mother's partner. The needs of male couples (such as mechanisms to protect their interests in surrogacy arrangements) are, of necessity, very different and quite palpably medical intervention offers them nothing: the 2008 Act made no attempt to make surrogacy arrangements more certain (even while it made parental orders after surrogacy available to all couples irrespective of gender-mix). Surrogacy arrangements remain unenforceable, and the financial aspects of these arrangements remain subject to judicial oversight.[84] There are sound reasons why the law should resist allowing surrogacy arrangements to become enforceable contracts,[85] but as we have seen the 2008 Act, by embracing a contract model for unregistered opposite-sex couples and unregistered female couples, does suggest that there is some room in the law's design of parenthood for enforceable contracts. And it is not obvious why the exclusion of the female connection to children (which disproportionately inhibits male couples seeking to become parents) should always require judicial approval while the termination of the male connection does not. Neither the law nor social policy can or should ignore the differing contributions men and women make to child creation but that does not mean that the existing disparity of treatment

81 Eijkholt, M., 'Procreative Autonomy and the Human Fertilisation and Embryology Act 2008: Does a Coherent Conception Underpin UK Law?' (2011) 11 *Medical Law International*, 93–126.

82 On procreative autonomy, see Brownsword, R., 'Happy Families, Consenting Couples, and Children with Dignity: Sex Selection and Saviour Siblings' (2005) 17 *Child and Family Law Quarterly*, 435–73. See also Zanghellini, A., 'Lesbian and Gay Parents and Reproductive Technologies: The 2008 Australian and UK Reforms' (2010) 18 *Feminist Legal Studies*, 227–51.

83 See Callus, note 9, above, at p. 364, who highlights the 'tangible incoherence between legislative developments following licensed ART [artificial reproductive technology] and common law stagnation for self-arranged artificial insemination'.

84 See note 46, above.

85 See Crawshaw, M., Blyth, E. and van den Akker, O., 'The Changing Profile of Surrogacy in the UK: Implications for National and International Policy and Practice' (2012) 34 *Journal of Social Welfare & Family Law*, 267–77.

between female couples and male couples should not be open to question. A better balance might be struck (for example) by removing judicial control over the financial rewards male couples are willing to offer.

More importantly, it needs to be recognised that men, whether coupled to other men or not, are increasingly embracing the role of parent – and this is to be encouraged. It is good social policy (for both men and women) to fashion a more gender-neutral view of parenting, that moves away from the ages-old allocation of parenting to the female domain. The cases discussed above might well be seen, in Smith's words, as 'a regressive effort to insert identified fathers into lesbian families'.[86] But it would be better to recognise them as attempts (if not altogether successful) to accommodate men's desire to fashion a new model of fatherhood which encompasses meaningful involvement in children's lives. Both men and women have a mutual interest in parenthood, even when parenting is primarily provided by a couple of only one gender. It would be a pity if the mutuality of interest in non-discrimination that exists for gay men and lesbians were to founder on an increasing disparity of interests in relation to parenthood and parenting. The Human Fertilisation and Embryology Acts encourage that disparity by medicalising the issue of same-sex parenting and by offering far more to women than to men. It is no surprise that the courts struggle to accommodate a new model of either parenthood or parenting, for this medicalisation of the issue inhibits the law from developing an understanding of what it means to be a parent unshackled from millennia-old perceptions of the roles that women and men *ought* to play in society's most important activity – the procreation and nurturing of children.

86 Smith, note 49, above, at p. 377.

Chapter 4
'Fetal Infants': At the Edge of Life?

Margot Brazier and John Harris*

Introduction

Birth, like love, changes everything: a woman who, a few hours before, retained exclusive control of her body and thus the fate of the fetus she carried, is now a mother with parental responsibility for her newborn. In many cases, though not all, a man who until the moment of birth was for legal purposes nigh on irrelevant becomes a father,[1] and acquires at least the chance to influence decisions about the baby's fate. Above all, in theory at least, the entity that as a fetus lacked legal personality is now a legal person to be protected in her own right, with, it is often argued, the same claims as her older brother or her parents. A 'bright line' is said to divide the fetus and the baby.[2] Amazing advances in neonatal medicine now enable more and more extremely premature babies to be resuscitated and kept alive to the joy of their lucky parents. Sadly, not all infants and parents are lucky and the infant survives for a short time but never goes home from the hospital, or lives, but is affected by severe disabilities. Parents and professionals have heartbreaking decisions to make about how far and how long they should struggle to prolong life. These human tragedies pose a host of legal and ethical dilemmas, three of which are addressed in this chapter: (1) How can we, and should we, make such a legal distinction between the fetus in the womb and the tiny neonate who makes it to birth? (2) Do we, and ought we to, assess the fate of the neonate exactly as we would make judgments about the care of her older sibling struck down by illness or injury? Is the 'bright line' between fetus and baby as radiant as it is claimed to be?[3] (3) As technology advances and science develops novel means to nurture the fetus, and perhaps even new understandings of what it is to be 'human' develop, may that 'bright line' fade into history?

Learning from Sheila McLean

It is impossible to choose a dilemma in medical law and ethics in relation to which one would not learn from Sheila McLean. The scope of her work in her amazing array of books and countless articles encompasses a vast canvass. She is no narrow specialist and on matters from birth to death she has made such a rich contribution to debates on law and medicine. Two factors guided our

---

* This chapter derives from a wider project funded by Wellcome 'The Human Body, Its Scope, Limits and Future' WT087349. We would like to thank Amel Alghrani for her invaluable comments on an earlier draft.

1 Or of course the mother's partner in a same sex couple becomes a second parent: ss. 43–4 of the Human Fertilisation and Embryology Act 2008.

2 Alghrani, A. and Brazier, M., 'What Is It? Whose Is It? Re-positioning the Fetus in the Context of Research' (2011) 70 *Cambridge Law Journal*, 51–82, at p. 52.

3 Alghrani and Brazier, note 2, above, at p. 53.

choice of the dilemma of the 'fetal infant'[4] in our tribute to her. After a gap of many years, the first author read again one of Sheila's seminal papers[5] in which she sought to find a compromise between the apparently implacable opponents in the debates about fetal status and abortion, debates in which the two current authors find ourselves opposed in the context of moral argument. Our 'war' offers us no joy and so we find in Sheila's paper a proposal that offers the tantalising prospect of a compromise which, as Sheila puts it, may not 'command the moral high ground' but might be 'a potentially practical step forward'.[6] Starting from Sheila's paper, we admit we have strayed into more general territory in reflecting on the dilemmas raised when an infant is born at the borderline of viability. Emulating Sheila, we are driven by a desire to copy the practical and scholarly way she approaches the most troubling questions in medical law. Sheila McLean has always been a scholar unafraid of getting her hands dirty addressing the thorniest of issues and applying a dose of pragmatism to ethical controversy. Thus as well as her published work, her lectures across the world, and all the students she has nurtured, Sheila has contributed in so many ways to policy-making nationally and internationally, and particularly in her beloved Scotland.

What struck the first author as she re-read 'Abortion Law: Is Consensual Reform Possible?' was how Sheila's arguments of 1990 in the context of abortion remain, and have become, relevant in different contexts. Sheila did not (and never expected to) reconcile the warring parties battling over the nature of the fetus and the rights of pregnant women. She did, however (as we believe she set out to), force all sides in the debate into uncomfortable reflection on the soundness of their own entrenched position. Years later, her arguments still command our attention. She casts light on problems of today and tomorrow. We focus on the innate problems, philosophical, legal and practical of the borderline that is birth. We examine decision-making about extremely premature neonates, whether born early by mischance or delivered early by design within a termination of pregnancy which, as proposed by Sheila, allows the woman to free herself of pregnancy while allowing the fetus a chance to survive.

Journey to Legal Life

Arbitrary age limits affecting rights and status are common in the law;[7] the boy aged 9 years and 364 days old cannot be charged with a criminal offence in England,[8] while his twin, born an hour before on the previous day and so 10 years old, can be hauled before the courts. At the stroke of midnight on her eighteenth birthday a girl in England is suddenly mature enough to wed, parental objections not withstanding. No such time limit has quite the same dramatic impact as the journey to birth. Once 'born alive' the baby acquires the legal personality that as a fetus, maybe only a few minutes before, it lacked.[9] Even if a wholly lawful decision has been made that the fetus should be aborted

4 A term used by the US scholar Nancy Rhoden, citing Hack, M., Fanaroff, A.A. and Merkatz, I.R., 'The Low-Birth-Weight Infant: Evolution of a Changing Outlook' (1979) 301 *New England Journal of Medicine*, 1162–5, at p. 1164: see Rhoden, N.K., 'The New Neonatal Dilemma: Live Births from Late Abortions' (1983–4) 72 *Georgetown Law Journal*, 1451–509, at p. 1465.

5 McLean, S.A.M., 'Abortion Law: Is Consensual Reform Possible?' (1990) 17 *Journal of Law and Society*, 106–23.

6 McLean, note 5, above, at p. 108.

7 See Lyons, B., 'Dying to Be Responsible: Adolescence, Autonomy and Responsibility' (2010) 30 *Legal Studies*, 257–78.

8 In England the age of criminal responsibility is 10.

9 *Paton v. British Pregnancy Advisory Service* [1979] QB 276, at 279.

should 'it' survive and be born alive, any active intervention to hasten death is in theory as much murder as killing any adult.[10] It may be lawful not to resuscitate the baby or to withdraw treatment, but only under conditions far more restrictive than those that allow for termination of pregnancy, even after 24 weeks' gestation. For just this reason, doctors usually strongly recommend that the woman undergoing termination of pregnancy after 21 weeks and 6 days should also consent to feticide.[11] The fetus must not be allowed to cross the 'bright line' to legal personhood.

It is this line itself that prompts the first dilemma about the status of the neonate, and for many people it makes no sense. John Harris put the case in his usual forthright style, asking: 'What do people think has happened in the passage down the birth canal to make it okay to kill the foetus at one end of the birth canal but not at the other?'[12] Sheila McLean makes the same point using less dramatic language: 'The distinction between full term handicapped babies and a late abortus is difficult to see'.[13] The distinction between an extremely premature infant and an abortus 'killed' at the same stage in gestation is harder still to grasp. Hence as Sheila and others have illustrated, the more extreme wings of the opposing parties in the everlasting debates on abortion join forces in condemning any legal rule that the fate of the fetus/infant depends on its location at the relevant minute in time. The anti-abortion camp concludes that any abortion after the point when a fetus could survive outside the womb should be unlawful. Their opponents ask rather why, in any logical world, we ban any form of neonaticide.[14] Sheila McLean, valiantly seeking to tease out a middle ground in the abortion wars, sought to distinguish between a claim to the right to be free of pregnancy – a claim that a woman retains the right to control of her body – and a claim that she has a right to demand fetal destruction. For different reasons, the second author of this chapter has asked and partially answered the same question.[15] The language of the English legislation that criminalised abortion, the antique Offences Against the Person Act 1861, prohibits procuring a miscarriage. The Abortion Act 1967 speaks of terminating pregnancy. Both Acts assume that ending the pregnancy and ending the life of the fetus are one and the same. McLean (writing in 1990) pointed out the error of that assumption in that in the later stages of pregnancy the developments in neonatal care allowed the fetus delivered early the chance of survival, a chance that is significantly better today. McLean pondered the scenario in which ectogenesis (an artificial womb) might make current debates on abortion 'obsolete'. If full ectogenesis should ever become reality so that the embryo never resided in a woman's womb then indeed the age old conflict between the rights and interests of woman and fetus ceases to be relevant, though as we shall see the 'war' over the status of the fetus is far from abated. More to the point for the moment is the development of partial ectogenesis where an artificial 'womb' can take over gestation in mid pregnancy. In a sense this has already happened. Extremely premature babies, from in one case 21 weeks 6 days,[16] can be supported in neonatal intensive care and survive.

---

10 But see Mason, J.K. and Laurie, G.T., *Mason and McCall Smith's Law and Medical Ethics*, 9th edn, Oxford, Oxford University Press, 2013, at pp. 350–51.

11 See Royal College of Obstetricians and Gynaecologists, *Termination of Pregnancy for Fetal Abnormality in England, Wales and Scotland*, 2010.

12 *Inter alia* in an interview with Sarah-Kate Templeton, *The Sunday Times*, 5 November 2006.

13 Note 5, above, at p. 118.

14 Giubellini, A. and Minerva, F., 'After Birth Abortion: Why Should the Baby Live?' (2013) 39 *Journal of Medical Ethics*, 261–3.

15 Harris, J., *Wonderwoman and Superman*, Oxford, Oxford University Press, 1992, ch. 7.

16 See the case of Amillia Taylor discussed in Alghrani, A., 'Regulating the Reproductive Revolution: Ectogenesis – A Regulatory Minefield?' in Freeman, M. (ed.) *Law and Bioethics*, Oxford, Oxford University Press, 2008, pp. 303–28, at p. 307.

Sheila McLean, in distinguishing between ending the pregnancy and ending the life of the fetus, advanced a number of propositions. From the point that the fetus is, to use her word, 'salvageable' the woman seeking to be relieved of a pregnancy should be advised and encouraged to consider a method of terminating the pregnancy that permits the maximum chance of fetal survival. Note, she never argues that the woman should be *compelled* to accept this option and she distinguishes the case of the 'handicapped foetus'.[17] Her argument raises two questions: (1) If the process of removing the fetus from its natural habitat (the womb) can be accomplished in a way that maximises survival chances and imposes no additional health risk or pain for the woman, on what basis can she claim a right to insist that the fetus be killed? As Singer and Wells note, we 'do not allow a mother to kill her newborn baby because she does not wish to keep it or hand it over for adoption'.[18] It does not suffice merely to counsel the woman not to kill the baby. (2) Why distinguish the 'handicapped foetus' from its unimpaired sibling?

Justifying Feticide?

Let us for a moment assume that procedures to terminate a pregnancy at a stage in gestation when the fetus has a chance, even a very small chance, of survival, can be performed in such a way as to maximise the chance of survival and at no additional risk or physical discomfort to the woman.[19] How then can we distinguish feticide from neonaticide? Given that babies can survive before the 24 week limit that in UK law narrows the grounds for termination, in theory a termination could be carried out at 23 weeks 6 days without evidence of fetal disability or grave risk to the woman's life or health.[20] Perhaps the woman did not discover her pregnancy till late in the day, or her circumstances have changed dramatically and she now feels that she cannot raise a child. After 24 weeks, in theory up to term, the woman may, if two medical practitioners certify that there is a substantial risk that if the child were born s/he would suffer from such physical or mental abnormalities as to be seriously handicapped, elect for a termination on ground of fetal handicap. However, that fetus may nonetheless stand a good chance of survival. The broad definition given to handicap within s. 1(1)(d) of the Abortion Act 1967 means that a pregnancy may lawfully be terminated when the fetus is affected by a condition which, were s/he to make it to birth, would not justify withholding life support, and there would be no doubt that the fetus must be admitted to neonatal intensive care.[21] In both such cases the strong likelihood is that to ensure the child is not born alive the termination will be preceded by feticide.

In our first example of the termination of a pregnancy at 23 weeks involving a fetus who (as far as can be known) is healthy, Sheila's paradigm case looks to be met. The woman who finds herself pregnant when she does not wish to be a mother should be free to rid herself of the pregnancy, but not to have the fetus killed. Sheila goes further and suggests that women might be asked to delay termination to increase the fetus's survival chances. In this example a wait, whether of 3 weeks or 26 weeks, would make a real difference to the chances of the child surviving and lessen

17 Note 5, above, at p. 118.

18 Singer, P. and Wells, D., 'Ectogenesis' in Gelfland, S. and Shook, J.R. (eds) *Ectogenesis: Artificial Womb Technology and the Future of Human Reproduction*, Amsterdam and New York, Rodopi, 2006, ch. 2.

19 Which is far from the case – see note 16, above, at p. 315.

20 Abortion Act 1967, ss. 1(1)(a).

21 See *Jepson v. The Chief Constable of the West Mercia Constabulary* [2003] EWHC 3318. And see Scott, R., 'Interpreting the Disability Ground of the Abortion Act' (2005) 64 *Cambridge Law Journal*, 388–412.

the risks of serious disability, but of course makes the legality of termination more problematic. So should feticide be permitted in such a scenario? The 1861 Act makes it an offence to procure a miscarriage and the 1967 Act provides a defence to terminating a pregnancy. Neither touch on the direct killing of the fetus; nothing in the 1967 Act expressly authorises feticide. Paradoxically, nothing in the 1861 Act expressly criminalises feticide. Its legality, if not morality, depends on case law establishing that given the fetus's lack of legal personality *in utero*, killing while it remains *in utero* is not homicide, albeit that if an attempt to kill is made and the child is born alive but later dies of its prenatal injury, the perpetrator may be convicted of homicide.[22] The European Court of Human Rights has so far declined to afford a right to life to the fetus.[23]

Sheila's argument is more one of morals than law; what the law might look like if her proposal were accepted rather than how it looks today. So let us test her case using the example of the healthy 23 week fetus. Four problems mar the beauty of the theory.

1. First, the very process of insisting that, while the woman may be freed of her pregnancy, she must accept all measures to promote live birth and be denied the option of feticide, necessarily means that the child is born not simply with only a small chance of survival, but that if she does survive she will live with a high chance of serious disability. The question becomes: is it ethical to promote a practice that creates a high risk of a child with serious disability?
2. The second matter derives from just that dilemma. A few more weeks *in utero* would lessen the risk of disability, so should women be invited or even required to accept a few more weeks of pregnancy before being afforded a lawful termination? They must wait for their 'reward', a guaranteed lawful termination. A woman in this situation should, as Judith Jarvis Thompson put it, accept a minimal Samaritan obligation.[24] But how long should this obligation endure? The optimal wait for the baby will be to term or close to term, maybe a further 10 to 15 weeks. The argument swiftly melds into the more general case put by those who oppose abortion: that a woman should carry an unwanted child to term and then be supported in placing the child for adoption.
3. Then there is a very practical issue. The 'successful' delivery of a living infant at 20, 22, 24 weeks may require a different and more burdensome (to the woman) mode of delivery, maybe a Caesarean section.[25] So far, the English courts have refused to compel women to undergo such surgery against their will.[26]
4. Finally, the crux of the case that a woman should be free to end her pregnancy but not to end the life of the fetus rests on the assumption that relief from the physical state of pregnancy is the likely motivation, at least for later abortions. This may be true in the rare cases where pregnancy poses grave risk to the life or physical health of the woman and such a woman may happily choose to be delivered in a manner that maximises the chances of healthy survival for both herself and her child. But what of the woman who discovers her pregnancy late, or

---

22 See *Attorney General's Reference (No 3 of 1994)* [1998] 1 AC 245; Fovargue, S. and Miola, J., 'Policing Pregnancy: Implications of Attorney General's Reference (No 3 of 1994)' (1998) 6 *Medical Law Review*, 265–6; Brazier, M., 'Parental Responsibilities, Foetal Welfare and Children's Health' in Bridge, C. (ed.) *Family Law: Towards the Millennium: Essays for P.M Bromley*, London, Butterworths, 1997, p. 263.

23 *Vo v. France* [2004] ECHR 326.

24 Thompson, J.J., 'A Defence of Abortion' in Dworkin, R.M. (ed.) *The Philosophy of Law*, Oxford, Oxford University Press, 1977, p. 112.

25 See note 16, above, at pp. 315–16.

26 *St George's Health Care NHS Trust v. S* [1998] 3 All ER 673 CA.

> simply changes her mind? Her motivation may be to avoid biological motherhood, to exercise her reproductive autonomy not to reproduce.[27] She does not, at this time, want her genetic child to come into existence. One group of interests that a woman ending a pregnancy might have centre on the interest in not producing offspring that she does not want, regardless of whether others want her to, or those others would like to rear any such unwanted child. Just as there may well be an interest in producing genetic offspring, there may be an equally powerful interest in *not* producing genetic offspring, requiring at least the same level of respect (whatever that is). What the substance of such claimed interests might amount to, or which might be the stronger, we will not investigate further here; we merely note that there seems to be the same initial plausibility in both the positive and the negative form of such a claim.

While it does not follow from any pro-choice or 'woman's right to choose' type of argument that she has a right or entitlement to end the life of the fetus *in utero*, such a claim might be founded on other legitimate interests that the mother has, depending on whether or not the fetus itself has any legitimate claims to life whilst *in utero*. Neither does it follow from the fact that it would be wrong to cause damage to a fetus *in utero* that would affect it adversely once 'out there' in the world, that such damage is wrongful if it is certain that the fetus will never make it into the world alive. Reluctantly, we find ourselves back in the very war we sought to avoid, the claims that should accrue to the fetus.

The Disabled Fetus

Sheila McLean states that her argument does not extend to the 'salvaging of the handicapped foetus'.[28] She notes that the courts have long sanctioned the selective non-treatment of full term handicapped babies.[29] She contends that termination on the grounds of fetal abnormality is 'permissible because of the needs of the foetus and not those of the mother'.[30] She reminds us that her argument 'is not dependent on the sanctity of life'.[31] As Sheelagh McGuinness[32] has so clearly shown, the problem with this exemption for the 'handicapped fetus' is that the fetal interests case is hard to make out. In practice, termination of disabled fetuses under s. 1(1)(d) of the Abortion Act is permitted for a range of disabilities that would never be seen as legitimate grounds to withdraw life sustaining treatment from a born infant. A *fetus* with Down's Syndrome may be killed by feticide after her mother decides she does not want this child. The *baby* with Down's, but no other impairments, must receive the same care as any healthy infant. Sheldon and Wilkinson[33] argue convincingly that s. 1(1)(d) allows de facto 'fetal euthanasia'. Neonatal euthanasia remains homicide.[34]

---

27 See *Evans v. UK* [2008] 46 EHRR 34, and see Alghrani, note 16, above, at pp. 313–15.

28 Note 5, above, at p. 118.

29 See also Harris, J., 'Ethical Problems in the Management of Some Severely Handicapped Children' (1981) 7 *Journal of Medical Ethics*, 117–24.

30 Note 5, above, at p. 118.

31 Note 5, above, at p. 118.

32 McGuinness, S., 'Law, Reproduction and Disability: Fatally Handicapped?' (2013) 21 *Medical Law Review*, 215–42.

33 Sheldon, S. and Wilkinson, S., 'Termination of Pregnancy for Reasons of Foetal Disability: Are There Grounds for a Special Exception at Law?' (2001) 9 *Medical Law Review*, 85–109, at p. 93.

34 Though note the strange case of Dr Munro: Dyer, C., 'Doctor Cleared of Act "Tantamount to Euthanasia"' (2007) 335 *British Medical Journal*, 67; Goodman, J., 'The Case of Dr Munro: Are There Lessons to Be Learnt?' (2010) 18 *Medical Law Review*, 564–77.

Crossing the Rubicon – Today

We move now to the legal fate of the neonate 'of woman born', and in particular, the baby born extremely prematurely. The neonatal period is conventionally defined as the first 28 days of life. The theory is straightforward. Once 'born alive' the neonate enjoys full legal personality. In its review of decision-making and fetal and neonatal care, the Nuffield Council on Bioethics put it this way: '[I]ndependent of gestational age, we consider the child of six days, six months or six years to be worthy of equal consideration'.[35] The baby of six minutes or six hours is in English law in theory as much of a legal person as the authors are at a somewhat greater age. The Rubicon has been crossed – though it should be noted that this metaphorical river, unlike its namesake in northern Italy, may be subject to geographical re-location when technology abolishes, or at least makes redundant, the concept of 'birth'. At such a time, maybe not very far in the future, we will be forced to reconceptualise the status of the emerging human individual, asking not whether it is viable in the sense of capable of living independent of its 'mother', but rather whether it is to be legally protected and what the reasons for such protection might amount to.

Meanwhile, today, relying as we still do on 'traditional' reproduction, neither the mother, nor both parents in concert, nor doctors, can seek to end the infant's life, even on grounds that would have justified its termination *in utero*. As the second author argued many years ago:

> In the case of abortion for example, if the mother is entitled to an abortion, her entitlement is to eject the fetus from her body, not to pursue it thereafter. So that her entitlement is not that it will die, only that it will be ejected from her body … it would seem doubtful that the mother had the right to pursue the fetus 'with an axe', so to speak, rather than let [others, who might be prepared to care for it] adopt it.[36]

He speaks here about bringing about a death that would occur after the removal of the fetus from the woman's body, assuming the moral parity of status between the *in utero* fetus and the being, of whatever nomenclature, pursued by an axe-wielding mother.

To return to the law, in making decisions about the care of her born infant the mother must act in the best interests of the infant, and if the father shares parental responsibility with her, both parents must give consent to, or agree to refuse treatment of, the infant.[37] The first and most important choice is whether the infant should be resuscitated and admitted to neonatal intensive care, and in the weeks that follow, if the infant is gravely ill, whether life-sustaining care should be withheld or withdrawn. Should the doctors caring for the infant believe that the parents are not acting in the infant's best interests, they may, and on occasion do, challenge the parents in the courts if attempts at mediation and persuasion have failed. If anyone acts to hasten the death of the infant, that amounts to murder in the same way as would similar action to hasten the death of any other person. And so, while (as we have seen) a woman could choose termination and feticide at 23 weeks' gestation simply because she discovered her pregnancy late and does not want to interrupt her studies, if the arrival of the baby catches her wholly unawares, she cannot seek to end its life. She may of course give the child up for adoption. In this sense the moment of birth does act as a

---

35 Nuffield Council on Bioethics, *Critical Care Decisions in Fetal and Neonatal Medicine*, London, 2006, at p. xvi and para. 2.19 (hereafter NCOB Report).

36 Note 15, above.

37 See Morris, A., 'Selective Treatment of Irreversibly Impaired Infants: Decision Making at the Threshold' (2009) 17 *Medical Law Review*, 347–76.

'bright line' and gives rise to the argument addressed above that it is illogical to rest so much on 'legal geography',[38] the chance of where the fetus or baby is located at the relevant moment in time.

The scenario above – a parent simply wishing to be rid of the newborn – while beloved of thought experimenters, is in essence just that, a thought experiment with little if any connection to the difficult decisions about withholding or withdrawing life sustaining treatment that parents and doctors have to make every day in neonatal intensive care units across the United Kingdom. In these real life decisions we ask whether the theory that the infant born extremely prematurely or an older neonate of a few days or weeks is granted the same status as her elder siblings translates into the reality that the neonate is granted just the same protection/status as the older child of six months or six years. We will suggest that she does not, and occupies in practice an intermediate status between the fetus and the healthy full-term baby. The second author might applaud such recognition of the absence of full personhood in this being that could be seen simply as an *ex utero* fetus. The first author would accord the baby moral status and see her as intrinsically enjoying the same claims to life and care as any other person. Yet both authors (albeit reluctantly) agree that in practice the infant is treated as not quite a fetus and not quite a baby; she exists, alas, in a degree of legal limbo, and that may be the best that society can do. A number of factors help to explain that legal limbo.

Although there are several judicial rulings on the treatment and care of infants and older children who are seriously ill and/or disabled, very few directly address the question as to whether a neonate (an infant of less than 28 days) born extremely prematurely should be admitted to neonatal intensive care or, later, whether life-sustaining treatment should be withdrawn. The jurisprudence makes no clear distinction as to age. The neonate below 28 days is simply one of that class of minors who can in no sense decide for herself.[39] Those judgments that do address disputes about the survival of a baby younger than 28 days old concern infants who are known to have at least some level of impairment or serious disability. In such cases, a diagnosis has been made that the baby has a condition that will affect its health and ability to function. What is in issue is how parents and doctors should respond. Should everything that can be done to prolong life be attempted? In attempting to set out the law as it applies to the extremely premature baby in relation to whom no certain prognosis of continuing illness or impairment can be made, one can proceed only by analogy, struggling to fit the general body of case law relating to older infants and children into a context which, if it fits at all, it fits only uncomfortably.

Why is this exercise so tough? The first hurdle is the line between still birth and live birth itself, the very location of the Rubicon. To make the transition from fetus (with no legal personality) to baby (with full legal personality) the baby must self-evidently be 'born alive'. The meaning of those two words is far from clear. Statute defines a stillbirth as a birth post 24 weeks' gestation of an infant wholly expelled from its mother who does not breathe or show any other sign of life.[40] So is a fluttering heartbeat before the cord is cut enough to constitute being born alive? If the infant emerges in apparently good condition but with immature lungs is she not 'born alive'? What of the baby born before 24 weeks who if born 'dead' is classified as miscarried but who if resuscitated has a chance of survival? Ancient case law looks at what might be meant by 'born alive'; nineteenth-century judges focused on evidence of the complete expulsion from the mother's body, independent circulation even if the infant never breathed and/or the placenta was not yet

38 See Wicks, E., 'Terminating Life and Human Rights: The Fetus and the Neonate' in Erin, C.A. and Ost, S. (eds) *The Criminal Justice System and Health Care*, Oxford, Oxford University Press, 2007, pp. 189–206.

39 See Brazier, M. and Cave, E., *Medicine, Patients and the Law*, 5th edn, London, Penguin, 2011, ch. 14.

40 Births and Deaths Registration Act 1953, as amended by the Stillbirth Definition Act 2002, s. 41.

delivered.[41] Those judgements, however, marked the division between liability for a criminal abortion for killing the fetus *in utero* and liability for homicide for killing the extruded fetus/baby.[42] The notion that a baby so sick it could not breathe could be resuscitated and live would have been seen as in the realms of fantasy. Case law on the meaning of the term 'capable of being born alive' in the Infant Life Preservation Act 1929 focuses on breathing but is contradictory. In *C v. S*[43] Sir John Donaldson MR speaks of 'capable of breathing either naturally or with the aid of a ventilator'. In *Rance v. Mid-Downs Health Authority*[44] Brooke J requires that the infant can breathe 'through its lungs alone, without deriving any of its living or power of living by or through any connection with the mother'.[45] The case law simply fails to meet the challenge of advances in medicine and neonatal care in 2015,[46] never mind a future that may allow for partial or complete ectogenesis. The extremely premature baby to whom modern medicine can offer a chance to live may on one interpretation of the law be 'born dead', and on another, the fetus, delivered well before it has today a chance to survive, may be 'born alive'. It is unsurprising that the legal spotlight does not shine brightly on the initial decision whether or not to resuscitate the baby who is born extremely prematurely. Parental preferences and clinical judgment will in nearly all cases be the determinant of the infant's fate.

Next, the consequences of extreme prematurity entail much that is unknown at the time initial decisions on resuscitation and admission to neonatal care must be made. The cases that reach the courts relating to the care of sick babies for the most part have the benefit of evidence of a particular condition or conditions on the basis of which a court can balance the benefits and burdens to the infant of interventions to prolong life. This 'balancing exercise' derives from one of the few cases that do deal directly with neonates: *Re B (A Minor)(Wardship: Medical Treatment)*.[47] B was born with Down's Syndrome and an intestinal obstruction. Simple surgery could remove the obstruction and B would then enjoy the then normal life-span of a child with Down's. Her parents refused consent but the Court of Appeal ordered that surgery proceed, describing the crucial question as whether 'the life of this child is demonstrably going to be so awful that in effect the child must be condemned to die or whether the life of this child is still so imponderable that it would be wrong for her to be condemned to die'. Note the emphasis on 'this child'. From these two words flow the problems in dealing with the care of the extremely premature infant born at the borderline of viability. In the second 2006 EPIcure Study,[48] of the babies delivered at 22 weeks, 152 showed signs of life at birth, 19 were admitted to neonatal intensive care and just three infants of the 19 admitted to intensive care survived to three years of age, one with serious, one with moderate and one with mild disability. Given that mild disability includes such minor impairments as a squint, survival for that lucky one in 19 would seem to outweigh any disability a squint entails. At 23 weeks, 339 babies showed signs of life at birth, 217 babies were admitted to neonatal intensive care, 63 survived to their third birthday, 17 of whom had some serious disability, 14 a moderate

---

41 *R v. Poulton* (1832) 5 C&P 329; *R v. Brain* (1834) 6 C&P 349.

42 *Attorney General's Reference (No 3 of 1994)* [1998] AC 245.

43 [1987] 1 All ER 1230, [1988] QB 135.

44 [1991] 1 QB 587.

45 [1991] 1 QB 587, at p. 619.

46 The NCOB Report recommended (at para. 9.11) that a consultation should take place to consider a new and more satisfactory definition of 'born alive'.

47 [1981] 1 WLR 1421.

48 EPIcure 2 studied survival and disability rates in infants born between 22 and 26 weeks + 6 days' gestation focusing in particular on the effect of advances in neonatal care since the earlier EPIcure 1 study in 1995: accessible at www.epicure.ac.uk.

disability and 32 had no impairment at all. But at birth who the lucky infants will be is largely imponderable.[49] There is little evidence about the likely outcome for 'this child'.

Both professional guidance[50] and the Nuffield Council Report *Critical Care Decisions in Fetal and Neonatal Medicine: The Ethical Issues* pay high regard to parental judgments of the best interests of the neonate, and the weight to be accorded to parental wishes correlates in some measure to the gestational age of the infant at birth. Thus the Nuffield Report proposes guidelines[51] on the resuscitation and admission to neonatal intensive care of extremely premature babies. The guidelines recommend (*inter alia*) that at 25 weeks' gestation the relatively high rate of survival and low rate of disability should result in the baby being admitted to neonatal intensive care, unless the baby is affected by some severe abnormality incompatible with any significant period of survival. Below 25 weeks' gestation, parents should be fully informed of the statistical evidence as to survival and disability. From 24 weeks to 24 weeks and 6 days' gestation, in the light of the evidence, the presumption should be that the baby will be admitted to neonatal intensive care unless doctors and parents 'are agreed that in the light of the baby's condition (or likely condition) it is not in his or her best interests to start intensive care'. From 23 weeks to 23 weeks and 6 days' gestation, precedence should be given to the wishes of the parents, and from below 22 weeks to 22 weeks and 6 days, the baby should be admitted to neonatal care only if the parents are adamant that the baby should be resuscitated and admitted to neonatal care after full counselling as to the low chances of survival and high risk of disability. The guidelines in effect grant the parents extensive powers to determine the best interests of their baby given that no definitive prognosis can be offered for that particular baby. The 'younger' the infant the greater the parental discretion appears to be. Moreover, the Nuffield Report expressly accepts that both the parents and the baby's immediate family have independent interests that should be given some weight.[52]

Best Interests, Parents and the Fetal Infant

There would appear at first sight to be nothing extraordinary about parental judgments taking centre stage in a decision about any sick child, be she six minutes or six years old. The neonate may be seen as being treated just like her older brother. But does the analogy hold good? Let us reflect for a moment on why the law does (not necessarily should) take account of what parents as opposed to doctors say about the best interests of a child. The parental claim to speak for the child is grounded not in status, that they are parents and the child is 'theirs', but on the responsibility for the welfare of that child imposed on them by the law. In *An NHS Trust v. B*[53] Holman J indicated that the parents' views 'may have particular value' to an understanding of the benefits and burdens to the child of proposed treatment or non-treatment derived from their knowledge of the child, his pleasures and pains. Their wishes as such and their own interests were not to be weighed in the balance. The parental role, it might be said, was as an advocate for the child. If a six-year-old child is critically ill and should he survive, he will be blind and tetraplegic, loving parents are likely to be well placed to understand the impact of such impairment on a child they know well. The bond

49 See note 10, above, at pp. 522–4.

50 British Association for Perinatal Medicine, *The Management of Extremely Preterm Infants at Less Than 26 Weeks from 26 Weeks Gestation: A Framework for Clinical Practice at the Time of Birth*, 2008 (hereafter BAPM Framework).

51 NCOB Report at paras 9.16–19: and see BAPM Framework, note 50, above.

52 NCOB Report, at para. 9.29.

53 [2006] EWHC 507 (Fam), at para. 16.

between parent and child will be well established. The parents of a newly born infant or neonate of a few days old who has spent her short existence in the bright lights and multiple machinery of a Neonatal Intensive Care Unit do not have that same knowledge of that infant. They may, and mostly will, have a fierce affection for their sick baby but are less well placed to speak for her. And yet they may be allowed a stronger voice than the parents of the older child. Why might this be?

The impact of caring for a child with serious disability on parents and the wider family is huge and social support is less than optimal. Allowing the parents to judge whether the prospect of days, weeks, months of watching to see if their baby will survive, of caring for him if he survives with serious disability and multiple health needs is a prospect they embrace, hoping for the better outcome or driven by their own religious or cultural values, might attract support. But put openly it flies in the face of what the law says for it prioritises parental interests. Tweak the argument a little. The baby born at 22 weeks' gestation, if she survives with serious disability, will to a large extent depend for her quality of life on her parents. Thus their ability and willingness to cope will radically affect the interests of that child: parental and child interests are intertwined. This was very much the stance taken by Butler Sloss P in *Re T* (1997),[54] the much criticised decision in which the Court of Appeal backed parents who refused a liver transplant for their dying two-year-old son. The parents argued that the pain, stress and probable repeat surgery outweighed the benefit of prolonging his life. According to Butler Sloss P:

> The mother and child are one for the purpose of this unusual case and the decision of the court to consent to the operation jointly affects the mother and it also affects the father. The welfare of the child depends on his mother.[55]

Re T, albeit followed in *LA v. SB, AB and MB*,[56] is often considered an aberrant decision[57] straying from the norm that the law looks to the exclusive interests of the child. We offer no comment on that controversy as it affects older children. We do suggest that guidance and practice in relation to the care of the extremely premature neonate indicates that parents are accorded a broader discretion to determine the fate of such infants than they will enjoy once the infant is older, even by a few weeks. Gestational age remains a factor even when the infant is free of the maternal womb. Arguments about whether viability should be recognised at 21, 23 or 24 weeks tell us little about the consequences for the care on the infant. At best there can only be a rather weak presumption of 'conditional viability'.

Crossing the Rubicon – the 'Day after Tomorrow'

What we describe above may offer a pragmatic way for the law and clinical practice to address the dilemmas posed by the 'fetal infant' but it is a compromise that is philosophically unsatisfactory, to say the least. The root cause of the problem is, as the second author has long argued, the fallacy of any notion of viability as the threshold for a change in moral status.[58] For Sheila McLean, much

---

54 [1997] 1 WLR 242.

55 [1997] 1 WLR 242, at 251.

56 [2010] EWHC 1744 (Fam).

57 See for example, Fox, M. and McHale, J., 'In Whose Best Interests?' (1997) 60 *Modern Law Review*, 700–709.

58 Here the discussion develops lines originating in: Regmi, S. and Harris, J., 'Ethics' in Rowlands, S. (ed.) *Abortion Care*, Cambridge, Cambridge University Press, 2014, pp. 16–23.

turned on what she describes as 'salvageability'. The law struggles with concepts of 'born alive' or 'capable of being born alive'. The clinician and the layperson speak of viability, the point at which a fetus might survive without maternal life support.

In his seminal paper on abortion, Roger Wertheimer characterises what he calls the liberal view on abortion in terms of viability. 'According to the liberal, the fetus should be disposable upon the mother's request until it is viable'.[59] A definition of 'viability' in the *Shorter Oxford English Dictionary* viz: 'Capable of living, able to maintain a separate existence' seems consistent with most modern uses of this term.[60] In the context of abortion this may be taken to mean that the fetus, if removed from the womb is capable of staying alive and maintaining an existence independent of the mother. Since (as we have seen above) the gestational age at which a fetus can, in a very few instances, survive after premature delivery has been reducing over the years, as Sheila argues, many of those uncomfortable about abortion but not opposed to all abortions ('the middle ground') commonly argue that this indicates that the age at which abortion may be legitimate also reduces. This is, of course, an argument that Sheila seeks to turn on its head in her attempt to advance the case that pro- and anti-abortion camps might unite in agreeing that once the fetus nears viability the woman should be permitted and encouraged to agree to a termination of pregnancy that allows the fetus a chance of survival. So time limits should be later, not sooner, to maximise the potential for this magic viability.

The appeal to the viability of the fetus once outside the womb is thus ubiquitous, but curious to the second author, not least because it lacks a shred of moral significance. The appeal of a viability 'test' as a compromise in the 'abortion wars' may be because many people feel comfortable with its policy implications, not necessarily because they either understand or accept it. Let us therefore examine further just what notions of viability might entail.

There are a number of ways the 'viability test' concerning the legitimacy of ending the life of an embryo or fetus might be interpreted. We will consider just three.

1. viability as independence
2. viability as entering the physical world, the world outside
3. viability as entering the social and moral world

All of these notions of viability share one big problem. A purported moral watershed seems not to refer to any feature of moral significance and appears to be technology and 'geography' or spatially dependent. In any context, it would be odd if the moral significance of a human individual varied with the technology available to sustain it, or with whether it was inside or outside the bodily envelope of another human being or entity.[61]

The second author comes back to his central ethical question (introduced above). What might have happened to alter the moral status of the emerging human individual in its (usually brief) transit down the birth canal which renders it much more vulnerable to having its life ended at one end of the birth canal but not at the other?[62] The moral justification for deploying technology to

59 Wertheimer, R., 'Understanding the Abortion Argument' (1971) 1 *Philosophy & Public Affairs*, 67–95.

60 *Shorter Oxford English Dictionary*, Volume II, Oxford, Clarendon Press, 1968 edn, p. 2352. This formulation is the second definition offered of viability in the dictionary and was in use in 1828.

61 Harris, J., 'Human Beings, Persons and Conjoined Twins: An Ethical Analysis of the Judgement in *Re A*' (2002) 9 *Medical Law Review*, 221–36.

62 Note 12, above. The interview with Sarah-Kate Templeton marks the first use of this example in print. John Harris has been using it in lectures since at least 1975.

make viable a developing human individual after an extremely premature birth must depend on the value, the moral status, or significance of the entity to be sustained by the technology. To put this point another way: it is the fact that the entity concerned is judged to be valuable, judged to have a valuable existence in the sense that their existence is worth preserving, their life worth saving, or worth continuing, that provides both the reason and the justification for attempting the rescue, for carrying out the life saving procedures, for putting the neonate on life support. An explanation of the motive for these would be entirely absent if the moral status of the entity was only determined *post hoc* by the fact of its having been the recipient of these measures.

Moreover, the plausibility of a legal status correlated with viability seems also dependent on the assumption or assertion of a moral status, a normative feature either of the transition itself or of something alleged to have happened during the transition.

Viability as Independence

It is not clear either what 'an existence independent of the mother' (or any other person or system) actually means, let alone what moral significance it has. Is it just physical separation that might indicate that the fetus/neonate has also separated itself from the rights to bodily integrity and self-determination of the mother? But why does the mother not also have her independence compromised by this symbiotic relationship? If you can sacrifice the baby in the womb to save the life of the mother why not the other way around? Why, if dependence in the sense of 'an independent existence' is the issue, does the mutual dependence not also compromise the moral significance of the mother? Why, in cases where continuing a pregnancy threatens the life of the mother (but the baby might de delivered alive *post mortem*), does the decision (always?) favour the mother?

A newborn infant may be 'separated' from its mother once the umbilical cord is cut, but it is hardly independent. It will be dependent on others for years, for nourishment, protection, shelter from the elements, rearing, education and so on. In its first few years, alienated from this dependency the infant will die as surely as will the extremely premature baby not admitted to neonatal care. We do not think that the human adult dependent on machines to stay alive or dependent on carers for her every need has a different moral or legal status on this account. Tony Bland did not lose the protection of the law simply because he was maintained 'alive' by machines.[63] And even as adults not so radically dependent, we humans are scarcely 'independent' in the sense required in a post industrial world. Others must provide us with water, electricity, light and other sources of power, and virtually all the products we use which require these things. Independence from others and from the products of others and of collectives is simply no longer attainable; we are dependent also on society. So if we are not talking of that sort of dependence, of what sort of dependence or independence are we talking and why is it of a significance that makes the difference between life and death?

Viability as Entering the Physical World, the World Outside

One of the arguments advanced to justify a focus on viability is that of 'geography'. The neonate, unlike the fetus, has entered the world outside. It is on its own, at least in the sense that it is no longer physically connected to another human being. It is no longer akin to Judith Jarvis Thompson's famous violinist, plugged into another. But does this matter? It is instructive to consider

63 *Airedale NHS Trust v. Bland* [1993] AC 789 (HL).

'uploading'. The idea behind this relatively new field, if not of inquiry at least of speculation, is that it might one day be possible to 'upload' human brain functioning to computers which have been programmed to generate neural networks automatically. This might enable 'survival' in some meaningful sense of the individual's consciousness, harnessed to a machine or functioning in a cyborg capable of locomotion and physical as well as digital interaction with the world and other entities, both human and of other sorts. If this proves possible, and many believe it will,[64] then combinations of more than one individual's brains may merge or coalesce in one entity harnessed to a method of locomotion, a cyborg, android or organic creature.

Sotola and Valpola propose some possible means of such coalescing minds:

> We present a hypothetical process of mind coalescence, where artificial connections are created between two or more brains. This might simply allow for an improved form of communication. At the other extreme, it might merge the minds into one in a process that can be thought of as a reverse split-brain operation. We propose that one way mind coalescence might happen is via an exocortex, a prosthetic extension of the biological brain which integrates with the brain as seamlessly as parts of the biological brain integrate with each other. An exocortex may also prove to be the easiest route for mind uploading, as a person's personality gradually moves away from the aging biological brain and onto the exocortex. Memories might also be copied and shared even without minds being permanently merged. Over time, the borders of personal identity may become loose or even unnecessary.[65]

They offer a definition of mind uploading:

> Mind uploads, or uploads for short (also known as brain uploads, whole brain emulations, emulations or ems) are hypothetical human minds that have been moved into a digital format and run as software programs on computers.[66]

In *2001: A Space Odyssey* Arthur C. Clarke noted, citing a non-fictional source:

> In the 1980s, Minsky and Good had shown how neural networks could be generated automatically – self replicated – in accordance with any arbitrary learning program. Artificial brains could be grown by a process strikingly analogous to the development of a human brain. In any given case, the precise details would never be known, and even if they were, they would be millions of times too complex for human understanding.[67]

Whatever one thinks either about the prospect or the feasibility of 'uploading' an individual's brain processes to a computer, possibly linked to, or part of, a cyborg, if it were the case that such a creature retained, or indeed developed afresh, brain functioning and personality of a level

64 Sandberg, A. and Boström, N., *Whole Brain Emulation: A Roadmap. Technical Report #2008-3*, Oxford, Future of Humanity Institute, Oxford University, 2008; Goertzel, B., 'Human-level Artificial General Intelligence and the Possibility of a Technological Singularity: A Reaction to Ray Kurzweil's *The Singularity Is Near*, and McDermott's Critique of Kurzweil' (2007) 171(18) *Artificial Intelligence*, 1161–73.

65 Sotola, K. and Valpola, H., 'Coalescing Minds: Brain Uploading-related Group Mind Scenarios' (2012) *International Journal of Machine Consciousness*, 1–20, available at: http://kajsotala.fi/Papers/CoalescingMinds.pdf (accessed 13 January 2015).

66 Sotola and Valpola, note 65, above.

67 Clarke, A.C., *2001: A Space Odyssey*, London, Orbit Books: Little Brown and Co, 1998, at p. 98.

required for personhood, a level previously described by one of the present authors,[68] then there are important sequelae. It seems highly unlikely that such creatures would be disqualified from personhood or human rights (or indeed post human rights)[69] solely on the grounds that they are linked inextricably (like mother and baby *en ventre sa mère*) to another entity: that is to say that because of such linkage they were simply not viable in their own right.[70]

Viability as Entering the Social and Moral World

The world in which we live and claim our own moral status is more than simply the physical environment in which we survive. Some have argued that socialisation, particularly co-operation and for most humans, the use of at least one natural language, are required for the development of personhood and with it full moral rights and status, but it does not follow that these are lost once social context is removed. Daniel Defoe's wonderful study of Alexander Selkirk's predicament via Robinson Crusoe[71] is a case in point. We should not confuse the necessary conditions for the development of rights, certain powerful sorts of interests or 'moral status' with the achievement of that status. So that while the conditions for the development of something are clearly important they are not to be confused with the thing itself, whatever that is. Entering the social and moral world is certainly for creatures that survive it, the start of something big. But it is not the same as that big something. This illustrates another dimension of the fallacy inherent in the 'potentiality argument', the suggestion that something (for example, an acorn) has a particular moral status in virtue of its potential to become something else (for example, an oak tree).[72] When that most moral of bears, Winnie the Pooh, trying to find something that Tiggers (animals who 'like everything') actually do like, offered to take Tigger round to Piglet's house to 'try some of Piglet's haycorns' for breakfast, he was not offering the moral equivalent of chopping down oak trees and thereby threatening the 'Hundred Aker Wood'. Even Pooh, acknowledged to be a bear 'of very little brain', knew this![73]

A Brave New World[74]

Sheila's paper, from which we have strayed by many a 'mile', postulates the development of partial ectogenesis whereby for the latter stages of gestation the fetus could be nourished and complete its

68 Harris, J.M., *Violence and Responsibility*, London, Routledge and Kegan Paul, 1980, ch. 1; Harris, J., *The Value of Life*, London, Routledge, 1985, ch. 1; Harris. J., 'The Concept of the Person and the Value of Life' (1999) 9 *Kennedy Institute of Ethics Journal*, 293–308; and Harris, J., 'Taking the "Human" Out of Human Rights' (2011) *Cambridge Quarterly of Healthcare Ethics*, 9–20.

69 Harris, 'Taking the "Human" Out of Human Rights', note 68, above.

70 Judith Thomson has of course described a case where this would be true: Thomson, J.J., 'A Defence of Abortion' (1971) 11 *Philosophy & Public Affairs*, 47–66. See also Karnein, A.J., *A Theory of Unborn Life*, Oxford, Oxford University Press, 2012.

71 http://www2.hn.psu.edu/faculty/jmanis/defoe/crusoe.pdf (accessed 13 January 2015).

72 Harris, *The Value of Life*, note 68, above, pp. 10–27.

73 Milne, A.A., *The House at Pooh Corner*, London, Methuen, 1974, pp. 18ff.

74 And we should recall that the use of this phrase by Shakespeare's Miranda in *The Tempest* made clear that the braveness of the world consisted in the fact that it 'has such creatures in't', and the suchness of the creatures was that they were adult (in fact Italian) men (Act 5 Scene 1). Proudfoot, R., Thomson, A. and Kasten, D.S. (eds) *The Arden Shakespeare*, Walton-On-Thames, Thomas Nelson and Sons, 1998, p. 1091, line 182.

development in an artificial environment that replicates as far as possible the maternal womb. We have argued that in a sense neonatal intensive care already constitutes a form of partial ectogenesis. But what of complete *ectogenesis*: the ability to gestate a human individual from fertilisation of egg by sperm (or by reprogramming cells to a toti-potent state) to 'birth', entirely outside a human body? If and when the possibility of complete ectogenesis becomes actual we will face a difficult question: will this also mean that the life of a zygote, embryo or fetus may never be ended during its progress from fertilisation to neonate? And the question cannot be evaded by appeals to the pregnant woman's autonomy and bodily integrity, for no woman will be pregnant. For the second author, the answer is simple. Without an acceptable account of when the emerging human individual acquires a moral status comparable to that of normal, fully conscious, adult humans, creatures with a set of powers and capacities that for all we know may be unique in the universe, there will be no coherent reason to protect its life in ways comparable to those in which your and the authors' lives are currently protected by law, morality and custom in most jurisdictions. The first author will have to decide if, absent a conflict with another individual (the pregnant woman), who is indubitably morally important, the zygote, embryo or fetus must be afforded the benefit of the doubt.[75]

In rejecting any moral significance in viability, the first author would go further arguing that viability does not start with conception, with formation of the zygote. At present, the possibility of complete ectogenesis viability as the 'capacity to maintain a separate existence' from a mother will cover all stages of human development because the 'emerging entity' will not need ever to have been in a human womb.[76] It will be difficult to resist pressure to regard as 'viable' not only the zygote but whatever has the capacity to become a zygote. This capacity is almost certainly possessed by any human cell appropriately treated, and of course with gametes of both genders, stored[77] or *in vivo*.

It is known, as already indicated, that virtually any human cell may be re-programmed to a pluripotent and probably to a totipotent stage, a stage equivalent to the zygote and that such cells may also be re-programmed into male and female gametes. These procedures, when the principle has been proved in humans, will have profound implications for our understanding of how many and what kind of parents a child may have and concerning whether birth itself will continue to feature as a stage, or as a necessary stage, in human reproduction.[78]

75 Brazier, M., 'Embryos' "Rights": Abortion and Research' in Freeman, M.D.A. (ed.) *Medicine, Ethics and the Law*, London, Stevens & Sons, 1988, pp. 9–22.

76 Alghrani, A., 'Viability and Abortion: Lessons from Ectogenesis' (2009) 4(6) *Expert Review of Obstetrics and Gynecology*, 625–34; Alghrani and Brazier, note 2, above; Alghrani, note 16, above; Alghrani, A., 'The Legal and Ethical Ramifications of Ectogenesis' (2007) 2 *Asian Journal of World Trade Organization & International Health Law and Policy*, 189–211.

77 Gulsuner, S., Walsh, T., Watts, A.C., et al., 'Spatial and Temporal Mapping of De Novo Mutations in Schizophrenia to a Fetal Prefrontal Cortical Network' (2013) 154(3) *Cell*, 518–29; Harris, J., 'Misleading Talk of "Three Parent Babies" Helps No One', *The Guardian* 19 September 2012, available at: http://www.guardian.co.uk/commentisfree/2012/sep/19/misleading-three-parent-babies-gene-therapy (accessed 13 January 2015); Hayashi, K., Ogushi, S. and Kurimoto, K., 'Offspring from Oocytes Derived from In Vitro Primordial Germ Cell-like Cells in Mice' (2012) 338 *Science*, 971–5; Easley, C.A., Phillips, B.T., McGuire, M.M., et al., 'Direct Differentiation of Human Pluripotent Stem Cells into Haploid Spermatogenic Cells' (2012) 2(3) *Cell Reports*, 440–46; Eguizabal, C., Montserrat, N., Vassena, R., et al., 'Complete Meiosis from Human Induced Pluripotent Stem Cells' (2011) 29 *Stem Cells*, 1186–95; Bourne, H., Douglas, T. and Savulescu, J., 'Procreative Beneficence and In Vitro Gametogenesis' (2012) 30 *Monash Bioethics Review*, 29–48.

78 Gonzales, C.P., Harris, J. and Testa, G., 'Multiplex Parenting: IVG and the Generations to Come' (2014) 40 *Journal of Medical Ethics*, 752–8; Testa, G. and Harris, J., 'Ethical Aspects of ES Cell-Derived Gametes' (2004) 305 *Science*, 1719.

It is, certainly according to the first author, almost impossible to act as if the embryo has moral and legal status even if we believe that it does. He has set out the arguments for this at length elsewhere.[79] Suffice it to note here two of these features: first that nature or the gods are profligate with embryonic life. Every live human birth costs on average the lives of four of its sibling embryos (in other words, pregnancy has an 80 per cent failure rate).[80] We do not perform funeral obsequies over the bodies of embryos washed out in the menstrual flow,[81] yet there are often embryos washed away in this particular flood. In the lab we can *divide* the early embryo into two or more cell clumps, each of these becoming a new embryo. We can then push these clumps together 'destroying' the, let us say, four embryos created by cell division, and all this without the loss of a single cell or indeed any other human material.

The issue of viability creates more problems than it solves given that so many types of entity may lay claim to be human precursors with the capacity to maintain an existence independent of the mother. Once maternal wombs, or any human womb at all, become unnecessary to the nurture of future human persons we can no longer rely on arbitrary lines in the sand, lines like birth, viability or conception, but rather must try to understand what really matters: what really confers the sort of moral status that we must protect and about which we should care?

Conclusion

The much-vaunted 'bright line' demarcating the fetus from the neonate is less than bright in practice and law. If we are honest, we must admit that we do not grant the extremely premature or very sick newborn the same legal protection as other older humans. She is treated as more than a fetus and less than most babies. But by being born she does acquire greater status than she enjoyed *in utero*. Thus Sheila's argument is seductive. If a pregnancy is to be terminated at a stage when the fetus might have chance, even a slim chance, of survival, the woman should be encouraged to allow the fetus that chance. If Sheila is right, then maybe the authors of this paper can declare a truce. Sadly, we suggest that as technology advances making a nonsense of many versions of viability, the conditions for the truce ebb away and whether 'pro-choice' or 'anti-abortion' each of us must develop a coherent account of why fetus or neonate matters or indeed why being human matters.

We end by again recording our debt to Sheila: for a highly distinguished and distinctive body of scholarship over so many years, for being a beacon of rationality and good sense in many contested and sometimes heated debates, for her important contributions to public life and finally for being the stimulus for two of her Manchester friends to re-visit one of the very many important problems Sheila has tackled so productively, and to spend some quality time debating with each other as well as with Sheila.

---

79 See Harris, J., *Enhancing Evolution*, Princeton, NJ and Oxford, Princeton University Press, 2007, ch. 10, pp. 160ff.

80 Robert Winston gave the figure of five embryos lost for every live birth some years ago in a personal communication. The literature is rather more conservative, making more probable a figure of three embryos lost for every live birth. Boklage, C.E., 'Survival Probability of Human Conceptions from Fertilization to Term' (1990) 35 *International Journal of Fertility*, 75–94. Also Leridon, H., *Human Fertility: The Basic Components*, Chicago, IL, University of Chicago Press, 1977. A figure of 70 per cent total embryo loss is confirmed by Macklon, N.S., Geraedts, J.P.M. and Fauser, B.C.J.M., 'Conception to Ongoing Pregnancy: The "Black Box" of Early Pregnancy Loss' (2002) 8(4) *Human Reproduction Update*, 333–43; Edmonds, D.K., Lindsay, K.S., Miller, J.F., et al., 'Early Embryonic Mortality in Women' (1982) 38(4) *Fertility and Sterility*, 447–53.

81 Though note that funerals are often held for still births born later in gestation.

PART II
Care

Chapter 5

Trust or Contract: How Far Does the Contemporary Doctor-Patient Relationship Protect and Promote Autonomy?

Graeme T. Laurie and J. Kenyon Mason

Introduction

The law has intervened extensively in the last 30 years in the name of autonomy enhancement and the protection of those with reduced mental capacity. It is, however, far from clear how much this has resulted in a net increase in the substantial trust that patients feel towards healthcare professionals – indeed, the opposite might be true. This chapter considers these developments against the backdrop of Sheila McLean's contributions on the topics of consent and autonomy. It argues that a failure by law and its institutions to grasp the nuances and contours of authentic autonomy has encouraged a pseudo-contractual doctor-patient dynamic in which patient abandonment is legally sanctioned and the spectre of paternalism remains. While recognising that law cannot prescribe trust, it nonetheless suggests ways in which law's future direction of travel could be more conducive to the promotion of a genuine therapeutic partnership.

The Changing Face of Medicine

Sheila McLean published her doctoral thesis in 1989[1] and it is now trite to say that its influence on medical practice in general was profound. The title – *The Patient's Right to Know* – clearly signalled that her particular interests lay in an analysis of the doctor-patient relationship within the therapeutic ambience which, as we will see, has failed to mature into an alliance, despite the increasing political and judicial attention devoted to the concept of patient autonomy.[2] McLean's ground-breaking contribution came during what can be seen as the developmental stages of a United Kingdom medical jurisprudence. It is a matter of history that, around the 1980s, the medical profession was under intense and critical review. This was partly self-induced by way of a number of scandals related to indefensible examples of malpractice.[3] The major impetus was, however,

1 McLean, S.A.M., *A Patient's Right to Know*, Aldershot, Dartmouth Publishing, 1989.

2 We do not mean to suggest that the patient experience today can simply be reduced to a straightforward binary 'doctor-patient' dynamic. In fact, the reality is that patients experience many encounters with a range of healthcare professionals in any journey through the healthcare system. Often, consent will be taken by a junior doctor, consultation by a different professional, perhaps diagnosis by another, and treatment by yet another. Notwithstanding, this simply compounds the concerns that we express in this chapter. We use the term 'doctor-patient relationship' merely as a shorthand that should be taken to encompass this reality.

3 The gauntlet was thrown down by Kennedy, I., *The Unmasking of Medicine*, London, George Allen and Unwin, 1981.

derived from a growing, and increasingly accepted, belief in individualism in general and the parallel, specifically medical, demand for self-determination based loosely on the patient's right to protection from untoward interference with his or her person – which is, effectively, a matter of assault.

However, the practice of medicine is by its very nature, based on personal interference. Thus, the distinction between a good and a bad doctor-patient relationship is defined – or refined – in the word 'untoward'. No-one would suggest that Dr Cameron of Tannochbrae[4] intended to *harm* his patients; his offence under the revisionist mantra was that of paternalism. Most doctors practising at a time when their pharmacopoeia was largely both homeopathic and herbal would have seen this as synonymous with the reputable principle of beneficence. Nevertheless, the medical profession fell foul of the public when it persisted in this stance in an era in which pharmacologically powerful drugs, and associated complex techniques, became freely available. Very rapidly then, 'untoward' treatment came to mean unconsidered treatment – that is to say, treatment which was given without, at the same time, giving the patient adequate opportunity to accept it or reject it. Thus was born the procedure-driven concept of informed consent which now constitutes the main pillar of medical jurisprudence in, at least, the greater part of the anglophone world – and this despite, in respect of the United Kingdom, the early, yet seemingly authoritative, words of Dunn LJ that: 'The concept of informed consent forms no part of English law'.[5] The unfortunate result of these terminological uncertainties has been that the right to informed choice of treatment and respect for autonomy have come to be regarded as synonymous. In our view, this is a misconception with worrying conceptual and practical consequences. McLean's understanding of consent could not have anticipated this collapse in the distinction between two related but distinguishable concepts which she attributes, broadly, to a differing jurisprudential interpretation of the meaning and purpose of 'informed consent' in the United States and the United Kingdom.[6] Another important distinction that McLean is keen for all to grasp is that between due and appropriate concern for a person and unwarranted paternalism: '… care must be taken to avoid opportunities for [the latter] to resurface where it interferes with autonomy'.[7] The line for McLean can be drawn thus: 'While there may be a role for beneficence … this is not the same as a justification for paternalism'.[8]

This chapter walks the fine lines between autonomy and consent, and beneficence and paternalism, as these have been drawn in the last 30 years, and against McLean's own analysis. We suggest that a failure to maintain sufficiently clear and bright lines, principally on the part of the courts, has led to a distortion of the doctor-patient relationship. Crucially, we contend that, today, this is a relationship of three parties – clinician, patient and the courts – in that the last police the parameters of the relationship dynamic and have, increasingly, taken it upon themselves to interfere in the name of autonomy in ways that might at times serve to undermine the all-important value of trust. While the medical profession in the United Kingdom has made considerable efforts to redress any imbalances in power – as demonstrated by the General Medical Council's guidance on *Tomorrow's Doctors* with its emphasis on effective communication and joint decision-making[9] – it

4 The archetypal general practitioner of the early to mid-twentieth century portrayed in the fictional BBC series *Dr Finlay's Casebook* (1960–70).

5 *Sidaway v. Board of Governors of the Bethlem Royal Hospital* [1984] QB 493 (CA), at 517.

6 McLean, S.A.M., *Autonomy, Consent and the Law*, London, Routledge Cavendish, 2010, at p. 40.

7 McLean, note 6, above, at p. 12.

8 McLean, note 6, above, at p. 15.

9 General Medical Council, *Tomorrow's Doctors* (2009, updated 2012), especially para. 15.

is far less clear that the same objective is being delivered by the law, especially by the way in which central notions of consent and autonomy are constructed and protected.[10]

Autonomy is a status whereby the human being is recognised as having the fundamental right, qua human, of control over his or her own body and the direction of his or her own life in both physical and intellectual senses. It is a quality, which – when present – indisputably merits respect. It is related to human dignity[11] which is an *inherent* quality, possessed of all persons and which exists irrespective of their ability to express it. Contrariwise, autonomy is contingent both on one's ability to recognise and to exercise it – and yet it is of no less fundamental importance for this fact. Consent, on the other hand, is a *means* to an end, that end being respect for the person and respect for their autonomy. It is an ethical and legal device or conduit by which we can achieve the desired end-point, but it is by no means the only way to do so. And yet, such is the sway which consent now holds over the discipline of medical law that this important distinction is often ignored. This error is compounded by the fact that it is consent rather than autonomy which emerges as the dominant paradigm of the two within the doctor-patient relationship – that is, that the means often comes to define the totality of the ends. Not only is this paradoxical and conceptually worrying, but it has profound practical consequences; once again, ones that we fancy were never intended or looked for by McLean when she wrote her seminal work.

From this prologue about conceptual confusion, the purpose of this chapter emerges as two-fold. First, we will explore what the collapse in the distinction between these central concepts has meant for medical law, arguing that it has impoverished both our understanding, and the very nature, of the doctor-patient relationship. This is true also with respect to the legitimate roles of those who play a part in the formation of the relationship – being both medical and judicial personnel. Second, we will argue for the reinstatement of the distinction between the roles of autonomy and consent, and for further clarification of the legitimate basis for beneficent as opposed to paternalistic interference, in order to reorient the way in which the relationship should be seen. These contributions depend on two different sets of circumstances: (i) when autonomy is present and accepted in the therapeutic relationship, and (ii) when it is disputed or open to question.

As to the former, we will demonstrate that the focus on consent to date has reduced the doctor-patient relationship to one that is driven by claims, rights and entitlements, and by concerns about breaches of duty and the pursuit of remedies; it has overlooked the importance of, and necessity for, trust as the basis for that relationship. We posit that the drift towards a pseudo-contractual, legalistic model should be resisted for the benefit of a genuine therapeutic alliance and for the betterment of medical law itself. As to the latter context, we will examine recent developments concerning the emerging legal category of the 'vulnerable adult', as driven by the English High Court and Court of Appeal. While this has been done in the name of facilitating autonomy, we argue that far more

10 More worryingly, the Francis report found that sustained and systemic communication failures that paid insufficient attention to patients and their needs contributed significantly to the unacceptable standards and outcomes in Mid-Staffordshire, see Francis, R., *Report of the Mid Staffordshire NHS Foundation Trust: Public Inquiry*, HC 947, 2013.

11 This paper cannot do justice to the role of dignity in medical law. Its pre-eminence arose with the over-used phrase 'death with dignity' which implies death free from pointless invasive therapy. It has subsequently been subject to multiple variations in meaning – see most recently C-34/10 *Brüstle v. Greenpeace eV* [2012] 1 CMLR 41 on the patentability of inventions involving commercial and industrial uses of embryos – so much so as to render the phrase 'human dignity' one that, in our view, is best avoided. Nonetheless, it is a favourite device of the European courts and has been described as forming the base of 'a kind of ethical last stand': Brownsword, R., 'Regulating Human Genetics: New Dilemmas for a New Millennium' (2004) 12 *Modern Law Review*, 14–39, at p. 20.

procedural attention must be paid to the limits of court powers over this category of person, lest the developments bleed into the medical domain and return clinicians to the role of paternalist.

Autonomy: The Patient's Protection

We have already pointed to the semantic confusion that currently exists as to the distinction between autonomy and consent and we re-emphasise that autonomy is a multifaceted quality of humanness, the protection of which is now accepted as the prime requirement of contemporary medical jurisprudence. Consent is not a complete reflection of that need. Fundamentally, the protection of a patient's autonomy as defined above lies in the criminal law of assault;[12] on this view, consent is no more than a device to protect the patient's autonomous right to accept or refuse the 'assaults' which are an integral aspect of modern medical practice. Thus, while it is undeniable that an intimate connection exists between consent and autonomy, the former represents no more than a secondary, or consequential, manifestation of the fundamental right. The two concepts are inseparable but they are not synonymous. In this section we explore some of the contours and the limits of consent as it is currently used in medical law, in both the therapeutic and research contexts. In particular, we posit that, whereas autonomy serves to *promote* the interests of the patient in general terms, the function of consent is limited to *protection* of his or her status against practices that drive the development of an unequal relationship.

Consent as an Aspect of Self-defence

Whether or not it is a derivative attribute only, the patient's practical *defence* of his or her autonomy lies in the primacy of *choice* as to medical interference – be it in the form of consent or refusal. Yet, it is one of the deep ironies about the groundswell of support for consent in the guise of patient empowerment that the reality is that the power that the patient derives is almost entirely negative: it is the right to say *no*. It is all too often forgotten that the doctor-patient relationship is one *between* supposedly autonomous individuals, and the courts have consistently ruled that the patient cannot *demand* treatment against the doctor's judgment.[13] From this, it follows that adoption of the mantra of consent is, in effect, an abrogation of autonomy. Moreover, refusal carries with it a rejection of opportunities proffered by the medical professionals, leading to a closing off of options and a restriction of possible life paths. This might indeed be what the patient chooses, but the scope of possible choice is limited to a binary yes/no and the so-called choice is reduced to the single option of rejection. We do not deny that such a choice can be liberating, but this is so only in the sense of a negative liberty: the right to respect for the integrity of the human persona. For us, then, one of the major and oft-heralded victories in the campaign for patient autonomy – reflected in the following case law dictum – has something of a hollow ring to it: 'This right of choice is not limited to decisions which others might regard as sensible. It exists notwithstanding that the reasons for making the choice are rational, irrational, unknown or even non-existent'.[14]

In the medical ambience, where a patient is faced with a choice between two therapeutic management proposals, the ability – or entitlement – to choose between the two is scarcely empowering unless it is assisted by the doctor as therapeutic partner. Yet, too often the patient is

12 As interpreted in *Chatterton v. Gerson* [1981] QB 432.

13 *R (Burke) v. General Medical Council* [2006] QB 273, (2006) 85 BMLR 1 (CA).

14 *Re T* [1993] Fam 95, at 102.

left alone in the name of autonomy to choose between options, the doctor having fulfilled his or her duty of establishing that the patient is in possession of the relevant facts and has capacity. Consent, if it is given, thus becomes a protector of the doctor rather than of the patient.[15] It is acquiescence with the proposed medical intervention, but it is scarcely patient-empowering beyond such limits. The enduring power remains one to say no – at any stage and for any reason[16] – but this may be of little assistance to the patient, or research participant, whose interests might be better served by a therapeutic or research alliance where the boundaries and contours of a relationship are negotiated on mutual terms. We suggest that patients and doctors alike are currently prevented from entering such an alliance by the constraints of consent as it has come to be constructed by these two key qualifying elements: capacity and informedness.

Capacity

Capacity is a factor that is *internal* to the patient, albeit that it is mostly judged by medical professionals. In law, it is a threshold device that is used to determine whether further (caring) intervention can legitimately be taken towards individuals who purport to say 'no' or who cannot speak for themselves. The default, as we know well, is that capacity is present in all mature adult persons. As such, there is no incentive to promote autonomy. Indeed, quite the opposite is true. Only if there is incapacity can an individual be treated non-consensually in their own best interests.[17]

McLean has revisited the subject as a whole in her recent monograph.[18] Very early in her presentation, she describes mental competence as the *sine qua non* of autonomy.[19] Certainly, many of the legal battles fought and won on the consent field over the last quarter century have been in and around questions of capacity. Case law[20] and legislation[21] now abound with attempts to define legal capacity and its role as a threshold mechanism for determining whether someone is *sufficiently* autonomous with respect to the *particular* decision they are facing to merit respect for any choices they purport to make.

We confess to being unimpressed with the majority of these templates which, of necessity, deal with the generality rather than the particular.[22] They do little more than recapitulate what most doctors would see as standard medical practice; as a result, the legal definition of capacity rests on the highly subjective opinions of individual practitioners. The answer to the broad question – has this adult person still got capacity? – is largely medically determined, but the legal consequence of a finding of capacity necessitates the unquestioning acceptance of any and all choices which are then made. As things stand, setting capacity as a legal threshold focuses all of our attention on the establishment of capacity and none on what happens thereafter. Indeed, there

15 Classically demonstrated in Lord Donaldson's famous dictum on the use of flak-jackets in *Re W (A Minor) (Medical Treatment)* [1992] 4 All ER 627.

16 *Re T*, note 14, above.

17 In Scotland, for adults, there must be 'benefit' after the Adults with Incapacity (Scotland) Act 2000. This formulation was preferred as less paternalistic than 'best interests'.

18 Note 6, above.

19 Note 6, above, at p. 17.

20 See Mason, J.K. and Laurie, G.T., *Mason and McCall Smith's Law and Medical Ethics*, 9th edn, Oxford, Oxford University Press, 2013, ch. 4.

21 Adults with Incapacity (Scotland) Act, Mental Capacity Act 2005, as amended, and Adults with Incapacity (Scotland) Act 2000, as amended.

22 Mason, J.K., 'Particularity and Medical Law' in Bankowski, Z. and MacLean, J. (eds) *The Universal and the Particular in Legal Reasoning*, Aldershot, Ashgate, 2007, pp. 235–46.

is a positive disincentive in law to explore with a patient how he or she might maximise their autonomy, through choices or otherwise. Once the Rubicon has been crossed, the doctor is not permitted to accompany the patient on his or her journey. Put bluntly, the law supports the potential abandonment of autonomous patients to the vagaries of their own choices. This is at considerable odds with what many patients would reasonably expect of their healthcare professionals. Moreover, it fails to reflect the possibility that we are all, in some sense, vulnerable and 'inevitably dependent' throughout our lives, and most especially when we are unwell.[23]

Informedness

Achieving autonomy does not only depend on the intrinsic quality of capacity. It can depend as much on the externally-driven provision of information about the nature and quality of choices that are to be made. Once again, this apparently leaves considerable control in the hands of the medical profession, and yet – despite the triumph of the clarion call for the patient's right to know – we would suggest that the legal result does little to promote either autonomy or a healthy therapeutic relationship.

Capacity and informedness must co-exist to create the autonomous patient. But this raises the question: how and how far does a patient have to be informed about a proposed medical intervention before his or her consent is valid? McLean published *The Right to Know* in the immediate aftermath of the House of Lords' decision in *Sidaway*.[24] This decision is remarkable in two important respects: first, it confirmed the application of the *Bolam*[25] principle to information disclosure cases in the UK and stated explicitly that the American doctrine of 'informed consent' had no place in our law. Second, there was no mention in the entirety of the judgement of the term *autonomy*. Such features were the strongest possible evidence to activists like McLean that medical paternalism was alive and well and that the battle for the patient's right to know remained to be fought. And fight they did. And win they did. Indeed, so far has the pendulum swung from *Sidaway* that the decision must now be considered as little other than anathema. In its place sit a wide range of purportedly patient-centred judgements,[26] best typified by the Supreme Court ruling in *Chester v. Afshar*[27] which, again with deep irony, had astonishingly similar facts to those of Mrs Sidaway and yet which produced an equally remarkable – and diametrically opposite – result. What is particularly remarkable about *Chester* is not only its blatant distortion of the rules of causation so as to enable the Court to find in favour of the claimant's argument that she was insufficiently informed, but also that the court appears to have brought us to the brink of a stand alone tort of affront to autonomy.[28]

---

23 See Fineman, M., *The Autonomy Myth: A Theory of Dependency*, New York, The New Press, 2005.

24 *Sidaway v. Board of Governors of the Bethlem Royal Hospital* [1985] AC 871.

25 *Bolam v. Friern Hospital Management Committee* [1957] 1 WLR 582 (negligence and relevance of recognised medical practice to standard of care).

26 See *Pearce v. United Bristol Healthcare NHS Trust* (1999) 48 BMLR 118; *Birch v. University College London Hospital NHS Foundation Trust* (2008) 104 BMLR 168; *Jones v. North West Special Health Authority* [2010] EWHC 178; and *Nicholas v. Imperial College Healthcare NHS Trust* [2012] EWHC 591.

27 *Chester v. Afshar* [2005] 1 AC 134. For discussion, see Meyers, D., '*Chester v. Afshar*: Sayanaro, Sub Silentio, *Sidaway*' in McLean, S.A.M. (ed.) *First Do No Harm*, Aldershot, Ashgate, 2006, ch. 16.

28 See Laurie, G., 'Personality, Privacy and Autonomy in Medical Law' in Whitty, N. and Zimmermann, R. (eds) *Rights of Personality in Scots Law: A Comparative Perspective*, Dundee, Dundee University Press, 2009, pp. 453–84. This seems to be largely in line with the ratio in *Rees v. Darlington Memorial Hospital NHS Trust* [2004] AC 309.

We are not concerned here to revisit the legal particularities of informedness in order to demonstrate the ways in which this feature of consent has developed. Rather, we are driven to point out the consequences for autonomy of this fixation on *informed* consent, albeit not in the US doctrinal sense. First, and most obviously, this conceptualisation implies that a consent that is insufficiently informed is not valid and, a fortiori, is not a genuine expression of autonomy. Yet, as the following examples show, this conclusion cannot be universalised across the whole spectrum of healthcare relationships. Secondly, a requirement of informedness can serve to undermine or even entirely thwart autonomy interests; this is, again, ironic since it is generally considered that consent processes are made procedurally robust precisely because they involve information giving. In particular, what this drive towards informedness to promote consent achieves, indirectly, is a potential undervaluing of circumstances where an otherwise autonomous individual might trust another party to 'do the right thing', be it with their being, their tissue or their data. We can choose to trust in circumstances where information is less than complete or, even, where the very provision of information is considered to be an affront in itself.

How Information Can Undermine Autonomy: (A) The Right Not to Know

One of us was inspired by McLean's work on the Right to Know to ask whether the converse claim was also sustainable, that is: is there a Right Not to Know?[29] The notion is perfectly understandable because we can all imagine circumstances in which we might prefer not to be told of a particular diagnosis or family trait if, say, nothing can be done about it. Is it not an equal entitlement under our claim to autonomy to reject information as it is to require it? We wager most of us would intuitively agree that this is, at least, not an unreasonable exercise of our autonomy. Moreover, in doing so we would have to recognise that this is about a lack of information and relies on us being able to trust those in possession of information *not* to disclose it. We have argued for the subtleties of this elsewhere.[30] Our contention that consent (or refusal) cannot do all of the work to protect our autonomy and other personal interests[31] is illustrated by the limited protection afforded by instruments such as the UNESCO Universal Declaration on the Human Genome and Human Rights (1997), Article 5c of which provides: 'The right of every individual to decide whether or not to be informed of the results of genetic examination and the resulting consequences should be respected'. Similarly, the Council of Europe Oviedo Convention on Human Rights and Biomedicine (1997), Article 10(2) states: 'Everyone is entitled to know any information collected about his health. However, the wishes of an individual not be so informed shall be observed'. These provisions are based on two challengeable assumptions: first, that a timely and effectively-informed opportunity to say 'No' is available; and, second, that a person can be informed that there is something to know about themselves without revealing the essence of the information itself! If we take seriously the idea that a genuine state of ignorance is valuable to our autonomous selves, then these formulations as matters of choice and control of information are deficient.

29 Laurie, G., 'Genetic Privacy: A Legal Perspective', Doctoral thesis under supervision of McLean, S.A.M., University of Glasgow, 1997; Laurie, G., *Genetic Privacy: A Challenge to Medico-legal Norms*, Cambridge, Cambridge University Press, 2002.

30 Laurie, G., 'Recognizing the Right Not to Know: Conceptual, Professional and Legal Implications' (2014) 42(1) *Journal of Law, Medicine and Ethics*, 53–63.

31 We posit, in fact, that this is a matter of protection of privacy interests, related to but also distinct from autonomy interests.

How Information Can Undermine Autonomy: (B) Broad Consent and Biobanks

It is clear, however, that the requirement of respect for autonomy goes deeper than that from many aspects. The extreme antithesis to individualistic autonomy can, perhaps, be epitomised in some such phrase as 'forgone autonomy' whereby the originator empowers the receptor to proceed on the assumption that specific consent has not been given but is encompassed within a general acquiescence with the circumstances. Such a situation arises when the originator does not – or cannot – know the full use to which the receptor is likely to put the material over which he or she has assumed control; the consent model then becomes difficult to apply as a means of justifying surrender of one's autonomy insofar as it seems to ignore the significance attached to 'informedness' in the concept of 'informed consent'. The exemplary situation is to be found in contribution to data and tissue research – or biobanks – in which, given that not even the controller of the bank can be certain of the future use of the material in his or her charge, application of the informed consent model is a virtual impossibility.[32] This has resulted in the literature and in practice in a flurry of attempts to reconceive and distinguish forms of consent variously as implied,[33] explicit,[34] informed,[35] specific,[36] broad[37] and generic.[38] But, if as we suggest, there should be a decoupling of consent from autonomy, where lies the alternative? In our view, there is no single answer but, in our search for that answer, we must first consider the precise circumstances in which one is pleading that autonomy rules.

Reconceptualising Autonomy in Practice – Alternative Models

From our above analysis, we suggest that there are two ways in which a patient's autonomy arises as a contentious issue. The first, which broadly reflects the status quo and which we tentatively describe as *defensive autonomy*, relates to the autonomous right to choose what is to be done to or with one's body. It is exemplified, as we have seen, by the respect that is due to our choices as to our medical management and is intimately bound to the consent model on which hangs much of the contemporary definition of autonomy. It is heavily dependent on two key thresholds being overcome: having the capacity to make choices and having adequate levels of information by which to make choices. Attempts to exercise one's autonomy beyond these limits are treated as

32 For in-depth discussion of this particular difficulty, see Harmon, S.H.E., 'Semantic, Pedantic or Paradigm Shift? Recruitment, Retention and Property in Modern Population Biobanking' (2008) 16 *European Journal of Health Law*, 27–43. For a proposed solution which emphasises robust governance mechanisms over consent-based approaches, see Laurie, G., 'Reflexive Governance in Biobanking: On the Value of Policy Led Approaches and the Need to Recognise the Limits of Law' (2011) 130(3) *Human Genetics*, 347–56.

33 Furness, P., 'Consent to Using Human Tissue: Implied Consent Should Suffice' (2003) 327(7418) *British Medical Journal*, 759–60.

34 Otlowski, M., 'Tackling Legal Challenges Posed by Population Biobanks: Reconceptualising Consent Requirements' (2012) 20 *Medical Law Review*, 191–226.

35 MacLean, A., 'From *Sidaway* to *Pearce* and Beyond: Is the Legal Regulation of Consent Any Better Following a Quarter of a Century of Judicial Scrutiny?' (2012) 20 *Medical Law Review*, 108–29.

36 Note 34, above, at p. 191.

37 Caulfield, T. and Kaye, J., 'Broad Consent in Biobanking: Reflections on Seemingly Insurmountable Dilemmas' (2009) 10 *Medical Law International*, 85–100.

38 Caulfield, T., 'Biobanks and Blanket Consent: The Proper Place of the Public Good and Public Perception Rationales' (2007) 1 *King's Law Journal*, 209–26.

suspect, flawed and non-deserving of respect. This having been said, it is precisely in the realm beyond autonomy that there have been considerable statutory legal reforms in the guise of the Mental Capacity Act 2005 and the Adults with Incapacity (Scotland) Act 2000 to determine how incapacitated persons should be treated. There now exist extremely robust procedural mechanisms by which we can place trust that patients will be treated in their own 'best interests' (or 'to their benefit' in Scotland) when autonomy and consent do not come into play. When they do, however, we suggest that a defensive need to obtain consent drives a culture of potential patient abandonment whereby individuals are left to their own devices to explore and exercise their autonomy. This casts consent as an aspect of control, albeit illusory in many cases. It follows that there is an expectation that control be facilitated.

Arguably, this has been compounded in recent years by the entry of the property model into the doctor-patient relationship.[39] Property is the paradigmatic legal device through which to exercise control. We pre-empted this more than a decade ago: 'The concepts of property and consent need not be mutually exclusive; indeed they should operate in tandem to ensure full and proper respect for individual rights'.[40] We did not anticipate, however, that an unlooked-for consequence of these parallel developments would be the increasing approximation of the doctor-patient relationship to something akin to pseudo-contract. We suggest that the metaphor of contract is pertinent in that it evokes a relationship characterised by an essentially oppositional dynamic focused on expectations of rights and entitlements, and with a growing cohort of remedies for non-performance and failure to satisfy, viz the apparent emergence of the stand-alone tort of affront to autonomy (above). The patient today, then, is entitled to information, is entitled to unquestioning respect for their refusals, is entitled to recognition of their property interests, and, ultimately, is entitled to be left alone entirely to determine his or her own *self* rule. This is, however, a view of autonomy in the most meagre of terms. It is a view that is likely to take the *care* out of the caring professions.

The alternative is to cast autonomy as *permissive* whereby the individual can legitimately and voluntarily surrender some aspect of his or her persona, as is typified by the originator entering the data- or bio-bank system or the organ transplant programme. On this interpretation, autonomy is no longer being used as a defensive shield but is, rather, being surrendered as an expression of community trust; and, again, consent fits uneasily into the resultant ethical pattern. The power to say no and withdraw usually remains (subject to the impracticalities of destroying data or samples) but, in this concept, there is no pretence of continuing control over said data or samples nor, indeed, of any necessary personal benefit. Indeed, the trusted surrender of autonomy might even bring risk, as in the example of recognising an interest in not knowing information about one's self: this can be a threat to privacy interests. Still, why should a pastiche of control – via consent – be the gold standard of our behaviour when our autonomy might be facilitated and exercised in ways which have no need for such control and are, instead, a reflection of our capacity and desire to trust? Developments in the law to date seem largely blind to these possibilities.

---

39 See Mason and Laurie, note 20, above, ch. 14 for discussion and literature.

40 Mason, K. and Laurie, G., 'Consent or Property? Dealing with the Body and Its Parts in the Shadow of Bristol and Alder Hey' (2001) 64 *Modern Law Review*, 710–29, at p. 727. See also, Harmon, S.H.E., 'A Penny for Your Thoughts, a Pound for Your Flesh: Implications for Recognizing Property Rights in Our Own Excised Body Parts' (2006) 7 *Medical Law International*, 329–54.

From Pseudo-contract to Trust

The relationship between trust and law is under-examined. Unlike the connections or disconnections between autonomy and trust explored by O'Neill and others,[41] law's role in the promotion of trusting dynamics – particularly those which encourage and facilitate autonomy to flourish – is relatively unchartered territory. An important and fundamental distinction, however, is that between what might be called *substantive* and *procedural* trust. Substantive trust refers simply to the situation when, as a matter of fact, a state of trust exists between parties. There is little that law can do directly to engender this. In contrast, there is much that law can do to promote procedural trust, that is, trust in systems and procedures of protection (and promotion) of interests, including those embodied in the mental capacity legislation, procedures for decision-making bodies such as the Court of Protection, and robust rules and approaches such as the presumption of capacity and the superlative of *best* interests when capacity is lacking. Procedural trust is founded on high degrees of certainty, transparency and a commitment to core values that ultimately guide decision-making.

While it can never guarantee substantive trust, procedural trust becomes particularly important when the law is still developing. Although we cannot know the end point that will eventually be reached, we ought to be able to trust that core values and precepts steer our course, and that auto-correction is possible when needed. This makes it all the more imperative that we are clear about what is at stake: particularly, what kind of autonomy we wish to support and promote, and which kinds of behaviour we accept or reject, such as McLean's fine line between beneficence and paternalism. Arguably, it is precisely because we have been less than clear in the past about the respective roles of consent and autonomy that we find ourselves in the position outlined above. If we seek, in the future, to promote and facilitate richer conceptualisations of autonomy, we must be able to rely on procedural trust in the systems and personnel involved – from within law and medicine alike.

An example from an area of developing law illustrates the issues very well. This is the recent resurrection of the inherent jurisdiction of the High Court in England and Wales in respect of the protection of vulnerable adults. Previously, the jurisdiction had been thought to have been extinguished by the passing of the Mental Capacity Act 2005. However, its enduring role is now said to be determinedly about facilitating the autonomy of this class of persons. The following analysis outlines the developments and offers commentary on this legal attempt to promote autonomy in light of lessons we have outlined above.

Autonomy: The Promotion of a Core Human Value

Common law and statute law have each been responsible for shaping two distinct aspects of autonomy in the last 30 years.[42] The common law has largely driven the consent-based developments outlined above, while statute has brought about extensive reforms to protect those persons who do not clear the threshold for competence, by introducing elaborate rules on determining capacity and best interests, and establishing the Court of Protection to deliver the protections of the Mental Capacity Act 2005 (MCA). These changes have served to delineate the outer limits of autonomous

41 O'Neill, O., *Autonomy and Trust in Bioethics*, Cambridge, Cambridge University Press, 2002; Manson, N.C. and O'Neill, O., *Rethinking Informed Consent in Bioethics*, Cambridge, Cambridge University Press, 2007.

42 The discussion now proceeds largely on the basis of English law. The position in Scotland is different and will be invoked only by way of comparative illustration.

action, albeit that the legislation requires attempts, so far as reasonably practicable, to encourage a person's participation;[43] and also efforts, so far as reasonably ascertainable, to take into account a person's wishes, feelings, beliefs and values.[44] The courts have made it very clear that the Act cannot be used to justify interventions based on professional concern about the outcome of an individual's decisions,[45] the jurisdiction of the Court of Protection only arises if capacity is lacking. As noted, however, capacity is largely an *internal* factor affecting a person, viz, s. 2(1) of the 2005 Act states:

> For the purposes of this Act, a person lacks capacity in relation to a matter if at the material time he is unable to make a decision for himself in relation to the matter *because of* an impairment of, or a disturbance in the functioning of, the mind or brain.[46]

Thus, although the Act extends far beyond purely medical cases in the same way that our autonomy is implicated in all aspects of our lives – including social care, welfare and beyond – many assessments of capacity will depend on medical evidence. But what is the legal and procedural position if there are reasons to doubt a person's capacity because of *external* factors, that is, not relating to the mind or brain?

Precisely this issue arose in *DL v. Local Authority and Others*, decided by the Court of Appeal in March 2012.[47] A local authority was concerned about the treatment of an elderly couple being cared for by their 50-year-old son. Allegations included threats, physical abuse, preventing his parents from leaving the house, and preventing carers and health professionals from visiting. The parents had capacity as defined under the 2005 Act, and so the Court of Protection had no jurisdiction to intervene. The local authority sought, instead, interim injunctive relief from the High Court, asking it to invoke its inherent jurisdiction that pre-dated the 2005 Act. The legal point at issue on appeal was summed up by McFarlane LJ in the opening paragraph of the judgment:

> The question for consideration is whether, despite the extensive territory now occupied by the MCA 2005, a jurisdictional hinterland exists outside its borders to deal with cases of 'vulnerable adults' who fall outside that Act and which are determined under the inherent jurisdiction.

Answering in the affirmative, the Court of Appeal endorsed a body of case law that had been developing largely through the efforts of Munby J. on his way to assuming Presidency of the High Court (Family Division). The key points of that jurisprudence, and the confirmation of the Court of Appeal, can be summed up as follows:

1. The inherent jurisdiction of the High Court endures with respect to adults whose autonomy has been compromised by external factors and when this leaves them outside the protection of the MCA. In particular, this can include persons:
   a) under constraint; or
   b) subject to coercion or undue influence; or

43 2005 Act, s. 4(4).

44 2005 Act, s. 4(6).

45 *York City Council v. C* [2013] EWCA Civ 478, [2014] 2 WLR 1, para. 53.

46 Emphasis added.

47 [2012] EWCA Civ 253, [2012] 3 WLR 1439, [2013] Fam 1.

c) for some other reason deprived of the capacity to make the relevant decision or disabled from making a free choice, or incapacitated or disabled from giving or expressing a real and genuine consent.[48]

2. The category of persons potentially caught by the jurisdiction is determinedly open-ended. As Munby J. said in *Re SA*:

   > ... I would treat as a vulnerable adult someone who, whether or not mentally incapacitated, and whether or not suffering from any mental illness, is or may be unable to take care of him or herself against significant harm or exploitation or who is deaf, blind, or dumb, or who is substantially handicapped by illness, injury or congenital deformation. This ... is not and is not intended to be a definition. It is descriptive not definitive.[49]

3. The jurisdiction is aimed at '... enhancing or liberating the autonomy of a vulnerable adult whose autonomy has been compromised by a reason other than mental incapacity ...'.[50] The Court of Appeal found there to be '... a sound and strong public policy justification for this',[51] and it was emphatic that 'either the jurisdiction exists or it does not' (in response to arguments that it is not possible to extrapolate from medical best interest cases to the general class of the vulnerable).[52] Its application therefore is dependent on the facts of any given case, and covers a gamut of circumstances, including medical, welfare, social care and marital cases. But importantly, and unlike the Court of Protection, the High Court cannot take decisions on behalf of such persons and in their best interests. It therefore raises questions about the nature and scope of the court's powers to intervene, and we consider this below.
4. The common law jurisdiction must complement the MCA and not undermine the will of Parliament with respect to that statute or any other legislative provision. It can be exercised to fill gaps[53] where it is necessary, lawful and proportionate to do so.[54]
5. The nature and scope of court powers are both specific and wide-ranging. Commending the approach of Macur J in *LBL v. RYJ and VJ*,[55] the Court of Appeal explained that exercise of the jurisdiction should reflect a 'facilitative, rather than dictatorial, approach' towards 'the re-establishment of the individual's autonomy of decision making in a manner which enhances, rather than breaches, their ECHR Article 8 rights'.[56] However, this is not limited to granting interim relief to remove an undue influence and allow a vulnerable person the space to makes their own decisions. For example, in *DL* injunctive relief was sought to

48 See *Re SA (Vulnerable Adult with Capacity: Marriage)* [2005] EWHC 2942 (Fam), [2006] 1 FLR 867, paras 76–9 per Munby J, entirely endorsed by the Court of Appeal in *DL*, note 47, above, at para. 54.

49 Note 48, above, at para. 82. Also, *A Local Authority and Mrs A* [2010] EWHC 1549, para. 79.

50 Note 47, above, at para. 54.

51 Note 47, above, at para. 63.

52 Note 47, above, at para. 55.

53 Munby J relied on the metaphor of the common law as 'the great safety net' to fill any gaps in protection of the vulnerable, as first stated by Lord Donaldson MR in *Re F (Mental Patient: Sterilisation)* [1990] 2 AC 1, CA; (1989) 86(10) LSG 42, and later endorsed by Dame Butler-Sloss P in *Re A Local Authority (Inquiry: Restraint on Publication)* [2004] Fam 96.

54 See *DL*, note 47, above, at paras 46–9, endorsing the earlier Court of Appeal ruling in *Westminster City Council v. C* [2008] EWCA Civ 198, [2009] 2 WLR 185 in which the judges confirmed strongly the jurisdiction as providing relief not otherwise available, and which in turn cited with approval the analysis and ruling of Munby J in *Re PS (An Adult)* [2007] EWHC 623.

55 [2010] EWHC 2665 (COP), para. 62.

56 Note 47, above, at para. 67. The CA considered compatibility with human rights at para. 66.

prevent the son from seeking to persuade or coerce his parents, and to restrain him from interfering with the provision of care and support. But the totality of the High Court's inherent powers extends much further, as seen in the case of *Westminster County Council v. C*,[57] where an earlier CA bench endorsed the use of the inherent jurisdiction to prevent removal of a vulnerable person[58] from the jurisdiction because of a questionable marriage in Bangladesh.

Space does not permit us to take issue with the question of whether this is a legitimate resurrection of an archaic jurisdiction.[59] Views on this can be found elsewhere.[60] Rather, we are concerned with the possible implications of these rulings and their scope, which is now confirmed as jurisdiction over a new category of person: the vulnerable – which is a 'categorisation' potentially applicable to almost every class of patient in a health context.[61] Moreover, we are keen to explore what this might mean for autonomy, using McLean's benchmark of the fine line between paternalism and beneficence. The Law Commission, for its part, stressed in 2011 that: '... the inherent jurisdiction cannot be used to compel a capacitated but vulnerable person to do or not do something which they have after due consideration, decided to do or not do ...'.[62] While supportive of the trump value of autonomy, this still does not tell us whether we can currently trust the courts to remain on the right side of the McLean line. We offer some considerations in this regard for courts and medical professionals alike.

Who Is Vulnerable?

The deliberately diverse and non-exhaustive category of vulnerable persons has potential application to any one of us, healthy or ill. This is not the same as saying that we have descended a slippery slope whereby the courts can override genuinely autonomous decisions,[63] but, rather that actual *or perceived* coercion of circumstances in any of our lives can attract the attention of the court and lead them, and those around us, to ignore our apparent choices, temporarily at least. The difficulty here has already been pointed out by McLean:[64] the question underlying the very definition of an autonomous decision '... is not *whether* we are influenced by external considerations but, rather, what is the *extent* of that influence'.[65] In pointing out that 'few decisions are totally free', McLean identifies that we are perpetually confronted by 'the underlying conundrum of how to translate

57 Note 54, above.

58 The 25-year-old man had autism and severe impairment of intellectual functioning.

59 Note, unlike the Children Act 1989 and the Family Law Act 1986, the Mental Capacity Act 2005 makes no explicit mention of, and places no express restriction on, any common law jurisdiction.

60 See Hewson, B., 'Neither Midwives nor Rainmakers: Why DL Is Wrong' (2013) *Public Law*, 451–9; Bridge, C., 'Inherent Jurisdiction' (2012) 42(Dec) *Family Law*, 1454–6; Hughes, R., 'The Inherent Jurisdiction over Vulnerable Adults' (2013) 3 *Private Client Business*, 132–9.

61 It is to be noted that, despite their titles, neither the Safeguarding Vulnerable Groups Act 2006 nor the Protection of Vulnerable Groups (Scotland) Act 2007 has any relevance to the present discussion, both dealing with the criminal law.

62 Law Commission, *Adult Social Care*, LC326, 2011, para. 9.80.

63 Note 47, above, at para. 32.

64 On coercion of circumstance, see J.K. Mason's review of McLean's book in (2011) 11 *Medical Law International*, at p. 307.

65 Note 6, above, at p. 62.

autonomy from aspiration into decisional reality'.[66] Central to this is a robust sense of what counts as evidence of undue influence or coercion.

Munby J in *Re SA* elaborated on this in some of his examples.[67] For instance, 'constraint' is represented by 'some significant curtailment of the freedom to do those things which in this country free men and women are entitled to do', while coercion or undue influence are typified by the Jehovah's Witness case *Re T*.[68] He noted:

> … where the influence is that of a parent or other close and dominating relative, and where the arguments and persuasion are based upon personal affection or duty, religious beliefs, powerful social or cultural conventions, or asserted social, familial or domestic obligations, the influence may, as Butler-Sloss LJ put it, be subtle, insidious, pervasive and powerful. In such cases, moreover, very little pressure may suffice to bring about the desired result.[69]

This suggests that autonomy is a fragile thing, potentially further undermined by a person's status as ill, deaf, dumb or blind, according to the case law (see above). But how, then, can autonomy be protected and promoted as part of a beneficent, as opposed to a paternalistic, approach of the courts or our carers? We suggest three important features when dealing with the evidence base: (1) adducing relevant evidence in a balance sheet, (2) determining whose evidence counts and (3) including the relevance of time.

1. In much the same way as we see the courts approaching a best interests test, the use of a balance sheet of considerations would be important in terms of helping to ensure that the full range of factors is taken into consideration. Vulnerability is likely to be brought about by the confluence of a range of factors, and it can depend as much on the behaviour of those around us and our own subjective state of being. A balance-sheet approach would promote clear articulation of, and justification for why, it is thought that the status of vulnerability had been reached – bearing in mind all the while that this category of person is, by law, mentally competent.
2. It matters very much *who* is giving evidence of vulnerability. For example, in *Re DL*, the Court of Appeal proceeded on the basis of the report of an independent social worker in whose opinion undue influence existed. This was so despite the fact that the son's version of events was not included. Unlike the position under the MCA in dealing with internal factors and likely to involve medical evidence, the external factors affecting vulnerability are subject to the vagaries of interpretation of a number of different persons – whose competence to do so is seldom defined. This makes it all the more incumbent on the courts to establish mechanisms to distinguish between opinion evidence, that simply disagrees with what are perceived to be 'bad' autonomous choices, and evidence that demonstrates that authentic autonomy is not being exercised.
3. The important point made by the Law Commission must be reiterated and recognised in court procedures to engender trust that they remain on the side of beneficence and not paternalism, viz, that there must be respect for a vulnerable person's decision to do or not to do something which, *after due consideration*, they have decided to do or not to do. In other

66 Note 6, above, at p. 65.

67 Note 48, above, at para. 78.

68 *Re T (Adult: Refusal of Treatment)* [1993] Fam 95. See also, *In re Z (Local Authority: Duty)* [2004] EWHC 2817 (Fam), [2005] 1 WLR 959.

69 Note 48, above, at para. 78.

words, time-frames are of crucial importance in setting limits on the inherent jurisdiction. This should impact both on the quality of any evidence that is brought forward – for example is this a recent or long-standing situation? – and also on the scope of any interim relief, that is, what amounts to a sufficient, and not excessive, time to allow for 'due consideration'?

What Does It Mean to Enhance or Liberate Autonomy?

We have already seen that the common law long ago established the absolute right for autonomous persons to make 'bad decisions'.[70] Whatever we might think of this as an ethical position, the legal question is whether this is the status that the inherent jurisdiction seeks to reinstate for vulnerable persons. We must assume that it is, given the formulation by Macur J in *LBL v. RYJ and VJ*, that was endorsed by the Court of Appeal in *Re DL*: '... the relevant case law establishes the ability of the court, via its inherent jurisdiction, to facilitate the process of unencumbered decision-making by those who they have determined have capacity free of external pressure or physical restraint in making those decisions'.[71] Furthermore, Munby J has said:

> The inherent jurisdiction can be invoked wherever a vulnerable adult is, or is reasonably believed to be, for some reason deprived of the capacity to make the relevant decision, or disabled from making a free choice, or incapacitated or disabled from giving or expressing a real and genuine consent.[72]

In the absence of any sense of what a 'real and genuine consent' for the person looks like, however, there is a real risk that there will be a blurring between cases that involve decisions with which others fundamentally disagree, and those which are examples of an actual absence of authentic autonomy. Moreover, authentic autonomy – question-begging though it is as a concept – is necessarily different for each of us. Some states of being, such as deafness or blindness, are permanent for most people who experience them. Many congenital deformations and illnesses will never go away. Some parents will genuinely prefer to live with their aggressive off-spring rather than never to see them again. All of this speaks to the importance of understanding what autonomy means for the people involved. This is not only a question for the courts. Indeed, a commitment to promoting autonomy requires early engagement with people about their values, preferences and options, most particularly in care and healthcare relationships. This can help to identify and promote the kind of autonomy that is meaningful for each person. For the courts' part, it suggests that there might be a role for an autonomy plan as part of any relief granted, such that there is a benchmark against which to determine when and if autonomy has been 'liberated' (to use the Court's own phraseology).

Moving into the realm of ethical conjecture, there is scope to consider how far beneficent promotion of autonomy implies on-going engagement with individuals about the range of options at their disposal. Rather than reverting to the legalistic position of *defensive autonomy* discussed above, this could support the flourishing of autonomous decision-making, even in cases where the ultimate outcome involves a decision with which many would disagree.[73]

---

70 Note 14, above, and text.

71 [2010] EWHC 2665 (COP), at para. 62.

72 Note 48, above, at para. 79.

73 See, for example, McCormack, B., Karlsson, B., Dewing, J. and Lerdal A., 'Exploring Person-centredness: A Qualitative Meta-synthesis of Four Studies' (2010) 24(3) *Scandinavian Journal of Caring Sciences*, 620–34.

What Are the Limits of the Jurisdiction?

An essential procedural safeguard, now standard as a result of the Human Rights Act 1998, is the importance of considerations of necessity and proportionality with respect to the protection and promotion of individual rights.[74] But what does autonomy demand of proportionality in this context? The courts have been at pains to point out that the inherent jurisdiction must not encroach on the will of Parliament, as manifested in the Mental Capacity Act and other legislation. Equally, it has been confirmed that the category of 'vulnerable person' extends to people suffering from mental incapacity and in respect of whom relief is not available under the MCA.[75] An example of this is found in the case of *Westminster City Council v. C*.[76] The matter in dispute related to the validity in English law of a marriage conducted by phone to Bangladesh, involving a profoundly autistic young man who was also affected by severe intellectual impairment. The local authority was concerned both with recognition of the marriage and by the prospect that the family might remove the vulnerable adult to Bangladesh. The trial judge supported the concerns and the parents appealed on the grounds of error of law, both as to a declaration of non-validity of marriage and challenging the assumed jurisdiction to act in such a case. Wall LJ in the Court of Appeal addressed the jurisdictional point head-on:

> I am also in no doubt that a combination of the inherent jurisdiction and the provisions of the 2005 Act is apt to confer jurisdiction on the High Court to make orders about where IC should live, including the decision as to whether or not it is in his interests to go and live in Bangladesh.[77]

As to the respective roles of the two areas of law, the Court of Appeal cited with complete approval the trial judge's finding that:

> No part of the 2005 [sic] deals with the issue of preventing the mentally incapacitated person from leaving the country … [I]n my judgment, save where to do so would be demonstrably inconsistent with the will of Parliament, the inherent jurisdiction remains alive, in appropriate cases, to meet circumstances unmet by the scope of the legislation. That is not, to state the obvious, an invitation to a court so to do unless it is lawful, necessary and proportionate so to do.[78]

The prospect of the *co-existence* of the two jurisdictions, and what that might mean for vulnerable persons and patients, is now open to serious question. It was raised in the medical context in the case of *A Local Authority v. Mrs A*.[79] This involved a couple, both of whom had learning

74 The human rights dimensions of these cases were discussed in *Local Authority X v. MM, KM* [2007] EWHC 2003 (Fam).

75 See Munby J, in *Re SA*, note 48, above, para. 83: 'The inherent jurisdiction is not confined to those who are vulnerable adults, however that expression is understood, nor is a vulnerable adult amenable as such to the jurisdiction. The significance in this context of the concept of a vulnerable adult is pragmatic and evidential: it is simply that an adult who is vulnerable is more likely to fall into the category of the incapacitated in relation to whom the inherent jurisdiction is exercisable than an adult who is not vulnerable. So it is likely to be easier to persuade the court that there is a case calling for investigation where the adult is apparently vulnerable than where the adult is not on the face of it vulnerable. That is all'.

76 [2008] EWCA Civ 198, [2009] Fam 11, [2009] 2 WLR 185.

77 At para. 54.

78 CA at para. 56, citing [2007] EWHC 3096 (Fam), at 121.

79 [2010] EWHC 1549 (Fam). Cf., *A Local Authority v. K* [2013] EWHC 242 (COP) involving a woman with Down's Syndrome and a more straight-forward application of best interests with respect to sterilisation

disabilities, and where the woman's desire, and ability to care, for another child was called into question because of her own inherent intellectual limits and the influence of her partner. The local authority was concerned by her refusal to use contraception and, initially, asked that force and restraint be authorised to require this. Acknowledging the practical difficulties in pursuing such a route, the court eschewed this prospect and ultimately made no order because it considered that the full range of options for the couple was yet to be explored.[80] Notwithstanding this, the ruling is important in at least two respects. First, Mrs A was judged to be incompetent within the terms of the Mental Capacity Act because of the co-existence of internal *and* external factors. As the judge said:

> In view of what I find to be the completely unequal dynamic in the relationship between Mr and Mrs A, I am satisfied that her decision not to continue taking contraception is not the product of her own free will … For these reasons, I am in no doubt that Mrs A presently lacks capacity to take a decision for herself about contraception.[81]

Second, the inherent jurisdiction was also held to pertain, and thus afforded power,

> … to prevent conduct by the dominant party which coerces or unduly influences the vulnerable party from making free decisions. The purpose, in respect of a capacitated but vulnerable adult, is to create a situation where he or she can receive outside help free of coercion, to enable him or her to weigh things up and decide freely what he or she wishes to do. In respect of an incapacitated adult, I consider the same should apply, except that the aim of providing him or her with relief from the coercion is first to gain capacity and, if achieved, then to enable him or her to reach a free decision.[82]

Most recently, in *XCC v. AA*,[83] Parker J seemed to confirm a cumulative rather than complementary relationship between the jurisdiction of the Court of Protection under the MCA and that of the High Court under the inherent jurisdiction. In circumstances similar to the *Westminster* case, the essential legal question concerned the recognition of a Bangladeshi marriage involving a vulnerable adult domiciled in the UK. Having established the incapacity of the adult – in terms of the 2005 Act – the court, nonetheless, felt able to provide relief in the form of a declaration of non-recognition of the marriage on the basis of the inherent jurisdiction; this particular outcome is not available under the legislation, but it was merited because '[i]t would be unjustifiable and discriminatory not to grant the same relief to incapacitated adults who cannot consent as to capacitous [sic] adults whose will has been overborne'.[84]

The court went further still in blurring the boundaries between the two jurisdictions. Because Part I of the 2005 Act concerning the relevant considerations to be taken into account about a person's best interests – such as their wishes, desires and preferences – does *not* pertain to the inherent jurisdiction, these did not operate as a constraining benchmark against which to limit that jurisdiction. Wider public policy considerations could be considered, such as the prospect that

---

and contraception and the importance of striking the right balance between 'protection and empowerment'.

80 The male partner indicated his willingness to allow A to have access to healthcare professionals to explore her choices.

81 At para. 73.

82 At para. 79.

83 [2012] EWHC 2183 (COP), [2013] 2 All ER 988, [2013] 2 FCR 401.

84 At para. 54.

the marriage was a vehicle to allow the Bangladeshi partner to enter the UK.[85] Finally, Parker J reiterated her earlier ruling that it is:

> … the duty of a doctor or other health or social work professional who becomes aware that an incapacitated person may undergo a marriage abroad, to notify the learning disabilities team of Social Services and/or the Forced Marriage Unit if information comes to light that there are plans for an overseas marriage of a patient who has or may lack capacity.[86]

If we examine this trend in case law relative to our concerns about facilitating autonomy and eliding the prospect of paternalism, there is much that raises concern as a matter of procedural trust, outlined above. The Court of Appeal in *DL* was adamant that it was not collapsing the distinction between incapable adults and those who are vulnerable.[87] And yet, these more recent rulings seem to do precisely this. It is possible to be mentally incapable for both internal *and* external factors (*Re A*), and it is possible to be, at the same time, caught by the provisions of the MCA as an incapable person and yet not have decisions bounded by the supreme safety consideration of one's own best interests (*XCC*).

It might make sense to argue that the category of 'vulnerable adult' necessarily encompasses everyone who is mentally incapable, except that the objectives of the law with respect to the two categories of patient have been explicitly stated to be quite different: those suffering from mental incapacity must be treated in their own best interests, while those who are capable and yet vulnerable must have their autonomy facilitated. But the impossibility of maintaining this supposedly clear bright line is revealed by persons whose vulnerable state is permanent. The persons affected by the declarations of non-recognition of marriage will never be in a position to marry. It is extremely concerning that best interests can be elided in terms of how they are treated under the law. We would argue that the important distinction as to the permanent or temporary nature of the source of vulnerability must be fully recognised if the common law is to continue to develop along these lines without further legislative intervention. We have argued above that an interim injunction must necessarily be time-limited if the objective of facilitating autonomy is to be realised. If this is an impossible objective, it cannot stand as the basis for an exercise of the jurisdiction. Contrariwise, if the essential nature of the inherent jurisdiction is, indeed, to be protective, then further elucidation of limiting parameters is required, such as a central role for best interests and full acceptance that beneficence is in play. Thus, we suggest that the law has now created three, and not two, categories of persons whose autonomy might be in doubt:

1. the *mentally incapable* caught by the MCA (whether this is for a cause that is temporary or permanent)
2. the *vulnerable person* whose condition is *temporary* (and for whom interim measures can be instituted to promote genuine and authentic future exercises of autonomy), and
3. the *vulnerable person* whose condition is *permanent* (and for whom facilitation of autonomy is possibly a misnomer). This last category is in the greatest need of attention and protection at the current time.

85 Paras 71–6.

86 Para. 96, albeit delivered as a postscript.

87 Note 47, above, at para. 15.

This is not to suggest that this last category of person cannot act autonomously in certain circumstances. Rather, it is a plea to recognise that *caring autonomy*[88] is required which will involve robust protection of their interests, as well as promotion of their overall well-being as part of a package of care.

What Is the Future for the Jurisdiction?

A final concern about these developments relates to the scope of relief that might be granted in the future. The Court of Appeal refused to limit this to interim measures. Furthermore, the marriage cases suggest that the jurisdiction does not only extend to orders against third parties, such as a non-interference injunction to create space for the vulnerable person. Instead, the jurisdiction might extend to actual control over the movements of the vulnerable persons themselves, including prohibition on leaving the country. It requires little imagination to contemplate where this might lead. For example, subject to a court being satisfied that a measure was necessary and proportionate (as might happen if all other options were exhausted), it could be used in the case of medical tourism and with respect to those seeking 'inappropriate' procedures abroad; or it might be extended to persons seeking assisted dying in foreign jurisdiction, and for whom the desperation of their situation is deemed to meet the criteria as operative external factors rendering them subject to the inherent jurisdiction. The liberty and human rights implications are considerable in such hypotheticals, and the practicalities might well mean that no court would attempt to go down such a route. Nonetheless, the re-emergence of the inherent jurisdiction in the extensive grey circumstances that we outline above requires considerable vigilance for the possible impacts – actual and perceived – that the prospect of its exercise might have on both autonomy and trust.

The very existence of the jurisdiction will raise dilemmas for healthcare professionals and others in care situations. The Law Commission pointed out in its report, *Adult Social Care*, that High Court proceedings are costly and time-consuming and 'an inappropriate way of dealing with emergency safeguarding cases'.[89] This might well be true, but the fact that this avenue is now open will necessarily mean that professionals working at the coal-face will be called upon to explore it. The High Court declaration of legality can be sought and obtained with relative ease.[90] Accordingly, the messages and concerns that we raise above are not only directed at the courts. The words of Munby J. in *Local Authority X v. MM and KM* must be taken seriously by all:

> ... The court must be careful to ensure that, in rescuing a vulnerable adult from one type of abuse, it does not expose her to the risk of treatment at the hands of the state which, however well intentioned, can itself end up being abusive of her dignity, her happiness and indeed of her human rights. That said, the law must always be astute to protect the weak and helpless, not least in circumstances where, as often happens in such cases, the very people they need to be protected from are their own relatives, partners or friends ... The emphasis must be on sensible risk appraisal, not striving to avoid all risk, whatever the price, but instead seeking a proper balance and being willing to tolerate

88 We borrow this expression from our doctoral graduate, Katri Löhmus, who developed the concept as part of her research: Löhmus, K., 'Caring Autonomy: Rethinking the Right to Autonomy under the European Court of Human Rights Jurisprudence', Doctoral thesis, University of Edinburgh, 2013.

89 Note 62, above, at para. 9.80.

90 See now, Practice Note, 'The Official Solicitor to the Senior Courts: Appointment in Family Proceedings and Proceedings under the Inherent Jurisdiction in Relation to Adults', March 2013. We envisage considerable practical difficulties for healthcare professionals in determining the *cause* of vulnerability and so the appropriate route to court, viz, Court of Protection or High Court.

> manageable or acceptable risks as the price appropriately to be paid in order to achieve some other good – in particular to achieve the vital good of the elderly or vulnerable person's *happiness*. What good is it making someone safer, if it merely makes them miserable?[91]

As to the future, the Department of Health has expressed scepticism about the role of the courts in exercising the inherent jurisdiction. For example, in a consultation for a new safeguarding power, it said:

> … we do not believe leaving such cases to be resolved on a case-by-case basis using the Court's inherent jurisdiction is a satisfactory solution. Resorting to the courts in every instance could increase the caseload of courts, result in differing outcomes, be expensive for local authorities and is likely to be extremely disempowering for individuals. If we establish that a proportionate and effective legislative solution could help resolve this issue, it would not be necessary to rely on case law to settle the matter.[92]

The Government's reply to the Law Commission's report recognised the resurrected inherent jurisdiction and confirmed that it had 'no further plans to legislate in this area at this time',[93] especially in light of the reforms that now appear in the Care Act 2014.[94] Reforms in the Care Act will not impact directly on the inherent jurisdiction and, instead, lay down a single over-arching principle of 'well-being' upon which local authority action relating to adult social care is to be organised. The Government has indicated that it prefers a single organising principle linked to key outcomes, rather than a more granular or detailed approach. Given this, and the uncertainties that it entails until put into practice, we contend that our contribution herein gives further specification and direction to the implementation of such a principle, particularly as it involves the promotion of individual well-being,[95] which explicitly include, inter alia, 'personal dignity (including treatment of the individual with respect), physical and mental health and emotional well-being and protection from abuse and neglect' of persons.[96]

Conclusion: A Focus on Relationships Not Rights

It may well be that the doctor-patient relationship suffers from the constraints imposed by its close association with a legal system and this may operate in diametrically opposed fashion. On the one hand, as McLean has put it:

> In an ideal world, judges would use the law to reinforce the fundamental value of patient autonomy. To the contrary, however, courts have devised a system that has arguably been overly

91 [2007] EWHC 2003 (Fam), at paras 118 and 120. Emphasis as in original.

92 Department of Health, *Consultation on a New Safeguarding Power*, 2012, para. 13.

93 Department of Health, *Reforming the Law for Adult Care and Support: The Government's Response to Law Commission Report 326 on Adult Social Care*, July 2012, para. 9.28.

94 For comment on the lead up to this legislation, see Ruck Keene, A., 'The Inherent Jurisdiction: Where Are We Now?' (2013) 3(1) *Elder Law Journal*, 88–92.

95 Section 1(1) of the Care Act 2014.

96 See ss. 1(1)(a), (b) and (c).

> concerned not with prioritising patient rights, but rather with balancing them with other, often policy based, considerations.[97]

The alternative view, which we support, starts with the premise that a consent-based relationship is based almost entirely on patients' rights. The language of rights, even when not unilateral, implies conflict and conflict inevitably attracts legal intervention and legalism. From very early times in the debate, we have been impressed by the view that the rights model is suspect in that: '[I]t can turn what may have been a caring and amicable [doctor-patient] relationship into an adversarial one, inimical both to constructive dialogue and [the patient's] own future health'.[98] Moreover, as we have argued throughout this chapter and as amply demonstrated by the second half of our discussion, consent cannot be the dominant framing device for the value that we place in autonomy. This sums up our main motive for seeking a more conciliatory or 'user friendly' model for a relationship which is, at least, under threat.

If doctors and carers are to take seriously McLean's passionate commitment to autonomy – and if they are to remain on the acceptable side of the beneficence/paternalism line in seeking to promote this – they would do well to consider the fundamental role of the value of trust in the carer relationship. There will always be reasons to refuse to respect refusals, and this is not in itself a problem because a trusting relationship is not one in which parties must always agree. It is, however, one in which we *care* about people's reasons,[99] and also one in which agreeing to disagree is a mutually recognised and important option in its own right. This is true whether we are involved in the process of giving information to facilitate autonomous choice, or creating spaces to do the same. On the route to actual trust in the doctor-patient relationship, we must be able to trust that the rules of engagement have our entire range of interests at heart.

---

97 Note 6, above, at p. 95.

98 Teff, H., *Reasonable Care: Legal Perspectives on the Doctor-Patient Relationship*, Oxford, Clarendon Press, 1994, at p. 115. Although old, this remains the quintessential 'middle of the road' monograph on the subject.

99 For discussion of the distinction between caring and caring *for*, see Herring, J., *Caring and the Law*, Oxford, Hart Publishing, 2012, pp. 15–16. Also, Herring, J., 'Forging a Relational Approach: Best Interests or Human Rights?' (2013) 13 *Medical Law International*, 32–54.

Chapter 6

Advance Directives and Surrogate Decision-Making: When Are Patients' Prior Wishes Not Determinative?

Loane Skene

Introduction

Professor Sheila McLean has visited Australia on many occasions and she has many friends and colleagues 'Down Under'. Many will recall her Kirby Oration at the Annual Conference of the Australian Institute of Health Law and Ethics (now the Australasian Association of Bioethics and Health Law) in Newcastle, New South Wales in 2002. Her topic was 'The Role of Law in Life and Death'.[1] This was a continuing theme in Professor McLean's research and writing, covering consent to medical treatment, refusal of treatment, end of life decision-making and, more specifically for the discussion in this chapter, advance directives. She advocated that advance directives should be followed by healthcare professionals.

In 2009, Professor McLean observed that, in England and Wales, the Mental Capacity Act 2005 'enshrines the concept of autonomy in statute, allowing individuals to choose to avoid a particular treatment that they would, for whatever reason, find unacceptable'; and that '[i]n Scotland, there is no statute that gives legal effect to advance directives, but there is a general view that they should be followed'.[2] She acknowledged that there may be 'doubt about the capacity of the individual to execute a valid directive'; and that doctors may 'seek a court decision about the validity of the directive', so that it would be lawful to provide life-sustaining treatment at least until the court's decision.[3] But she supported the right of patients such as Kerrie Wooltorton and Ms B to refuse treatment and to be allowed to die.[4] It will be recalled that Ms Wooltorton had swallowed antifreeze on a number of previous occasions and had accepted treatment but she refused it on the occasion in question;[5] Ms B, tetraplegic and ventilator-dependent, refused ventilation and a court affirmed her right to do so.[6]

Advance directives are commonly believed to ensure that patients' wishes about their future treatment will be given effect if the patient is later not competent to make decisions. However, in

---

1 Professor McLean presented two other papers at the conference: 'Current Debates on Assisted Reproductive Technology in the UK'; and 'Handling Concerns about Retained Organs and Tissue: The Scottish Experience'. I mention these papers as a reminder of the breadth of her interests and scholarship.

2 McLean, S.A.M., 'Are Advance Directives Legally Binding or Simply the Starting Point for Discussion on Patients' Best Interests? Ethical View' (2009) 339 *British Medical Journal*, http://www.bmj.com/content/339/bmj.b4695 (accessed 13 January 2015).

3 Note 1, above.

4 McLean, S.A.M., 'Live and Let Die' (2009) 339 *British Medical Journal*, 837.

5 See 'Sheila McLean on Advance Directives and the Case of Kerrie Wooltorton', *BMJ Blogs*, 1 October 2009.

6 *Ms B v. NHS Hospital Trust* [2002] 2 All ER 449. As McLean observed, 'the court even levied a small fine on the doctors involved for failing to comply with [Ms B's] wishes': note 4, above.

the common law and legislation, there are many ways a patient's wishes may be overridden. This is arguably even more the case in Australia than in the United Kingdom. This chapter reports the findings of an extensive survey in three Australian states of physicians' knowledge of the law, and their practical decision-making. The survey suggests that physicians rely more on their clinical judgment than on legal principles in making decisions about the withdrawal of treatment. Similarly, surrogate decision-makers are generally required by Australian legislation to act in a patient's 'best interests', rather than making a 'substituted judgment' of what the patient would have wanted, even if the patient's wishes are legally required to be considered in the process. Legislation authorises urgent treatment without consent and courts and tribunals can review and authorise treatment in other cases. In these circumstances, one may question the effectiveness of many directives and other legal strategies in giving effect to patients' wishes when they are no longer competent. The chapter focuses on Australian law as there has been legislation in Australia on these topics for many years, and draws comparisons with the law in the UK.

In Australia, as in the UK, autonomy, also called self-determination, has been acknowledged by the common law as the predominant principle in medical decision making.[7] In *Rogers v. Whitaker*,[8] the leading Australian case on 'informed consent', the High Court endorsed 'the paramount consideration that a person is entitled to make his own decisions about his life'.[9] In a later New South Wales case, the judge accepted that patients can make binding decisions in advance refusing treatment they do not want (in that case dialysis).[10] There has also been legislation in Australia predating the Mental Capacity Act 2005 by many years to give legal effect to patients' advance directives and to decisions made on behalf of patients by formally appointed surrogate decision-makers.[11]

Thus, from an ethical and common law perspective (and in Australia in legislation), it has been long recognised that patients themselves, not their doctors, should decide about medical treatment, though the patient will obviously consider medical advice in making the decision. As discussed in the case law, doctors may understand the medical issues – the patient's history, the features of particular medical conditions and treatment options. However, patients know their own values, which will ultimately determine the treatment they are prepared to undergo.[12] Patients have to assess for

7 The principles stated by the House of Lords in *Airedale National Health Service Trust v. Bland* [1993] AC 789 have been approved in a number of Australian cases (see, for example, *Hunter and New England Area Health Service v. A* [2009] NSWSC 761 (McDougall J), at [17] and [18]). Lord Goff said in *Bland* (at 863–4) that doctors must give effect to the wishes of '… an adult patient of sound mind [who] refuses, however unreasonably, to consent to [life-sustaining] treatment … even though [the doctors] do not consider it to be in his best interests to do so. … [and] the fundamental principle … of the sanctity of human life' must yield to that of self-determination. See also discussion on the current law in Australia: Victorian Law Reform Commission (VLRC), Final Report 24, *Guardianship*, 2012, http://www.lawreform.vic.gov.au/projects/guardianship-final-report (accessed 13 January 2015), ch. 13, 'Medical Treatment', paras 13.6–12.

8 [1992] HCA 58, (1992) 175 CLR 479 (HCA).

9 Quoting these words from King CJ's judgment in *F v. R* (1983) 33 SASR 189, at 193.

10 *Hunter and New England Area Health Service v. A* [2009] NSWSC 761.

11 Medical Treatment Act 1988 (Vic.); Guardianship Act 1987 (NSW); Powers of Attorney Act 1998 (Qld); Medical Treatment (Health Directions) Act 2006 (ACT); Consent to Medical Treatment and Palliative Care Act 1995 (SA); Natural Death Act 1988 (NT); Directions for Medical Treatment Bill 2005 (Tas.); Acts Amendment (Consent to Medical Treatment) Bill 2006 (WA). Differences between the states' provisions regarding consent to treatment are noted in the VLRC Final Report, note 7, above, paras 13.41–50. See also, *National Framework for Advance Care Directives*, September 2011, available on the website of the Australian Health Ministers Advisory Council: http://www.ahmac.gov.au/cms_documents/AdvanceCareDirectives2011.pdf (accessed 13 January 2015).

12 See *Rogers v. Whitaker* [1992] HCA 58, (1992) 175 CLR 479 (HCA), at [14].

themselves their willingness to take risks and bear pain or physical restrictions; and their life goals. The state, 'the community' and paternalistic, if well-meaning, physicians are not entitled to determine the medical treatment that competent adult patients will have. The same ideas are reflected in the Australian legislation. In the state of Victoria, the Preamble to the Health Services (Conciliation and Review) Act 1987 (Vic.) states that one of the 'guiding principles ... [to be promoted] in the Victorian health care system' is 'an environment of informed choice in accepting or refusing treatment ...' (para. (f)). Under s. 16(2), if a 'provider' of health services acts unreasonably by not following the guiding principles, a complaint may be made to the Health Services Commissioner.

A patient's right to autonomy does not extend to a right to be given any particular treatment, but rather to choose one of the options that is offered by the treating physician or, more usually, to refuse particular treatment that they do not want. Thus in the English case of *R (Burke) v. GMC*,[13] the Court of Appeal held that a patient did not have a right to require that he must be provided with food and water if he later became incompetent and unable to communicate. There has also been a number of Australian cases stating that a patient's relatives have no legal right to have treatment provided for the patient against medical advice.[14] The treatment to be provided would be decided by reference to clinical judgment about what was appropriate in the circumstances.

A patient's right to make his or her own medical decisions includes the right to consent or to refuse in advance.[15] Refusal of treatment in advance is more problematic than consent in advance. If treatment has been refused but the circumstances change, and the patient is unable to communicate, treatment cannot then be given even if the patient might have wanted the treatment. The patient might then die. For example, Jehovah's Witnesses can legally refuse blood transfusions before an operation and, if they are later incompetent, their advance directive is binding and must be followed by the physicians who are treating them, even if the person did not imagine a life-threatening situation when earlier refusing the transfusion. An advance directive cannot be legally overridden by physicians deciding that an emergency has arisen and that treatment is necessary to save the patient's life, nor to avoid a serious risk to the patient's physical or mental health. Treating a patient who has refused treatment in advance may be a battery (sometimes called an assault or trespass) for which the physician could be sued, even if the patient has suffered no injury and the patient's life has, in fact, been saved by the treatment. The bodily violation of being given treatment the patient has refused is an actionable wrong in itself.[16]

The level of information and understanding that a patient must have in order to be assessed as competent and to give a refusal of treatment that is later binding has been the subject of some controversy in recent Australian cases. Freckelton has analysed four of these cases and concluded

---

13 [2005] EWCA Civ 1003.

14 For example, in *Messiha v. South East Health* [2004] NSWSC 1061, the court endorsed the withdrawal of treatment including artificial ventilation and feeding from a 75-year-old man with severe hypoxic brain damage after cardiac arrest despite family objection. See also *In the Application of Herrington; Re King* [2007] VSC 151 (unreported, Williams J, 24 April 2007), in which the court would not order treatment the relatives wanted to be provided.

15 At common law, one can generally both consent and refuse in advance. The Australian legislation discussed in this chapter generally deals with a patient's right to refuse treatment in advance, though the South Australian, Western Australian and Queensland statutory schemes provide for advance refusal and consent.

16 *Malette v. Shulman* (1987) 47 DLR (4th) 18 (Can Ont CA) (patient successfully sued for trespass); compare *Ms B v. NHS Hospital Trust* [2002] 2 All ER 449 (fine imposed); *X v. The Sydney Children's Hospital Network* [2013] NSWCA 320, at [12] ('both a criminal offence and a tort', citing *Department of Health and Community Services (NT) v. JWB (Marion's case)* (1992) 175 CLR 218, at 234; *Schloendorff v. Society of New York Hospital*, 105 NE (1914) 92, at 93).

that 'a measure of uncertainty persists in respect of persons who have reached a decision about rejecting nutrition, hydration or medication without full provision of information to enable the patient to make such a decision' with judges in some cases imposing a more stringent test than those in other cases. He believes the more stringent test will in future be required by the law, 'given the importance of the issue'.[17] If that occurs, there may be greater scope for physicians to assess patients as incompetent if they are confused or have limited understanding of their condition and options for treatment. Decisions can then be made by someone else, a surrogate decision-maker.

Cases in which a patient has *refused* the treatment in advance, must of course be distinguished from a case where the patient has *neither consented to, nor refused*, the treatment. If treatment is provided when the patient is not able to consent, or has not been asked to consent, the treatment might be described as '*non-voluntary*', meaning that no consent has been obtained. However, providing treatment in such a case may still be lawful. That is certainly true when there is an emergency, both in the UK and in Australia; and the principle may extend further. In England some years ago, in the case of *Re F*,[18] involving the proposed sterilisation of a mentally incompetent patient, Lord Goff endorsed a principle of 'necessity', based on the patient's best interests, to justify withdrawing treatment from an incompetent patient.[19] The principle of necessity would apply, he said, where 'the action taken ... [was] such as a reasonable person would in all the circumstances take, acting in the best interests of the assisted person'.[20] However, that approach, so far as it is based on accepted medical practice, seems to elide principles in the law of trespass (treatment requires consent) and negligence (the physician's standard of care)[21] and several judges have ruled that it would not be accepted in Australian common law.

Nicholson CJ said in *Re Marion*[22] in the Family Court of Australia, that he was '... unable to see how a test that may be appropriate in considering whether a medical procedure has been carried out with reasonable care can be applied to circumstances where the medical procedure is to be carried out without the consent of the patient'.[23] Mason CJ and Dawson, Toohey and Gaudron JJ said in the High Court of Australia appeal in the same case, 'The House of Lords decision in *Re F* was influenced by the particular jurisdictional framework ... the court had no jurisdiction to authorise sterilisation'.[24] McHugh J also said in the High Court in the same case, 'Whatever may be the position in England, the approach of their Lordships is not consistent with the common law of Australia'.[25] One reason, of course, is that in Australia, the courts did have jurisdiction to review these cases, both at common law and under the guardianship legislation. This means that although treatment may be given without consent in an emergency, Australian physicians may need to be more cautious in other cases. There may be scope to 'presume' consent in some circumstances but if there has been an earlier refusal of treatment by the patient or a surrogate decision-maker, they should adopt the statutory procedure for administering treatment that is described below.[26]

---

17 Freckelton, I., 'Patients' Decisions to Die: The Emerging Australian Jurisprudence' (2011) 18 *Journal of Law and Medicine*, 427–38, at p. 438.

18 *Re F (Mental Patient: Sterilisation)* [1990] 2 AC 1.

19 *Re F*, note 18, above, at 75. See also *Bland*, note 7, above, at 867.

20 *Re F*, note 18, above, at 75.

21 As I remarked in 2008: Skene, L., *Law and Medical Practice*, 3rd edn, Sydney, LexisNexis Butterworths, 2008, at p. 93.

22 *Re Marion* (1990) 14 Fam LR 427.

23 *Re Marion*, note 22, above, at 441.

24 *Re Marion*, note 22, above, at 462.

25 *Re Marion*, note 22, above, at 462–3.

26 Procedures vary from state to state. The legislation is listed above, note 11.

The Australian legislation certainly emphasises the right of patients to refuse treatment they do not want. In Victoria, for example, the Medical Treatment Act 1988 (Vic.) prescribes the procedure for executing a formal Refusal of Treatment Certificate, in the precise form set out in a Schedule to the Act. If a person completes this form and it is witnessed by a registered medical practitioner and another person, a physician who provides the treatment that has been refused may be charged with the offence of 'medical trespass' under the Act, as well as being sued for trespass at common law. If a Refusal of Treatment Certificate has been properly executed and witnessed, the treatment must not be provided;[27] it is no defence that the treatment is given in an emergency to save a person's life or to avoid a serious risk to the person's health. A Refusal of Treatment Certificate does not currently require to be registered even when death will result from the refusal; but the Victorian Law Reform Commission has recommended that it should be possible to register Refusal of Treatment Certificates with an online system.[28] In England and Wales, there are additional measures for the applicability of an advance decision if death is a prospect: Mental Capacity Act 2005, ss. 25(5) and (6).

Australian legislation enables a range of surrogate decision-makers to make medical decisions for patients who are not able to make their own decisions.[29] These include a tribunal or court, or a guardian appointed by a tribunal or court, or someone appointed by the patient,[30] or even a close relative or carer (the 'person responsible'[31]), though the decisions that can be made by a 'person responsible' are limited.[32] People may also provide written instructions concerning the treatment they would want in particular circumstances (an 'instructional directive'[33]).

---

27 Guardianship and Administration Act 1986 (Vic.), s. 41. The Medical Treatment Act 1988 (Vic.) also provides for an agent appointed by the patient according to the procedure specified in the Act to sign a Refusal of Treatment Certificate on behalf of the person who appointed the agent; and the state (through the Civil and Administrative Tribunal (VCAT)) may appoint a guardian to refuse treatment, if the person has not refused treatment under the Act, or appointed an agent to refuse treatment. The agent or guardian may then sign a Refusal of Treatment Certificate, but that can be reviewed by a court, unlike an individual's own Refusal of Treatment Certificate, which is binding if it applies in the circumstances. It should be noted that, in Queensland, a health provider who does not comply with an advance health directive is protected from liability if he or she has reasonable grounds to believe that a direction in the directive is uncertain or inconsistent with good medical practice: Powers of Attorney Act 1998 (Qld), s. 103(1).

28 VLRC Final Report, note 7, above, Recm. 203; see also VLRC, Consultation Paper 10, *Guardianship*, February 2011 (VLRC Consultation Paper), http://www.lawreform.vic.gov.au/projects/guardianship/guardianship-consultation-paper (accessed 13 January 2015), paras 8.142–3.

29 See legislation listed at note 11, above.

30 In Victoria, this may be an 'agent' appointed by an enduring power of attorney (medical treatment) under the Medical Treatment Act 1988 (Vic.); or an 'enduring guardian' appointed under the Guardianship and Administration Act 1986 (Vic.).

31 See Guardianship and Administration Act 1986 (Vic.), s. 37. This section sets out a 'hierarchy' of people who may decide, with those appointed by the patient for particular decisions generally having priority, provided they are 'reasonably available and willing and able to make a decision': s. 37(1). The VLRC has recommended a simpler hierarchy for health decision makers, with the first being the patient's 'co-decision maker': VLRC Final Report, note 7, above, Recm. 208.

32 For example, in Victoria, a 'person responsible' can consent to treatment but cannot refuse life-sustaining treatment. However, an 'agent' appointed by the patient under the Medical Treatment Act 1988 (Vic.) can refuse life-sustaining treatment.

33 VLRC Consultation Paper, note 28, above, para. 9.2. This Paper also noted other methods for improving communication of patients' wishes, such as the five steps of the 'Respecting Patients' Choices' programme: paras 9.59–64.

The law therefore seems relatively clear both in the UK and in Australia regarding patient autonomy, the circumstances in which treatment may be given without consent and a patient's right to refuse treatment, including refusing in advance. Also, under the Australian legislation, surrogate decision-makers are specifically required to take account of the patient's prior wishes.[34] One might therefore expect that physicians would feel themselves legally bound to follow the prior wishes of patients who have refused particular treatment, especially when those wishes have been expressed in documents that appear to be legally binding. However, that is not necessarily the case.

Physicians' Practice in Making End-of-life Decisions

An extensive empirical study that is currently being undertaken in Australia casts doubt on the effectiveness of the various legal developments in ensuring that patients' prior wishes are followed in practice. The study is being led by researchers at the Queensland University of Technology.[35] It is designed to investigate physicians' knowledge of the law in New South Wales, Victoria and Queensland, and their practice in taking account of the law when providing end-of-life care, especially in making decisions about withdrawal of treatment from adults who lack capacity. The results are still being analysed but it seems from the preliminary findings that many physicians seem not to understand or follow the law on advance directives and their legal obligations in dealing with surrogate decision-makers.[36] The principal guide of many physicians in making decisions is their clinical judgment.

The study commenced with three focus groups being established (a total of 17 doctors), one for each state). Following the focus groups, a pilot survey was developed which, for maximum representativeness, was sent to physicians in a wide range of specialties involved in end of life care: palliative medicine, geriatric medicine, renal medicine, intensive care, respiratory medicine, emergency medicine and medical oncology. The legal questions in the survey were validated by independent legal experts in the three states. The survey set out a number of medical scenarios, followed by questions to investigate the physicians' knowledge of the law concerning advance care directives (ACDs) and their attitude to them. The response rate was between 24 per cent and 52 per cent for the different specialities.

The responses to question 8 of the survey were especially significant for the issues discussed in this chapter. Respondents were asked whether they would commence antibiotics for a 53-year-old AIDS patient with a valid ACD in which he refused antibiotics if a life-threatening infection arose. He had consented to other treatment. With antibiotics, he could live for some time; without them he would die. His family wanted him to be treated.[37] Respondents who said that they would

34 For example, the Guardianship and Administration Act 1986 (Vic.), s. 28(2)(e); s. 38(a) (in determining whether a proposed medical procedure would be in a patient's 'best interests', the first matter to be taken into account is 'the wishes of the patient, so far as they can be ascertained'); ss. 42HA(6)(c), 42U.

35 Professors Ben White and Lindy Willmott. The study is entitled 'Withholding and Withdrawing Life-sustaining Treatment from Adults Who Lack Capacity: The Role of Law in Medical Practice': see White, B.P., Willmott, L., Parker, M., et al., 'Should Law Have a Role in End of Life Care?' (2012) 42(9) *Internal Medicine Journal*, 966–8.

36 The following account of the survey and preliminary findings is based on a presentation by Professor White at the Annual Conference of the Australasian Association of Bioethics and Health Law in Sydney in 2013, 'Does Law Matter? Medical Decision-making at the End of Life'. Professors White and Willmott have kindly read this section of the chapter.

37 The facts were, of course, more detailed. Also, I have quoted only a few questions in the survey.

commence antibiotics despite the ACD were then asked to select a reason for making this decision: 'I do not have to follow the ACD because it is inconsistent with what is clinically indicated'; 'the ACD is relevant to my decision making but other factors are more relevant'; 'the ACD is not relevant to my decision making because I don't believe ACDs are appropriate to determine treatment'; 'the ACD does not have legal effect'; 'Other – please specify'. The physicians who said they would not commence antibiotics were also given a range of reasons: 'The most important consideration is following the patient's wishes'; 'The most important consideration is that the law requires me to follow the ACD'; 'Both of the above considerations are equally important'; 'Other – please specify'.

A large majority of respondents in each state said that they would commence antibiotics despite the valid ACD. However, their reasons differed. Many appeared not to know the law, or the law was not the predominant or a significant reason for their decision. Factors given greater weight in decision making included: 'Patient's expected quality of life after proposed treatment'; 'Whether treatment is clinically indicated'; 'Your personal ethical principles'; and 'Following the patient's ACD'.

This fascinating study has significant implications for the law in this area. The authors 'estimate that almost 40,000 adult deaths occur nationally each year following a medical decision to withhold or withdraw treatment'[38] and in making these decisions, physicians are often 'acting in significant medico-legal roles', such as assessing a patient's mental capacity and communicating with potential surrogate decision-makers.[39] But the issues may be more complex and nuanced than may first appear. It is possible that the physicians who seem at first glance to be unaware of the law's emphasis on patient autonomy, or deliberately decide not to follow it, may be acting not only with understandable compassion, but also in accordance with other legal principles. To make this case, one must consider the circumstances in which a competent adult patient's prior wishes may lawfully not be followed.

Circumstances in which Patients' Prior Wishes May Lawfully Not Be Followed

There are many circumstances in which a patient's general right to decide in advance about treatment may be undermined. These are considered in turn.

Patients' Statements about Future Treatment May Be Interpreted as Not Applying in the Circumstances

Any statement about a patient's wishes or advance directive may be open to interpretation as to its meaning and the circumstances in which it was intended to apply. For example, if a patient has said, 'when I am terminally ill', it may be decided that the patient has not yet reached that stage, so the directive does not apply. Similarly, if the patient has refused 'life-sustaining measures', that may be interpreted as referring to measures such as mechanical ventilation and artificial nutrition and hydration, and not to routine care like antibiotics. Or, it might be said that the patient had anticipated a routine procedure, such as a birth or hysterectomy, not one in a life-threatening

38 These cases will not generally involve a formal refusal of treatment by, or on behalf of, the patient. In most, agreement will be reached after discussion between the physician, other medical carers, the patient and family members about the appropriate treatment to be provided.

39 Note 35, above.

situation. The patient's refusal would then not cover those circumstances and it would be justifiable either to ignore it or to allow a surrogate decision-maker to consent to a treatment, such as a blood transfusion.[40]

These arguments can be particularly appreciated in the case of unanticipated findings during surgery. Patients who are told that they have cancer and, on the basis of that knowledge, refuse 'CPR (cardio-pulmonary resuscitation) if I stop breathing' might take a different view if the surgery reveals that the suspected cancer is in fact a benign intestinal blockage that could be readily removed by surgery, with the patient then able to live a long and healthy life.[41] Even if the patient's life is likely to be subject to some impairment, the patient may still prefer to live that life than to die at that time. It is no wonder that physicians are sometimes tempted to interpret advance directives in light of later developments, especially if a surrogate decision-maker can decide after a patient has been assessed as incompetent.

In Victoria, physicians may decide not to follow a patient's prior wishes even if the patient has followed the statutory process for refusing treatment, though it is harder for physicians to ask surrogate decision-makers to decide about treatment if the patient has executed a valid Refusal of Treatment Certificate. Registered medical practitioners who witness Refusal of Treatment Certificates attest to the fact that the patient is suffering from a particular condition, is of sound mind, has been given relevant information, 'appeared to understand that information' and 'clearly expressed or indicated a decision' to refuse all treatment, or treatment of a particular kind.[42] But even in such cases, it may be possible for physicians to decide that giving a blood transfusion if a patient suffers a haemorrhage is treating a different condition from the one for which the patient was first admitted to hospital, so that it is not covered by the patient's Refusal of Treatment Certificate. A surrogate decision-maker can then be involved, since the patient is incompetent to decide, with the possibility also of applying to a tribunal or court to review the case. This enables more flexibility in decision-making, especially in light of changing circumstances, but it may undermine the patient's autonomy in the initial refusal of treatment.

Patients May Be Assessed as Lacking 'Competence' or 'Capacity' so that Surrogate Decision-makers Can Decide

If a person is assessed as not being competent, or not having capacity,[43] to make a particular decision, the person's decision will not be determinative. The assessment of whether a person is

---

40 That happened in the Victorian case *Qumsieh v. GAB and Pilgrim* (1998) 14 VAR 46, [1998] VSCA 45, in which a woman was given a blood transfusion after childbirth despite her earlier statements that she did not want such treatment; also in an American case, *In the Matter of Alice Hughes*, 611 A 2d 1148 (NJ Sup Ct App Div, 1992), in which a pregnant woman's refusal of a blood transfusion was overridden.

41 Compare Powers of Attorney Act 1998 (Qld), s. 103(1), note 27, above, which supports doctors treating a patient without consent in such circumstances.

42 Medical Treatment Act 1988 (Vic.), s. 5; Sch. 1: Refusal of Treatment Certificate. 'Medical treatment' is defined in the Act to exclude the administration of 'palliative care', which is defined to include the reasonable provision of food and water and pain relief: s. 3. Those measures are therefore not covered by the Refusal of Treatment Certificate and can be provided. However, a patient could refuse even those measures at common law. With regard to information, see note 20, above, and accompanying text.

43 The term 'competence' has been used for many years in the common law. It comprises two elements – the capacity to make a decision and the ability to communicate the decision in some way: VLRC Consultation Paper, note 28, above, at para. 9.23. The Victorian Guardianship and Administration Act 1986 refers to an inability to make decisions because of a 'disability'. The terms of reference for the VLRC Final Report

competent to consent to treatment, or to refuse it, is the responsibility of the treating physicians. If their assessment of the person's competence to decide is later questioned, they may face potential legal liability. If they have assessed the person as not competent and provided treatment the person has refused, they may be liable in battery if the court finds that the person was competent and the refusal should therefore have been followed.[44] Alternatively, if they assessed the person as competent to refuse the treatment and did not provide it, they may be liable in negligence for failing to provide the treatment if the court finds the person was not competent to refuse the treatment. Naturally, this uncertainty and risk may cause physicians to be cautious in assessing competence and it would be no surprise if they examined a patient's reasons for refusing proposed treatment, or the failure to provide any reasons, and on that basis concluded that the person was not competent to decide. As soon as that assessment has been made, the person's wishes are no longer determinative, though they may still be taken into account.[45] The physicians can lawfully provide urgent treatment at once and then consult a surrogate decision-maker with regard to further decisions.

This procedure may be illustrated by the Victorian Guardianship and Administration Act 1986 (Vic.), Part 4A. If a person is 'incapable of understanding the general nature and effect of the proposed procedure or treatment' or of indicating whether he or she consents, a 'person responsible' (defined to include a spouse, carer or relative as well as formally appointed decision-makers[46]) may consent to the procedure (ss. 36, 37, 42H).[47] The determination that a patient is not competent therefore has important consequences for the patient's autonomy in relation to treatment at that time.

Patients have been assessed as not competent on various grounds. Some have suffered from a medical condition that impaired their decision-making capacity, like anorexia nervosa, which English judges have regarded in a number of cases as undermining patients' ability to make an informed choice.[48] In other cases, patients have had delusions that prevented them accepting what was happening to them, or what treatment could offer them.[49] Those patients have been readily accepted as incompetent; though interestingly, patients who have rejected treatments on religious grounds, as Jehovah's Witnesses do with blood transfusions, have not been assessed as incompetent on that ground.[50]

---

included whether the terms 'capacity' and 'vulnerability' might be considered, rather than the legislation being based on a person being unable to decide because of a disability. The VLRC has recommended that this should not be changed: VLRC Final Report, note 7, above, p. xxvi. For the information required for competence, see note 20, above, and accompanying text.

44 Note 19, above. Under Australian law, if a patient is assessed as not competent, consent should ordinarily be sought from a surrogate decision-maker, unless urgent treatment is needed – in that case, treatment could be given under the emergency principle without consent from anyone. The emergency principle is preserved in the legislation; for example, Guardianship and Administration Act 1986 (Vic.), s. 42A.

45 Note 34, above.

46 Note 31, above.

47 Though possibly not if the patient is likely to be able to decide personally 'within a reasonable time': s. 42HA, another provision designed to safeguard the patient's autonomy.

48 For example, *Re E (Medical Treatment: Anorexia)* (Rev 1) [2012] EWHC 1639 (COP) (Court ruled that a 32-year-old woman lacked capacity to refuse treatment and authorised force feeding).

49 For example, *Re MB* (1997) 38 BMLR 175 (CA) (patient held unable to refuse caesarean section because of her fear of the anaesthetist's needle). Compare *Re C (Adult: Refusal of Treatment)* [1994] 1WLR 290, [1994] 1 All ER 819 (CA) (patient held competent to refuse amputation despite bizarre beliefs).

50 For example, *Qumsieh v. GAB and Pilgrim* (1998) 14 VAR 46, [1998] VSCA 45, in which the patient was treated without her consent but not on the basis that she was incompetent because of her religion; *The Sydney Children's Hospital Network v. X* [2013] NSWSC 368 in which a blood transfusion was authorised for

In many of the cases in which competence has been an issue, one would very likely agree with the physician's assessment that the patient was not competent in the circumstances (especially now that legislation provides for a surrogate decision-maker to decide about proposed treatment). However, where there is scope for physicians to find that a person who seems to be making an unreasonable decision is not competent, there may be concern that the person's autonomy may be too readily overridden. One factor in assessing a person as incompetent could be an assumption that no ordinary person who is acting 'reasonably' would decide in the way the patient has done and that the patient is therefore not competent. Such a view is, of course, quite understandable but it seems to ignore Lord Donaldson's widely quoted statement in *Re T (Adult: Refusal of Medical Treatment)*,[51] a case in which the patient refused a blood transfusion:

> Every adult is presumed to have [the] ... capacity to decide his own fate and should be allowed to do so unless that presumption is rebutted ... The patient's right of choice exists *whether the reasons for making that choice are rational, irrational, unknown or even non-existent.*[52]

Legislation on the Process of Surrogate Decision-making May Undermine Patients' Prior Wishes

As noted earlier, Australian legislation enables a range of surrogate decision-makers to make medical decisions for patients who are not able to make their own decisions, including tribunals or courts; a guardian appointed by a tribunal or court; someone appointed by the patient; or even a close relative or carer (the 'person responsible'), though the decisions that can be made by a 'person responsible' are limited.[53] These surrogate decision-makers are required to act in the patient's best interests and the legislation requires them to take account of the patient's prior wishes so far as they are known in determining the person's best interests.[54] To that extent, the patient's autonomy is intended by the legislation to be maintained as far as possible when the patient is no longer competent.

Despite this, however, the availability of the procedures for surrogate decision-making may have the result that a person's wishes are more readily overridden than before these provisions were introduced. Given the difficulty in assessing patients' competence in some cases, the liability risks if the wrong assessment is made, and time and resource constraints in hospitals, physicians may turn to surrogate decision-makers in cases that are not straightforward. They can then be confident that the surrogate decision-maker is likely to act 'reasonably', taking account of changes in the patient's circumstances. Due weight may be given to the patient's wishes but the surrogate

---

a 17-year-old patient but Gzell J at [48] recognised that the patient could lawfully refuse a transfusion when he became an adult 10 months later. Gzell J said at [49] 'The sanctity of life in the end is a more powerful reason for me to make the orders than is respect for the dignity of the individual'. On appeal (*X v. The Sydney Children's Hospital Network* [2013] NSWCA 320), Bastin J. said at [64] 'religious beliefs are internationally accepted as an aspect of an individual's fundamental autonomy with which the state cannot interfere and should not disregard' (citing several human rights instruments). The reasoning of the trial judge and the orders he made were upheld: [68], [74].

51 [1993] Fam 95, [1993] 3 WLR 782.

52 [1993] Fam 95, at 112, [1993] 3 WLR 782, at 796 (emphasis added); cited with approval in *X v. The Sydney Children's Hospital Network* [2013] NSWCA 320, at [64] with regard to 'minority religious beliefs' (Bastin J).

53 For example, the 'person responsible' can consent to treatment for the represented person but not refuse life-sustaining treatment.

54 Note 34, above.

is likely to be easier to deal with and, if not, it is probably easier to have a surrogate's decision reviewed by a court or tribunal than those of the patient.[55]

The risk that patients' autonomy may be undermined by surrogate decision-making applies even if they have appointed their own surrogate decision-maker. Surrogates must consider the patient's wishes (assuming that the patient has indicated wishes that are relevant in the later situation) but they are not bound to follow them. That issue was raised by the Victorian Law Reform Commission in its recent review of the guardianship legislation.[56] The Commission suggested in its Consultation Paper that, instead of being required to act in a patient's 'best interests', surrogate decisions could be replaced by a 'substituted judgment' approach, which 'requires a substitute decision-maker to make the decision that the person themselves would have made if they had the capacity to do so'.[57] That suggestion was supported in most responses.[58]

The Commission also canvassed a number of other reforms in its community consultation process to 'provide greater accountability and more scrutiny of decision-making arrangements',[59] including clearer statements of the responsibilities of surrogate decision-makers and an oath or declaration when they commence them, training, reporting requirements, a registration scheme for the appointment of surrogate decision-makers and notification of their activation, random investigation and auditing of appointees, and civil penalties for abuse of powers. Many of these measures have been recommended in the Commission's final report.[60]

Legislation Authorises Urgent Treatment Without Consent, Unless Refused in Advance by the Patient

Even if there is no surrogate decision-maker, both the common law and legislation enable treatment to be given without consent, unless there is a valid advance directive refusing that treatment.[61] In Victoria, if there is no advance directive refusing treatment, the Guardianship and Administration Act 1986 enables treatment to be given without consent in an emergency (s. 42A); or, even if it is not an emergency, the treatment is considered necessary in the patient's best interests.[62]

Courts and Tribunals Can Review and Authorise Medical Treatment

Courts and tribunals (like the Victorian Civil and Administrative Tribunal) have always played an important role in the oversight of medical decision-making and that has been increased under

55 The review process in Victoria is described in the VLRC Final Report, note 7, above, at para. 13.40.

56 VLRC Consultation Paper, note 28, above, p. 177, Question 41, 'Should the wishes expressed in a document making a personal appointment be binding, or should they merely be matters that the personally appointed decision-maker must consider?'

57 VLRC Consultation Paper, note 28, above, p. 27; paras 4.19, 5.72; ch. 17. See also para. 5.73 considering the 'history of the person' as well as the person's wishes.

58 VLRC Final Report, note 7, above, para. 13.83.

59 VLRC Consultation Paper, note 28, above, Executive Summary, p. 27.

60 VLRC Final Report, note 7, above, Executive Summary, paras 46–7; 68–74; List of Recommendations, pp. xxxiii–lxxxv.

61 Such as a Refusal of Treatment Certificates in Victoria, see note 27, above.

62 Guardianship and Administration Act 1986 (Vic) ss. 42K, 42L; a notice in the prescribed form must be given within three days to the Office of the Public Advocate (s. 42K(1)(c)) and, if the 'person responsible' has refused the treatment, the doctor must delay the commencement of the treatment to give the surrogate decision-maker time to have the decision reviewed. Both of these sections are subject to s. 41, which gives priority to the patient's Refusal of Treatment Certificate, even in an emergency.

the legislation. This structure may be readily justified because of the potential conflicts of interest between the patient and the surrogate decision-maker. However, the decisions of surrogate decision-makers are more open to review than those of patients themselves. As noted earlier, a competent adult patient is legally entitled to make even unwise decisions that seem to an outsider not to be in the patient's best interests.[63] The only way that those decisions can be overridden is by interpreting the decision as not applying in the circumstances that have later arisen; or by deciding that the patient is not competent.

When a decision is made by a surrogate decision-maker, on the other hand, it can be challenged in a court or tribunal on the basis that the surrogate decision-maker was not acting in the best interests of the patient. That includes not taking account of the patient's wishes, so far as they are known,[64] but, under the legislation, the responsibility of the surrogate decision-makers is not simply to give effect to the patient's autonomy. They must also consider other matters relating to the patient's best interests. This means that the patient's wishes may be overridden. This is another matter on which the Victorian Law Reform Commission has recommended changes to strengthen the autonomy of incompetent patients. The Commission's final report notes the importance of the United Nations Convention on the Rights of Persons with Disabilities, the Victorian Charter of Human Rights and Responsibilities Act 2006, and the changing approach in the community to people with disabilities[65] so that greater emphasis is placed on 'promoting the participation of people with disabilities in decisions that affect them'.[66] It proposes a wider range of decision-making processes, including 'supported decision making' and 'co-decision making'[67] to assist people with disabilities to make their own decisions and to have them followed, as well as substitute decision-making.

Conclusion

It can be seen from this discussion that, in Australia, there are many situations in which it is legally justifiable for a patient's advance wishes not to be followed, despite the legislation and case law emphasising the right of competent adult patients to refuse treatment that they do not want, including refusal in advance. The practice of physicians who appear not to be acting in accordance with an incompetent patient's ACD in making decisions about end-of-life care should be assessed in the light of those exceptions. For example, the survey of physicians' clinical practice that has been described in this chapter has found in early analysis that a large majority of those who responded would commence antibiotics in certain circumstances, despite a valid ACD from the patient refusing antibiotics if a life-threatening infection arose. Many of the physicians said that they would base their decisions on clinical factors and their own personal ethical principles rather than the law. Those findings may lead to concern that the physicians' emphasis on 'medical interests', perhaps viewed in the light of the physicians' ethical principles, may detract from a more holistic view of patients' overall interests, especially their right to have their autonomy respected, that is widely accepted in medical law and ethics.

However, as this chapter has argued, it is possible that the physicians who seem at first glance to be unaware of the law's emphasis on patient autonomy, or who deliberately decide not to follow the law, may be acting not only with understandable compassion, but also in accordance with other

63 Compare Lord Donaldson's statement in text to note 52, above.

64 Note 34, above.

65 VLRC, Final Report, note 7, above, pp. xxi–xxii.

66 VLRC, Final Report, note 7, above, p. xiii.

67 VLRC, Final Report, note 7, above, Glossary, pp. xiv–xix; ch. 9.

legal principles, even if those principles were not articulated in the survey. These include: the scope to interpret the meaning of the ACD and the circumstances in which it was intended to apply; the assessment of the patient as lacking 'competence' or 'capacity' so that surrogate decision-makers can decide about treatment; and the increased flexibility of decision-making if decisions are made by surrogate decision-makers who must take account of the patient's earlier expressed wishes in determining the patient's best interests but are not bound by the patient's wishes.

Moreover, the perceived undermining of patients' autonomy is not necessarily objectionable. Although individual autonomy and minimal state interference are the predominant values with competent adult patients, there may be a place for other values when the patient is no longer competent, such as communitarian ethics or the ethics of care. In the Australian case of *Hunter and New England Area Health Service v. A*,[68] McDougall J referred to the 'relevant but in some cases conflicting interests' of autonomy and 'the interest of the State in protecting and preserving the lives and health of its citizens'.[69] In Victoria, as in other jurisdictions, people who are mentally ill and need treatment that they cannot receive in the community may be involuntarily detained and treated.[70] Certain alcoholic and drug-dependent people may also be compulsorily detained and treated.[71] Patients who are trying to commit suicide may be lawfully prevented from doing so under common law and statutory provisions.[72] It is possible that such situations could be met by assessing the person as incompetent so that a surrogate decision-maker can be appointed. But even in the absence of such an approach, one might accept that if people like those are not treated because they will not or cannot consent, they will be deprived of treatment that they need. Similarly, one might accept that patients who make ACDs while they are competent cannot anticipate all the circumstances that may arise later, such as unexpected findings, new treatments and even an understanding of how they may be able to cope with a disability.[73] Physicians often cite their experience of patients who initially refused procedures like the amputation of a gangrenous leg but have later been grateful despite the amputation, once they have become accustomed to an artificial leg; and fit young patients rendered paraplegic and ventilator-dependent after a sporting accident may adjust to their state despite passing through a stage of wanting the treatment withdrawn. If patients' directions must always be followed, those patients may miss out on treatment they might otherwise have wanted if more fully informed about them.

Legislation such as the Victorian Guardianship and Administration Act, and the scope it provides for review of medical decisions, offers a compromise between respecting patients' competent decisions and safeguarding their welfare. Some people may regard the availability of surrogate decision-making, in itself, as an easy option for physicians to undermine a patient's autonomy by too readily assessing the patient as lacking capacity so that his or her wishes can be overridden. Others see this as an appropriate safeguard of the patient's medical interests at a time of

68 [2009] NSWSC 761.

69 [2009] NSWSC 761, at [5]; see also, *The Sydney Children's Hospital Network v. X* [2013] NSWSC 368 (Gzell J, note 50, above).

70 The Victoria Mental Health Act 2014, Division 3, ss. 19–22, allows people to make advance statements about their wishes for medical treatment if they should later become mentally ill: http://www.legislation.vic.gov.au/Domino/Web_Notes/LDMS/PubStatbook.nsf/f932b66241ecf1b7ca256e92000e23be/0001F48EE2422A10CA257CB4001D32FB/$FILE/14-026aa%20authorised.pdf (accessed 13 January 2015). See also: Disability Act 2006 (Vic).

71 Alcoholics and Drug-dependent Persons Act 1968 (Vic.), ss. 11 and 12.

72 See, for example, Crimes Act 1958 (Vic.), s. 463B.

73 The information required before an ACD is valid is a moot point in Australia – see note 37, above, and accompanying text.

uncertainty. The recent reviews of the law in this area by the Victorian Law Reform Commission[74] and other bodies,[75] taking account of changing attitudes to people with disabilities and international human rights instruments, are likely to result in more nuanced procedures to promote autonomy, while enabling the patient to be treated in some circumstances despite an ACD.

---

74 The VLRC Final Report, note 7, above, was tabled in Parliament on 18 April 2012 and recommends many changes to the guardianship legislation. However, most of the provisions described in this chapter would be retained, including those in the Medical Treatment Act, which would be incorporated in the new guardianship legislation: VLRC Final Report, paras 200, 201.

75 The recent report from the Australian Law Reform Commission is about '… ensuring people with disability have an equal right to make decisions for themselves'. It embodies the notion of 'supported decision-making', including full recognition of advance statements. See Australian Law Reform Commission, *Equality, Capacity and Disability in Commonwealth Laws: Final Report*, ALRC Report 124, August 2014, available at: https://www.alrc.gov.au/sites/default/files/pdfs/publications/alrc_124_whole_pdf_file.pdf (accessed 13 January 2015).

Chapter 7

Disability and Healthcare: Some Philosophical Questions

Robin Downie

Introduction

I have been privileged to be a member of several national committees chaired by Sheila McLean. She was unfailingly able to identify the key issues in any topic and to involve all members in discussion and in writing papers to assist in the final committee report. This was always done with good humour. Committee meetings were never my *forte* but I always looked forward to the ones chaired by Sheila because I knew that time would not be wasted and that she would steer us all to reach helpful conclusions. I also benefited from sharing some teaching with her in the Glasgow University MPhil in Law and Ethics in Medicine. Again, this was a course enormously enjoyed by the doctors and other healthcare professionals who took part.

Sheila's interests are wide and one of them concerns the rights of the disabled.[1] This is the topic that I shall discuss, as a philosopher rather than a lawyer. Sheila always claims that she is no philosopher, but she has a sharp mind for conceptual issues, and the topic of disability and its relationship to healthcare certainly raises conceptual issues.

Definitions

Any discussion of the relationship between disability and healthcare must begin by attempting to make it clear what is meant by 'disability'. But we must first face the objection that there is no such condition. For example, it might be said that people can be 'differently abled'. That might mean that if you are blind you will develop other senses, such as hearing, to a higher degree than the sighted population. This is common among blind musicians. Some associations for the deaf have taken a different line and argued that the difference between those who can hear and those who are deaf is a cultural one, that there is a 'deaf culture'.[2] They point to their sign language and the shared experiences which go with a shared language and take this as evidence that they are simply culturally different rather than disabled.[3] Other groups again use terms such as 'challenged' – visually challenged, intellectually challenged and so on, or they might speak of 'learning difficulties'. Others again might argue that if the groups in question encounter problems in their daily lives the problems are created by society and social arrangements which do not facilitate their lives, for example by providing adequate ramps and other appropriate provisions.

---

1 McLean, S.A.M. and Williamson, L., *Impairment and Disability: Law and Ethics at the Beginning and End of Life*, Abingdon, Routledge-Cavendish, 2007.

2 Padden, C.A. and Humphries, T.L., *Inside Deaf Culture*, Cambridge, MA, Harvard University Press, 2005.

3 Levy, N., 'Deafness, Culture, and Choice' (2002) 28 *Journal of Medical Ethics*, 284–5.

This kind of argument can be developed and made more plausible if a distinction is drawn between 'impairment' and 'disability', as Sheila McLean and Laura Williamson do in their book.[4] It can be argued that people might be physically impaired but are disabled only if society fails to offer facilities and services which will counteract the disability. In terms of this approach 'impairment' is an individual concern but 'disability' is a social concern.

It is easy to understand and sympathise with what lies behind all such attempts. They show a laudable desire to get away from the harsh terminology of the past, and to stress that the groups in question are human beings with human dignity. Nevertheless, disability is real and re-description will not change its reality. This bedrock must be agreed if government agencies are to be persuaded to create arrangements and the public to pay taxes to enable disabled groups to have worthwhile lives.

But to claim that disability is real is not to say what it is, and there are formidable problems in deciding what it is. It might be said that an easy way round the problem is to say that disability is any condition which entitles someone to a government disability allowance. But this is not a convincing approach. Allowances or benefits are variable depending on a given government's welfare policy and the state of the economy in the country. The fact that Disability Discrimination Acts in the UK have developed in 1995 and 2005 and been superseded by the Equality Act 2010 seems to suggest that there is not one timeless correct Platonic Form of a definition, but rather that definitions have changed as a result of changes in public attitudes and political policies. To bring this out I shall examine the most recent definition offered in the Equality Act 2010.

A person is disabled according to this Act if he or she has 'a physical or mental impairment' that has a 'substantial' and 'long-term' negative effect on the person's ability to 'carry out normal day-to-day activities'.[5] The Act defines 'substantial' as 'more than minor or trivial'[6] and guidance produced by the UK Government's Office for Disability Issues gives the example of taking much longer than it usually does to complete daily tasks like getting dressed.[7] By 'long-term' it means 12 months or more,[8] and the Guidance gives the example of a breathing condition that develops as a result of a lung infection.[9] 'Progressive conditions', or those which get worse over time, count as disablement, and there are special rules about recurring or fluctuating conditions such as arthritis. Some conditions are not covered by the definition. We are told by the Guidance that these include addiction to non-prescribed drugs or alcohol (see further below). This definition and the covering explanations raise some interesting questions. The definition uses the word 'normal', a weasel word if ever there was one. It glosses 'normal' in terms of 'completing daily tasks like getting dressed', but for many people their daily tasks include much more than that. We might therefore ask: Normal for whom and according to whose standards? We are told that a 'progressive condition' or 'one that gets worse over time' can be classed as a disability. Old age seems to fit this kind of progression, and of course 'age discrimination' is often condemned alongside disability discrimination. Again, colour blindness might be thought by some to be a disability; it would make impossible some kinds of 'normal' life. But it is excluded as a disability by the Act, according to the Guidance.

Surprisingly, HIV infection, cancer and multiple sclerosis are 'automatically' covered by the Act.[10] It is easy to see why multiple sclerosis is included, but someone with HIV infection or

4 Note 1, above.

5 Equality Act 2010, s. 6(1).

6 Equality Act 2010, s. 212(1).

7 *Equality Act 2010: Guidance*, at p. 15. Available at: http://odi.dwp.gov.uk/docs/wor/new/ea-guide.pdf (accessed 13 January 2015).

8 Equality Act 2010, Sch. 1, Pt 1, para. 2(1).

9 *Equality Act Guidance*, note 7, above, at p. 26.

10 Equality Act 2010, Sch. 1, Pt 1, para. 6(1).

some cancers may well be able to carry out normal daily activities, but they are 'automatically' included. On the other hand, the Guidance makes clear that addiction to non-prescribed drugs or alcoholism is excluded. But some addicts and alcoholics are likely to have extreme cravings which have a substantial and long-term effect on a 'normal' life. The Act stresses that disability concerns 'effects', such as difficulty in performing daily tasks, rather than underlying causes. But alcoholism and drug addiction may have serious effects on a 'normal' life, and cancer is not an 'effect' but an underlying condition. The main difficulty with the 2010 Act is that it tries to give a definition, or a set of necessary and sufficient conditions for disability, but is then obliged for political, financial or other reasons to include certain conditions which do not seem to fit the definition and to exclude others which do seem to fit.

But we need not yet give up the attempt to find a definition. Wittgenstein has argued that it is not possible to find necessary and sufficient conditions for many words. His example is of the idea of a 'game'; there is no set of conditions which can cover, for example, both football and the card game 'patience'. Nevertheless, we can recognise both as games because they have the sort of resemblance to each other that members of the same family might have. Similarly it might be said that there are 'family resemblances' among the members of the different groups who see themselves as in different ways disabled.[11] This approach is certainly less prescriptive than a definition which stipulates that to be disabled a person must possess a given set of features. But when we begin to consider what the family resemblances are we hit difficulties. Compare the problems of someone who has Down's Syndrome with those of a person in a wheelchair, or who is blind, or who has HIV infection. Are there any features they have in common, or even family resemblances among their characteristics? With a small amount of assistance from the social services, or indeed friends, families or partners, they could lead 'normal' or indeed distinguished lives, whether as cabinet ministers, pianists or poets. It is this that encourages many to say that disability is a misleading category.

It might be helpful to compare the concept of disability with that of disease, because the problems of defining disease have similarities to those of defining disability. Since the time of Aristotle there have been attempts to classify diseases in terms of the features they may have in common. This biological approach is the dominant one at the moment and its popularity has been increased by the spectacular rise of genetics. Thus the search in medical science is to isolate the gene or the faulty gene 'for' a given disease. Diseases thereby become objective occurrences independent of the experiences of those who have the disease. As distinct from this there is a view that diseases are cultural phenomena – what counts as a disease in one culture – obesity, say – may be seen as a sign of success in another. Again, some kinds of sexual behaviour may be seen in some cultures as conditions appropriately treated by psychiatrists, and in others simply as morally bad behaviour. The misleading assumption in this controversy is that there is one correct definition of disease. But perhaps different definitions are useful for different purposes. A definition which is useful for, say, evolutionary biology, may not be of interest to a clinician. The Equality Act 2010 is less about defining disability for its own sake, and more about discouraging discrimination.

Taking this pragmatic approach we might suggest that if someone has a physical or mental condition such that the person would benefit from some assistance then the assistance should be provided. But what sort of assistance? There are two answers often given to this question. One is to the effect that what is needed is medical assistance, that disability is a clinical problem affecting some individuals. This is often called the 'medical model' of disability. The other answer is that disability may not be a problem at all, or if it is, it is a social problem requiring social rather than

---

11 Wittgenstein, L., *Philosophical Investigations*, Oxford, Blackwell, 1953, paras 65–75.

medical solutions. This is known as the 'social model' of disability.[12] There would certainly be legal and financial implications – involving rights and responsibilities – depending on which model is adopted, but I shall not investigate these. Rather I shall suggest some considerations which do or might influence supporters of the social model when they minimise the importance of medical interventions in the management of disability.

Medical and Social Models of Disability

One argument might be that nature should be left to take its course, that to try to alter by medical means what we are born with is to act like God. People should simply play the hand they are dealt by nature, and society should make that optimally possible. In other words, it is up to society to create the conditions that will enable someone to have a fulfilling life no matter what their physical or mental condition. In its extreme form this argument is highly unpersuasive – it would rule out medical treatments for diseases of any kind. But a slightly different and modified version of the argument criticises the desire which parents might have for a perfect child. I shall deal with this argument later in the section on genetics, but note here that using medical means to minimise disability must be distinguished from genetic manipulation aimed at perfection.

A second argument might be that medicine is increasingly inclined to colonise all areas of human life. Some conditions are such that either they should not be treated at all, or if they are to be treated it should be by other professions.[13] Now there is some force in the claim that healthcare has adopted too wide a remit and it is relevant to consider how this has come about. The central point is that medicine has adopted the very broad role of promoting the 'best interests' of patients.[14] This aim is at such a high level of generality that it is impossible to disagree with it, and it does not distinguish the practices of medicine from many other activities, such as education, or the making of social policy. Can the aim be made more precise?

An obvious first move in the direction of precision is to expand 'interests' or 'benefit' to 'health' interests and benefit. But this move requires some clarification of the concept of health. Traditionally doctors understood health, or their role in preserving it, in a negative way – they attempted to remove impediments to health. Today that is still the major aim that guides decision making in medicine, and I shall suggest that it should remain so. But aims and decision making in medicine have been made more complex since the World Health Organization (WHO) in 1946 put forward the notorious definition of health as: '[a] state of complete physical, social and mental well-being, and not merely the absence of disease or infirmity'.[15] How far can this idealistic account of health be grafted on to the traditional aim of medicine, and what is its relevance to disability? Put another way, this is the question of whether medicine should be confined to the removal of impediments to health or whether, more ambitiously, its role should be extended to promote health as defined by the WHO – what is called 'positive health' or well-being.

---

12 Oliver, M., *Understanding Disability: From Theory to Practice*, Basingstoke, Macmillan, 1996.

13 Glasziou, P., Moynihan, R., Richards, T. and Godlee, F., 'Too Much Medicine; Too Little Care: Time to Wind Back the Harms of Over-diagnosis and Over-treatment' (2013) 347 *British Medical Journal*, http://www.bmj.com/content/347/bmj.f4247 (accessed 13 January 2015).

14 Medical Schools Council, *The Consensus Statement on the Role of the Doctor*, 2008, available at: http://www.medschools.ac.uk/Publications/Pages/Role-of-the-Doctor-Consensus-Statement.aspx (accessed 13 January 2015).

15 World Health Organization, *Constitution*, New York, 1946. Available at: http://www.who.int/governance/eb/who_constitution_en.pdf (accessed 13 January 2015).

Two arguments can be used to suggest that medicine should be confined to the removal of impediments to health. The first is that there is more than a hint of paternalism about the suggestion that we need medicine to guide us to a state of physical and mental well-being, or that doctors are experts in happiness. Happiness or well-being is such an individual thing that there cannot be experts on it. Health – often thought to be the area of medical expertise – is not always a necessary condition of well-being. Someone may be in a terminal condition in a hospice but be surrounded by friends and at peace with the world. The second argument for limiting the remit of medicine is that, to be economically realistic, the aims of medicine should be confined to treating disease and infirmity to the extent that that can be done by medicine. Other professions can concern themselves with offering advice and training to promote physical fitness and overall well-being. It should be noted of course that the view that doctors should be concerned only with 'best interests' in the sense of removing impediments to health is quite compatible with the view that they should be positive in their approach to patients. Honest but sensitive communication is required with a frank and courteous manner, coupled with the realisation that medicine cannot solve every problem.[16]

What implications does a narrow view of the aims of medicine have on disability? Certainly the narrow view of medicine can still include the treatment of such disorders as HIV infections, cancers, multiple sclerosis and clinical depression. All these problems are recognised by the 2010 Act as 'disabilities'. Medicine can also be involved in the amelioration of other disabling conditions with devices such as hip or knee replacements. These conditions are what we might term 'internal' to the person and medicine here has a primary role. But supporters of the social model of disability are correct in arguing that there are limits to what medicine can do, or should try to do, in the treatment of disability; many forms of disability give rise to social or 'external' problems and require 'external' or social solutions.

The conclusion of this section then is that setting up the medical and the social models of disability as if they were exclusive alternatives is misleading. It is easy to select conditions which would support either point of view. Some conditions may require or benefit from constant medical attention, medication for clinical depression or the like, while others, say a person in a wheelchair, require ramps and good equipment for getting around. This suggests that a joined-up approach will work best. Indeed, there are large and developing industries of bioengineering or biotechnology which sit midway between what is medical and what is infrastructure improvement, such as electronic devices which assist communication. McLean and Williamson neatly sum up the false either/or when they say '… the medical model tends to overlook the role of bias and discrimination and the social model exhibits a tendency to deny that disability has any roots in physical and mental impairment'.[17]

Equality, Equity and Utility

Disability groups assert their rights to equal access to healthcare, public buildings, educational institutions, eligibility for employment and availability of support and carer services. These rights are widely accepted in principle by the Disability Discrimination Acts of 1995 and 2005. The Equality Act 2010 was a further attempt to meet some of the criticisms of disability groups.[18] But

16 McLean, S.A.M. and Mason, J.K., *Legal and Ethical Aspects of Healthcare*, London and San Francisco, CA, Greenwich Media, 2003, ch. 4.

17 Note 1, above, at p. 35.

18 Note 5, above.

underlying the full implementation of at least some of the rights there is a tension that is present in all public policies: between the respective claims of social utility and individual rights. This tension is particularly acute when agencies deal with the rights of disability groups since they can reasonably claim that they start off with a double disadvantage. I shall explore this tension as a way of highlighting the issues in disabled groups' claims for more equality of treatment.

An important principle which ought to guide, if not wholly determine, government policy in any field is utility, or the maximising of benefit for the majority of a population. This general principle turns into specific economic tools such as cost/benefit analysis or quality-adjusted life years and is presented to the public as 'value for money'. But it is obvious that this ought not to be the only guiding principle. For example, suppose a doctor or a social worker is faced with a disabled client who might benefit from an expensive drug, and/or requires hours of social work time. In terms of maximising benefit to the community at large it might be better to ignore the needs of such people and spend the resources on those whose need is less severe but who might benefit more. But this policy seems wrong in that it ignores the rights of individuals to equal consideration. No one ought to be regarded simply as expendable for the sake of the good of others.

This notion of 'equal consideration', however, needs more examination. In some contexts the demand for equal consideration is simply a demand for consistency of treatment between one person and another. In other words, it is a demand that people be treated in accordance with a rule which can be formulated. But the demand for consistency seems to clash with the more personalised side to casework. Professionals involved in casework stress the inapplicability of general rules because of the uniqueness of individual situations. On the other hand, where benefits are being distributed clients and patients in disabled groups are keen to demand consistency, using terms such as 'post code lottery', where that means that allocation of assistance seems based on arbitrary geographical distinctions. Consistency seems to be a necessary condition for the distribution of medical or social benefits to disabled groups if such distribution is to be seen as fair. But consistency is certainly not sufficient for fairness. After all, a principle such as 'Never spend time with anyone who is disabled' could be applied consistently. To get nearer the moral principle of equal consideration we need some way of ruling out such possibilities.

It is tempting to try to do this by saying that what is required is not consistency but an actual equality of treatment. But this is not satisfactory either. As pointed out above, caseworkers and clinicians stress that some people need much more help than others within patient and disability groups, and no one thinks it reasonable to spend the same amount of time and money whatever the problem. What is required is that all differences of treatment be based on a criterion which will group like cases together, and distinguish unlike cases, for morally appropriate reasons. This principle of justified differences in treatment is usually called a principle of equity. Equity is not the same as equality, since it requires not only that like cases should be treated equally but also that unlike cases should be treated unequally.[19] Equity presupposes a criterion for justifiable differences in the way people are treated. In the context of disability this criterion will be need (although in other contexts criteria such as merit, or ability to benefit, might be relevant).

But this analysis highlights the problem of what is to be meant by the term 'need', a term which it is easy to pass over since it is so familiar in this kind of discussion. A 'need' arises from a desire or an aim to reach a certain goal; that which is needed is instrumental for attaining the goal. But what is the goal? Some economists propose a very wide goal, and define need as a 'capacity

---

19 It is unfortunate that 'health inequalities' has become a standard term since it runs together different issues such as opportunity, outcome, and neglect of risk factors.

to benefit'.[20] According to this definition people 'need' from health and social services anything that might benefit their health and well-being. This would entail not only regular investigation and treatment of any factors which might impact on health but also the idea that everyone needs to be assured of good housing, lack of deprivation, rewarding employment and so on. Disability groups might well say 'Yes, that is what we do need!' But there is the problem of resources and their allocation not only for the health of non-disability groups, but also for other areas requiring spending from the public purse, such as education, defence and the arts. It is therefore arguable that 'capacity to benefit' is too broad a definition of need.

The American ethicists, Beauchamp and Childress, suggest a narrower definition of 'need' as 'that without which one will be fundamentally harmed'.[21] This provides a minimum level for the relief of needs. It suggests care and protection for those who cannot manage on their own, but it does not suggest provision for special education. It must be remembered that the US takes a much narrower view of what the state should provide by way of health and welfare benefits than would be acceptable in the UK. It is likely, perhaps it is inevitable, that those charged with making a 'needs assessment' in individual cases will base their judgments on criteria varying between the wider and the narrower account of needs. In the context of scarce resources we shall probably never be free of disputes both about government policies and about 'post code lotteries'.

There is a further contentious issue within the context of social equality. Whereas most disability groups would agree with the idea of equity as distinct from strict equality in the allocation of health and welfare goods and services, there may be another context in which they might argue for strict equality. The issue here concerns equality of opportunity. It is plausible to argue that all disabled groups should have equality with those who are not disabled in respect of opportunity for whatever goods life can offer, such as education, employment, access to medical services and so on. Now 'equality of opportunity' is a slogan with which it is difficult to disagree in the abstract but it can have problems when applied in the context of disability.

Consider first access to medical services. In some medical contexts there is no problem. Everyone can and should have equal access to their GP, although disabled groups claim that this does not always happen.[22] But consider scarce resources such as kidney transplants or expensive life-prolonging drugs and treatments. How do disabled groups fare here? Granted the reality of scarce resources there is really no escape from some form of rationing, whatever politicians may say, or whatever is their preferred term – 'prioritising' or the like – or preferred method of rationing. Discussions about the allocation of public funds for healthcare usually apply to two areas – macro-allocation and micro-allocation.[23] Macro-allocation decisions determine what treatments and care the publicly funded healthcare services should provide, and how much of them; and micro-allocation concerns discrimination among individuals to determine who should receive the greater share of scarce resources within a given area of healthcare. Consider first some problems of macro-allocation. How do disabled groups fare in the contest for macro-allocation of healthcare resources?

The benefits of healthcare (understood in the negative sense discussed above) fall into three categories: the prolongation of life; the relief of distressing symptoms arising from physical and

---

20 Edgar, A., Salek, S., Shickle, D. and Cohen, D., *The Ethical QALY: Ethical Issues in Healthcare Resource Allocations*, Haslemere, Euromed Communications, 1994, at p. 4.

21 Beauchamp, T.L. and Childress, J.F., *Principles of Biomedical Ethics*, 4th edn, Oxford, Oxford University Press, 1994, p. 330.

22 British Medical Association, *Disability Equality within Healthcare: The Role of Health Professionals*, London, 2007, ch. 3.

23 Randall, F. and Downie, R.S., *The Philosophy of Palliative Care: Critique and Reconstruction*, Oxford, Oxford University Press, 2006, pp. 183–95.

mental illness; care and support with the activities of daily living when this becomes necessary because of physical or mental infirmity or disability. Granted that background, it is usual for macro-allocation decisions to be guided by three criteria: the characteristics of the population to be served; the characteristics of the treatments and services; moral principles of justice.

If we begin with population characteristics it is obvious that economically deprived nations will prioritise provision of food, shelter, basic hygiene and preventive measures against infectious diseases. They will be unable to afford expensive life-prolonging treatments such as renal dialysis. It would clearly be wrong in contexts such as these to spend money on expensive life-prolonging treatments rather than the basics of food and inexpensive vaccinations and antibiotics. Secondly, the benefits, harms and risks of treatments and patients' after-care are relevant here. Outcomes are important in the assessment, but there are huge difficulties in attempts to quantify net benefit and represent it on a single numerical scale. One attempt to do this was the Quality Adjusted Life Year (QALY).[24] The QALY measure has been much criticised in detail and in main principle, not least by disability groups, who can use the 'double disadvantage argument'.[25] The main principle is best discussed, thirdly, in the context of moral principles of justice.

As we have seen, the relevant principle of justice in this context is equity – equals should be treated equally and unequals unequally in proportion to their relevant inequality. In other words, we should treat people in the same way (equally) unless there are relevant differences. This moral principle can be in conflict with utility, which in this context is usually expressed as efficiency – attaining the maximum output from the input of resources. The problem here is that people, especially politicians, respond very positively to the concept of efficiency. But they ignore the point that efficiency is not an absolute free-standing goal; it is relative to a given end. This takes us back to the aims of healthcare mentioned above. At the moment in Western societies the emphasis is on the prolongation of life. Enormous sums are spent on chemo-therapies which may (or may not) prolong life for a few months. A Health Board that refuses this kind of expenditure is liable to be faced with a media campaign. But what is ignored is the opportunity cost. If millions are to be spent on treatments which may prolong life for short periods, what groups in society will be deprived of resources for care and support? Disability groups may well have a case for arguing that their claims for an equitable share of the macro-allocation of funds or healthcare are edged out in favour of resources for life-prolonging treatments.

I shall turn now to problems of micro-allocation. The necessity to discriminate between individuals in order to determine who receives the greater share of scarce resources is an unpleasant but unavoidable reality. It is a sphere in which judgments are necessary. Such judgments require a technical component and a moral component. As in macro-allocation, there must be a balance between equity and efficiency or utility, with the added need to obtain the patient's consent to treatment. With all patients, but especially with disabled groups, there is a need to allocate not only drugs and treatments but also time. There is a natural tendency to give the most time to the patient (or relative) who is most assertive in demanding that time. But a policy of allocating time according to demand is clearly unjust, for less assertive patients may benefit more from professional time, and may be harmed by being allocated insufficient time, in terms of both medical attention and supportive caring.

The language used to describe micro-allocation, particularly in the media, tends to exacerbate emotional reactions: differentiation between individuals can be portrayed as discrimination. This

---

24 Williams, A., 'Priority Setting in Private and Public Health Care: A Guide through the Ideological Jungle' (1988) 7 *Journal of Health Economics*, 173–83.

25 See also Whitehead, S. and Shehzad, A., 'Health Outcomes in Economic Evaluation: The QALY and Utilities' (2010) 96(1) *British Medical Bulletin*, 5–21.

is particularly the case when the treatment is described as 'life-saving', a term which suggests that if society does not provide such treatments it is failing to save lives. Sometimes the treatments so described are very expensive – hundreds of thousands of pounds per annum with marginal benefit. But the term 'life-saving' with regard to medical treatment is misleading in most cases. If a curative treatment for an otherwise terminal illness can be given to a child or young person one might reasonably argue that the treatment is life-saving. But most such treatments simply prolong life for a short time at considerable expense and with unpleasant side effects for the patient. The important point here is the opportunity cost. If someone is receiving very expensive treatments of marginal benefit, someone else may not be getting treatment or support. Unfortunately, it may often be individuals who are disabled.

The two principles governing the allocation of scarce resources – equity and utility – apply at the micro-level as well as the macro-level. But in reaching a judgment on individual cases a clinician can be guided to some extent by criteria which derive from these broad principles but are more specific. The most obvious of these more specific criteria is medical utility, or the expectation of medical benefit from the treatment. For example, if only one kidney is available and there are two potential recipients, the likelihood of success in the transplant is as relevant as the length of time the transplant might add to the life of each patient. For example, if one patient is diabetic the chances of success of the transplant are less, so if other clinical features are similar then the transplant should go to the non-diabetic patient. How should medical utility impact on disability in micro-allocation?

Groups who deny the reality of disability can hardly try to use it as a relevant factor in claiming priority for scarce resources. But if we grant the reality of disability, how should it affect decision-making in the context of micro-allocation? A lot will turn on the nature of the disability. In some cases, for example cases of severe mental disorder, the patient may not understand what is happening and treatments may increase distress. So in some cases medical utility will apply. But in other cases it can be argued that if we use the criterion of equity then disability on its own should not be a determining factor in allocating scarce resources. The disabled person has already been disadvantaged by nature or accident and should not be further discriminated against.

There is another problem which arises within the area of equality. As was said above, most people respond favourably to the idea of equality of opportunity, but equality of opportunity does not necessarily lead to equality of outcome. Some disabled groups are not going to achieve equal outcome without a large degree of positive discrimination in their favour. This issue arises particularly in employment. But here we must remember the issue with which this section began. A state must weigh the benefits of overall social utility with individual rights. How far can positive discrimination be justified to promote equal satisfactions? Once again officials and politicians will be faced with the claims of disability pressure groups in the context of limited resources.

A study by the Joseph Rowntree Foundation[26] sums up what many disabled people want from service planning:

- recognition of access needs
- recognition of the impact of impairment and disabling barriers
- being treated as a 'whole person'
- flexible services that respond to individual and changing needs
- being listened to and treated with respect
- easy access to services, including preventative and early intervention services

---

26 Morris, J., *'One Town for My Body, Another for My Mind': Services for People with Physical Impairments and Mental Health Support Needs*, London, Joseph Rowntree Foundation, 2004.

No one could fault these demands, but the problem in meeting them is that they are much the same as the demands of non-disabled persons, and there will inevitably need to be judgments in the meeting of these demands, granted a limited budget. In other words, the conclusion is that in conditions of scarcity there is no possibility of avoiding contentious decisions. The issues are too complex to be decided by algorithms. Youth and age, and persons with different kinds of disability, will all compete for scarce resources.

Public Attitudes

It is often alleged by disability groups that the attitude of the general public towards people with disability is callous or hostile or in other ways inappropriate. On the other hand it has been said that public attitudes changed as a result of the Paralympics in London, and the general public now have much more understanding of disability and are impressed with what can be achieved despite disability.[27] This view was widely held after the Games, and no doubt there is some truth in it. But it has two problems. The first is that the improvement in public attitudes came as a result of saturation coverage of the Games in TV and newspapers. It is, however, well-known that public attitudes manipulated in this way are short-lived rather than deeply rooted or permanent. The second problem concerns the type of disability. Wheelchair athletes and basketball players are easy to admire and identify with, but various kinds of mental disorder are less attractive. To understand these differences it may be helpful to offer an account of what an attitude is.

A broad account of an attitude would define it as any mental state which has what philosophers call an 'intentional object'.[28] Bodily states such as sensations just happen, but attitudes are always directed to some state of affairs in the world. For example, if someone stands on my foot my attitude towards him/her will be determined by whether I see the incident as an accident, as the result of negligence or as deliberate. And if I think it is deliberate, my attitude will be further refined if I think that the point was either to injure me or to warn me that my conversation was becoming tactless. My varying understanding of the situation will determine the emotional content of my attitude.

How disabled people are seen and therefore the nature of attitudes to them will depend on the kind of disability and beliefs about how it was acquired. For example, it would be surprising if public attitudes to a disabled ex-serviceman in a wheelchair were anything but favourable. On the other hand, attitudes to persons suffering from obesity or HIV infection might be less favourable because these attitudes may be affected by the belief, whether true or not, that disabilities resulting from these conditions are matters of personal responsibility. The difficult cases are the ones where the disability shows itself in ways which many people find physically or emotionally embarrassing or even repellent. For example, many people find muttering or shouting or eating in an off-putting manner more than they can face. They may well understand that the disability is not at all the fault of the person but they cannot handle the situation in which they may be confronted by it. The public is often criticised for this kind of reaction, but there may be a built-in recoil from certain physical manifestations, and it takes training and experience to overcome this. And quite apart

27 See Hawkes, R., 'The Paralympics Have the Power to Change Attitudes Towards Disabled People', 6 September 2012, at: http://blogs.lse.ac.uk/politicsandpolicy/paralympics-disabled-people-hawkes/ (accessed 13 January 2015).

28 Searle, J.R., *Intentionality: An Essay in the Philosophy of Mind*, Cambridge, Cambridge University Press, 1983.

from instinctive reactions, people may simply not know how to behave. This can vary from the traditional 'Does he take sugar?' to attempts to avoid disabled people altogether.

There is another side to this. Genuine efforts to be of assistance may be rejected by a disabled person and be seen as patronising. It is not easy for the non-trained person to get it right. Familiarity with the disabled person may sometimes be as useful as training in establishing an appropriate attitude. The mother of a child with Down's Syndrome will be familiar with the child and his/her behaviour and may be surprised if visitors seem ill at ease. Without advice, visitors may simply not know how to behave or what to say. There is no easy solution to the problem of public attitudes, but obviously education about disabilities will help.[29] Government agencies may also have a role here, as perhaps may the law.

Genetics

Genetics is now a rapidly developing area of medical and general science. It has a bearing on disability in two main medical procedures: Pre-Natal Screening Diagnosis (PND) and Pre-implantation Genetic Diagnosis (PGD).[30] In the case of PND potential parents who are at risk of giving birth to a child with a disability arising from a genetic defect may request that the embryo *in utero* be checked for the presence of defective genes. Risk factors here may include family histories of such disorders or perhaps age, as the likelihood of some disabilities, such as Down's Syndrome, increases with age. If a genetic defect is discovered the only remedy at the moment is termination of pregnancy. For that reason some potential parents would not wish PND even if at risk.

To avoid the distress of termination many parents at risk prefer PGD. Embryos can be tested *in vitro* for a range of disorders. The parents are then given the choice of whether to agree to implantation or not. Four ethical issues arise here. The first arises for those who hold that an embryo has distinctively human rights qua its status as a person and that these will be violated by the discarding of so-called defective embryos. This position is often adopted by those who have certain religious beliefs and argument is not likely to alter the conviction.

The second ethical issue concerns the charge that to terminate or not implant because the child when born may have a disability is to imply that disabled people now alive do not have lives worth living. This conclusion does not follow; nothing is implied about the lives of existing disabled people. Suppose, however, we grant for the sake of argument that some disabled people might be offended because they perceive such an implication. Does it follow that PGD should not be offered? In answering this question we must place the alleged offence taken by some disabled people in the context of a parent considering PGD. From the parents' perspective it will certainly be preferable if a child is not disabled, for many obvious reasons, such as the lives of their other children, their own lives and careers and the funding of support services. It is plausible to argue that from an ethical perspective a choice based on such substantial matters will outweigh the alleged feelings of offence of some disabled people. It is not clear in any case, as claimed above, that such a choice in any way reflects adversely on existing people who are disabled.[31]

The third possible charge is that reproduction is a gift and that any form of selection or manipulation turns the child into a commodity. In other words, the argument is that it is wrong to

29 Carel, H., *Illness: The Cry of the Flesh*, Stocksfield, Acumen Publishing, 2008.

30 The Scottish Pre-implantation Genetic Diagnosis and Screening Service, *A Framework for Decision Making* (2011). Available at: http://www.nsd.scot.nhs.uk/documents/pgdframework.pdf (accessed 13 January 2015).

31 *Parliamentary Inquiry into Abortion on the Grounds of Disability*, 2013. Available at: http://www.abortionanddisability.org (accessed 13 January 2015).

choose traits of an offspring, no matter how well-intentioned the aim might be.[32] In reply we might argue that if what is proposed is simply screening for aneuploidy or serious Mendelian disorders then the objection, however sincerely voiced, seems to exaggerate when it suggests that clinicians or scientists are turning a child into a commodity. On the other hand, it may be the case that genetic counsellors and others do not always provide sufficient information on the support available to the parents of disabled children and underestimate the rewards which parents of disabled children find in caring for them.

But the charge of manipulation can be restated in a way which constitutes the fourth objection I shall consider, namely, that the manipulation involved in PGD is at least the first step towards a policy of eugenics.[33] Eugenics, several steps down the slope, arrives at policies practised in Nazi Germany. These policies advocated the killing or the sterilisation of the disabled and other groups held to be 'degenerates'. It was claimed that 'degenerates' had 'bad genes' which would weaken the race. One interesting feature of this criticism is that it moves the argument away from the unanswerable questions which arise in the standard abortion debate about the moral status of the embryo to a controversy on selecting embryos for different indications. Here we must distinguish between medical and non-medical indications, while allowing that there is a fair amount of overlap between the two sorts of indication.

Medical indications may be the identification of genes suggesting the likelihood of late onset conditions, such as Alzheimer's disease or late onset breast cancer. An objection here might be that medical research is proceeding fast and by the time a child reaches the late onset age there may well be cures available. Nevertheless, it is easy to have sympathy for parents who do not wish to take the chance that cures will be available, at least for some late onset conditions, and for whom the prospect of their child suffering in any way is too much to contemplate.

Non-medical indications are of three kinds: selection for sex; selection for human leukocyte antigen matching with existing children so that the second child may be a source of stem cells for the first child; and selection for such matters as intelligence or beauty.

There are three common reasons given for selection for sex. Firstly, there are certain inherited diseases, such as Duchenne muscular dystrophy, which affect only males. A woman at risk of passing on the defective gene for this may wish to avoid giving birth to a male child. Granted my preceding arguments, sex selection for this purpose seems ethically acceptable. Secondly, some ethnic groups prefer male children. This does not seem a valid consideration for the use of scarce resources; certainly it would be strenuously rejected by feminist groups. Thirdly, some parents wish sex selection to balance their families. Robertson has argued that '... gender variety in one's children seems to be a legitimate desire ...'.[34] In discussing this we must contrast the background economics. Robertson is arguing in the context of a healthcare system in the US which is funded privately or through insurance cover. In the UK the funding for healthcare comes from the taxpayer and is limited. Granted that important difference, it does not seem legitimate to use a scarce and expensive service simply to satisfy a parental desire of this kind. But let us suppose parents are willing to pay privately for the service. Is it then ethically acceptable? It seems to me to fall into the category of the less desirable kind of genetics – the kind which may be categorised as 'eugenics'. I shall discuss it further in considering the other main non-medical indications for PGD.

---

32 See Kass, L.R., 'Triumph or Tragedy: The Moral Meaning of Genetic Technology' (2000) 45 *American Journal of Jurisprudence*, 1–16.

33 Harris, J., 'Is Gene Therapy a Form of Eugenics?' (1993) 7 *Bioethics*, 178–87.

34 Robertson, J.A., 'Ethics and the Future of Preimplantation Genetic Diagnosis' (2005) 10(1) *Reproductive Biomedicine Online*, 97–101.

Turning now to the second non-medical indication, or borderline medical indication: the selection of an embryo to provide an organ or cell transplant to a sibling affected by a fatal disease such as Fanconi anaemia. Only zygotes that are compatible with the existing child are implanted. This use of PGD came to be known as the creation of the 'saviour sibling'. A saviour sibling is said to be the solution to any disease requiring hematopoietic stem cell transplantation.[35] The usual objection to this procedure is that the child concerned is being used as a means to benefit other children. More precisely, there may be adverse psychological effects on a child if it comes to think it has been born not for its own sake but to benefit a sibling. The general argument is weak; we all use each other as a means all the time, and society would cease to exist if we didn't! The second formulation of the Kantian imperative is that persons should not be used only as a means but always at the same time as an end.[36] In more detail it is up to the parents to make clear to the sibling saviour that it is valued and loved for its own sake. There is no reason to think that parents would do other than treat all their children as ends. The service is available for this purpose in the US and to a more limited extent in the UK.

The third non-medical indications are such matters as selection for intelligence, beauty or athletic ability. At the moment selection for such features is beyond the reach of genetics, but the science is developing swiftly. Is selection for such aims ethically acceptable? Non-medical reasons of this kind seem to me to fall squarely within the category of eugenics, and to represent the commodification of children to satisfy parental whims. The same argument would apply to the desire of some deaf parents to select for deafness. It is true that parents in any case try to mould their children by way of education and pressures of all kinds. But there is a difference in category between rational means of influencing behaviour such as education and causal means such as genetic modification. Fortunately this use of PGD is not possible at the moment. I would add that the desire to balance a family by using PGD for sex selection seems to me to be another undesirable use of PGD. It is one thing to use PGD to create a saviour sibling to save the life of a child, but it is another to sex select to satisfy a parental whim.

Before leaving the topic of genetics I shall note some arguments in favour of PGD. Firstly, PGD offers the alternative of screening embryos rather than foetuses and thus it avoids the psychological problems of termination of pregnancy. Secondly, many couples who are at risk of conceiving an embryo liable to diseases such as Tay Sachs, sickle cell or cystic fibrosis may choose not to attempt a family to avoid having a child with a disorder. PGD offers the possibility of a conception which will result in a child without such disabilities. Nevertheless, Tom Shakespeare is probably right when he says: 'There is a marked disparity between the generally upbeat, confident rhetoric of the genetics establishment and its media apologists, and the gloomy, hostile and suspicious reactions of disabled people and their organisations'.[37]

Consent and Mental Capacity (Incapacity)

A central concept in any medical treatment is consent, about which a great deal has been written over the past half century. It has long been central to medical law and ethics that a patient must

35 Bennett, B., 'Symbiotic Relationships: Saviour Siblings, Family Rights and Biomedicine' (2005) 19(3) *Australian Journal of Family Law*, 195–212.

36 Kant, I., *Groundwork of the Metaphysic of Morals*, London, Hutchinson's University Library, 1953, ch. 2.

37 Shakespeare, T., 'Choices and Rights: Eugenics, Genetics and Disability Equality' (1998) 13 *Disability and Society*, 665–82, at p. 671.

give and may withhold consent for medical treatment. What lies behind this is the idea that patients know their own best interests better than doctors do. This of course is questionable – we don't always know what in the long run are our best interests. But we always know what we currently do or do not want, and that is enough to justify the refusal of consent. This is not, however, sufficient to justify the insistence that a certain treatment be provided. Whatever may be the case in the US or elsewhere, there is no doubt that in the UK a doctor's view on whether treatment should or should not be provided does and ought to trump the patient's wishes.[38] Nevertheless, it remains important that discussions should take place and out of them should emerge joint decision-making.

How does consent operate when the patient is disabled? In many cases consent can be applied in standard ways. There is no reason why a patient who is in a wheelchair or is blind or deaf will be unable to receive the appropriate information and agree or not to the proposed treatment. If there is a problem it may be because relatives urge the patient to accept (or refuse) a treatment for non-clinical reasons. A more serious problem arises, however, when the disability concerns the mental capacity of the patient. Indeed, there are several problems.

First, someone lacking mental capacity to give consent may have made an advance statement refusing in advance certain treatments in certain conditions, and indicating their wishes, preferences and values. This situation might arise when a person foresees that he/she may be overtaken by incapacity, such as dementia, and takes the legally recognised step of writing an advance decision[39] or living will. Problems with this can arise if the wording is ambiguous or open to more than one interpretation. For example the statement might say that its writer, if lacking capacity, does not wish life-prolonging treatments, but does wish symptom control. But some treatments appropriate for symptom control may also have the effect of prolonging life. Again, doubts may arise about the validity of the document. When was it written? Was it signed and witnessed? Doctors, fearing subsequent complaints by relatives or litigation, will naturally wish to be assured that the document is legally valid, especially if it is refusing life-prolonging treatment.

Secondly, the person lacking capacity may have appointed in advance a person to consent or refuse on their behalf. The assumption is that the person will know the wishes and values of the person lacking capacity. Here there can be problems if relatives disagree, and the proxy decision maker may not want the responsibility of refusing life-prolonging treatment even if it is known that that would have been the preference of the patient. Legal systems vary on these points and it is not possible to generalise on the legal position.

Most commonly there will be no advance statement and no one appointed to take decisions. This situation is covered in English law by the Mental Capacity Act 2005, and in Scottish law by the Adults with Incapacity (Scotland) Act 2000. This legislation stipulates that when a patient lacks capacity decisions are to be made by the physician in the best interests of the patient. Ethical problems can arise here if the physician disagrees with the relatives as to what should be done. Of course, relatives may know the values and wishes of the patient and these can provide helpful information. This position is especially contentious in cases where the patient is disabled. Relatives may feel emotionally attached to a disabled person or have a sense of guilt; alternatively, they may have a desire to be free of a burden. All these factors may affect their judgments. The onus is on the doctor to reach a joint decision with the relatives and this may not be easy. But even if the patient lacking capacity is disabled the doctor has the legal right to make the decision in the light of the available information.

38 See, for example, the case of *Burke v. GMC* [2004] EWHC 1879 (Admin), [2005] EWCA Civ 1003.

39 See for example in England and Wales: Mental Capacity Act 2005, ss. 24–6.

Carers

No account of the problems of disability would be complete without acknowledging the central role of carers in providing support – although 'support' is too weak a word to do justice to what is sometimes round-the-clock nursing, guiding and general minding of someone with a disability.[40] The carer is often a family member and is unpaid, although in some countries government grants are available. The carers may be parents looking after children or children looking after parents or siblings looking after each other. The support provided can be part-time or, with severe disability, full-time. It is not surprising that the majority of carers are female, and that there is considerable incidence of ill-health, such as depression, among carers.[41]

Disability groups have long been vocal in their demands for services and support and of course much of this has to be provided by carers. It is therefore not surprising that carers themselves are now well organised and are able to draw public attention to their voluntary work and form themselves into groups for mutual support and to lobby politicians. Disabled groups who criticise parents for having a termination of pregnancy because a test indicates that their child will be severely handicapped might consider whether they are themselves implying that the life of the mother of the severely handicapped baby is not worthwhile. Certainly, the carer of a severely handicapped child might consider her life to be worthwhile, but the worthwhileness cannot consist in having a career or much life outside the home.

The life of a family member devoted to caring for a disabled child or parent suffering from dementia is certainly one of genuine altruism. But sometimes there is another side to it, perhaps especially one which affects the mothers of disabled children. The mother of a disabled child, for example, one with Down's Syndrome, can develop a very strong attachment to the child. This may be a necessary condition for the devoted care required. But it is also possible that devoted care can become possessive and over-protective, and this may interfere with progress towards an independent or less dependent life. Every virtue carries its own temptations and this is true even of the supreme altruism of the caring mother of a disabled child.

Conclusion

There is clearly a range of issues around the broad topic of disability and healthcare, including uncertainty as to what constitutes disability. It is very tempting for pressure groups and similar bodies to concentrate on single issues, such as a given range of disabilities, and to fail to see that their plan would not fit other sorts. Moreover, approaches which view disability as an entirely social issue may not be in the interests of all categories of disabled people. Humane policies require co-operation among the various agencies concerned with disability – social and medical – and the policies must rest on informed and supportive public attitudes.

---

40 The role of carers is discussed in www.nuffieldbioethics.org/dementia 2010 (accessed 13 January 2015), especially ch. 7.

41 A useful website is: http://www.carersuk.org/help-and-advice (accessed 13 January 2015).

Chapter 8

Bioethics through the Telescope: Institutional Ethics in the NHS

Christopher Newdick

Introduction

Much of the study of contemporary bioethics concerns issues we observe through the microscope. Its patient-specific focus reflects Beauchamp and Childress' four ethical principles of autonomy, non-maleficence, beneficence and justice.[1] The best text-books also emphasise, for example, the individual rights expressed by autonomy, medical negligence, informed consent, confidentiality, life and death issues and reproductive rights – and this is fine beyond a certain point. But these principles which say so much about my rights today, do not say enough about community interests both now but in the future. They fail to place bioethics arising within the *system* of healthcare on which our rights and duties are founded. By contrast, the 'telescopic' dimension of the subject embraces much wider factors, for example what factors predispose us to illness, rights of *access* to care and the nature of the institutions which respond to need. These deserve attention because they also shape our rights to care.[2] Matters of this nature are important to anyone whose healthcare is not based solely on a private contractual arrangement and are becoming increasingly important. Contemporary pressures on public finances make the point. Between 1948 and 2009, spending on the NHS expanded almost every year, amounting today to over £100 billion.[3] For the next 10 years or so, however, when many other public service budgets are being cut, the best we can expect for the NHS is flat funding. However, as our 'obesogenic' society[4] requires more care for diabetes, and an ageing population requires more care in later life, real terms investment will steadily decline. NHS England forecasts that 'continuing with the current model of care will result in the NHS facing a funding gap between projected spending requirements and resources available of around £30bn between 2013/14 and 2020/21', that is, over 20 per cent of projected costs for 2020/21.[5] Starkly put, our current model of care is unsustainable. Painful and unfamiliar decisions are inevitable and 'entitlement rights' have to be assessed. For example, in England

1 Beauchamp, T. and Childress, J., *Principles of Biomedical Ethics*, 7th edn, Oxford, Oxford University Press, 2012.

2 See Daniels, N., *Just Health: Meeting Health Needs Fairly*, Cambridge, Cambridge University Press, 2008, p. 81, discussing socioeconomic status as a 'determinant' of health status. See also Prainsack, B. and Buyx, A., *Solidarity: Reflections on an Emerging Concept in Bioethics*, London, Nuffield Council on Bioethics, 2011, ch. 3.

3 Harker, R., *NHS Funding and Expenditure*, House of Commons Library, SN/SG/724, 2012, available at: www.nhshistory.net/parlymoney.pdf (accessed 13 January 2015).

4 Swinburn, B.A., Sacks, G., Hall, K.D., et al., 'The Global Obesity Pandemic: Shaped by Global Drivers and Local Environments' (2011) 378 *The Lancet*, 804–14, at p. 804.

5 NHS England, *The NHS Belongs to the People: A Call to Action*, London, 2013, p. 15. See also: http://www.england.nhs.uk/wp-content/uploads/2013/07/nhs_belongs.pdf (accessed 13 January 2015), p. 11.

(but not Scotland or Wales), successive governments have turned to the principles of markets and competition between hospitals to wring greater efficiency from the NHS. The Mid Staffordshire Hospital Inquiries (discussed below), however, describe a picture of callous neglect of patients, exacerbated by the drive to respond to market forces. These matters provoke *threshold* questions which the four principles do not confront. For that we need a telescope to examine matters from a different vantage point.

Sheila McLean contributed to this understanding in a practical sense in the advice she provided to Health Boards on making difficult decisions for whole communities of people.[6] Her advice requires us to think about bioethics from a broader perspective: given the general commitment of the NHS to promote social welfare, what structures best support (or hinder) that objective? If the NHS is an example of patients sharing in an exercise in social collaboration, how do the rights and interests of other patients modify the expectations of individuals in isolation? The subject addresses individual patients, systems management, resource allocation and government itself. This chapter discusses some of these questions by considering (1) the ethics of access to care, (2) institutional ethics and the unintended systemic pressures that influence hospital care, illuminated by the Mid Staffordshire Inquiries, (3) institutional ethics in healthcare markets in England, and (4) public health ethics and the tension between the individualism expressed by traditional Hippocratic ethics and the assumption of mutuality, reciprocity and citizenship inherent in social welfare systems. It argues for bioethics to include a broader canvass of concerns in addition to the relationship between doctor and patient.

The Ethics of *Access* to Care

Let us start with rights of access to care. From a purely clinical perspective, every medical need merits an appropriate response and resource constraints should never stand in the way. For some time, the European Court of Justice (ECJ) took the same view and construed EU law to guarantee hospital care abroad if it could not be provided at home.[7] But this is fanciful. It is blind to the hard choices required of any system in which demand exceeds supply. Within public systems committed to notions of healthcare solidarity, such an individualistic approach to welfare rights has never been feasible. Today, public services austerity intensifies fundamental questions about health service priorities. For example, if hard choices are unavoidable, is cancer or neonatal care more important than mental health or community care? Is geriatric care as important as paediatric care? As between *clinicians*, should we spend more on doctors, or nurses; on GPs or hospitals? Within *hospitals*, should we invest more on computer imaging systems, accident and emergency, intensive care, or cardio-vascular care? Or should we change things completely and invest properly in *preventive* and community care to stop people becoming ill in the first place? Doing the same as before has often been less controversial than 'disinvesting' from existing services and changing priorities, so the most significant influence on NHS commissioning policy has been past practice and acute hospitals have always commanded the lion's share of the budget. We might think more

6 McLean, S.A.M., Williamson, L., Devlin, B. and Blair, A., *Ethico-Legal Decision-Making in Healthcare*, Glasgow, University of Glasgow, 2004.

7 See Newdick, C., 'Citizenship, Free Movement and Health Care: Cementing Individual Rights by Corroding Social Solidarity' (2006) 43 *Common Market Law Review*, 1645–68; and Somek, A., *Solidarity Decomposed: Being and Time in European Citizenship*, University of Iowa Legal Studies Research Paper 13, 2007, pp. 1–59. Although the ECJ seems to have retreated from this extreme position more recently: see *Commission v. France* (2010) ECJ, C-512/08.

hospitals are a good thing but when the NHS was founded, 48 per cent of people died before the age of 65. That figure is now 18 per cent and chronic illnesses make huge additional demands upon the NHS.[8] A system originally designed for short-term and acute illness in hospital has failed to adapt to long-term conditions needing a range of different treatments in the community. Whereas almost all of the Labour government's investment in the NHS after 2000 went into acute NHS care, the core business of the NHS has become the complex needs of elderly patients.[9] Much of the work of hospitals should be transferred to primary and community care so that more is done long before patients reach the crisis which requires highly resource-intensive admission to hospital wards specialising in single episodes of illness.[10] How should we manage the difficult choices required?

In contrast to the individualistic response of the ECJ, judicial review in the UK has been sympathetic to a communitarian response to resource allocation which balances the interests of whole communities of people.[11] At present, these principles have been developed only in respect of individual treatments, rather than decisions involving long-term and strategic planning. Nevertheless, the response is founded on procedural rights which acknowledge the 'political' nature of the choices required and guarantees a transparent decision-making processes. The courts have not specified exactly how these procedures should work, but they are codified in the English *NHS Constitution*[12] which requires NHS 'commissioners' of care to observe a number of fundamental principles. First, commissioners must publish the process by which choices are made. The process should demonstrate the factors taken into account in decision-making and concede that some treatments will not be available, say because they are very expensive and produce little therapeutic benefit. The Scottish *Charter of Patients' Rights and Responsibilities* agrees: 'Your health board must make informed decisions about how best to share out the resources it has to meet its area's needs. This means it will not necessarily be able to provide every treatment for every patient'.[13]

Second, those denied access to treatment are entitled to know why.[14] This requires the creation of a *general* ethical framework within which commissioners can make decisions in respect of *particular* treatments. The policy in respect of particular treatments should normally have the benefit of a well-informed standing committee composed of clinicians, managers and lay advice. The decision should be based on a thorough appraisal of the evidence of its clinical and cost effectiveness. Transparency demands that both the general ethical framework and the particular treatment *policy* be made available on the Internet or in writing. If it is impossible to provide all the treatments we need, then fairness demands that the system treats patients equally, fairly and consistently. Third, the system must be sensitive enough to accommodate *exceptional*

8 See generally, *Ready for Ageing*, HL Paper 140, 2013, annex 13, The Stationary Office, London, a report of the Select Committee on Public Service and Demographic Change, at para. 213, available at: http://www.publications.parliament.uk/pa/ld201213/ldselect/ldpublic/140/140.pdf (accessed 13 January 2015).

9 *Ready for Ageing*, note 8, above, annex 13.

10 The English system, misleadingly called 'payment by results', still incentivises hospitals to admit as many patients as possible. Controversial 're-configuration' decisions should be held to account under a model based on 'accountability for reasonableness'. See Daniels, note 2, above, ch. 4.

11 Newdick, C., *Who Should We Treat?*, 2nd edn, Oxford, Oxford University Press, 2005; and Syrett, K., *Law, Legitimacy and the Rationing of Health Care*, Cambridge, Cambridge University Press, 2007.

12 National Health Service, England, 2013, principle 7, p. 4.

13 Charter of Patient Rights & Responsibilities, pp. 5–6, given effect by the Patient Rights (Scotland) Act 2011, s. 1.

14 The English NHS Constitution is given statutory effect in the National Health Service Commissioning Board and Clinical Commissioning Groups (Responsibilities and Standing Rules) Regulations 2012, SI 2996, Parts 7–9.

circumstances.[15] Say I suffer from a condition for which treatment is not normally available because it is too expensive. I should have the opportunity to demonstrate that my circumstances are so different from those of other patients that I should be regarded as an exception. This is easier to imagine if I am biologically different in the sense that treatment that is ineffective in others will cure me. It is more problematic if my claim is based on my *social*, or non-clinical circumstances, for example that my disease is terminal and I have children to resettle.[16] Here too, patients are entitled to a written explanation and a right of appeal to ensure the rules of natural justice have been properly observed. The second and third 'transparency' principles are set out in the *NHS Constitution*. (Curiously they are not discussed in the Scottish *Charter*.)

As we move away from particular treatments toward *institutional* arrangements (that is, the macro-issues of resource allocation), the process becomes increasingly political. For example, do we have too many doctors, should we permit waiting lists to lengthen, how should we expand community care? As we move the focus away from individual patients, so the clinical input at one stage of the process is joined by political and democratic input at the other.[17] These strategic questions involve choices which are not especially *clinical* in nature. More work is required, especially as NHS resources become more constrained, to understand how these public-centred ethics should be evaluated. At present, our ethical response to these tensions has been limited to the claims of individual patients seeking access to particular treatments. Yet the challenge is to reconfigure entire components of the NHS to promote the interests of the community as a whole. Take preventive care. We urgently need a sustained response to 'avoidable' diseases to reduce the burden of illness, both on individuals themselves and the NHS as a whole. Yet this entails disinvesting from hospitals and redirecting resources to, for example, community care and pre-school education. If we fail to take these steps, the NHS will progressively contract and end up as a last resort service. I consider the difficulty this presents below. These decisions involve the public interest and, indeed, the rights of future generations where the politics of democratic legitimacy are probably more relevant than the ethics of individual autonomy.

Institutional Ethics and the Quality of Treatment

So far I have considered the dynamic between the NHS and the community. Let us now consider the tensions within hospitals themselves. The need to do so is amply illuminated by two inquiries into Mid Staffordshire Foundation Trust by Robert Francis QC in 2010 and 2013.[18] Both of the major political parties in England have committed themselves to market forces as the 'invisible hand' guiding the NHS.[19] A central component of that commitment has been the creation of Foundation

15 See generally *R v. NW Lancashire HA, ex p A, D & G* (2000) 53 BMLR 148.

16 In *R (Condliff) v. North Staffordshire PCT* [2011] EWCA Civ 910 the health authority successfully argued that the difficulties of providing a fair and consistent framework for non-clinical factors justified excluding them from 'exceptionality' review.

17 See Newdick, C., 'The Positive Side of Health Care Rights' in McLean, S.A.M. (ed.), *First Do No Harm: Law Ethics and Healthcare*, Aldershot, Ashgate, 2006, pp. 573–86; and Coggon, J., *What Makes Health Public?*, Cambridge, Cambridge University Press, 2012.

18 See (a) *Independent Inquiry into Care Provided by Mid Staffordshire NHS Foundation Trust*, January 2005–March 2009, London, HC375, 2010 and (b) *Report of the Mid Staffordshire NHS Foundation Trust Public Inquiry*, London, HC 898, 2013.

19 See generally, Le Grand, J., *The Other Invisible Hand: Delivering Public Services Through Choice and Competition*, Princeton, NJ, Princeton University Press, 2007.

Trust hospitals which are granted additional institutional autonomy if they achieve economic and quality targets set by government. Clinical quality is often assessed by reference to 'targets', for example as to waiting times in accident and emergency departments and for admission for elective care. The two inquiries revealed, however, that the drive to achieve Foundation Trust status created an environment that tolerated appalling suffering that may have caused between 400 and 1,200 deaths between 2005 and 2009.[20] Targets had been achieved by reducing investment in staff and forcing patients through the system without sufficient nursing care. The result left vulnerable patients at extreme risk of serious harm.

The stories told in the second volume of the first Mid Staffordshire report make difficult reading. Medicines were not administered; patients were left without food and water, not taken to the toilet, told to relieve themselves in their beds and not cleaned afterwards and left for hours on commodes. Those who complained were met with indifference, or hostility. Systems did not exist to pass concerns up through the tiers of hospital management so the board was either ignorant of, or ignored, circumstances on the clinical wards. There was a disconnection between the hospital's clinical and managerial leadership. This happened because financial targets dominated the hospital's management agenda so that nursing levels were cut without proper regard to the impact on care. Clearly, the hospital board and individual clinicians should be held responsible for that, either for institutional negligence, or within the *Bolam* principle. Equally, this happened because of pressure from the Department of Health and Strategic Health Authorities to prioritise the financial targets required for Foundation Trust status which paid insufficient attention to the consequences for patients.[21] Auditors and inspectors too were subject to the same influence and this helps explain why a hospital suffering such financial stress could win Foundation Trust status, giving it greater autonomy from government, despite systemic failings in clinical care well known to large numbers of patients, relatives and staff.[22]

The influence of central targets in Mid Staffordshire suggest circumstances of institutional 'capture' of the hospital by government itself and this is not unique to Mid Staffordshire. Maidstone & Tunbridge Wells Hospital[23] and Stoke Mandeville Hospital[24] were subject to similar criticism by the Healthcare Commission, and the Health Services Ombudsman published a similarly critical report about the experience of hospital for older people in 2011.[25] Elderly and vulnerable patients are most often the victims. An unintended consequence of the drive to achieve Foundation Trust status was the growth of a managerial disregard for patients. Management looked upwards to their political masters, but not down into the hospital itself. Complaints were discouraged so that

---

20 *Independent Inquiry into Care Provided by Mid Staffordshire NHS Foundation Trust*, note 18, above, at p. 352. The figure is disputed because it represents the number in excess of that which might be expected of hospitals elsewhere.

21 *Report of the Mid Staffordshire NHS Foundation Trust Public Inquiry*, vol. I, note 18, above, at para. 2.118. The same finding was made by the Healthcare Commission in its Stoke Mandeville and Maidstone & Tonbridge Wells reports, see notes 23 and 24, below.

22 The GMC estimated between 120 and 150 doctors must have known what was happening. See *Annual Accountability Hearing with the General Medical Council*, House of Commons Health Committee, HC 1429, Session 2010–12, para. 42.

23 *Investigation into Outbreaks of Clostridium Difficile at Maidstone and Tunbridge Wells NHS Trust*, London, Healthcare Commission, 2007.

24 *Investigation into Outbreaks of Clostridium Difficile at Stoke Mandeville Hospital, Buckinghamshire Hospitals NHS Trust*, London, Healthcare Commission, 2006.

25 *Care and Compassion: Report of the Health Service Ombudsman on Ten Investigations into NHS Care of Older People*, London, HC 778, 2011.

clinicians became blind to the evidence before their eyes. In one example in which a hospital consultant wrote a critical report of the circumstances surrounding a patient's death, the hospital's legal advisors persuaded him to change his conclusions specifically to protect the hospital's reputation. The intention was to conceal the mistake to promote the hospital's self-interest.[26] Clearly, in a service established only to promote public interests, this is a problem. And beyond the hospital itself, governmental anxiety about reputation-management led to a harsh and insensitive attitude to the problems confronted by NHS managers.[27] If the Department of Health under-values its managers, then the attitude of hospital managers towards patients and staff is likely to be affected too. Speaking implicitly to government, the Berwick report noted in its recommendations following the Mid Staffordshire inquiry:

> Fear is toxic to both safety and improvement ... Time and again, we see the harvest of fear in the Mid Staffordshire story, a vicious cycle of over-riding goals, misallocation of resources, distracted attention, consequent failures and hazards, reproach for goals not met, more misallocation and growing opacity as dark rooms with no data came to look safer than ones with light.[28]

How can we develop a notion of institutional ethics to cope with these insidious pressures? Lord Nolan's recommendations, in 1994, for standards of selflessness, integrity, objectivity, accountability, openness, honesty and leadership[29] conveys the nature of the duties owed by public servants. Some of the institutional ethics advocated by Nolan and Francis are contained in the *NHS Constitution*, that is, that the NHS is 'effective and focused on patient experience',[30] that 'the system of responsibility and accountability ... should be transparent and clear to the public',[31] the NHS will 'monitor and make efforts to improve'[32] and so on. But these fine words have had little impact. The challenge is not the principles themselves, but finding evidence they are working. Inescapably, we need to devise procedures and encourage a culture which foster trust between patient and institution. Hospital boards should regularly meet in public and publish their minutes. They should encourage complaints and deal with them openly. Specific attention should be given to the duty of candour when things go wrong.[33] In addition, patients should be given greater opportunity to record their experience of the NHS, a principle absent from the Charters, Constitutions and many codes of conduct. Impressive national regulatory bodies like the Healthcare Commission, Care Quality Commission and Monitor are not close enough to the patient experience. An articulate account of the patient voice would be more effective in cementing the Nolan principles at institutional level. As the Berwick report said, we should treasure and learn from information on risks and the

26 *Report of the Mid Staffordshire NHS Foundation Trust Public Inquiry*, note 18, above, at para. 22.49.

27 The perception of bullying is discussed in the *Report of the Mid Staffordshire NHS Foundation Trust Public Inquiry*, vol. II, note 18, above, para. 19.286. See also *Gibb v. Maidstone and Tunbridge Wells NHS* [2010] EWCA Civ 678 and the critical comments of Sedley LJ as to the way in which the Department of Health dealt with a senior manager, at [42].

28 *A Promise to Learn – A Commitment to Act*, National Advisory Group on the Safety of Patients in England, London, 2013, at p. 9.

29 See *Standards in Public Life*, Cm 2850-I, 1994.

30 Note 12, above, at p. 3, Principle 3.

31 Note 12, above, at p. 4, Principle 7.

32 Note 12, above, at p. 7.

33 *Report of the Mid Staffordshire NHS Foundation Trust Public Inquiry*, HC 947, vol. III, 2013, para. 22.162–4.

things that have gone wrong, in particular the 'voices of patients, carers, and staff'.[34] If the major problem in Mid Staffordshire was the disconnection between clinicians and managers, transparent comparisons of patient satisfaction between hospitals could provide a shared agenda of common concerns which would be difficult to ignore. This is an application of informed consent principles at an institutional level to illuminate the nature of the care provided in hospitals and could give these meta-ethics a more secure foundation.

Note, however, adopting Hirschman's typology, that the capacity to 'voice' concern is not the same as encouraging 'exit'.[35] 'Voice' promotes institutional engagement with the public without necessarily threatening the viability of the service; it encourages individuals to engage constructively with public bodies to illuminate and improve the services provided. By contrast, 'exit' is more aggressive. By encouraging individuals to locate alternative providers, it threatens to destabilise the viability of the institution itself. Indeed, by encouraging people to abandon a service and go elsewhere, exit may undermine the capacity of an articulate voice to express concern.[36] Some will argue that a system committed to the invisible hand of competition and market forces should close unpopular hospitals. Equally, many patients do not have such a choice of hospital. Elderly and infirm patients require hospitals nearby and remoter areas of the country suffer disproportionate loss if a local hospital closes. We should understand how institutional structures intended to promote patients' rights to exit may also threaten concern for equality of access to the NHS and the fair distribution of public services.

Institutional Ethics and Healthcare Markets

The tension between selfless public service and private self-interest brings us to public services served by *private* business. I have noted the preference of UK governments south of the border for market-based responses to institutional design. What is the role of private, commercial interests in respect of social solidarity? Many of us may feel instinctively uneasy about encouraging private interests to profit from the misfortunes of disease. Far better that public-spirited staff commit themselves to the NHS as a vocation. Equally, the experience of Mid Staffordshire and the other reports of NHS care suggest we cannot place blind faith in our commitment to public service. For example, if we all have better information on which to compare hospitals so remedial steps can be taken, then at least one element of competition has been conceded. Even with this concession, the NHS in England has taken an approach very different from that north of the border. Scotland admits the more limited private involvement of GPs as private contractors, pharmaceutical companies and private care homes. There, however, the involvement of commerce largely stops. By contrast, successive English governments have committed the NHS to inviting private hospitals and clinics to compete with NHS hospitals for NHS patients. The theory is that competition drives value for money and that treating patients as consumers will improve the experience of the NHS by shortening waiting times and improving the quality of care.

---

34 *A Promise to Learn – A Commitment to Act*, note 28, above, p. 10. Identical recommendations were made by Professor Sir Ian Kennedy in *Learning from Bristol*, Cm 5207, 2001, pp. 365–6, para. 30-3.

35 Hirschman, A., *Exit, Voice and Loyalty*, Cambridge, MA, Harvard University Press, 1970, at pp. 33–4.

36 See Vincent-Jones, P., *The New Public Contracting: Regulation, Responsiveness, Relationality*, Oxford, Oxford University Press, 2006, p. 213, discussing the impact of middle-class parents leaving state education in favour of private schools.

Whether this will work is disputed because the evidence that competition drives quality is equivocal.[37] Clearly, the Scots and Welsh are not convinced by the English 'experiment'. So, in the absence of clear evidence, let us put that question aside and ask instead how the public service ethos discussed by Nolan and Francis applies to private commercial interests. Specifically, should private interests ever be subject to judicial review, the Human Rights Act or the Freedom of Information Act? How should doctors who take profits from a private business account to patients for any conflict of interest? Should the same 'selfless' duties of disclosure of adverse incidents apply even if it would damage shareholder interests? For those with Bevanite instincts, the law is not encouraging. In England, the courts have consistently emphasised the private, commercial rights engaged in this arrangement. The idea is that private companies also have duties to shareholders. They have offered their services to the NHS for profit and are no different from a supermarket. It would be illegitimate to impose obligations upon them as if they were public bodies. If judicial review applies at all, it is only in the most superficial sense. For example, in one case the question arose whether a private water company had a duty to fluoridate its water supplies because, as many acknowledged, it was in the public interest to do so. But the company objected that it was a socially controversial thing to do and more trouble to the company than it was worth. It argued it was entitled to give full regard to its private interests in avoiding complaints and possible litigation. The court agreed.[38] Unless statute curtailed its powers in this regard, it was within its private right to do so. Similarly, the Human Rights Act 1998, which applies to public authorities, does not apply to private residential and nursing homes.[39] This is so even when they are charities and derive almost all of their work from providing services to publicly-funded residents on behalf of local authorities. Only Baroness Hale and Lord Bingham support the idea that private businesses providing public services should be subject to similar public duties when they step into the public authority's shoes. In truth, the difference between these views is based more on instinct than legal logic, but it is most unattractive that public and human rights should vary according to the nature of the hospital provider in which we receive our NHS care.

One answer to this problem of balancing public and private rights is to insert specific clauses into the contracts by which private businesses have been engaged, requiring the provider to observe the Human Rights Act provisions. However, it is a second-best solution because it is a contract between public authority and private provider only, to which the patient or resident is not a party. One suspects that many public authorities will not have the time or resource to support an individual patient's human rights claims. Nor is the private provider subject to judicial review (any more than Tesco, or the Royal Bank of Scotland). The extent to which our public law remedies have been eroded in England by the 'de-nationalisation' of the NHS is striking.[40] One possible solution to this problem is to use the Contracts (Rights of Third Parties) Act 1999 to give patients and residents enforceable contractual rights of their own under these contracts. On the other hand, we should not assume public authorities have the bargaining power to insist upon such a clause. If private companies say 'No: take it or leave it', governments committed to engaging private providers in the NHS may have little choice in the matter.

A similar concern arises in connection with conflicts of interest in the NHS in England. As in Scotland, GPs are engaged as private contractors running their own partnerships for profit (much like

37 Reviewing the literature, see Bevan, G. and Skellern, M., 'Does Competition between Hospitals Improve Clinical Quality? A Review of Evidence from Two Eras of Competition in the English NHS' (2011) 343 *British Medical Journal*, http://www.bmj.com/content/343/bmj.d6470 (accessed 13 January 2015).

38 *R v. Northumbrian Water Ltd, ex p Newcastle and North Tyneside HA* [1999] Env LR 715.

39 *YL v. Birmingham City Council* [2007] UKHL 27.

40 See the illuminating study by Vincent-Jones, *The New Public Contracting*, note 36, above.

small firms of solicitors doing mostly publicly-funded work). In Scotland, the Health Boards which commission care are still public authorities wholly subject to public law supervision. However, the English reforms of 2012 have given GPs responsibility for commissioning NHS services in Clinical Commissioning Groups (CCGs). GPs have legitimate private interests. Enterprising GPs on CCG boards may commission care from nursing homes, or clinics offering NHS, or cosmetic services in which they have their own commercial interests. Conflicts of interest are inevitable. How should patients be protected from abuse and exploitation?[41] The law of informed consent is not helpful because it offers a remedy in the law of negligence which assumes the patient has been damaged. Without personal injury, informed consent is irrelevant. Clearly, conflicts of interest give rise to a very different concern based on trust and confidence between doctor and patient. Given the judicial response to the nursing home cases above, we should probably presume that conflicts of this nature are not unlawful and the question is only how they should be managed. Again, we have to resort to professional good practice and Department of Health guidelines. None addresses the matter satisfactorily. The GMC says patients should be informed, but is a notice on the surgery notice-board acceptable?[42] The BMA says patients should *never* have concerns about conflicts of interest,[43] and a Department of Health *Code of Conduct*[44] suggests general disclosure principles, but leaves their interpretation to individual CCGs. None discusses remedies for breach. Clearly, we are very far from understanding how standards of public accountability should apply to private interests.

Equality and Public Health Ethics

Let us return to lifestyle trends and the increase in type 2 diabetes and the various illnesses associated with it, such as coronary heart disease, cerebro-vascular disease and musculo-skeletal disease. The cost of treating obesity and its related conditions is estimated to increase from £4.2 million to £9.7 million by 2050 (when real terms investment in the NHS is falling), with costs to the wider economy of £49.9 million.[45] The government's Office for Budget Responsibility (OBR) estimates that our current expectations of public expenditure will be 'unsustainable' by 2050.[46] One response is behavioural so we take more exercise and eat more fruit and vegetables, but how does this resonate with traditional notions of personal autonomy and tabloid headlines about the nanny state? If that were not controversial enough, the results of such a policy could take 20 years to reduce healthcare costs. There is nothing especially *clinical* about decisions like this. Given bioethics' primary focus on the individual, public health has never had much influence in the NHS. In England, new duties have been imposed on the Secretary of State, the NHS Commissioning Board and Clinical Commissioning Groups to reduce inequalities between people and 'Health

41 The problem is more familiar to the US. See Rodwin, M.A., *Conflicts of Interest and the Future of Medicine*, New York, Oxford University Press, 2011.

42 General Medical Council, *Good Medical Practice*, London, 2013, para. 79.

43 British Medical Association, *Ensuring Transparency and Probity*, London, 2011.

44 NHS Commissioning Board, *Code of Conduct*, London, 2012.

45 Government Office for Science, *Foresight: Tackling Obesity*, 2nd edn, London, 2013, 40, that is, to increase from 6 per cent to 13.9 per cent of total NHS costs.

46 Office of Budget Responsibility, *Fiscal Sustainability Report 2012: Executive Summary*, London, 2012, paras 48–50, attributable mainly to health, pensions and social care costs.

England' has also been created with a public health remit within local authorities.[47] Combining the sharply rising costs of 'lifestyle' diseases with a prolonged period of NHS austerity, this is perhaps the most pressing of all the ethical challenges that confront modern welfare systems.

Traditional notions of autonomy hesitate to discuss the ethical responsibilities we owe to ourselves and others.[48] For example, on the right of the political spectrum, some have an instinctive distrust of government and fear that public welfare has an enfeebling and enervating effect on individual self-reliance and initiative.[49] Such a view might acknowledge the wide disparities we observe in health status so heavily influenced by social determinants, that is, that the poorest classes suffer a disproportionate burden from diseases of affluence.[50] Equally, it may view them as a matter of individual choice and responsibility in which the state has no business to interfere. If I wish to eat and drink to excess and to take insufficient exercise, is this a matter for me and my autonomy alone? Or does it raise issues of citizenship, both because the institutional duty of equality is not being observed effectively, and because my morbidity imposes burdens on others? Sheila MacLean invites us to reconsider this one-dimensional view of autonomy, citing John Stuart Mill: 'As soon as any part of a person's conduct affects prejudicially the interests of others, society has jurisdiction over it'.[51] This raises the debate about the nature of 'harm' and when such a jurisdiction exists, but it also encourages us to think about duties of citizenship. As she says, by removing us from society, extreme claims for individualism and autonomy decontextualise the lives we live.[52] Once we re-establish the context, as Sen says, we should accept a community-duty to promote the *capabilities* of all its members equally.[53] The duty arises in the present with respect to health inequality, but as the OBR forecasts, it also concerns the sustainability of current spending patterns in the NHS. So there is also a pressing concern for the future and our impact upon future generations of people who (if they could do so) might be alarmed at the manner in which our behaviour today threatens the viability of the NHS. These concerns present a severe challenge to traditional notions of autonomy and invite us to consider the extent to which it is legitimate to influence behaviour which traditional bioethics might otherwise have regarded as the autonomous product of free will.

The more autonomy is understood to be a component of citizenship and to describe the relationship *between* individuals, the more it involves the compromises of politics and democracy which accommodate the interests of others.[54] Once we accept this idea, we can discuss the extent to which measures are required to modify behaviour. In truth, we are very far from doing so. Should the response be directed primarily at individuals on the basis that we are responsible for our own

---

47 See National Health Service Act 2006, ss. 1C, 13G, 14T and 73A inserted by the Health and Social Care Act 2012, ss. 4 (Secretary of State), 23 (NHS Commissioning Board), 26 (Clinical Commissioning Groups) and 30 (local authorities).

48 See Beauchamp, D., 'Community: The Neglected Tradition of Public Health' (1985) 15 *Hastings Center Report*, 28–36.

49 See Epstein, R., 'In Defense of the "Old" Public Health: The Legal Framework for the Regulation of Public Health' (2004) 69 *Brooklyn Law Review*, 1421–70; and Fitzpatrick, M., *The Tyranny of Health: Doctors and the Regulation of Lifestyle*, London, Routledge, 2005.

50 Marmot, M., *Fair Society, Healthy Lives*, London, The Marmot Review, 2010, at para. 2.5.

51 McLean, S.A.M., *Autonomy, Consent and the Law*, London, Routledge-Cavendish, 2010, p. 16, citing Mill, J.S., *On Liberty*, 1869. See also Brazier, M., 'Do No Harm: Do Patients Have Responsibilities Too?' (2006) 65 *Cambridge Law Journal*, 397–422.

52 MacLean, note 51, above, at p. 14.

53 Sen, A., *The Idea of Justice*, London, Allen Lane, 2009.

54 See generally, Dworkin, G., *The Theory and Practice of Autonomy*, New York, Cambridge University Press, 1988, and Gaylin, W. and Jennings, B., *The Perversion of Autonomy*, 2nd edn, Washington, DC, Georgetown University Press, 2003.

health? Dworkin has suggested that people who opt to be unhealthy should not have the same access to healthcare as those whose condition is caused by brute bad luck.[55] Similarly, Sunstein and Thaler propose a policy of 'nudging' people toward, for example, a healthier diet and opportunity for exercise.[56] 'Nudge' focuses on individual behaviour, rather than social structures. However, Marmot's *social determinant of health* model suggests there is limited scope for such a policy. He found that 'health inequalities do not arise by chance, and they cannot be attributed simply to genetic makeup, "bad", unhealthy behaviour, or difficulties in access to medical care ... Social and economic differences in health status reflect, and are caused by, social and economic inequalities in society'.[57] If social status plays the dominant role in public health, then attention should be directed there first. This strongly suggests that nudging individuals will not make much difference. There are so many possible responses. Supermarkets, for example, keep detailed records of our purchasing patterns. Should we use incentives to promote public health policy by reminding consumers of the alternative products available on the shelves?[58] Should we reward local education authorities for changing behaviour through school clubs, or hospitals for collaborating with GPs to keep patients *out* of hospital, or town planning authorities for encouraging pedestrian and cycle ways?[59] These are difficult concerns which deserve greater attention but they point to a more prominent role for government in promoting community health.

Conclusion

Bioethics through the telescope does not contradict traditional, microscopic notions of ethics, but it argues they must be understood within a context. It puts the individual into a social and institutional setting, together with the additional tensions this introduces. The solutions to the questions that arise here are often assisted by the messy compromises of politics, rather than immutable principles of ethics alone. When modern social welfare systems depend on how we invest in each other's health, we need a clearer conception of the rights and duties we owe to each other – especially in today's economic climate. Communitarianism provides a starting point for the debate.[60] Whilst it lacks the analytical purity of traditional bioethics, it is capable of freeing itself from conceptual avatars with little actual connection to the structures and constraints of modern institutions. Should we be troubled by the suggestion that well-understood bioethical principles should adapt to accommodate the more consequentialist concerns of economics and politics? The need to do so is emphasised by Sen and others who urge greater acceptance of what has been

55 Dworkin, R., *Sovereign Virtue: The Theory and Practice of Equality*, Cambridge, MA, Harvard University Press, 2000, ch. 2.

56 Thaler, R.H. and Sunstein, C.R., *Nudge: Improving Decisions about Health, Wealth and Happiness*, London, Penguin Books, 2009.

57 Marmot, note 50, above, p. 16.

58 This raises again the question of *corporate citizenship*, that is, the idea that private business has non-commercial public duties. See generally, Frank, R.H., *The Darwin Economy: Liberty, Competition, and the Common Good*, Princeton, NJ, Princeton University Press, 2011; and Prosser, T., 'Regulation for Social Solidarity' (2006) 33 *Journal of Law and Society*, 364–87.

59 Using public opinion surveys as to what is 'acceptable', see Ipsos Mori, *Understanding Society: How Do We Change Behaviour?*, London, 2013.

60 See generally, Sandell, M.J., *Liberalism and the Limits of Justice*, 2nd edn, New York, Cambridge University Press, 1998; Gaylin and Jennings, note 54, above.

called 'non-ideal' theory,[61] which says of ideal-type analysis that it '"purifies" thought by eradicating supposedly irrelevant, mundane, or trivial conceptual features'.[62] However, the cost of doing so is that it portrays an 'alien place, reflective only of an incomplete picture of the important aspects of the society we live in'.[63] This understanding is crucial to enable us to respond to the institutional constraints which will modify our expectations of public welfare systems. It will also permit us to adapt the certainties of Beauchamp and Childress' four principles by acknowledging how the strength of a community helps us to confront the challenges of the future together.

61 See, for example, Sen, note 53, above, at pp. 5–12; Schneider, C.E., *The Practice of Autonomy: Patients, Doctors and Medical Decisions*, New York, Oxford University Press, 1998, p. xv; and Powers, M. and Faden, R., *Social Justice, the Moral Foundations of Public Health and Health Policy*, New York, Oxford University Press, 2006, p. 31.

62 Coggon, note 17, above, at p. 210.

63 Coggon, note 17, above, at p. 213.

PART III
Liability

Chapter 9

Clinical Negligence and Poor Quality Care: Is Wales 'Putting Things Right'?

Vivienne Harpwood

Introduction

The NHS in Wales, in common with other jurisdictions, is experiencing unprecedented numbers of clinical negligence claims. A range of solutions has been sought throughout the world to address the need to compensate patients who suffer injuries in the course of medical treatment, while keeping control over the escalating cost of redress. In 2011, Sheila McLean chaired a Working Group tasked with investigating the potential benefits of a no-fault compensation system for patients in Scotland alongside existing clinical negligence arrangements. Her carefully considered report contains a section dealing with the proposed solution in Wales for handling low value claims. Her committee advised on the key principles and design criteria that might be adopted for a no-fault compensation scheme, and recommended the introduction of a scheme based on a modified version of the model currently in operation in Sweden.[1] In the same year, a far more conservative approach was introduced in Wales through a new system which had recently been implemented following the NHS [National Health Service] Redress (Wales) Act 2006, entitled *Putting Things Right*, aimed at dealing with lower value claims alongside concerns raised by staff and complaints by patients about poor quality care. McLean's Report indicates that lawyers and policy makers in Wales and Scotland recognise that it is not only financial compensation that is required, but also the restoration of individuals who have suffered harm to the position they had been in prior to the injury, as far as this is possible.[2] This chapter explains the origins and rationale of the new system in Wales, and attempts at this very early stage to assess its success to date. It also considers the implications for other jurisdictions in the light of the Francis Inquiry Report in 2013 on events at Mid Staffordshire.

The Structural Context

The constituent countries of the UK are becoming increasingly diverse in their approaches to the delivery and structure of their National Health Service responsibilities, as is exemplified by the legislative frameworks for healthcare in each country. Since the media focus tends to be centred on England, developments in Wales are little-known and seldom discussed outside the Principality, so it is necessary to describe the background to the reforms in Wales at this stage.

1 Scottish Government, *No Fault Compensation Review Group, Report and Recommendations*, Volume 1, February 2011 (hereinafter referred to as the McLean Report).

2 McLean Report, Introduction.

Under the arrangements for devolution, a separate Assembly for Wales was created by the Government of Wales Act 2008 after a referendum was passed accepting the proposals made soon after New Labour came into power. However, there was no provision in that Act for separation of the legislature from the executive. The Welsh Assembly assumed the statutory powers and duties of the Secretary of State for Wales, but in practice the Assembly delegated most of its executive powers to the Assembly Ministers. The Assembly also assumed a large number of powers to make law by means of secondary legislation, but it had no power at that stage to make any primary legislation. A Commission appointed in 2002 to review the operation of devolution in Wales recommended that the Assembly should be replaced by two separate bodies – an executive and a legislature, and that by 2011 the Assembly should be able to make primary legislation for Wales.[3]

On 3 March 2011, a referendum on extending the law-making powers of the National Assembly for Wales was held in Wales, and there was a majority vote in favour of allowing the Assembly to make laws on all matters in the 20 subject areas for which it already had powers – which include health. Therefore the Assembly is now able to make laws without the requirement that there should be agreement by the Westminster Parliament, subject to standing orders. This is similar to the existing UK system in Westminster where Bills can be introduced by Government or private members. However, only the UK Parliament is able to make laws in areas that are not devolved, such as defence and taxation. The UK Parliament will not make laws for Wales on subjects concerning which the Welsh Government already has powers, without obtaining the agreement of the Welsh Government that it can do so. Despite this simplified approach, there is still a complex patchwork of legislation and delegated legislation relating to Wales.

Devolution has enabled the NHS in Wales to take what in many respects is a radically different approach to that in England, while remaining true to the basic principles on which the NHS was founded. The vision for the present structure of healthcare services in Wales was explained by Edwina Hart, the then Welsh Health Minister, as bringing to an end the internal market in NHS services in Wales, ensuring that within each of seven geographical areas, one organisation would deliver all healthcare services, allowing for greater uniformity in the approach to delivering healthcare. Wales was prepared to take time in the development of these services to guarantee that there would be an NHS structure in place that would endure for the next 20 to 30 years. Since 2010, the Welsh structure has been based on a framework for delivering healthcare through seven Local Health Boards, with NHS Trusts being responsible for delivering ambulance services and certain tertiary services.

Policy variations between England and Wales have resulted not only in completely different structures for healthcare delivery, but also in differences of emphasis and changed priorities in relation to healthcare. To take but a few examples, Wales has a new system for dealing with people suffering from mental illness, introduced by the Mental Health Measure 2009, much of which has been in force since 2012. Although the Mental Health Act 1983 remains in force in Wales, the Mental Health Measure makes a number of important changes to the way people with psychiatric problems can access and receive primary and secondary mental health services. Prescriptions have been free of charge in Wales since April 2007, as have dental check-ups for all residents under the age of 25 and over the age of 60. Car parking at hospitals in Wales is free of charge. Welsh NHS patients are being given a voice in Wales through Community Health Councils, which have

3 The formal arrangements for this were set out in 2005 in a White Paper entitled *Better Governance for Wales*, and the Government of Wales Act 2006 established a second devolution settlement for Wales. This created a complex legal framework that envisaged a third and subsequent settlement, enabling a referendum to be held in the future without further recourse to Parliament, to secure the granting of full primary law making powers to the Assembly.

been retained, and through extended advocacy arrangements for the people in hospital who are suffering from mental illness. There are different NHS complaints systems in England from Wales and different approaches to organ donation, specifically in recent legislation introduced in Wales to implement a system of presumed consent.[4]

The approach in Wales to handling concerns and claims now differs in many respects from that in England, and it is the new system, introduced in 2011, based on a policy document entitled *Putting Things Right* which lies at the heart of the discussion in this chapter.

Common Problems

Despite variations in healthcare policy between England and Wales, all the UK countries share many common problems, which include serious concerns about pressures on 'accident and emergency' departments and out-of-hours provision for patients who seek treatment outside the normal working day for general practitioners. There is also disquiet about waiting-lists for surgery in the light of increasing demands for unscheduled care and the shortage of doctors in the UK as a whole. These factors can create a climate in which it is more likely that mistakes will be made, some of which will inevitably cause harm to patients, and there are common problems involving errors made in healthcare settings. Inhumane treatment and the avoidable deaths of some patients in certain NHS hospitals, which became a national scandal, resulted in the Francis Inquiry and subsequent Report, published in February 2013.[5] Although this focused on events at the Mid Staffordshire NHS Trust in England, the other UK countries are anxious to learn lessons from the Report and its recommendations. Coupled with the issues highlighted in this Report are concerns about the rising cost of defending claims and compensating patients injured in the course of healthcare.

Concerns, Complaints and Clinical Negligence Claims

Wales, in common with other jurisdictions in Europe and the United States of America, is experiencing an unprecedented rise in the volume of claims for clinical negligence, coupled with an increasing number of complaints about healthcare treatment and services. Data analysed by the Working Group chaired by Sheila McLean indicated that the volume of claims and compensation payments have risen in Scotland over the past decade in parallel with those in other jurisdictions.[6] Over the past three years, payments to claimants in Wales have doubled, mirroring figures in England,[7] to reach a total of £89m in the three-year period to April 2010.[8] This resulted in an increase of £16m in funds paid by the Welsh Government to the Welsh Risk Pool.[9] Another

4 The Human Transplant (Wales) Act 2013.

5 The final report of the Mid Staffordshire NHS Foundation Trust Public Inquiry was published on 6 February 2013.

6 Farrell, A.M., Devaney, S. and Dar, A., *No Fault Schemes for Medical Injury: A Review*, Interim Report, p. 13.

7 See Clinical Negligence Scheme for Trusts, *Annual Report and Accounts 2012/13*, Claim Trends, p. 14.

8 Figures obtained by the *Western Mail* newspaper from the Welsh Risk Pool on a FOI request in May 2013.

9 The Welsh Risk Pool undertakes a similar role to the Clinical Negligence Scheme for Trusts in England, administering a programme funded through contributions by NHS organisations which form its

worrying feature of the present system is that the cost of defending claims frequently exceeds the value of the claim itself.

As in other UK jurisdictions, the reasons for these recent developments are complex, and have been attributed to numerous factors, including the popularity of 'no-win, no-fee' cases, higher awards to take account of increased life expectancy of claimants, and the high cost of care and specialist equipment, particularly for those who suffered brain injuries at birth. Over the past 30 years, societal change and attitudes to compensation have resulted in a culture in which many patients who suffer injury in the care of the NHS expect to be compensated.

Scotland, like England and Wales, currently has a system that covers compensation by the state for clinical negligence claims against NHS employees, including medical, dental and nursing staff, and Health Boards fund the defence of claims, being protected against disproportionate losses by the mandatory Clinical Negligence and Other Risks Indemnity Scheme (CNORIS). As in the other UK countries, General Practitioners (GPs) and other primary care contractors are separately insured. Liability for Health Boards is handled by the Central Legal Office.[10]

The Attempt at a Solution in Wales

Although there has been no attempt to introduce comprehensive reform in Wales, a new scheme has recently been implemented under the NHS Redress (Wales) Measure 2008 which promotes early settlement of lower value claims. The history of this legislative development is interesting,[11] and can be traced back to August 2001, when the Chief Medical Officer published *Call for Ideas*,[12] inviting patients, NHS staff, the public and other key stakeholders to express views on the way in which the NHS should handle clinical negligence incidents in the future. His recommendations for reform were published in 2003 in *Making Amends*,[13] a Consultation Paper stating proposals for reforming the system for dealing with clinical negligence in the NHS.

The NHS Redress Act 2006 gives effect to the proposal in Recommendation 1 that an NHS Redress Scheme should be introduced to instigate appropriate investigations when things go wrong, and to provide remedial treatment, rehabilitation and care where needed, with suitable explanations and apologies, and financial compensation if necessary in certain cases. The proposed system would therefore combine complaints handling with compensation and remedial treatment.

---

membership. The Welsh Risk Pool is funded by the Welsh Assembly, and repays compensation money paid out by Welsh NHS bodies in cases where settlements are over £25,000.

10 See Stephen, F., Melville, A. and Krause, T., *A Study of Medical Negligence Claiming in Scotland*, Scottish Government, June 2012.

11 The legal powers are contained in ss. 113, 115 and 195 of the Health and Social Care (Community Health and Standards) Act 2003; ss. 187 and 206 of the National Health Service (Wales) Act 2006 and ss. 1 to 7, 9, 11 and 12 of the NHS Redress (Wales) Measure 2008. The relevant sections of the NHS Redress (Wales) Measure 2008 are commenced by the NHS Redress (Wales) Measure 2008 (Commencement) Order 2011. The Commencement Order was made on 2 February 2011, and s. 113(2), (3) and (4) of the Health and Social Care (Community Health and Standards) Act 2003 was finally brought into force by the Health and Social Care (Community Health and Standards) Act 2003 Commencement (Wales) (No. 5) Order 2011.

12 See *Call for Ideas*, 2001, UK Government: http://webarchive.nationalarchives.gov.uk/20130107105354/http://www.dh.gov.uk/prod_consum_dh/groups/dh_digitalassets/@dh/@en/documents/digitalasset/dh_4078009.pdf (accessed 13 January 2015).

13 Available at: http://webarchive.nationalarchives.gov.uk/20130107105354/http://www.dh.gov.uk/prod_consum_dh/groups/dh_digitalassets/@dh/@en/documents/digitalasset/dh_4060945.pdf (accessed 13 January 2015).

The 2006 Act provides for a 'scheme' to be established to enable the settlement of certain claims without the need for court proceedings. Section 1 of the Act states:

> (1) The Secretary of State may by regulations establish a scheme for the purpose of enabling redress to be provided without recourse to civil proceedings in circumstances in which this section applies.
>
> (2) This section applies where under the law of England and Wales qualifying liability in tort on the part of a body or other person mentioned in subsection (3) arises in connection with the provision, as part of the health service in England or of qualifying services.

In terms of the qualifying liability in tort, the Act refers broadly to personal injury or loss arising out of a breach of a duty of care owed to any person in connection with the diagnosis of illness, or the care or treatment of any patient and in consequence of any act or omission by a healthcare professional. It does not apply in connection with primary care. The Act establishes the parameters of the cases to which any such scheme can apply, stating which bodies can be members of a scheme, and giving the Secretary of State power to make regulations governing the detailed rules for the operation of the scheme. To that extent this is a framework Act, annoyingly avoiding specifying details of the schemes that can be made under it.

The powers given to the Secretary of State include the power to place new duties on scheme members and the Commission for Healthcare Audit and Inspection (then known as the Healthcare Commission, and replaced later by the Healthcare Commission and the Commission for Social Care Inspection, and finally by the Care Quality Commission in 2009)[14] to consider whether cases or complaints fall within a redress scheme and if so, to take appropriate action. The 'redress' envisaged by the Act is clarified to some extent in section 3, by stating[15] that a scheme must provide for redress *ordinarily* to comprise –

> (a) the making of an offer of compensation in satisfaction of any right to bring civil proceedings in respect of the liability concerned,
> (b) the giving of an explanation,
> (c) the giving of an apology, and
> (d) the giving of a report on the action which has been, or will be, taken to prevent similar cases arising.

In addition,[16] a scheme may, in particular –

> (a) make provision for the compensation that may be offered to take the form of entry into a contract to provide care or treatment or of financial compensation, or both;
> (b) make provision about the circumstances in which different forms of compensation may be offered.

A scheme can specify the matters in respect of which financial compensation may be offered, and provide details about the assessment of the amount of financial compensation, also specifying an upper limit on the amount of financial compensation that may be included in an offer under the

14 Health and Social Care Act 2008, s. 1.
15 NHS Redress Act 2006, s. 3(2).
16 NHS Redress Act 2006, s. 3(3).

scheme. Under s. 3(5)(b), if a scheme does not specify a limit, it must specify an upper limit on the amount of financial compensation that may be included in such an offer in respect of pain and suffering; and s. 3(5)(c) provides that it may not specify any other limit on what may be included in such an offer by way of financial compensation.

Wales took the initiative before England to construct a scheme, and the Welsh Assembly Government established the *Putting Things Right* project which considered the way in which the NHS in Wales handles concerns, and made recommendations for dealing effectively with such issues, using methods of investigation that were proportionate and would lead to appropriate remedies for patients and service users. The work undertaken in advance of the new scheme included a review of a pilot project in Wales entitled *Speedy Resolution*, for dealing with uncomplicated claims against the NHS, valued between £5,000 and £15,000 which had been in existence since 2005. That scheme had been introduced in response[17] to a report by the Auditor General for Wales[18] which had pinpointed administrative problems within the existing system, and fears for the future of the NHS in the light of financial projections based on the rising number of clinical negligence claims.

The *Speedy Resolution Scheme* shared many of the objectives of the scheme proposed under the NHS Redress Measure, as it had been designed to provide a quick, proportionate and fair means of resolving low value claims in Wales for clinical negligence, and it also aimed at dealing with concerns about the rising costs of defending claims, about the time taken to settle and the need to provide adequate explanations to patients who suffered harm. The *Speedy Resolution Scheme* also encouraged NHS bodies to provide explanations to patients who had expressed concerns about their care, and apologies where appropriate, advising the use of action plans as a means of learning from mistakes and reducing the number of future claims.

An evaluation of this scheme by stakeholders concluded that it had proved beneficial in some respects to both claimants and defendants.[19] The scheme was considered, on balance, to have provided a realistic alternative to litigation, offering certain benefits, particularly in reducing costs and in establishing a structured framework for dispute resolution and dealing with claims in a timely fashion. The view was that:

> An obvious benefit provided by the Scheme is that in those claims where compensation is paid to a claimant the relationship between the award and costs is more proportionate when compared to non-Scheme claims. To this extent the Scheme is meeting with one of its objectives: of providing a proportionate means of resolving low value straightforward clinical negligence claims against the NHS in Wales.

The researchers concluded that the scheme was 'meeting its objective of providing a quick, proportionate and fair resolution of straightforward low value clinical negligence claims' was generally fit for purpose, and should continue to apply in Wales. However, the evidence on time-scales indicated a problem in connection with procedural delay in respect of the admission stage. Delay at this point would ultimately contradict the notion of 'speedy resolution', and the delays in obtaining medical reports gave still greater cause for concern, prejudicing the overall objective of meeting the 61-week overall timescale.

---

17 National Auditor Office, *Clinical Negligence in the NHS in Wales*, February 2001.

18 *Clinical Negligence in the NHS in Wales*, note 17, above.

19 See *Evaluation of the Speedy Resolution Scheme*, 2008, available at http://www.wales.nhs.uk/sites3/Documents/420/WAG%20Speedy%20Resolution%20Scheme%20-%20July%202008.pdf (accessed 13 January 2015).

Despite these reservations, the Speedy Resolution Scheme paved the way for the introduction of *Putting Things Right*. Welsh Ministers obtained framework powers under the NHS Redress Act 2006 which enabled the enactment of the NHS Redress (Wales) Measure 2008, following a period of consultation to look specifically at the principles behind the measure over the summer of 2007. The measure was an important landmark in legal development for Wales, since it was the first such legislation of the Welsh Government to reach the statute book. The measure allowed Welsh Ministers to create subordinate legislation containing details of the processes for dealing with low value cases in which, after an initial investigation, it was determined that there may be negligence. The Regulations made under the measure and supporting guidance came into force on 1 April 2011.

The Structure of the Redress Scheme

Under the Welsh scheme, which is still entitled *Putting Things Right*, and under its accompanying Regulations, the arrangements are applicable to NHS organisations and GPs, in respect of the receiving, handling and investigation of 'concerns', but if there is any compensation to be paid where an investigation determines that there may be a qualifying liability in tort, they do not apply to GPs. The policy behind the proposed reforms acknowledged that the previous system was expensive, defensive, complex and riddled with inconsistencies. The evidence also suggested that the system had an adverse effect upon NHS staff morale and the confidence of patients and the public. Patients were often dissatisfied with the lack of explanations and apologies following an incident. The new scheme has a single point of entry, enabling one system to deal both with all concerns (including complaints), and claims in cases where compensation is estimated to be less than £25,000, and it has enabled the NHS in Wales to overhaul its complaints system and the management and investigation of concerns.

'Concerns' comprise complaints, incidents and claims, and under the scheme, all three of these have to be investigated by the 'responsible body' (a Local Health Board or hospital trust). This process is overseen by a 'responsible person' who must not be an executive of the Board, and it is administered by a suitably qualified manager of the Health Board. An 'incident' is defined as 'any unexpected or unintended incident which did lead to or could have led to harm for a patient'.[20] This broad definition includes 'near misses', but patients need only be informed where an initial investigation reveals that there has actually been moderate or severe harm. What constitutes moderate or severe harm is decided in accordance with guidance from the Welsh Government.[21]

Notification of concerns may be made by a wide range of individuals under the Regulations,[22] including anyone affected, or likely to be affected by the action, omission or decision of the body in question, a non-executive director of the organisation, a member of the staff or a partner in the organisation. There are time limits for notifying concerns, which are fixed at 12 months from the date of the incident or the date of knowledge of the person notifying the concern,[23] but concerns can be investigated outside that timeframe where certain criteria are met, and three years have not elapsed since the incident. The scheme replaces the Welsh NHS complaints procedure established in 2003, and co-exists for the time being alongside the Speedy Resolution Scheme (until that scheme reaches the end of its natural life, in cases worth between £5,000 and £15,000).

20 The National Health Service (Concerns, Complaints and Redress Arrangements) (Wales) Regulations 2011, No. 704 (W.108), s. 2.

21 2011 Regulations, s. 12(7).

22 2011 Regulations, reg. 12.

23 2011 Regulations, reg. 5:15.

A detailed account of the Regulations that set out the processes under the Redress Scheme is beyond the scope of this chapter, and a brief summary of the main points is set out below, but of particular interest is the system of grading of concerns according to severity, and the setting of the parameters of the investigation to be carried out by the NHS with the involvement of the person who notified the concern, so keeping the patient at the centre of the process, in line with more general recent NHS policy requirements. Redress may be an apology, an explanation, financial compensation, remedial care and/or treatment, or any combination of these.

Qualifying Liability

If the responsible body is notified about a concern that includes an allegation that some form of injury or harm has, or may have been, caused, the investigator must consider whether a 'qualifying liability' may exist, and a duty will arise in this respect to consider financial or other redress, as long as the estimated compensation does not exceed £25,000.[24] In effect, since this approach retains the need to prove clinical negligence on the basis of the traditional formula, and in order to achieve appropriate outcomes, a good understanding of the law of negligence is required on the part of employees of Health Boards in operating the scheme. All the elements need to be understood – duty of care, breach of duty, factual causation, remoteness of damage and quantum.

The arrangements for redress are set out in Part Six of the Regulations, which covers general damages, special damages, sums due, if any, to the Compensation Recovery Unit, and the cost of any treatment that may be necessary. This aspect of the Regulations has proved challenging, because relatively inexperienced NHS staff have been required to make an assessment as to whether there is a qualifying liability, on the basis of the *Bolam* test,[25] as modified by the case of *Bolitho v. City and Hackney Health Authority*,[26] decided 40 years later, and to consider the question of quantum and issues surrounding the Compensation Recovery processes.

Clearly, a substantial training period was required to ensure that staff responsible for handling complaints acquired the necessary understanding of the law, and competence in forensic investigation and analysis to deal with these matters appropriately. Good communication skills are also required to inform patients, where necessary, about the implications of the qualifying liability in tort at the earliest opportunity, and to provide the explanations and apologies which are actively encouraged under the scheme.

Free Legal Advice for Patients

The Regulations relating to redress allow for legal advice to be made available to patients free of charge, as long as it is provided from firms of solicitors who have a solicitor who is a recognised member of the Law Society or one of the Action against Medical Accidents (AvMA) Clinical Negligence Panels. For some time, solicitors have provided advice and support to patients bringing

24 Reg. 44 sets the limit for the financial element of redress at £25,000. This is for special and general damages. Reg. 44(2) provides that if, on investigation, it transpires that quantum exceeds £25,000, redress, in accordance with the Regulations, must not be offered. The regulation provides that the compensation awarded will be assessed on the common law basis. The Welsh Ministers also have the power to issue a compensation tariff.

25 *Bolam v. Friern Hospital Management Committee* [1957] 1 WLR 583, which established that a doctor who acts in accordance with a responsible body of medical opinion is not negligent.

26 [1997] 3 WLR 1151.

complaints about NHS services in England and Wales under the NHS complaints procedure, partly because of the requirement that if 'Before The Event' (BTE) Insurance and public funding is to be obtained for claims, patients should first pursue the complaints procedure. All new concerns and complaints against the NHS in Wales, whatever their value, are subject to the Regulations, and if, in the event, damages fall within the parameters of redress, the patient is likely to take the route available to them under the scheme. This development provides a welcome advantage to patients, but can be worrying for legal advisors who may not always be able to recoup their costs. The NHS organisation concerned must also ensure that if medical experts need to be instructed, they are instructed jointly by the Welsh NHS organisation and the person who notified the concern. There are special arrangements in place for dealing with redress where there are also English NHS organisations involved.

Communicating with Patients

Regulation 26 makes it clear that once it becomes apparent that there is or may be a qualifying liability, the body concerned must produce an interim report summarising the nature and substance of the matter or matters notified in the concern and describing the investigation that has been undertaken so far, explaining why there may be a qualifying liability. This is helpful from the complainant's perspective as a copy of any relevant medical records must be provided together with an explanation about the availability of access to legal advice and about the availability of advocacy and support services.

The procedure to be followed to determine whether or not a qualifying liability exists must be explained, as must the procedure for making an offer of redress if a qualifying liability is found to exist. A copy of the investigation report must be made available to the person seeking redress, and details must be provided about the right to notify the concern to the Public Services Ombudsman for Wales. Perhaps more significantly, the person seeking redress must be afforded the opportunity to discuss the contents of the interim report with the 'responsible person' or a person acting on his or her behalf. Under normal circumstances, this stage must be completed within a strict time scale.

Clearly, people expressing concerns are at a distinct advantage under this new system. They are likely to be provided expeditiously with the information they need about potential legal liability, and are informed that they are entitled to legal advice free of charge. Thus 'concerns' must be followed up expeditiously by NHS organisations, and what might previously have been treated purely as a complaint may now result in the payment of compensation in some circumstances.

A New Culture of Openness

The Welsh Government was keen to establish what it described in the context of dealing with concerns about treatment and care, as emphasising that staff at all levels should be encouraged to apologise when necessary for adverse outcomes and should offer explanations about what had occurred.[27]

---

27 NHS Wales, *Interim Guidance on the Handling of Concerns in the NHS Wales Structure*, September 2009, p. 5, available at http://www.wales.nhs.uk/sites3/documents/932/INTERIM%20GUIDANCE%20PDF%20VERSION.pdf (accessed 27 January 2015).

As has been articulated in so many NHS policy documents published in the UK, NHS organisations in Wales were urged to work to establish a culture which is patient and user focused, as opposed to process driven. Ironically, many of the recommendations made in the Francis Report reiterate what is contained in the explanatory notes to the NHS (Wales) Measure, prompting a culture of openness and timely and efficient investigation of concerns, with the provision of support for staff and a means by which lessons can be learned from mistakes. Such rhetoric can be found in a wide range of NHS policies issued since the late twentieth century. These include the report of the first major review of the NHS Complaints system entitled *Being Heard*,[28] the Report of the Bristol Inquiry[29] and *Making Amends*.[30]

In implementing the new process, while no specific 'duty' of candour was introduced, the Welsh government was anxious to reassure NHS employees, emphasising that staff can be confident that 'investigations will be fair and impartial and that [staff] will be supported throughout the process'. To balance this, an investigation was conducted into the level of support to be made available to people wishing to raise concerns, with the intention of building up on the National Patient Safety Agency's 'Being Open' policy which had already been adopted across the NHS in Wales, and was being re-launched by the NPSA in the autumn of 2009.[31]

The Redress Position in England

In England, the NHS Redress Act implemented few of the recommendations made in *Making Amends*. Some years ago, Lord Darzi of Denham, in response to a question in the House of Lords[32] about the implementation of the Act, emphasised that significant work around complaints reform would be implemented in April 2009.[33] He said that this would lay the general foundations of redress, in its wider sense, and explained:

> The NHS Redress Act 2006 is a piece of framework legislation that will need to be enacted through secondary legislation. The department has continually believed that putting in place the appropriate secondary legislation for this piece of work will require considerable stakeholder involvement to discuss the detail around the working of any scheme.

He continued:

---

28 Department of Health, *Being Heard: Report of the Review Committee on NHS Complaints Procedures*, D106/BH/1.5m HSSH J07 3274, July 1994.

29 Department of Health, *Report of the Public Inquiry into Children's Heart Surgery at the Bristol Royal Infirmary 1984–1995: Learning from Bristol*, 2001.

30 Department of Health, *Making Amends: A Consultation Paper Setting Out Proposals for Reforming the Approach to Clinical Negligence in the NHS*, 2003.

31 The National Patient Safety Agency (NPSA) developed a policy on openness and honesty following patient safety incidents involving patients, their families and/or carers receiving an apology and an explanation. The policy encouraged open, honest communication as soon as possible after a patient safety incident, and recommended that all NHS Trusts should have developed a policy adapted to local requirements by June 2006. It did not provide the opportunity for financial redress.

32 In response to a question by Lord Gregson, Hansard 18 March 2009: Column WA49.

33 Note 32, above.

> The department considers it is currently more important to embed the general principles of wider redress across the National Health Service – those of apologies and explanations, a spirit of openness, a culture of learning from mistakes and robust investigation – rather than focusing on financial redress only for those cases which are of low monetary value which satisfy set principles in tort law; and where financial compensation would be appropriate.

He avoided providing any more detail, simply using the familiar rhetoric about 'putting the patient or service user at the heart of any complaints process' and making the commitment that only after the principles in the new complaints scheme are embedded across health and social care organisations, could the details of redress in relation to clinical negligence be considered further.

The NHS in England has not made any regulations to date to introduce the redress scheme, a position that has been severely criticised. In its Patient Safety report the Health Select Committee declared that it was 'appalled' by the lack of progress and apparent failure of the government to make any plans to introduce the required regulations.[34] It went so far as to recommend that the government should adopt a more radical approach by following the example of New Zealand in abandoning clinical negligence litigation to achieve more openness.[35]

Evaluating *Putting Things Right*

Although it is still too early to evaluate in depth the operation of the new scheme in Wales, it is possible to make some initial observations, based on minutes of Local Health Board meetings and general data about claims and complaints in their areas. To place the reform in context, it should be noted that the changes introduced by *Putting Things Right* needed to be implemented during a period of continuing adjustment by the Health Boards in Wales to a new structural framework for the administration of healthcare.

From the patients' perspective, the unified system for reporting incidents, complaints and claims as concerns should alleviate the stress involved in expressing their dissatisfaction, and should also mean that patients receive an explanation and apology at a relatively early stage, together with an action plan aimed at avoiding similar mistakes in future.[36] The complexities of the tort system can be avoided in low value claims, so that patients who are distressed or anxious do not have to face the additional anxiety of the legal process. However, the use of the traditional conceptual framework for determining the issue of a qualifying liability could operate to the disadvantage of patients who seek monetary redress. It is impossible to know whether patients who approach a solicitor in the first instance are immediately informed about the *Putting Things Right* process.

From the clinician's point of view, the retention of the *Bolam/Bolitho* test as the basis for determining whether there is a qualifying liability could be seen as an advantage, since that approach continues to afford a relatively solid defence to clinical negligence liability. That being the case, there is a disincentive to openness in respect of errors, and an argument arises that the use of the new scheme could raise issues about a possible breach of Art. 6 of the European Convention on Human Rights which guarantees that in the determination of his civil rights and obligations '... everyone is entitled to a fair and public hearing within a reasonable time by an independent and impartial tribunal

---

34 House of Commons, Health Select Committee, *Patient Safety*, Volume 1, 2009, para. 97.

35 *Patient Safety*, note 34, above, paras 96 and 98.

36 See Lloyd-Bostock, S. and Mulcahy, L., 'The Social Psychology of Making and Responding to Hospital Complaints: An Account Model of Complaint Processes' (1994) 16 *Law and Policy*, 123–47.

established by law'. The continued focus on the performance of the clinician, as opposed to the system as a whole, threatens the efforts of the Welsh Government to encourage a culture of openness.

Management of the new processes required a change of culture to ensure that there was transparency of approach, and NHS Employers signed up around the same time, to the Speaking Up Charter[37] launched on 15 October 2012, setting out commitments to fostering a culture of openness and transparency and to enable 'whistle blowers' as well as patients to raise concerns over safely without fear of discrimination. Yet another initiative based on initial findings of the *Inquiry into Events in Mid-Staffordshire NHS Trust*, this policy was promoted because staff needed to feel supported to raise concerns safely and confidently in the knowledge that 'taking action quickly and comprehensively has to be a top priority'.

Separately, under the 1000 Lives Programme, an encouraging development in Wales has been the regular and routine use of 'Patients' Stories' as training and awareness tools for staff and Health Board members, which feed into the processes under the new system for redress. These presentations are made by a variety of staff members, or by patients and their supporters, and a culture of learning without blaming can be observed, as a result of which it would appear that there is greater willingness on the part of clinicians to acknowledge mistakes.[38]

Another bonus for Health Boards in Wales has been the extensive training undertaken to ensure that staff who would be operating the scheme had the necessary skill and knowledge to deal appropriately with the issues that would arise. Despite this, however, it has been noted that there are many instances of referrals by staff to the lawyers employed by Legal and Risk Services for advice and support in their decision-making.[39] An increase of up to 60 per cent in the number of complaints about healthcare throughout Wales was reported soon after the scheme was introduced, and many were accompanied by solicitors' letters and requests for redress. Reporting of concerns and complaints was initiated by patients and their relatives in almost equal numbers,[40] but the Community Health Councils also played an important part in the process.

Anecdotal evidence suggests that the duty on Health Boards to offer compensation when it is determined that a qualifying liability exists, has already resulted in a rise in compensation payments to claimants. In one health board, an overspend on Patient Care and Safety was identified for the first quarter of 2013 as being wholly attributable to increased costs for clinical negligence and personal injury claims. However, there is evidence that costs have been substantially reduced in respect of lower value clinical negligence claims, a factor which might balance out the rise in compensation payments to some extent.

Similar trends are reported throughout Wales. To take the figures reported in just one Local Health Board, Cwm Taf, which is responsible for the delivery of services in the South Wales Valleys, in the two years since the new system was established a number of developments were reported. In 2012, in addition to higher value claims, the Health Board identified 36 cases where there had been a breach of duty of care which may have resulted in harm up to the value of £25,000, and at that stage, although responses had been provided, consideration of redress was still on-going. The Health Board did conclude six cases during the year and the costs involved in these redress cases were claimant's costs of £1,907, defence costs of £3,773 and compensation of £16,622.[41]

---

37 'NHS Employers', 24 April 2013, policy launched on 15 October 2012.

38 NHS Wales, *1000 Lives Campaign, Guidance on the Use of Patients' Stories*.

39 Personal Communication to author from Legal and Risk Services.

40 The Cwm Taf Local Health Board Papers September 2013 Concerns report indicates that 39 per cent of complaints were made by patients and an equal number by relatives.

41 Concerns Annual Report 2013.

There was a reduction in legal costs under the scheme. In the second year of the operation of the redress system, the same Health Board identified 21 lower value cases where there had been a breach of duty of care which may have resulted in harm, some of which had originated in the previous year. The Health Board settled nine cases that were opened during 2012/13 and a further 14 cases from the previous year. The costs of redress cases were as follows:

Cases opened in:	**Defence costs**	**Claimants' costs**	**Damages**
2011/12	£2,300	£26,302	£44,850
2012/13	£2,340	£3,840	£25,278

This picture is encouraging, as in previous years, the legal costs involved in defending low value claims was disproportionately high in comparison with the amount paid by way of compensation. The McLean Report noted a similar situation:[42]

> [T]he cost to NHS Health Boards in adverse fees, CLO chargeable costs, and outlays has risen quite significantly as have the sums paid out in adverse costs. Indeed the latter two items taken together are on average higher than the award .... In recent years costs have been much greater than the awards made for these low value awards.

An obvious major criticism of the system in Wales lies in the fact that the organisation responsible for causing harm to the patient is also responsible for determining whether a concern gives rise, or might give rise, to a qualifying liability.[43] However, given the depth and scale of monitoring by clinical governance committees, Health Boards, community health councils, coroners, the Public Service Ombudsman for Wales, the Wales Audit Office and Healthcare Inspectorate Wales, it would be difficult for an organisation to avoid an admission of liability where one would be justified.

Another consideration when the scheme was established was the arrangement for fees for legal advice to be capped according to guidance by the Welsh Assembly Government,[44] which follows recommendations made by a joint working group comprising representatives of legal firms dealing with clinical negligence and from the Welsh Health Legal Service and of Local Health Boards.[45] While this guidance and the fact that a formal tort claim remains open to patients should ensure that expert advice is of sufficiently high quality, there is a concern that not all expertly qualified solicitors in this field are prepared to work for the fees set in the guidance.[46]

42 McLean Report, para. 2.23.

43 Farrell, A. and Devaney, S., 'Making Amends or Making Things Worse? Clinical Negligence Reform and Patient Redress in England' (2007) 27(4) *Legal Studies*, 630–48.

44 Welsh Assembly Government, *Putting Things Right: Guidance on Dealing with Concerns from the 1st April 2011*, 2nd Version, 2012. Available at: http://www.cwmtafuhb.wales.nhs.uk/opendoc/189754&88F3BFFD-C37D-E941-DE35A87211BBFED4 (accessed 13 January 2015). Updates and developments as of late 2014 are available here: http://www.wales.nhs.uk/sites3/home.cfm?orgid=932 (accessed 13 January 2015).

45 Welsh Assembly Government, Legal Advice Working Group on 'Putting Things Right', Final Report, 2008.

46 Ferguson, A. and Braithwaite, E., 'Putting Things Right in Wales' (2012) 18 *Clinical Risk*, 6–8. Moreover, it has been estimated that £119,000 was spent in 2012–13 on expert medical advice to support health boards in Wales in administering the scheme.

A workshop held by the Welsh Government in December 2012 provided some initial feedback on the operation of *Putting Things Right*, based on information provided by the Welsh Risk Pool, the Public Services Ombudsman for Wales, Community Health Councils and Health Boards. Among the problems identified at that point were inconsistencies in the decisions across Wales about whether cases fell within the 'qualifying liability' criteria, problems with assessing quantum, delays in responding to concerns, lack of engagement with patients and/or their supporters when seeking an expert opinion, as well as the poor quality of some responses and staffing problems in some Health Boards. However, there was also evidence at the workshop of good practice across Wales. All Health Boards had set up Redress panels to decide what form of redress would be appropriate, and there was evidence of shared learning and the implementation of lessons to improve the quality and safety of patient care. Perhaps the greatest benefit afforded by the new system is that redress is now considered for all patients who suffer harm whether or not they initiate a claim, and NHS England is awaiting a fuller analysis before introducing a scheme of its own.

The More Radical Recommendations in the McLean Report

What characterises the Welsh scheme for redress is the retention of the basic law of negligence, and the need to establish that there would be liability in negligence before compensation can be offered. While the scheme allows for claimants to be paid compensation where that is considered appropriate by officers in a Health Board, the system in Wales which takes the onus away from the patient in claims of low value, nevertheless falls short of what was described in the McLean Report when the Regulations were still in draft form: 'The Welsh measure is an administrative alternative to litigation which does not require the claimant to prove fault or liability, and so could be considered to fall within a wide definition of no fault compensation'.[47]

In effect, *Putting Things Right* is indeed little more than an administrative solution, the operation of which is still to be evaluated in depth. It is not remotely as radical a solution as that proposed by McLean and her Committee after exploring the true 'no-fault' schemes in other jurisdictions which are applicable to all patients, focusing on those in New Zealand and Sweden. The research report and review[48] identified common elements of no-fault schemes, all of which require eligibility criteria to be satisfied and place caps or limits on the extent to which cover is provided, and result in lower compensation payments being made, but in a relatively timely fashion. The preference expressed in the McLean Report was for a modified version of the Swedish system, operational since 1975[49] as a voluntary scheme, and later as a statutory scheme in 1996, which is confined to medical injury and allows parallel recourse to the courts. The Report recommended that any financial compensation would be based on need rather than on a tariff, and any award made under the no-fault scheme should be deducted from an award made later as a result of litigation.

The Swedish scheme has been received positively by consumers, and surveys indicate that 50 per cent of responses are positive.[50] Those who are unhappy about the Swedish scheme complain that it does not operate as expeditiously as they would like (though the time-scales involved

47 McLean Report, para. 2.37.

48 McLean Report, para. 3.3.

49 As long ago as 1978 the *Pearson Report* in the UK recommended consideration of a no-fault system for compensating medical accidents, but such a system has been repeatedly rejected by the Government on the grounds of its likely cost. *Royal Commission on Civil Liability and Compensation for Personal Injury* 2 (Chairman: Lord Pearson), Report, Cmnd 7054 (3 vols), London, HMSO, 1978.

50 McLean Report, para. 3.29.

are very much shorter than those encountered in the UK litigation systems), and that there is insufficient discussion with patients. Human rights issues were examined by the Committee and members were satisfied that all necessary criteria would be satisfied by the introduction of a no-fault compensation scheme of the type proposed.

Conclusion

As long ago as 2001, *Making Amends*[51] reviewed the origins, strengths and weaknesses of medical litigation, analysed the issues and concerns which arise from it, and suggested reform. In very familiar words, the aim of those proposals was stated as addressing the need to ensure that: 'The emphasis of the NHS is directed at preventing harm, reducing risks and enhancing safety; there is a better co-ordinated response to harm resulting from health care, including investigation, support, remedial treatment and care where needed and fair recompense'. Another of the aims was to produce a system of redress that is affordable and reasonably predictable in its operation, which would act as an incentive for healthcare organisations to improve quality of care and patient safety.

Many years later, after a long series of inquiries, investigations, policy documents and proposals, it is clear that there is no perfect solution to the problems that are inevitably inherent in any process based on the traditional negligence litigation formula. Although the processes and procedures embedded in *Putting Things Right* have yet to be evaluated in detail, it is at least an attempt to deal with some of the many criticisms that have been made of the clinical negligence system in the UK over many years. Nevertheless, if justice in its broadest sense is to be achieved for patients, coupled with an efficient system for dealing with concerns and learning lessons from mistakes, despite obvious resource problems, a more radical solution similar to that proposed by the McLean Report in Scotland is greatly to be preferred for Wales. Her model represents a move away from the more traditional individualistic approach to a more communitarian and distributed notion of justice.

51 Note 31, above.

Chapter 10
No-Fault Compensation for Medical Injury: Principles, Practice and Prospects for Reform

Anne-Maree Farrell*

Introduction

Professor Sheila McLean's interest in the issue of no-fault compensation schemes for medical injury, including the principles that should guide their establishment, is a longstanding one.[1] In addition to her wide-ranging expertise in matters of medical law and ethics, this made her an eminently suitable choice on the part of the Scottish Government to chair the No Fault Compensation Review Group (NFCRG).[2] The Group was established in 2009 to examine the potential benefits for patients in Scotland of a no-fault compensation scheme for injury resulting from medical treatment, and to consider whether it should sit alongside the existing medical negligence system.[3] The Report setting out the NFCRG's findings and recommendations was published in 2011 (McLean Report),[4] and a further consultation on the Report has now been completed.[5] At the time of writing, the Scottish Government has yet to respond to the consultation and announce whether it intends to implement the Report's recommendations.

---

* In the period 2009–2010, a group of academics then based at the University of Manchester (Professor Frank Stephen, Dr Sarah Devaney, Dr Angela Melville and myself) were retained to provide research support to the No Fault Compensation Review Group (NFCRG). I would like to acknowledge the work and support provided by my colleagues on the project, as well as the assistance provided by Sandra Falconer and colleagues at the Scottish Government Health and Social Care Directorate.

1 See for example, McLean, S.A.M., 'Accident Compensation Liability Without Fault: The New Zealand Experience' (1985) 7(1) *The Journal of Social Welfare Law*, 31–45; McLean, S.A.M., 'Can No-Fault Analysis Ease the Problems of Medical Injury Litigation?' in McLean, S.A.M. (ed.) *Compensation for Damage: An International Perspective*, Aldershot, Dartmouth, 1993, pp. 75–90; McLean, S.A.M. (ed.), *Law Reform and Medical Injury Litigation*, Aldershot, Dartmouth, 1995.

2 The Scottish Government had previously indicated its initial support for establishing a no-fault scheme for medical injury in the wake of the findings from a consultation on a Patients' Rights Bill in Scotland, see the Scottish Government Healthcare Policy and Strategy Directorate, *Patients' Rights: A Public Consultation on a Patients' Rights Bill for Users of the NHS in Scotland*, Edinburgh, 2008.

3 In doing so, it was required to take into account cost implications, consequences for healthcare staff, quality and safety of care, wider implications for the system of justice and personal injury liability, and evidence as to how no-fault compensation for medical injury operated in other countries, see: *No Fault Compensation Review Group, Report and Recommendations, Volume 1*, February 2011, available at: http://www.scotland.gov.uk/Topics/Health/Policy/No-Fault-Compensation/ReviewGroupVol1 (accessed 13 January 2015) (hereinafter referred to as the McLean Report).

4 Note 3, above.

5 *Consultation on Recommendations for No-Fault Compensation in Scotland for Injuries Resulting from Clinical Treatment*, available at: http://www.scotland.gov.uk/Publications/2012/08/4456 (accessed 13 January 2015).

Two important themes (among others) run through Professor McLean's published research on the topic, as well as the McLean Report itself: first, the importance of a principled approach to designing and implementing such schemes; and second, a critical appreciation of the fact that this is a complex and difficult area of civil justice reform. It sits alongside a number of government-sponsored reports across a range of countries on no-fault schemes, dating back to the late 1960s,[6] as well as a voluminous academic literature in the area.[7] The Report offers one of the most recent and cogent analyses of the social, political, economic and legal issues at stake in establishing no-fault schemes, albeit restricted to medical injury.[8] As such, it provides a useful and insightful springboard for exploring what principles should underpin the design and implementation of no-fault schemes for medical injury, as well as providing an opportunity to review critically key aspects of existing schemes with a view to assessing the prospects for reform in Scotland. Drawing on a restorative justice model, it is argued in this chapter that a principled approach to establishing a no-fault scheme for medical injury requires that a redress package is offered which is responsive to what patients say they want as a result of suffering harm through medical treatment. This should involve paying adequate financial compensation; providing appropriate apologies and explanations; and facilitating professional accountability and lesson-learning in order to enhance patient safety and improve healthcare outcomes. Where this is not possible within the no-fault scheme itself, then I would concur with the findings in the McLean Report that, at the very least, a more 'joined-up' approach needs to be developed, which links the scheme to independent complaints procedures and professional disciplinary bodies.[9] Ensuring that this redress package is provided offers the best chance of ensuring patient satisfaction with the scheme in the long term. Even if such reforms are implemented, the question remains as to whether aspiration will ever match reality. Based on a review of current schemes for medical injury in this chapter, it is suggested that the full implementation of the redress package recommended in the McLean Report is likely to remain elusive in practice.

---

6 In particular, there was a flurry of reports on the issue of no-fault compensation schemes for personal injury in a number of countries in the 1960s and 1970s. See, for example, New Zealand Royal Commission of Inquiry into Compensation for Personal Injury, *Compensation for Personal Injury in New Zealand: Report of the Royal Commission of Inquiry*, Wellington, Government Printer, 1967 (Woodhouse Report); Pearson, the Right Honourable Mr Justice, *Royal Commission on Civil Liability and Compensation for Personal Injury*, Cmnd 7054-1, London, HMSO, 1978 (Pearson Report); *Compensation and Rehabilitation in Australia: Report of the National Committee of Inquiry*, Canberra, AGPS, 1974 (Australian Woodhouse Report). More recently see, for example, the following report in relation to no-fault compensation schemes for medical injury: Chief Medical Officer (CMO), *Making Amends: A Consultation Paper Setting Out Proposals for Reforming the Approach to Clinical Negligence in the NHS*, London, Department of Health, 2003; and *Report of the Expert Group on Financial and Other Support*, March 2003, Chair: Lord Ross, Commissioned by Scottish Executive (Lord Ross's Report), available at: http://www.scotland.gov.uk/Resource/Doc/47034/0024918.pdf (accessed 13 January 2015).

7 For an overview of selected literature in relation to no-fault compensation schemes for medical injury, see Farrell, A.M., Devaney, S. and Dar, A., *No-Fault Compensation Schemes for Medical Injury: A Review*, No Fault Compensation Review Group, Report and Recommendations, Interim Report, February 2010, ch. 6, available at: http://www.scotland.gov.uk/Resource/0039/00394407.pdf (accessed 13 January 2015).

8 I acknowledge that different terminology is used to describe no-fault schemes that deal with harm caused through medical treatment. For the purposes of this chapter, I intend to make use of the term 'medical injury' when referring to harm suffered as a result of medical treatment (broadly construed), although I note that the recently closed consultation on the McLean Report refers to no-fault compensation for 'injuries resulting from clinical treatment', see note 5, above.

9 McLean Report, at pp. 53–4.

In order to examine these arguments, the chapter begins with a brief overview of the available empirical evidence about what patients want in terms of redress, before proceeding to consider what principles and goals should inform no-fault schemes for medical injury. Thereafter, key themes in the literature on no-fault schemes are examined by reference to the arguments made about what injured patients want in terms of redress. Examples are drawn predominantly from the no-fault scheme for personal injury in New Zealand, as well as the more restricted scheme for medical injury which operates in Sweden. The final section offers some concluding comments on the prospects for reform and establishment of a no-fault scheme for medical injury in Scotland.

What Patients Want: A Redress Package

The McLean Report emphasises the importance of offering a redress package as part of a no-fault scheme that is responsive to what patients have said they want when things go wrong as a result of medical treatment. In this regard, the Report was picking up on empirical data that had been gathered in the United Kingdom (UK) and elsewhere on the issue. In the early 1990s, a seminal piece of empirical research was published which examined what injured patients wanted in terms of redress. It found that patients who had suffered a medical injury wanted an explanation and an apology for what went wrong, financial compensation, and for their treating doctors to be held to account for what happened to them. They also wanted lessons to be learned and reforms implemented where necessary, so that what happened to them did not happen to other patients in the future.[10] In the early 2000s, proposals were put forward to establish a scheme to provide a redress package for injured patients, which included explanations, apologies, compensation and lesson-learning.[11] The UK government eventually agreed to establish a National Health Service (NHS) Redress Scheme to provide this package in relation to claims with an upper limit of £20,000.[12] To date, the Scheme has not been implemented in England, although Wales has now implemented its own scheme for claims up to a maximum of £25,000.[13]

---

10 See Vincent, C., Young, M. and Phillips, A., 'Why Do People Sue Doctors? A Study of Patients and Relatives Taking Legal Action' (1994) 343 *The Lancet*, 1609–13. The components of this redress package for injured patients has also been confirmed more recently as a result of empirical research undertaken in Australia, see Iedema, R. and Piper, D., 'Do Patients Want and Expect Compensation Following Harm?' (2013) 116 *Precedent*, 48–51, at p. 48. More specifically on the need for open disclosure following medical injury by healthcare professionals, see Iedema, R., Allen, S., Britton, K., et al., 'Patients' and Family Members' Views on How Clinicians Enact and How They Should Enact Open Disclosure: The "100 Patient Stories" Qualitative Study' (2011) 343 *British Medical Journal*, http://www.bmj.com/content/343/bmj.d4423 (accessed 13 January 2015).

11 CMO, *Making Amends*, note 6, above.

12 See NHS Redress Act 2006, c. 44. For an analysis of the Act and a critique of how the Scheme was likely to work in practice, see Farrell, A.M. and Devaney, S., 'Making Amends or Making Things Worse? Clinical Negligence Reform and Patient Redress in England' (2007) 27(4) *Legal Studies*, 630–48. Note that the National Health Service Litigation Authority (NHSLA) has proposed that a fixed costs pilot scheme be instituted for clinical negligence claims in England valued up to £25,000, see Hyde, J., 'Pilot Aims to Limit Clinical Negligence Solicitors' Fees', *Law Gazette*, 20 May 2013.

13 See the National Health Service (Concerns, Complaints and Redress Arrangements) (Wales) Regulations 2011, No. 704 (W.108); Ferguson, A.L. and Braithwaite, E., 'Putting Things Right in Wales' (2012) 18 *Clinical Risk*, 6–8; and Chapter 9 of this volume: Harpwood, V., 'Clinical Negligence and Poor Quality Care: Is Wales "Putting Things Right"?'.

As part of the NFCRG's deliberations, an empirical research study was also commissioned to enquire into the views of Scottish patients who had suffered a medical injury. The findings from the study identified patient grievances as involving 'an often complex and overlapping mix of concerns about communication breakdown, poor staff attitudes, inadequate general care and generally feeling disempowered'.[14] Many patients had indicated that they had initially sought to have their grievances dealt with via established complaint procedures. While gaining access to such procedures was generally not perceived as problematic, patients were often dissatisfied with the outcomes, citing insufficiency in explanations provided and the fact that there was little evidence that lessons had been learned from what had happened to them. Unable to obtain what they wanted from their treating doctors, hospitals or complaints procedures, injured patients sometimes then decided to pursue medical negligence claims.

The decision to pursue such claims was therefore usually the final step in an extended process for such patients. The study concluded that the establishment of a no-fault scheme for medical injury would not necessarily fully address the full gamut of patient grievances arising from a medical injury, if its main aim was simply to provide financial compensation. If the scheme was limited in this way, then it was likely to result in ongoing problems, such as a lack of patient satisfaction and trust in their doctors and in the healthcare more generally. It was also stressed that if such a scheme was to be successful, then it needed to address both clinical and non-clinical aspects of the medical treatment and its aftermath for injured patients.[15]

A Principled Approach to No-Fault Schemes for Medical Injury

Claims alleging negligence resulting in personal injury in tort and delict systems are predicated on the fact that claimants are able to establish that a person or body owed them a duty of care, that this duty was breached, and that the breach caused them to suffer damage. Where negligence is proved and therefore fault established, the goal is to restore claimants to the position they were in prior to suffering personal injuries, through an award or settlement of financial compensation. This is often justified on the grounds of corrective justice. Deterrence is also said to be a by-product of the finding of fault in the tort and delict systems, as those likely to be held liable make suitable adjustments to prevent the negligent event from happening again.[16]

This fault-based approach has been the subject of sustained critique by both academic and policy-makers alike. Although an in-depth examination of the voluminous literature and reports on the issue is outside the scope of this chapter, it is useful briefly to summarise some of the more influential arguments that have been raised as part of this critique, in order to place political and stakeholder support for no-fault schemes in context. First, it has been argued that the fault principle is unjust in separating out those entitled to compensation due to accidental injury and those who are not. Second, the compensation awarded does not bear an appropriate, if any, relationship to the degree of fault. Third, there is little evidence of deterrence or lesson-learning so as to prevent similar events occasioning personal injury occurring in the future. Fourth, such claims only provide

14 Stephen, F., Melville, A. and Krause, T., *A Study of Medical Negligence Claiming in Scotland*, Research Findings No. 113/2012, Government Social Research, Scotland, p. 1, available at: http://www.scotland.gov.uk/Resource/0039/00394437.pdf (accessed 13 January 2015).

15 Note 14, above.

16 For an overview and critique of the philosophies and principles underpinning tort law, see Owen, D.G. (ed.), *Philosophical Foundations of Tort Law*, Oxford, Oxford University Press, 1995; Postema, G.J. (ed.), *Philosophy and the Law of Torts*, Cambridge, Cambridge University Press, 2001.

for awards of financial compensation and fail to deal with other crucial non-financial aspects of redress, in particular the need for rehabilitation. Fifth and finally, the adversarial legal culture which structures the conduct of such claims in tort and delict systems exacerbates rather than resolves conflict between the parties. The worst excesses of such culture contribute to excessive delay, a failure to resolve claims in a timely manner, a lack of transparency, unwanted burdens being placed on courts' resources and high legal costs.[17]

In addition, the conduct of medical negligence claims have been singled out for giving rise to a number of problematic issues, including the significant disproportion between costs and awards of compensation especially in low value claims; excessive delay in resolving claims; the pursuit of claims without merit and the unwarranted defence of claims; a lower success rate than would be found in other personal injury claims; and the entrenched suspicion and lack of cooperation exhibited between parties involved in such claims.[18] The perceived deficiencies of the fault-based approach for dealing with personal injuries have led to repeated calls across a range of countries for 'no-fault' schemes to be established as an alternative form of redress for injured patients.[19]

For present purposes, let us assume political and stakeholder support for such reform in the case of medical injury: which principles should guide such reform? The McLean Report recommended that the following principles should apply: accessibility, fairness, appropriateness of compensation, timeliness of adjudication and cost effectiveness.[20] Facilitating access to justice is a key aspect of accessibility, as is ensuring that there is fair, independent and timely adjudication of claims made under such schemes. The goal of appropriate compensation should be to restore patients, as far as possible, to the position they were in prior to suffering the medical injury.[21] The McLean Report also recommended that there should be a focus on the need for non-financial support as part of a principled approach to such a scheme. Although the NFCRG's terms of reference were fairly circumscribed, the Group nevertheless emphasised that there were a number of other 'desirable' goals that should be taken into account in establishing such a scheme, including the importance of rehabilitation, improving complaints procedures, and facilitating a change in culture to bring about lesson-learning to improve healthcare outcomes.[22] As stated previously, this also aligns with what injured patients have said they want in terms of redress.

Indeed, the principles recommended by the NFCRG to underpin the establishment of a no-fault scheme for medical injury in Scotland have their historical legacy in those espoused in the seminal Woodhouse Report,[23] which led to the establishment of the New Zealand no-fault scheme in the

17 For an overview of the arguments on this issue, see Atiyah, P., *The Damages Lottery*, Oxford, Hart Publishing, 1997; Cane, P., *Atiyah's Accidents Compensation and the Law*, 8th edn, Cambridge, Cambridge University Press, 2013. See also Lunney, M. and Oliphant, K., *Tort Law: Text and Materials*, 5th edn, Oxford, Oxford University Press, 2013, at pp. 952–69.

18 See for example, The Right Honourable the Lord Woolf, Master of the Rolls, *Access to Justice: Final Report* 170, HMSO, 1996, ch. 15; CMO, *Making Amends*, note 6, above. For a critical examination of these issues, see Harpwood, V., *Medicine Malpractice and Misapprehensions*, London, Routledge-Cavendish, 2007.

19 For a recent call for reform, see Weisbrot, D. and Breen, K.J., 'A No-Fault Compensation System for Medical Injury Is Long Overdue' (2012) 197(5) *Medical Journal of Australia*, 296–8, cf. Rait, J.L., 'How Do We Best Compensate for Accidental Medical Injuries?' (2012) 197(5) *Medical Journal of Australia*, 299–300.

20 McLean Report, para. 5.2.

21 This is in line with the longstanding tort law principle regarding awards of financial compensation for personal injury, see *Lim v. Camden & Islington Area Health Authority* [1980] AC 174, at 187, per Lord Scarman.

22 McLean Report, at paras 5.5, 6.4, 6.8, 6.14, 6.23–4.

23 Note 6, above.

1970s. Two important principles underpinning the scheme were 'comprehensive entitlement' and 'community responsibility'. Comprehensive entitlement was conceptualised as including both financial and non-financial redress. There was a particular emphasis on the need for rehabilitation, given the perceived failure on the part of the tort system to address this issue effectively.[24] Although the concept of community responsibility was not well elaborated upon in the Woodhouse Report, the justification for the no-fault scheme clearly drew on distributive justice principles to underline the importance of collective social responsibility for citizens who had suffered accidental personal injury.[25] It is an approach that finds support in the McLean Report in its justification of a more restricted no-fault scheme for medical injury:

> [S]eeking compensation for medical injury presents special legal problems and on these grounds alone special consideration could be justified. In addition, we concluded that healthcare was a social responsibility; when something goes wrong it is not unreasonable to argue that society should pick up the bill to put it right in as much as this is possible.[26]

Such a justification recognises the complex and difficult issues faced in establishing liability in medical negligence claims, as well as the fact that healthcare is seen as a collective social responsibility in Scotland, underpinned by the NHS. Although those in favour of equality of coverage for all individuals who have suffered accidental personal injury have criticised more restrictive no-fault schemes, such as those limited to medical injury, the reality is that these restrictive schemes have now been operating in several countries for some time, covering personal injuries caused through employment related accidents, pharmaceuticals, and vaccinations respectively. In fact, New Zealand represents one of the few examples of an expansive approach to covering accidental personal injuries in a no-fault scheme. However, even the New Zealand scheme has been subject to criticism over its failure to ensure equality of coverage.[27] In the end, the search for a principled justification for more restrictive no-fault schemes must necessarily take account of political imperatives, national historical and social trajectories, and questions of affordability in practice.[28]

More broadly (and importantly), the findings and recommendations in the McLean Report reveal a principled commitment to providing redress to injured patients that is not just based on distributive justice grounds, but incorporates what I would suggest is a restorative justice approach. I have argued elsewhere that no-fault schemes underpinned by a commitment to this approach are likely to offer a more responsive approach to what injured patients want in terms of redress.[29] Although restorative justice has most often been applied in the criminal justice context, it potentially has much to offer in terms of providing a principled approach to guide no-fault schemes for medical injury. It emphasises the importance of accepting responsibility towards those who have suffered harm unjustly at the hands of another. This can take numerous forms,

---

24 Robinson, M.A., *Accident Compensation in Australia: No-Fault Schemes*, Sydney, Legal Books, 1987, at pp. 59–60.

25 McLean, S.A.M., 'Accident Compensation Liability Without Fault', note 1, above, at pp. 32–3; Robinson, note 24, above, at pp. 58–9.

26 McLean Report, at para. 4.2.

27 Fitzjohn, J. and Studdert, D., 'A Compensation Perspective on Error Prevention: Is the ACC Medical Misadventure Scheme Compensating the Right Sort of Injury?' (2001) 114 *New Zealand Medical Journal*, 432–4.

28 Davis, P.B., Lay-Yee, R., Briant, R. and Scott, A., 'Modeling Eligibility under National Systems of Compensation for Treatment Injury' (2006) 31(2) *Journal of Health Politics, Policy and Law*, 295–319.

29 Farrell and Devaney, note 12, above, at p. 632.

including offering apologies and explanations, repairing harm that has been caused or accepting accountability through mechanisms of public and private governance. Where the state is involved, it should be seen as having a particular responsibility for ensuring the accountability of such processes, including facilitating access to appropriate mechanisms that uphold the rule of law. This may include the provision of legal advice and representation, as well as ensuring that rights and due process are protected.[30]

Reviewing No-Fault Schemes for Medical Injury

As part of its work, the NFCRG undertook to examine a number of existing no-fault schemes for medical injury. My colleagues and I prepared a literature review of such schemes for the Group, covering schemes operating in New Zealand, the Nordic countries (Sweden, Norway, Denmark and Finland) and the limited schemes that had been established in Florida and Virginia for birth-related neurological injury.[31] As part of the review, background interviews were conducted with a number of key stakeholders in both New Zealand and Sweden. While such a review could not hope to capture fully how the schemes worked in practice,[32] we were able to analyse a significant amount of both normative and empirical published research in the area. This enabled us to examine the advantages and disadvantages of such schemes, and to identify a number of key themes for consideration by the Group.[33] In the following section, I critically examine some of these key themes, evaluating them by reference to whether they are likely to contribute to a responsive redress package for patients who have suffered a medical injury.

Access to Justice

Access to justice is a widely used term within legal and other literature, however, it is subject to differing interpretations depending on pre-existing assumptions and perspectives, as well as context.[34] For present purposes, access to justice is defined as incorporating both procedural and substantive justice, as well as promoting 'equality of arms' in relation to accessing no-fault schemes for medical injury.[35] The question of whether greater access to justice is achieved through the establishment of no-fault schemes needs to take account of issues relating both to the quality and quantity (that is, financial compensation) of justice provided to injured patients. It could be argued that both may differ depending on the overarching principles which underpin the scheme,

---

30 See Braithwaite, J., *Restorative Justice and Responsive Regulation*, Oxford, Oxford University Press, 2002; Braithwaite, J., 'Accountability and Responsibility through Restorative Justice' in Dowdle, M. (ed.) *Public Accountability: Designs Dilemmas and Experiences*, Cambridge, Cambridge University Press, 2006, pp. 33–51.

31 Farrell, A.M., Devaney, S. and Dar, A., *No-Fault Compensation Schemes for Medical Injury: A Review*, No Fault Compensation Review Group, Report and Recommendations, Volume II, February 2010, available at: http://www.scotland.gov.uk/Topics/Health/Policy/No-Fault-Compensation/ReviewGroupVol1 (accessed 13 January 2015).

32 McLean Report, para. 3.5.

33 Farrell, Devaney and Dar, note 7, above, para. 1.16.

34 Bottomley, S. and Bronnitt, S., *Law in Context*, 4th edn, Sydney, Federation Press, 2012, ch. 5.

35 Rhode, D.L., *Access to Justice*, New York, Oxford University Press, 2004, at pp. 5–6; Sommerlad, H., 'Reflections on the Reconfiguration of Access to Justice' (2008) 15(3) *International Journal of the Legal Profession*, 179–93, at p. 190.

which in turn may structure access, eligibility criteria, level and type of compensation awarded, provision of medico-legal advice, and adjudication processes. Even where there is political support for no-fault schemes, the question of affordability in the long term may prove to be the ultimate arbiter in determining access to justice for injured patients, as well as whether a fully responsive redress package is made available.

Easy, Quick and Low Cost Access

Differing viewpoints have been offered within the relevant literature as to whether no-fault schemes for medical injury encourage greater access to justice. It has been suggested that such schemes are likely to provide a clearer 'road map' in terms of how to go about making a claim, with quicker times to resolution than would be seen in claims made under the tort and delict systems. Empirical evidence available from both the New Zealand and the Swedish schemes reveals the relative ease with which patients can lodge claims at minimal or no cost, which in the case of the former scheme includes assistance being provided by 'registered health professionals'.[36] Many claims relate to relatively minor injuries, or are otherwise low value claims. The claims are processed by claims handlers and this assists in keeping costs low at this initial stage. In Sweden, for example, 99.9 per cent of claims for medical injury are resolved through this administrative process, usually involving one claims handler and a medical qualified doctor who provides expert advice based on a review of the claimant's medical records.[37] Where the claims involve relatively minor injuries, then determination regarding coverage is usually made within a short period of time. However, claims based on medical injuries are often more complex, particularly in terms of establishing causation, which is still required to be satisfied under no-fault schemes. This means that determining coverage may take longer, lasting between six and nine months in the case of the Swedish and New Zealand schemes, respectively.[38]

The Phenomenon of Under-claiming

Notwithstanding claims that no-fault schemes do provide greater access to justice than is the case under tort and delict systems, it is clear that the phenomenon of under-claiming also exists under such schemes. The available empirical evidence from both the New Zealand and Swedish schemes is that there is significant under-claiming by those who would potentially be eligible for cover under the schemes. In Sweden, it has been estimated that only 10 per cent of those eligible to make a claim under the no-fault scheme in fact do so.[39] With respect to the New Zealand scheme, injured patients from ethnic minorities, those who are socio-economically disadvantaged and the elderly are the groups that are least likely to make a claim, despite potential eligibility.[40] In such circumstances, claims that broader access to justice will be achieved for injured patients under no-

36 Farrell, Devaney and Dar, note 7, above, at para. 2.24 and pp. 41–2.

37 Kachalia, A., Mello, M.M., Brennan, T.A. and Studdert, D.M., 'Beyond Negligence: Avoidability and Medical Injury Compensation' (2008) 66(2) *Social Science and Medicine*, 387–402; McLean Report, at para. 3.32.

38 Farrell, Devaney and Dar, note 7, above, at para. 2.26; McLean Report, at para. 3.29.

39 See Johansson, H., 'The Swedish System for Compensation of Patient Injuries' (2010) 115(2) *Uppsala Journal of Medical Sciences*, 88–90; McLean Report, at para. 3.28.

40 Bismark, M.M., Brennan, T.A., Davis, P.B. and Studdert, M., 'Claiming Behaviour in a No-Fault System of Medical Injury: A Descriptive Analysis of Claimants and Non-Claimants' (2006) 185(4) *Medical Journal of Australia*, 203–7; Bismark, M.M., Brennan, T.A., Paterson, R.J., et al., 'Relationship between

fault schemes cannot be taken at face value. As a result, how best to ensure that all patients who may be eligible for coverage have the requisite capacity, knowledge and support to access their potential entitlements under such schemes, requires more detailed consideration.

Eligibility

Designing eligibility criteria is crucial in terms of determining the nature and scope of access (to justice) to no-fault schemes for medical injury. In tort and delict systems, there is a need to establish both substandard care and causation in order to be 'eligible' for compensation in medical negligence claims. Given the difficulties in establishing liability in such claims, there is scope when designing no-fault schemes to offer an expansive approach to determining eligibility which sets a lower or alternative threshold for injured patients seeking redress, and this evidences a commitment in practice to providing greater access to justice. Approaches to eligibility criteria differ as between no-fault schemes, however, with some offering a more expansive approach and others less so. In the case of the NHS Redress Scheme in Wales, eligibility is determined by reference to a 'qualifying liability in tort', meaning that the same criteria for establishing liability in tort claims (that is, substandard care) must also be satisfied before injured patients may be entitled to coverage under the scheme.[41]

In the Swedish scheme, the concept of 'avoidability' is used instead of negligence to determine eligibility. It is an alternative standard which sits at a mid-point between negligence and strict liability. Patients are eligible if they have experienced injuries that could have been avoided under optimal circumstances. What this means is that the injuries would have not occurred in the hands of the best healthcare professional (HCP) or health system, which is known as the 'experienced specialist' rule. The Swedish scheme sets the higher standard of 'excellent care', as opposed to 'acceptable care', which is used in the other Nordic schemes.[42] Eligibility is also determined by reference to specific categories of injuries, with treatment and diagnostic injuries accounting for at least 85 per cent of all claims.[43] In contrast, the New Zealand scheme has had differing approaches to determining eligibility over time with respect to medical injuries. For many years, the concept of 'medical misadventure' was used, which was interpreted restrictively and imported a fault-based element in order to determine eligibility. In 2005, reforms were implemented to replace this criterion with 'treatment injury', which removed any fault-based element. The term 'treatment' has been interpreted broadly, and it is intended to cover injuries suffered in the treatment process,

---

Complaints and Quality of Care in New Zealand: A Descriptive Analysis of Complaints and Non-Complaints Following Adverse Events' (2006) 15 *Quality and Safety in Health Care*, 17–22.

41 See *National Health Service (Concerns, Complaints and Redress Arrangements) (Wales) Regulations 2011*, Part 6. For a critique of this restricted approach to determining eligibility and its impact on access to justice under the (yet to be implemented) NHS Redress Scheme in England, see Farrell and Devaney, note 12, above, at p. 634.

42 Espersson, C., *The Patient Injury Act: A Comment*, 2000, available at: http://www.patientforsakring.se/resurser/dokument/engelska_artiklar/Comments_on_the_Patient_Injury_Act.pdf (accessed 13 January 2015); Kachalia et al., note 37, above.

43 Hellbacher, U., Espersson, C. and Johansson, H., *Patient Injury Compensation for Healthcare-Related Injuries in Sweden*, Stockholm, Visby, 2007, available at: http://www.patientforsakring.se/resurser/dokument/engelska_artiklar/Patient_Injury_Compensation_for_Helthcare-Related_Injuries.pdf (accessed 13 January 2015); Farrell, Devaney and Dar, note 7, above, at para. 3.17.

resulting from both preventable and unpreventable adverse events.[44] Having reviewed eligibility criteria in these existing no-fault schemes, the McLean Report recommended an expansive approach, suggesting that eligibility should simply be based on a clear description of what injuries are ineligible. It was further suggested that all medical treatment injuries which occur in Scotland should be covered, as well as ensuring that it extended to injuries incurred as a result of treatment provided by all registered HCPs in Scotland, and not just those employed by the NHS.[45] The Scottish Government's response to these recommendations on eligibility is awaited with interest.

Causation

The need to establish causation in relation to medical negligence claims in tort and delict systems is often the most difficult aspect of making such claims. In such systems, there is a requirement that a claimant establish, on the balance of probabilities (that is, slightly more than 50 per cent), that the alleged negligence in question caused the injury.[46] Pre-existing medical conditions, patients presenting with complex or a range of different medical conditions, or even simply the loss of chance of a better outcome,[47] are just some of the issues that have made establishing causation in medical negligence claims so difficult.[48] Favourable expert evidence to establish (substandard care and) causation is vital to the success of such claims, as is advice from those with specialist legal expertise in the relevant field.[49]

Establishing that the medical treatment in question (broadly construed) 'caused' the patient's injury remains an additional and crucial eligibility criterion in existing no-fault schemes for medical injury, and this will also be the case in the event that a Scottish scheme is established. In the circumstances, the McLean Report noted the importance of patients being able to obtain relevant specialist advice in relation to accessing such a scheme, although further detail on the nature and scope of funding arrangements for this advice is needed.[50] Whether a Scottish government will be prepared to fund the provision of expert medico-legal advice as part of a no-fault scheme for medical injury is open to question, particularly where other schemes either do not provide such funding, or are only prepared to do so at relatively low, fixed cost rates.[51] Whatever approach is

44 Manning, J., 'Treatment Injury and Medical Misadventure' in Skegg, P.D.G. and Paterson, R. (eds) *Medical Law in New Zealand*, Wellington, Thomson Brookers, 2006, at pp. 698–9; Farrell, Devaney and Dar, note 7, above, at paras 2.10–17.

45 McLean Report, at para. 7.

46 For an overview of the particular difficulties experienced in establishing causation in tort law, see Goldberg, R. (ed.), *Perspectives on Causation*, Oxford, Hart Publishing, 2011.

47 On causation in medical negligence claims involving the loss of a chance, see *Hotson v. East Berkshire Area Health Authority* [1987] AC 750; *Gregg v. Scott* [2005] 2 AC 176; in Australia, see *Tabet v. Gett* [2010] HCA 12.

48 Goldberg, R., 'Medical Malpractice and Compensation in the UK' (2012) 87 *Chicago-Kent Law Review*, 131–61, at pp. 150–56.

49 Farrell and Devaney, note 12, above, at p. 636.

50 McLean Report, p. 6.

51 This was the approach suggested in the case of the NHS Redress Scheme in England: see Farrell and Devaney, note 12, above, at p. 635. On the broader issues faced in funding and costs associated with medical negligence claims, see Jackson, the Honourable Lord R., *Review of Civil Litigation Costs: Final Report*, London, The Stationery Office, 2010, ch. 23 (Jackson Report). Subsequently, the UK government announced that it would remove public funding for medical negligence claims in England and Wales, except in limited circumstances. The changes were implemented via the Legal Aid, Sentencing and Punishment of Offenders Act 2012, c.10 (henceforth: LASPO) and came into effect on 1 April 2013. In Scotland, there is limited legal

taken, access to independent medico-legal advice for injured patients to assist in dealing with eligibility criteria, particularly on causation and assessing whether offers of financial compensation are appropriate, should be seen as an important aspect of ensuring the quality of (access to) justice in no-fault schemes for medical injury.

Other Eligibility Criteria

It is important to keep in mind that there may also be other criteria that patients must meet to be eligible for coverage under no-fault schemes. Such criteria may include covering only certain types of medical injury; needing to reach a certain threshold level of injury or percentage of disability before coverage is reached; or imposing specified time limits for making claims under the scheme. Meeting these additional criteria, along with the difficulties in establishing causation, operate in practice to screen out a significant number of claims for medical injury under no-fault schemes. This is evidenced by the fact that only 50 per cent of claims on average are accepted under the Swedish scheme, and 60 per cent on average in the New Zealand scheme under what are considered to be very broad eligibility criteria.[52] In short, there is a need to be cautious about claims that no-fault schemes for medical injury are likely to provide greater and easier access to justice for patients than would pursuing claims under tort and delict systems. Instead, a more complex picture presents itself. While proving substandard care may no longer be required, and it may be much easier to identify institutions and administrative mechanisms in order to assist with the (easy) submission and quicker resolution of claims, specific eligibility criteria and the perennial problem of needing to establish causation, may still operate in practice to exclude coverage of a significant proportion of injured patients under such schemes.

Adjudication Processes

In the UK context, the arguments regarding both access to, and the quality of, justice under no-fault schemes for medical injury, are necessarily mediated by existing legal obligations under the European Convention on Human Rights (ECHR). The McLean Report succinctly identified a number of problematic issues in this regard: first, whether a no-fault scheme would be likely to breach Article 6 of the Convention, namely the right to a fair and public hearing; and second, whether a move from a system of determination of liability to one of determination that harm had occurred gives rise to any particular conflict with existing ECHR obligations. Additionally, we could add whether the *procedure* for determining coverage under a no-fault scheme itself potentially gives rise to problems with ensuring compatibility with the right to a fair hearing.[53]

The McLean Report concluded that in order to ensure both substantive and procedural compatibility with human rights obligations, it would be important that any no-fault scheme for medical injury established in Scotland provide for a right to appeal to the courts from decisions regarding coverage under the scheme.[54] The courts would need to have full jurisdiction on matters of law, as well as the power to quash the initial decision and have it remitted for a new hearing and

---

aid funding available for medical negligence claims: see http://www.slab.org.uk/public/civil (accessed 13 January 2015). This was also acknowledged to be a problem in the McLean Report at paras 2.6–9.

52 See Farrell, Devaney and Dar, note 7, above, at para. 2.37 (New Zealand); para. 3.19, p. 41 (Sweden).

53 McLean Report, at para. 4.4.

54 The relationship between no-fault schemes and compatibility with the ECHR was also examined in proposals to establish the NHS Redress Scheme in England and Wales: see CMO, *Making Amends*, note 6, above, at ch. 7.

decision by an impartial body. This would need to take place in the event that the court itself did not review the initial decision. It was emphasised that for Article 6 to be satisfied, there would also need to be independence in adjudication, as well as an 'equality of arms' between parties.[55] The Report also pointed out that issues of fairness in the determination of coverage under a no-fault scheme was not necessarily confined to ensuring compatibility with Article 6, but also included the right to seek judicial review of an initial decision regarding coverage under administrative law. It was acknowledged, however, that this was likely to be an expensive option for patients to pursue and had the potential to undermine the system as a whole.[56]

While countries with current legal obligations under the ECHR would have difficulty in removing the right to litigate, including the right of claimants to seek a fair hearing before the courts or other independent tribunal, the McLean Report also observed that the right to litigate is one that is entrenched in Scotland. Therefore, any attempt to remove the right could potentially result in a political and public backlash. In the circumstances, any move in this direction would need to be carefully considered.[57] In contrast, the right to litigate in relation to personal injury claims, including those caused through medical treatment, was largely removed in New Zealand (with some very limited exceptions) as a result of the establishment of its no-fault scheme in the 1970s.[58] Although this has become an acceptable part of the New Zealand social and political fabric over time, high-profile episodes of medical malpractice have led patients and their families to seek redress in other ways, most notably through the use of the criminal law.[59] In the mid-1990s, an independent patient complaints process was established through the New Zealand Health and Disability Commissioner (HDC), which was accompanied by the creation of a Code of Rights.[60] It has been argued that both initiatives have proved crucial in managing patient concerns and enhancing confidence in the national health system.[61]

Financial Compensation

Where liability has been successfully established in medical negligence claims under tort and delict systems, the aim is to restore claimants to the position they were in prior to suffering injury through an award of financial compensation.[62] This compensation may include both pecuniary and non-pecuniary losses. Although there are well-established heads of damage that may be claimed, the total amount of financial compensation awarded is tailored to the individual circumstances

---

55 McLean Report, at para. 4.8.

56 McLean Report, at paras 4.11–12.

57 McLean Report, at para. 5.4(b)(iv).

58 For further information on the limited circumstances in which the right to litigate is preserved under the New Zealand no-fault scheme, see Farrell, Devaney and Dar, note 7, above, at para. 2.4; and more generally, the Accident Compensation Act 2001 No. 49 (New Zealand).

59 Merry, A.F., 'When Are Errors a Crime? Lessons from New Zealand' in Erin, C. and Ost, S. (eds) *The Criminal Justice System and Health Care*, Oxford, Oxford University Press, 2007, at pp. 67–97.

60 For an overview of the work of the Health and Disability Commissioner, see http://www.hdc.org.nz (accessed 13 January 2015). The full title of the Code of Rights is the Code of Health and Disability Services Consumers' Rights. In force since 1996, it affirms the right of New Zealand healthcare consumers to receive an appropriate standard of care, see http://www.hdc.org.nz/the-act--code/the-code-of-rights (accessed 13 January 2015).

61 Paterson, R., 'The Patients' Complaints System in New Zealand' (2002) 21(3) *Health Affairs*, 70–79, at pp. 76–8.

62 Note 21, above.

of the claimant. As previously noted, the empirical evidence available in relation to what injured patients want reveals that financial compensation is but one of the elements sought as part of a redress package.[63] Although payment of financial compensation is central to the operation of existing no-fault schemes, the categories of compensation offered differ as between such schemes. In turn, this may also differ from what is available in the case of successful medical negligence claims made under tort and delict systems.

There are several reasons why this may be so. In the first instance, it may depend on the goals underpinning a particular no-fault scheme. For example, rehabilitation is a key goal under the New Zealand scheme and therefore it was not considered necessary to include claims for non-pecuniary losses. Instead, the focus is on medical and similar expenses, loss of income and earning capacity, as well as payments for permanent impairment where certain threshold levels are met.[64] Even where pecuniary losses are covered under no-fault schemes, caps or tariffs may be imposed, irrespective of individual need or effect. As is the case in Sweden, awards of financial compensation under its no-fault scheme for medical injury may even be seen as merely a 'top-up', in the context of generous national social security provision for injured patients.[65]

All these factors may contribute to a lack of equivalence between awards of compensation under no-fault schemes and those awarded under tort and delict systems for the same injury, with awards under the former being consistently lower.[66] While the McLean Report acknowledges the importance of ensuring adequate and supportive social security provision alongside any no-fault scheme for medical injury to be established in Scotland,[67] the political reality is that Scotland (and indeed the rest of the UK for that matter), is unlikely to enjoy the type of generous social security provision currently enjoyed in the Nordic countries any time soon. It therefore raises the question as to whether Scottish claimants would be amenable to receiving lower awards of compensation than they would in the courts, in return for potentially easier access and quicker resolution of their claims under a no-fault scheme for medical injury. This feeds into the more challenging question about the quality of justice and redress that injured patients should be entitled to receive under a no-fault scheme.

Affordability

The question of affordability looms large when examining the viability (or otherwise) of no-fault schemes in the long term. Expanded eligibility criteria, heightened public profile and perceived ease of accessibility may result in a large increase in the number of claims lodged with such schemes. In turn, this may contribute to significant administrative or transaction costs associated with processing claims under such schemes.[68] Although this has been acknowledged as an issue in the Swedish scheme, transaction costs remain comparatively low overall. Those associated with birth-related neurological injury for example are estimated to be approximately 10 per cent of the

---

63 Note 14, above.

64 Farrell, Devaney and Dar, note 7, above, at paras 2.45–70.

65 McLean Report, at para. 3.32.

66 Bismark, M.M. and Paterson, R.J., 'No-Fault Compensation in New Zealand: Harmonizing Injury Compensation, Provider Accountability and Patient Safety' (2006) 25 *Health Affairs*, 278–83.

67 McLean Report, at p. 6, para. 7.

68 This was noted to be the case in Sweden, see the McLean Report, at para. 3.30. In relation to the New Zealand scheme, a growth in relatively minor claims for medical injury was observed when eligibility was expanded in 2005, changing from the more restrictive criterion of 'medical misadventure' to 'treatment injury': see Farrell, Devaney and Dar, note 7, above, at para. 2.37.

overall costs of medical negligence claims brought for the same injury in England.[69] In contrast, concerns have repeatedly been raised over the long-term affordability of the New Zealand scheme, particularly given the high costs of rehabilitation and other associated liabilities.[70] It is interesting to note that notwithstanding successive proposals to establish a no-fault scheme in England, UK governments have baulked at introducing such a scheme due to the likely high administrative costs and concerns about long-term affordability.[71]

While accepting that long-term affordability is a very important issue in terms of ensuring the viability of no-fault schemes, there is also a need to consider the quality of access to justice that is being provided under schemes, where increasing restrictive eligibility criteria are used to effectively exclude coverage for a significant number of what may be deserving claims (see above). Designing a no-fault scheme that is restrictive in terms of eligibility, as well as predominantly focused on keeping the financial bottom line as low as possible, is unlikely to offer the sort of redress package sought by injured patients. In addition, a rationale for establishing a no-fault scheme simply on the basis of a comparison between the administrative costs of processing claims under such schemes and the costs of medical negligence claims is not a principled response to the quality of justice that may (or may not) be provided under such schemes, given the factual and legal complexities that often arise in cases of medical injury. In short, quality of justice cannot and should not be separated from affordability issues in the design and implementation of no-fault schemes for medical injury, particularly if the goal is to provide a redress package that is responsive to what patients want.

Professional Accountability and Learning from Medical Error

One of the oft-asserted arguments within the existing literature is that the adversarial culture that structures the conduct of medical negligence claims in tort and delict systems hinders, or at least removes the incentive to repair, the relationship between patients and their doctors (or other HCPs) where things have gone wrong. Instead, it is argued that the establishment of a no-fault scheme would promote relationships between patients and doctors which were less defensive;[72] would ease the financial pressure experienced by doctors with regard to escalating insurance premiums; and would remove the ever present threat of litigation hanging over doctors.[73] Notwithstanding

69 McLean Report, para. 3.32.

70 Accident Compensation Corporation, *Annual Report 2013*, pp. 20–21, available at: www.acc.co.nz (accessed 13 January 2015); Morrison, S., 'The New Zealand No-Fault Accident Compensation Scheme: The Financial Viability of the NZ Model' (2013) 114 *Precedent*, 39–42.

71 Indeed, the UK government is yet to implement the NHS Redress Scheme in England, notwithstanding the fact that the legislative framework for the scheme has been in place since 2006 (see NHS Redress Act 2006). For further details concerning the scheme, see Farrell and Devaney, note 12, above.

72 The issue of defensive medicine, whether it exists and the extent of the problem, is a subject of debate in the relevant literature, see for example Kessler, D. and McClellan, M., 'Do Doctors Practice Defensive Medicine?' (1996) 111(2) *The Quarterly Journal of Economics*, 353–90; Studdert, D.M., Mello, M.M., Sage, W.M., et al., 'Defensive Medicine among High-Risk Specialist Physicians in a Volatile Malpractice Environment' (2005) 293(21) *Journal of the American Medical Association*, 2609–17. Although it has been claimed that defensive medicine exists in the UK, the empirical evidence is weak (see CMO, *Making Amends*, note 6, above), where much of the evidence relied upon is anecdotal or referenced from the United States.

73 In the McLean Report, at para. 2.21, it is noted that while the volume of medical negligence claims rose in the 1990s in Scotland, there has been a declining trend since 1999. Awards of compensation and costs of claims have risen more or less steadily over the period 1999–2009 in absolute terms. Interestingly, the number of settled claims in 2009 was only slightly higher than 10 years previously, even with account being

claims made by the medical profession in this regard, the available empirical evidence points to injured patients not taking the decision to pursue litigation lightly. As previously mentioned, it is a decision that is usually taken at the end of a process where apologies or explanations from their treating doctors had not been forthcoming or were not considered sufficient, or where there was dissatisfaction with the outcomes of investigations or complaints processes.[74] In short, the doctor-patient relationship had in a good number of cases become problematic or had otherwise broken down as a result of patients' difficulties in obtaining the information or explanations they needed, and in holding their treating doctors to account for what had happened to them. This fits with other empirical evidence that identifies the opportunity to hold their treating doctors to account as being one of the key elements in the redress package sought by injured patients, in addition to learning lessons from what happened to them to improve patient safety and healthcare outcomes for other patients in the future.[75]

In contrast to the limitations of tort and delict systems, it has been suggested that there is much potential in no-fault schemes for promoting a joined-up approach to facilitating professional accountability, as well as instituting professional and institutional learning from medical error.[76] The question is whether a no-fault scheme for medical injury is likely to achieve this goal in practice. The evidence which exists in this regard is not promising. In the Nordic countries, the issue of professional accountability is considered to be entirely separate from the operation of their no-fault schemes.[77] Although the birth-related neurological injury schemes operating in Virginia and Florida were designed to address the concerns of obstetricians about the financial and professional burdens they faced, given the rising numbers of claims against them, the available evidence points to the schemes having had little impact on improving quality and safety in obstetric practice.[78]

As mentioned previously, it has also been suggested that the reform of both disciplinary procedures for HCPs and independent complaints procedures in New Zealand have enhanced professional accountability.[79] However, the positive contribution of its no-fault scheme to this issue is less clear. What data has been published in relation to (preventable) adverse events in New Zealand has shown that the rate is similar to that found in other national settings, such as Australia and the United States, which allow medical negligence claims under their tort systems.[80] Although the scheme continues to collect data on adverse events in medical care, a lack of financial and other

taken of inflation. In England, medical negligence claims remained steady and even declined in the mid-2000s, following institutional reform leading to the centralised defence of such claims through the NHSLA. More recently, there has been a year-on-year increase in claims, although the reasons for this increase are unclear: see NHSLA, *Report and Accounts 2012–2013*, p. 14, available at: www.nhsla.com (accessed 13 January 2015).

74 Stephen, Melville and Krause, note 14, above.

75 Note 14, above.

76 McLean Report, at paras 6.23–24.

77 There are a number of independent initiatives that have been taken to improve patient safety and learn from medical error in Sweden. See Essinger, K., *The Swedish Medical Injury Insurance, Report 2009–02–20*, available at http://www.patientforsakring.se/resurser/dokument/engelska_artiklar/Report_on_the_Swedsih_Medical_Injury_Insurance.pdf (accessed 13 January 2015).

78 Sloan, F.A., Whetten-Goldstein, K. and Hickson, G.B., 'The Influence of Obstetric No-Fault Compensation on Obstetricians' Practice Patterns' (1998) 17(3) *The American Journal of Obstetrics and Gynecology*, 671–6.

79 Paterson, R., 'Regulation of Health Care' and 'Assessment and Investigation of Complaints' in Skegg, P.D.G. and Paterson, R. (eds) *Medical Law in New Zealand*, Wellington, Thomson Brookers, 2006, pp. 3–22 and 593–612 respectively.

80 Davis, P.B., Lay-Yee, R., Briant, R., et al., *Adverse Events in New Zealand's Public Hospitals: Principal Findings from a National Survey*, Wellington, Ministry of Health, 2001.

resources has meant that there has not been a systematic approach to linking such data to lesson-learning.[81] One is left to conclude that although the potential exists for enhanced professional accountability and lesson-learning through no-fault schemes, it has generally not been realised in practice. Therefore, the question remains as to exactly how best to incentivise doctors to engage in safe practice with patients and whether no-fault schemes should have a role (and, if so, what role) in this regard.

Conclusion

The McLean Report recommended that a no-fault compensation scheme for medical injury be introduced in Scotland and provided a useful and insightful springboard in this chapter for examining the principles that should underpin the design of such schemes. A review of existing schemes was also undertaken, with a particular focus on those operating in Sweden and New Zealand. In designing a no-fault scheme for medical injury that was likely to be responsive to what patients want in terms of redress, the review identified the importance of taking account of issues such as ease of access, eligibility, causation, adjudication processes and affordability, as well as the importance of professional accountability and lesson-learning to improve patient safety and healthcare outcomes. The findings from the review also revealed that there is a need to be cautious about broad ranging, aspirational claims as to what can be achieved through no-fault schemes for medical injury. Rhetoric does not match reality in the absence of generous national social security provision and a more integrated approach to dealing with (negligent) adverse events in healthcare. In the circumstances, such schemes are unlikely on their own to offer a panacea to the long-running problem of how best to redress the harm caused to patients through medical treatment.

81 Oliphant, K., 'Beyond Misadventure: Compensation for Medical Injuries in New Zealand' (2007) 15(3) *Medical Law Review*, 357–91, at p. 390; Farrell, Devaney and Dar, note 7, above, at paras 2.81, 2.83.

PART IV
Regulation

Chapter 11

Research Participants and the Right to be Informed

Deryck Beyleveld and Roger Brownsword

Introduction

Introducing *Autonomy, Consent and the Law*,[1] Sheila McLean remarks that if the law is 'to facilitate or protect the capacity of an autonomous person to make an autonomous choice – one that reflects his or her own values – it is necessary to develop standards that can ensure meaningful patient participation in healthcare decisions'.[2] And, the development of such standards, McLean suggests, 'is generally said to be the function of the legal doctrine of consent'.[3] However, having analysed a sweep of English medical law (focusing on end-of-life questions, pregnancy, genetics and organ transplantation), McLean claims that the jurisprudence of (informed) consent is less than fully congruent with the idea that the autonomy of the patient is focal. Indeed, McLean concludes: 'In building the rules around consent to treatment, courts have stopped short of ensuring that people are fully informed and therefore truly able to weigh their decisions and act in a self-determining manner'.[4]

Following McLean, we would say that, were autonomy to be regarded as focal, it would be for each individual patient, not for clinicians, to decide whether a suitable available treatment should be commenced, modified or discontinued, and which of such treatments to have. Guided by such an autonomy model, (informed) consent would translate in the following way. If a patient refuses to consent to a procedure (for example, a pregnant woman refuses to consent to a Caesarean section or a person refuses assisted nutrition and hydration[5]), then she should not be subjected to the procedure; conversely, if a person consents to the administration of a drug (for example, a drug that will end her life), then the drug should be administered. But, as this example shows, there may be other considerations, such as the good of other patients and society's perceptions of the value of human life, which prevent the views of the individual patient from being the sole concern. McLean's point is that, if consent is to serve the autonomy of a patient, it must be designed to track and reflect that particular patient's will (however seemingly 'irrational' or 'unreasonable') rather than operate in accordance with its own rules.[6]

---

1 McLean, S.A.M., *Autonomy, Consent and the Law*, Abingdon, Routledge-Cavendish, 2010.

2 McLean, note 1, above, at p. 3.

3 McLean, note 1, above, at p. 3.

4 McLean, note 1, above, at p. 216.

5 Of course, there is a question mark about whether ANH is appropriately characterised as a form of medical treatment: see McLean, S.A.M., 'From *Bland* to *Burke*: The Law and Politics of Assisted Nutrition and Hydration' in McLean, S.A.M. (ed.) *First Do No Harm: Law, Ethics and Healthcare*, Aldershot, Ashgate, 2006, pp. 431–46.

6 See McLean, note 1, above, at p. 98: 'It is generally agreed that the corollary of the right to consent to treatment is the right to refuse it. While choosing to accept recommended therapy can be an affirmation of the patient's autonomy, so too can be his/her decision to avoid or reject it. Both are about self-determination or control over our lives … [w]hile rejecting treatment may seem in some cases to be irrational … there may be reasons – possibly unknown to healthcare professionals – that lead people to make the decision not to accept it'.

According to McLean, the autonomy of patients is compromised not only when their consent or refusal of consent is egregiously ignored but also when they make decisions that 'are based on misunderstandings or on overt or covert denial of choice resulting from withholding of information that *would* have been important to that particular patient …'.[7] Following up this latter claim, we might inquire how far the foreground 'informational' doctrines of English medical law serve the background idea that the patient's autonomy is fundamental. This prompts McLean to review the well-known common law cases on disclosure of risk.[8] However, we might extend this line of inquiry. For example, in the context of experimental procedures, we might ask whether the law requires clinicians to inform patients in a way that facilitates the latter making their own treatment decisions.[9] If the law permits a clinician to withhold information about a procedure in order to steer the patient towards a treatment decision that health-care professionals would generally endorse, this suggests that a thread of paternalism remains in the law; and, by contrast, if the law permits a clinician to withhold information about a procedure in order to steer the patient towards a treatment decision that health-care professionals would generally regard as far too risky, this raises quite different concerns about the safety of patients. Either way, the autonomy of patients is compromised.

In this chapter, our interest is in the analogous question of the responsibilities of *researchers* to inform *participants* in a way that respects the autonomy of the latter. If participation is to be on an informed basis, there are many questions to be answered – for example, questions that relate to the purpose (or purposes) of the study, whether the research processes or products might be patented (and commercialised), whether and how the privacy of participants and the confidentiality of their information will be respected, whether participants will remain identifiable (and linkable to the samples and data that they provide), whether participants have proprietary rights in relation to their samples and data, and so on. Much could be written about each of these questions. However, our present interest is in the responsibilities of researchers to return autonomy-relevant findings to their (identifiable) participants – in short, the question is whether there will be (and should be) any individualised feedback of health-related findings made by the researchers. For example, if a researcher realises that a particular participant has a life-threatening aneurysm, would the law be deviating from an autonomy-centred focus if it did not require the finding to be disclosed – or, at any rate, would this be a deviation if the participant had either already consented to the return of findings or had not indicated that there should be no return of findings?

Currently, this line of inquiry is of intense interest because it takes us to one of the most complex and contested issues in the ethics and governance of biobanks. There is no single definition of biobanks, and myriad examples now exist, domestically and internationally, of collections that are of recent origin as well as historical, in some cases going back many decades. A common feature, however, is that these are collections of biosamples, personal data, scans and images, and so on. While some might be held for clinical care purposes, their wider value lies in their role as a research resource. The central question here – a question that Catherine Heeney and Michael Parker rightly single out as '[o]ne of the most hotly debated' in the context of modern biobanking practice – is 'whether there is an obligation to feedback research results to participants'.[10] Suppose,

7 McLean, note 1, above, at p. 61.

8 McLean, note 1, above, at pp. 73–86. The leading case in English law is *Sidaway v. Bethlem Royal Hospital Governors and Others* (1985) 1 BMLR 132.

9 Compare the Nuffield Council on Bioethics, *Novel Neurotechnologies: Intervening in the Brain*, London, June 2013, 111–13.

10 Heeney, C. and Parker, M., 'Ethics and the Governance of Biobanks' in Kaye, J., Gibbons, S.M.C., Heeney, C., et al., *Governing Biobanks*, Oxford, Hart Publishing, 2012, at pp. 282, 295. See, too,

for example, that researchers, who are conducting genetic analysis on biobanked materials, identify a particular mutation for breast cancer in a sample provided by an identifiable participant. Do the researchers have an obligation to inform the participant; or, to turn this round, does the participant have a right to be informed? If it is claimed that the participant does have such a right, a host of further questions need to be addressed, including questions about the scope of the right, its weight in relation to any competing rights, whether researchers owe feedback responsibilities also to third parties (such as relatives of the participant), how the information is to be conveyed to the participant, how the right might be affected by an explicit 'no feedback' policy at the biobank, and whether the right to be informed also implies a right that researchers actively 'look out for' potentially clinically significant findings.[11]

Responding to the headline question of whether researchers have a responsibility to feed back to individual participants those findings that might be clinically significant, we are guided by a rights-based ethic, specifically an ethic that is rooted in the seminal work of Alan Gewirth.[12] According to Gewirthian ethics, in a community of rights, agents are categorically required to respect the generic conditions of agency – for present purposes, particularly the conditions of physical and psychological well-being that are essential before an agent has any prospect of successfully engaging in purposive activity (whatever the agent's purpose, whatever the activity). The generic rights that agents directly hold against one another are both negative (against unwilled acts of interference with the generic conditions) and positive (for acts of assistance in support of their generic conditions provided that this is consistent with the agent's will and does not threaten equally or more important generic rights of those providing assistance). It follows that our blunt – we emphasise that this is extremely blunt – response to the central question is that, where the information in question relates to an agent's generic conditions, then researchers do have feedback responsibilities to their individual participants.

This chapter is in three principal parts. First, we sketch the context for the present debate about the informational responsibilities of researchers, particularly analysing the significance of a biobank's 'no feedback' policy and the plausibility of a participant's claim that they have a 'reasonable expectation' that feedback will be provided. Secondly, we outline the key features of the Gewirthian view of positive rights and its justification. Thirdly, we apply this ethic of rights to a number of illustrative scenarios where the question is whether Gewirthian-guided researchers would do the right thing by giving (or not giving) feedback to a participant; and, at the same time, we draw out the implications for anonymisation (as a strategy to protect participant privacy) if this has the consequence that researchers are thereby disabled from identifying participants who have a right to be informed.

The Context

Why is it that the question of the informational responsibilities of researchers should have become so 'hot'? It is not that biobanks are new. However, large population-wide biobanks, established as a resource to be curated for access and use by the research community (much like a library) are new;

---

the Presidential Commission for the Study of Bioethical Issues, *Anticipate and Communicate: Ethical Management of Incidental and Secondary Findings in the Clinical, Research, and Direct-to-Consumer Contexts*, Washington, DC, 2013.

11 For a recent discussion, see Gliwa, C. and Berkman, B.E., 'Do Researchers Have an Obligation to Actively Look for Genetic Incidental Findings?' (2013) 13 *American Journal of Bioethics*, 32–42.

12 Gewirth, A., *Reason and Morality*, Chicago, IL, University of Chicago Press, 1978.

and the possibility of undertaking (and understanding the import of) quite detailed genotyping and sequencing is assuming much greater prominence. Moreover, where the studies are of a longitudinal nature, with researchers needing periodically to recontact participants (for example, for further samples or data to be supplied, or for remeasurement, and so on), it is in the nature of the project that clinically significant findings can be returned to individual participants. If feedback can be given by biobanks and their researchers (or researchers who use the resource), the question then is whether it ought to be given.

In many biobanks, the general rule is that 'no feedback' will be given to participants. However, in two respects 'no feedback' is open to misunderstanding. The 'no feedback' notice notwithstanding, there might actually be some findings that are returned to participants.

First, even where the declared policy is one of 'no feedback', this usually refers to the position once participants' samples and data have been 'banked'. Prior to that point, some health-related information might be given to participants. For example, at the point of enrolment, participants might be given their blood pressure or bone density readings, or their BMI score, and so on; and, there might also be some advice about incidental observations as when a participant might be advised to check out a suspicious-looking mole with their doctor. However, once the samples and data have been collected and 'banked' for the use of researchers, the 'no feedback' policy signals that the general rule is that there will be no individual feedback arising from the findings made by researchers (general findings, of course, will be disseminated in the usual way).

The second misunderstanding is more subtle. When a biobank declares that its policy is 'no feedback', this might mean quite literally that there is no feedback, that there is an absolute rule against feedback. Here, 'no feedback' is intended to signify that participants have no right to feedback and that researchers have a duty not to inform; in no circumstances will even clinically significant results of research undertaken on the banked materials be returned to individual participants. However, 'no feedback' might be intended less literally, signalling something more specific, namely that the researchers do not accept any obligation to give feedback. This latter reading is designed to counter participants who assert that they have a right to be informed and that, concomitantly, the researchers have matching obligations. While such a reading is intended to shield researchers against claims for feedback made by participants, it does not preclude the giving of feedback, but, whether or not participants are informed, is exclusively for the biobanks and their researchers to decide. If the latter is the policy of the biobank, the relevant discretion might be structured in more than one way – for example, by adopting defaults of various kinds, reserving some feedback questions for case-by-case determination, and so on; and, in practice, some feedback (drawing on research on banked materials) might be given.

In the light of these remarks, consider the 'no feedback' policy of the Avon Longitudinal Study of Parents and Children (ALSPAC) the well-known longitudinal study of parents and their children in the Bristol area. ALSPAC declares its policy on disclosure of biomedical information to participants in the following terms:[13]

> The policy is that information shall not, as a general rule, be disclosed to participants.
>
> This general policy should only be set aside when it is reasonably certain that the benefits of disclosure clearly outweigh any possible risks to the participants or their families. This in turn will arise when three conditions are met:

13 Available at: www.bristol.ac.uk/alspac/researchers/data-access/ethics/ (accessed 13 January 2015).

1. That an item of data gives clear, unequivocal information of an existing or future health problem.
2. That the health problem identified is amenable to treatment of proven benefit
3. That the participant has indicated beforehand that they wish to be informed if such a problem is identified.

While the function of the 'no feedback' notice at ALSPAC is to scotch any idea that participants have a right to feedback, this does not rule out the possibility of informing individual participants about clinically significant findings. On this view, although participants have no *right* to be informed as such, they might nevertheless be informed if they have signalled this *preference* and provided that the researchers judge that there is a net benefit in giving individual feedback.

One of the points made in support of the ALSPAC policy (and, likewise, biobanks that have a similar policy) is that participants understood when they enrolled that there would be no feedback. In other words, the policy is supported inter alia by the following considerations:[14]

- Individuals have consented to participate in the study on the clear understanding that all measures are for research purposes only and not to inform decisions about their health. To emphasise this, it is often stated explicitly in the information given to participants.
- As a corollary, it is frequently repeated that the tests that participants undergo are not a check on their health, and that if participants are worried they should go to their own doctors.
- The relationship between researcher and participant differs from that between doctor and patient. Crucially the duty of care is different. The primary concern of a researcher is not to the health of a participant but to acquire information for the benefit of humankind.

There is no doubt that the ALSPAC ethics committee is seeking to do the right thing but the question is whether, from a rights-based perspective, this paternalistic policy is appropriate.

Heeney and Parker come close to answering this question. Noting that one 'no feedback' strategy is, in effect, to manage the expectations of participants, they say:

> One route would be to make it clear to participants and health professionals at the time of consent that there will be no feedback of research results. There are a number of arguments supporting this including its potential for greater clarity about consent and about the distinction between research and clinical care and the fact that feedback assumes some sort of infrastructure in which the connection with participants is maintained to the extent that they can still be contacted and told to seek medical advice, for example.[15]

However, as the authors remark, this approach has fallen out of favour in those cases where research might 'produce very clear evidence of a serious harm which might be avoided by an easily available intervention and where there exists something akin to a duty of easy rescue'.[16] In other words, if our premise is that participants have a positive right to be informed (possibly akin to a positive right to be rescued where this is straightforward and not difficult for the rescuer), we are less likely to judge that biobanks do the right thing by withholding clinically significant findings. Moreover, even if a 'no feedback' policy has been 'communicated' to participants, we might wonder whether its significance has been fully appreciated; and we might judge that, regardless of the biobank's

14 Again, drawing on the ALSPAC policy, note 13, above.

15 Heeney and Parker, note 10, above, at p. 296.

16 Heeney and Parker, note 10, above, at p. 296.

declared policy, participants 'reasonably expect' to be given feedback where a biobank holds clinically significant, serious and actionable information about a particular individual.[17]

These observations invite two lines of inquiry. First, on what basis might we defend the premise that participants have a positive right to be informed? Secondly, how does the idea of 'reasonable expectation' play in this context? We respond to the first question in the next part of the chapter; and we close the present part by making some short remarks in response to the second question.

One of the striking features of much of our ethical and regulatory thinking (notably in relation to the interest in privacy) is that the recognition of a right hinges on the question of whether we judge that a person has a 'reasonable expectation' that his or her particular interests will be respected and protected. If a participant's claim to have feedback hinges on whether it is based on a reasonable expectation to have feedback, then the question is: by reference to what standard or practice or to whose authority is the expectation judged to be a reasonable one?

First, the participant might invoke relevant background rules of law. There has been much discussion of whether a participant might succeed against a researcher in a tort claim for wrongful non-disclosure.[18] The consensus is that English law does not clearly support such a claim; and, if the legal test turns on whether it is 'fair, just, and reasonable' to place researchers under a feedback responsibility, this seems merely to restate the original question of whether the claimant's expectation is a reasonable one.

Where a biobank declares a 'no feedback' policy which is clearly notified to participants, if anything, this further weakens the participant's tort claim. However, where 'no feedback' signals that the biobank reserves a discretion to give feedback, a participant might argue in a judicial review that the discretion has been exercised improperly. If successful, the claimant might compel the researchers or biobank to reconsider their decision; but, of course, a claim of this kind would only get off the ground if the policy set by the biobank and its administration were judicially reviewable.

Secondly, the participant might claim that the researchers had formally or informally signalled that feedback would be given. Where a biobank has a well-advertised 'no feedback' policy, this kind of claim would be unlikely to succeed. However, if the policy had not been signalled, then the claim would turn on whether the participant could show on the facts that an undertaking to provide feedback had been given. In principle, unless the background law prohibited researchers from giving feedback, their voluntary assumption of a responsibility to give feedback would be a strong ground for claiming a reasonable expectation of feedback.

Thirdly, the participant might rely on a general attitude that there should be some reciprocity in the relationship with researchers: participants assist researchers in various ways in return for which researchers should assist participants by giving appropriate feedback. There does seem to be evidence that at least some (and, quite possibly, many) participants sign up with the expectation that there will be reciprocation.[19] However, the fact that others share one's own expectation does

17 Compare, for example, Wolf, S., Crock, B.N., Van Ness, B., et al., 'Managing Incidental Findings and Research Results in Genomic Research Involving Biobanks and Archived Data Sets' (2012) 14 *Genetics in Medicine*, 361–84; and Knoppers, B.M., Deschênes, M., Zawati, M.H. and Tassé, A.M., 'Population Studies: Return of Research Results and Incidental Findings Policy Statement' (2012) *European Journal of Human Genetics*, 245–7.

18 Seminally, see Johnston, C. and Kaye, J., 'Does the UK Biobank Have a Legal Obligation to Feedback Individual Findings to Participants?' (2004) 12 *Medical Law Review*, 239–67.

19 Bovenberg, J., Meulenkamp, T., Smets, E. and Gevers, S., *Always Expect the Unexpected: Legal and Social Aspects of Reporting Biobank Research Results to Individual Research Participants*, Nijmegen, Radboud University, Centre for Society and Genomics, 2009; Beskow, L.M., Namey, E.E., Cadigan, R.J., et al., 'Research Participants' Perspectives on Genotype-Driven Research Recruitment' (2011) 6(4) *Journal of*

not make anyone's expectation *reasonable*. Possibly, the claim for reciprocity might be grounded in some other way – for example, in the way that Henry Richardson relies on the relationship of 'entrustment' between participants and researchers;[20] but it is not enough that the de facto expectation is widely held by participants.

Fourthly, the participant might rely on the settled custom and practice at other biobanks or in a certain sector of research (or, indeed, in clinical practice as genetic analysis becomes routine). For example, it might be that researchers who work with MRI scans might consider it best practice to return incidental findings to their participants. Accordingly, where there are such practices and where the claimant participant is dealing with researchers at a biobank with no declared policy on feedback, the unstated assumption (and expectation) that there will be feedback might look perfectly reasonable. However, where 'no feedback' is the declared rule, contrary custom and practice notwithstanding, the argument that there is a reasonable expectation of feedback is seriously weakened.

What these appeals to reasonableness have in common is that they rely on a range of contingent factors being set in the right way. If the law supports a claim to feedback, if researchers voluntarily assume a responsibility to give feedback, if custom and practice supports giving feedback, and the like, then the participant's claim will get to first base; and, other things (such as the notification of the biobank's policy) being equal, the participant's expectation will show as a reasonable one. Where 'reasonable expectation' is the test, then the participant will be judged to be entitled to be informed.

By contrast, a participant might claim to have a reasonable expectation of being given feedback because a right to be informed is grounded in reason – not in contingent legal provisions or promises or custom and practice. Quite simply, if a participant has such a reason-based right to be informed, it would be reasonable (to put the claim at its lowest) to expect to be informed. The question, to which we now turn, is how such a right might be rationally grounded.

A Rationally-Grounded Right to Be Informed

According to Gewirth, agents[21] categorically ought to accept the Principle of Generic Consistency (PGC) – which requires them to grant generic rights (rights to the generic conditions of agency GCAs) to all agents.[22] The reason why the PGC is categorically binding on agents is that it is dialectically necessary for agents to accept it, which is to say that an agent (any agent – call him 'Albert') fails to understand what it is to be an agent (hence implicitly contradicts the idea that he is an agent) if he does not accept it. In essence, for the PGC to be dialectically necessary it is necessary and sufficient for three propositions to be true, which are:

1. If doing X or having Y is necessary for Albert to pursue or achieve his chosen purpose E, then Albert ought to do X or act to secure Y or else give up pursuit of E, which is to say that the Principle of Hypothetical Imperatives of Instrumental Reason (PHI) is dialectically necessary.

Empirical Research on Human Research Ethics, 3–20; and Wellcome Trust and Medical Research Council, *Assessing Public Attitudes to Health Related Findings in Research*, London, April 2012.

20 Richardson, H.S., *Moral Entanglements: The Ancillary-Care Obligations of Medical Researchers*, New York, Oxford University Press, 2012.

21 Those capable of acting for reasons. In effect, those who have the capacity to do things voluntarily in order to achieve purposes that they have chosen.

22 See note 12, above.

2. It is possible for there to be GCAs.
3. If it is dialectically necessary for Albert to accept that he ought to do Z, then it is dialectically necessary, not only for every other agent (say Brenda) to accept that she ought to do Z, but for Albert to accept that he ought to act in accord with the principle that Brenda ought to do Z unless this would prevent Albert from acting in accordance with the principle that Albert ought to do Z.

From (1) and (2) it follows that it is dialectically necessary for Albert to accept:

4. I (Albert) ought to defend my possession of the GCAs unless I am willing to accept the generic damage to my ability to pursue or achieve my purposes (generic damage being damage to my ability to pursue or achieve every purpose I might have) that will result from my non-possession of the GCAs.

For the sake of brevity, we will express (4) as the proposition that it is dialectically necessary for Albert to accept that he ought to defend his possession of the GCAs from interference against his will.

If (3) is also true, then it follows from (4) that it is also dialectically necessary for Albert to accept that he ought to defend Brenda's possession of the GCAs from interference that is against her will, provided only that doing so does not prevent him from defending his own possession of the GCAs from interference against his will (and vice versa). But this is equivalent to it being true that the PGC is dialectically necessary for all agents.

We submit that (1) and (2) are clearly true. (1) is true because it is analytic. (2) is true because its truth follows simply from the coherence of the idea that there might be GCAs. The contentious proposition is (3). We will not, here, attempt to explain why we believe (3) to be true also.[23] This is because, for present purposes, it will suffice for us to establish that the English legal system ought to comply with the PGC *on the assumption* that it recognises that all human beings are equal in dignity and rights. This is because the proposition that human beings are equal in dignity and rights is one that the English legal system currently purports to uphold,[24] and when this proposition is combined with propositions (1) and (2) then acceptance of the PGC follows (not as dialectically necessary) but as contingent upon acceptance of the proposition that human beings are equal in dignity and rights.[25]

---

23 See Beyleveld, D., *The Dialectical Necessity of Morality: An Analysis and Defense of Alan Gewirth's Argument to the Principle of Generic Consistency*, Chicago, IL, University of Chicago Press, 1991, for a comprehensive defence of the argument for the dialectical necessity of the PGC. For a recent specific defence of (3), see Beyleveld, D., 'Williams' False Dilemma: How to Give Categorically Binding Impartial Reasons to Real Agents' (2013) 10 *Journal of Moral Philosophy*, 204–26.

24 It does so by the Human Rights Act 1998, which requires English law to be interpreted in conformity with the substantive rights of the European Convention on Human Rights (ECHR) if it is at all possible to do so. The Preamble to the ECHR, states that it is a first step to give effect to the rights declared in the Universal Declaration on Human Rights 1948 (UDHR). Article 1 of the UDHR states that all human beings are equal in dignity and rights. Granted, the Human Rights Act permits departure from the ECHR. On this basis, the acceptance of the principle that human beings are equal in dignity and human rights seems to be a qualified one. However, it is arguable that departure from this principle remains unqualified as acceptance of the substantive rights of the ECHR cannot even be qualified acceptance if Article 1 of the UDHR is not accepted in an unqualified manner. This is because Article 1 UDHR in part defines what it is to be a human right.

25 For more detail see Beyleveld, D., 'The Principle of Generic Consistency as the Supreme Principle of Human Rights' (2011) 13 *Human Rights Review*, 1–18.

Now, whether justified as dialectically necessary or as dialectically contingent upon the acceptance of human rights, the generic rights prescribed by the PGC are clearly rights under the will-conception. The duty that Albert has to defend Brenda's GCAs is, by the nature of the right he must recognise she has, one that she may release him from by her will (provided only that doing so will not generically damage other agents against their will). However, if Brenda is to exercise her will in relation to acts or decisions that might affect her possession of the GCAs she clearly needs to know what the effect of these acts might be on this possession and also about the alternatives that are available. In other words, she must be granted a right to be informed.

The generic rights are also, clearly, both positive and negative. Albert has a right that Brenda not act to interfere with Albert's possession of the GCAs against his will, and also a right that she assist him to secure his possession of the GCAs when he cannot do so by his own unaided efforts, if she can assist without disproportionate risk to her own possession of the GCAs.[26] This is simply because in order to defend his possession of the GCAs, Albert needs to have them; so he needs assistance when he cannot defend his own possession as much as he needs non-interference. He, thus, must have the same attitude towards assistance to secure the GCAs that he needs and desires as he must have to interference with his GCAs that is against his will. So, if Albert ought to defend Brenda's possession of the GCAs from interference against her will, he ought also to assist her to secure that possession when she cannot do so for herself and she so wishes, and so on.

Applications of a Participant's Right to Be Informed

If participants have a (Gewirthian-based) prima facie right that researchers inform them about matters that bear on their GCAs, such as their individual health and well-being, then it is clear why there should be feedback when the information is potentially life-saving, when the burden of informing is low, and when the participant is not otherwise able (or likely) to access the information. However, there are still many questions about the right and about the hard cases that might arise. In this part of the chapter, we address five such further questions.

Participant's Consent

The first question concerns the relationship between A's right to be informed and whatever consent A may give or withhold to the researchers' proposed arrangements for feedback or 'no feedback'. Clearly, if A has a right to have feedback, and if A wishes to have feedback, then it is not strictly necessary for A to consent to having feedback. That said, in a context where it is possible that A might not wish to have feedback, getting A to confirm consent to feedback leaves no doubt that A does wish to stand on his right.

---

26 While non-possession of a GCA has a generic effect on an agent's ability to act, that is, it negatively affects that ability whatever the agent's purposes, this effect can be more or less immediate, more or less capable of amelioration, and more or less severe. For example to kill someone has an immediate, not ameliorable, effect of maximum severity. It stops the agent from attempting to act, from maintaining the capacity to act and from improving the capacity to act. A disease might eventually kill someone but might be treatable. Ill health might reduce one's ability to act successfully in a generic way but the extent to which it has this effect can vary. See Gewirth, *Reason and Morality*, note 12, above, 48–63. Because this is so, the generic rights are ranked in a hierarchy according to their 'needfulness' for action, and this ranking is to be used to determine when a generic risk is proportionate or disproportionate.

As controller of the right (such as the right to be informed by B), A has three options in relation to the operation of the right. They are as follows:

a. A may require B to inform him (A insists on B performing the duty);
b. A may prohibit B from informing him (A in effect exercises a 'right not to know'[27]); or
c. A may permit B to inform or not to inform him, at B's choice.

Where A opts for (c), A consents to B not informing him; and where B then acts within the terms of this authorisation, B does no wrong to A (relative to A's right to be informed).[28] Provided that A's agreeing to 'no feedback' is equivalent to A consenting not to be informed, then the position is as in (c).

What about case (b), where A signals that there is to be no feedback? Harking back to McLean's thesis, if the researchers are to respect A's autonomy, and the particular setting that A has chosen for the operation of the right to be informed, they will give no feedback. If they do so, because they judge (paternalistically) that this is in A's best interests, they (and the law if it supports such action) have failed to keep faith with respect for the agent's autonomy.

While it is tolerably clear what researchers should do when A's position is known, it is much more problematic when the will of a participant is not known. For example, where a research project began before feedback became such a hot topic, participants might not have been asked the right questions. In such a context of uncertainty, how should researchers proceed? It would be easy if the researchers could recontact each of the participants to establish their will in relation to feedback. There might be a few cases where this is possible. However, we assume that there will be many cases where it is simply not possible to establish the participant's position, including cases where this is not possible without giving the game away. Where this is so, how should researchers proceed?

A plausible default position for the research community is to inform a participant if the return of the finding is clinically treatable and possibly life-saving. To give feedback in such circumstances is analogous to treating a person rendered unconscious in an accident when it is not known whether that person wants to be treated but when, at the same time, without the treatment the person will be seriously damaged or will die. Indeed, the default for feedback might be further elaborated according to whether the condition is life-threatening and the treatment low risk. If feedback is given in these circumstances, and if the participant would have wanted feedback (and now welcomes it), then all is well. However, the problem with this particular case of uncertainty is that the researchers do not know what the participant would have wanted and when, following the default, they give feedback, the participant might not welcome it. If so, the researchers have acted in a way that is out of line with the participant's right to be (not) informed. However, there is no easy option. If researchers guess wrong, they either give feedback that is potentially life-saving but not in line with the participant's will, or – and this is hardly an attractive alternative – they withhold feedback in line with the participant's will and do nothing to assist the participant's health.[29]

If a default of the kind just sketched looks defensible where the finding is clinically treatable, what about the case where it is not treatable? In this kind of case, it becomes more plausible for researchers to suppose that the individual participant really might not wish to know. Indeed, even some participants who have signed up for feedback might not wish to know; but, of course, there

---

27 See McLean, note 1, above, at pp. 178–80 (in the context of autonomy and genetic information).

28 See Beyleveld, D. and Brownsword, R., *Consent in the Law*, Oxford, Hart Publishing, 2007.

29 Compare the shape of the analysis in Beyleveld, D. and Brownsword, R., 'Emerging Technologies, Extreme Uncertainty, and the Principle of Rational Precautionary Reasoning' (2012) 4 *Law, Innovation and Technology*, 35–65.

will be others who value this feedback in order to put their affairs in order or maximise what is left of their lives. Again, researchers are on the horns of an impossible dilemma: if they get it wrong, either they give feedback to a participant who would not have wanted to know and who derives no benefit from the information given, or they withhold feedback from a participant who would have wished to know and who would have valued the information (bad news though it is).

The lesson to be taken from this seems to be that researchers need to talk participants through the different kinds of feedback that might be given (whether it is treatable, whether treatment would be burdensome and so on) and then ask participants to indicate how they wish to exercise their right to be informed. No doubt, the indications given at enrolment can be reviewed or refreshed periodically; and, if participants have on-line access to their own password-protected feedback files, then they can edit their files in accordance with their latest wishes.

Unclear Information: Genetic Markers

'No feedback' policies often are justified by saying that the researchers do not wish to return false positive findings and cause participants unnecessary anxiety and distress. As biobanks facilitate various kinds of genetic analysis, there will be many markers the clinical significance of which is unclear. If the researchers cannot say with confidence what the significance of the marker is, is 'no feedback' the right policy?

Clearly, if participants have a right to be informed, 'no feedback' cannot be the right policy simply because the researchers so decide; it can only be the right policy if this is the will of the participant – and this simply continues the discussion of the previous section. Picking up that discussion, the pertinent question is about the kind of conversation that researchers need to have with their prospective participants.[30] Information needs to be given, in an accessible form, about the best understanding that researchers have about the link between particular genetic markers and their impact on the health of the individuals concerned. This conversation will reveal different levels and degrees of uncertainty, most importantly uncertainties about the nature of the link between the marker and the expression of particular diseases. In all probability, the genetics community (both researchers and clinicians) will rapidly develop guidelines placing each particular marker in one of three categories: for return; to be considered for return; and not for return.[31] Where such a recommended feedback scheme is in place, it might be presented to prospective participants as 'non-negotiable', as applicable subject to 'opt-out', or as an option available by 'opt-in'.

In this vein, the American College of Medical Genetics and Genomics has recently recommended that, in the context of *clinical* exome and genome sequencing, there should be a (reviewable) list of variants that should always be returned to patients.[32] Variants on this minimum list, the College estimates, will be included in about 1 per cent of sequencing reports. Summarising its proposal, the College says:

---

30 For some helpful remarks on the rapidly changing context of genomics and its bearing on feedback to participants, see Parens, E., Appelbaum, P. and Chung, W., 'Incidental Findings in the Era of Whole Genome Sequencing?' (2013) 43(4) *Hastings Center Report*, 16–19.

31 See Wolf et al., note 17, above.

32 Green, R.C., Berg, J.S., Grody, W.W., et al., 'ACMG Recommendations for Reporting of Incidental Findings in Clinical Exome and Genome Sequencing', available at: http://www.acmg.net/docs/ACMG_Releases_Highly-Anticipated_Recommendations_on_Incidental_Findings_in_Clinical_Exome_and_Genome_Sequencing.pdf (accessed 13 January 2015). (Note: updated Recommendations as of 14 November 2014 available at: https://www.acmg.net/docs/Survey_Results_Secondary_findings.pdf, accessed 13 January 2015) See, too, Parens et al., note 30, above.

> [T]he Working Group has recommended that when a report is issued for clinically indicated exome and genome sequencing, a minimum list of conditions, genes and variants should be routinely evaluated and reported to the ordering clinician who can place them into the context of that patient's medical and family history, physical examination and other laboratory testing. We have recommended that these findings be reported without seeking preferences from the patient and family and without limitation due to the patient's age … The Working Group recognizes that this list should, and will, evolve as further empirical data are collected on the actual penetrance of these variants, and on the health benefits and costs that might follow from their disclosure as incidental findings.[33]

Recognising that its recommendations 'may be seen to violate existing ethical norms regarding the patient's autonomy and "right not to know" genetic risk information',[34] the College defends its position in the following terms:

> [Given that the minimum list] is weighted toward conditions where prevalence may be high and intervention may be possible, we felt that clinicians and laboratory personnel have a fiduciary duty to prevent harm by warning patients and their families about certain incidental findings and that this principle supersedes concerns about autonomy, just as it does in the reporting of incidental findings elsewhere in medical practice.[35]

So long as patient autonomy is reduced to patient *preferences*, the College's position might be justifiable. However, if patients have a Gewirthian based *right* not to know, the College's position, however well-meaning, is irrational.

What if a patient, having been told about the return of incidental findings where variants are on the minimum list, objects and wishes to exercise their right not to know? According to the College, the only options for such a patient (with, as the College would have it, such preferences) are either to 'decline clinical sequencing if they judge the risks of possible discovery of incidental findings to outweigh the benefits of testing'[36] or to agree to the clinical sequencing on the College's standard minimum list terms. If the NHS were to adopt this approach in its 100,000 genomes project,[37] we take it that it would not only be Gewirthians who would protest about such a violation of patients' rights to be treated.

Returning to the context of *research*, suppose that the terms and conditions for participation in a particular study were to adopt a non-negotiable feedback policy along the lines of the College's minimum list. For prospective participants, the choice is to participate on these terms or not at all. If a prospective participant, not wishing to have such feedback, was then excluded from the study, would this be a violation of his or her rights? Although concerns are sometimes expressed about willing participants being unfairly excluded, and although exclusion would frustrate one of the would-be participant's projects, there would be no violation of the agent's generic rights.

---

33 Green et al., note 32, above, at pp. 19–20.

34 Green et al., note 32, above, at p. 11. See recently, Chadwick, R., Levitt, M. and Shickle, D. (eds) *The Right to Know and the Right Not to Know: Genetic Privacy and Responsibility*, 2nd edn, Cambridge, Cambridge University Press, 2014.

35 Green et al., note 32, above, at p. 11.

36 Green et al., note 32, above, at p. 11.

37 http://www.guardian.co.uk/science/2012/dec/10/1000000-peoples-dna-mapped (accessed 13 January 2015).

Whether there was some violation of a contingent right would depend on the context, on what was reasonably expected, and the like.

Informing Third Parties

In the context of third-party interests, McLean observes quite correctly that '[j]ust as genetic information may devastate those who willingly seek it out, so too it may harm those who did not search for it but who are provided with it nonetheless in their purported interests'.[38] This prompts the following question: Do researchers have a responsibility to inform third parties (for example, genetically-related members of a participant's family) where they have findings that bear on the health and well-being of the latter? If the question were put to an English court, it is quite likely that, even if the liability of researchers to participants had been recognised, liability to third parties would be denied – judges would simply be too nervous about over-extending liability and burdening researchers. Moreover, liability would probably be denied on the ground that the relationship between researchers and third parties, unlike that between researchers and participants, lacked sufficient proximity. However, from a Gewirthian perspective, there is no obvious reason to deny third parties positive rights against researchers, including a right to have individual feedback arising from the research project – whatever a lack of 'proximity' might mean to common lawyers, it does not resonate in the same way for Gewirthians. Nevertheless, as McLean's remarks foreshadow, even from this perspective there are some complex issues of principle and practice.

To start with one of the issues of principle: what is the position if the participant has exercised their right not to know? Clearly, the participant (unless specially authorised to act for third parties) has no right to exercise the rights of third parties: if the participant elects to have no feedback, this cannot entail that there is no feedback for third parties. Therefore, it is perfectly possible that, while a participant elects to have no feedback, a third party might have elected to have feedback if they had been asked. This gives rise to two questions: first, what is the right thing for researchers to do where they cannot give feedback to a third party (whose position on feedback is not known) without informing a participant who has elected to have no feedback; and, secondly, if the views of third parties are registered when participants are enrolled, does this mean that some prospective participants might be unfairly excluded because they cannot accept the feedback policy in relation to third parties?

The first question returns us to our discussion on consent. There, we suggested that a defensible default for researchers might be to give feedback to a participant whose will is not known where the condition is clinically treatable. Other things being equal, this might also be a plausible default in relation to a third party. However, we are now assuming two complicating factors: one is that researchers cannot give feedback to the third party without violating the participant's rights (the participant having elected not to be informed);[39] and the other is that, without knowing the position of the third party, giving feedback might or might not be in line with the will of the third party. At best, researchers would violate the rights of the participant and inform the third party in a way that is in line with the latter's will. At worst, they would act in a way that was in line with neither the

38 McLean, note 1, above, at p. 222.

39 This has the makings of a question of competing or conflicting rights of the kind that we discuss in the next sub-section below. If the participant and the third party each rely on a 'right to be informed' (one not wanting to be informed, the other wanting to be informed), the question is one of competing rights; if, however, we characterise the participant's right as a different 'right not to be informed', the question is one of conflicting rights – a case of the participant's 'right not to be informed' coming into conflict with the third party's 'right to be informed'.

will of the participant rights-holder nor that of the third-party rights-holder. On balance, respecting the rights and the known will of the participant seems like the more defensible default.

The second question, concerning the exclusion of prospective participants, takes us back to our recent discussion about genetics and the minimum list. There, we suggested that there is no generic right to participate; but there might be context-dependent contingent rights. Here, there is no reason to change that view.

Conflicting and Competing Rights

Rights theories are commonly rejected on the ground that they cannot handle questions of conflicting or competing rights. We should note that there is a difference between competing rights (where each agent, A and B, pleads the same right R, for example, in relation to a scarce resource) and conflicting rights (where agents A and B each plead a different right); but critics maintain that rights theory collapses when presented with either kind of case. Certainly, unless a rights theory holds that conceptually rights cannot conflict (in which case rights are recognised rather sparingly and then specified very precisely) there has to be a strategy for dealing with conflicts. Briefly, where rights compete, the spirit of Gewirthian ethics is to try to give priority to the agent whose need (as expressed by the right) is the greater; and, where rights conflict, the strategy is to try to give priority to the right that ranks as more important relative to the generic rights of agents.

To start with competing rights, consider again a hypothetical case in which a participant has exercised her right to be informed by indicating that she does not wish to have feedback (for example, about a predisposition to cancer) but a related third-party has exercised the same right by registering a wish to have feedback. Where it is not possible to inform the third-party without also informing the participant, it is not at all obvious which right should prevail. Possibly the context will indicate that the generic needs of one agent are greater than those of the other; but, on the face of it, their needs are much the same. If there really is nothing to choose between the parties, it might be necessary to resort to some secondary and contingent considerations – for example, the view in the community might be that, because the participant is actually assisting the researchers, it is only fair that the researchers should tip the balance in her favour.

Moving on to conflicting rights, those who favour a 'no feedback' policy often point out, quite correctly, that giving feedback involves opportunity costs for the researchers. The more time that researchers spend on feedback, the less time that they will spend on the research project and the longer it will take for, say, a new drug or diagnostic test to be developed. Suppose that this is presented as a conflicting rights issue, with the participant's right to have feedback opposed by the rights of agents generally to have beneficial health-related research come to fruition. However, barring some exceptional circumstances, agents surely do not have a *generic* right that others undertake health-care research, let alone research that is tailored to their particular needs. If this is correct, the generic right to be informed prevails. Granted, if we examine the way in which a particular research study is funded, we might detect certain expectations about the delivery of health-care benefits. Even so, these contingent expectations cannot overcome generic rights unless the rights-holders have consented. It seems likely, therefore, that the generic right to be informed is going to be difficult to overcome when supposedly conflicting rights are set against it.

Relationship with Privacy and Anonymisation

Article 1 of Directive 95/46/EC, to which the UK gives effect via the Data Protection Act 1998, requires the processing of personal data to be consistent with fundamental rights and freedoms of data subjects (those whose personal data is being processed), especially the right to privacy. Recital 26 of the Directive states that the principles of data protection do not apply to data rendered anonymous, by which it means data rendered so that the data subject cannot be identified from it directly or indirectly (for example by use of a code) by anyone without disproportionate effort. Article 8 of the Directive prohibits the processing of sensitive personal data (which includes data on the health of the data subject), unless certain conditions are satisfied. Now, according to the jurisprudence of the European Court of Human Rights, Article 8 of the European Convention on Human Rights (ECHR) (the privacy right) is engaged whenever data on a person's health is processed without the explicit consent of the data subject.[40] This means, though this is not clear from either the Directive or the Data Protection Act, that data on a person's health may not be processed without the explicit consent of the data subject unless conditions laid down in Article 8.2 ECHR are satisfied if the instruments in question are to be compatible with the Convention.

Recital 26 of the Directive has, however, led many, including the UK's Information Commissioner,[41] to consider that privacy is fully protected by rendering personal data anonymous and that doing so places the data outside of the remit of the Directive. However, there are circumstances in which rendering personal data anonymous (in the way that Recital 26 of the Directive specifies) will violate the right to privacy, or if not that, then some other fundamental right, unless the consent of the data subject is obtained.[42] From what we have argued in this chapter, this is fully in line with what the PGC requires, and will include cases where the data, if it can still be connected to the patient, could be used to treat the patient, or warn the patient of a serious health-threatening risk, while rendering the data anonymous renders this impossible.

In relation to this, it should be noted that rendering data anonymous is itself, per both the Directive and the UK Act, a process performed on personal data, which means that it is something that needs the consent of the patient, in relation to which, where anonymisation is contemplated, the patient needs to be informed of the consequences of anonymisation (including whatever consequences this might have in relation to the right to be informed).

Conclusion

To return to our starting point, in an important contribution to the jurisprudence of medical law, McLean charts the failure to bring informed consent into alignment with the requirements of autonomy. We take it to be implicit in her critique, first, that respecting the autonomy of persons (whether patients or research participants) is fundamentally right and, secondly, that it would not be appropriate to remedy the legal pathology by weakening our valuation of autonomy.

---

40 See the case of *M.S. v. Sweden* (1997) 28 EHRR 313, paras 34–5.

41 See the Information Commissioner's guidance of 2012 'Data Protection: Anonymisation: Managing Data Protection Risk Code Of Practice', especially at 11, available at: https://ico.org.uk/media/1061/anonymisation-code.pdf (accessed 19 January 2015).

42 To be sure, the Information Commissioner recognises that, especially in medical research the use of personal data might be necessary (see note 41, above, at 13). But the Information Commissioner confuses matters by asserting at 3 in the summary to the guidance (available at: https://ico.org.uk/media/for-organisations/documents/1042731/anonymisation_code_summary.pdf, accessed 19 January 2015) that while there are circumstances in which the ECHR will render it inappropriate to use anonymised data, these do not affect the Data Protection Act 1998. This is false because the Data Protection Directive (see Article 1.1), and, therefore the UK Act (if properly implemented) exist to protect the rights of individuals under the Convention in relation to the processing of personal data. Processing that violates the ECHR will also violate the Directive.

Reading McLean's critique from our Gewirthian perspective, we share her vision of flourishing agency – that is, the vision of agents acting autonomously in the sense that they freely choose and pursue their own projects and purposes. However, none of this is possible without the generic conditions of agency being secured and respected. Accordingly, the moral imperative for the law is to ensure that, in all its articulations – in its primary respect for autonomy and well-being as well as in its treatment of informed consent – it is compatible with the generic needs of agency.

The question of whether researchers should give clinically significant feedback to their participants brings into focus the positive (informational) rights of agents in relation to their generic needs.[43] If the law is to keep faith, not only with the autonomy of agents, but more fundamentally with the protection of the generic conditions that are presupposed by the myriad autonomous choices made by agents, it cannot routinely accept that 'no feedback'[44] is a legitimate position for researchers to specify in their protocols. If a failure to give a participant feedback is also a failure to respond to the generic needs of the agent in question, then the law should require the withholding of feedback to be justified by reference to one or more of three kinds of reasons: (i) that the right to be informed is not engaged – for example, because giving feedback is 'disproportionate' relative to the researcher's own generic needs, or the participant is in a position to gain the information without any acts of assistance; (ii) that giving feedback would be contrary to the will (consent) of the participant; or (iii) that giving feedback to the participant would be to infringe an even more important right of another agent. The law has good reasons to take seriously the claim that researchers have a responsibility to give feedback; but there can also be good reasons for judging that, in a particular case, the giving of feedback is not required or even permitted.[45]

43 Throughout *Autonomy, Consent and the Law*, McLean maintains that there is no deep opposition between individual and relational conceptions of autonomy, that agents might freely choose to act in a way that recognises their responsibilities to, so to speak, 'connected' others. From a Gewirthian view, it is clearly the case that agents might freely choose to act in this way. However, the optionality of such 'relational' action should not be taken out of context: where the generic rights (both negative and positive) of other agents are engaged, autonomy is necessarily circumscribed by agency responsibilities.

44 In either of the senses that we identified in the section 'Context' above.

45 Roger Brownsword wishes to make it absolutely clear that this chapter, exploring the implications of Gewirthian ethics for giving feedback to research participants, is co-authored in his personal capacity and in no sense represents the views of the the UK Biobank Ethics and Governance Council.

Chapter 12

Children, Cosmetic Surgery and Perfectionism: A Case for Legal Regulation?

Jean V. McHale

Introduction: The Rise and Rise of Perfectionism

The first years of the twenty-first century have seen a huge expansion in the use of cosmetic procedures. From the exceptional face-lift procedure that used to be the purview of the rich (conducted quietly in Harley Street), today cosmetic surgery and related procedures have become mainstream. The use of breast enlargements and botox is increasingly seen as a life-style choice. Cosmetic procedures are used by some citizens as a means of postponing the ageing process. For others, the use of such procedures is very much a means of making themselves 'look' better or 'feel' better. New and enhanced surgical techniques and procedures have been accompanied by the rise of providers offering cut-price surgery to an increasingly mobile patient population. From 'botox parties' to 'cosmetic surgery holidays', the landscape has radically changed. Of course, perfectionism is by no means the exclusive concern of this century. From Ancient Greece and the celebration of the idealised male form, what constitutes the 'perfect' human form has varied over time and social context.[1] Perfectionism in human forms is innately culturally determined, and this is reflected by the diversity today of images of putative perfect form across cultures and jurisdictions. The broader trends in such imagery and the debates concerning their legitimacy have been the extensive work of sociologists and feminist theorists in recent times.[2]

The influence of cultural norms accompanied with advances in clinical technologies has proved to be a powerful cocktail. The movement towards uniformity in the human form, it being a means through which individuals may be perceived as being able to gain legitimacy and cultural acceptance, has nonetheless worrying undertones and consequences, albeit that to a certain extent the phenomenon is inevitable. The individual or sub-group may be the subject of stigma and discrimination, and indeed of persecution, for failing to conform to the accepted norm. Events such as the compulsory sterilisation of adults in the USA and Nazi Germany continue to cast a long shadow.[3] The ease of dissemination of information via the Internet has, moreover, changed the dialogue concerning body image. Images of exceptionally beautiful, and increasingly digitally enhanced, people form part of common cultural representations. This can be seen as particularly problematic when this contributes to shape children's preconceptions of what exactly is 'normal'.

A further dimension to the enhancement debate is the issue of safety. What was downplayed at the end of the last century, and in the early years of the last decade in relation to cosmetic procedures, was the question of risk. Cosmetic surgical procedures can come at a very high price

1 See for example Jenkins, I.D. and Turner, V., *The Greek Body*, London, The British Museum Press, 2009.

2 Davis, K. *Reshaping the Female Body: The Dilemma of Cosmetic Surgery*, London, Routledge, 1995; Woolf, N., *The Beauty Myth*, London, Vintage Books, 1991.

3 See for example Lombardo, P.A., *A Century of Eugenics in America: From the Indiana Experiment to the Human Genome*, Bloomington, IN, Indiana University Press, 2011.

if things go wrong. This was illustrated starkly, recently, by the problems experienced by women who were the recipients of Poly Implant Prosthesis (PIP) breast implants.[4] This provoked an international scandal involving the use of low-grade silicon in implants, gravely endangering the health of women who unknowingly had been in receipt of the implants. Such concerns regarding the safety of such implants and related correspondence led to a recent report in the UK chaired by Professor Bruce Keogh.[5]

A single chapter would not be sufficient to attempt to address thoroughly all of the related issues. Rather, here the focus is upon one particularly challenging aspect of the debate concerning regulation in this area, namely, the use of cosmetic surgery and minors. There has been a gradual rise in access to such procedures by adolescents on both sides of the Atlantic.[6] In 2013, the American Society of Plastic Surgeons reported that the most common cosmetic surgical procedures for teenagers were ear correction, nose reshaping, breast reduction, correction of breast asymmetry and gynecomastia (reduction of excessive breast tissue in teenage boys).[7] The most common non-surgical procedures were laser hair removal, microdermabrasion and chemical peels. In some senses none of this is new: the dialogue around 'perfect children' has generated heated ethical debate since the advent of IVF technology and pre-implantation genetic diagnosis.[8] However, perfecting before conception has now been translated into perfecting *once* born. Is this simply going too far? Has a concern to promote individual autonomy simply reached its limits in this context? What is conspicuous though by its absence from recent reviews of cosmetic surgery in the UK is any attempt to ban the practice itself. This might seem a radical step to address the risks of cosmetic surgery, but it is something that has been under consideration for some time in the Antipodes. Concern in the southern hemisphere has centred upon the impact of the drive to 'perfectionism' in relation to adolescents, and the rising use of cosmetic procedures on young people driven by a perceived 'body beautiful' culture. Such concerns have led not simply to a lively debate upon these issues but actual legislation regulating these questions. If these concerns are so real and so pertinent, should the UK then follow its Australian cousins and statutorily regulate or indeed ban the use of invasive cosmetic procedures upon minors? Is this really instead a question of autonomy – something which should be left to the individual to determine – or are children and adolescents themselves at least different in these circumstances? Where should the boundaries lie?

This chapter first examines the normalising of perfectionism as evidenced through what appears to be increased social acceptability of bodily modification for cosmetic purposes, in general, and in the context of children and adolescents, specifically. Secondly, it examines whether a case for the regulation or prohibition of cosmetic surgery concerning children and adolescents can be made, and

4 Latham, M., '"If It Ain't Broke, Don't Fix It?" Scandals, Risk and Cosmetic Surgery Regulation in the UK and France' (2014) 22(3) *Medical Law Review*, 384–408.

5 See Keogh, B., *Poly Implant Prothèse (PIP) Breast Implants: Final Report of the Expert Group*, London, Department of Health, 18 June 2012.

6 Larson, K. and Gosain, A.K., 'Cosmetic Surgery in the Adolescent Patient' (2012) 129(1) *Plastic & Reconstructive Surgery*, 135e–141e.

7 American Society of Plastic Surgeons, *Plastic Surgery for Teenagers Briefing Paper* (2013), available at: http://www.plasticsurgery.org/news/briefing-papers/plastic-surgery-for-teenagers.html (accessed 13 January 2015).

8 See for example Harris, J., *Wonderwoman and Superman: Ethics of Human Biotechnology*, Oxford, Oxford University Press, 1992; Savulescu, J., 'Procreative Beneficence: Why We Should Select the Best Children' in Holland, S. (ed.) *Arguing About Bioethics*, London, Routledge, 2012, pp. 74–82; Karpin I. and Savell, K., *Perfecting Pregnancy: Law, Disability, and the Future of Reproduction*, Cambridge, Cambridge University Press, 2012.

it explores issues around societal harm. Thirdly, it examines if such procedures should be restricted wholly or in part then before considering what possible regulatory models could be adopted.

Normalising Perfectionism

The normalisation of cosmetic procedures might be a source of fascination, or of humour, or it might simply be an interesting distraction. For many years, however, such procedures were largely the provenance of the very wealthy. The questions were, to that extent, contained. But it is the mainstreaming of such procedures that can be seen as changing the nature of the debate. New and enhanced surgical procedures and treatments have been accompanied by the rise of cut-price providers offering treatments to what is an increasingly mobile patient population. The clinician seen as saviour, through the slash of the knife, is now easily able to provide succour. As Sheila McLean wrote in her book *Old Law, New Medicine*: 'the translation of dissatisfaction into illness, the tendency to turn to medicine for the cure of social and economic dysfunction, have done us no favours'.[9]

Furthermore, as she goes on to comment in the same volume, '[t]he technological impulse or imperative has come to dominate or control … those who are indisputably ill',[10] and as she says this can distort the very humanity it seeks to assist. Of course it is easy to condemn the recipients of cosmetic surgery and to vilify their choices, and indeed as McLean and others have noted elsewhere it can be argued that in the case of a competent adult this is simply a case of an individual making what is an autonomous choice. As McLean has recently cautioned in the light of the PIP implant issue against denying people 'the liberty to do what they want with their own bodies', she recognises that '… they have to be made aware of the risks'.[11] There are, however, interesting questions as to the regulation (and indeed the lack of such regulation) in this area in the UK, and as to the law's response to disability in the context of medicine more generally. Will we soon reach the point where the cosmetically unenhanced can be seen as the 'new disabled'? As Sheila McLean and Laura Wilkinson have noted in their book *Impairment and Disability*,[12] there are two models – two competing approaches to disability. The first is that of the 'medical model'. The second is that of the 'social model'. Of course, as they rightly highlight, these two models are far less distinct and different than they might be viewed at first sight. Clinical approaches to what constitutes disability are informed by the social debate in this area. Clinicians do not operate in a vacuum unencumbered by social and cultural influences. Their perceptions of disability are also informed by cultural and social norms. But, perhaps here lies a major challenge. If such cultural influences define and delineate our understanding in this way, then to what extent might this in turn help to redefine such procedures as being 'normal' in the future? As asked above: will the cosmetically unenhanced become the new *disabled*?

As part of the evidence to the Keogh review a research report was produced assessing the implications of such procedures upon younger recipients.[13] Some of its findings make very uncomfortable reading:

---

9 McLean, S.A.M., *Old Law, New Medicine*, London, Pandora Press, 1998, at p. xi.

10 McLean, note 9, above, at p. 21.

11 Allan, V., 'The Beauty Bomb', *The Sunday Herald*, 8 January 2012, available at: http://www.heraldscotland.com/comment/columnists/the-beauty-bomb.16382838 (accessed 13 January 2015).

12 McLean, S.A.M. and Williamson, L., *Impairment and Disability: Law and Ethics at the Beginning and End of Life*, London, Routledge-Cavendish, 2007.

13 Creative Research, *Regulation of Cosmetic Interventions: Research among Teenage Girls*, 2013.

> For these girls … there is recognition that cosmetic interventions, particularly of the less serious, non-surgical type, have often because so normalised that girls are often surprised to find that procedures such as teeth whitening are classed as cosmetic procedures at all. While cost is a barrier to the more expensive surgical procedures, unsurprisingly at their age, this does not mean that they feel people do not have access to them; it is recognised that many ordinary people desire and manage to find the money to have them and this includes members of their own family as well as friends.[14]

The Report further goes onto state:

> The girls readily admit the pressure regarding their appearance that they feel in their daily lives as they are scrutinised and judged by their peers, and they compare themselves (and others) with the ideal and perfect images presented in the media by celebrities. The pressure to compete with peers as well as envy of celebrities' appearance and the accompanying lifestyle, combines with increasing awareness of the potential to change the way you look, and the solutions available to do so.[15]

As the report notes, in Essex, influenced by television programmes such as *The Only Way is Essex*, there was particular evidence of girls contemplating a range of procedures 'when they are old enough'.[16] Ultimately, however, the questions of adolescents and of cosmetic surgery were not discussed in the Keogh Report itself. Rather the focus of the report, understandably given its remit in relation to examining the implications of the PIP scandal, was upon those issues which were central to the backdrop as to why the Expert Group had been set up initially, namely issues of safety in relation to a range of cosmetic procedures.

While there is some evidence of increase in availability and take up of cosmetic procedures in relation to minors, one problem here is the extent to which there is research concerning the sheer number of such procedures in the UK. There is currently no central collection of such information. Moreover, such procedures are almost invariably undertaken in the private sector, thus some caution is needed. Notwithstanding, the question can be asked once again: is there a (growing) case for regulation or indeed total prohibition of such procedures in relation to minors? In some jurisdictions there are already strong calls for this, and in others legislation already exists, as we shall see below. The approach taken by some members of the medical profession and policy makers in the Antipodes is illustrated by the comments made by the President of the Cosmetic Physicians Society of Australasia who said in July 2013: 'Children should not receive cosmetic or surgical procedures of any kind unless there are compelling medical or psychological reasons'.[17]

Possible analogies can be drawn here with the debates concerning the developments in relation to genetics where it has been suggested by McLean and others that the rise in genetic testing could lead to what might be, in effect, an uninsurable, unemployable underclass.[18] Will it happen in the future that those who are cosmetically unenhanced become a new effectively unemployable underclass? Certainly, the pressure to conform to a certain norm is translating through into the courts in the area of discrimination litigation as highlighted by a notable employment tribunal action

---

14 *Regulation of Cosmetic Interventions*, note 13, above, p. 2, para. 1.2.2.

15 *Regulation of Cosmetic Interventions*, note 13, above, p. 2, para. 1.2.2.

16 *Regulation of Cosmetic Interventions*, note 13, above, p. 2, para. 1.2.2.

17 Carroll, L., 'Doctors Seek Ban on Cosmetic Surgery for Under 18s', *Sydney Morning Herald*, 22 July 2013, available at: http://www.smh.com.au/lifestyle/beauty/doctors-seek-ban-on-cosmetic-surgery-for-under18s-20130721-2qcp8.html (accessed 13 January 2015).

18 See McLean, note 9, above, at p. 175.

by the BBC TV presenter Miriam O'Reilly. O'Reilly successfully brought an age discrimination case against the BBC.[19] In evidence to this tribunal it was suggested that O'Reilly's manager had suggested that the presenter undertake cosmetic enhancements (which she did not do).

If the normalisation of the pursuit of perfection in relation to children and adolescents is, indeed, a serious concern, then it is suggested that we should at least be willing to explore the prospect of regulation. But where, precisely, should the boundaries lie here? This question is addressed in the next section.

Children, Adolescents and Cosmetic Surgery: A Case for Regulation?

There is at present no general overarching regulation of the performance of cosmetic surgery upon children and adolescents. That does not mean, however, that the law is not concerned with such procedures at all; indeed, as closer examination of such issues illustrates, the law does serve to delineate the boundaries of this area. Here we consider what cosmetic procedures a child or their parents can consent to at present, and what current legal regulation exists. Secondly, we consider whether there is a case for such regulation, either in its current form or extended to address issues that accompany the growth of the practices, as outlined above.

Much of the discussion around the formation of health law in the UK has centred on the importance of respect for decision-making autonomy. However, decisional autonomy concerning consent to treatment only goes so far in English law. The nature of consent is circumscribed. For example, English law does not allow an individual to consent to the infliction of harm, however grave.[20] It should be noted that specific surgical procedures are subject to the criminal law, for example, female genital mutilation is criminalised under the Prohibition of Female Genital Mutilation Act 2003. In relation to cosmetic and related procedures there are two examples of specific criminal prohibitions. First, let us consider the use of sunbeds. Concern in the 2000s arose in relation to the use of sunbeds. Tanning was seen as increasingly fashionable and this led to a large increase in the availability of tanning salons. At the same time, clinicians became concerned at the development of skin cancers linked to sunbed use and the rise in such cancers in young people. Such concerns led to legislation in the form of the Sunbeds (Regulation) Act 2010. Section 2 provides that there is a duty upon persons who carry on a 'sunbed business' that no person under 18 uses a sunbed on the 'relevant' premises to which it relates. In addition, the Act provides that no offers should be made to make a sunbed available for use on such premises by persons under 18. The Act does, however, recognise that there are some skin conditions for which sunbed treatment would be recommended. Consequently, it is provided that use of sunbeds are not subject to such regulation under section 3(1) of the legislation if:

> (a) the use is for the purpose of medical treatment provided under the supervision or direction of a registered medical practitioner, and
> (b) the sunbed is a dedicated sunbed in, or provided by, a healthcare establishment.[21]

---

19 *O'Reilly v. BBC and Another*, 2200423/2010.

20 *R v. Brown* [1994] 1 AC 212.

21 s. 3(1) Sunbeds (Regulation) Act 2010. Healthcare establishments include hospitals as defined under s. 275 of the National Health Service Act 2006.

The only other direct statutory ban in relation to cosmetic procedures is in relation to tattoos. The Tattooing of Minors Act 1969 prohibits the tattooing of persons under the age of 18. Section 1 of the Act provides:

> It shall be an offence to tattoo a person under the age of eighteen except when the tattoo is performed for medical reasons by a duly qualified medical practitioner or by a person working under his direction, but it shall be a defence for a person charged to show that at the time the tattoo was performed he had reasonable cause to believe that the person tattooed was of, or over, the age of eighteen and did in fact so believe.

In contrast, the performance of other cosmetic procedures on children or adolescents is in practice subject to self-regulation of clinicians.[22] However, that does not necessarily mean that the performance of certain cosmetic procedures upon minors would necessarily fall within the category of procedures which can be consented to in English law, whether by the minor or by her or his parents. This raises the question as to whether cosmetic surgery is the type of procedure to which minors are able to give consent themselves, or indeed whether their parents are able to consent lawfully to such procedures on their behalf. Undertaking medical procedures without consent may lead to a prosecution in relation to common law offences of assault and battery, or one of the offences under the Offences Against the Person Act 1861. In the case of children, consent to treatment may be given by children themselves if they have decision-making capacity or consent can be given by the person with parental responsibility if the child lacks decision-making capacity, or if they themselves are unwilling or unable to make that decision. The Family Law Reform Act 1969, section 8, provides that minors over 16 may consent to surgical, medical and dental treatment. In the House of Lords in *Gillick v. West Norfolk and Wisbech Area Health Authority*[23] it was held that the test for determining decision-making capacity related to whether a child has attained sufficient maturity and, inter alia, whether the decision is in their own best interests.[24] While children over the age of 16, or those under 16 who are *Gillick* competent, can consent if they have capacity, should they refuse consent their rights to decision-making autonomy are circumscribed. The decision of a competent minor to refuse treatment can be overridden either by the child's parents or by the court exercising its inherent jurisdiction to act in the best interests of the child.[25] But whether consent can be given to cosmetic surgery remains uncertain.

Does, and indeed should, cosmetic surgery constitute 'proper medical treatment'?[26] Cosmetic surgery itself, as we have seen, covers a broad spectrum – from the removal of birthmarks, to cleft palate surgery and on to breast augmentation. Some of these procedures may be thought to fall within this category, whether all these procedures can be so classified is, however, an entirely separate issue. Are these 'acceptable harms' or rather is this something that the law can and should directly regulate? Can such procedures be seen as inflicting undue harm and not constituting 'proper' medical treatment?

Specific harms may be pointed to here: first and foremost, harm to the individual child. The performance of surgery may itself cause harm physical pain and suffering and other consequent

22 See Latham, note 4, above, at p. 15.

23 [1986] AC 112, [1986] 1 FLR 229, [1985] UKHL 7.

24 [1985] 3 All ER 402.

25 See further *Re R (A Minor) (Wardship: Medical Treatment)* [1992] 1 FLR 190 and *Re W (A Minor) (Consent to Medical Treatment)* [1993] 1 FLR 1.

26 In *Attorney General's Reference (No 6 of 1980)* Lord Lane CJ held that 'reasonable surgical interference' fell outside the criminal law. See also *Airedale NHS Trust v. Bland* [1993] 1 All ER 821.

trauma. Cosmetic procedures, as we have seen earlier in this chapter, can be very risky indeed. Nonetheless, many other surgical procedures are clearly risky but are nonetheless regarded as involving risks that are worth taking within the sphere of an individual's autonomous choosing. The balance choice is to prefer the (perceived) benefit of the procedure over the risks which arise consequent upon the performance of surgery.

This might also be seen to be the case in relation to certain 'cosmetic' procedures. Take the removal of a birth mark, for example. This may be seen as 'cosmetic' in that its presence by itself may not be thought to impact directly on the physical health of the child. However, the continued presence of the birthmark might impact upon the health of the child in other ways, for example if the child suffers bullying in relation to their appearance and this causes psychological distress. In turn, psychological harm may translate into damage to physical health. Thus, it could be argued that removal of the birthmark would be clearly therapeutic. Would the same argument apply, however, in relation to breast implants in a situation in which a teenager is bullied because they have small breasts? Should cosmetic procedures be sanctioned to enable a person to better 'fit in' to society? How does, for example, this argument translate in relation to an adolescent with Down's Syndrome where undertaking surgery might leave the individual less visibly affected by disability?[27]

In such a situation do we need to consider not only the potential harms to the individual but also broader societal harms which might result from sanctioning such an action? For society, the NHS or indeed parents to condone/support/fund such cosmetic procedures could be seen as an endorsement of the view that a child or adolescent is somehow defective, subnormal or less than perfect. This, in turn, could be seen as a movement down the slippery slope towards an increasingly homogenised society. It could, ultimately, be seen as condoning unacceptable discriminatory attitudes and behaviour.

Furthermore, in a situation in which parents or courts are required to give consent for such procedures to be undertaken can it be truly said that such procedures are in the best interests of the minor? Brazier and Cave have suggested that such surgery could be said not to be in a child's best interests.[28] On the other hand, they admit that this may be context dependent and that such procedures may be justifiable in particular circumstances. An example is of surgery in relation to 'bat ears'. It is suggested that this would involve a balancing test between the pain of the surgery and whether a child would be taunted over their physical appearance.

Thirdly, while a mature minor can give consent in principle, we must ask whether this would truly be voluntary consent. While in cases such as *Gillick* the courts have demonstrated recognition and respect for children's decision-making autonomy in principle, whether a minor *actually* has such decision-making autonomy in a specific situation becomes a decision-relative test. The graver the decision and the resultant consequences, this might work against a minor being found to actually have decision-making capacity to make this particular decision. Some procedures have major long-term consequences, and yet might not be lifesaving. Furthermore to what extent is it the case that the social and cultural context would suggest that such decisions were not truly autonomous?

If the decision to undergo cosmetic surgery is impacted in such a way by cultural and social norms, and those norms in turn are defined by commercial or clinical pressures, then to what extent are the decisions that are made, once again, truly autonomous choices? Now, of course, admittedly the same argument could be applied to many choices in day-to-day life that we still recognise as being made autonomously. Consider, for example, the debates around obesity and the impact

27 See further Jones, R.B., 'Parental Consent to Cosmetic Facial Surgery in Down's Syndrome' (2000) 26 *Journal of Medical Ethics*, 101–2.

28 Brazier, M.R. and Cave, E., *Medicine, Patients and the Law*, 5th edn, London, Penguin, 2011.

of the food industries upon such perceived autonomous choices. Nonetheless, the difficulty of identifying what might be an autonomous choice does not mean that the validity of what constitutes an autonomous choice in this context should not be subject to further scrutiny.

Regulation of Cosmetic Procedures Concerning Minors: Options for Reform

As we have seen above, the growth of cosmetic procedures and their use by minors poses considerable challenges. There needs to be an active debate on this issue by policy makers and wider society. It is also conceded that some apparently 'cosmetic' procedures might be justified for therapeutic reasons. But, if it is accepted in relation to minors that the prospect of harm here is such that respect for individual and parental decision-making autonomy might legitimately be overridden, then a further issue arises: what approach should be taken? Various options are available.

First, we could trust to professional self-regulation. The clinician could be left as gatekeeper with the ability to restrict availability and access to such procedures. Such an argument can be summed up as: 'We should essentially leave it to and trust individual doctors'. This has the advantage of recognising that some of these decisions can indeed be problematic and ethically complex, and the solution as to the desirability of surgery can vary from case to case. But would this be enough? It is submitted that it would not be. Medical self-regulation in the past has not proved unproblematic and there has indeed been a much-chequered history.[29] Moreover, many cosmetic procedures in relation to which specific public policy issues may arise are those which would normally be undertaken in the private sector. The rise and rise of private sector medicine raises many challenges for the provision of healthcare in general. The rise of healthcare as a business stretches notions of professional ethical codes. Comparisons with other areas of business such as banking sadly illustrate that on occasions professional ethics and profit are uneasy bedfellows. Turning down a patient may simply be bad for business. In addition, concerns around the ethics and efficacy of cosmetic procedures in other contexts have led consistently to calls for regulation in this area, heightened by recent scandals. As the Keogh Report commented: 'Previous attempts at self-regulation in the industry have failed, largely because voluntary codes have meant that only the best in this disparate sector commit themselves to better practice, while the unscrupulous and unsafe carry on as before'.[30] The problem at present is that there is simply no comprehensive regulation of practitioners in this area.

This leads us neatly to the second possible option here. We could require that cosmetic surgery in general, and cosmetic surgery procedures upon minors in particular, should be subject to specific overarching statutory regulation. This would have the advantage of addressing three critical issues: (1) the safety of products used, for example the implants themselves, (2) the question of the safety of the particular practitioners, and (3) the safety of the particular patients. And yet it must be remembered that there is already broader engagement with the question of the safety of the *products* themselves at EU level. The existing EU Medical Devices Directives are to be subject to reform through the introduction of a new Regulation.[31] This Regulation tightens up some of

---

29 Stacey, M., *Regulating British Medicine: General Medical Council*, Chichester, John Wiley, 1992; Davis, M., *Medical Self-Regulation: Crisis and Change*, Aldershot, Ashgate, 2007.

30 Keogh, note 5, above, at p. 5.

31 Council Directive 93/42/EEC of 14 June 1993 concerning medical devices [1993] OJ L169/1 (as amended). Commission, 'Proposal for a Regulation of the European Parliament and of the Council on Medical Devices, and Amending Directive 2001/83/EC, Regulation (EC) No 178/2002 and Regulation (EC) No 1223/2009' COM (2012) 542 final.

the issues concerning quality and safety. But simply regulating products remains a fragmented approach concerning cosmetic procedures, albeit a necessary one. So one option would be to go further and to establish a specific statutory framework for the regulation of cosmetic procedures as well as products. There have been attempts to do this in the past. For example, the MP Anne Clwyd introduced the Regulation of Cosmetic Surgery Bill into Parliament in 2004. Some statutory regulation of clinics themselves was introduced through the Care Standards Act in 2000 accompanied by set national minimum standards. The function of oversight of such clinics was taken over by the Care Quality Commission established under the Health and Social Care Act 2008. The introduction of legislation was something that – while mooted – was not taken forward in the Keogh review. Keogh proposed that there must be a register of providers. In addition there should be accredited qualifications developed and also that there should be specific standards on formal certification, training by a committee that has now been established by the Royal College of Surgeons: the Inter-speciality Committee on Cosmetic Surgery.[32] The Report also recommended that the Parliamentary and Health Service Ombudsman powers be extended to the private sector.[33]

Cosmetic surgeons themselves have supported some degree of regulation of their practice. In 2012 cosmetic surgeons recommended that there should be restrictions, for example, on advertisements for persons under the age of 18.[34] A major question remains, however, in relation to the rise of the non-professional/unqualified practitioner in relation, for example, to the administration of such things as dermal fillers. There are consequent questions of competence, of safety and of administration, along with the lack of an effective audit trail and aftercare. A statutory framework would enable questions of professional competence, product safety and issues of ethics to be addressed through a single structure.

A possible model would be statutory frameworks such as those established by the Human Fertilisation and Embryology Act 1990 and the Human Tissue Act 2004. The formula employed in these statutes is to set up an overarching regulatory body – in the case of the former, the Human Fertilisation and Embryology Authority (HFEA), and the latter, the Human Tissue Authority (HTA) – chaired by a respected independent figure with public standing. Secondly, such a statutory framework can specifically provide that certain activities are subject to regulation – usually through a licensing scheme – and kept under review. As with the HFEA and HTA, this could also lead to the licensing of premises where such activities were undertaken. A new Authority could also be involved in the licensing of practitioners. Practitioners could be required to meet specified levels of professional competence to undertake their role and this could be subject to re-validation and licensing.

In the case of minors, specific safeguards could be put into place. So for example, as in the case of live organ donation under the Human Tissue Act, such transplants from a child donor could require specific approval. Here currently judicial approval is required alongside approval from a special three-person expert panel of the Human Tissue Authority. This type of model could be utilised in relation to serious invasive cosmetic procedures. Alternatively, the decision could simply be left to a three-person expert panel of the regulatory body. Entrenched at the heart of the legislation regulating decisions related to children could be a provision requiring that the welfare of the child was paramount and all such procedures would be assessed in relation to what was the child's best interests.

---

32 See further Keogh, note 5, above, at p. 7.

33 Keogh, note 5, above, at p. 8.

34 See British Association of Aesthetic Plastic Surgeons, 'Mary Had a Little Lipo? Protect Children from Surgery Ads', available at: http://baaps.org.uk/about-us/press-releases/1420-mary-had-a-little-lipo-protect-children-from-surgery-ads (accessed 13 January 2015).

While this may facilitate consistency and effective decision-making, such radical legislative reform would require the political will to drive it forward; yet, as we have seen in the aftermath of the Keogh Report, such regulation does not appear likely in the near future. The Keogh Report suggested a series of regulatory measures some of which rely on self-regulation, though others go beyond this; nonetheless, the Expert Group did not propose comprehensive statutory regulation. It recommended instead that there should be greater oversight of private medicine in this area by a special Ombudsman. All cosmetic surgeons are to be given approved training. The Royal College of Surgeons is to set standards. One of the major problems of this area is that of the business dimension. Keogh said there needed to be an advertising Code of Conduct which could address concerns regarding the use of such things as promotional cut-price surgery offers. More formal training is also to be required of beauticians who inject fillers and so on. However, this still remains a piecemeal approach and none of these recommendations specifically addresses the question of children and adolescents.

There is, however, a third option which could be taken, though possibly combined with elements of option two: that of specific statutory regulation of cosmetic surgery procedures concerning children. We saw earlier that there were a number of possible identifiable harms in relation to the inclusion of children in cosmetic surgery procedures but that the law as it stood was fundamentally too uncertain to address these issues. This could take several forms. There could be specific statutory regulation of such procedures with a regulatory body such as that suggested above in relation to such procedures in general. Alternatively, or in addition, this could be combined with the use of the criminal law.

Would the criminal law be a helpful option here? In particular, what about a criminal law prohibition upon the use of cosmetic procedures concerning minors? First, the surgical risks of such procedures might not be seen as justifiable when taken in the context of the rationale for the performance of such procedures. All surgery inevitably involves risks. And yet, while arguments for respecting individual autonomy and personal liberty – however unwise to the outsider – may demand respect in relation to adults, as we saw above it can be argued that children should be viewed differently. There is a precedent for this approach. As has been noted, the rise of the body beautiful culture and the extent to which teenagers were going under the knife caused particular concerns in Australia in the 2000s. In 2008 this led to statutory reform in the state of Queensland. The performance of cosmetic surgery procedures on minors was criminalised under the Public Health Act 2005. Such procedures are subject to a fine of some $150,000 or up to two years in prison. The statute sets out what is considered a 'cosmetic procedure'. It is defined in section 213A as including abdominoplasty, foreheadplasty, liposuction or liposculpture, resurfacing of the skin by removal of the epidermis, and penetration of the papillary dermas, insertion of facial contour implants, mammoplasty, genioplasty, insertion of permanent injectable fillers, rhinoplasty and porcelain veneer of teeth. Interestingly other procedures, some of which are considered controversial and have led to debate in the past, are not included; these include, circumcision of the penis, correction of disfiguring scarring resulting from a medical condition, illness or trauma, and removal of a tattoo. In addition some specific 'cosmetic procedures' are sanctioned for medical purposes to correct deformities, congenital abnormalities or physical effect of a medical condition, illness or trauma.

As can be seen, then, the statute did not criminalise all such activities. In some circumstances such procedures were regarded as legitimate. The Public Health Act 2005 section 213B of that state provides that an action will not be an offence if committed in a situation in which a person 'believes, on grounds that are reasonable in the circumstances, that performance of the procedure is in the best interests of the child'. In establishing such a belief the following criteria also needed to have been taken into account:

- ... views of the child (including the reasons the procedure is wanted), taking into account the child's maturity and understanding of the procedure, its risks, limitations and consequences;
- ... views of the parent, including whether the parent supports the procedure;
- ... the child's physical and psychological health ...;
- ... timing of the procedure, including whether waiting until the child is an adult is preferable.

The Queensland statute can be seen to take a balanced approach, recognising that in some instances procedures may be justified while at the same time targeting many general forms of cosmetic surgery. It is unclear at present as to what precise impact the legislation has had in Queensland. Any legislation would need to carefully delineate which procedures were included. Still, the Queensland statute does provide a useful model here. As can be seen there are exceptions for certain procedures such as male circumcision. This is a highly controversial issue itself involving charged debates concerning bodily integrity.[35] It is submitted that a statute engaging with cosmetic surgery questions may not be the best place to engage with such an issue. If the Queensland approach was followed, a grey area would develop concerning what should fall into the category of those procedures that are to be sanctioned and this would need to be carefully interpreted to avoid the legislation being undermined. Practitioners in the area, both medical and non-medical, would need to be educated as to the impact of the legislation. Moreover, to be effective such legislation would need to be effectively monitored. This then takes us back to the whole question of an oversight body, as such would be ultimately needed regardless of the kinds of sanctions imposed.

Conclusion

As Shelia McLean and Gerry Maher so eloquently highlighted in their book, medical decisions themselves are fundamentally very complex. It is impossible to critique effectively medical practice and outside its context to recognise the part played by other factors whether law, morals or social considerations.[36] Any amendment of the law in this area is likely to prove exceedingly controversial. But it is submitted that this is one issue that we do need to address as part of a thorough reconsideration of the law applying to the kinds of choices that children can take with respect to their bodies. The relationship between choice and vulnerability in decision-making may clearly prove a problematic one. Nonetheless, there do appear to be clearly identifiable harms in this context. There is, first, the risk of the procedure itself and the consequences of undertaking serious cosmetic surgery with consequent problems in undertaking revocation of such surgery upon individuals whose bodies are still growing. Secondly, broader societal harms might arise from the message that we are sending out to children. Yes, there is clearly a question here in relation to older persons and the use of cosmetic procedures, but in the case of children there is a very challenging issue concerning the vulnerability of children bombarded with unreal images of body perfectionism. And, of course, there is the ultimate question of whether regulation would work at all? Would the adolescent and parent denied surgery in the UK simply hop on Eurostar or EasyJet and receive treatment elsewhere? The last few years have been characterised by the rise and rise of health tourism. Here, as in any other area of healthcare, attempts to regulate may be frustrated by the ability to travel and access a global market in healthcare. But that does not

35 See Fox, M. and Thomson, M., 'Reconsidering "Best Interests": Male Circumcision and the Rights of the Child' in Milos, M. (ed.) *Human Rights and Circumcision*, New York, Springer, 2009, 15–31.

36 See further McLean, S.A.M. and Maher, G., *Medicine, Morals and the Law*, Aldershot, Gower, 1983.

mean that we should not address this issue. It is too easy to assume that globalisation means that resistance in the form of regulation is futile.

It is suggested that there does need to be a reflective debate upon such issues in the UK. It is also recognised that any such debate and indeed regulation will be challenging. But perhaps the tipping point has been reached and the time has come for regulation – even perhaps the outright prohibition of cosmetic procedures concerning children and adolescents – to be placed squarely on the agenda.

Chapter 13

Legal Regulation of New Technologies: Re-thinking Xenotechnologies in the Twenty-first Century

Marie Fox*

Introduction

A central preoccupation of contemporary health law is how law should respond to new technologies.[1] Indeed some commentators have even proposed that 'Law and Technology' may now comprise a new legal sub-discipline of interest to property, environmental, human rights, tort and international trade lawyers, as well as health lawyers.[2] New technologies currently attracting public concern and legal attention include nanotechnology,[3] neurotechnology,[4] and genetic and other forms of enhancement technology.[5] In common with past technological innovations each is seen as holding out tremendous promise, but this hope is accompanied by significant risks that fuel demands for regulation. Yet, as Barbara Koening has argued, over time these technological innovations frequently become routine so that ethico-legal concerns about the technology tend to fade.[6] Such a process can be traced, for instance, in the widespread use and subsequent normalisation of IVF technologies;[7] although as Sarah Franklin's recent history of IVF and stem cells reminds us, a certain ambivalence continues to characterise our response to these technologies.[8] In the case of certain biotechnologies, however, law and other forces may conspire to prevent the technology becoming

---

* I would like to acknowledge the helpful feedback from the editors and other participants at the workshop preceding this volume.

1 Brownsword, R. and Goodwin, M., *Law and the Technologies of the Twenty-First Century*, Cambridge, Cambridge University Press, 2012; Brownsword, R. and Yueng, K. (eds) *Regulating Technologies: Legal Futures, Regulatory Frames and Technological Fixes*, Oxford, Hart Publishing, 2008.

2 Brownsword and Goodwin, note 1, above, at p. 3.

3 Deissie, H.T., 'Taming Matter for the Welfare of Humanity: Regulating Nanotechnology' in Brownsword and Yueng, note 1, above, at pp. 327–56; Stokes, E., 'Nanotechnology and the Products of Inherited Regulation' (2012) 39 *Journal of Law and Society*, 93–112; Lee, R.G. and Petts, J., 'Adaptive Governance for Responsible Innovation' in Owen, R., Heintz, M. and Bessant J. (eds) *Responsible Innovation*, London, Wiley, 2013, pp. 143–64.

4 Brownsword, R., 'Regulating Brain Imaging: Challenge and Opportunity' (2009) 3 *Frontiers in Human Neuroscience*, 1–2; Nuffield Council on Bioethics, *Novel Neurotechnologies: Intervening in the Brain*, London, 2013.

5 Harris, J., *Enhancing Evolution: The Ethical Case for Making Better People*, Princeton, NJ, Princeton University Press, 2007.

6 Koenig, B., 'The Technological Imperative in Medical Practice: The Social Creation of a "Routine" Treatment' in Lock, M. and Gordon, D. (eds) *Biomedicine Examined*, London, Kluwer, 1988, pp. 465–96.

7 Thompson, C., *Making Parents: The Ontological Choreography of Reproductive Technologies*, Cambridge, MA, MIT Press, 2005.

8 Franklin, S. *Biological Relatives: IVF, Stem Cells and the Future of Kinship*, Durham, NC, Duke University Press, 2013.

routine, so that the concerns they have historically evoked remain potent, although the particular form these concerns take may change through time. This chapter uses xenotransplantation as a case study in legal regulation, tracing a regulatory history which saw xenotechnologies[9] become the subject of intense regulatory attention in the mid 1990s, but recede from public view over the past 20 years, even as scientific innovation in this field has continued apace. Throughout this period Sheila McLean's work has played a pivotal role in shaping legal thinking about this technology in the UK, at a time when leading scientists in the field were working in this jurisdiction and, as with IVF, when the UK was perceived to be in the regulatory vanguard in framing responses to xenotechnologies. Reflecting her prominence in shaping the field of health law more broadly,[10] McLean has contributed both to policy formation as a key member of UKXIRA (the regulatory body established to oversee this technology) while also offering a searching ethico-legal critique of the practice, notably in a commissioned co-authored report which was controversially supressed by the Department of Health,[11] and subsequently published as the seminal monograph in the field in 2005.[12] In light of the developments in the decade following publication of *Xenotransplantation: Law and Ethics*, I suggest that the failure of successive governments to implement McLean and Williamson's proposals have contributed to the current unsatisfactory regulatory vacuum, demonstrating the prescience of McLean's vision. However, I contend that the time for advocating legislation with the express purpose of regulating xenotransplantation along the lines that McLean and Williamson proposed may now have passed, and that there is a need to frame new regulatory approaches fit for purpose in the twenty-first century. Although xenotransplantation has faded from the regulatory agenda, as attention has switched to the technologies noted above,[13] nevertheless productive scholarship on xenotransplantation has occurred, notably in the disciplines of anthropology and sociology. In this chapter I suggest that in framing an appropriate response to xenotechnologies in a changing regulatory environment[14] legal scholars should take seriously the questions posed, and learn from the insights and methodologies drawn from other disciplines. Such scholarship has raised important questions about the values that should underpin technological innovation which are to date largely ignored in legal discussions of how to regulate innovative techniques such as

9 As I have argued elsewhere, the range of technologies encompassed under the umbrella term 'xenotransplantation' make it more appropriate to speak of a range of technologies rather than a unified practice – see Fox, M., 'Rethinking the Animal/Human Boundary: The Impact of Xenotechnologies' (2005) 26 *Liverpool Law Review*, 149–67. In similar vein Haddow et al. adopt the term 'xeno-practices' – see Haddow, G., Bruce, A., Calvert, J., et al., 'Not "Human" Enough to Be Human, But Not Animal Enough to Be "Animal": The Case of the HFEA, Cybrids and Xenotransplantation in the UK' (2010) 29 *New Genetics and Society*, 3–17.

10 Fox, M. and Murphy, T., 'The Body, Bodies, Embodiment: Feminist, Legal Engagement with Health' in Davies M. and Munro V. (eds) *The Ashgate Research Companion to Feminist Legal Theory*, Farnham, Ashgate, 2013, pp. 249–66, at pp. 249–50.

11 Townsend, M., 'Doubts on Pig Organ Transplants Ignored', *The Observer*, 29 June 2003, available at: http://www.theguardian.com/politics/2003/jun/29/health.healthandwellbeing (accessed 13 January 2015).

12 McLean, S.A.M. and Williamson, L., *Xenotransplantation: Law and Ethics*, Aldershot, Ashgate, 2005.

13 In this regard it is worth noting that xenotransplantation is not even indexed in Brownsword and Goodwins' *Law and the Technologies of the Twenty-First Century*, note 1, above.

14 Brownsword and Goodwin, note 1, above, at p. 27 define the regulatory environment as 'a context that has a certain coding for action, a coding that signals whether various acts are permitted (even required) or prohibited, whether they will be viewed positively or neutrally, whether they incentivised or disincentivised, whether they are likely to be praised or criticised, even whether they are possible or impossible and so on'.

what it means to be human,[15] and how technologies serve to redefine the meaning of medicine, health and kinship.[16]

The Promissory Potential of the Xeno Era

The story of xenotechnologies – which may be broadly defined as the transplantation of body parts between different species, comprising both whole organ transplants and the use of animal cells or tissues – has a long genealogy dating back on some accounts to the mid-seventeenth century.[17] Periodically since that time interest in xenotransplantation has been rekindled only to fade away, and as Lesley Sharp has shown, xenotransplantation served to underpin, but was then eclipsed by, the success of allotransplantation.[18] Notable, albeit failed, experiments in xenotransplantation involving primate transplants to humans marked the middle years of the twentieth century, and culminated in the infamous 'Baby Fae' case in which a 14-day old human infant was given a baboon heart transplant and survived for 21 days before dying of heart failure caused by acute organ rejection. Negative reactions to this scandal caused interest in xenotransplantation to wane. However, approximately 20 years ago in the mid 1990s, the procedure became the focus of acute media, policy and legal attention, starting with a report by the Nuffield Council on Bioethics published in 1996, which noted: 'Recent developments suggest that transplantation teams are making progress in controlling the immune response to animal transplants in order to prevent rejection … it is looking increasingly probable that many of the biological obstacles to xenotransplantation will eventually be overcome'.[19]

Nik Brown and Sian Beynon-Jones have criticised the Nuffield Council's uncritical acceptance of a series of announcements the previous year by the (now defunct) British Biotech firm Imutran, to the effect that it would imminently be in a position to transplant whole pig organs to humans following preclinical experiments with primates, and accused it of a panicked response to commercial predictions, never validated by peer review which were subsequently revealed to be, at best, hopelessly optimistic.[20] Yet, in retrospect, it is apparent that at this historical juncture the promissory scientific claims made by key scientific stakeholders were more likely to be accepted because this was an era in which the trials being conducted and the regulatory responses being devised was marked by a number of special features. Sharp has argued persuasively that globally the mid 1990s marked the end of a 30-year period dating back to the mid 1960s which can now be 'celebrated as a golden era of bold surgical efforts'.[21] Certainly in the UK, in this period predating the Alder Hey

15 See, for example Fuller, S., *Humanity 2.0: What It Means to Be Human Past, Present and Future*, Houndsmills, Palgrave, 2011.

16 See, for example, Brown, N. and Webster, A., *New Medical Technologies and Society: Reordering Life*, Cambridge, Polity Press, 2004.

17 For details of this history see, McLean and Williamson, note 12, above, ch. 2; Persson, A. and Welin, S., *Contested Technologies: Xenotransplantation and Human Embryonic Stem Cells*, Lund, Nordic Academic Press, 2008, ch. 2.

18 Sharp, L.A., *The Transplant Imaginary: Mechanical Hearts, Animal Parts and Moral Thinking in Highly Experimental Science*, Berkeley and Los Angeles, CA, University of California Press, 2013.

19 Nuffield Council on Bioethics, *Animal-to-Human Transplants: The Ethics of Xenotransplantation*, London, 1996.

20 Brown, N. and Beynon-Jones, S., '"Reflex Regulation": An Anatomy of Promissory Science Governance' (2012) 14 *Health, Risk & Society*, 223–40, at p. 227.

21 Sharp, note 18, above, at p. 52.

and Bristol organ retention scandals of the late 1990s, public concerns about transplantation were for the most part limited to the question of how to increase the supply of human organs which was radically outstripped by demand. Concerns that were shortly to emerge about how organs were taken and used in the absence of consent and about inappropriate commodification of body parts were relatively muted at this point, as hope in new technologies to address infertility, organ failure and a range of other medicalised problems was at its height. Alarm about the growing shortage of suitable human organs for transplantation purposes, coupled with awareness of the limitations of artificial organs, led to xenotransplantation being touted as a possible solution to the crisis,[22] and to biotechnology companies investing considerable sums in the technique.[23] In response, a number of high-profile reports were commissioned. The Nuffield Council report in 1996 (hereafter 'the Nuffield Report') was swiftly followed by a report Ian Kennedy produced for the Department of Health (hereafter 'the Kennedy Report') which was equally accepting of the views of scientific stakeholders,[24] while at the supranational level the Council of Europe published a 'State of the Art Report' in 1997.[25] With hindsight it is ironic that these reports canvassing regulatory responses appeared at precisely the moment when this period of intensely visible activity in the xeno field was actually drawing to a close, and it is now possible to characterise both UK reports, as well as academic responses to them, as products of a particular time, whose authors were responding to a regulatory environment which has since altered significantly.

As Thérèse Murphy and Gearoid O'Cuinn have observed, legal discussions about how to regulate technology typically focus on 'the force of law as prohibiting or enabling, on law's capacity to protect and promote (whether that be protecting and promoting new health technologies, or the rights and dignity of individuals where these are seen to be threatened by such technologies, real or potential)'.[26] In practice they argue that this tends to mean that '… new health technologies produce calls for more law and, from others, for less law. There tends to be lots of talk of law acting as limit and, equally, lots of talk of the limits of law';[27] however, there is less consideration of the values or purposes of law. Certainly this 'more law' view was the vision of law that underpinned both the Nuffield and Kennedy reports. The 'more law' stance is particularly evident in the emphasis in the Kennedy Report on the centrality of law to the regulatory scheme it proposes: '[S]ome form of regulatory system is essential. This system must be founded in law as the nature of our concerns regarding the protection of animal welfare and the control of risk to humans through, in particular infection, are such as to make legal regulation essential'.[28]

This conclusion followed from an extensive overview of the legal provisions – at both national and EU level – that were then in place to govern the procedure. The Kennedy Advisory Group agreed that these provisions contained important lacunae, with the result that it was uncertain how far the law protected the welfare of both animal and human subjects:

22 On the construction of this crisis see Sharp, note 18, above, ch. 2.

23 Persson and Welin, note 17, above, ch. 5.

24 Department of Health, *Animal Tissue into Humans: A Report by the Advisory Group on the Ethics of Xenotransplantation*, London, 1996 (Kennedy Report).

25 Council of Europe, *Xenotransplantation: State of the Art*, Strasbourg, 1997.

26 Murphy, T. and O'Cuinn, G., 'Taking Technology Seriously: STS as a Human Rights Method' in Flear, M.L., Farrell, A.-M., Hervey, T.K. and Murphy, T. (eds) *European Law and New Health Technologies*, Oxford, Oxford University Press, 2013, pp. 285–308, at p. 289.

27 Note 26, above, at p. 304.

28 Kennedy Report, note 24, above, at para. 8.3.

> [The] existing legal framework is inadequate to answer our concerns about risks to patients and the wider population … we recommend that the legislation which we propose take account of [the highly regarded regulatory procedures which exist to govern other aspects of healthcare] so as to ensure that a similar structure is put in place to regulate any procedure involving xenotransplantation.[29]

While the Nuffield Report agreed that some 'regulatory framework' was necessary to guarantee the safety and quality of animal organs and tissue[30] and to allay public concerns,[31] it was more open as to the legal status of the regulatory entity, suggesting that a non-statutory body akin to the Gene Therapy Advisory Committee, which oversees ethical approval of gene therapy clinical trials, might suffice. The Kennedy Report, however, was categorical that its proposed 'National Standing Body' must have statutory backing: 'We state here our view that *new, specific primary legislation* to regulate xenotransplantation is required in the interests of patients, public health and animal welfare'.[32]

Acknowledging pressure on the Parliamentary timetable, it conceded that a non-statutory body would suffice in the short term but *only* until legislation could be enacted. Equally, it was clear that a Code of Practice or other non-statutory guidance was simply not adequate. The Kennedy Report proceeded to outline the onerous and specialist duties that should be entrusted to this statutory body. These were to include standard-setting and overview tasks; advising on research to be carried out (in relation to infection risks, immunology and physiology) and assessing whether it was safe and ethical for trials on humans to begin; defining measures to measure public health risks; setting animal welfare standards in conjunction with the Home Office; and devising arrangements for long-term surveillance and follow up of xenotransplant recipients. The proposed statutory body was also to be responsible for implementation measures such as approving and licensing clinical sites and animal facilities and approving applications for clinical trials subject to various conditions and keeping under review developments in the field.[33] This list of statutory functions is strikingly similar to those carried out by the Human Fertilisation and Embryology Authority (HFEA), and in terms of membership, the Kennedy Advisory Group's recommendations echo those of the Warnock Committee in proposing that to command public respect, along with that of animal welfare groups and the medical scientific community, '… its membership must reflect an appropriate range of expertise and interests'.[34] These recommendations for a statutory body with wide-ranging powers were generally applauded by commentators at the time,[35] and the failure of the Labour Government to give legislative backing to the interim regulatory body – UKXIRA – established in the wake of the Nuffield and Kennedy reports, lies at the heart of McLean and Williamson's critique of the legal governance of xenotransplantation in their monograph. In an analysis clearly informed by McLean's experience of serving on UKXIRA during its tenure from 1997 to 2007, they argue that its regulatory role was hampered by its status as a non-departmental public body. Specifically its inability to impose sanctions meant that in order to secure compliance it needed to 'work in co-operation with industry and its impact and success as an advisory body [were] dependent

---

29 Kennedy Report, note 24, above, at para. 8.67.

30 Kennedy Report, note 24, above, at para. 6.32.

31 Kennedy Report, note 24, above, at para. 6.38.

32 Kennedy Report, note 24, above, at para. 9.2.

33 Kennedy Report, note 24, above, ch. 9.

34 Kennedy Report, note 24, above, ch. 9.

35 Fox, M. and McHale, J., 'Xenotransplantation: The Ethical and Legal Ramifications' (1998) 6 *Medical Law Review*, 42–61.

upon good relations with industry'.[36] In addition, McLean and Williamson criticised UKXIRA for lacking a clear remit to consider the ethical issues associated with xenotransplantation in a 'strategic, thoroughgoing' manner, instead addressing these issues in a 'relatively cursory' fashion.[37] In their view this resulted in part from the somewhat limited conception of the ethical issues posed by xenotransplantation, as laid out in the Kennedy Report.[38] In a more radical critique of UKXIRA, Beynon-Jones and Brown accuse it of following Kennedy and Nuffield in uncritically accepting the views of scientific stakeholders and failing to interrogate spurious scientific claims.[39] In the monograph's conclusion McLean and Williamson were unequivocal. Given the uncertainties and risks generated by xenotransplantation for putative human recipients, animals used as 'donors', the broader public and future generations, and the limited remit and powers of UKXIRA, they echoed Kennedy in insisting that: 'Statutory backing for the regulatory body is imperative. Not only does it give the regulator "teeth", but a statutory remit would build into the system the safeguards which come from the compatibility requirement with the Human Rights Act 1998'.[40]

Their recommendations for regulating the procedure have effectively become orthodoxy in the field. Thus, a similar approach was advocated by Sara Fovargue who concluded her 2012 monograph by arguing that: 'a specialist xenotransplantation regulatory authority should be established in every county *before* clinical use, in order to protect individual and public health'.[41] Whether such bodies should be placed on a statutory footing is left unclear, but in a subsequent essay Fovargue argues that the criminal law may justifiably be used to ensure compliance with surveillance schemes deemed necessary to protect individual and public health from the risks posted by xenotransplantation and that a dedicated xenotransplant statute is necessary for this purpose.[42]

Certainly, the subsequent fate of the non-statutory UKXIRA suggests that McLean and Williamson were correct to argue that a statutory footing for the regulator was necessary. While the Coalition Government's so-called 'Bonfire of the Quangos' in 2010, which aimed at tackling the budget deficit by abolishing or merging hundreds of quangos,[43] demonstrated that statutory backing was no guarantee of longevity, it is worth noting that in the health field the statutory HFEA

---

36 McLean and Williamson, note 12, above, at p. 112.

37 McLean and Williamson, note 12, above, at pp. 112, 113.

38 McLean and Williamson, note 12, above, at pp. 266–7. Jean McHale and I shared these concerns that the debates as played out in Nuffield and Kennedy were bounded, with the result that some of the most troubling moral issues, such as the right of humans to co-opt animal bodies for experimental medical purposes were obscured or downplayed.

39 Beynon-Jones, S.M. and Brown, N., 'Time, Timing and Narrative at the Interface Between Technoscience and Policy' (2011) 38 *Science and Public Policy*, 639–47.

40 McLean and Williamson, note 12, above, at p. 272.

41 Fovargue, S., *Xenotransplantation and Risk: Regulating a Developing Biotechnology*, Cambridge, Cambridge University Press, 2012, at p. 243.

42 Fovargue, S., 'Bioethical Conflict and Developing Biotechnologies: Is Protecting Individual and Public Health from the Risks of Xenotransplantation a Matter for the (Criminal) Law?' in Alghrani, A., Bennett, R. and Ost, S. (eds) *Bioethics, Medicine and the Criminal Law*, Cambridge, Cambridge University Press, 2012, pp. 140–56.

43 See *Public Bodies Reform: Proposals for Change*, 2010, available at: http://webarchive.nationalarchives.gov.uk/20121015000000/http://www.direct.gov.uk/prod_consum_dg/groups/dg_digitalassets/@dg/@en/documents/digitalasset/dg_191543.pdf (accessed 13 January 2015); Porter, A., 'Quango Cuts: 177 Bodies to Be Scrapped Under Coalition Plans', *The Daily Telegraph*, 24 September 2010, available at: http://www.telegraph.co.uk/news/politics/8021739/Quango-cuts-177-bodies-to-be-scrapped-under-coalition-plans.html (accessed 13 January 2015).

and Human Tissue Authority (HTA) were ultimately spared abolition or merger,[44] while the Human Genetics Commission (which like UKXIRA was a non-departmental public body) was abolished following the review of public bodies. By that stage UKXIRA was already history having been unceremoniously disbanded in January 2007. Compounding concerns about the regulatory vacuum following the demise of UKXIRA was the Government's failure to offer a convincing justification for its somewhat ad hoc abolition, which seemed to reflect the lack of any coherent rationale for the regulation of health technologies.[45] Announcing the decision, health minister Andy Burnham pointed to significant regulatory developments since the deliberations of the Kennedy Report. Whereas the Advisory Group had concluded that the definition of 'medicinal products' in the relevant EU directive did not encompass xenotransplantation, and that general oversight by RECs (Research Ethics Committees) was inadequate for this task, Burnham highlighted the impact of the 2003 EU Directive on medicinal products (Commission Directive 2003/63/EU) and the subsequent Medicines for Human Use (Clinical Trials) Regulations 2004, contending that 'they make specific provision for xenotransplantation proposals'.[46] In this way the Government could be read as favouring a 'less law' strategy which sought to normalise xenotechnologies as simply another form of clinical research that could be entrusted to a range of existing regulatory bodies without the need for specialist expertise. Thus, following the abolition of UKXIRA the assessment of the safety and efficacy of xenotransplantation clinical trials fell to the Medicines Healthcare Products Regulatory Agency (MHRA) while the ethics of such trials was to be entrusted to Research Ethics Committees; and experimental treatments (that is, those 'where a clinician offers a particular course of treatment tailored to a particular patient's needs; either a brand new treatment or a new use of a drug or product licensed for use in other ways') were to be assessed by the Clinical Governance Committee of what were then NHS Trusts and referred to either a Research Ethics Committee or the Gene Therapy Advisory Committee (GTAC) where the xenogeneic product is genetically modified. Although it is true that the 2004 Regulations did indeed go some way to addressing the gaps identified by the Kennedy Committee, in a paper criticising the decision to disband UKXIRA, McLean and I, writing with Laura Williamson, condemned the strategy. In the first place, although changes to the governance structure of RECs had standardised their procedures and imposed more stringent obligations on researchers, our view was that general RECs lacked the necessary expertise to regulate xenotransplantation adequately, and additionally it was problematic to add this task to their already onerous workload. Furthermore, entrusting decision-making on this issue to Research Ethics Committees and other bodies charged with regulating what may be done to humans risks a still greater downplaying of animal welfare.[47] Furthermore, we argued that regulatory gaps were likely to remain in a complex and fragmented EU scheme not explicitly devised to cover xenotransplantation.[48] More recently, in a detailed doctrinal analysis of European medicinal products legislation, Beynon-Jones and Brown have illustrated that in the process of incorporating xenotechnologies within the definition of 'medicinal products', European medicinal products legislation effectively erases the animal source, thereby downplaying both the risks that such species border-crossing entails and rendering invisible the animal suffering and sacrifice

44 Sample, I., 'Two Health Regulators Spared Axe but Face Efficiency Review', *The Guardian*, 25 January 2013, available at: http://www.theguardian.com/society/2013/jan/25/two-health-regulators-spared-axe (accessed 13 January 2015).

45 Williamson, L., Fox, M. and McLean, S.A.M., 'The Regulation of Xenotransplantation in the United Kingdom After UKXIRA: Legal and Ethical Issues' (2007) 34 *Journal of Law & Society*, 441–64.

46 Written Statements, Tuesday 12 December 2006. Hansard Column WS177, WS182.

47 Williamson, Fox and McLean, note 45, above, at pp. 458–9.

48 Williamson, Fox and McLean, note 45, above, at pp. 450–54.

which lies at the heart of these practices.[49] Other critiques have lamented the 'short termism' of the Government's policy in abolishing a specialist advisory body, and in fact the reason for dispensing with UKXIRA seems attributable less to the improved system of research regulation that Burnham highlighted than to what Brown and Beynon-Jones refer to as the 'dramatic collapse of expectations within the British xenotransplantation industry' following the news in 1999 that the Roslin Institute was terminating its xenotransplantation programme, followed by the announcement of Imutran's imminent closure.[50] Thus, in media reports following the announcement that the interim body was to be scrapped, a Department of Health spokesperson attributed the decision to a lack of interest in scientific research into the procedure:

> At the time UKXIRA was established it was thought xenotransplantation could prove to be a potential solution to the shortage of organ transplants. However, research has not developed as it was thought at that time and it doesn't look likely it will offer solutions in the short to medium term.[51]

Yet as Beynon-Jones and Brown note, notwithstanding this collapse in hopes concerning the future of xenotransplantation, and its widespread characterisation as a 'failed' technology, xenotechnology research has continued. As their work demonstrates, scientific activity – albeit without any public fanfare – has continued on a scale comparable to that of the mid 1990s when xenotechnologies were at the forefront of regulatory attention, and potential new uses for these technologies are continually uncovered.[52] Against this backdrop McLean and Williamson's concern that certain types of xenotransplants had already been taking place in the UK and that this was problematic without statutory oversight has been lent added weight by the abolition of UKXIRA. Whatever the regulator's shortcomings, with its abolition has vanished the only specialist forum for generating specialist knowledge and advice and informing public debate. Moreover, given that the 'cyclical nature of innovation is a constant feature' of scientific progress, Haddow and her colleagues at Edinburgh argue that it was premature to conclude that the scientific promise of xenotransplantation was exhausted and that a specialist regulatory body was no longer necessary.[53] Specifically, they highlight the desirability of a regulatory body capable of regulating human/animal hybrid bodies, and they conclude that, given the regulatory void that has existed since UKXIRA's demise, consideration should be given to reconvening the body (or a similar body) to regulate entities that elude neat classification as human or animal.[54] In sum, given the ontological and practical challenges posed by xenotechnologies, too little had changed by 2006 to justify a departure from the Kennedy Report's conclusion that: 'given the complexity of the issues presented by xenotransplantation, we are persuaded that trials should not be left only to local consideration and that proposals for clinical trial of xenotransplantation should be considered by a national body'.[55] In turn the absence of such a national body has surely contributed to the way in which xenotransplantation has receded still further from public attention and continues to elude ethico-legal scrutiny or debate.

49 Beynon-Jones and Brown, note 39, above.

50 Beynon-Jones and Brown, note 39, above, at p. 229.

51 Curtis, P., 'Ethicists Fear Free for All in Human-animal Transplants', *The Guardian*, 13 January 2007.

52 Beynon-Jones and Brown, note 39, above.

53 Haddow et al., note 9, above, at p. 10.

54 Haddow et al., note 9, above, at p. 16.

55 Kennedy Report, note 24, above, at para. 8.74.

What, if Anything, Is Special about Xenotechnologies?

Nevertheless, while continuing to believe that it was regrettable that in the late 1990s a regulatory opportunity was missed to put in place a dedicated statutory body that could have shaped debates in this field, I am hesitant when it comes to endorsing the more recent calls for statutory intervention along the lines advocated by Fovargue, or calls for a resurrection of a body akin to UKXIRA, as supported by Haddow et al. Since the 1990s the regulatory environment has altered significantly, and I would argue that it is worth questioning whether biotechnological developments, the nature of the debates they generate, and the surrounding political context in which they play out have shifted to the point where a new regulatory paradigm is now necessary. A key aspect of this query concerns the issue of why a particular technology merits particular legal attention and a specialist regime. As we saw above, the model for the Kennedy Report's mooted national body was the HFEA, and Emily Jackson has pointed out in this context that it 'is worth asking why fertility treatment is subject to this special regulatory regime'.[56] She notes that in the late 1980s and early 1990s justifications for a specialist regulatory scheme for fertility treatment pertained to possible health risks posed by the techniques, concern about the moral status of the embryo, and ethical questions to which the technologies give rise – such as who should qualify for access to treatment. Ultimately, she concludes that the most convincing rationale for a specialist regulatory regime is now largely historical, since the novel and controversial nature of these technologies in the 1970s and 1980s meant that a specialist regulatory regime was then warranted. Arguably since xenotransplantation remains controversial, and because – in part due to the absence of a dedicated body to monitor and advise on developments – we are no closer to being in a position to evaluate or safeguard against the risk it poses, this could be taken to support the case for a dedicated legal regime.

The two most compelling reasons for making such a case pertain to the order of risk that xenotechnologies pose, and to the particular anxieties that it induces. Legal commentators tend to identify the public health risks of the practice as the most compelling reason to regulate,[57] citing risks beyond the immediate parties to the procedures. In both the Kennedy and Nuffield reports it was ultimately the fear of the unknown and unquantifiable risks to patients, their contacts and the broader public which persuaded them of the need for regulation. This would aim to ensure that xenotransplant recipients would be aware of risks, that they would be adequately monitored, and that trials would not proceed until these risks could be judged sufficiently safe to run – a point which both reports concluded had not been reached in 1996. In this regard the Kennedy Report clearly stated that with the 'current state of knowledge it is not acceptable to move to clinical trials involving humans'.[58] As Fovargue and Ost summarise, in their detailed consideration of the unknowable risks the technologies pose:

> On the basis of the available evidence, moving to clinical trials presents uncertain risks of a grave nature, the main one being an infectious disease pandemic. Xenotransplantation poses manufactured risks, risks created by scientific progress and of which we have no prior experience; thus calculating the probability of their occurrence is especially difficult.[59]

56 Jackson, E., *Medical Law: Text, Cases and Materials*, 3rd edn, Oxford, Oxford University Press, 2013, at p. 776.

57 McLean and Williamson, note 12, above, at pp. 179–85; Fovargue, note 41, above, at pp. 45–57; Fovargue S. and Ost, S., 'When Should Precaution Prevail? Interests in (Public) Health, the Risk of Harm and Xenotransplantation' (2010) 18 *Medical Law Review*, 302–29.

58 Kennedy Report, note 24, above, at para. 4.58.

59 Fovargue and Ost, note 57, above, at p. 325.

They conclude that because of the exceptional nature of these risks, xenotransplantation clinical trials are different to other trials and that the state should take action to prohibit clinical xenotransplantation. Although more equivocal about a ban, back in 2005 McLean and Williamson observed that 'it may not be overstating the case to suggest that xenotransplantation is unique in the history of medical innovation',[60] so that a dedicated legal regime is required.

The uniqueness to which they point pertains not only to the magnitude of third party risks but also to the fact that xenotransplantation generates deep-seated anxieties about species integrity and the nature of the human. Elsewhere I have sought to demonstrate the multiple challenges to species, generational and bodily boundaries that are mounted by xenotechnologies.[61] Notwithstanding the efforts of the scientific community, as reflected in the Kennedy and Nuffield reports, to nullify such concerns by pointing to continuities in the use of animal parts in human medicine,[62] the transplantation of foreign tissue from another species into the human body is radically disordering because of the ontological and boundary challenges it poses by conjoining bodies from different species. Thus, as geographer Gail Davies notes: '[a] new ontological order is … proposed … which troubles the application of established ethical principles to new forms of life that are seen as different from existing human or animal bodies … xenotransplantation is disordering on several fronts …'.[63]

Maneesha Deckha has suggested that this troubling of species lines generates what she terms 'species anxiety' 'because the humans involved become "animalized" and thus absorb the subordinate status assigned in Western cultures to nonhumans in general'. For her, because 'xenotechnologies urge us to revisit the boundary lines around species identity that we have currently drawn' and thereby expose their contingency, they threaten the whole edifice of human identity upon which Western law is founded.[64]

However, acknowledging that xenotechnologies are in many respects exceptional[65] does not determine that in the twenty-first century they should be regulated by a dedicated legal regime, and I would argue that a combination of biotechnological developments and changes to the regulatory environment now mean that the case for a separate xenotransplantation regulatory regime is less compelling that it was in the 1990s.

In the first place other technological developments in the field of embryology, notably the ability to create trans-species or inter-species embryos in the wake of amendments contained in the 2008 Human Fertilisation and Embryology Act, seem to pose a more radical challenge than xenotransplantation does to the human/animal species divide.[66] In echoes of the claims made by

60 McLean and Williamson, note 12, above, at p. 93.

61 Fox, note 9, above.

62 Indeed Lesley Sharp has argued that scientists working in the field actively strive to legitimise transpecies hybridity – Sharp, L., 'Imagining Transpecies Kinship in Xenotransplantation' (2011) 8 *Sites*, 12–31.

63 Davies, G., 'The Sacred and the Profane: Biotechnology, Rationality and Public Debate' (2006) 38 *Environment and Planning*, 423–44, at p. 434.

64 Deckha, M., 'Holding onto Humanity: Animals, Dignity and Anxiety in Canada's Assisted Human Reproduction Act' (2009) 5 *Unbound*, 21–54, at pp. 32–3, 35. See also Fox, note 9, above.

65 Indeed Joanna Bourke asserts that 'in its breach of bodily boundaries … it can be seen as the ultimate in biopolitics' – Burke, J., *What It Means to Be Human*, London, Virago, 2011, at p. 359.

66 Brown, N., 'Besting the Embryo: The Metrics of Humanness in the Transpecies Embryo Debate' (2009) 4 *Biosocieties*, 147–63; Fox, M., 'Legislating Interspecies Embryos' in Deazley, R. and Smith, S. (eds) *The Legal, Medical and Cultural Regulation of the Body: Transformation and Transgression*, Aldershot, Ashgate, 2009, pp. 95–126.

scientists in the xenotransplantation debates, such legislative changes were largely prompted by scientific claims that the creation of trans-embryos using cow or rabbit eggs offered a solution to the shortage of human eggs being donated to create embryos for research purposes. As Alex Sharp has noted, law can readily integrate the xenotransplant recipient into the legal or symbolic order, given that s/he remains recognisably ontologically and morphologically human.[67] By contrast, the potential of trans-embryos for boundary, bodily and species disruption is significantly more profound, since scientists may increase the human composition of trans embryos dramatically, thus dismantling traditional concepts of personhood as well as species.[68] They thus embody, as Sharpe has argued, a double breach of nature and law:

> They involve a breach of nature because the process of their creation entails mixing human and animal. They involve a breach of the law because mixing of this kind introduces a profound challenge to key legal distinctions ... The confusion that human/animal hybrid [embryos] introduce to the law can be considered to be of the most profound kind.[69]

Consequently, as UK law sanctions more radical forms of hybridity, by permitting the creation of an assortment of what it terms 'human admixed embryos' in s. 4 of the Human Fertilisation and Embryology Act 2008, the xenotransplant recipient becomes normalised, and it might be questioned whether the anxieties of mixing, contamination and pollution of the human which xenotechnologies raise now seem less acute than they did 20 years ago. In turn, this might suggest that the need to regulate, or indeed ban, xenotechnologies in order to allay public anxieties is less pressing.

Changes to the regulatory environment itself may be as significant as the relative normalisation of xenotechnologies. A number of changes are worth noting since the time of the Kennedy and Nuffield deliberations. First, in practical terms there now seems to exist a greater scepticism about the value of quangos and regulatory bodies. Both the review of public bodies discussed above, coupled with the questions which surface periodically concerning the future of existing statutory bodies such as the HFEA and HTA, suggest that there is likely to be little enthusiasm on the part of governments of any political persuasion for the creation of new or revived regulatory bodies, especially where doing so would also entail finding time in an already crowded Parliamentary agenda. Furthermore, legal scholars have highlighted the limitations of traditional risk assessments that have underpinned regulatory control and have advocated a shift away from conventional 'command and control' regulatory measures backed by sanctions for breach in favour of new and more adaptive legal frameworks for the governance of innovation in biotechnology and other fields.[70] Relatedly, the growing attention paid since the 1990s to the need for global health governance and regulatory regimes which transcend the borders of the nation state means that it is increasingly the case that national legislation is regarded as inadequate to police the use of innovative technologies. This may be particularly true in a field such as xenotransplantation, where the proliferation of relatively small biotech start-ups, such as the Cambridge-based Imutran, who were heavily invested in the technology,[71] could relatively easily be moved or merged. The movement of global capital

---

67 Sharpe, A., *Foucault's Monsters and the Challenges of Law*, London, Routledge, 2011, at p. 140.

68 Kopinski, N.E., 'Human-Nonhuman Chimera: A Regulatory Proposal on the Blurring of Species Lines' (2003–4) *Boston College Law Review*, 619–66, at p. 622.

69 Sharpe, note 67, above, at p. 138.

70 Lee and Petts, note 3, above; Wynne, B., 'Uncertainty and Environmental Learning: Reconceiving Science and Policy in the Preventive Paradigm' (1992) *Global Environmental Change*, 111–27.

71 Persson and Welin, note 17, above, ch. 5.

makes it virtually impossible for a national statutory body to regulate effectively global companies and their subsidiaries[72] within the confines of national borders, suggesting that to govern effectively global enterprises across borders some form of legal transnationalism is called for.[73] As we have seen above, the growing influence of European law in this field was cited as one justification for abolishing UKXIRA and it is clear that EU law is having an important impact on governance of biotechnologies.[74] However, given the different drivers for European regulation with the premium placed on the necessity of ensuring safety, standardisation and efficiency in order to create stable markets, it is clear that in the European context, as Beynon-Jones and Brown have demonstrated, there is much less of a premium on risk. The downplaying or erasure of the risks from animal biotechnologies that they highlight in the European governance also points to the likely futility of calls for a new national regulatory body to address xenotechnologies.

Conclusion

In the past the UK has been in the vanguard of both scientific and regulatory developments in the field of biotechnology, particularly in the fields of embryo research and assisted conception, where the enactment of legislation following Warnock's deliberation was seen as a largely successful approach which has subsequently been kept under review in a way which at least allows for a degree of public consultation and impact.[75] However, even in the field of reproductive technologies notable regulatory gaps, such as the separate and manifestly inadequate scheme for regulation of surrogacy, persist.[76] Moreover, this regime too faces the challenge of how its agenda squares with EU law and how it can regulate across borders. Had a statutory body along the lines of the HFEA been created to govern xenotransplantation research in the 1990s it would have been possible to present the UK as also taking a lead on regulation of this issue. Even had the regulatory trigger for such a body ultimately turned out to be grounded in spurious scientific claims about the feasibility of a move to whole organ transplantation from animal sources, this would not necessarily have undermined the case for such a body. Since even its critics acknowledge that UKXIRA discharged certain of its functions, including the generating of an information base on the risks and feasibility of different forms of xenotransplantation, and liaison with representatives of the industries as well as international organisations in the field creditably,[77] there is little doubt that a better resourced, dedicated, central agency would have had a useful role to play, not least in ensuring a better information base for decision-making in the field. The existence of such a body would have provided us with information we currently lack about scientific developments and perhaps offered some mechanism for evaluating risks that we are currently no better placed to

72 Imutran was owned by Novartis, the Swiss pharmaceutical giant.

73 Cotterell, R., 'Spectres of Transnationalism: Changing Terrains of Sociology of Law' (2009) 36 *Journal of Law and Society*, 481–500.

74 Flear et al., note 26, above; Hervey, T. and McHale, J., *European Health Law*, Cambridge, Cambridge University Press (forthcoming 2015).

75 Fox, M., 'The Human Fertilisation and Embryology Act 2008: Tinkering at the Margins' (2009) 17 *Feminist Legal Studies*, 333–44.

76 See for example Brunet, L., Carruthers, J., Davaki, K., et al., *A Comparative Study on the Regime of Surrogacy in EU Member States*, Brussels, European Parliament, 2013, available at: http://www.europarl.europa.eu/RegData/etudes/etudes/join/2013/474403/IPOL-JURI_ET(2013)474403_EN.pdf (accessed 13 January 2015).

77 For details see McLean and Williamson, note 12, above, at pp. 98–104.

assess than we were two decades ago. However, with little appetite existing for such a body given the shifts in the regulatory environment outlined above, I would argue that legal scholars now need to think more critically about regulatory responses to such technological developments and address what is special about types of research that have historically been subject to special regulatory regimes, and to consider whether the current legislative scheme for regulating biotechnologies is defensible or as Williamson, McLean and I contended unacceptably ad hoc.[78] Of course, any attempt to frame a coherent and joined-up approach to regulation, even on a national level is likely doomed to failure, and as noted above a transnational approach to biotechnologies now seems to be called for. At the very least, however, we need to learn from past regulatory failure. In this regard Beynon-Jones and Brown point to the history of xenotransplantation regulation in the UK as demonstrating 'the imminent, near term and reactive relationship [of the policy] community to the future of the fields it seems to regulate'.[79] Such a charge is equally applicable to law, as is Beynon-Jones and Browns' conclusion that it is necessary to critically interrogate scientific narratives and 'to explore the economics and professional interests served through rhetorics of hope and promise' as played out in debates around biotechnologies. Their advocacy of a more reflexive approach to regulation chimes with the work of legal scholars such as Lee and Petts who contend that current 'processes of governance allow little opportunity for reflection on the purposes of and motivations of science and innovation', and fail to pay heed to the importance of setting societal priorities for the future.[80] Lee and Petts argue that regulators need to engage with scientists but in that process be more attentive to the purposes and motivations of research and development, in fields such as nanotechnology. In the case of xenotechnologies and other transbiologies which fragment, splice and reconfigure bodies at surgical and cellular levels, such reflection may also confront us with the deeper and troubling issues, which were almost wholly absent from regulatory debates, about how and why we value human exceptionalism and bodily or species integrity. Applied to the regulatory sphere such reflection may, for instance, call into question whether retaining a distinctively *Human* Fertilisation and Embryology Authority is defensible. Certainly as Nik Brown has demonstrated, in making judgments about which entities get to count as human and thus fall within the remit of such a regulatory scheme we are currently reduced to impoverished and ultimately meaningless metric calculations about degree of humanness, given our failure to consider the need for more hybrid regulatory structures.[81] Heeding Murphy and O'Cuinns' call for legal scholars to move beyond the somewhat reductionist debate about whether more or less law is needed,[82] it seems that, as they propose, a more sustained engagement with science and technology scholarship would allow us to take up the questions of hybridity, purification and what it means to be human. In the process this might prompt a rethinking of why it is currently the case that the 'regulatory institutions, agencies and bodies that govern [transbiologies] have certain species-centric qualities outlooks and histories',[83] and how in the early stages of the twenty-first century we can fashion new systems of governance better fit to regulate research on human and non-human animals.

---

78 Williamson, Fox and McLean, note 45, above, at p. 463.

79 Beynon-Jones and Brown, note 39, above, at p. 225.

80 Lee and Petts, note 3, above, at p. 160.

81 Brown, note 66, above.

82 Murphy and O'Cuinn, note 26, above.

83 Beynon-Jones, S.M. and Brown, N., 'Where the Wild Things Are: The EU Regulation of Transpecies Bioscience' in Flear et al. (2013), note 26, above, pp. 343–61, at p. 343.

Chapter 14

The Human Genome Revolution: Sheila McLean's Quest for Intellectual Rigour and Reproductive Liberty

Mark Henaghan*

Introduction

The scientific importance of the discovery of the human genome cannot be over emphasised. Some 'heralded' the subsequent sequencing of the human genome 'as one of the most important scientific endeavors of our time'.[1] Others said that attempting to map the human genome was 'the most ambitious scientific project ever undertaken',[2] and that it represented 'science's final frontier'.[3] Even after the sequencing of the human genome was declared to be complete in 2003, the scientific community remained captivated by the human genome and continues to produce a substantial volume of research in this field.

However, the human genome is about much more than just science. Although human genome research is scientific in nature, the far-reaching consequences of the work are 'of a universal character' and affect humanity as a whole.[4] As Article 1 of the Universal Declaration on the Human Genome and Human Rights states, '[t]he human genome underlies the fundamental unity of all members of the human family, as well as the recognition of their inherent dignity and diversity. In a symbolic sense, it is the heritage of humanity'.[5] Genomic research profoundly affects all aspects of human life, from conception until death, and raises fundamental questions about what it means to be a human being:

> [I]t is clear that everything from basic survival to status may be affected by genetic knowledge. Our genetic inheritance may predict whether we are conceived, implanted or carried to term. It may also predict how we live our lives, how we view ourselves, our relationships with family and many others, and affect how we make decisions at the end of our lives.[6]

---

* Thank you to Ruth Ballantyne, Professional Practice Fellow, Faculty of Law, University of Otago, Dunedin, New Zealand, for her significant research and editorial assistance with this chapter.

1 Chial, H., 'DNA Sequencing Technologies Key to the Human Genome Project' (2008) 1 *Nature Education*, 219.

2 McLean, S.A.M. and Giesen, D., 'Legal and Ethical Considerations of the Human Genome Project' (1994) 1 *Medical Law International*, 159–75, at p. 161.

3 McLean, S.A.M., 'Mapping the Human Genome: Friend or Foe?' (1994) 39 *Social Science and Medicine*, 1221–7, at p. 1221.

4 McLean and Giesen, note 2, above, at p. 171.

5 Universal Declaration on the Human Genome and Human Rights, art. 1.

6 McLean, S.A.M., 'Interventions in the Human Genome' (1998) 61 *Modern Law Review*, 681–96, at p. 687.

As a result of the successful charting of the human genome and the significant amount of research that followed, humankind has been 'genetically laid bare as never before'.[7]

Sheila McLean was one of the first legal academics to recognise the wider legal and ethical implications of human genome research, and was at the forefront of the movement calling for careful debate about the variety of issues raised by genetic research. As she said in 1998:

> A great responsibility falls on the shoulders of those who create and manipulate the techniques and technologies which produce these effects, but one also falls on the community to engage with them in a manner which is informed and mature … Mature ethical and legal responses are urgently needed if the good that genetics offers is not to be outweighed by the bad.[8]

This chapter charts McLean's significant contribution to the field of human genomics. It considers her original quest for the ethical and legal implications of genetic research to be analysed in a balanced way and with, what she calls 'intellectual rigour'.[9] The chapter closely examines her denouncement of overly moralistic reasoning and her pursuit of future human genomic policies based instead upon comprehensive deliberation, not only by scientists and academics, but by the community as a whole. The chapter then explores (and structurally echoes) McLean's burgeoning academic progression from a call for proper debate about the abstract possibilities raised by genomic research, to her appeal for reproductive liberty, incorporating John Stuart Mill's harm principle, in the context of the concrete realities of genomic reproductive developments. This examination illustrates not just McLean's scholastic trajectory, but also her steadfast repudiation of high-minded moral reasoning as a legitimate decision-making device. The chapter concludes with a discussion of her invaluable role in the New Zealand Human Genome Project as an international collaborator and shows her unremitting desire for policy formation to be underpinned by proper debate and libertarian reproductive freedoms, rather than appeals to vague moral ideals.

McLean and the Human Genome

Right from the beginning of the so-called human genomic revolution, before the sequencing of the human genome was even complete, McLean's work was instrumental in calling for concentrated legal and ethical debate about the issues raised by the human genome. She also quickly recognised the importance of community engagement with such important issues. As early as 1994, McLean called for the democratisation of genomic scientific knowledge. As McLean and Dieter Giesen said, '[a]s scientists scale ever greater heights of knowledge and understanding, human society … must be involved and empowered'.[10] McLean argued that wide-ranging discussions were required – regardless of how the human genome was to be classified – because the research posed significant ethical and moral dilemmas for the whole of society. At stake was the 'very identity of the human individual'.[11] As McLean said in the *Modern Law Review*:

> Whether or not one views the genetic revolution as benign, evil or neutral, one thing is clear: there is a perceived need to master and control the Leviathan which genetic science is creating. Equally,

7 McLean, note 6, above, at p. 682.
8 McLean, note 6, above, at p. 696.
9 McLean, note 6, above, at p. 684.
10 McLean and Giesen, note 2, above, at p. 159.
11 McLean and Giesen, note 2, above, at p. 159.

> attempts to regulate genetic knowledge and techniques to maximise the benefits and minimise the potential harms must take place in an atmosphere, and from a perspective, which show balance and intellectual rigour.[12]

McLean's concept of 'intellectual rigour'[13] focused on avoiding unduly parochial perspectives and remaining open to a wide variety of scientific and ethical possibilities, rather than merely parroting preconceived ideas about right and wrong.[14] As she put it:

> For debate to be valuable it must be firmly based in knowledge and understanding, engaged in without prejudice, removed from the parochialism which may obliterate or obfuscate the concerns of the poorer world, mindful of other species on the planet and driven by strength not fear.[15]

This fits within her call for 'sophisticated debate' on such issues:[16]

> It is important, therefore, that comment on genetics and its potential is couched in terms which both respect the science and explore the ethics ... If we are to harvest the good and avoid the bad of genetics, it is essential that an informed, intelligent and sophisticated debate is undertaken.[17]

McLean argued that such debate should start from an understanding of what human genomic research actually tells us about ourselves, rather than starting out imagining the worst-case scenario. Accordingly, she called for negative moral rhetoric to give way to 'healthy scepticism'.[18] She put it thus:

> A preliminary to any assessment of the impact of intervention in the human genome must, therefore, be consideration of what genetics actually tell us about ourselves and others. This enquiry must be conducted in an atmosphere of healthy scepticism but free from the excesses of rhetoric which blunt the edges of the issues and lead to the triumph of the superficial over the thoughtful.[19]

The 'excesses of rhetoric' referred to here are frequently found in overly moralistic arguments.[20] Moral and ethical ideals are inherently subjective and personal. As philosopher Jim Flynn noted, when making decisions we ultimately look within ourselves and we 'find certain moral ideals acceptable and other moral ideas loathsome'.[21] While, there is nothing wrong with this approach to personal decision-making per se, individuals should be suspicious of those who attempt to become self-appointed stewards of humanity's moral wellbeing by elevating their own individual sense of morality to an illusion of objectivity. McLean acknowledged that an individual's sense of morality

---

12 McLean, note 6, above, at p. 684.

13 McLean, note 6, above, at p. 684.

14 See generally McLean, note 6, above, at pp. 695–6.

15 McLean, note 6, above, at pp. 695–6.

16 McLean, S.A.M., 'The Gene Genie: Good Fairy or Wicked Witch?' (2001) 32 *Studies in History and Philosophy of Biological and Biomedical Sciences*, 723–39, at p. 724.

17 McLean, note 16, above, at p. 724.

18 McLean, note 6, above, at p. 684.

19 McLean, note 6, above, at p. 684.

20 McLean, note 6, above, at p. 684.

21 Flynn, J.R., *How to Defend Humane Ideals: Substitutes for Objectivity*, Lincoln, NE and London, University of Nebraska Press, 2000, at p. 170.

has its place in human genome research. However, she noted that one should not be permitted to hide behind the rhetoric of ethics, because individual morality alone is not a 'sufficiently robust reason' to prevent others from making their own decisions about such a fundamental humanistic issue:[22]

> The bald assertion that something is unethical is insufficient to make it so. We may say we don't like something, but to dress up our distaste in the language of ethics is to do significant harm to the language of ethics and its intellectual and conceptual content. We may believe something to be immoral – that is a product of our own intuitions and social and cultural upbringing – and this is essentially unchallengeable. However, the moral intuitions of individuals do not form a sufficiently robust reason to deny those who do not share them the right to take advantage of whatever is disapproved of.[23]

This powerful and insightful statement automatically renounces the power of those who profess to know, based on their own individual moral intuitions and/or putative greater ethical knowledge, what is right or wrong for the rest of society.

While it is clear that making decisions for society based on individual moral ideals is inappropriate, especially when applied to fundamentally important and personal issues such as those raised by genomic medicine, attempting to make decisions based predominantly on a claim to shared notions of morality or ethics (if reaching a suitable degree of consensus on such matters is even possible) is also ill-advised for two reasons. First, such an approach would inappropriately subscribe to the idea that might is automatically right. History has shown that the majority does not always hold the most defensible moral and ethical views. The historically poor treatment of native and indigenous peoples around the world provides a particularly poignant example of just how wrong the opinion of a majority of society can be on a particular issue at a given time. Secondly, what originally begins as a shared understanding of moral and ethical principles, often does not remain shared for long. Additional historic examples clearly illustrate that moral and ethical principles are not static and have an inherently impermanent nature. They are in a constant state of flux and are continuously reimagined over time. As McLean has noted, 'whether or not something is "right" may change depending on the ethical and intellectual infrastructure on which it builds, or on the time at which it is proposed to undertake it'.[24] For example, until 1986 it was a criminal offence in New Zealand under the Crimes Act 1961 for men to engage in consensual sexual activities together.[25] However, fast-forward to 2013 when New Zealand became the thirteenth country in the world to allow same sex marriage. Indeed, New Zealand now permits two individuals to marry 'regardless of their sex, sexual orientation, or gender identity'.[26] This indicates that individuals and groups of individuals' moral and ethical views evolve over time.

On this basis, ethical and moral principles should not themselves dictate what regulatory or legislative policies should be created to deal with issues arising from the human genome. Consequently, one would expect that policies created to deal with the practical application of human genome research would be informed and deliberately shaped by intellectual debate and evidence, rather than moralistic ideals. However, as McLean and Elliston state: '[w]hile we might wish to believe that public policy is based on proven facts and shaped in a rational and deliberative manner,

22 McLean, S.A.M., 'What Is Wrong with Reproductive Cloning?' (2002) *Genetics Law Monitor*, 6–9, at p. 8.

23 McLean, note 22, above, at pp. 7–8.

24 McLean, note 16, above, at p. 724.

25 See Homosexual Law Reform Act 1986.

26 See Marriage (Definition of Marriage) Amendment Act 2013, s. 5.

this is by no means a given'.[27] Likewise, as Edward Page notes, policies can be considerably more subjective:

> Insofar as they arise from conscious reflection and deliberation, policies may reflect a variety of intentions and ideas: some vague, some specific, some conflicting, some unarticulated. They can … even be the unintended or undeliberated consequences of professional practices or bureaucratic routines.[28]

Crafting satisfactory policies to contend adequately with the rapidly developing world of human genomics is no easy feat. New possibilities resulting from human genome research create an array of value choices that require proper consideration before adequate policies can be created to deal with such significant issues. Consequently, each policy decision needs to be recognised for what it is: one subjective choice (hopefully based on rigorous intellectual debate) from a group of potential choices, rather than the objective answer handed down from on high. Allowing individuals or decision-makers to hide the ethical and moral framework behind the choices being made is not the answer.

Even after legislators and/or regulators have crafted their chosen policy, a gap remains between the expression of the policy, its interpretation and its practical application. On that basis, there is a need, not just for vigorous intellectual debate about the appropriate stance to take in terms of new genomic technologies, but also for more detailed discussions about the possible practical applications of any policies formulated from those initial debates. Legislators and/or regulators must also recognise the need to monitor and assess such policies frequently lest the moral climate, and the social environment, change over time.

McLean and Reproductive Liberty

The scientific discoveries generated by the sequencing of the human genome have had (and continue to have) a momentous bearing on humanity as a whole. The genetic knowledge stemming from this research has generated seemingly endless possibilities.[29] McLean contends that these new opportunities are exciting, declaring '[w]hat we *can* do is amazing; what we *will* be able to do, almost unimaginable – almost, but not quite, that is. The science fiction of only a few years ago is our present day reality'.[30] Medical science has been one of the most significantly affected fields, whereby '[t]he combination of assisted reproduction and genetics, so-called 'reprogenetics',

27 McLean, S.A.M. and Elliston, S., 'Conclusion' in McLean, S.A.M. and Elliston, S. (eds) *Regulating Pre-Implantation Genetic Diagnosis: A Comparative and Theoretical Analysis*, London and New York, Routledge, 2013, pp. 224–38, at p. 228.

28 Page, E.C., 'The Origins of Policy' in Moran, M., Rein, M. and Goodin R.E. (eds) *The Oxford Handbook of Public Policy*, Oxford, Oxford University Press, 2006, pp. 207–27, at p. 207.

29 Some researchers believe that the Human Genome Project and the potential resulting scientific developments have been over-hyped. As Holtzman and Marteau state: 'Although we do not contend that the genetic mantle is as imperceptible as the emperor's new clothes were, it is not made of the silks and ermines that some claim it to be. Those who make medical and science policies in the next decade would do well to see beyond the hype.' See Holtzman, N.A. and Marteau, T.M., 'Will Genetics Revolutionize Medicine?' (2000) 343(2) *The New England Journal of Medicine*, 141–4, at p. 144. See also Hall, S.S., 'Revolution Postponed' (2010) 303 *Scientific American*, 60–67.

30 McLean, note 16, above, at p. 723.

has heralded a revolution in reproductive choice',[31] which has 'radically alter[ed] the face of reproductive decision-making'.[32] As a result of this 'reproductive revolution' many difficult questions have emerged. As McLean said:

> The so-called revolutions in human genetics and assisted reproduction – perhaps especially when combined – provide remarkable diagnostic and therapeutic potential. However, these apparent forces for good also raise ethical and sometimes legal questions which can shape the responses of both individuals and states as to how, when and to whom they should be made available.[33]

As the possibilities generated by human genome research became concrete advancements in medical technology, McLean's arguments also progressed. Her original quest for 'intellectual rigour' in debating the ethical and legal consequences of human genome sequencing, generally, became a search for freedom in terms of how individuals could use new assisted human reproduction technologies.[34] However, she continued to express her frustration at the constant resort to morality as a tool to unduly limit the personal choices of individuals. As McLean and Elliston said, as recently as 2013:

> [T]he knee-jerk response to innovation is often to use the law to impose moral values, even though these values may change over the years and may, in any case, be illegitimate. In addition, while it is clearly the case that individuals will be guided by their own moral values, it is less clear that concerns for 'public opinion' or some aggregation of supposed moral values are in themselves sufficient justifications for preventing others, who do not share these values, from making choices that *for them* are morally appropriate.[35]

McLean presents reproductive liberty as an alternative discourse in response to her continued negation of such overly moralistic reasoning. McLean advocates reproductive freedom in a libertarian context, whereby access to modern procreative technologies developed by virtue of ever-increasing scientific understandings of the human genome should be dependant on individual choice, rather than questions of externally-imposed morality, so long as that individual's choices do not harm others. Thus, McLean has argued:

> [W]hen technology is available, it should be distributed without discrimination and – most importantly – that its use should not be unnecessarily interfered with unless it can be shown that harm would result from failing to curb people's access to it.[36]

In terms of reproductive liberty, this means that 'in the absence of evidence of harm, people should be free to make their own decisions about whether and when to reproduce and what kind of children to have'.[37] McLean openly acknowledges that her views in this regard are influenced by notable

31 McLean, S.A.M., *Modern Dilemmas Choosing Children*, Edinburgh, Capercaillie Books, 2006, at p. 9.

32 McLean, note 31, above, at p. 9.

33 McLean and Elliston, note 27, above, at p. 1.

34 McLean, note 6, above, at p. 684.

35 McLean and Elliston, note 27, above, at p. 237.

36 McLean, note 31, above, at p. 211.

37 McLean and Elliston, note 27, above, at p. 228.

libertarian John Stuart Mill and his formulation of the harm principle.[38] As Mill famously said in *On Liberty*:

> The object of this Essay is to assert one very simple principle ... That principle is, that the sole end for which mankind are warranted, individually or collectively, in interfering with the liberty of action of any of their number, is self-protection. That the only purpose for which power can be rightfully exercised over any member of a civilized community, against his will, is to prevent harm to others. His own good, either physical or moral, is not sufficient warrant. He cannot rightfully be compelled to do or forbear because it will be better for him to do so, because it will make him happier, because, in the opinion of others, to do so would be wise, or even right.[39]

When applied to human assisted reproductive technology, Mill's harm principle provides a simple solution to a wide array of complex problems. It allows individuals to access not just current technologies, but also reproductive techniques and technologies as they are developing, without the need for detailed legal and regulatory policies to be in place, as long as such approaches do not cause harm to other individuals. This maximises the freedom and individual choice, which McLean seeks.[40] It also allows individuals to reap the benefit of scientific discoveries quickly in this fast-moving and fundamentally important field. McLean argues that such libertarian principles should be preferred over more conservative and restrictive approaches because they result in the least coercive results for the individuals involved. According to McLean and Elliston:

> One major problem with the anti-liberal approach is that it imposes the views of one group on another. The liberal approach, on the other hand, coerces nobody and provides liberty for those who wish to exercise it in ways that others would not choose to.[41]

For example, if a couple who both carry the gene for cystic fibrosis seek to have a child without this genetic disorder via *in vitro* fertilisation (IVF) by screening out affected embryos using pre-implantation genetic diagnosis (PGD) there are two options.[42] First, we could allow the particular couple to exercise their reproductive liberty (with the guidance of the appropriate medical professionals), regardless of the fact that some (uninvolved) members of society dislike PGD because they believe such a procedure is tantamount to 'playing God'. This would enhance the couple's sense of freedom and, most importantly, allow them to have a child that did not have to suffer the debilitating and eventually terminal consequences of cystic fibrosis. This option does not

---

38 McLean, note 31, above, at p. 211.

39 Mill, J.S., *On Liberty*, 2nd edn, London, John W. Parker and Son, 1859, at pp. 21–2.

40 This way of approaching freedom encompasses Isaiah Berlin's concept of negative liberty, which is premised on the enhancement of individual choice through the reduction of external interference. This can be directly contrasted with positive liberty, which enhances individual freedom based on an entitlement to resources. See Berlin, I., 'Two Concepts of Liberty' in Berlin, I., *Four Essays on Liberty*, Oxford, Oxford University Press, 1969, pp. 118–72. To use IVF as an example, liberty in a negative sense would prevent medical professionals and legislators from unduly limiting an individual's access to IVF. Whereas positive liberty would suggest a commitment to provide access to funds to ensure that an individual could actually access IVF procedures.

41 McLean and Elliston, note 27, above, at p. 237.

42 For detailed ethical analysis of PGD, see Snelling, J., 'Parental Preferences and Procreative Choices: Reproductive Liberty and the Regulation of Preimplantation Genetic Diagnosis', PhD Thesis, University of Otago, 2012.

prevent anybody from doing something that they strongly wish to do, and it also does not force anybody to do anything that they do not choose to do. The only people unhappy with this decision are those who disagree with this procedure from an ethical point of view. These individuals are uninvolved with, and unaffected by, the decision as they do not have to live with the consequences in any direct, meaningful way.

The second option is to acquiesce to others' personal sense of morality and prevent the particular couple from exercising their reproductive liberty.[43] This decision would leave the couple in a very difficult position. They would either have to choose not to have a biological child at all, possibly resulting in a significant sense of loss and sadness, or try to conceive a child naturally (if that was indeed possible for the couple) and risk that child being born with cystic fibrosis.[44] This would reduce not just the couple's quality of life, but also the life expectancy of their resulting child. The trade-off must consider all of this individual hardship and difficulty with the claims of some members of society happy who are not even directly affected by the couple's procreative choices.

McLean would argue that the second option is unduly coercive and inhibits the couple's ability to have a family of their choosing for an insufficiently defensible reason. McLean and Elliston caution against attempts to limit individual choice, saying '[t]he mere fact that we *can* limit choice is not a sufficient justification for doing so'.[45] A satisfactory rationalisation before the suppression of freedom and choice is especially important in reproductive matters. Decisions about founding a family are of fundamental importance to the individual or couple involved and, as such, are enshrined in the Universal Declaration of Human Rights (among other international legal instruments).[46] As McLean notes: '[r]eproductive liberty is of immense value to all of us; perhaps no more so than for those who struggle to conceive naturally, or for whom choosing certain characteristics in their future offspring is of great importance'.[47]

Mill's harm principle, as adopted by McLean, would require evidence of some foreseeable and sufficiently tangible harm resulting from the couple's decision to use IVF and PGD before their choice to do so would be restricted. However, before evidence of alleged harm can be gathered and assessed, one must contemplate exactly what counts as 'harm'. McLean and Elliston note that the notion of harm necessarily contains subjective elements. As they explain:

> While proponents of the precautionary principle would point to the lack of evidence as requiring a cautious approach, a liberal account would prioritise reproductive liberty unless and until evidence of harm is found. How a risk-benefit analysis is calculated will, of course, depend on which interests and concerns are prioritised. This, in turn, as we have seen in relation to making public

43 It is not that those members of society who are opposed to the use of such procreative technologies should be entirely ignored, but rather that the couple's claim – in terms of harm – is much greater in magnitude than those who seek to prevent such technologies from being used. The couple's claim is stronger simply because of the more significant personal impact the resulting decision potentially will have upon their lives. The individuals who disapprove of such technologies are not personally affected in any real way by the couple's decision.

44 It is recognised that the couple could, arguably, adopt a child. However, this would not provide the biological connection with their child that this particular couple seeks. For more information about the value attributed to genetic parenthood, see for example, Purewal, S. and Van Den Akker, O., 'The Socio-cultural and Biological Meaning of Parenthood' (2007) 28(2) *Journal of Psychosomatic Obstetrics & Gynecology*, 79–86; and Meyer, D.D., 'Parenthood in a Time of Transition: Tensions between Legal, Biological, and Social Conceptions of Parenthood' (2006) 54 *The American Journal of Comparative Law*, 125–44.

45 McLean and Elliston, note 27, above, at p. 229.

46 Universal Declaration of Human Rights, art. 16.

47 McLean, note 31, above, at p. 221.

> policy, will depend on many factors, including the personal morality of legislators and regulators and their views as to what is, and is not, acceptable or important.[48]

Does 'harm' consist purely of physical detriment, or should other types of harm such as emotional distress and economic deprivation count? For example, it is clear that smoking is a physical harm to those exposed to it – directly and indirectly. There is a raft of medical evidence that an individual who chooses to smoke around others (especially children) risks causing physical harm to them. On this basis, devotees of Mill's harm principle would prevent individuals from smoking in the proximity of others.[49] However, what of the harm caused to the individual who chooses to smoke? Some may argue that because the individual's choice to smoke only harms himself or herself, their choice should not be unduly restricted.

However, this all depends on exactly how harm to others is defined. Those completely opposed to smoking would argue that the individual's choice to smoke does physically harm others, albeit indirectly. This is based on evidence that people who choose to smoke are more likely to suffer from health problems, often requiring expensive medical and surgical care. The realities of public health systems with finite amounts of resources mean that the smoker's medical treatment comes at the cost of another's ability to access timely medical treatment of their own. An individual's decision to smoke can also be economically harmful to others because public health systems are primarily funded out of taxpayers' money. Other people such as employers could suffer economic harm due to a loss of productivity caused by the smoking individual becoming unwell. Emotional harm may also be caused to the smoking individual's family if that individual becomes unwell and/or dies prematurely.

Discerning the tangible harm caused by smoking is not especially difficult and can frequently be seen with the naked eye. However, not all kinds of physical harm are this easy to pin down. For example, is being intentionally brought into the world deaf a form of physical harm? This question was fiercely debated after a deaf, female, same-sex couple from the United States intentionally used a sperm donor suffering from congenital deafness to conceive a deaf child. The couple did not see deafness as a kind of harm, or even as a disability. Rather they viewed being deaf 'as defining their cultural identity' and regarded 'signing' as 'a sophisticated, unique form of communication'.[50] Is this choice an acceptable use of reproductive freedom, given that reproductive liberty '... cannot be regarded as an absolute right'.[51] Would it have made a difference if the couple had used IVF and PGD procedures to create their deaf child? Would it have made a difference if they had used these techniques intentionally to create an intellectually disabled child, or a child suffering from cystic fibrosis?

Such arguments depend on the result of a balancing exercise as to whether it is more harmful for a child to be intentionally born with a disability, or more harmful for the child to never have been born at all. McLean argues that '[a]s the embryo is not an "other" it cannot be harmed, and the child it may become will generally not be harmed by the fact of being born'.[52] Likewise, regarding deafness specifically, Melissa Fahmy states 'the child in question is not injured or made worse off by the selection or resulting birth, given that the only alternative for the child would be not to

48 McLean and Elliston, note 27, above, at p. 234.

49 The University of Otago in New Zealand, which on 1 January 2014 took steps to become a completely smoke-free campus, employed such an approach. See University of Otago, 'Smoke-Free Campus' (1 January 2014), www.otago.ac.nz/smokefree/index.html (accessed 13 January 2015).

50 Savulescu, J., 'Deaf Lesbians, "Designer Disability", and the Future of Medicine' (2002) 325 *British Medical Journal*, 771–3, at p. 771.

51 McLean, note 31, above, at p. 215.

52 McLean, note 31, above, at p. 219.

exist at all'.[53] The point here is not to attempt to resolve these long-standing dilemmas. Rather, these examples clearly illustrate that the classification and parameters of harm need to be carefully considered alongside the principles of reproductive liberty.

Ultimately, whether or not an individual's choice causes harm to others must be based on an agreed definition of harm and strong evidence of that harm. The focus cannot be on hypothetical harms that could possibly be caused in extreme cases. As McLean and Elliston have argued:

> The use of speculative fears, even those that are alleged to be shared by society at large, to dictate the terms on which individuals may exercise choice should always engender the utmost caution. This is especially true where what is involved is the choice to engage in what is an area of private and highly significant decision-making: Namely, whether to seek to establish a family, and in some cases, what kind of family to have ... The tactic is to home in on the most extreme example that could be imagined and then use it to show the danger of the enterprise being permitted at all, even if the basis for objection is entirely speculative and rests on assumptions of dubious validity. What this form of argument does, then, is to seek to engage people's innate anxieties about just where science may take us. Additionally it appeals to a latent sense of discomfort with the reproductive enterprise being structured or manipulated as opposed to 'natural'.[54]

Others have joined McLean's appeal for an evidence-based harm analysis when considering new developments in the assisted human reproduction field. Indeed, the House of Commons Science and Technology Committee in the United Kingdom has said that '[r]eproductive and research freedoms must be balanced against the interests of society but alleged harms to society, too, should be based on evidence'.[55]

Where there is insufficient evidence to assess whether a reproductive choice is harmful or not, McLean believes that the individual involved should be able to make their own choice, with assistance from the appropriate medical professionals. If, and only if, harm can be proven, McLean and Elliston accept that applicable legal or regulatory intervention may be required.[56] Any regulatory or legislative intervention ultimately deemed necessary should be underwritten by libertarian principles and should not be unduly influenced by hypothetical possibilities or a further resort to vague moralistic discourse. As McLean and Elliston state, 'the importance of reproductive liberty should be the primary moral principle underpinning regulatory responses; not speculative fears, knee-jerk reactions, moral distaste or unreflective majoritarianism'.[57]

The downside of the libertarian harm principle approach, as advocated by Mill and McLean, is that significant harms may not be immediately obvious. This means that by the time the risk of harm is recognised and suitable evidence has been gathered, it may be too late to prevent the harm. For example, if in 20 years from now it is discovered that children conceived via IVF suffer from significantly higher rates of mental illness than children born as a result of natural conception, the harm to those children cannot be retrospectively remedied. If the harm is sufficiently serious, the law may eventually intervene to prevent IVF from occurring in the future, and this will protect future children. However, it will not help those children who have already suffered harm. Other more long-term harms might not just affect individuals, but humanity as a whole. For example, if discarding

53 Fahmy, M.S., 'On the Supposed Moral Harm of Selecting for Deafness' (2011) 25 *Bioethics*, 129.

54 McLean and Elliston, note 27, above, at pp. 235–6.

55 House of Commons Science and Technology Committee, *Human Reproductive Technologies and the Law: Volume 1*, London, The Stationary Office, 2005, at p. 22.

56 McLean and Elliston, note 27, above, at p. 238.

57 McLean and Elliston, note 27, above, at p. 238.

particular embryos to avoid certain genetic conditions leads, over time, to less diversity in the human gene pool, this might cause irreversible harm to future generations. As nature shows, a reduction in a species' level of diversity increases the likelihood of eventual extinction.[58] As McLean states:

> Genetic science undoubtedly holds out the promise of great advantages in the struggle with illness and disease. However, it also poses significant ethical and moral dilemmas, not only for those at the coal-face of research and experimentation but also for society and for mankind as a whole. This area of scientific progress will profoundly affect the lives of present and future members of society, bringing into question the very identity of the human individual and intruding upon the snail's pace of evolution in a decisive and probably irreversible manner.[59]

This longer-term possibility might therefore be a clear reason to proceed with caution – as the precautionary principle allows us to do; and to keep laws, regulations and policies under constant and regular review to allow for timely modifications if required.

McLean and the New Zealand Human Genome Project

Many countries (both separately and collaboratively) researched the human genome and its implications for genomic medicine. In New Zealand, the Human Genome Project (Te Kaupapa Rangahau Ira Tāngata), which was generously funded by the New Zealand Law Foundation, carried out an extensive examination of the new reproductive choices created by human genome research developments and considered the legal, ethical and cultural implications of those choices from different theoretical and methodological lenses.[60]

The project was entrusted to the University of Otago, Faculty of Law. However, given the fundamental importance of the project, some international expertise was required. Sheila McLean was selected to be one of the project's international expert advisors because of her outstanding contribution to the fields of the human genome and reproductive liberty, and for her impressive research reputation. She made an immense contribution to the project for the following three years and was an integral part of the large research team involved.[61] Her call for 'intellectual rigour'[62] and her constructions of reproductive liberty are evident throughout the four research reports produced during the project. These reports made policy recommendations to the New Zealand government

58 See Sax, D.F. and Gaines, S.D., 'Species Diversity: From Global Decreases to Local Increases' (2003) 18 *Trends in Ecology and Evolution*, 561–6.

59 McLean and Giesen, note 2, above, at p. 159.

60 See the following four research reports which were published as books during the project: Henaghan, M. (ed.) *Choosing Genes for Future Children: Regulating Preimplantation Genetic Diagnosis*, Dunedin, Human Genome Research Project, 2006; Henaghan, M. (ed.) *Genes, Society and the Future: Volume I*, Dunedin, Human Genome Research Project, 2007; Henaghan, M. (ed.) *Genes, Society and the Future: Volume II*, Dunedin, Human Genome Research Project, 2007; and Henaghan, M. (ed.) *Genes, Society and the Future: Volume III*, Wellington, Human Genome Research Report, Brookers, 2009.

61 McLean's contribution to the project far exceeded the original brief in that she also co-supervised several PhDs after the project ended that arose from researchers who had been involved with the project. A notable example was Dr Jeanne Snelling's PhD thesis, which considers deeply philosophical questions and arguments about reproductive autonomy in a systematic and intellectually precise manner and is a testament to McLean's support and abilities in this field. See Snelling, note 42, above.

62 McLean, note 6, above, at p. 684.

and relevant regulatory bodies.[63] From the very beginning of the project, McLean's long-held beliefs as to the importance of broad intellectual debate underpinned the policy recommendations resulting from the project. As the first research report, *Choosing Genes for Future Children: Regulating Preimplantation Genetic Diagnosis*, noted:

> The best way to develop good regulatory policy is to consider as many viewpoints as possible in a fair and even-handed manner. The final decision to regulate or not is for the government to consider, decide and act. Our task is to present the viewpoints and regulatory options with compassion and to analyse them as best we can without bias.[64]

This shows an intellectual drive for a concentrated debate of the fundamental issues involved, alongside respect for the ultimate decision-making power of the government.

The project also began from the premise that there is no completely objective way to decide what is ethically 'right' in terms of genomic medicine and reproductive liberty, which is clearly influenced by McLean's own research in this area. As Henaghan and McLean state:

> There is an incommensurable diversity of human goods and no overriding objective criterion to definitively rank them. If there are no rational grounds for insisting that one view of the good is superior to those of others, then forced suppression of a particular belief or practice leads to the loss of something humanly valuable.[65]

This statement fits neatly alongside McLean's own beliefs in reproductive liberty and Mill's harm principle, in that unless something will demonstrably harm others, it should not be unduly restricted. There is an acknowledgment that there is a 'tension between, on the one hand, individual freedom and privacy to make reproductive choices and, on the other hand, social solidarity and responsibility to ensure that human dignity is not eroded or undermined'.[66] Notwithstanding, the project openly '... critiques majority positions which unjustifiably or inconsistently erode family choices'.[67]

The project ultimately made policy recommendations on a broad variety of issues including: pre-implantation genetic diagnosis (PGD), genetic testing of new-borns and children, genetic testing of ethnic groups, new genetic testing technologies, and possible insurance implications of genetic knowledge. McLean contributed to the majority of these issues and the resulting recommendations during her role as one of the project's overseas collaborators. Her involvement significantly enhanced the depth of analysis found in both the research undertaken and the reports ultimately produced, and her impressive international reputation considerably increased the impact of the project.

Conclusion

McLean has made a significant contribution to human genome research and reproductive liberty throughout her career. She has consistently denounced excessively moralistic reasoning during her

---

63 See Henaghan (2006); Henaghan, *Vol. I* (2007); Henaghan, *Vol. II* (2007); and Henaghan (2009), all note 60, above.

64 Henaghan, M. and McLean, S.A.M., 'Main Findings' in Henaghan (2006), note 60, above, at p. 3.

65 Henaghan and McLean, note 64, above, at p. 3.

66 Henaghan and McLean, note 64, above, at p. 9.

67 Henaghan and McLean, note 64, above, at p. 13.

original quest for 'intellectual rigour'[68] when debating the sequencing of the human genome, and in her later pursuit of libertarian focused reproductive freedom, which gainfully employed Mill's harm principle. Throughout the developing trajectory of her arguments, McLean retained her focus on the fundamental importance of reproductive matters and the extremely personal nature of decisions about such matters. The clarity and strength of this analysis of reproductive liberty has created a dynamic setting for individual freedom and choice to flourish in an area otherwise susceptible to over-regulation and 'worst-case scenarios'. McLean's work illustrates a mastery of both the scientific realities and the ensuing ethical conflict generated by genomic developments, and has been widely disseminated to scientists, academics, policy makers and the general public. Her contribution to the New Zealand based Human Genome Project highlighted not just the depth of her arguments, but the international esteem in which her work is held.

Whichever way we look at reproductive liberty and the limits imposed by the harm principle, one must remember what is at stake for the people involved: '[t]hose who want access to reprogenetics technologies have a reason – probably a very good one – for wanting to do so'.[69] At some point we need to trust that the individuals seeking reproductive freedom (and the medical professionals trained to help them) will make the choice that is *right* for *them*. As McLean and Elliston state:

> In the long run, it does not seem unreasonable to trust people to make decisions that are appropriate for them and their families in conjunction with their medical advisers ... there is no reason to suppose that the decisions they make will be harmful, immoral or unethical.[70]

Unless individual choices are proven to be harmful to others, it is difficult to see why society should unduly restrict the formation of other individuals' families. This is not to say that everyone will agree with each other's reproductive decisions, but as Mclean has rightly argued, we can '... disapprove of decisions made by others without taking it upon ourselves to prevent them from being made'.[71]

68 McLean, note 6, above, at p. 684.
69 McLean, note 31, above, at p. 222.
70 McLean and Elliston, note 27, above, at p. 237.
71 McLean, note 31, above, at p. 219.

PART V
Issues at the End of Life

Chapter 15

In Word, or Sigh, or Tear:[1] Depression and End-of-Life Choices[2]

Colin Gavaghan

Introduction

Although debates about the (legal and moral) status of voluntary euthanasia (VE) and assisted suicide (AS) seem as intractable as ever, it may be that the terrain on which they are played out has recently shifted. While earlier exchanges were often characterised by 'first order' arguments between the relative importance of (typically) autonomy and the relief of suffering, on the one hand, and the value of life or importance of not killing, on the other, much of the recent discourse has been characterised by what may be seen as 'second order' concerns. That is to say, both sides agree about which ethical principles matter, but disagree about how these principles are promoted, or contravened, by the practices in question. Opponents of reform, then, may agree with supporters that autonomy and beneficence are important ethical values, while disagreeing that they will be promoted by allowing the practices of voluntary euthanasia and assisted dying.

Often, the points of divergence concern putatively 'vulnerable' people. Thus, again, while we might agree that autonomy is important, we might disagree that people in this particular category are capable of acting autonomously, or at least fear that their autonomy will be seriously compromised by their circumstances. Equally, the concern might be that their best interests and future happiness will not be best served by allowing them to act on their current preferences.

This shift of focus can be seen in the context of the recently-revived New Zealand debate on assisted dying, where John Kleinsman, Director of the Nathaniel Centre – the New Zealand Catholic Bioethics Centre – was at pains to point out that: 'I am, in all honesty, not interested in imposing my religious views on anyone'; but rather, his argument against assisted dying '... centres on safety and protection of those who are vulnerable'.[3] In a recent polemic against proposed law reform in Scotland, journalist Kevin McKenna has issued a similar warning: 'Many people who take their own lives do so because of depression. Society has not yet begun to consider urging those suffering from depression to kill themselves and have done with it'.[4]

In this chapter, I intend to focus on this last category of people: those whose autonomy and safety are often thought to be threatened by legalised VE/AS because they have been diagnosed with, or at least suspected of being affected by, a depressive disorder. Although there has been considerable

---

1 The title comes from Samuel Taylor Coleridge's 1802 poem, *Dejection: An Ode*, the second stanza of which begins as follows: 'A grief without a pang, void, dark, and drear, / A stifled, drowsy, unimpassioned grief, / Which finds no natural outlet, no relief, / In word, or sigh, or tear'.

2 Thanks are due to Simon Connell, John McMillan and Jeanne Snelling for helpful comments on this chapter.

3 Kleinsman, J., 'Legal Euthanasia Kills Justice for All', *Sunday Star Times*, 6 May 2012.

4 McKenna, K., 'Scotland's Assisted Suicide Bill Is an Offence to Our Human Dignity', *The Observer*, 1 February 2014.

recent disagreement about the precise diagnostic boundaries of such conditions, there is substantially greater consensus that they present a particular concern for end-of-life decision-making.

The significance of depression to VE/AS – and perhaps to end-of-life choices more generally – can be seen in two contexts. First, questions surround the role of depression as a *qualifying condition* for VE or AS. Those jurisdictions that have permitted these practices have generally sought to constrain their availability to people affected by certain kinds of health conditions. As discussed below, such restrictions have given rise to questions as to whether, and if so in what circumstances, depression may render a person eligible for legally sanctioned assistance, and a considerable body of case law has grown up around such questions.

At the same time, controversy exists around the role of depression as an *excluding condition* with regard to competent choices. The presence, actual or suspected, of such disorders is often thought to invalidate, or at least cast doubt upon, competence to make autonomous choices. Even the generally pro-reform Falconer Commission did '… not consider that a person with depression, whose judgement might be significantly impaired as a result of this depression, should be permitted to take such a momentous decision as ending their own life'.[5]

This chapter explores the relationship between depressive disorder and end-of-life decisions in both of these contexts. Drawing on and developing themes touched on by Sheila McLean in 2007,[6] it also examines this issue against the backdrop of what some commentators see as an expanding definition of 'depression' that threatens to pathologise a range of thoughts and wishes common among terminally or chronically ill people. While it is beyond my remit (and probably my expertise) to take an informed position on the desirability of this 'diagnostic inflation', it seems important to consider its likely implications for decisions as to legal capacity to consent to, and eligibility to be provided with, VE or AS.

A (Brief) History of Depression

Though use of the term 'depression' in this context is relatively recent, its roots can – with some reservations[7] – be traced to early writings about 'melancholia'. 'If fear and sadness continue long', noted Hippocrates in his Aphorisms, 'the person is melancholic'.[8] The term derives from the belief of ancient Greek physicians that the condition was caused by an imbalance of bodily fluids, or humours: the term derives from the Greek words *melas* (black) and *kholé* (bile).

A slight detour in the Middle Ages saw the concept become entangled with the Christian Church's notion of *accidie*, and become associated with the sin of sloth.[9] Otherwise, two aspects of the Hippocratic approach persisted until the Renaissance: the attribution of melancholia to humoral

5 *Commission on Assisted Dying* (Falconer Report), London, Demos, 2011, at p. 28.

6 McLean, S.A.M., *Assisted Dying: Reflections on the Need for Law Reform*, London, Routledge-Cavendish, 2007.

7 The assumption that depression is the direct linear successor of melancholia has been challenged, with Jennifer Radden warning that 'The conclusion that there is but one unchanging condition identified as melancholia in the past and renamed depression in our own era represents a troubling oversimplification', in 'Is This Dame Melancholy? Equating Today's Depression and Past Melancholia' (2003) 10(1) *Philosophy, Psychiatry, & Psychology*, 37–52, at p. 3.

8 Sprengell, C., *The Aphorisms of Hippocrates and the Sentences of Celsus*, 2nd edn, London, 1735, at p. 200.

9 Wolpert, L., *Malignant Sadness: The Anatomy of Depression*, London, Faber and Faber, 2006, at p. 4; Blazer, D.G., *The Age of Melancholy: 'Major Depression' and Its Social Origin*, New York, Routledge, 2005, at pp. 43–6.

imbalance,[10] and the 'clustering of traits around the poles of sadness and fear'.[11] References to 'depression' in this context can be traced to the seventeenth and eighteenth centuries; Samuel Johnson and George Eliot certainly used it in much the way we do today.[12]

During the nineteenth century, the term 'depression' came increasingly into use, though often to describe a symptom rather than a condition; 'the basic diagnostic term was still usually *melancholia* or *melancholy*'.[13] By the beginning of the twentieth century, however, the terms 'depression' and 'melancholia' were coming to be used more or less synonymously,[14] with the former term gaining increasing favour among medical professionals.[15] Emil Kraepelin's work was highly influential in the formative years of 'scientific' psychiatry, and this was no less true regarding his approach to depression. An important facet of Kraepelin's approach to mental illness was a distinction between 'endogenous' and 'exogenous' disorders[16] – that is, those with an identifiable external cause, and those that, with no such identifiable cause, were deemed to originate internally.[17]

This binary approach became the dominant one for the early part of the twentieth century, where exogenous aetiology developed into the concept of 'reactivity',[18] but it came to be challenged in more recent times by those who saw both 'exogenous/melancholic' and 'endogenous/neurotic' depression as lying along a continuum.[19] This, in turn, led to a major shift in how depression was perceived and diagnosed; the dominant approach, as explained below, now defines it by reference to symptoms rather than causes. This move was controversial at the time and, as I discuss later in this chapter, remains so today.

It is not clear whether depression or melancholia were always regarded as threats to autonomy. According to Charles F. McKhann:

> [T]he concept has evolved throughout the nineteenth century and into the twentieth that suicide is a manifestation of mental disturbance and that the individual is not responsible for his or her action. … This principle grew out of the observation that many suicides occurred in patients who had severe manic depressive (biphasic) disorders, those who were under severe emotional stress, and those who had suffered psychological trauma.[20]

---

10 Wolpert, note 9, above, at p. 6.

11 See Radden, note 7, above, at p. 38.

12 Jackson, S.W., *Melancholia and Depression: From Hippocratic Times to Modern Times*, New Haven, CT, Yale University Press, 1986, at p. 5.

13 Jackson, note 12, above, at p. 6.

14 See Blazer, note 9, above, at p. 48.

15 Jackson, note 12, above, at p. 6.

16 Kraepelin, E., *Psychiatrie: ein Lehrbuch für Studirende und Aertze*, 6th edn, Leipzig, Barth Verlag, 1899. Reprinted as Quen, J.M., Metoiu, H. and Ayed, S. (eds), *Psychiatry: A Textbook for Students and Physicians*, Canton, MA, Science History Publications, 1990. In fact, the dichotomous classification of depression was originally introduced by Paul Möbius, but it was the more influential works of Kraepelin that served to popularise the concepts; Jackson, note 12, above, at p. 212.

17 As Stanley Jackson explains, the precise meaning of, and distinctions between, these terms was the source of some confusion, with 'exogenous' variously defined as 'external to the brain' or attributable to identifiable and measurable causes. Jackson, note 12, above, at p. 212.

18 Jackson, note 12, above, at p. 212.

19 Parker, G., 'Classifying Depression: Should Paradigms Lost Be Regained?' (2000) 157(8) *American Journal of Psychiatry*, 1195–203; Horwitz, A.V. and Wakefield, J.C., *The Loss of Sadness: How Psychiatry Transformed Normal Sorrow into Depressive Disorder*, Oxford, Oxford University Press, 2007.

20 McKhann, C.F., *A Time to Die: The Place for Physician Assistance*, New Haven, CT, Yale University Press, 1999, at p. 69.

The standard definitions today are to be found in the Diagnostic and Statistical Manual of the American Psychiatric Association (DSM-V), and the World Health Organization's International Classification of Diseases (ICD-10). These differ in certain respects, but common to both are what we might call the 'core' symptoms of lowered or 'depressed' mood,[21] and diminished capacity for enjoyment or pleasure. Other symptoms are commonly, but not invariably, associated with the condition, such as tiredness or reduced energy, disturbed sleep patterns, loss of appetite, weight loss, reduction in libido, feelings of worthlessness or low self-esteem, and ideas of 'excessive' guilt.

ICD-10 subdivides depressive episodes into 'mild', 'moderate' and 'severe'.[22] A 'mild' episode is one in which 'two or three' of the generic symptoms are present, with four or more indicating a 'moderate' episode. A 'severe' episode is one in which:

> ... several of the above symptoms are marked and distressing, typically loss of self-esteem and ideas of worthlessness or guilt. Of particular relevance for present purposes, suicidal thoughts and acts are common and a number of 'somatic' symptoms are usually present.[23]

DSM-V requires that at least five of the typical symptoms be present, including at least one of the core symptoms.[24] Depressive episodes may or may not be accompanied by psychotic symptoms, such as '... hallucinations, delusions, psychomotor retardation, or stupor so severe that ordinary social activities are impossible'.[25]

Definitional Controversy

Debates around the 'pathologisation' of normal human experience are not new. For over half a century, Thomas Szasz, Ivan Illich and their successors have railed against 'the medicalization of life'[26] and the 'tyranny of pharmacracy'.[27] The practice of psychiatry and the 'myth of mental illness'[28] has been a particular focus for these impassioned polemics. While the echoes of the general 'anti-psychiatry' critique can still be heard from time to time, most of today's critiques are more focused on particular examples of putative medical, psychiatric and pharmacological overreach. Many psychiatric conditions are argued to be dramatically over-diagnosed and over-medicated – either at the behest of a greedy pharmaceutical industry, or by a state bent on

---

21 *International Statistical Classification of Diseases and Related Health Problems 10th Revision* (ICD-10), 2010, Chapter V: 'Mental and Behavioural Disorders', available at: http://apps.who.int/classifications/icd10/browse/2010/en (accessed 13 January 2015); American Psychiatric Association, *Diagnostic and Statistical Manual of Medical Disorders*, 5th edn (DSM-V), 2013, 'Depressive Disorders'.

22 ICD-10, note 21, above, at F32.

23 ICD-10, note 21, above, at F32.2.

24 DSM-V, note 21, above, 'Depressive Disorders'.

25 ICD-10, note 21, above, at F32.3.

26 Illich, I., 'The Medicalization of Life' (1975) 1 *Journal of Medical Ethics*, 73–7.

27 Szasz, T., 'The Therapeutic State: The Tyranny of Pharmacracy' (2001) 5(4) *The Independent Review*, 485–521.

28 Szasz, T., *The Myth of Mental Illness: Foundations of a Theory of Personal Conduct*, revised edn, New York, HarperCollins, 1974.

greater social control[29] – if not invented outright for the purposes of manufacturing demand for 'treatments'.[30]

'Clinical depression' has not been insulated from these sorts of controversies. 2007 saw the publication of two prominent critiques of perceived over-diagnosis. In the *British Medical Journal*, professor of psychiatry Gordon Parker argued that: 'A low threshold for diagnosing clinical depression, however, risks treating normal emotional states as illness, challenging the model's credibility and risking inappropriate management'.[31]

In similar terms, Allan Horwitz and Jerome Wakefield argued:

> … that the recent explosion of putative depressive disorder, in fact, does not stem primarily from a real rise in this condition. Instead, it is largely a product of conflating the two conceptually distinct categories of normal sadness and depressive disorder and thus classifying many instances of normal sadness as mental disorders.[32]

Such critiques gained momentum and publicity when the American Psychiatric Association (APA) published its draft reforms of the DSM, reforms which soon attracted allegations of diagnostic inflation. In particular, the proposal to extend a diagnosis of major depression to situations of bereavement elicited strong criticism. The British Psychological Society had this to say:

> [W]e are concerned that clients and the general public are negatively affected by the continued and continuous medicalisation of their natural and normal responses to their experiences; responses which undoubtedly have distressing consequences which demand helping responses, but which do not reflect illnesses so much as normal individual variation.[33]

Allen J. Francis, a psychiatrist and Chair of the committee which produced the previous edition of the DSM, spoke out in even starker terms, claiming: 'Making grief a mental disorder will be a bonanza for drug companies, but a disaster for grievers. The decision is also self destructive for DSM 5 and further undermines the credibility of APA. Psychiatry should not be mislabeling the normal'.[34]

Although it is not my intention in this chapter to take sides in the debate over putative diagnostic inflation, this discussion of the controversy around it is relevant for my purposes. For one thing, it illustrates that 'clinical depression' is a contested diagnosis, with many fuzzy borders. If a diagnosis

---

29 Francis Fukuyama has argued against what he sees as the over-diagnosis of attention deficit hyperactivity disorder among school-aged boys, arguing that 'Ritalin has come to play the role of an overt instrument of social control', in Fukuyama, F., *Our Posthuman Future: Consequences of the Biotechnology Revolution*, New York, Farrar, Straus and Giroux, 2002, at p. 46.

30 Fishman, J.R., 'Manufacturing Desire: The Commodification of Female Sexual Dysfunction' (2004) 34(2) *Social Studies of Science*, 187–218.

31 Parker, G., 'Is Depression Overdiagnosed? Yes' (2007) 335 *British Medical Journal*, 328, http://www.bmj.com/content/bmj/335/7615/328.full.pdf (accessed 19 January 2015).

32 See Horwitz and Wakefield, note 19, above, at p. 6.

33 The British Psychological Society, *Response to the American Psychiatric Association: DSM-5 Development*, June 2011, at p. 11. See: http://apps.bps.org.uk/_publicationfiles/consultation-responses/DSM-5%202011%20-%20BPS%20response.pdf (accessed 13 January 2015).

34 Frances, A.J., 'Last Plea to DSM 5: Save Grief from the Drug Companies', *Psychology Today*, 3 January 2013. See: http://www.psychologytoday.com/blog/dsm5-in-distress/201301/last-plea-dsm-5-save-grief-the-drug-companies (accessed 13 January 2015).

of 'depression' is to serve either as a qualifying or an excluding criterion for assisted dying, then eligibility for such assistance will often depend on where the psychiatric profession chooses – and it is, unquestionably, a choice – to set those borders.

Later in the chapter, I consider the current professional criteria in more detail, with a view both to considering how well they fit with legitimate concerns around end-of-life choices, and also to point out the danger of potential definitional circularity. First, though, I consider the dual role of depression in the context of end-of-life choices.

Depression as a Qualifying Criterion

Those jurisdictions which allow assistance at the end of life often limit this option to those who satisfy certain qualifying criteria. This might involve an objective test, such as that the person is terminally ill and predicted to die within a certain period of time, or a subjective test, typically some variant on the requirement for intolerable or unacceptable suffering.

Whether depression will satisfy the qualifying criteria will depend on the jurisdiction in question. In jurisdictions such as the Netherlands which require only 'lasting and unbearable' suffering,[35] the question has arisen as to whether this suffering must be somatic[36] in origin, or whether psychiatric suffering[37] could suffice. In 1994, the Dutch Supreme Court decided that non-somatic suffering could form the basis for a defence for performing euthanasia. In the widely discussed *Chabot* decision, it held:

> A claim of necessity can … not be excluded simply on the ground that the patient's unbearable suffering, without prospect of improvement, does not have a somatic cause and that the patient is not in the terminal phase. … the cause of the suffering does not detract from the extent to which suffering is experienced.[38]

However, when the suffering was non-somatic in origin, additional safeguards were put in place, specifically the requirements:

- that the applicant must have been examined by an independent colleague; and
- that the applicant cannot have refused any 'realistic' therapeutic alternative.

35 Termination of Life on Request and Assisted Suicide (Review Procedures) Act 2002, Article 2(1)(b). Belgium's Law on Euthanasia 2002 is similar, requiring 'persistent and unbearable physical or mental suffering that cannot be alleviated'.

36 'Somatic', which is also derived from Greek, means 'of the body'. In medical terms, it is usually contrasted with mental illnesses, though it should not be forgotten that mental illnesses may themselves have bodily causes.

37 For the purposes of this chapter, 'psychiatric' suffering may be taken to be that variety of non-somatic suffering that results from a diagnosed mental illness. This may be contrasted with 'existential' suffering, which is that variety of non-somatic suffering which has no such diagnosed cause.

38 From English translation of Supreme Court decision in Griffiths, J., 'Assisted Suicide in the Netherlands: The Chabot Case' (1995) 58 *Modern Law Review*, 232–48, at p. 237.

Whether these additional safeguards are sufficient,[39] or indeed necessary,[40] has been a ground of some contention. In the wake of the judgment, it was also widely predicted that it was only a matter of time before the courts were called upon to decide whether severe unhappiness that did not satisfy the criteria for 'clinical depression' would qualify.[41]

In 2002, the Supreme Court was faced with precisely this question. Unlike the patient in Chabot's case, GP Philip Sutorius had not diagnosed his patient as suffering from depression or any other 'medically classified disease or disorder'. Rather, Edward Brongersma was affected by loneliness, 'feelings of senselessness, physical deterioration, and a long-standing wish to die not associated with depression'.[42] For the Dutch Supreme Court, this was a step too far. The defence of necessity was rejected; merely being 'tired of life' is not sufficient for the purposes of Dutch law.[43]

The law in Switzerland has recently become the focus of considerable judicial attention with regard to non-somatic suffering and the putative 'right to die', with two cases reaching the European Court of Human Rights.[44] In theory, Swiss law is amongst the more liberal with regard to assisted dying, in that inciting or assisting suicide are only offences when carried out 'for selfish motives'.[45]

In practice, the most humane and effective means of suicide are considerably more tightly regulated. Under Swiss federal medicine laws, the lethal substances most suitable for these purposes are available only in accordance with a medical prescription. And both case law[46] and the professional medical guidelines by which Swiss doctors are bound allow them only to issue such prescriptions where:

> (1) the patient's illness makes it likely that death is close, (2) other options for support have been discussed and, where appropriate, put into place, and (3) the patient is capable of discernment, his or her wish appears to be carefully considered, is not the result of external pressure and is to be regarded as final, which must be verified by an independent third party who need not necessarily be a doctor. (Federal Court, translation from ECtHR, para. 16)

It appeared, then, that it would only be those near the end of life who would be able to avail themselves of physician-assisted suicide (PAS); and no other route is readily available for

---

39 'However well any legislation is hedged about with guidelines and protections against abuse, the slippery slope predicts an inevitable extension of these practices to other, more vulnerable, groups, such as those who are demented, mentally ill, chronically disabled, frail, dependent, and elderly – and perhaps even simply unhappy'. Ogilvie, A.D. and Potts, S.G., 'Assisted Suicide for Depression: The Slippery Slope in Action?' (1994) 309(6953) *British Medical Journal*, 492–3, at p. 493.

40 'The Court … does not explain why rejection of treatment stands in the way of necessity in the case of non-somatic suffering, whereas it is pretty well established that this does not apply to somatic suffering'. Griffiths, note 38, above, at p. 243.

41 'It will be interesting to see whether the Dutch courts will hold assistance with suicide justifiable in several categories of cases in which the person concerned is not "sick" at all (for example the case of very elderly persons who are incapacitated in various ways and simply "tired of life")'. See Griffiths, note 38, above, at p. 246.

42 Griffiths, J., Weyers, H. and Adams, M., *Euthanasia and Law in Europe*, Portland, OR, Hart Publishing, 2008, at p. 36.

43 Sheldon, T., 'Being "Tired of Life" Is Not Grounds for Euthanasia' (2003) 326(7380) *British Medical Journal*, 71, http://www.bmj.com/content/326/7380/71.3 (accessed 19 January 2015).

44 *Haas v. Switzerland* (2011) App. No. 31322/07 (ECHR); *Gross v. Switzerland* (2013) App. No. 67810/10 (ECHR).

45 Swiss Penal Code, Article 115.

46 *Zurich Case*, Entscheid der 3 Kammer VB Nr 9900145 (1999) (Zurich Administrative Court).

those who want to access lethal drugs. The reality, as Isra Black has explained, may have been somewhat different:

> … empirical evidence from the Swiss right-to-die organisations before and after the *Zurich Case* has revealed a relatively low yet significant prevalence of PAS among individuals with non-fatal conditions, without corresponding criminal and/or professional proceedings.[47]

The applicant in the *Haas* case[48] had suffered from '… a serious bipolar affective disorder for about 20 years. During this period he has twice attempted suicide and has stayed in psychiatric hospitals on several occasions'.[49] Starting in 2004, he attempted to obtain assistance in ending his life, and approached several psychiatrists with a view to receiving a prescription of a lethal substance, specifically sodium pentobarbital.[50] When none of the psychiatrists was willing to provide such a prescription, Haas turned first to the Swiss courts, claiming that his right to control the timing and manner of his death (under Article 8 of the European Convention on Human Rights) was being infringed by this requirement.

Having been unsuccessful at first instance, Mr Haas appealed in 2006 to the Federal Court. The appeal was rejected. It is interesting to consider in detail the Court's ruling. First, it held that – contrary to what the earlier case law seemed to require – mental illness and psychological suffering could provide a legal basis for assistance with dying:

> It must not be forgotten that a serious, incurable and chronic mental illness may, in the same way as a somatic illness, cause suffering such that, over time, the patient concludes that his or her life is no longer worth living. The most recent ethical, legal and medical opinions indicate that in such cases also the prescription of sodium pentobarbital is not necessarily precluded or to be excluded on the ground that it would represent a breach of the doctor's duty of care ….[51]

Second, it acknowledged that 'the greatest restraint must be exercised' when providing assistance in such cases. In particular:

> [I]t is necessary to distinguish between a desire to die as the expression of a psychological disorder which can and must be treated, and a wish to die that is based on the considered and sustained decision of a person capable of discernment ('pre-suicide assessment'), which must be respected as applicable.[52]

---

47 Black, I., 'Existential Suffering and the Extent of the Right to Physician-Assisted Suicide in Switzerland' (2014) 22(1) *Medical Law Review*, 109–18, at p. 110.

48 *Haas*, note 44, above.

49 *Haas*, note 44, above, at para. 7.

50 It might be asked why Mr Haas could not have ended his life without assistance. Unlike, for example, Dianne Pretty and Debbie Purdy, he was not physically incapacitated. Indeed, one of the Swiss Government's arguments before the European Court was that '[t]here were numerous other solutions available to able-bodied persons wishing to commit suicide' (*Haas*, note 44, above, at para. 38). There is no doubt a good deal that could be said on this subject, but for the moment I will confine myself to the observation that, for those without ready access to, and knowledge of, toxic substances, it may be more difficult than generally realized to find what Mr Haas described as 'the only dignified, certain, rapid and pain-free method of committing suicide' (at para. 33).

51 *Haas Entscheid*, 2A48/2006 (3 November 2006) (CH Federal Supreme Court) [6.3.2], at 6.3.5.1. Translation from *Haas*, note 44, above, at para. 16.

52 *Haas Entscheid*, note 51, above, at 6.3.5.1. Translation from *Haas*, note 44, above, at para. 16.

The key consideration was whether 'the wish to die is based on an autonomous and all-embracing decision'.[53] Since the 'question of whether the conditions have been met in a given case cannot be examined without recourse to specialised medical – and particularly psychiatric – knowledge', 'a thorough psychiatric examination thus becomes necessary'.[54]

Although this ruling seemed to have widened the criteria for assisted suicide (in this case, with the help of a physician), it did not satisfy Mr Haas, who regarded the requirement to undergo medical examination as both an interference with his Art 8 right, and a practically insurmountable obstacle to achieving assistance,[55] and he appealed this decision to the European Court of Human Rights. The Court, while expressing sympathy for Haas's 'wish to commit suicide in a safe and dignified manner and without unnecessary pain and suffering',[56] found in favour of the Swiss Government. In particular, it held:

> [T]he regulations put in place by the Swiss authorities, namely the requirement to obtain a medical prescription, pursue, *inter alia*, the legitimate aims of protecting everybody from hasty decisions and preventing abuse, and, in particular, ensuring that a patient lacking discernment does not obtain a lethal dose of sodium pentobarbital.[57]

The more recent *Gross* decision[58] concerned a situation that was, on the face of it, very similar to that in *Haas*. Aldo Gross had also attempted to take her own life, and had also received psychiatric in-patient care in the aftermath. Like Mr Haas, she sought a quick and humane means to end her own life, and approached various psychiatrists seeking a prescription for sodium pentobarbital. Gross's case differed in that she was not suffering from any recognised illness at all, but only from a persistent desire to die. Unsurprisingly, she had been unable to persuade the physicians she consulted to issue her with a prescription for lethal drugs. Although satisfied as to her decision-making capacity, they regarded themselves as constrained by the fact that she was not suffering from any illness.

As with Mr Haas, Ms Gross was unsuccessful before the domestic courts, and ultimately brought her case to the European Court of Human Rights. By a narrow majority, the Court held against the Swiss Government, on the grounds that: 'Swiss law, while providing the possibility of obtaining a lethal dose of sodium pentobarbital on medical prescription, does not provide sufficient guidelines ensuring clarity as to the extent of this right'.[59] In a ruling somewhat redolent of that of the House of Lords in Debbie Purdy's case,[60] the European Court of Human Rights required the Swiss Government:

> ... to issue comprehensive and clear guidelines on whether and under which circumstances an individual in the applicant's situation – that is, someone not suffering from a terminal illness – should be granted the ability to acquire a lethal dose of medication allowing them to end their life.[61]

---

53 *Haas Entscheid*, note 51, above, at 6.3.5.1. Translation from *Haas*, note 44, above, at para. 16.

54 *Haas Entscheid*, note 51, above, at 6.3.5.2.

55 It should be noted that the validity of this latter concern was called into some doubt by the ECtHR, where the majority were 'not convinced that it was impossible for the applicant to find a specialist who would have been prepared to assist him'. *Haas*, note 44, above, at para. 60.

56 *Haas*, note 44, above, at para. 56.

57 *Haas*, note 44, above, at para. 56.

58 *Gross*, note 44, above.

59 *Gross*, note 44, above, at para. 67.

60 *R (on the application of Purdy) v. Director of Public Prosecutions* [2009] UKHL 45.

61 *Gross*, note 44, above, at para. 69.

In doing so, however, the Court was careful to stress that the substantive content of those guidelines was largely a matter for the Swiss Government to decide.[62] As Isra Black has observed, this could see Ms Gross's 'victory' transpiring to be a pyrrhic one, because:

> … the Government might respond with clear guidance that PAS for non-fatal conditions (with the exception of mental disorders meeting the *Haas* conditions) or, more narrowly, for existential suffering, is not responsible medical practice.[63]

The 'fuzzy edges' that previously seem to have allowed Swiss physicians to 'provide … PAS [physician assisted suicide] to elderly individuals with apparent existential suffering, ostensibly without censure' will now have to be made clearer. It is at least possible that this will be done in such a way as to render the situation more, rather than less, restrictive for those whose wish for PAS is borne of existential suffering.

The two jurisdictions best known for allowing euthanasia or assisted suicide, then, either already have, or are probably about to adopt, positions that accept 'clinical' depression as a qualifying criterion, but draw the line at 'mere' existential suffering. This attempt to draw clear distinctions between 'psychiatric' and 'existential' non-somatic suffering has elicited critical responses, from at least two directions. For opponents of euthanasia, its provision to 'clinically depressed' people is problematic. Herbert Hendin described the *Chabot* case as 'especially troubling, as it marked Dutch acceptance of depressed suicidal patients as eligible for assisted suicide or euthanasia. Depressed patients', he warned, 'with or without medical conditions who did not respond quickly to treatment could be vulnerable'.[64]

Opponents have also expressed fears that accepting non-somatic suffering as a ground for euthanasia will lead invariably to a situation wherein euthanasia will be provided on demand to anyone who is merely unhappy.[65] The requirement that the applicant be 'medically ill', we might fear, will be readily circumvented, and indeed may provide an incentive for sympathetic medics to provide pseudo-diagnoses. As well as circumventing the spirit of the law, this might risk contributing to the 'diagnostic inflation' of mental illness.

For some supporters of AS/VE, on the other hand, the distinction is at best arbitrary, and at worst irrational and inhumane. Regardless of which of the two most frequently advanced arguments for legalisation – autonomy or beneficence – is followed, nothing of ethical significance hangs on the presence of absence of a recognised 'medical illness'. Thus, Griffiths and Weyers have argued that: 'By trying to draw a line between suffering that is medically classifiable and other forms of suffering the court seems to choose the route of repression. It seems doubtful whether the demarcation will survive in practice'.[66]

Although in profound disagreement as to how the situation should be improved, both sides seem to be in agreement in doubting that the distinction between 'clinical' depression and 'mere' unhappiness is particularly clear or likely to withstand challenge. One of the more overt exponents of this view is Julian Savulescu, who has argued that Edward Brongersma '… was in fact suffering

62 *Gross*, note 44, above, at para. 69.

63 See Black, note 47, above, at p. 117.

64 Hendin, H., 'Seduced by Death: Doctors, Patients, and the Dutch Cure' (1994) 10(2) *Issues in Law & Medicine*, 123–69, at p. 129.

65 See Ogilvie and Potts, note 39, above, at p. 493. See also Delacey, T.C., 'Euthanasia, Innocence and the Slippery Slope' (Winter 1995) *Policy*, 36–9, at p. 39.

66 Griffiths, Weyers and Adams, note 42, above, at pp. 49–50.

from the commonest terminal disease: ageing. … We do not consider it to be a disease because of the way we have arbitrarily defined the concept of disease'.[67]

As I discussed above, the view that the boundaries of disease – and in particular, depressive disease – have been defined arbitrarily is by no means an uncommon one. Even among those who do not consider the definition wholly arbitrary, it is widely recognised that the boundary between 'clinical' depression and 'mere' unhappiness can be somewhat fuzzy. If there is merit in this critique, then it seems that an approach to euthanasia that accepts 'depressive illness' as a qualifying condition, but not non-pathological 'existential suffering', is likely to be problematic.

Furthermore, for those concerned about the capacity of euthanasia applicants to make autonomous decisions, it may be seen as somewhat anomalous that those diagnosed with psychiatric illness will be permitted to choose to die with assistance, while those with no such diagnosis will not.

In 2010, Dutch media reported on the formation of an organisation – 'Out of Free Will' – dedicated to campaigning for the right to assisted suicide for 'All Dutch people over 70 years of age who feel tired of life'. Although widely depicted as a radical initiative to expand the availability of euthanasia, it is interesting to note that the group seeks to limit such a right to situations where: 'The suicide assistants must make sure the death wish is more than a rash impulse, *the product of depression*, or the symptom of another illness, and that the patient has considered the consequences of his actions for those who will survive him'.[68]

If the presence of depression is at least to serve as a red flag for problems with mental capacity, then the 'Out of Free Will' proposal may be seen as having certain advantages over the current position of Dutch law. Can we, though, assume that such a red flag response would be justified? As I discuss in the next section, the precise relationship between depressive illness and decision-making capacity is not straightforward.

Depression as an Excluding Criterion

Concerns about the influence of depression on decision-making capacity (henceforth simply 'capacity') lie at the heart of the second role depression can play in discussions and proposals about euthanasia. The moderate form of the argument here is that any proposals to allow euthanasia must be drafted so as to protect depressed (or at least seriously depressed) people from harmful or non-autonomous choices. In practice, this may mean excluding any depressed people from being able to avail themselves of VE/AS.

The extreme form of the argument is that the threat to depressed people is of such a nature and magnitude that it counts as a strong reason against allowing VE/AS at all. What both the moderate and extreme versions rely on, then, is an assumption that allowing (at least some) depressed people to access euthanasia would be a bad outcome.

The moderate version can be seen in the report of the generally pro-reform Falconer Commission:

> Although the distinction between 'appropriate sadness' and depression in the context of terminal illness is complex, the Commission does not consider that a person with depression, whose

---

67 Savulescu, J., 'A Simple Solution to the Puzzles of End of Life? Voluntary Palliated Starvation' (2014) 40 *Journal of Medical Ethics*, 110–13, at p. 110.

68 Jesma, F., 'Citizens Group Argues "Right to Die"', 8 February 2010, available at: http://vorige.nrc.nl/international/Features/article2478619.ece/Citizens_group_argues_right_to_die (accessed 13 January 2015) (emphasis added).

> judgement might be significantly impaired as a result of this depression, should be permitted to take such a momentous decision as ending their own life.[69]

The phrasing of this finding is somewhat ambiguous as to whether the phrase 'whose judgement might be significantly impaired' is a restrictive or non-restrictive clause. That is, is it being assumed that people with depression have suspect judgment merely by virtue of being depressed, or is the report alluding to a subset of depressed people of whom this might be said, and towards whom more care should be shown?

In either event, the draft legislation to which the report gave rise spoke only of 'recognising and taking account of the effects of depression or other psychological disorders that may impair a person's decision-making'.[70] This suggests an intention that a diagnosis of depression will function as a warning flag rather than a Stop sign; as an indicator of a need for particular scrutiny of an applicant's decision-making capacity, rather than an assumption that it is lacking. Whether it would be interpreted in that way in practice is, of course, another question.

Another more recent legislative proposal – Margo MacDonald's Assisted Suicide (Scotland) Bill,[71] introduced in November 2013 – appeared to take a harder line on the issue. In the section headed Capacity, the Bill laid out standard criteria for decision-making capacity (which are discussed in the next section), but supplemented this with a requirement that the person 'is not suffering from any mental disorder (within the meaning of section 328 of the Mental Health (Care and Treatment) (Scotland) Act 2003 …) which might affect the making of the request'.[72] Note that this was more than a requirement for greater scrutiny of the standard criteria for capacity; rather, it appeared to be stating that, even if those other criteria are satisfied, the presence of any mental disorder which *might* affect the making of the request would exclude them from eligibility. In contrast to Lord Falconer's Bill, this is a Stop sign rather than a warning flag.

Each of these initiatives, then, takes the moderate view that assisted dying legislation can be enacted in a manner that would afford adequate protection to depressed and other mentally ill people, but they diverge with regard to the precise role a diagnosis should play. It is possible that these are built in as political compromise – to appease and mollify in the face of concerns like those considered earlier. But there is also a kernel of ethical substance to this: if there is reason to doubt the capacity of depressed people then is this not a reasonable protection?

In evaluating this suggestion, I will consider two other questions. First, are there reasons to believe that depressed people are, as a rule, likely to have absent or diminished capacity? And second, are there reasons to think that the standard test for capacity is inadequate to respond to the phenomenon of depression?

In the final section, I will consider the possibility that there are reasons other than concern for capacity or autonomy to treat depressed individuals as a discrete class for these purposes.

---

69 See Falconer Report, note 5, above, at p. 28.

70 Assisted Dying Bill 2013, Clause 8(1)(a)(ii).

71 Unlike abortion, euthanasia and assisted suicide are not 'reserved' matters in terms of the Scotland Act 1998. Therefore, the Scottish Parliament is free to legislate on these issues.

72 Section 12. The 2003 Act does not contain an exhaustive list of 'mental disorders', but it seems clear that depression would qualify. See Patrick, H., *Mental Health, Incapacity and the Law in Scotland*, Edinburgh, Tottel Publishing, 2006, at para. 11.14.

Depression and Decision-making Capacity

Depression – at least in its more serious forms – can qualify as a mental disorder,[73] and as such might fall within the provisions of mental health legislation. This may mean that depressed people are subject to compulsory detention, assessment or treatment, though typically this will be limited to treatment for the mental disorder. It does not follow that depressed people are incompetent to make decisions about medical treatment more generally. The Common Law has long recognised that these are separate questions.[74]

Whether a depressed individual satisfies the criteria for capacity will depend on the individual person, the decision to be made, and the laws of the jurisdiction in question. Although details vary between jurisdictions, legal tests for capacity tend to involve four common elements:

- the ability to *understand* – this includes both understanding of information relevant to the decision,[75] and also the reasonably foreseeable consequences of that decision;[76]
- the ability to *retain* information long enough to make a decision;[77]
- the ability to *use* relevant information to reach a decision;
- the ability to *communicate* a decision.[78]

Capacity, then, at least as it is understood in the Common Law world, is a process-based test. It relies upon the abilities to make a decision in a certain kind of way, and is not – at least in theory – concerned with the content of the decision made. As Buchanan and Brock put it, '[a]n adequate standard of competence will focus primarily not on the content of the patient's decision but on the *process* of the reasoning that leads up to that decision'.[79] This approach is consistent with value pluralism, and with the traditional liberal ideal that the state should, where possible, be neutral as between different conceptions of the good life. Provided they are capable of understanding what is involved in the decision, the values and priorities of individual patients should be respected, even where they are idiosyncratic or, to most people, quite irrational.[80] All that matters is that someone is capable of making a decision in light of their free and settled (and I will return to that last qualifier in due course) values; the actual content of those values is not, or should not be, a concern for courts or doctors.

---

73 'We do not doubt that reactive depression (not merely a transient sense of being "a little down" or "fed up with everything") is capable of amounting to mental disorder'. *St George's Health Care NHS Trust v. S* [1998] 3 WLR 936, per Judge, LJ at p. 961.

74 *In re C (Adult: Refusal of Treatment)* [1994] 1 WLR 290. For a recent example, see *Newcastle upon Tyne Hospitals Foundation Trust v. LM* [2014] EWHC 454 (COP). This concerned a refusal of a blood transfusion by a Jehovah's Witness who had 'a background history of depression and paranoid schizophrenia and in the past had received compulsory treatment'. Having heard evidence from her treating doctors, Jackson J held that '[t]here was no evidence that mental illness had interfered with her decision-making'. The refusal was legally valid.

75 See, for example, Mental Capacity Act 2005, s. 3(1)(a), and Adults with Incapacity (Scotland) Act 2000, s. 1(6)(d).

76 Mental Capacity Act 2005, s. 3(4).

77 Section 3(3) of the Mental Capacity Act makes it clear that '[t]he fact that a person is able to retain the information relevant to a decision for a short period only does not prevent him from being regarded as able to make the decision'.

78 Mental Capacity Act 2005, s. 3(1)(d); Adults with Incapacity (Scotland) Act 2000, s. 1(6)(c).

79 Buchanan, A.E. and Brock, D.W., *Deciding for Others: The Ethics of Surrogate Decision Making*, Cambridge, Cambridge University Press, 1990, at p. 50.

80 *In re T* [1992] 3 WLR 782; *Re MB* [1997] 2 FLR 426, (1997) 38 BMLR 175 (CA).

Depression *can* impact upon all of the standard elements of capacity. There are, certainly, instances of depression that are accompanied by psychotic features, 'hallucinations, delusions, psychomotor retardation, or stupor so severe that ordinary social activities are impossible'.[81] Such features may well see the standard capacity test failed at the first hurdle. Furthermore, as one team of leading researchers in this area have explained: 'There appears to be little disagreement that major depression can have an impact on cognitive functions related to decision making. Impairments may exist in concentration ..., information processing, and reasoning, among others'.[82] To say that depression *can* result in these problems, though, is not to say that it invariably, or even usually, does so. As noted in a recent meta-analysis, the literature around this area 'is small and heterogeneous and so conclusions can only be tentative'.[83] However, such research as has been conducted suggests that, while depression can have an impact, most depressed people retain 'adequate' levels of decision-making capacity.

Applebaum and Grisso's research on capacity and mental illness has been influential in this regard.[84] They compared the performance of cohorts of people with depression and schizophrenia with cohorts without diagnosed mental illness, on a range of 'functional abilities that the courts are likely to consider relevant'.[85] While recognising that decision-making capacity is task-specific,[86] the study design was intended to identify 'functions associated with ... [the] main legal standards for competence'.[87] Specifically, Applebaum and Grisso were concerned with understanding treatment disclosures, perceptions of disorder, thinking rationally about treatment, and expressing a choice.

The study concluded that '76% of the depression group performed in the "adequate" range ... across all decision-making measures', leading the authors to conclude that '... the justification for a blanket denial of the right to consent to or refuse treatment for persons hospitalized because of mental illness cannot be based on the assumption that they uniformly lack decision-making capacity'.[88] Of course, questions could be asked about the definition of 'adequate' adopted by Applebaum and Grisso – a definition that they acknowledge was ad hoc. Furthermore, the authors acknowledged that conclusions about capacity were somewhat tenuous outwith the context of a particular jurisdiction and a particular decision.[89] Nonetheless, the results are significant in emphasising several points. First, there was wide degree of variation between depressed participants in terms of their performances on the various measures. Second, many of the depressed participants performed at least as well as the non-mentally-ill control group, while 'a significant portion performed at or above the mean for persons without mental illness'.[90]

---

81 See ICD-10, note 21, above, at F32.3.

82 Appelbaum, P.S., Grisso, T., Frank, E., et al., 'Competence of Depressed Patients for Consent to Research' (1999) 156(9) *American Journal of Psychiatry*, 1380–84, at p. 1380.

83 Hindmarch, T., Hotopf, M. and Owen, G.S., 'Depression and Decision-making Capacity for Treatment or Research: A Systematic Review' (2013) 14(1) *BMC Medical Ethics*, http://www.biomedcentral.com/1472-6939/14/54 (accessed 13 January 2013).

84 Applebaum, P.S. and Grisso, T., 'The MacArthur Treatment Competence Study. I Mental Illness and Competence to Consent to Treatment' (1995) 19(2) *Law and Human Behavior*, 105–26.

85 Applebaum and Grisso, note 84, above, at p. 119.

86 Applebaum and Grisso, note 84, above, at p. 119.

87 Applebaum, P.S. and Grisso, T., 'The MacArthur Treatment Competence Study. II Measures of Abilities Related to Competence to Consent to Treatment' (1995) 19(2) *Law and Human Behavior*, 127–48, at p. 146.

88 Appelbaum, P.S. and Grisso, T., 'The MacArthur Study Treatment Competence Study. III Abilities of Patients to Consent to Psychiatric and Medical Treatments' (1995) 19(2) *Law and Human Behavior*, 149–74, at p. 171.

89 Appelbaum and Grisso, note 88, above, at p. 170.

90 Appelbaum and Grisso, note 88, above, at p. 171.

A more recent London-based study of depressed people admitted to a psychiatric hospital arrived at a similar figure, finding an estimated 31 per cent prevalence of incapacity with regard to decisions about future treatment for depression.[91] If these studies are reliable, then there is little empirical basis for abandoning the presumption of capacity[92] when dealing with depressed people – though there may very well be cause for greater caution and scrutiny than with non-depressed people.

This conclusion, and the studies from which it derives, relate to capacity as it is generally understood in medical law. That is, it relates to the abilities of depressed people to understand, retain and use information. Yet the distinct phenomenon of depression has led some writers to question the adequacy of that account; to question whether the example of depression shows that something is missing from the standard account. One possibility is that the standard tests for capacity pay insufficient account to reality-distorting effects attendant on 'pathological pessimism'.[93]

Pessimism and Information Processing

Behavioural scientist Abraham Rudnick has explored this concern, noting that depression could 'disrupt appreciation of the benefits of treatment due to undervaluing positive outcomes while focusing on negative outcomes of treatment and thus skewing the weights given to treatment outcomes in favour of treatment risks'.[94] Discussing the possible implications of depression in a criminal law context, Fernandez, Coverdale and Brookbanks have spoken of the danger that 'a depressed person may fail to recognise the viability of other options when negatively perceiving the future or even when having difficulty seeing a future'.[95]

On one level, this sort of 'information processing' impairment may come close to a cognitive deficit, of the sort involved in a standard capacity evaluation. If a patient's estimate of the likelihood of a procedure's success differs markedly from what the best evidence suggests, then we may doubt that they are capable of 'understanding' the information needed to make the choice. Yet at the same time, we may wonder whether this serves to set apart the depressed patient from the non-depressed majority. The ability of human beings to gauge probabilities with any accuracy has long been called into question. In particular, there is a substantial body of evidence claiming to show that we are, overwhelmingly, biased towards optimism. We often, for instance, unrealistically weigh our own prospects more favourably than those of other people: '… over two decades of research on comparative risk judgments suggest that people systematically tip the scale in their own favor, predicting their outcomes will be brighter than that of their peers'.[96]

---

91 Owen, G.S., Richardson, G., David, A.S., et al., 'Mental Capacity to Make Decisions on Treatment in People Admitted to Psychiatric Hospitals: Cross Sectional Study' (2008) 337 *British Medical Journal*, http://www.bmj.com/content/bmj/337/bmj.39580.546597.BE.full.pdf (accessed 19 January 2015).

92 This presumption is recognised in various jurisdictions; see Mental Capacity Act 2005 s. 1(2) (England and Wales); Adults with Incapacity (Scotland) Act 2000: Code of Practice (2008), at 1.1 (Scotland); Health and Disability Commissioner (Code of Health and Disability Services Consumers' Rights) Regulations 1996 ('the Code of Patient Rights'), right 7(2) (New Zealand).

93 Beck, A.T., Rush, A.J., Shaw, B.F. and Emery, G., *Cognitive Therapy of Depression*, New York, Guilford Press, 1987, at p. 75.

94 Rudnick, A., 'Depression and Competence to Refuse Psychiatric Treatment' (2002) 28 *Journal of Medical Ethics*, 151–5, at p. 152.

95 Fernandez, P., Coverdale, J. and Brookbanks, W., 'Implications of Autonomy for Forensic Consequences of Extended Suicide' (2002) 9(2) *Psychiatry, Psychology and Law*, 146–50, at p. 148.

96 Shepperd, J.A., Carroll, P., Grace, J. and Terry, M., 'Exploring the Causes of Comparative Optimism' (2002) 42 *Psychologica Belgica*, 65–98, at p. 65. It is interesting to note that the authors of this paper attribute

A more general unrealistic optimism has also been widely detected. As Tali Sharot has described:

> People hugely underestimate their chances of getting divorced, losing their job or being diagnosed with cancer; expect their children to be extraordinarily gifted; envision themselves achieving more than their peers; and overestimate their likely life span (sometimes by 20 years or more).[97]

Recent research in which Sharot has been involved has raised the intriguing possibility that depressed people may in fact be less biased and more realistic when processing new information. A group of people affected by major depressive disorder and a control group were each presented

> … with a short description of one of 70 adverse life events and asked to estimate how likely this event was to occur to them in their lifetime. They were then presented with the average probability of that event occurring to a person living in the same sociocultural environment.[98]

Whereas the non-depressed participants 'updated their beliefs to a greater extent in response to desirable, compared with undesirable, information', no such difference was found for the depressed group. The researchers claim that this raises the possibility that what are often seen as 'negativity biases' among depressed people may in fact be better characterised as 'realism relative to an objective standard or by an absence of a positivity bias relative to healthy individuals'.[99]

It does not follow from this that we should seek to divest ourselves of any optimism biases. 'Mild to moderate positivity biases' have been shown to 'reduce stress and anxiety', 'enhance a motivation to obtain desired goals', 'enhance individual and group success'. Furthermore, 'all else being equal, it seems that optimists live longer, recover faster from diseases … and earn more'.[100] All of these factors may well provide good, beneficence-driven reasons to try to treat or ameliorate the symptoms of depression. That, however, is a separate matter from what I am considering here. Depression, and a pessimistic world view, may be bad for us in all sorts of ways, but they are not obviously bad for our decision-making and information-processing capacities.

Appreciation and Value Impairment

Another possible problem relates to what has been referred to variously as motivational or value impairment,[101] evaluative understanding[102] or appreciation. Applebaum, Grisso, et al. refer to the possibility that '[d]ecreased motivation to protect one's interests, perhaps associated with feelings of hopelessness, may alter the nature of patients' treatment decisions'.[103] Likewise Fernandez,

---

'comparative optimism' more to an unrealistically negative view of other people's prospects, rather than an unrealistically sunny view of our own!

97 Sharot, T., 'The Optimism Bias', *Time*, 28 May 2011. For a fuller account of this theory, see *The Optimism Bias: Why We're Wired to Look on the Bright Side*, New York, Random House, 2012.

98 Korn, C.W., Sharot, T., Walter, H., et al., 'Depression Is Related to an Absence of Optimistically Biased Belief Updating about Future Life Events' (2014) 44(3) *Psychological Medicine*, 579–92, at p. 584.

99 Korn et al., note 98, above, at p. 579.

100 Korn et al., note 98, above, at p. 589.

101 Brock, D.W., 'Patient Competence and Surrogate Decision-Making' in Rhodes, R., Francis, L.P. and Silvers, A. (eds) *The Blackwell Guide to Medical Ethics*, Oxford, Blackwell Publishing, 2007, pp. 128–41, at p. 130.

102 Fernandez et al., note 95, above.

103 Appelbaum et al., note 82, above, at p. 1380.

Coverdale and Brookbanks have spoken of the danger that 'excessive pessimism, or even a perception of doom along with feelings of guilt and worthlessness, may cause the individual to question her personal worth and attribute less value to the welfare of others, including children'.[104] Dan Brock has described the depressed person as 'value impaired'. While acknowledging that '[t]here may be no failure in their understanding or reasoning about this outcome', he argues that 'mental illness ... distorts what they value from what it would otherwise be can result in incompetence to decide about treatment'.[105]

Though they express themselves in slightly different ways, what seems common to these approaches is a concern not with information processing, but with the outcome weighting – not, this time, with the *likelihoods* of different outcomes coming about, but with their importance or desirability. The impairment, if there is one, relates to what the person cares about, or how much they care about it.

Yet as Rudnick also notes, '... giving value to outcomes that significantly affect one's life (and death) may be considered part of normal decision making (and hence of competence)'.[106] It is safe to say that human beings vary significantly in the manner in which we rank and prioritise good and bad outcomes. In the absence of some objective measure of how much someone *ought to* value particular outcomes, it is difficult to see how someone's decision-making could be adjudged objectively deficient in this regard. Does it follow that how much someone cares about a risk or an outcome is a matter of entirely personal preference? Would it always be wrong, for example, to attempt to persuade someone that they ought to care more about something? In Robert Heinlein's award-winning 1973 science fiction novel *Time Enough for Love*, the family of the ancient protagonist Lazarus Long adopts various strategies to persuade him that his life is still worth living. Are they wrong to do so?

In the next section, I will consider the possibility that there are beneficence-based reasons why such an attempt may at least be permissible. But my focus here is on autonomy, and capacity to make decisions. Can 'value impairment' undermine those attributes? If so, and if depression often results in this kind of value impairment, then this may have significant implications for the question of whether depressed people are able to make autonomous decisions.

It seems likely that further probing may sometimes be merited. It may be justifiable, for instance, to seek a level of internal consistency in someone's reasoning process. Do their stated hopes, fears and values correspond with the decision they have taken? It is, we might think, possible for someone to be simply mistaken about how their choices align with their values, as when someone whose greatest fear is hurting his family makes a choice that – unknown to him – will have the effect of causing them great distress. It is also possible that someone can simply be mistaken as to what their values demand; someone who is a devout adherent to a particular religion may be misinformed as to what the tenets of that religion actually require, and it is possible that demonstrating this to them could see them change their decision.[107] But where choices appear to align with stated values and priorities, it is less clear that there is a credible challenge to autonomy.

Does this commit us to respecting the suicidal choice of Charles McKhann's hypothetical 'teenager who despairs over a dissolved love affair'? May we not agree with McKhann that

104 Fernandez et al., note 95, above, at p. 148.

105 Brock, note 101, above, at p. 130.

106 Rudnick, note 94, above, at p. 152.

107 Possible, but not inevitable. As my colleague Rex Ahdar points out, respect for religious views must entail respect for the religious views that an individual happens to hold, even where they depart from the orthodoxy of their stated denomination. Ahdar, R. and Leigh, I., *Religious Freedom in the Liberal State*, 2nd edn, Cambridge, Cambridge University Press, 2013, at pp. 196–7.

intervention in such a case may be justifiable?[108] Or what of someone whose wish to die manifests during a period of acute grief? Again, the beneficence-derived justification for such intervention will be considered in the next section, but what of the effects of acute and transient depression on autonomy?

Certainly, a degree of stability in one's values or preferences may be thought a reasonable prerequisite of autonomy.[109] If faced with someone who flutters from one preference to another from hour to hour, we may reasonably wonder whether they have anything like a settled value system at all.[110] Indeed, a degree of such stability has sometimes been expressly required by the courts when dealing with end-of-life decisions. In Ms B's case, Dame Butler-Sloss addressed the question of possible ambivalence in the patient's wish to end life-sustaining treatment, though she was careful not to suggest that this would too readily undermine capacity: 'In my view, ambivalence may be relevant if, and only if, the ambivalence genuinely strikes at the root of the mental capacity of the patient'.[111]

As Butler-Sloss may have been aware, it could be a mistake to set too high a bar when it comes to stability of values and preferences. As Rudnick acknowledges, this kind of thinking could be taken too far, so as 'to imply that individuals cannot competently change their preferences, which is absurd, as preferences do and should change, depending upon circumstances, critical reflection, and personal development'.[112] While acknowledging the case for treating depressed patients as incompetent '[i]f their decision is not consistent with their earlier decisions', Gerben Meynen went on to note: '... I think it is fair to state that new situations may very well yield new decisions and behavioral responses. People should be free to choose new responses to the challenges they face'.[113]

Quite how free any of us may be to choose our responses is an interesting question, but it is certainly true that challenging our adverse circumstances can elicit responses that can seem quite out of keeping with a person's previous character. Often this will be in the form of tapping into reserves of strength that were hitherto unknown. It may see them come to value that which they had previously taken for granted. As Beauchamp and Childress observe (while discussing the work of Agnieza Jaworska):

> A patient might request a highly invasive treatment at the end of life against his previous judgment about his best interests because he has come to a conclusion that surprises him: he cares more about living a few extra days than he had thought he would. Despite his long-standing and firm view that he would reject such invasive treatments, he now accepts them.[114]

---

108 McKhann, note 20, above, at pp. 47–8.

109 As the authors of one influential text on decision making put it, 'a competent decision-maker also requires a *set of values* or *conception of what is good* that is at least minimally consistent, stable, and affirmed as his or her own'. Buchanan and Brock, note 79, above, at p. 25.

110 Indeed, we might even wonder whether we are dealing with a single person at all. On some views, continuity of personal identity is contingent upon a certain degree of continuity of certain mental properties. This view is articulated (though not in fact shared) by David DeGrazia: 'for A at one time and B at a later time to be the same person, there must be sufficient psychological continuity (exemplified by memories, intentions and their fulfillment, and enduring desires and beliefs) between them'. See DeGrazia, D., 'Advance Directives, Dementia, and the "Someone Else Problem"' (1999) 13(5) *Bioethics*, 373–91, at p. 378.

111 *Ms B v. An NHS Hospital Trust* [2002] EWHC 429 (Fam), at para. 35.

112 Rudnick, note 94, above, at p. 153.

113 Meynen, G., 'Depression, Possibilities, and Competence: A Phenomenological Perspective' (2011) 32 *Theoretical Medicine and Bioethics*, 181–93, at p. 188.

114 Beauchamp, T.L. and Childress, J.F., *Principles of Biomedical Ethics*, 7th edn, Oxford, Oxford University Press, 2009, at pp. 103–4.

This, they suggest, 'is not uncommon in medical contexts'.[115] Religious conversions may be rarer than they once were, but they are far from unknown, right up to the deathbed.[116] It would, presumably, be quite unthinkable to deny a lifelong Jehovah's Witness a blood transfusion when he needs and wants one, simply because that preference seems out of keeping with the 'settled' values he had previously displayed!

It is also possible that someone may simply decide, after a long period of stoicism and struggle, that they have had enough. This need not be a betrayal of their previous values, but rather, a result of the reality that reserves of energy and determination are not infinite. It may be true that a choice that seems to emanate from values quite different from those consistently held by the patient throughout the greater part of his life is a choice that should be subject to greater scrutiny. But that which we most value can change throughout our lives, and that fact alone need not undermine respect for those values at any given time.

The fact that a depressed person appears to abandon previously held values, then, or to express concerns and wishes that seem 'out of character', may give reason for closer scrutiny of their capacity. But I suggest that such changes do not, in themselves, demonstrate incapacity. People change their minds, and people faced with grave or arduous situations may change their minds quite dramatically. Provided the changed values are themselves relatively stable and consistent, they may well be better seen not as a symptom of a disease process, but of a very human response or adaptation to a radically new situation.

Finally, it is worth remembering that some instances of depression are far from transient or fleeting, and the decisions made while in that state may be long-standing. The patients in the *Chabot* and *Haas* cases, considered earlier, had well-established, stable and long-standing wishes to die. Even were we to require a fairly high degree of stability from end-of-life choices, it is far from obvious that all, or even most, people with depression would fail to satisfy this criterion.

Beneficence-based Concerns: 'You'll Thank Us Later'

I have suggested that while the presence of depression may provide a reason to scrutinise a patient's decision-making capacity more carefully, it does not necessarily in itself provide a reason to assume that such capacity is impaired. Is it possible, though, that other sorts of ethical concerns arise when decisions are made by depressed people – decisions, perhaps, rooted in concerns for beneficence? I have argued that the mere likelihood that someone will later change their mind does not in itself invalidate their current exercise of autonomy, but their welfare is another matter.

This, rather than concern with autonomy *per se*, may have been what lay behind the objection of Mr G in the *Ms B* case, when he spoke of the likelihood that his patient would, if kept alive, 'come ... to appreciate in greater depth the value of life to them. This tends to arise most often as the person leaves hospital for life in the community'. Herbert Hendin bases his opposition to euthanasia partly on such concerns: 'Depression, anxiety, and the wish to die are often the first reactions to the prospect of serious illness and possible death. Exploring and treating this demoralizing triad can change the decision whether to live with illness'.[117] He supports this contention with a vivid

115 Beauchamp and Childress, note 114, above, at p. 104.

116 For a recent critical discussion, see Myth 18 of Blackford, R. and Schüklenk, U., *50 Great Myths About Atheism*, West Sussex, Wiley-Blackwell, 2013, at p. 54.

117 Hendin, note 64, above, at p. 126.

account from his own practice. His patient had experienced a major depressive episode after her husband's sudden death. She had attempted suicide, and been hospitalised on several occasions:

> Her condition was incurable, she insisted, and suicide was the only solution. She would not consider treatment but came for a few sessions, and I remained in touch with her and her family to see how she was doing. … Two more distressing years were followed by a nearly fatal suicide attempt, from which she awoke after several days of coma to tell her daughter that she was finished with suicide. She agreed to see me but could only tell me that she had had a dream in which her husband came to her and said, 'That's enough – you've put yourself and everyone else through enough suffering'. She claimed she woke the following morning free of her depression. When I spoke to her a year later and to her daughter a few years after that, they told me that she was living by herself, had made a new social life, and was no longer depressed or suicidal. Under a system that permitted legalized assisted suicide in her case, long before her recovery this patient would have ended her life with the concurrence of her family and the assistance of her doctor.[118]

Should Hendin really have allowed his patient to die? Or did his duty of beneficence mean that he was right to thwart her suicidal efforts? It is not difficult to see the appeal of the latter approach. Only an autonomy fundamentalist, it may be thought, would object to an exercise in paternalism when the outcome would be an additional many years of worthwhile life. This concern also found support from the House of Lords' Select Committee:

> Society already makes strenuous efforts to frustrate attempted suicides on the basis that the person who has attempted to take his or her [life] may well think better of it at a later date, and we have been told by a number of those who gave evidence to us that people who ask for assistance to die frequently change their minds either because they have received better palliative care or simply because they have re-assessed and come to terms with their situation.[119]

There are at least two responses we might offer to this approach, the first principled, the second empirical. The principled approach would simply assert the pre-eminence of autonomy over beneficence when the two principles come into conflict. This would involve accepting that even a predictably massive gain in terms of beneficence would be out-weighed by any exercise in autonomy, even one which reflects views that the patient is unlikely to hold for long.

This is, in fact, already the approach accepted at Common Law with regard to treatment-refusing decisions, as clearly demonstrated in a series of court judgments.[120] In the final analysis, autonomy trumps beneficence. And to extend the playing-card metaphor a little, even a '2' of autonomy would trump an 'Ace' of beneficence. This is not a state of affairs that has met with universal acclaim,[121] but it is nonetheless an accurate statement of the law, at least in England and Wales.

An alternative response to the appeal from beneficence would derive from doubts as to the accuracy with which such predictions can be made. It is true that depression is *sometimes* transient or treatable. Perhaps we may even say 'often' or 'usually'. But it is not *always* the case, and

---

118 Hendin, note 64, above, at p. 130.

119 House of Lords Assisted Dying for the Terminally Ill Select Committee, First Report, 2005, at para. 253.

120 *Ms B v. An NHS Hospital Trust* [2002] EWHC 429 (Fam); *St George's Health Care NHS Trust v. S* [1998] 3 WLR 936; *Re MB* [1997] 2 FCR 541.

121 Foster, C., *Choosing Life, Choosing Death: The Tyranny of Autonomy in Medical Ethics and Law*, Portland, OR, Hart Publishing, 2009.

psychiatrists are not necessarily well-placed to predict whether a particular episode will last for a short time, a long time or forever. Furthermore, it is not invariably the case that a depressed person's wish to die ends when the depressive episode does.

Melinda Lee has explored the presumption 'that once the problem has cleared, the patient will look at treatment decisions differently', and the related presumption that 'a person whose wishes were overridden in such circumstances would feel relieved later that such paternalistic steps were taken'. Her conclusion was that: '[r]ecent research has challenged that presumption by showing depressed patients don't necessarily choose to hasten death in the first place and they often make the same decisions after they recover from depression'.[122] Overriding a patient's autonomous choice on the basis that they will definitely be glad of it later is one thing; overriding their choice on the basis that they will *probably*, or *possibly*, be glad of it is quite another. The metaphor here would not be a low-value autonomy card trumping a high-value beneficence card. It would be more like refusing to exchange a low-value autonomy card for a yet-to-be-drawn beneficence card that may or may not be a higher value.

It would also, we might think, be a mistake to calculate 'beneficence' only by reference to the quality of life of the person once free from depression. In Hendin's case study, he refers to '[t]wo more distressing years' before the patient could enjoy life again. While the distress involved in those years may not outweigh the gain from many subsequent happy years, neither can it be discounted from any consequentialist calculation. For a patient with a terminal diagnosis, or of a very advanced age, the prospect of two years of distress being outweighed by anything thereafter may seem remote.

Finally – and this is perhaps less of an argument than an observation – we might wonder whether the argument from benevolent paternalism applies to a great many more patients and situations than envisioned here. If the argument is simply based on the belief that the patient's welfare is better promoted by overriding his present wishes, and instead following doctors' predictions about what will be to their benefit, then why should this be particularly true in relation to VE or AS, or indeed to end-of-life decisions at all? I will return to this last observation in my concluding remarks.

Conclusion: 'Never Kill Yourself When You Are Suicidal'[123]

The assumption that people affected by depression are endangered by laws permitting assisted suicide or euthanasia is so wide-spread as to be practically ubiquitous. Even those convinced by the arguments for allowing such options more generally are concerned to restrict them in such a way as to 'protect' depressed people by excluding them from their remit. For others, the perceived impossibility of guaranteeing such protection provides a compelling reason to reject such permissive laws.

Sheila McLean has been one of the very few writers in this area to challenge this assumption. While stressing the importance of ensuring that available treatment for depression would be offered, she has sought to distinguish this from the assumption that 'this would change people's minds about wanting an assisted death'.[124] In this chapter, I have sought to address a number of questions around

122 Lee, M., 'The Case of the Depressed Patient', Markkula Center for Applied Ethics blog, Winter 1997.

123 Shneidman, E.S., 'Approaches and Commonalities of Suicide' in Diekstra, R.F.W. (ed.) *Suicide and Its Prevention: The Role of Attitude and Imitation*, World Health Organization, 1989, pp. 14–36, at p. 32.

124 McLean, note 6, above, at p. 40.

the role of depression in end-of-life choices, and particularly in discussions about euthanasia and assisted suicide. It is now time to seek to draw some conclusions from these enquiries.

First, those jurisdictions that have permitted VE/AS have tended to adopt the position that, while suffering derived from psychiatric illness can justify the provision of assistance, requests made in such circumstances will be subject to certain additional requirements, such as the necessity to have exhausted other treatment options. 'Mere' existential suffering or chronic unhappiness that is not associated with a recognised psychiatric disorder will not, it seems, be sufficient.

As I suggested above, this means that, for legal purposes, a great deal hangs on the distinction between 'clinical' depression, and non-pathological unhappiness, a distinction that is much contested even within psychiatry. It is considerably more questionable whether anything of ethical significance hangs upon it. Regardless of whether support for VE/AS derives from respect for autonomy or utilitarian considerations, it is not clear why the satisfaction of the diagnostic criteria for depression should make a difference to someone's eligibility.

Indeed, I argue that the requirement for such a diagnosis is, at best, arbitrary, and at worst, perverse, since it renders eligible those at greater risk of decision-making impairment, while disqualifying those with no such risk factors. Furthermore, it may create an incentive for well-intentioned psychiatrists to predicate diagnostic decisions on whether or not they wish to assist a patient to access VE/AS. If there are good reasons to allow VE/AS in cases of non-somatic suffering – and I believe that there are – then there are good reasons to extend that to all causes of non-somatic suffering; drawing arbitrary lines around certain causes runs the risk of over-medicalising the issue.

With regard to depression's role as an excluding condition, the picture is not so clear. In the context of VE/AS, several recent proposals, and much recent writing, have sought to exclude depressed people from making such decisions. On the 'moderate' version of this position, that would mean introducing mechanisms to ensure that depressed people could not access VE/AS. The 'extreme' version would hold that, since we cannot be certain that such measures would prove effective, VE/AS should not be permitted at all. Yet it is difficult to reconcile either position with how Common Law jurisdictions currently deal with the possible effect of depression in end-of-life decisions. Certainly, the extreme position is not one that generally characterises the law's response to refusals of life-sustaining treatment. Indeed, the right to refuse such treatment is a common element throughout the European Union and Anglo-American legal systems. Even the moderate thesis seems too strong in that context; as I have shown, the mere presence of a depressive disorder will not, in itself, be enough to undermine someone's right to refuse life-saving treatment.

Of course, it may be argued that 'passive' assistance in dying, in the form of withholding or withdrawing life-sustaining medical treatments, is of a different ethical and legal order to 'active' assistance, in the form of VE or AS. Whatever the validity of that distinction in general terms (and it is highly contested in ethics, and somewhat blurred in law), its relevance to the issue of depression is spurious. If there is a danger that depression may lead people to choose death in circumstances that raise problems for autonomy or beneficence, then that seems no less likely to be true in a 'passive' than an 'active' context, however much those may differ in other respects.

So, from the perspective of risk and 'vulnerability', the position of depressed people seeking to access 'active' assistance seems no different from those seeking to exercise 'passive' rights; if depression does not provide a compelling reason to prevent the latter, then the same must apply to the former. But of course, the situations could be brought into line in one of two ways: by allowing both, or allowing neither. Is the influence of depression on capacity such as to presumptively invalidate decisions taken by such people? My review of the literature casts considerable doubts on the case for so doing. Using a standard notion of decision-making capacity, in line with current law and practice, the evidence suggests that a considerable majority of people with depression satisfied the criteria. Most cases of depression are not accompanied by psychotic symptoms, and most affected people still have the abilities to understand, retain and use information. Indeed, some recent research has raised the intriguing prospect that depressed people are better at predicting outcomes than their 'healthy', but unrealistically optimistic, counterparts.

But is the standard account of capacity fit for purpose, or does the example of depression reveal it to be deficient? I explored several features of depression that may be thought to support such a challenge, and perhaps the most compelling challenge relates to the stability of a depressed person's values, and their consistency with what the person valued in their non-depressed state. It is not unreasonable to be concerned about the authenticity or validity of decisions made in a period of acute depression when those differ substantially from the settled preferences previously exhibited. It may well be consistent with respect for autonomy to require that decisions made in such circumstances are subject to greater levels of scrutiny. Yet even here, we should be careful of assuming too readily that changed values or priorities are a symptom of mental illness. People change their minds, and people faced with extreme decisions or situations may act in ways that surprise even themselves.

Likewise, when considering beneficence or welfare-based concerns, care should be taken to avoid certain tempting but unfounded assumptions. Not all depression is treatable, and not all cases of successful treatment result in abandoning of the desire to die. The patients in the *Chabot* and *Haas* cases, though depressed, had harboured strong and consistent desires to die for many years. Forcing them to endure further suffering in the hope that they may someday get better and thank us for keeping them alive risks offending principles of autonomy and beneficence, and is very much out of step with how law responds to other cases of treatment refusal. This is not to say that there are *never* instances of apparent choice that are in fact the product of mental illness rather than autonomous decision-making. It is just to say that we should be careful not to assume too much in this regard.

Finally, we must end with a note of warning about definitional circularity. As I explained at the outset, one of the standard diagnostic criteria for depressive illness is suicidal ideation.[125] It should be obvious that problems can arise when the psychiatrists who are asked to evaluate a patient's competence to make a choice also regard that very choice as a symptom of mental illness.[126] A wish for death may very well raise a warning flag, indicating closer scrutiny of competence. Such decisions are, to state the obvious, final (though no more so than refusals of life-saving treatment); and while most depressed people may retain decision-making capacity, the evidence points to a substantial minority whose capacity is substantially impaired. But a closer scrutiny of capacity is not the same thing as a presumption of incapacity. None of the evidence or arguments evaluated here seems to me to merit this presumptive conclusion.

There may be very good beneficence-based reasons why the psychiatric profession should regard suicide prevention as an important objective. There may also be very good reasons why, increasingly, what would previously have been thought of as 'normal sadness' is being brought within the definition of 'depression'; if suffering can be alleviated, we might think it churlish to withhold support because that suffering is not 'pathological' in nature. But not all desires to die are the product of, or even evidence of, mental illness or incapacity. Concern for vulnerable people is a valid and valuable perspective in any discussions around law reform, but care should be exercised lest it become a guise for illiberal paternalism.

---

125 ICD-10, note 21, above, at F32.2; DSM-V, note 21, above, 'Major Depressive Disorder: Diagnostic Criteria', A9.

126 A point eloquently put in McLean, note 6, above, at p. 41.

Chapter 16
Assisted Dying: Humanity or Autonomy?

Tom Campbell

Introduction

Sheila McLean has made a very considerable contribution to the ongoing debate about the legalisation of 'assisted dying',[1] a term which is used to cover both assisted suicide (when one person provides the means for another person to commit suicide) and voluntary euthanasia (when one person brings about the death of another at the latter's request). In a number of articles[2] and a major book[3] McLean has argued in a balanced yet forceful manner for a legal process which gives individuals control over the time and manner of their own deaths. This autonomy-based right, she says, overrides such harms to other people as are likely to result from legalising the practice of assisted dying. This proposal is radical with respect to legal reform in that it includes no conditions, such as the poor health or suffering of the person receiving assistance, other than their mental competence. It is also radical philosophically in that its justification relies almost exclusively on the value of autonomy without involving other valued objectives, such as the relief of suffering.

In this body of work McLean draws on her extensive knowledge of relevant comparative law, and her formidable skills in normative jurisprudence, whilst demonstrating an impressive knowledge of end-of-life medical practice in a variety of countries. Without entering into detail on the wide range of empirical and legal matters relevant to issues of assisted dying, this chapter takes up some of the more philosophical aspects of McLean's assessment of the ethical issues at stake. It questions elements of her autonomy-based moral justifications for a permissive approach to assisted dying, while largely concurring with her procedural recommendations for law reform. The aim is to support her telling contribution to this debate while suggesting modifications to its philosophical basis, which, on my view, ought to be oriented more to justifications of law reforms which focus primarily on the relief of suffering and only secondarily on the ethical importance of autonomy with respect to assisted dying.

---

1 For the 'ongoing debate', see Jackson E. and Keown, J., *Debating Euthanasia*, Oxford, Hart Publishing, 2012, and also White, B. and Willmott, L., 'How Should Australia Regulate Voluntary Euthanasia and Assisted Suicide?' (2012) *Journal of Law and Medicine*, 410–38.

2 McLean, S.A.M., 'Live and Let Die' (2009) 339 *British Medical Journal*, 837; Elliston, S.J. and McLean, S.A.M., 'Death, Decision Making and the Law' (2004) *Juridical Review*, 265–93; McLean, S.A.M., 'The Rights to Life: Euthanasia' in Smith, R.K.M. and van den Anker, C. (eds) *The Essentials of Human Rights*, London, Hodder Arnold, 2005, pp. 242–4; McLean, S.A.M., 'Assisted Dying: The View from the United Kingdom' in Birnbacher, D. and Dahl, E. (eds) *Giving Death a Helping Hand: Physician-Assisted Suicide and Public Policy: An International Perspective*, Dordrecht, Springer, 2008, pp. 113–28; McLean, S.A.M. and Morgan, D., 'Choosing Death or Life: Law, Medicine and Patients' Rights' (2009) *Juridical Review*, 129–48.

3 McLean, S.A.M., *Assisted Dying: Reflections on the Need for Law Reform*, London, Routledge-Cavendish, 2007.

The first part of the chapter explores McLean's justification of assisted dying and identifies what she considers to be a desirable legal framework for such practices. The second part compares 'humanity' and 'autonomy' as rival candidates for providing the basis of the moral justification for permitting assisted dying. The chapter then develops a humanitarian position which incorporates only what may be called 'instrumental autonomy'. It next discusses the eligibility criteria for receiving assistance in dying best suited to a humanity-based mode of assisted dying regulation and offers some ideas as to how they might be administered so as to protect the interests of those involved. The chapter concludes by suggesting that law reforms along the lines proposed by McLean are better grounded in a humanitarian moral justification in which considerations of autonomy feature mainly on account of their instrumental efficacy in protecting the interests of certain categories of vulnerable people.

McLean's Justification of Assisted Dying

Since suicide is no longer an offence in most developed countries, including the UK, and since an increasing number of people in similar jurisdictions are living longer as a result of modern medical treatment, but often experience a very poor and sometimes miserable quality of life during that prolongation, it is a logical step to make provision for those who are in this situation and wish to end their lives, but who are not in a position, or do not wish, to fulfil this choice unassisted. This step requires the law to permit what would otherwise be criminal conduct on the part of those who advise or help someone to die. Going beyond the existing negative liberty right to commit suicide, as established by the abolition of legal prohibitions of suicide, it also requires assuring freedom from prosecution for those who provide assistance either by facilitating the suicide or by intervening directly to bring about the death of the person seeking assistance. In the absence of people willing to assist dying, there could also be a requirement for the persons choosing to die to have a positive claim right to such assistance as they need to implement their choice to die, establishing correlative duties on some others to provide such assistance. McLean's own recommendations for law reform encompass legislating a negative liberty right for the providers of assisted dying but do not go so far as to commend a positive claim right to such assistance.

McLean reaches this position via the libertarian principle, derived from the work of John Stuart Mill,[4] that a person's liberty, or self-determination, should not be limited by law with respect to any action which is private in that it does not cause harm to anyone else.[5] If no harm to others occurs, then there is no moral justification for placing legal limits on a person's conduct. Where harm to others does result, then liberty may be restricted but only if the harm is sufficiently serious to justify such intervention. McLean does not contend that assisted dying does not produce some adverse consequences for third parties that may be classified as 'harms', such as significant financial and psychological disadvantage. Rather, her case is based on the contention that assisted dying has substantially greater moral significance for the person who dies than for those who are affected by that death. This enables her to deal with the standard range of criticisms that arise from the observation that any intended human death is likely to cause some harm to others, and is therefore typically a public rather than a purely private matter.

4 Mill, J.S., 'On Liberty' in Lindsay, D.A., *Utilitarianism, Liberty and Representative Government*, London, Everyman, 1910, pp. 65–172.

5 McLean, note 3, above, at p. 3.

McLean's position is based on a strong commitment to the moral priority of autonomy in relation to matters which primarily concern a person's private interests, even when this may have some detrimental consequences for others.[6] She reaches her conclusion on assisted dying by affirming the core prima facie case for respecting every competent person's autonomy in relation to their own life and death, and deals with counter arguments by showing that, when these are properly analysed and subjected to empirical scrutiny, they do not carry the moral weight necessary to override the autonomy-based right to die. For instance, McLean responds to the contention that assisted dying can sometimes have a deleterious effect on relatives, so that it is not strictly a private matter relating only to the personal interests of the person whose life is at stake, by pointing out the much greater interests individuals have in their own existence. This, she suggests, has already been acknowledged in the legalisation of suicide, indicating that, if such criticisms of assisted dying were sound, they would be equally compelling with respect to legally permitting those suicides which do not involve the assistance of others.

In the course of her reflections McLean deals with a number of confusions which commonly feature in the right to die debate. Thus, she accepts that there are powerful considerations centring on the common law principle of the 'sanctity of life', which affirms the duty not to kill another human being, based on the high intrinsic value of human life. She notes, however, that even religious believers, who take the 'sanctity' of life to derive from the fact that life is a gift of God, accept a right of self-defence, including, in some circumstances, killing a life-threatening attacker. More generally, she notes that 'the law has simultaneously restated the importance of the sanctity of human life while at the same time respecting the decisions made by people to reject that life by according dominance to the principle of respect for autonomy'.[7] In this way she interprets the sanctity of life as no more than 'a brake on treating human life in a casual way' that 'protects people from having their lives unwillingly removed'.[8]

Another confusion to which McLean draws our attention is the argument that the social origins of all moral values adopted by individuals presupposes the social nature of human life and thus conflicts with the isolationist self-centred perspective of those promoting individual autonomy.[9] She rightly rejects the contention that, because an individual's choices are in part the product of their socialisation, their choices may properly be limited by the values dominant in that society. McLean goes on to commend a less self-centred 'relational rather than an atomizing version'[10] of autonomy, in which the autonomous person takes into account the needs and interests of others when making her decisions, a factor which plays a significant role in the reasons that govern the conduct of autonomous individual agents, including those who, in certain circumstances, choose to die.

McLean reinforces her position by reference to the unfairness of excluding those who, for various reasons, are unable or unwilling to kill themselves, from the benefits that arise from having the liberty to do so. One of these benefits is that access to assisted dying enables individuals to undergo medical treatment which extends their lives without taking the risk that it might keep them alive to a stage when they are not able to commit suicide without assistance, which means that they do not have to forego this extra life in order to be in unaided control of the manner and timing of their death.[11]

---

6 McLean, note 3, above, at pp. 27–43.

7 McLean, note 3, above, at p. 30.

8 McLean, note 3, above, at p. 30.

9 Thus, Somerville, M., *Death Talk: The Case Against Euthanasia and Physician-Assisted Suicide*, Montreal, McGill University Press, 2001, at p. 42.

10 McLean, note 3, above, at p. 33.

11 McLean, note 3, above, at pp. 17ff.

Other more diffuse considerations, which apply to assisted dying but not to self-administered suicide, relate to the effects of an assisted dying system on the practice of health practitioners.[12] These centre on the problems that arise when professionals who are thought of, and think of themselves, as caregivers and healers are officially involved in ending rather than prolonging human lives. Medical practitioners in general are unwilling to be publicly associated with assisted dying as distinct from palliative care and there is strong resistance amongst most health professions to any prospect of being required to take part in assisting dying as a treatment within their normal duties of patient care. This latter scenario is not commended by McLean and therefore does not present an immediate problem for her position, provided there are adequate sources of assistance available to meet the needs of those seeking assisted dying.

To the unwillingness of health professions to be involved in assisted dying must be added concerns about public attitudes towards the providers of health services, which could arise if the legalisation of assisted dying were to generate anxiety and distrust of physicians on the part of patients. This concern has more to do with how patients view health professionals rather than how health professionals view themselves. McLean's responses to these considerations depends in part on a contextual analysis of the important moral and political distinction between acts and omissions, according to which people are rightly held responsible for their active conduct but only in a specific range of circumstances should they be held responsible for their failures to act. On this basis killing is (nearly always) wrong but letting someone die, in the absence of any special relationship, may not be. McLean argues that the medical duty of care towards a patient renders the distinction between act and omission morally irrelevant with respect to the provision of healthcare to existing patients by those who owe them a duty of care. In this context, letting die is morally no different from active killing.[13] On this analysis, there is no reason for people to be more anxious about the latter than the former. This may not, of course, actually quell patient anxieties, any more than would be the case if there was transparency with respect to the current medical practice of routine termination of what are seen as futile treatments for dying persons, and with respect to the administration of medicines which hasten death while also relieving suffering under the cover of the principle of double effect, which, in effect, permits killing as a foreseen side effect of administering lethal doses of sedatives.[14]

On the basis of these moral considerations, particularly those relating to achieving parity between those who are able and those who are not able, or are unwilling, to commit suicide unaided, the legislative proposals put forward by McLean allow assisted dying for competent persons through abolishing existing offences relating to the provision of assisted dying, thus extending the existing negative liberty right to bring about the end one's life to those who are not able to do so for practical or personal reasons. This differs from most proposals for law reform, which confine the extension of such a right only to those who are judged to be terminally ill and are medically assessed as having an unacceptable quality of life.[15] McLean finds such requirements unacceptable

12 McLean, note 3, above, at pp. 55–61.

13 McLean, note 3, above, at pp. 96–107. McLean's position on this is thereby not vulnerable to the powerful defence of the act/omissions distinction in McGee, A., 'Ending the Life of the Act/Omission Dispute: Causation in Withholding and Withdrawing Life-sustaining Measures' (2011) 31 *Legal Studies*, 467–91.

14 See Otlowski, M., *Voluntary Euthanasia and the Common Law*, Oxford, Clarendon Press, 1997.

15 For an example, see the Private Member's Bill introduced in the Tasmanian Parliament in 2013: http://www.parliament.tas.gov.au/bills/Bills2013/61_of_2013.htm (accessed 13 January 2015). The Bill, entitled *Voluntary Assisted Dying*, was narrowly defeated. It proposed legislating for physician assisted dying where this involves unsolicited voluntary requests; medical confirmation of competence (tested on verbal communication and absence of a psychiatric or psychological disorder); medically informed consent;

because, under such a regime, the procedures involved in assisted suicide do not adequately respect the person's autonomy and effectively give the power of veto to medical practitioners, thereby significantly reducing the scope of the individual's control over their own life and death. She resists this 'medicalisation' of assisted dying through the adoption of medical criteria for eligibility, on the grounds that it is for the patients not their medical practitioners to decide on whether their lives are worth living.[16]

McLean deals with these physician-centred obstacles to patient autonomy by excluding the eligibility conditions of terminal illness and health-related suffering as necessary preconditions, and also by extending the range of persons who may assist in dying beyond medical practitioners, who would no longer have a gate-keeping role in decision-making in connection with assisted dying. Here McLean points to the Swiss model of assisted suicide in which, apart from the testing of the mental competence of the individual concerned, the only eligibility requirement is that the assisting persons do not stand to benefit from providing that assistance.[17] This demedicalises the eligibility criteria for assisted suicide, provides some protection against unwarranted pressures being placed on vulnerable individuals, and creates a safe and dignified environment for the procedures involved in assisted dying.

However, McLean's proposal makes the controversial assumption that any competent adult person should be eligible to request assistance in dying. In a succinct summation of her position she answers the criticism that 'it cannot be acceptable that anyone, irrespective of their medical condition, should be allowed to seek and obtain an assisted death'[18] with the response: 'why not? If that same person had the emotional or physical capacity to commit suicide their choice would not be second-guessed and they would commit no crime'.[19] This follows through the logic of her commitment to autonomy by endorsing a demedicalised and largely deregulated procedure for assisted dying.

Humanity or Autonomy?

Compelling as McLean's recommendations for radical liberalisation of assisted dying may be, they do not reflect the views of the substantial majority of those in liberal democracies, who support a more restricted scope for assisted dying.[20] For most people the predominant focus is on the strong

---

physician-confirmed terminal illness (defined as that of an adult in advanced stages of an incurable and progressive medical condition involving suffering); there being no alternative way to relieve the patients suffering adequately and to the satisfaction of the patient; and the termination being self administered or administered by the person's medical practitioner, after concurring second opinions have been obtained.

16 McLean, note 3, above, at pp. 76f., 185f., 198f.

17 McLean, note 3, above, at p. 201. See, Fischer, S., Huber, C.A., Imhof, L., et al., 'Suicide Assisted by Two Swiss Right-to-die Organisations' (2008) 34 *Journal of Medical Ethics*, 810–14.

18 This summarises the view presented in Finnis, J., 'Euthanasia, Morality, and Law' (1998) 31 *Loyola of Los Angeles Law Review*, 1123–46.

19 McLean, note 3, above, at p. 199. See also p. 41: 'On what basis can we challenge the rights of non-terminally ill people to make an autonomous choice to die?'

20 Usually said to be about 80 per cent. See, for instance, Clery, E., McLean, S. and Phillips, M., 'Quickening Death: The Euthanasia Debate' in Park, A., Curtice, J., Thomson, K., et al., *British Social Attitudes: The 23rd Report*, London, Sage, 2007, pp. 35–54; and YourLastRight.com, 'Australian Public Desire for Legalisation of Assisted Dying in Restricted Circumstances', 2012, available at: http://www.dwdnsw.org.au/documents/2013/POLL%20WHITE%20PAPER%202012.pdf (accessed 13 January 2015).

desire to avoid both pointless and painful extensions of life, while still having full access to such healthcare as is available. The primary situations which are anticipated with dread are being kept alive in distressing and sometimes painful circumstances. The hoped-for alternative is a dignified and relatively painless death over which they have some control. From this perspective, assisted dying is not seen as being on a par with suicide in other contexts. Rather, it is fuelled by awareness that in many cases medical practice itself can give rise to the need for assistance in dying. Not unreasonably, therefore, what are viewed by the public as the most compelling, but not the sole, reasons for legalising assisted dying are absent if we are not dealing with the problem of prolonging lives in a way which involves either a miserable or a comatose existence.

Interestingly, McLean herself gives much of her attention to autonomy issues that arise within medical contexts and involve the forms of suffering which occur in terminal situations. An important part of her argument for the importance of assisted dying is that it facilitates individuals' control over their lives not just generally but, most evidently, when confronted with serious medical conditions. She commends excluding illness-related suffering and terminal illness as conditions of eligibility for assisted dying on the grounds that this reduces the autonomy of the individual because it makes the successful fulfilment of their end-of-life choices contingent on a medical opinion as to whether the eligibility conditions are satisfied in their case. Yet the relevance of suffering, especially suffering involved in terminal illness, in practice features centrally in the reasons she gives as to why it is so important for individuals to have the right to legally permitted assistance in dying. The amelioration of unacceptable indignity and misery at the end of life, some of which is a direct although unintended result of progress in medical treatments, emerges as the chief underlying justification for legalising assisted dying. Her prime concern with the exclusion of those medical factors from the content of the law relating to assisted dying focuses on the importance of securing the legal capacity of the person principally involved effectively to protect their medically salient interests. To achieve this it is necessary, she argues, to exclude medical criteria, such as the existence of a 'terminal illness' and hence remove the need for medical judgment for the determination of eligibility for assisted dying.

Sound as this line of argument is in itself, it opens the way for legalising assisted dying for persons who choose to die on the basis of non-medical reasons, some which appear to rest on quite trivial grounds. This runs counter to the high value traditionally placed on human lives. This in turn raises concerns that some people without serious illness may be subject to the influence of those who have a vested interest in the outcome, or share controversial and extreme views as to the value of human life and the significance of suicide. Without questioning the importance of autonomy as it arises in the right to reject medical treatment, or the right to seek assistance in extending the right-holder's life, it is highly questionable to approve of a system that permits assistance in dying to anyone who requests it, for whatever reason. Autonomy, outside the context of significant and ongoing suffering, seems an inadequate basis for assisting someone's suicide or bringing about their death. It is the relief, or ending, of suffering that motivates others to assist in someone else's dying. This humanitarian justification is central to the case for legalising assisted dying.[21]

The tension between autonomy- and humanity-based justifications for assisted dying might be avoided by subordinating 'humanity' to 'autonomy'. Those who think purely in terms of autonomy can, on libertarian assumptions, argue for a right to die, if necessary with assistance, solely on the basis of the individual's moral entitlement to take their own lives, provided they do not at the same time inflict serious harm on others. When challenged to say why assisted dying is so commonly

21 See Singer, P., *Rethinking Life and Death: The Collapse of Our Traditional Ethics*, Oxford, Oxford University Press, 1995.

associated with the relief of suffering, the libertarian may answer that it is not the relief of suffering that is the basis of the justification, but simply the result of having an entitlement to autonomy in private matters. On this view, autonomy remains the decisive moral basis for justifying the legality of suicide and, by extension, the right of those requiring or desiring to die, for whatever reason, to be assisted in so doing. Release from suffering is just one of the many reasons that may be given and must be accepted as an exercise in human autonomy.

This would appear to be McLean's considered position. When discussing her rejection of standard limitations on the exercise of autonomy in dying, such as the precondition of having a terminal illness, usually in combination with significant or intense suffering, she argues:

> If it is the case that everyone, and not just those more obviously 'in need', can lay claim to the same right to seek assisted dying, then so be it. That most of the permissive laws around the world that place restrictions on accessibility is a commentary on the laws; not on the philosophical basis for the argument.[22]

However, the philosophical basis of assisted dying is contested. In response to those who prioritise autonomy over humanity, it is argued that this subordination should be reversed, so that, in the context of assisted dying, autonomy is valued only as a means to avoid suffering. Approaching assisted dying from this humanitarian perspective, it is justified as a means to the termination of suffering, with autonomy entering the scenario simply as a means to achieving this end. This explains the focus of the euthanasia debate on the unmanageable suffering involved in some illnesses, not all of which can be satisfactorily dealt with through palliative care, and the important roles of relatives and physicians in providing assistance to those fearing or experiencing distress.

This humanitarian position is enhanced by concern for the wellbeing of persons who are not sufficiently competent to be candidates for voluntary assisted dying. They too, despite their lack of capacity, have a suffering-based claim for effective assistance which is independent of their lack of autonomy. How this should be institutionalised is a different issue, but humanitarians can view their position as superior to that of the autonomy approach, in so far as it provides a common basis for taking action to assist in the dying of competent and non-competent persons in great distress. This is not to say that humanity trumps autonomy when applied to competent persons, for the absence of a request will always be overriding in the case of a competent person.

A further rationale for adopting humanity rather than autonomy as the moral foundation for permitting assisted dying arises in the case of physician assisted dying which involves voluntary euthanasia, that is, active intervention to end the life of a patient. Here the focus shifts to the moral reasons why physicians should or should not be legally permitted to assist dying as part of their medical practice. On the autonomy model, according to which a person's repeated requests to be assisted in dying may be granted without legal repercussions, provided there is no conflict of interest involved, there seems to be no reason why a physician should become involved in cases where the choice to die is made on account of, for instance, a bereavement, a personal financial disaster, boredom or the limitations of old age, where there is no medical reason for the person's request to assistance in dying. While it is not suggested that a physician should have a legal duty to kill patients on their request, it is morally appropriate for physicians to assist in a dying because they have the skills to make sure it is as successful and as painless as possible. However, it is not

22 McLean, note 3, above, at p. 42.

persuasive to suggest that they should become involved purely in order to respect the autonomy of the person making the request to die, whatever that person's reasons might be.[23]

Autonomy, from the Humanitarian Perspective

Contention over the autonomy basis for justifying assisted suicide invites further consideration as to what sort of autonomy is involved in justifiable assisted dying, and how this does or does not relate to the reasons prompting the request to die. More detail is therefore needed as to how autonomy and suffering are intertwined as rationale for assisted dying.

A wide variety of different conceptualisations of autonomy are in play with respect to assisted dying. In its most general meaning, autonomy is a matter of individuals having control over their own lives.[24] However, there are many different types of autonomy and different reasons for promoting and valuing these different aspects of autonomy. As a social and political concept, autonomy has two ingredients: the absence of external obstacles, including legal ones, which prevent agents from doing what they choose, and the presence of internal capacities of agents to make choices and to carry them out. The existence of both these ingredients is a matter of degree and thresholds for each have to be specified before any precise statements about the existing or desired autonomy of any agent can be made. This means that the moral significance of autonomy varies with the sort of choices at stake and the nature of the external and internal obstacles to the realisation of these choices.

Three types of autonomy are particularly relevant to assisted dying. The first concerns the value human beings place on making their own choices, just for its own sake, in relative abstraction from what sort of choices are involved and requiring only a measure of critical reflection. This type of autonomy involves a process of independent thought, a measure of decision-making on the basis of reasoning, and the opportunity to act on the basis of this decision. Having such choices and acting accordingly can be satisfying, enjoyable and worthwhile in itself, and can engender a sense of freedom and fulfilment, independently of its moral content. This may be called personal autonomy.[25]

A second type of autonomy is a more specific version of the first with a very different flavour and significance. It concerns the value placed on *moral* agency, that is autonomy in relation to moral evaluations and moral actions for which the agent may properly be held responsible. This Kantian mode of autonomy is both a moral right and a moral duty. It is closely related to the exercise of free will, and is usually alleged to be distinctive to humans as a species and central to the intrinsic value of human life, and therefore deserving of respect and encouragement. It centres on how people ought to act in relation to the wellbeing of others, but also concerns duties towards themselves. This may be called moral autonomy.[26]

---

23 However, where a doctor-patient relationship already exists, it is usually appropriate that a physician be involved in providing medical assistance for their patients on the basis of a humane concern for their wellbeing.

24 Another view is that there is no identifiable general meaning for the wide range of uses attributable to the word 'autonomy'. See Arpaly, N., *Unprincipled Virtue: An Inquiry into Moral Agency*, Oxford, Oxford University Press, 2004.

25 See Taylor, J.S. (ed.) *Personal Autonomy*, Cambridge, Cambridge University Press, 2005. The term is usually contrasted with both moral autonomy and political autonomy, and is interpreted in a variety of different ways. Here I adopt a content-neutral view of autonomy requiring only a minimalist understanding of the autonomous individual's capacity to decide things for herself after reflection.

26 See Hill, T., 'The Kantian Conception of Autonomy' in Christman, J. (ed.) *The Inner Citadel: Essays on Individual Autonomy*, New York, Oxford University Press, 1989, pp. 91–108. Also Dworkin, G., *The Theory and Practice of Autonomy*, New York, Oxford University Press, 1988.

A third type of autonomy exists when individuals have the internal capacity and external circumstances, including legal provisions, that enable them to protect what they value by giving them the means to effectively protect and further their interests. It routinely involves having a measure of control over the conduct of others which provides a form of valuable independence, and is treasured for its results. This may be called instrumental autonomy.[27]

Each of these autonomies serves rather different functions and directs our attention to the types and range of choices involved and the different reasons for deeming them to be important. Thus, personal autonomy points to the sheer pleasure of choice and action concerning whatever takes our fancy. Its value is intrinsic to it and largely independent of what the choices are about. Its importance is a matter for individuals to assess for themselves, this itself being a matter of individual choice. The importance such freedom of choice has for individuals varies considerably from person to person but is a factor normally highly valued by individuals in liberal societies as a vital part of an enjoyable and satisfying life.

Moral autonomy, on the other hand, is not about open-ended choosing. It calls for the exercise of moral judgments concerning moral goals, rights and obligations. Where moral autonomy is at issue, there is a duty on the part of agents to make such judgments and to act on them. On a Kantian analysis, moral goodness requires individual moral agents to make up their own minds about moral right and wrong, particularly with respect to how they manage their lives and behave towards other people, and to act accordingly. In consequence humans, as moral agents, are morally accountable for their choices and actions.

Instrumental autonomy is different again, for it concerns the provision of means for individuals to protect and further their interests, often in competitive but also in cooperative situations, which may include their interest in benefiting or not harming others. Here the choices that count vary with what is important to the individual, although there are many things which are important to nearly all human beings, including life itself. Because instrumental autonomy matters for the protection and furtherance of the interests of persons and the achievement of their desires, it forms a major part of utilitarian ethics as a means for minimising suffering.

This characterisation of distinct but overlapping types of autonomy enables us to clarify what is at stake in the assisted dying debate. The debate is not much concerned with the minimalist account of personal autonomy, that is, with reasoned choice for its own sake. Yes, choice per se is sometimes good in itself and the wider the range of choice the better, at least in the eyes of most people, so there is a prima facie reason for maximising choice within the constraints of feasibility, whatever these choices may be. But, if the outcome of these choices affects others substantially then choice for its own sake may be readily overridden, depending on the moral weight of competing interests. In consequence, the value of personal autonomy does not appear to be by itself commensurate with the importance of choice in relation to termination of life. Further, having the choice of killing yourself or the choice of being killed by another can hardly be seen as adding to the totality of choices, given that death puts an end to all further choice. And so, while personal autonomy provides reasons for extending freedom from external controls and promoting collaborative conduct in the fulfilment of choice-dependent actions, there are no powerful context-independent reasons for ensuring that people get what they want merely because they want it, whatever it happens to be.

---

27 For the role of autonomy in protecting the individual from the state, see Feinberg, J., *The Moral Limits of the Criminal Law: Harm to Self*, vol. 3, Oxford, Oxford University Press, 1986. Instrumental autonomy may be seen as a form of political autonomy because of the element of interpersonal power it represents.

In the case of moral autonomy, the situation is very different, since it concerns engaging with moral issues, and therefore calls for justifications which go beyond self-interest and personal wishes. Some of these moral questions arise with respect to the choice of life or death. There are moral justifications for and against committing suicide, at least in some situations. To that extent there are moral reasons for moral agents to have that choice. A number of examples, involving self-sacrifice and the prevention of harm to others, suggest that such justifications for suicide are available in some circumstances. If we adopt a conception of morality that includes duties to self, then there are further matters which it is the individual moral agent's duty to consider. In both cases, within the liberal tradition, these matters are of primary significance to the individual whose life is at stake, which means that there is at least a prima facie case for the individual concerned having the moral right, and perhaps a moral duty, to act on the basis of their own evaluation of the situation in so far as it concerns only themselves.

The high intrinsic value of moral autonomy provides strong reasons for respecting the views of persons who are considering ending their own lives or seeking to have assistance in so doing. It may even be argued that, as moral agents, they are morally bound to make such choices for themselves, as well as for others, so that we ought to respect and encourage them to make their life or death decision in moral terms. Certainly it is disrespectful to moral agents to say that they cannot take into account the interests of others when making difficult choices about their own lives. That said, if we are dealing with people in stressful situations, it seems oppressive to insist that they conduct themselves as fully moral agents who ought to make a considered moral choice as to how they handle their distressing circumstances. Where a moral choice is made in these circumstances, this does add a moral weight to the case for offering and legally permitting assistance, a case that is not present in the case of intrinsic autonomy. Nevertheless, where the life of an individual is at stake, protecting that life, rather than respecting the moral autonomy of that individual, is likely to be the morally overriding factor. In stressful situations, considerations of moral autonomy do not readily generate a negative liberty right or duty to participate on the part of those whose assistance is needed to carry out such an act.

Instrumental autonomy, that is the capacity of individuals effectively to further and protect their own interests, is the most relevant type of autonomy for assisted dying. Assisted dying arises paradigmatically in the case of persons who need the assistance of others with respect to pressing matters that relate to their own fundamental interests. This context gives instrumental autonomy great importance. In contrast, personal autonomy has relatively little weight in such a context. Assisted dying has little or nothing to do with promoting (or ending) choice for its own sake. Moral autonomy is more relevant than personal autonomy, for moral duty applies to all aspects of human life. However, for persons in the sort of circumstances envisaged for assisted dying, while they are able to be influenced by moral considerations and do frequently consider their moral duties to others, moral autonomy loses much of its relevance. The focus is more on the moral duties of others than the person contemplating death.

On this analysis, the sort of autonomy which relates most clearly to assisted dying is one whose justification is primarily related to the relief of suffering both in terms of pain and the misery which results from grave illness with little or no prospect of relief. Here, autonomy is not required for its own sake or to fulfil the role of moral agents but to serve the interests of the person concerned. Instrumental autonomy is arguably a necessary means by which some individuals can do what is necessary to protect their interests, usually in distressing medical circumstances. In this case, it is the consequences of autonomy that provide the moral basis for assisted dying which explains both how and why autonomy features so prominently in the assisted dying debate without being its moral foundation.

Eligibility Criteria, and Their Application

If the principal role of autonomy in assisted dying is to serve and protect the interests of persons in their own deaths, it makes sense to identify dealing with suffering as the prime interest to be taken into account when designing the rules for a regulatory scheme. This suffering need not be confined to the pain accompanying an illness but may include emotional distress arising from illness or other causes, including normal psychological responses to adverse situations. Hence instrumental autonomy is deeply involved in the humanitarian perspective on assisted dying, and its implementation fits making such humanitarian considerations the prime policy objectives.

This does not, however, necessarily take us back to what McLean regards as the 'medicalisation' of assisted dying, for it need not be the case that the humanitarian approach requires evidence of terminal illness causing untreatable suffering as the eligibility criterion for assisted dying. While factors such as suffering are relevant to the justification of institutionalising assisted dying, these need not be made an explicit legal precondition for the provision of such assistance. Release from suffering may be the overall purpose of assisted dying legislation but the rules involved can be instrumental in reducing suffering without making suffering a criterion of eligibility for assisted dying. The logic of this is that, while dealing with suffering is the purpose of the institutionalisation of assisted dying, this is served best by respecting the applicant's request for assistance without requiring an external review of the applicant's judgment as to why the request is being made. Medical supervision of the suicide process itself is appropriate, and information concerning medical diagnoses and prognostications should be made available to anyone contemplating suicide for medical reasons. Even in medical circumstances, however, medical opinion is not determinative of whether suffering of a particular sort or intensity is a rational justification for the legitimacy of assisted dying.[28] That is a matter for individual judgment on the part of the applicants in the light of their views as to what is a worthwhile life.

The factual assumptions underlying this sort of instrumentality is that competent people do not seek assisted dying without good reasons and these good reasons routinely relate to prolonged suffering usually associated with ongoing physical or mental illnesses, often exacerbated by other types of financial and personal circumstances. Together with this comes the importance of enabling the individual to come to their own decision as to what is bearable or what is worthwhile without subjecting their judgment to external expert opinion. Suffering in the broad sense of enduring misery, and indeed pain itself, is not something that an external observer can reliably calculate. Nor are there special skills to help us determine how much and what sort of suffering is to count as 'severe' or 'unbearable'. These are matters that depend on the subjective judgment of the individual involved. Moreover, not all suffering relevant to assisted dying arises from a medical condition (however widely the term 'medical' is defined). Therefore, making judgments of this type dependent on the subjective views of external observers greatly diminishes the instrumental autonomy of those seeking assisted dying.

For these reasons, those whose sufferings and lives are at stake should be the arbiters of whether or not their situation is sufficiently awful to justify having access to assistance in dying. However, in making their decision, the effectiveness of their autonomy may depend on access to such information as is available concerning their medical or other circumstances. But the fact that access to medical expertise of this sort may be an important element in the process whereby the applicant makes her life or death decision does not mean that the person with that expertise should determine whether the person requesting assistance meets the eligibility requirements.

28 A point repeatedly made in McLean, note 3, above, pp. 199–200.

Thus far, this analysis assumes the mental competence of the person whose life is at stake. However, on both humanitarian and autonomy-based approaches, there has to be some sort of check as to the capacity of the individuals involved to make an adequately reasoned decision about their future. That is a precondition for the effectiveness of instrumental autonomy. A brief outline is therefore required as to how an external determination of competence may be instituted without undermining the role of necessary instrumental autonomy in assisted dying.

Determination of competence requires an authoritative panel of experts to assess the mental competence of the person seeking assistance in dying. Such a review panel could have a number of overlapping functions, going beyond assessing the general mental competence of the applicant, to a more specific rationality test with respect to the reasons given for seeking assisted dying, which can include a further cognate function of checking whether there is any undue influence or coercion at issue with respect to family, friends or any healthcare institutions involved. A suitably constituted review panel could be required to deal with crucial issues that bear on the voluntariness of the request being made, covering these three elements of general competence, the rationality of the specific request, and the possibility of undue influence. Such a panel would require expertise in psychology, psychiatry and counselling, and could have a legal chairperson with the specific duty of safeguarding the interests of the applicant. If appropriate, the applicant's medical practitioner could be consulted on any medical history that is relevant to the competence and voluntariness of the application.

The expert review panel would not be called upon to assess the degree of suffering involved, but would be required to determine whether the state of mind of the applicant for assistance is that of a competent person with understandable reasons for choosing to die, and having the capacity to understand medical diagnoses and prognostications or other circumstances that are relevant to a decision that death is a preferred option to continuing with life. While focusing mainly on the conditions of instrumental autonomy, the panel would also be able to give cognisance to the personal and moral autonomy of the applicant concerning what sort of life is worth living. The competence-based eligibility criteria applied would require tests of competence in which the burden of proof is on those who doubt the competencies in question. If the applicant has been given the opportunity to be provided with any relevant medical or other experts, and is able to express his or her reasons for requesting assisted dying, then there would be no further hurdles to be cleared.

Currently, in those jurisdictions with a legal framework for assisted dying, such as the Netherlands, Belgium, Oregon and Washington,[29] the crucial decision-maker to act on a person's request is that person's medical practitioner who must consult with another independent medical practitioner. This is understandable given these systems' medical conditions of eligibility. Once these are revised so as to better enable any persons who wish assistance in dying (while having safeguards in place to make sure that they are mentally competent and not under undue influence from others), the way is open to have review panels whose qualifications and specified roles are suited to respecting the instrumental autonomy of those involved and hence serve the ultimate humanitarian purpose of such a legal framework.

This brief schematic outline of a possible regulatory regime does no more than indicate the sort of arrangements that should be considered for the protection of individuals from undue pressures while giving them the sort of access to assisted dying that is commensurate with their situation,

29 Thus in the Netherlands and Belgium the person's physician is the key figure. He/she has to consult another, independent, physician who must see the patient and can consult with a psychiatrist if this is deemed appropriate. In Oregon and Washington it is similar, but with more stress on assessing competence, and in some cases patients are referred for counselling. See Lewis, P., *Assisted Dying and Legal Change*, Oxford, Oxford University Press, 2007.

as they perceive it to be. At the same time, the panel would assist in the identification of those rare cases where there are no intelligible reasons to support an application for assisted dying. The review panel is envisaged also as being a body to which relatives and others whose assistance is sought by those wishing to die can go for advice and, if appropriate, permission to provide the necessary assistance.

Within this model, no healthcare professional would be legally obliged to take part in assisted dying. Yet, specialists involved in the care of patients would normally be legally privileged as persons permitted to provide lethal treatment to competent persons under their care when so requested by those persons, once they have been judged competent by a review panel. In cases of assisted suicide, those who do no more than provide the means for suicide would be excluded from prosecution.

Such a regime for facilitating assisted dying has the advantage that it can normally take place in a context where palliative care is available for those who wish to take advantage of it, while those for whom this is either not effective or not desired may opt for assisted dying. This would go a long way to dealing with that priority group for whom palliative care does not effectively reduce chronic suffering. An important part of such a reform would be to give relatives and friends who are asked to assist in dying a place to go for consideration and advice, rather than relying on prosecutorial guidelines to exclude the possibility of being charged with murder.[30]

This brief discussion of the eligibility requirements and regulatory oversight of assisted dying within a humanitarian framework which incorporates a substantial measure of instrumental autonomy sketches the sort of model which would best serve its humanitarian objectives. As it turns out, this model is closely aligned in structure to that proposed by McLean, although founded on a significantly different rationale from her autonomy-based perspective.

Conclusion

Whatever the reforms that are eventually introduced, the fierce and contentious debate on the legitimisation of assisted dying will not be easily resolved. The plight of a small minority of stricken persons for whom death is a vital option is a pressing concern and is likely to remain so. Meanwhile, there continues to be growing anxieties and distress amongst a much larger group who witness the deaths of their near relatives and have forebodings as to what their own future may hold. Nevertheless, in the absence of evidence concerning any serious danger of entering on

30 The nearest existing institutionalised norms in England for legitimising assisted dying are to be found in the Crown Prosecution Service guidelines which, as originally promulgated, advised that there be no prosecutions where the applicant's request is voluntary and there is no conflict of interest involved. See *Policy for Prosecutors in Respect of Cases of Encouraging or Assisting Suicide* (2010), available at: http://www.cps.gov.uk/publications/prosecution/assisted_suicide_policy.html (updated October 2014) (accessed 13 January 2015). The original version of the policy arose from the finding in *R (on the application of Purdy) v. DDP* [2009] UKHL 45 in which the House of Lords instructed the Director of Public Prosecutions (DPP) to publish a policy identifying the factors he will take into account in cases of assisted suicide. Debbie Purdy had sought judicial review against the decision of the DPP who declined to provide such guidelines. She had wanted her husband to accompany her to Switzerland where she could lawfully arrange for her assisted suicide. See Keown, J., 'Purdy: Assisted Suicide by Judicial Legislation?' (2009) *New Law Journal*, 1340–41, and also White, B. and Downie, J., 'Prosecutorial Guidelines for Voluntary Euthanasia and Assisted Suicide: Autonomy, Public Confidence and High Quality Decision-Making' (2012) 36 *Melbourne University Law Review*, 656–705.

a slippery slope towards disrespect for human life, a largely libertarian regime of assisted dying, focused on enabling assisted dying for those competent persons who see it as their least undesirable option, is likely to be the best model for achieving humane care in accordance with the wishes of those experiencing or fearing a quality of life that is, in their view, worse than death. The main point of this chapter is that such a regime is most securely founded on humanitarian justifications.

Yet there will still be concern about what McLean refers to as what 'protects people from having their lives unwillingly removed'.[31] The prime argument against assisted dying is that it will put pressure on another group of vulnerable people to opt for dying when this is not what they really want for themselves.[32] No review panel will spot all instances of such undue pressure. This is not, however, in itself a sufficient reason for failing to move from a covert system of informal and haphazard medical discretion, which is made viable only because of a systematic failure to apply existing law relating to assisted dying.

It is understandable that current reform proposals incorporate the common view that assisted dying be conditional on the judgment of others that there is a terminal illness, the discomforts of which cannot be satisfactorily alleviated by palliative care. However, what is suggested here is that any satisfactory reform must leave competent individuals to decide, in the light of such expert advice as they wish to have, and their own assessment of their situation. This is not because the justification of assisted dying is directly based on the personal or moral autonomy of the individual involved, but because the option of assisted dying comes in almost entirely as a mechanism which enables people to protect themselves against enduring unacceptable life-prolonging procedures in situations where they would be better off dead. Similar considerations apply where the suffering of the individual that generates thoughts of suicide is not based principally, or indeed at all, on medical matters.

The restricted rules on eligibility and their associated regulatory procedures outlined above as the preferred implementation of a legal reform based on humanitarian considerations are in procedural content very similar to the recommendations made by McLean on the basis of autonomy considerations. There are, however, important differences arising from a humanitarian basis. It provides a more secure moral basis for legal reform, and would significantly affect the design and operation of an assisted dying regime so as to make it more palatable to those involved. It is, however, a practical point in favour of this proposal that it accommodates many of the procedural recommendations promoted by McLean, albeit on a rather different philosophical basis. Such a system, however it is justified in terms of background moral goals, would deal much better with the plight of that relatively small percentage of people who would prefer assisted dying to a prolonged and miserable or terminally comatose quasi-existence, while not confining its availability to them alone. Combining strong instrumental autonomy rights and an alert human rights focus on the situation of other minority groups is likely to provide the best humanitarian outcomes.

---

31 McLean, note 3, above, at p. 30.

32 For the human rights dimensions of assisted dying, see Campbell, T., 'Euthanasia as a Human Right' in McLean, S.A.M. (ed.) *First Do No Harm: Law, Ethics and Healthcare*, Aldershot, Ashgate, 2006, pp. 447–60.

References

Journal Articles

Alghrani, A., 'The Legal and Ethical Ramifications of Ectogenesis' (2007) 2 *Asian Journal of World Trade Organization & International Health Law and Policy* 189–211.

——, 'Viability and Abortion: Lessons from Ectogenesis' (2009) 4(6) *Expert Review of Obstetrics and Gynecology* 625–34.

——, and Brazier, M., 'What Is It? Whose Is It? Re-positioning the Fetus in the Context of Research' (2011) 70 *Cambridge Law Journal* 51–82.

Almack, K., 'Seeking Sperm: Accounts of Lesbian Couples; Reproductive Decision-making and Understanding the Needs of the Child' (2006) 20 *International Journal of Law Policy and the Family* 1–22.

Annas, G., 'Fairy Tales Surrogate Mothers Tell' (1988) 16 *Law, Medicine and Ethics* 27–33.

Appelbaum, P.S., and Grisso, T. 'The MacArthur Treatment Competence Study. I Mental Illness and Competence to Consent to Treatment' (1995) 19(2) *Law and Human Behavior* 105–26.

——, and Grisso, T., 'The MacArthur Treatment Competence Study. II Measures of Abilities Related to Competence to Consent to Treatment' (1995) 19(2) *Law and Human Behavior* 127–48.

——, and Grisso, T., 'The MacArthur Treatment Competence Study. III Abilities of Patients to Consent to Psychiatric and Medical Treatments' (1995) 19(2) *Law and Human Behavior* 149–74.

——, Grisso, T., Frank, E., O'Donnell, S., and Kupfer, D.J., 'Competence of Depressed Patients for Consent to Research' (1999) 156(9) *American Journal of Psychiatry* 1380–84.

Bainham, A., '"Truth Will Out": Paternity in Europe' (2007) 66 *Cambridge Law Journal* 278–82.

Beauchamp, D., 'Community: The Neglected Tradition of Public Health' (1985) 15 *Hastings Center Report*, 28–36.

Bennett, B., 'Symbiotic Relationships: Saviour Siblings, Family Rights and Biomedicine' (2005) 19(3) *Australian Journal of Family Law* 195–212.

Beskow, L.M., Namey, E.E., Cadigan, R.J., Brazg, T., Crouch, J., Henderson, G.E., Michie, M., Nelson, D.K., Tabor, H.K., and Wilfond, B.S., 'Research Participants' Perspectives on Genotype-Driven Research Recruitment' (2011) 6(4) *Journal of Empirical Research on Human Research Ethics* 3–20.

Bevan, G., and Skellern, M., 'Does Competition between Hospitals Improve Clinical Quality? A Review of Evidence from Two Eras of Competition in the English NHS' (2011) 343 *British Medical Journal*, http://www.bmj.com/content/343/bmj.d6470 (accessed 13 January 2015).

Beyleveld, D., 'The Principle of Generic Consistency as the Supreme Principle of Human Rights' (2011) 13 *Human Rights Review* 1–18.

——, 'Williams' False Dilemma: How to Give Categorically Binding Impartial Reasons to Real Agents' (2013) 10 *Journal of Moral Philosophy* 204–26.

——, and Brownsword, R., 'Emerging Technologies, Extreme Uncertainty, and the Principle of Rational Precautionary Reasoning' (2012) 4 *Law, Innovation and Technology* 35–65.

Beynon-Jones, S.M., and Brown, N., 'Time, Timing and Narrative at the Interface Between Technoscience and Policy' (2011) 38 *Science and Public Policy* 639–47.

Bezanson, R.P., 'Solomon Would Weep: A Comment on In the Matter of Baby M and the Limits of Judicial Authority' (1988) 16 *Law, Medicine and Ethics* 126–30.

Bismark, M.M., Brennan, T.A., Davis, P.B., and Studdert, M., 'Claiming Behaviour in a No-Fault System of Medical Injury: A Descriptive Analysis of Claimants and Non-Claimants' (2006) 185(4) *Medical Journal of Australia* 203–7.

——, Brennan, T.A., Paterson, R.J., Davis, P.B., and Studdert, D.M., 'Relationship between Complaints and Quality of Care in New Zealand: A Descriptive Analysis of Complaints and Non-Complaints Following Adverse Events' (2006) 15 *Quality and Safety in Health Care* 17–22.

——, and Paterson, R.J., 'No-Fault Compensation in New Zealand: Harmonizing Injury Compensation, Provider Accountability and Patient Safety' (2006) 25 *Health Affairs* 278–83.

Black, I., 'Existential Suffering and the Extent of the Right to Physician-Assisted Suicide in Switzerland' (2014) 22(1) *Medical Law Review* 109–18.

Blyth, E., 'The UK's Human Fertilisation and Embryology Act 1990 and the Welfare of the Child: A Critique' (1995) 3 *International Journal of Children's Rights* 417–38.

Boklage, C.E., 'Survival Probability of Human Conceptions from Fertilization to Term' (1990) 35 *International Journal of Fertility* 75–94.

Bourne, H., Douglas, T., and Savulescu, J., 'Procreative Beneficence and In Vitro Gametogenesis' (2012) 30 *Monash Bioethics Review* 29–48.

Bowman, D.M., and Ludlow, K., 'Assessing the Impact of a "For Government" Review on the Nanotechnology Regulatory Landscape' (2012) 38 *Monash University Law Review* 168–212.

Brandon Chen, Y.Y., and Flood, C.M., 'Medical Tourism's Impact on Health Care Equity and Access in Low- and Middle-Income Countries: Making the Case for Regulation' (2013) 41 *Journal of Law, Medicine and Ethics* 286–300.

Brazier, M., 'Do No Harm: Do Patients Have Responsibilities Too?' (2006) 65 *Cambridge Law Journal* 397–422.

Bridge, C., 'Inherent Jurisdiction' (2012) 42(Dec) *Family Law* 1454–6.

Brown, N., 'Besting the Embryo: The Metrics of Humanness in the Transpecies Embryo Debate' (2009) 4 *Biosocieties* 147–63.

——, and Beynon-Jones, S., '"Reflex Regulation": An Anatomy of Promissory Science Governance' (2012) 14 *Health, Risk & Society* 223–40.

Brownsword, R., 'Regulating Human Genetics: New Dilemmas for a New Millennium' (2004) 12 *Medical Law Review* 14–39.

——, 'Happy Families, Consenting Couples, and Children with Dignity: Sex Selection and Saviour Siblings' (2005) 17 *Child and Family Law Quarterly* 435–73.

——, 'Regulating Brain Imaging: Challenge and Opportunity' (2009) 3 *Frontiers in Human Neuroscience* 1–2.

Burns, T.A., 'When Life Is an Injury: An Economic Approach to Wrongful Life Lawsuits' (2003) 52 *Duke Law Journal* 807–39.

Callus, T., '"Wrongful Life" à la Française' (2001) 5 *Medical Law International* 117–25.

——, 'A New Parenthood Paradigm for Twenty-first Century Family Law in England and Wales?' (2012) 32 *Legal Studies* 347–68.

Campbell, A., 'Conceiving Parents Through Law' (2007) 21 *International Journal of Law Policy and the Family* 242–73.

Campbell, M., 'Conscientious Objection, Health Care and Article 9 of the European Convention on Human Rights' (2011) 11 *Medical Law International* 284–304.

——, Sahin-Hodoglugil, N.N., and Potts, M., 'Barriers to Fertility Regulation: A Review of the Literature' (2006) 37 *Studies in Family Planning* 87–98.

Carpenter, B.C., 'Sex Post Facto: Advising Clients Regarding Posthumous Conception' (2012) 38 *American College of Trust & Estate Counsel Law Journal* 187–228.

Caulfield, T., 'Biobanks and Blanket Consent: The Proper Place of the Public Good and Public Perception Rationales' (2007) 1 *Kings Law Journal* 209–26.

——, and Kaye, J., 'Broad Consent in Biobanking: Reflections on Seemingly Insurmountable Dilemmas' (2009) 10 *Medical Law International* 85–100.

Chial, H., 'DNA Sequencing Technologies Key to the Human Genome Project' (2008) 1 *Nature Education* 219.

Cook, R.J., 'Human Rights and Maternal Health: Exploring the Effectiveness of the Alyne Decision' (2013) 41 *Journal of Law, Medicine and Ethics* 103–23.

——, and Dickens, B.M., 'Upholding Pregnant Women's Right to Life' (2012) 117 *International Journal of Gynecology and Obstetrics* 90–94.

Cotterell, R., 'Spectres of Transnationalism: Changing Terrains of Sociology of Law' (2009) 36 *Journal of Law and Society* 481–500.

Crawshaw, M., Blyth, E., and van den Akker, O., 'The Changing Profile of Surrogacy in the UK: Implications for National and International Policy and Practice' (2012) 34 *Journal of Social Welfare & Family Law* 267–77.

Davies, G., 'The Sacred and the Profane: Biotechnology, Rationality and Public Debate' (2006) 38 *Environment and Planning* 423–44.

Davis, P.B., Lay-Yee, R., Briant, R., and Scott, A., 'Modeling Eligibility under National Systems of Compensation for Treatment Injury' (2006) 31(2) *Journal of Health Politics, Policy and Law* 295–319.

Deckha, M., 'Holding onto Humanity: Animals, Dignity and Anxiety in Canada's Assisted Human Reproduction Act' (2009) 5 *Unbound* 21–54.

DeGrazia, D., 'Advance Directives, Dementia, and the "Someone Else Problem"' (1999) 13(5) *Bioethics* 373–91.

Delacey, T.C., 'Euthanasia, Innocence and the Slippery Slope' (Winter 1995) *Policy* 36–9.

Des Jarlais, D.C., 'Harm Reduction: A Framework for Incorporating Science into Drug Policy' (1995) 85(1) *American Journal of Public Health* 10–12.

Dickens, B.M., and Cook, R.J., 'The Legal Status of In Vitro Embryos' (2010) 111 *International Journal of Gynecology and Obstetrics* 91–4.

——, and Cook, R.J., 'Conscientious Commitment to Women's Health' (2011) 113 *International Journal of Gynecology and Obstetrics* 163–6.

Diduck, A., '"If Only We Can Find the Appropriate Terms to Use the Issue Will Be Solved": Law, Identity and Parenthood' (2007) 19 *Child and Family Law Quarterly* 458–80.

Douglas, G., 'The Intention to be a Parent and the Making of Mothers' (1994) 57 *Modern Law Review* 636–41.

Dyer, C., 'Doctor Cleared of Act "Tantamount to Euthanasia"' (2007) 335 *British Medical Journal* 67.

Easley, C.A., Phillips, B.T., McGuire, M.M., Barringer, J.M., Valli, H., Hermann, B.P., Simerly, C.R., Rajkovic, A., Miki, T., Orwig, K.E., and Schatten, G.P., 'Direct Differentiation of Human Pluripotent Stem Cells into Haploid Spermatogenic Cells' (2012) 2(3) *Cell Reports* 440–46.

Edmonds, D.K., Lindsay, K.S., Miller, J.F. Williamson, E., and Wood, P.J., 'Early Embryonic Mortality in Women' (1982) 38(4) *Fertility and Sterility* 447–53.

Eguizabal, C., Montserrat, N., Vassena, R., Barragan, M., Garreta, E., Garcia-Quevedo, L., Vidal, F., Giorgetti, A., Veiga, A., and Izpisua Belmonte, J.C., 'Complete Meiosis from Human Induced Pluripotent Stem Cells' (2011) 29 *Stem Cells* 1186–95.

Eijkholt, M., 'Procreative Autonomy and the Human Fertilisation and Embryology Act 2008: Does a Coherent Conception Underpin UK Law?' (2011) 11 *Medical Law International* 93–126.

Elliston, S.J., and McLean, S.A.M., 'Death, Decision Making and the Law' (2004) *Juridical Review* 265–93.

Epstein, R., 'In Defense of the "Old" Public Health: The Legal Framework for the Regulation of Public Health' (2004) 69 *Brooklyn Law Review* 1421–70.

Erdman, J.N., 'Access to Information on Safe Abortion: A Harm Reduction and Human Rights Approach' (2011) 34 *Harvard Journal of Law & Gender* 413–62.

——, 'Harm Reduction, Human Rights, and Access to Information on Safer Abortion' (2012) 118 *International Journal of Gynecology and Obstetrics* 83–6.

——, Grenon A., and Harrison-Wilson, L., 'Medication Abortion in Canada: A Right-to-Health Perspective' (2008) 98 *American Journal of Public Health* 1764–9.

——, DePiñeres, T., and Kismödi, E., 'Updated WHO Guidance on Safe Abortion: Health and Human Rights' (2013) 120 *International Journal of Gynecology and Obstetrics* 200–203.

Everett, K. and Yeatman, L., 'Are Some Parents More Natural Than Others?' (2010) 22 *Child and Family Law Quarterly* 290–309.

Fahmy, M.S., 'On the Supposed Moral Harm of Selecting for Deafness' (2011) 25 *Bioethics* 129.

Farrell, A.M., and Devaney, S., 'Making Amends or Making Things Worse? Clinical Negligence Reform and Patient Redress in England' (2007) 27(4) *Legal Studies* 630–48.

Fenstad, J.E., 'Relationships Between the Social and Natural Sciences' (1995) 3 *European Review* 61–71.

Ferguson, A.L., and Braithwaite, E., 'Putting Things Right in Wales' (2012) 18 *Clinical Risk* 6–8.

Fernandez, P., Coverdale, J., and Brookbanks, W., 'Implications of Autonomy for Forensic Consequences of Extended Suicide' (2002) 9(2) *Psychiatry, Psychology and Law* 146–50.

Finnis, J., 'Euthanasia, Morality, and Law' (1998) 31 *Loyola of Los Angeles Law Review* 1123–46.

Fischer, S., Huber, C., Imhof, L., Mahrer Imhof, R., Furter, M., Ziegler, S.J., and Bosshard, G., 'Suicide Assisted by Two Swiss Right-to-die Organisations' (2008) 34 *Journal of Medical Ethics* 810–14.

Fishman, J.R., 'Manufacturing Desire: The Commodification of Female Sexual Dysfunction' (2004) 34(2) *Social Studies of Science* 187–218.

Fitzjohn, J., and Studdert, D., 'A Compensation Perspective on Error Prevention: Is the ACC Medical Misadventure Scheme Compensating the Right Sort of Injury?' (2001) 114 *New Zealand Medical Journal* 432–4.

Flannery, M.T., '"Rethinking" Embryo Disposition upon Divorce' (2013) 29 *Journal of Contemporary Health Law and Policy* 233–82.

Fovargue, S., and Miola, J., 'Policing Pregnancy: Implications of Attorney General's Reference (No 3 of 1994)' (1998) 6 *Medical Law Review* 265–96.

——, and Ost, S., 'When Should Precaution Prevail? Interests in (Public) Health, the Risk of Harm and Xenotransplantation' (2010) 18 *Medical Law Review* 302–29.

Fox, M., 'Rethinking the Animal/Human Boundary: The Impact of Xenotechnologies' (2005) 26 *Liverpool Law Review* 149–67.

——, 'The Human Fertilisation and Embryology Act 2008: Tinkering at the Margins' (2009) 17 *Feminist Legal Studies* 333–44.

——, and McHale, J., 'In Whose Best Interests?' (1997) 60 *Modern Law Review* 700–709.

——, and McHale, J., 'Xenotransplantation: The Ethical and Legal Ramifications' (1998) 6 *Medical Law Review* 42–61.

Frances, A.J., 'Last Plea to DSM 5: Save Grief from the Drug Companies' *Psychology Today* 3 January 2013.
Freckelton, I., 'Patients' Decisions to Die: The Emerging Australian Jurisprudence' (2011) 18 *Journal of Law and Medicine* 427–38.
Freedman, L.R., and Stulberg, D.B., 'Conflicts in Care for Obstetric Complications in Catholic Hospitals' (2013) 4 *American Journal of Bioethics (AJOB) Primary Research* 1–10.
Furness, P., 'Consent to Using Human Tissue: Implied Consent Should Suffice' (2003) 327(7418) *British Medical Journal* 759–60.
Giubellini, A., and Minerva, F., 'After Birth Abortion – Why Should the Baby Live?' (2013) 39 *Journal of Medical Ethics* 261–3.
Glasziou, P., Moynihan, R., Richards, T., and Godlee, F., 'Too Much Medicine; Too Little Care: Time to Wind Back the Harms of Overdiagnosis and Overtreatment' (2013) 347 *British Medical Journal*, http://www.bmj.com/content/347/bmj.f4247 (accessed 13 January 2015).
Gliwa, C., and Berkman, B.E., 'Do Researchers Have an Obligation to Actively Look for Genetic Incidental Findings?' (2013) 13 *American Journal of Bioethics* 32–42.
Goertzel, B., 'Human-level Artificial General Intelligence and the Possibility of a Technological Singularity: A Reaction to Ray Kurzweil's *The Singularity Is Near*, and McDermott's Critique of Kurzweil' (2007) 171(18) *Artificial Intelligence* 1161–73.
Goldberg, R., 'Medical Malpractice and Compensation in the UK' (2012) 87 *Chicago-Kent Law Review* 131–61.
Gomperts R.J., Jelinska, K., Davies, S., Gemzell-Danielsson, K., and Kleiverda, G., 'Using Telemedicine for Termination of Pregnancy with Mifepristone and Misoprostol in Settings Where There Is No Access to Safe Services' (2008) 115 *British Journal of Obstetrics and Gynaecology* 1171–8.
Gonzales, C.P., Harris, J., and Testa, G., 'Multiplex Parenting: IVG and the Generations to Come' (2014) *Journal of Medical Ethics*, http://jme.bmj.com/content/early/2014/03/07/medethics-2013-101810.full (accessed 6 March 2015).
Goodman, J., 'The Case of Dr Munro: Are There Lessons to Be Learnt ?' (2010) 18 *Medical Law Review* 564–77.
Gostin, L.O., Buckley, G.J., and Kelley, P.W., 'Stemming the Global Trade in Falsified and Substandard Medicines' (2013) 309 *Journal of the American Medical Association* 1693–4.
Green, R.C., Berg, J.S., Grody, W.W., Kalia, S.S., Korf, B.R., Martin, C.L., McGuire, A.L., Nussbaum, R.L., O'Daniel, J.M., Ormond, K.E., Rehm, H.L., Watson, M.S., Williams, M.S., and Biesecker, L.G., 'ACMG Recommendations for Reporting of Incidental Findings in Clinical Exome and Genome Sequencing' (2013) 15 *Genetics in Medicine* 565–74.
Griffiths, J., 'Assisted Suicide in the Netherlands: The Chabot Case' (1995) 58 *The Modern Law Review* 232–48.
Gulsuner, S., Walsh, T., Watts, A.C., Lee, M.K., Thornton, A.M., Casadei, S., Rippey, C., and Shahin, H., 'Spatial and Temporal Mapping of De Novo Mutations in Schizophrenia to a Fetal Prefrontal Cortical Network' (2013) 154(3) *Cell* 518–29.
Hack, M., Fanaroff A.A., and Merkatz, I.R., 'The Low Birth Weight Infant: Evolution of a Changing Concept' (1979) 301 *New England Journal of Medicine* 1162–65.
Haddow, G., Bruce, A., Calvert, J., Harmon, S., and Marsden, W., 'Not "Human" Enough to Be Human, But Not Animal Enough to Be "Animal": The Case of the HFEA, Cybrids and Xenotransplantation in the UK' (2010) 29 *New Genetics and Society* 3–17.
Hall, S.S., 'Revolution Postponed' (2010) 303 *Scientific American* 60–67.

Harder, L., and Thomarat, M., 'Parentage Law in Canada: The Numbers Game of Standing and Status' (2012) 26 *International Journal of Law Policy and the Family* 62–87.
Harmon, S.H.E., 'A Penny for Your Thoughts, a Pound for Your Flesh: Implications for Recognizing Property Rights in Our Own Excised Body Parts' (2006) 7 *Medical Law International* 329–54.
——, 'Semantic, Pedantic or Paradigm Shift? Recruitment, Retention and Property in Modern Population Biobanking' (2008) 16 *European Journal of Health Law* 27–43.
Harris, J., 'Ethical Problems in the Management of Some Severely Handicapped Children' (1981) 7 *Journal of Medical Ethics* 117–24.
——, 'Is Gene Therapy a Form of Eugenics?' (1993) 7 *Bioethics* 178–87.
——, 'The Concept of the Person and the Value of Life' (1999) 9 *Kennedy Institute of Ethics Journal* 293–308.
——, 'Human Beings, Persons and Conjoined Twins: An Ethical Analysis of the Judgement in *Re A*' (2002) 9 *Medical Law Review* 221–36.
——, 'Stem Cells, Sex, and Procreation' (2003) 12 *Cambridge Quarterly of Healthcare Ethics* 353–71.
——, 'Taking the "Human" Out of Human Rights' (2011) *Cambridge Quarterly of Healthcare Ethics* 9–20.
Hayashi, K., Ogushi, S., and Kurimoto, K., 'Offspring from Oocytes Derived from In Vitro Primordial Germ Cell-like Cells in Mice' (2012) 338 *Science* 971–5.
Hendin, H., 'Seduced by Death: Doctors, Patients, and the Dutch Cure' (1994) 10(2) *Issues in Law & Medicine* 123–69.
Herring, J., 'Forging a Relational Approach: Best Interests or Human Rights?' (2013) 13 *Medical Law International* 32–54.
Hewson, B., 'Neither Midwives nor Rainmakers: Why DL Is Wrong' (2013) *Public Law* 451–9.
Hindmarch, T., Hotopf, M., and Owen, G.S., 'Depression and Decision-making Capacity for Treatment or Research: A Systematic Review' (2013) 14(1) *BMC Medical Ethics*, http://www.biomedcentral.com/1472-6939/14/54 (accessed 13 January 2013).
Holtzman, N.A., and Marteau, T.M., 'Will Genetics Revolutionize Medicine?' (2000) 343(2) *The New England Journal of Medicine* 141–4.
Horsey, K., 'Challenging Presumptions: Legal Parenthood and Surrogacy Arrangements' (2010) 22 *Child and Family Law Quarterly* 449–74.
Hughes, R., 'The Inherent Jurisdiction over Vulnerable Adults' (2013) 3 *Private Client Business* 132–9.
Hyde, J., 'Pilot Aims to Limit Clinical Negligence Solicitors' Fees' *Law Gazette* 20 May 2013.
Iedema, R., Allen, S., Britton, K., Piper, D., Baker, A., Grbich, C., Allan, A., Jones, L., Tuckett, A., Williams, A., Manias, E., and Gallagher, T.H., 'Patients' and Family Members' Views on How Clinicians Enact and How They Should Enact Open Disclosure: The "100 Patient Stories" Qualitative Study' (2011) 343 *British Medical Journal*, http://www.bmj.com/content/343/bmj.d4423 (accessed 13 January 2015).
——, and Piper, D., 'Do Patients Want and Expect Compensation Following Harm? (2013) 116 *Precedent* 48–51.
Illich, I., 'The Medicalization of Life' (1975) 1 *Journal of Medical Ethics* 73–7.
Johansson, H., 'The Swedish System for Compensation of Patient Injuries' (2010) 115(2) *Uppsala Journal of Medical Sciences* 88–90.
Johnston, C., and Kaye, J., 'Does the UK Biobank Have a Legal Obligation to Feedback Individual Findings to Participants?' (2004) 12 *Medical Law Review* 239–67.

Jones, R.B., 'Parental Consent to Cosmetic Facial Surgery in Down's Syndrome (2000) 26 *Journal of Medical Ethics* 101–2.

Kachalia, A., Mello, M.M., Brennan, T.A., and Studdert, D.M., 'Beyond Negligence: Avoidability and Medical Injury Compensation' (2008) 66(2) *Social Science and Medicine* 387–402.

Kass, L.R., 'Triumph or Tragedy: The Moral Meaning of Genetic Technology' (2000) 45 *American Journal of Jurisprudence* 1–16.

Keown, J., 'Purdy: Assisted Suicide by Judicial Legislation' (2009) *New Law Journal* 1340–41.

Kessler, D., and McClellan, M., 'Do Doctors Practice Defensive Medicine?' (1996) 111(2) *The Quarterly Journal of Economics* 353–90.

Khan, K.S., Wojdyla, D., Say, L., Gulmezoglu, A.M., and Van Look, P.F., 'WHO Analysis of Causes of Maternal Deaths: A Systematic Review' (2006) 367(9516) *The Lancet* 1066–74.

Knoppers, B.M., Deschênes, M., Zawati, M.H., and Tassé, A.M., 'Population Studies: Return of Research Results and Incidental Findings Policy Statement' (2012) *European Journal of Human Genetics* 245–7.

Kopinski, N.E., 'Human-Nonhuman Chimera: A Regulatory Proposal on the Blurring of Species Lines' (2003–4) *Boston College Law Review* 619–66.

Korn, C.W., Sharot, T., Walter, H., Heekeren, H.R., and Dolan, R.J., 'Depression Is Related to an Absence of Optimistically Biased Belief Updating about Future Life Events' (2014) 44(3) *Psychological Medicine* 579–92.

Krieger, N., 'Who and What Is a "Population"? Historical Debates, Current Controversies, and Implications for Understanding "Population Health" and Rectifying Health Inequities' (2012) 90 *Milbank Quarterly*, 634–81.

Laing, J.A., and Oderberg, D.S., 'Artificial Reproduction: The "Welfare Principle" and the Common Good' (2005) 13 *Medical Law Review* 328–56.

Larson, K.B.A., and Gosain, A.K., 'Cosmetic Surgery in the Adolescent Patient' (2012) 129 *Plastic & Reconstructive Surgery* 135e–141e.

Latham, M., '"If It Aint Broke, Don't Fix It?" Scandals, Risk and Cosmetic Surgery Regulation in the UK and France' (2014) 22(3) *Medical Law Review* 384–408.

Laurie, G., 'Reflexive Governance in Biobanking: On the Value of Policy Led Approaches and the Need to Recognise the Limits of Law' (2011) 130(3) *Human Genetics* 347–56.

——, 'Recognizing the Right Not to Know: Conceptual, Professional and Legal Implications' (2014) 42(1) *Journal of Law, Medicine and Ethics* 53–63.

Levy, N., 'Deafness, Culture, and Choice' (2002) 28 *Journal of Medical Ethics* 284–5.

Lloyd-Bostock, S., and Mulcahy, L., 'The Social Psychology of Making and Responding to Hospital Complaints: An Account Model of Complaint Processes' (1994) 16 *Law and Policy* 123–47.

Lozano, R., Wong, H., Foreman, K.J., Rajaratnam, J.K., Naghavi, M., Marcus, J.R., Dwyer-Lindgren, L., Lofgren, K.T., Phillips, D., Atkinson, C., Lopez, A.D., and Murray, C.J.L., 'Progress Towards Millennium Development Goals 4 and 5 on Maternal and Child Mortality: An Updated Systematic Analysis' (2011) 378(9797) *The Lancet* 1139–65.

Lyons, B., 'Dying to Be Responsible: Adolescence, Autonomy and Responsibility' (2010) 30 *Legal Studies* 257–78.

McCandless, J., and Sheldon, S., 'The Human Fertilisation and Embryology Act (2008) and the Tenacity of the Sexual Family Form' (2010) 73 *Modern Law Review* 175–207.

McCormack, B., Karlsson, B., Dewing, J., and Lerdal A., 'Exploring Person-centredness: A Qualitative Meta-synthesis of Four Studies' (2010) 24(3) *Scandinavian Journal of Caring Sciences* 620–24.

McGee, A., 'Ending the Life of the Act/Omission Dispute: Causation in Withholding and Withdrawing Life-sustaining Measures' (2011) 31 *Legal Studies* 467–91.

McGuinness, S., 'Law, Reproduction and Disability: Fatally Handicapped?' (2013) 21 *Medical Law Review* 215–42.

Macklon, N.S., Geraedts, J.P.M., and Fauser, B.C.J.M., 'Conception to Ongoing Pregnancy: The "Black Box" of Early Pregnancy Loss' (2002) 8(4) *Human Reproduction Update* 333–43.

MacLean, A., 'From *Sidaway* to *Pearce* and Beyond: Is the Legal Regulation of Consent Any Better Following a Quarter of a Century of Judicial Scrutiny?' (2012) 20 *Medical Law Review* 108–29.

McLean, S.A.M., 'Accident Compensation Liability Without Fault: The New Zealand Experience' (1985) 7(1) *The Journal of Social Welfare Law* 31–45.

——, 'Abortion Law: Is Consensual Reform Possible?' (1990) 17 *Journal of Law and Society* 106–23.

——, 'Mapping the Human Genome: Friend or Foe?' (1994) 39 *Social Science and Medicine* 1221–7.

——, 'Interventions in the Human Genome' (1998) 61 *Modern Law Review* 681–96.

——, 'The Gene Genie: Good Fairy or Wicked Witch?' (2001) 32 *Studies in History and Philosophy of Biological and Biomedical Sciences* 723–39.

——, 'What Is Wrong with Reproductive Cloning?' (2002) *Genetics Law Monitor* 6–9.

——, 'De-Regulating Assisted Reproduction: Some Reflections' (2006) 7 *Medical Law International* 233–47.

——, 'Live and Let Die' (2009) 339 *British Medical Journal*, 837.

——, 'Are Advance Directives Legally Binding or Simply the Starting Point for Discussion on Patients' Best Interests? Ethical View' (2009) 339 *British Medical Journal*, http://www.bmj.com/content/339/bmj.b4695 (accessed 13 January 2015).

——, and Giesen, D., 'Legal and Ethical Considerations of the Human Genome Project' (1994) 1 *Medical Law International* 159–75.

——, and Morgan, D., 'Choosing Death or Life: Law, Medicine and Patients' Rights' (2009) *Juridical Review* 129–48.

——, and Ramsey, J., 'Human Rights, Reproductive Freedom, Medicine and the Law' (2002) 5 *Medical Law International* 239–58.

Mason, K., and Laurie, G., 'Consent or Property? Dealing with the Body and Its Parts in the Shadow of Bristol and Alder Hey' (2001) 64 *Medical Law Review* 710–29.

Maxwell, N.G., 'The Kansas Case of *KMH*: US Law Concerning the Legal Status of Known Sperm Donors' (2008) 4 *Utrecht Law Review* 135–61.

Meyer, D.D., 'Parenthood in a Time of Transition: Tensions between Legal, Biological, and Social Conceptions of Parenthood' (2006) 54 *The American Journal of Comparative Law* 125–44.

Meynen, G., 'Depression, Possibilities, and Competence: A Phenomenological Perspective' (2011) 32 *Theoretical Medicine and Bioethics* 181–93.

Millbank, J., 'The Limits of Functional Family: Lesbian Mother Litigation in the Era of the Eternal Biological Family' (2008) 22 *International Journal of Law Policy and the Family* 149–77.

Morris, A., 'Selective Treatment of Irreversibly Impaired Infants: Decision Making at the Threshold' (2009) 17 *Medical Law Review* 347–76.

——, and Saintier, S., 'To Be or Not To Be: Is That the Question? Wrongful Life and Misconceptions' (2003) 11 *Medical Law Review* 167–93.

Morrison, S., 'The New Zealand No-Fault Accident Compensation Scheme: The Financial Viability of the NZ Model' (2013) 114 *Precedent* 39–42.

Newdick, C., 'Citizenship, Free Movement and Health Care: Cementing Individual Rights by Corroding Social Solidarity' (2006) 43 *Common Market Law Review* 1645–68.

Ogilvie, A.D., and Potts, S.G., 'Assisted Suicide for Depression: The Slippery Slope in Action?' (1994) 309(6953) *British Medical Journal* 492–3.

Oliphant, K., 'Beyond Misadventure: Compensation for Medical Injuries in New Zealand' (2007) 15(3) *Medical Law Review* 357–91.

Otlowski, M., 'Tackling Legal Challenges Posed by Population Biobanks: Reconceptualising Consent Requirements' (2012) 20 *Medical Law Review* 191–226.

Owen, G.S., Richardson, G., David, A.S., Szmukler, G., Hayward, P., and Hotopf, M., 'Mental Capacity to Make Decisions on Treatment in People Admitted to Psychiatric Hospitals: Cross Sectional Study' (2008) 337 *British Medical Journal*, http://www.bmj.com/content/bmj/337/bmj.39580.546597.BE.full.pdf (accessed 19 January 2015).

Parens, E., Appelbaum, P., and Chung, W., 'Incidental Findings in the Era of Whole Genome Sequencing?' (2013) 43(4) *Hastings Center Report* 16–19.

Parker, G., 'Classifying Depression: Should Paradigms Lost Be Regained?' (2000) 157(8) *American Journal of Psychiatry* 1195–203.

——, 'Is Depression Overdiagnosed? Yes' (2007) 335 *British Medical Journal* 328, http://www.bmj.com/content/bmj/335/7615/328.full.pdf (accessed 19 January 2015).

Paterson, R., 'The Patients' Complaints System in New Zealand' (2002) 21(3) *Health Affairs* 70–79.

Petersen, K., 'Abortion Laws and Medical Developments: A Medico-legal Anomaly in Queensland' (2011) 18 *Journal of Law and Medicine* 594–600.

Petersen Z., Myers, B., van Hout, M.-C., Plüddemann, A., and Parry, C., 'Availability of HIV Prevention and Treatment Services for People Who Inject Drugs: Findings from 21 Countries' (2013) 10 *Harm Reduction Journal*, http://www.harmreductionjournal.com/content/10/1/13 (accessed 13 January 2013).

Prosser, T., 'Regulation for Social Solidarity' (2006) 33 *Journal of Law and Society* 364–87.

Purewal, S., and Van Den Akker, O., 'The Socio-cultural and Biological Meaning of Parenthood' (2007) 28(2) *Journal of Psychosomatic Obstetrics & Gynecology* 79–86.

Radden, J., 'Is This Dame Melancholy? Equating Today's Depression and Past Melancholia' (2003) 10(1) *Philosophy, Psychiatry, & Psychology* 37–52.

Radin, M., 'Market-inalienability' (1987) 100 *Harvard Law Review* 1849–937.

Rait, J.L., 'How Do We Best Compensate for Accidental Medical Injuries?' (2012) 197(5) *Medical Journal of Australia* 299–300.

Ranous, J.S., and Sherrin, J.J., 'Busting the Blessing Balloon: Liability for the Birth of an Unplanned Child' (1975) 39 *Albany Law Review* 221–51.

Reich, W.T., 'The Wider View: André Helleger's Passionate, Integrating Intellect and the Creation of Bioethics' (1999) 9 *Kennedy Institute of Ethics Journal* 25–51.

Rhoden, N.K., 'The New Neonatal Dilemma: Live Births from Late Abortions' (1983–4) 72 *Georgetown Law Journal* 1451–509.

Robertson, J.A., 'Ethics and the Future of Preimplantation Genetic Diagnosis' (2005) 10(1) *Reproductive BioMedicine Online* 97–101.

Rosettenstein, D.S., 'Defining a Parent: The New Biology and the Rebirth of the *Filius Nullius*' (1981) 131 *New Law Journal* 1095–96.

Ruck Keene, A., 'The Inherent Jurisdiction: Where Are We Now?' (2013) 3(1) *Elder Law Journal* 88–92.

Rudnick, A., 'Depression and Competence to Refuse Psychiatric Treatment' (2002) 28 *Journal of Medical Ethics* 151–5.

Ruger, J.P., 'Global Health Justice' (2009) 2 *Public Health Ethics* 261–75.

Sandel, M., 'The Case Against Perfection, What's Wrong with Designer Children, Bionic Athletes and Genetic Engineering' (2004) *The Atlantic* 1 April.

Savulescu, J., 'Deaf Lesbians, "Designer Disability", and the Future of Medicine' (2002) 325 *British Medical Journal* 771–3.

——, 'A Simple Solution to the Puzzles of End of Life? Voluntary Palliated Starvation' (2014) 40 *Journal of Medical Ethics* 110–13.

Sax, D.F., and Gaines, S.D., 'Species Diversity: From Global Decreases to Local Increases' (2003) 18 *Trends in Ecology and Evolution* 561–6.

Scott, R., 'Interpreting the Disability Ground of the Abortion Act' (2005) 64 *Cambridge Law Journal* 388–412.

Sedgh, G., Singh, S., Shah, I.H., Åhman, E., Henshaw, S.K., and Bankole, A., 'Induced Abortion: Incidence and Trends Worldwide from 1995 to 2008' (2012) 379 *The Lancet* 625–32.

Sepper, E., 'Taking Conscience Seriously' (2012) 98 *Virginia Law Review* 1501–75.

Shakespeare, T., 'Choices and Rights: Eugenics, Genetics and Disability Equality' (1998) 13 *Disability and Society* 665–82.

Sharp, L., 'Imagining Transpecies Kinship in Xenotransplantation' (2011) 8 *Sites* 12–31.

Shaw, D., and Cook, R.J., 'Applying Human Rights to Improve Access to Reproductive Health Services' (2012) 119 *International Journal of Gynecology and Obstetrics* S55–9.

Sheldon, S., 'Fragmenting Fatherhood: The Regulation of Reproductive Technologies' (2005) 68 *Modern Law Review* 523–53.

——, and Wilkinson, S., 'Termination of Pregnancy for Reasons of Foetal Disability: Are There Grounds for a Special Exception at Law?' (2001) 9 *Medical Law Review* 85–109.

Sheldon, T., 'Being "Tired of Life" Is Not Grounds for Euthanasia' (2003) 326(7380) *British Medical Journal* 71, http://www.bmj.com/content/326/7380/71.3 (accessed 19 January 2015).

Shepperd, J.A., Carroll, P., Grace, J., and Terry, M., 'Exploring the Causes of Comparative Optimism' (2002) 42 *Psychologica Belgica* 65–98.

Sherris, J., Bingham, A., Burns, M.A., Girvin, S., Westley E., and Gomez, P.I., 'Misoprostol Use in Developing Countries: Results from a Multicountry Study' (2005) 88 *International Journal of Gynecology and Obstetrics* 76–81.

Shetty, P., 'India's Unregulated Surrogacy Industry' (2012) 380(9854) *The Lancet* 1633–4.

Sloan, F.A., Whetten-Goldstein, K., and Hickson, G.B., 'The Influence of Obstetric No-Fault Compensation on Obstetricians' Practice Patterns' (1998) 17(3) *The American Journal of Obstetrics and Gynecology* 671–6.

Smith, L., 'Is Three a Crowd? Lesbian Mothers' Perspectives on Parental Status in Law' (2006) 18 *Child and Family Law Quarterly* 231–52.

——, 'Tangling the Web of Legal Parenthood: Legal Responses to the Use of Known Donors in Lesbian Parenting Arrangements' (2013) 33 *Legal Studies* 355–81.

Snyder, J., Crooks, V., Johnston, R., and Kingsbury, P., 'Beyond Sun, Sand, and Stitches: Assuming Responsibility for the Harms of Medical Tourism' (2013) 27(5) *Bioethics* 233–42.

Sommerlad, H., 'Reflections on the Reconfiguration of Access to Justice' (2008) 15(3) *International Journal of the Legal Profession* 179–93.

Sotola, K., and Valpola, H., 'Coalescing Minds: Brain Uploading-related Group Mind Scenarios' (2012) *International Journal of Machine Consciousness* 1–20.

Stokes, E., 'Nanotechnology and the Products of Inherited Regulation' (2012) 39 *Journal of Law and Society* 93–112.

Studdert, D.M., Mello, M.M., Sage, W.M., DesRoches, C.M., Peugh, J., Zapert, K., and Brennan, T.A., 'Defensive Medicine among High-Risk Specialist Physicians in a Volatile Malpractice Environment' (2005) 293(21) *Journal of the American Medical Association* 2609–17.

Stumpf, A.E., 'Redefining Mother: A Legal Matrix for New Reproductive Technologies' (1986) 96 *Yale Law Journal* 187–208.

Sutherland, E., 'From "Bidie-in" to "Cohabitant" in Scotland: The Perils of Legislative Compromise' (2013) 27 *International Journal of Law Policy and the Family* 143–75.

Swinburn, B.A., Sacks, G., Hall, K.D., McPherson, K., Finegood, D.T., Moodie, M.L., and Gortmaker, S.L., 'The Global Obesity Pandemic: Shaped by Global Drivers and Local Environments' (2011) 378 *The Lancet* 804–14.

Szasz, T., 'The Therapeutic State: The Tyranny of Pharmacracy' (2001) 5(4) *The Independent Review* 485–521.

Testa, G, and Harris, J., 'Ethical Aspects of ES Cell-Derived Gametes' (2004) 305 *Science* 1719.

Thomson, J.J., 'A Defence of Abortion' (1971) 11 *Philosophy & Public Affairs* 47–66.

Vincent, C., Young, M., and Phillips, A., 'Why Do People Sue Doctors? A Study of Patients and Relatives Taking Legal Action' (1994) 343 *The Lancet* 1609–13.

Walker, S.E.P., 'Potential Persons and the Welfare of the (Potential) Child Test' (2014) 14 *Medical Law International* 157–71.

Weisbrot, D., and Breen, K.J., 'A No-Fault Compensation System for Medical Injury Is Long Overdue' (2012) 197(5) *Medical Journal of Australia* 296–8.

Wertheimer, R., 'Understanding the Abortion Argument' (1971) 1 *Philosophy & Public Affairs* 67–95.

White, B., and Downie, J., 'Prosecutorial Guidelines for Voluntary Euthanasia and Assisted Suicide: Autonomy, Public Confidence and High Quality Decision-Making' (2012) 36 *Melbourne University Law Review* 656–705.

——, and Willmott, L., 'How Should Australia Regulate Voluntary Euthanasia and Assisted Suicide?' (2012) *Journal of Law and Medicine* 410–38.

——, Willmott, L., Parker, M., Cartwright, C., and Williams, G., 'Should Law Have a Role in End of Life Care?' (2012) 42(9) *Internal Medicine Journal* 966–8.

Whitehead, S., and Shehzad, A., 'Health Outcomes in Economic Evaluation: The QALY and Utilities' (2010) 96(1) *British Medical Bulletin* 5–21.

Williams, A., 'Priority Setting in Private and Public Health Care: A Guide through the Ideological Jungle' (1988) 7 *Journal of Health Economics* 173–83.

Williamson, L., Fox, M., and McLean, S.A.M., 'The Regulation of Xenotransplantation in the United Kingdom After UKXIRA: Legal and Ethical Issues' (2007) 34 *Journal of Law & Society* 441–64.

Wise, J., 'Global Operation Tackles Internet Trade in Fake Drugs' (2012) 345 *British Medical Journal*, http://www.bmj.com/content/345/bmj.e6724?hwshib2=authn%3A1421229240%3A20150113%253A14af6725-f749-4233-8cf9-394370500a0d%3A0%3A0%3A0%3AWxpgibju4%2FZDuimqQtqOwA%3D%3D (accessed 13 January 2015).

Wolf, S., Crock, B.N., Van Ness, B., Lawrenz, F., Kahn, J.P., Beskow, L.M., Cho, M.K., Christman, M.F., Green, R.C., Hall, R., Illes, J., Keane, M., Knoppers, B.M., Koenig, B.A., Kohane, I.S., Leroy, B., Maschke, K.J., McGeveran, W., Ossorio, P., Parker, L.S., Petersen, G.M., Richardson, H.S., Scott, J.A., Terry, S.F., Wilfond, B.S., and Wolf, W.A., 'Managing Incidental Findings and Research Results in Genomic Research Involving Biobanks and Archived Data Sets' (2012) 14 *Genetics in Medicine* 361–84.

World Health Organization, 'The International Committee for Monitoring Assisted Reproductive Technology (ICMART) and the World Health Organisation (WHO) Revised Glossary on ART Terminology' (2009) 24 *Human Reproduction* 2683–7.
Wynne, B., 'Uncertainty and Environmental Learning: Reconceiving Science and Policy in the Preventive Paradigm' (1992) *Global Environmental Change* 111–27.
Yamin, A.E., 'Applying Human Rights to Maternal Health: UN Technical Guidance on Rights-based Approaches' (2013) 121 *International Journal of Gynecology and Obstetrics* 190–93.
Zampas, C., and Lamačková, A., 'Forced and Coerced Sterilization of Women in Europe' (2011) 114 *International Journal of Gynecology and Obstetrics* 163–6.
Zanghellini, A., 'Lesbian and Gay Parents and Reproductive Technologies: The 2008 Australian and UK Reforms' (2010) 18 *Feminist Legal Studies* 227–51.

Books, Book Chapters and Reports

Accident Compensation Corporation, *Annual Report 2013*.
Ahdar, R., and Leigh, I., *Religious Freedom in the Liberal State*, 2nd edn, Cambridge, Cambridge University Press, 2013.
Alghrani, A., 'Regulating the Reproductive Revolution: Ectogenesis – A Regulatory Minefield' in Freeman, M. (ed.) *Law and Bioethics*, Oxford, Oxford University Press, 2008, 303–28.
American Psychiatric Association, *Diagnostic and Statistical Manual of Mental Disorders*, 5th edn, 2013.
Arpaly, N., *Unprincipled Virtue: An Inquiry into Moral Agency*, Oxford, Oxford University Press, 2004.
Atiyah, P., *The Damages Lottery*, Oxford, Hart Publishing, 1997.
Australian Health Ministers Advisory Council, *National Framework for Advance Care Directives*, 2011.
Beauchamp, T.L., and Childress, J.F., *Principles of Biomedical Ethics*, 7th edn, Oxford, Oxford University Press, 2013.
Beck, A.T., Rush, A.J., Shaw, B.F., and Emery, G., *Cognitive Therapy of Depression*, New York, Guilford Press, 1987.
Benatar, S., and Brock, G. (eds), *Global Health and Global Health Ethics*, Cambridge, Cambridge University Press, 2011.
Berlin, I., 'Two Concepts of Liberty' in Berlin, I., *Four Essays on Liberty*, Oxford, Oxford University Press, 1969, 118–72.
Beyleveld, D., *The Dialectical Necessity of Morality: An Analysis and Defense of Alan Gewirth's Argument to the Principle of Generic Consistency*, Chicago, IL, University of Chicago Press, 1991.
Beynon-Jones, S.M., and Brown, N., 'Where the Wild Things Are: The EU Regulation of Transpecies Bioscience' in Flear, M.L., Farrell, A.-M., Hervey, T.K., and Murphy, T. (eds) *European Law and New Health Technologies*, Oxford, Oxford University Press, 2013, 343–61.
——, and Brownsword, R., *Consent in the Law*, Oxford, Hart Publishing, 2007.
Blackford, R., and Schüklenk, U., *50 Great Myths About Atheism*, West Sussex, Wiley-Blackwell, 2013.
Blazer, D.G., *The Age of Melancholy: 'Major Depression' and Its Social Origin*, New York, Routledge, 2005.

Blyth, E., and Potter, C., 'Paying for It? Surrogacy, Market Forces and Assisted Conception' in Cook, R., Sclater, S.D., and Kaganas, F. (eds) *Surrogate Motherhood: International Perspectives*, Oxford, Hart Publishing, 2003, 227–42.

Bottomley, S., and Bronnitt, S., *Law in Context*, 4th edn, Sydney, Federation Press, 2012.

Bovenberg, J., Meulenkamp, T., Smets, E., and Gevers, S., *Always Expect the Unexpected: Legal and Social Aspects of Reporting Biobank Research Results to Individual Research Participants*, Nijmegen, Radboud University, Centre for Society and Genomics, 2009.

Braithwaite, J., *Restorative Justice and Responsive Regulation*, Oxford, Oxford University Press, 2002.

——, 'Accountability and Responsibility through Restorative Justice' in Dowdle, M. (ed.) *Public Accountability: Designs Dilemmas and Experiences*, Cambridge, Cambridge University Press, 2006, 33–51.

Brazier, M., 'Embryos' "Rights", Abortion and Research' in Freeman, M.D.A. (ed.) *Medicine, Ethics and the Law*, London, Stevens & Sons, 1988, 9–22.

——, 'Parental Responsibilities, Foetal Welfare and Children's Health' in Bridge, C. (ed.) *Family Law: Towards the Millennium: Essays for P.M Bromley*, London, Butterworths, 1997, 263–95.

——, and Cave, E., *Medicine, Patients and the Law*, 5th edn, London, Penguin, 2011.

Bristow, J. (ed.), *Britain's Abortion Law: What It Says, and Why*, London, BPAS, 2013.

British Association for Perinatal Medicine, *The Management of Extremely Preterm Infants at Less Than 26 Weeks from 26 Weeks Gestation: A Framework for Clinical Practice at the Time of Birth*, 2008.

British Medical Association, *Disability Equality within Healthcare: The Role of Health Professionals*, London, 2007.

——, *Ensuring Transparency and Probity*, London, 2011.

British Psychological Society, *Response to the American Psychiatric Association: DSM-5 Development*, 2011.

Broberg, G., and Roll-Hansen, N., *Eugenics and the Welfare State: Sterilization Policy in Denmark, Sweden, Norway and Finland*, East Lansing, MI, Michigan State University Press, 1996.

Brock, D.W., 'Patient Competence and Surrogate Decision-Making' in Rhodes, R., Francis, L.P., and Silvers, A. (eds) *The Blackwell Guide to Medical Ethics*, Oxford, Blackwell Publishing, 2007, 128–41.

Brown, N., and Webster, A., *New Medical Technologies and Society: Reordering Life*, Cambridge, Polity Press, 2004.

Brownsword, R., and Goodwin, M., *Law and the Technologies of the Twenty-First Century*, Cambridge, Cambridge University Press, 2012.

——, and Yueng, K. (eds), *Regulating Technologies: Legal Futures, Regulatory Frames and Technological Fixes*, Oxford, Hart Publishing, 2008.

Bruinius, H., *Better for All the World: The Secret History of Forced Sterilization and America's Quest for Racial Purity*, New York, Vintage Books, 2007.

Brunet L., Carruthers, J., Davaki, K., King, D., Marzo, C., and McCandless, J., *A Comparative Study on the Regime of Surrogacy in EU Member States*, Brussels, European Parliament, 2013.

Buchanan, A.E., and Brock, D.W., *Deciding for Others: The Ethics of Surrogate Decision Making*, Cambridge, Cambridge University Press, 1990.

Burke, J., *What It Means to Be Human*, London, Virago, 2011.

Burleigh, M., and Wippermann, W., *The Racial State: Germany 1933–1945*, Cambridge, Cambridge University Press, 1991.

Campbell, T., 'Euthanasia as a Human Right' in McLean, S.A.M. (ed.) *First Do No Harm: Law, Ethics and Healthcare*, Aldershot, Ashgate, 2006, 447–60.
Cane, P., *Atiyah's Accidents Compensation and the Law*, 8th edn, Cambridge, Cambridge University Press, 2013.
Carel, H., *Illness: The Cry of the Flesh,* Stocksfield, Acumen Publishing, 2008.
Chadwick, R., Levitt, M., and Shickle, D. (eds) *The Right to Know and the Right Not to Know: Genetic Privacy and Responsibility*, 2nd edn, Cambridge, Cambridge University Press, 2014.
Chief Medical Officer, *Making Amends: A Consultation Paper Setting Out Proposals for Reforming the Approach to Clinical Negligence in the NHS*, London, Department of Health, 2003.
Clarke, A.C., *2001: A Space Odyssey*, London, Orbit Books: Little Brown and Co, 1998.
Clery, E., McLean, S., and Phillips, M., 'Quickening Death: The Euthanasia Debate' in Park, A., Curtice, J., Thomson, K., Phillips, M., and Johnson, M. (eds) *British Social Attitudes: The 23rd Report*, London, Sage, 2007, 35–54.
Coggon, J., *What Makes Health Public?*, Cambridge, Cambridge University Press, 2012.
Cohen, I.G., 'Medical Outlaws or Medical Refugees? An Examination of Circumvention Tourism' in Hodges, J.R., Turner, L., and Kimball, A.M. (eds) *Risks and Challenges in Medical Tourism: Understanding the Global Market for Health Services*, Santa Barbara, CA, Praeger, 2012, 207–29.
Cook, R.J., and Cusack, S., *Gender Stereotyping: Transnational Legal Perspectives*, Philadelphia, PA, University of Pennsylvania Press, 2010.
Cook, R.J., Dickens, B.M., and Fathalla, M.F., *Reproductive Health and Human Rights: Integrating Medicine, Ethics and Law*, Oxford, Clarendon Press, 2003.
Cook, R.J., Erdman, J.N., and Dickens, B.M., *Abortion Law in Transnational Perspective: Cases and Controversies*, Philadelphia, PA, University of Pennsylvania Press, 2014.
Cook R.J., and Undurraga, V., 'Article 12' in Freeman, M.A., Chinkin, C., and Rudolf, B. (eds) *The UN Convention on the Elimination of All Forms of Discrimination against Women: A Commentary*, Oxford, Oxford University Press, 2012, 311–34.
Council of Europe, *Xenotransplantation: State of the Art*, Strasbourg, 1997.
Daniels, N., *Just Health: Meeting Health Needs Fairly*, Cambridge, Cambridge University Press, 2008.
Davis, K., *Reshaping the Female Body: The Dilemma of Cosmetic Surgery*, London, Routledge, 1995.
Davis, M., *Medical Self-Regulation: Crisis and Change*, Aldershot, Ashgate, 2006.
Davis, P.B., Lay-Yee, R., Briant, R., Schug, S., Scott, A., Johnson, S., and Bingley, W., *Adverse Events in New Zealand's Public Hospitals: Principal Findings from a National Survey*, Wellington, Ministry of Health, 2001.
de Mora, R., *Eliminating Maternal Deaths from Unsafe Abortion in Uruguay: The Experience of Iniciativas Sanitarias*, UNFPA, 2011.
Deissie, H.T., 'Taming Matter for the Welfare of Humanity: Regulating Nanotechnology' in Brownsword, R. and Yueng, K. (eds) *Regulating Technologies: Legal Futures, Regulatory Frames and Technological Fixes*, Oxford, Hart Publishing, 2008, 327–56.
Department of Health, *Being Heard: Report of the Review Committee on NHS Complaints Procedures*, D106/BH/1.5m HSSH J07 3274, July 1994.
——, *Animal Tissue into Humans: A Report by the Advisory Group on the Ethics of Xenotransplantation*, London, 1996.
——, *Review of the Common Law Provisions Relating to the Removal of Gametes and of the Consent Provisions of the Human Fertilisation and Embryology Act 1990*, 1998.

——, *Report of the Public Inquiry into Children's Heart Surgery at the Bristol Royal Infirmary 1984–1995: Learning from Bristol*, 2001.
——, *Making Amends: A Consultation Paper Setting Out Proposals for Reforming the Approach to Clinical Negligence in the NHS*, 2003.
——, *Consultation on a New Safeguarding Power*, 2012.
——, *Reforming the Law for Adult Care and Support: The Government's Response to Law Commission Report 326 on Adult Social Care*, 2012.
——, *Abortion Statistics for England and Wales 2012*, 2013.
Department of Health and Social Security, *Report of the Committee of Inquiry into Human Fertilisation and Embryology* ('The Warnock Report'), Cmnd. 9314, London, HMSO, 1984.
Dickens, B.M., 'Wrongful Birth and Life, Wrongful Death Before Birth, and Wrongful Law' in McLean, S.A.M. (ed.) *Legal Issues in Human Reproduction*, London, Gower Medico-Legal Series, 1989, 80–112.
——, 'Ethical Issues Arising from the Use of Assisted Reproductive Technologies' in Vayena, E., Rowe, P.J., and Griffin, P.D. (eds) *Current Practices and Controversies in Assisted Reproduction*, Geneva, WHO, 2002, 333–48.
——, 'Conscientious Objection: A Shield or a Sword?' in McLean, S.A.M. (ed.) *First Do No Harm: Law, Ethics and Healthcare*, Aldershot, Ashgate, 2006, 337–51.
——, 'The Right to Conscience' in Cook, R.J., Erdman, J.N., and Dickens, B.M. (eds) *Abortion Law in Transnational Perspective: Cases and Controversies*, Philadelphia, PA, University of Pennsylvania Press, 2014, 210–38.
Drummond, S.G., *Fruitful Diversity: Revisiting the Enforceability of Gestational Carriage Contracts*, Research Paper no. 25/1013, Osgoode Hall Law School, York University, 2013.
Dworkin, G., *The Theory and Practice of Autonomy*, New York, Cambridge University Press, 1988.
Dworkin, R., *Sovereign Virtue: The Theory and Practice of Equality*, Cambridge, MA, Harvard University Press, 2000.
Edgar, A., Salek, S., Shickle, D., and Cohen, D., *The Ethical QALY: Ethical Issues in Healthcare Resource Allocations*, Haslemere, Euromed Communications, 1994.
Essinger, K., *The Swedish Medical Injury Insurance, Report 2009–02–20.*
Falconer Report: *Commission on Assisted Dying*, London, Demos, 2011.
Farrell, A.M., Devaney, S., and Dar, A., *No-Fault Compensation Schemes for Medical Injury: A Review*, No Fault Compensation Review Group, Report and Recommendations, Volume II, 2010.
Feinberg, J., *The Moral Limits of the Criminal Law: Harm to Self*, vol. 3, Oxford, Oxford University Press, 1986.
Fineman, M., *The Autonomy Myth: A Theory of Dependency*, New York, The New Press, 2005.
Fitzpatrick, M., *The Tyranny of Health: Doctors and the Regulation of Lifestyle*, London, Routledge, 2005.
Flynn, J.R., *How to Defend Humane Ideals: Substitutes for Objectivity*, Lincoln, NE and London, University of Nebraska Press, 2000.
Foster, C., *Choosing Life, Choosing Death: The Tyranny of Autonomy in Medical Ethics and Law*, Portland, OR, Hart Publishing, 2009.
Fovargue, S., *Xenotransplantation and Risk: Regulating a Developing Biotechnology*, Cambridge, Cambridge University Press, 2012.
——, 'Bioethical Conflict and Developing Biotechnologies: Is Protecting Individual and Public Health from the Risks of Xenotransplantation a Matter for the (Criminal) Law?' in Alghrani,

A., Bennett, R., and Ost, S. (eds) *Bioethics, Medicine and the Criminal Law*, Cambridge, Cambridge University Press, 2012, 140–56.
Fox, M., 'Legislating Interspecies Embryos' in Deazley, R. and Smith, S. (eds) *The Legal, Medical and Cultural Regulation of the Body: Transformation and Transgression*, Aldershot, Ashgate, 2009, 95–126.
——, and Murphy, T., 'The Body, Bodies, Embodiment: Feminist, Legal Engagement with Health' in Davies M. and Munro V. (eds) *The Ashgate Research Companion to Feminist Legal Theory*, Farnham, Ashgate, 2013, 249–266.
——, and Thompson M., 'Reconsidering "Best Interests": Male Circumcision and the Rights of the Child' in M. Milos (ed.) *Human Rights and Circumcision*, New York, Springer, 2009, 15–31.
Francis Report: *Report of the Mid Staffordshire NHS Foundation Trust: Public Inquiry*, HC 947, 2013.
Frank, R.H., *The Darwin Economy: Liberty, Competition, and the Common Good*, Princeton, NJ, Princeton University Press, 2011.
Franklin, S. *Biological Relatives: IVF, Stem Cells and the Future of Kinship*, Durham, NC, Duke University Press, 2013.
Fukuyama, F., *Our Posthuman Future: Consequences of the Biotechnology Revolution*, New York, Farrar, Straus and Giroux, 2002.
Fuller, S., *Humanity 2.0: What It Means to Be Human Past, Present and Future*, Houndsmills, Palgrave, 2011.
Gaylin, W., and Jennings, B., *The Perversion of Autonomy*, 2nd edn, Washington, DC, Georgetown University Press, 2003.
General Medical Council, *Tomorrow's Doctors*, 2009, updated 2012.
——, *Good Medical Practice*, London, 2013.
Gewirth, A., *Reason and Morality*, Chicago, IL, University of Chicago Press, 1978.
Goldberg, R. (ed.), *Perspectives on Causation*, Oxford, Hart Publishing, 2011.
Government Office for Science, *Foresight: Tackling Obesity*, 2nd edn, London, 2013,.
Griffiths, J., Weyers, H., and Adams, M., *Euthanasia and Law in Europe*, Portland, OR, Hart Publishing, 2008.
Guttmacher Institute, *Facts on Induced Abortion Worldwide: Worldwide Incidence and Trends*, 2012.
Harker, R., *NHS Funding and Expenditure*, House of Commons Library, SN/SG/724, 2012.
Harpwood, V., *Medicine Malpractice and Misapprehensions*, London, Routledge-Cavendish, 2007.
Harris, J., *Violence and Responsibility*, London, Routledge and Kegan Paul, 1980.
——, *The Value of Life*, London, Routledge, 1985.
——, *Wonderwoman and Superman: Ethics of Human Biotechnology*, Oxford, Oxford University Press, 1992.
——, *Enhancing Evolution*, Princeton, NJ and Oxford, Princeton University Press, 2007.
Healthcare Commission, *Investigation into Outbreaks of Clostridium Difficile at Stoke Mandeville Hospital, Buckinghamshire Hospitals NHS Trust*, London, 2006.
——, *Investigation into Outbreaks of Clostridium Difficile at Maidstone and Tunbridge Wells NHS Trust*, London, 2007.
Health Service Ombudsman, *Care and Compassion: Report of the Health Service Ombudsman on Ten Investigations into NHS Care of Older People*, London, HC 778, 2011.
Heeney, C., and Parker, M., 'Ethics and the Governance of Biobanks' in Kaye, J., Gibbons, S.M.C., Heeney, C., Parker, M., and Smart, A., *Governing Biobanks*, Oxford, Hart Publishing, 2012, 282–301.

Hellbacher, U., Espersson, C., and Johansson, H., *Patient Injury Compensation for Healthcare-Related Injuries in Sweden*, Stockholm, Visby, 2007.

Henaghan, M. (ed.), *Choosing Genes for Future Children: Regulating Preimplantation Genetic Diagnosis*, Dunedin, Human Genome Research Project, 2006.

—— (ed.), *Genes, Society and the Future: Volumes I and II*, Dunedin, Human Genome Research Project, 2007.

—— (ed.), *Genes, Society and the Future: Volume III*, Wellington, Human Genome Research Report, Brookers, 2009.

Herring, J., *Caring and the Law*, Oxford, Hart Publishing, 2012.

Hervey, T., and McHale, J., *European Health Law*, Cambridge, Cambridge University Press (forthcoming 2015).

Hill, T., 'The Kantian Conception of Autonomy' in Christman, J. (ed.) *The Inner Citadel: Essays on Individual Autonomy*, New York, Oxford University Press, 1989, 91–108.

Hirschman, A., *Exit, Voice and Loyalty*, Cambridge, MA, Harvard University Press, 1970.

Horwitz, A.V., and Wakefield, J.C., *The Loss of Sadness: How Psychiatry Transformed Normal Sorrow into Depressive Disorder*, Oxford, Oxford University Press, 2007.

House of Commons Health Committee, *Annual Accountability Hearing with the General Medical Council*, HC 1429, Session 2010–12.

House of Commons Science and Technology Committee, *Human Reproductive Technologies and the Law: Volume 1*, London, The Stationary Office, 2005.

House of Lords, *Ready for Ageing*, HL Paper 140, The Stationary Office, London, 2013.

Human Rights Watch, *Uruguay: New Abortion Law Breaks Ground for Women's Rights*, 2012.

International Federation of Gynecology and Obstetrics (FIGO), *Ethical Guidelines on Conscientious Objection*, 2005.

International Statistical Classification of Diseases and Related Health Problems 10th Revision (ICD-10), 2010.

Ipsos Mori, *Understanding Society: How Do We Change Behaviour?*, London, 2013.

Jackson, E., *Medical Law: Text, Cases and Materials*, 3rd edn, Oxford, Oxford University Press, 2013.

——, and Keown, J., *Debating Euthanasia*, Oxford, Hart Publishing, 2012.

Jackson Report: *Review of Civil Litigation Costs: Final Report*, London, The Stationery Office, 2010.

Jackson, S.W., *Melancholia and Depression: From Hippocratic Times to Modern Times*, New Haven, CT, Yale University Press, 1986.

Jenkins, I.D., and Turner, V., *The Greek Body*, London, The British Museum Press, 2009.

Joffe, C., *Doctors of Conscience: The Struggle to Provide Abortion before and after Roe v. Wade*, Boston, MA, Beacon Press, 1995.

Jonsen, A., *The Birth of Bioethics*, New York, Oxford University Press, 1998.

Justinian, *Digest*, II.

Kant, I., *Groundwork of the Metaphysic of Morals*, London, Hutchinson's University Library, 1953.

Karnein, A.J., *A Theory of Unborn Life*, Oxford, Oxford University Press, 2012.

Karpin I., and Savell, K., *Perfecting Pregnancy: Law, Disability, and the Future of Reproduction*, Cambridge, Cambridge University Press, 2012.

Kennedy, I., *The Unmasking of Medicine*, London, George Allen and Unwin, 1981.

——, *Learning from Bristol*, Cm 5207, 2001.

Keogh, B. *Poly Implant Prothesis (PIP) Breast Implants: Final Report of the Expert Group*, Department of Health, 18 June 2012.

Kevles, D.J., *In the Name of Eugenics: Genetics and the Uses of Human Heredity*, Berkeley, CA, University of California Press, 1986.

Kleegman, S.J., and Kaufman, S.A., *Infertility in Women*, Philadelphia, PA, F.A. Davis, 1966.

Koenig, B., 'The Technological Imperative in Medical Practice: The Social Creation of a "Routine" Treatment' in Lock, M. and Gordon, D. (eds) *Biomedicine Examined*, London, Kluwer, 1988, 465–96.

Kraepelin, E., *Psychiatrie: ein Lehrbuch für Studirende und Aertze*, 6th edn, Leipzig, Barth Verlag, 1899.

Laurie, G., 'Genetic Privacy: A Legal Perspective', Doctoral thesis, University of Glasgow, 1997.

——, *Genetic Privacy: A Challenge to Medico-legal Norms*, Cambridge, Cambridge University Press, 2002.

——, 'Personality, Privacy and Autonomy in Medical Law' in Whitty, N. and Zimmermann, R. (eds) *Rights of Personality in Scots Law: A Comparative Perspective*, Dundee, Dundee University Press, 2009, 453–84.

Law Commission, *Adult Social Care*, LC326, 2011.

Le Grand, J., *The Other Invisible Hand: Delivering Public Services Through Choice and Competition*, Princeton, NJ, Princeton University Press, 2007.

Lee, R.G., and Petts, J., 'Adaptive Governance for Responsible Innovation' in Owen, R., Heintz, M., and Bessant J. (eds) *Responsible Innovation*, London, Wiley, 2013, 143–64.

Leridon, H., *Human Fertility: The Basic Components*, Chicago, IL, University of Chicago Press, 1977.

Lewis, P., *Assisted Dying and Legal Change*, Oxford, Oxford University Press, 2007.

Lõhmus, K., 'Caring Autonomy: Rethinking the Right to Autonomy under the European Court of Human Rights Jurisprudence', Doctoral thesis, University of Edinburgh, 2013.

Lombardo, P.A., *A Century of Eugenics in America: From the Indiana Experiment to the Human Genome*, Bloomington, IN, Indiana University Press, 2011.

Luker, K., *Abortion and the Politics of Motherhood*, Berkeley, CA, University of California Press, 1984.

Lunney, M., and Oliphant, K., *Tort Law: Text and Materials*, 5th edn, Oxford, Oxford University Press, 2013.

Lynch, H.F., *Conflicts of Conscience in Health Care: An Institutional Compromise*, Cambridge MA, MIT Press, 2008.

McKhann, C.F., *A Time to Die: The Place for Physician Assistance*, New Haven, CT, Yale University Press, 1999.

McLean, S.A.M. (ed.), *Legal Issues in Human Reproduction*, London, Gower Medico-Legal Series, 1989.

——, *A Patient's Right to Know*, Aldershot, Dartmouth, 1989.

——, *Law Reform and Human Reproduction*, Aldershot, Dartmouth, 1992.

——, 'Can No-Fault Analysis Ease the Problems of Medical Injury Litigation?' in McLean, S.A.M. (ed.) *Compensation for Damage: An International Perspective*, Aldershot, Dartmouth, 1993, 75–90.

—— (ed.), *Law Reform and Medical Injury Litigation*, Aldershot: Dartmouth, 1995.

——, *Review of the Common Law Provisions Relating to the Removal of Gametes and of the Consent Provisions, in the Human Fertilisation and Embryology Act 1990*, London, Department of Health, 1998.

——, *Old Law, New Medicine*, London, Pandora Press, 1999.

——, 'The Rights to Life: Euthanasia' in Smith, R.K.M. and van den Anker, C. (eds) *The Essentials of Human Rights*, London, Hodder Arnold, 2005, 242–4.
——, 'From *Bland* to *Burke*: The Law and Politics of Assisted Nutrition and Hydration' in McLean, S.A.M. (ed.) *First Do No Harm: Law, Ethics and Healthcare*, Aldershot, Ashgate, 2006, 431–46.
——, *Modern Dilemmas Choosing Children*, Edinburgh, Capercaillie Books, 2006.
——, *Assisted Dying: Reflections on the Need for Law Reform*, London, Routledge-Cavendish, 2007.
——, 'Assisted Dying: The View from the United Kingdom' in Birnbacher, D. and Dahl, E. (eds) *Giving Death a Helping Hand: Physician-Assisted Suicide and Public Policy: An International Perspective*, Dordrecht, Springer, 2008, 113–28.
——, *Autonomy, Consent and the Law*, Abingdon, Routledge-Cavendish, 2010.
——, and Elliston, S., 'Conclusion' in McLean, S.A.M. and Elliston, S. (eds) *Regulating Pre-Implantation Genetic Diagnosis: A Comparative and Theoretical Analysis*, London and New York, Routledge, 2013, 224–38.
——, and Maher, G., *Medicine, Morals and the Law*, Aldershot, Gower, 1983.
——, and Mason, J.K., *Legal and Ethical Aspects of Healthcare*, London and San Francisco, CA, Greenwich Media, 2003.
——, and Williamson L., *Xenotransplantation: Law and Ethics*, Aldershot, Ashgate, 2005.
——, and Williamson, L., *Impairment and Disability: Law and Ethics at the Beginning and End of Life*, Abingdon, Routledge-Cavendish, 2007.
——, Williamson, L., Devlin, B., and Blair, A., *Ethico-Legal Decision-Making in Healthcare*, Glasgow, University of Glasgow, 2004.
Manning, J., 'Treatment Injury and Medical Misadventure' in Skegg, P.D.G. and Paterson, R. (eds) *Medical Law in New Zealand*, Wellington, Thomson Brookers, 2006, 679–724.
Manson, N.C., and O'Neill, O., *Rethinking Informed Consent in Bioethics*, Cambridge, Cambridge University Press, 2007.
Marmot, M., *Fair Society, Healthy Lives*, London, The Marmot Review, 2010.
Mason, J.K., *Medico-Legal Aspects of Reproduction and Parenthood*, 2nd edn, Aldershot, Ashgate/Dartmouth, 1998.
——, *The Troubled Pregnancy: Legal Wrongs and Rights in Pregnancy*, Cambridge, Cambridge University Press, 2007.
——, 'Particularity and Medical Law' in Bankowski, Z. and MacLean, J. (eds) *The Universal and the Particular in Legal Reasoning*, Aldershot, Ashgate, 2007, 235–46.
——, and Laurie, G.T., *Mason and McCall Smith's Law and Medical Ethics*, 9th edn, Oxford, Oxford University Press, 2013.
Medical Schools Council, *The Consensus Statement on the Role of the Doctor*, 2008.
Merry, A.F., 'When Are Errors a Crime? Lessons from New Zealand' in Erin, C. and Ost, S. (eds) *The Criminal Justice System and Health Care*, Oxford, Oxford University Press, 2007, 67–98.
Meyers, D., '*Chester v. Afshar*: Sayanaro, sub silentio, *Sidaway*' in McLean, S.A.M. (ed.) *First Do No Harm: Law, Ethics and Healthcare*, Aldershot, Ashgate, 2006, 255–72.
Mill, J.S., *On Liberty*, 2nd edn, London, John W. Parker and Son, 1859.
——, 'On Liberty' in Lindsay, D.A., *Utilitarianism, Liberty and Representative Government*, London, Everyman, 1910, 65–172.
Milne, A.A., *The House at Pooh Corner*, London, Methuen, 1974.
Morris, J., *'One Town for My Body, Another for My Mind': Services for People with Physical Impairments and Mental Health Support Needs*, London, Joseph Rowntree Foundation, 2004.

Murphy, T., and O'Cuinn, G., 'Taking Technology Seriously: STS as a Human Rights Method' in Flear, M.L., Farrell, A.-M., Hervey, T.K., and Murphy, T. (eds) *European Law and New Health Technologies*, Oxford, Oxford University Press, 2013, 285–308.

National Advisory Group on the Safety of Patients in England, *A Promise to Learn – A Commitment to Act*, London, 2013.

National Committee of Inquiry on Compensation and Rehabilitation in Australia, *Compensation and Rehabilitation in Australia: Report of the National Committee of Inquiry*, Canberra, AGPS, 1974.

New Zealand Royal Commission of Inquiry into Compensation for Personal Injury, *Compensation for Personal Injury in New Zealand: Report of the Royal Commission of Inquiry*, Wellington, Government Printer, 1967.

Newdick, C., *Who Should We Treat?*, 2nd edn, Oxford, Oxford University Press, 2005.

——, 'The Positive Side of Health Care Rights' in McLean, S.A.M. (ed.) *First Do No Harm: Law Ethics and Healthcare*, Aldershot, Ashgate, 2006, 573–86.

NHS Commissioning Board, *Code of Conduct*, London, 2012.

NHS England, *The NHS Belongs to the People: A Call to Action*, London, 2013.

Norrie, K., 'From Decriminalisation to Marriage: Changing Judicial, Political and Religious Attitudes in the United Kingdom to Gay and Lesbian Families' in Petersen, H., Villaverde, J.M., and Lund-Andersen, I. (eds) *Contemporary Gender Relations and Changes in Legal Cultures*, Copenhagen, DJØF Publishing, 2013, 181–210.

Nuffield Council on Bioethics, *Animal-to-Human Transplants: The Ethics of Xenotransplantation*, London, 1996.

——, *Critical Care Decisions in Fetal and Neonatal Medicine*, London, 2006.

——, *Novel Neurotechnologies: Intervening in the Brain*, London, June 2013.

——, *Donor Conception: Ethical Aspects of Information Sharing*, London, 2013.

Office of Budget Responsibility, *Fiscal Sustainability Report 2012: Executive Summary*, London, 2012.

Oliver, M., *Understanding Disability: From Theory to Practice*, Basingstoke, Macmillan, 1996.

O'Neill, O., *Autonomy and Trust in Bioethics*, Cambridge, Cambridge University Press, 2002.

Otlowski, M., *Voluntary Euthanasia and the Common Law*, Oxford, Clarendon Press, 1997.

Owen, D.G. (ed.), *Philosophical Foundations of Tort Law*, Oxford, Oxford University Press, 1995.

Padden, C.A., and Humphries, T.L., *Inside Deaf Culture*, Cambridge, MA, Harvard University Press, 2005.

Page, E.C., 'The Origins of Policy' in Moran, M., Rein, M., and Goodin R.E. (eds) *The Oxford Handbook of Public Policy*, Oxford, Oxford University Press, 2006, 207–27.

Paterson, R., 'Regulation of Health Care' in Skegg, P.D.G. and Paterson, R. (eds) *Medical Law in New Zealand*, Wellington, Thomson Brookers, 2006, 3–22.

——, 'Assessment and Investigation of Complaints' in Skegg, P.D.G. and Paterson, R. (eds) *Medical Law in New Zealand*, Wellington, Thomson Brookers, 2006, 593–612.

Patrick, H., *Mental Health, Incapacity and the Law in Scotland*, Edinburgh, Tottel Publishing, 2006.

Pearson Report: *Royal Commission on Civil Liability and Compensation for Personal Injury*, Cmnd 7054-1, London, HMSO, 1978.

Persson, A., and Welin, S., *Contested Technologies: Xenotransplantation and Human Embryonic Stem Cells*, Lund, Nordic Academic Press, 2008.

Porta, M., Greenland, S., and Last, J.M. (eds), *A Dictionary of Epidemiology*, 5th edn, Oxford, Oxford University Press, 2008.

Postema, G.J. (ed.), *Philosophy and the Law of Torts*, Cambridge, Cambridge University Press, 2001.

Powers, M., and Faden, R., *Social Justice, the Moral Foundations of Public Health and Health Policy*, New York, Oxford University Press, 2006.

Prainsack, B., and Buyx, A., *Solidarity: Reflections on an Emerging Concept in Bioethics*, London, Nuffield Council on Bioethics, 2011.

Public Bodies Reform: Proposals for Change 2010, available at: http://webarchive.nationalarchives.gov.uk/20121015000000/http://www.direct.gov.uk/prod_consum_dg/groups/dg_digitalassets/@dg/@en/documents/digitalasset/dg_191543.pdf, accessed 13 January 2015.

Quen, J.M., Metoiu, H., and Ayed, S. (eds), *Psychiatry: A Textbook for Students and Physicians*, Canton, MA, Science History Publications, 1990.

Randall, F., and Downie, R.S., *The Philosophy of Palliative Care: Critique and Reconstruction*, Oxford, Oxford University Press, 2006.

Regmi, S., and Harris, J., 'Ethics' in Rowlands, S. (ed.) *Abortion Care*, Cambridge, Cambridge University Press, 2014, 16–23.

Review of the Common Law Provisions Relating to the Removal of Gametes and of the Consent Provisions of the Human Fertilisation and Embryology Act 1990, London, Department of Health, 1998.

Rhode, D.L., *Justice and Gender: Sex Discrimination and the Law*, Cambridge, MA, Harvard University Press, 1989.

——, *Access to Justice*, New York, Oxford University Press, 2004.

Richardson, H.S., *Moral Entanglements: The Ancillary-Care Obligations of Medical Researchers*, New York, Oxford University Press, 2012.

Robinson, M.A., *Accident Compensation in Australia: No-Fault Schemes*, Sydney, Legal Books, 1987.

Rodwin, M.A., *Conflicts of Interest and the Future of Medicine*, New York, Oxford University Press, 2011.

Ross Report: *Report of the Expert Group on Financial and Other Support*, Scottish Executive, 2003.

Royal College of Obstetricians and Gynaecologists, *Termination of Pregnancy for Fetal Abnormality in England, Wales and Scotland*, 2010.

Royal Commission on Civil Liability and Compensation for Personal Injury (Chairman: Lord Pearson), Report, Cmnd 7054 (3 vols), London, HMSO, 1978.

Sandberg, A., and Boström, N., *Whole Brain Emulation: A Roadmap. Technical Report #2008–3*, Oxford, Future of Humanity Institute, Oxford University, 2008.

Sandell, M.J., *Liberalism and the Limits of Justice*, 2nd edn, New York, Cambridge University Press, 1998.

Savulescu, J., 'Procreative Beneficence: Why We Should Select the Best Children' in Holland, S. (ed.) *Arguing About Bioethics*, London, Routledge, 2012, 74–82.

Schneider, C.E., *The Practice of Autonomy: Patients, Doctors and Medical Decisions*, New York, Oxford University Press, 1998.

Scottish Government, *No Fault Compensation Review Group, Report and Recommendations, Volume 1*, 2011.

Scottish Government Healthcare Policy and Strategy Directorate, *Patients' Rights: A Public Consultation on a Patients' Rights Bill for Users of the NHS in Scotland*, Edinburgh, 2008.

Searle, J.R., *Intentionality: An Essay in the Philosophy of Mind*, Cambridge, Cambridge University Press, 1983.

Sen, A., *The Idea of Justice*, London, Allen Lane, 2009.

Sepper, E., *Contraception and the Birth of Corporate Conscience*, Washington University in St. Louis School of Law Legal Studies Research Paper No.13-07-01, July 2013.

Shakespeare, W., *The Tempest*, in Proudfoot, R., Thomson, A., and Kasten, D.S. (eds) *The Arden Shakespeare*, Walton-On-Thames, Thomas Nelson and Sons, 1998.

Sharot, T., *The Optimism Bias: Why We're Wired to Look on the Bright Side*, New York, Random House, 2012.

Sharp, L.A., *The Transplant Imaginary: Mechanical Hearts, Animal Parts and Moral Thinking in Highly Experimental Science*, Berkeley and Los Angeles, CA, University of California Press, 2013.

Sharpe, A., *Foucault's Monsters and the Challenges of Law*, London, Routledge, 2011.

Sheldon, S., *Beyond Control: Medical Power and Abortion Law*, London, Pluto, 1997.

——, 'The Abortion Act 1967: A Critical Perspective' in Lee, E. (ed.) *Abortion Law and Politics Today*, London, Macmillan, 1998, 43–58.

Shneidman, E.S., 'Approaches and Commonalities of Suicide' in Diekstra, R.F.W. (ed.) *Suicide and Its Prevention: The Role of Attitude and Imitation*, World Health Organization, 1989, 14–36.

Singer, P., *Rethinking Life and Death: The Collapse of Our Traditional Ethics*, Oxford, Oxford University Press, 1995.

——, and Wells, D., 'Ectogenesis' in Gelfland, S., and Shook, J. (eds) *Ectogenesis: Artificial Womb Technology and the Future of Human Reproduction*, Amsterdam and New York, Rodopi, 2006, 9–26.

Skene, L., *Law and Medical Practice*, 3rd edn, Sydney, LexisNexis Butterworths, 2008.

Snelling, J., 'Parental Preferences and Procreative Choices: Reproductive Liberty and the Regulation of Preimplantation Genetic Diagnosis', PhD Thesis, University of Otago, 2012.

Somek, A., *Solidarity Decomposed: Being and Time in European Citizenship*, University of Iowa Legal Studies Research Paper 13, 2007.

Somerville, M., *Death Talk: The Case Against Euthanasia and Physician-Assisted Suicide*, Montreal, McGill University Press, 2001.

Sprengell, C., *The Aphorisms of Hippocrates and the Sentences of Celsus*, 2nd edn, London, 1735.

Stacey, M., *Regulating the General Medical Council*, Chichester, John Wiley, 1992.

Stephen, F., Melville, A., and Krause, T., *A Study of Medical Negligence Claiming in Scotland*, Research Findings No. 113/2012, Government Social Research, Scotland.

Strathern, M., 'Still Giving Nature a Helping Hand? Surrogacy: A Debate about Technology and Society' in Cook, R., Sclater, S.D., and Kaganas, F. (eds) *Surrogate Motherhood: International Perspectives*, Oxford, Hart Publishing, 2003.

Syrett, K., *Law, Legitimacy and the Rationing of Health Care*, Cambridge, Cambridge University Press, 2007.

Szasz, T., *The Myth of Mental Illness: Foundations of a Theory of Personal Conduct*, revised edn, New York, HarperCollins, 1974.

Taylor, J.S. (ed.), *Personal Autonomy*, Cambridge, Cambridge University Press, 2005.

Teff, H., *Reasonable Care: Legal Perspectives on the Doctor-Patient Relationship*, Oxford, Clarendon Press, 1994.

Thaler, R.H. and Sunstein, C.R., *Nudge: Improving Decisions about Health, Wealth and Happiness*, London, Penguin Books, 2009.

Thompson, C., *Making Parents: The Ontological Choreography of Reproductive Technologies*, Cambridge, MA, MIT Press, 2005.

Thompson, J.J., 'A Defence of Abortion' in Dworkin, R.M. (ed.) *The Philosophy of Law*, Oxford, Oxford University Press, 1977, 112–28.

Victorian Law Reform Commission, Consultation Paper 10, *Guardianship*, 2011.
——, Final Report 24, *Guardianship*, 2012.
Vincent-Jones, P., *The New Public Contracting: Regulation, Responsiveness, Relationality*, Oxford, Oxford University Press, 2006.
Warnock Report: *Committee of Inquiry into Human Fertilisation and Embryology*, Cmnd 9314, 1984.
Wellcome Trust and Medical Research Council, *Assessing Public Attitudes to Health Related Findings in Research*, London, April 2012.
Welsh Assembly Government, *Putting Things Right: Guidance on Dealing with Concerns from the 1st April 2011*, 2nd Version, 2012.
Weston, K., *Families We Choose: Lesbians, Gays, Kinship*, New York, Columbia University Press, 1998.
Wicks, E., 'Terminating Life and Human Rights: The Fetus and the Neonate' in Erin, C.A. and Ost, S. (eds) *The Criminal Justice System and Health Care*, Oxford, Oxford University Press, 2007, 189–206.
Williams, G., *The Sanctity of Life and the Criminal Law*, London, Faber and Faber, 1958.
Wittgenstein, L., *Philosophical Investigations*, Oxford, Blackwell, 1953.
Woolf Report: *Access to Justice: Final Report*, 1996.
Wolpert, L., *Malignant Sadness: The Anatomy of Depression*, London, Faber and Faber, 2006.
Woodhouse Report (Australia): *Compensation and Rehabilitation in Australia: Report of the National Committee of Inquiry*, Canberra, AGPS, 1974.
Woodhouse Report (New Zealand): New Zealand Royal Commission of Inquiry into Compensation for Personal Injury, *Compensation for Personal Injury in New Zealand: Report of the Royal Commission of Inquiry*, Wellington, Government Printer, 1967.
World Health Organization, *Constitution*, New York, 1946.
——, *Report of a WHO Technical Consultation on Birth Spacing*, WHO/RHR/07.1, Geneva, WHO, 2007.
——, UNICEF, UNFPA, The World Bank, *Trends in Maternal Mortality: 1990–2008*, Geneva, WHO, 2010.
——, *Unsafe Abortion: Global and Regional Estimates of the Incidence of Unsafe Abortion and Associated Mortality in 2008*, 6th edn, 2011.

Index

For Product Safety Concerns and Information please contact our EU representative GPSR@taylorandfrancis.com Taylor & Francis Verlag GmbH, Kaufingerstraße 24, 80331 München, Germany

Batch number: 10726294

Printed by Printforce, the Netherlands